Feasting on History

Columbia Studies in International and Global History

Columbia Studies in International and Global History
CEMIL AYDIN, TIMOTHY NUNAN, AND DOMINIC SACHSENMAIER, SERIES EDITORS

This series presents some of the finest and most innovative work coming out of the current landscapes of international and global historical scholarship. Grounded in empirical research, these titles transcend the usual area boundaries and address how history can help us understand contemporary problems, including poverty, inequality, power, political violence, and accountability beyond the nation-state. The series covers processes of flows, exchanges, and entanglements—and moments of blockage, friction, and fracture—not only between "the West" and "the Rest" but also among parts of what has variously been dubbed the "Third World" or the "Global South." Scholarship in international and global history remains indispensable for a better sense of current complex regional and global economic transformations. Such approaches are vital in understanding the making of our present world.

> Zeyneb Hale Eroglu, *Muslim Transnationalism in Modern China: Debates on Hui Identity and Islamic Reform*
>
> Pierre Singaravélou, trans. Stephen W. Sawyer, *Tianjin Cosmopolis: An Alternative History of Globalization*
>
> Jie-Hyun Lim, trans. Megan Sungyoon, *Victimhood Nationalism: History and Memory in a Global Age*
>
> Sandrine Kott, *A World More Equal: An Internationalist Perspective on the Cold War*
>
> Julia Hauser, *A Taste for Purity: An Entangled History of Vegetarianism*
>
> Hayrettin Yücesoy, *Disenchanting the Caliphate: The Secular Discipline of Power in Abbasid Political Thought*
>
> Anne Irfan, *Refuge and Resistance: Palestinians and the International Refugee System*
>
> Michael Francis Laffan, *Under Empire: Muslim Lives and Loyalties Across the Indian Ocean World, 1775–1945*
>
> Eva-Maria Muschik, *Building States: The United Nations, Development, and Decolonization, 1945–1965*
>
> Jessica Namakkal, *Unsettling Utopia: The Making and Unmaking of French India*
>
> Michael Christopher Low, *Imperial Mecca: Ottoman Arabia and the Indian Ocean Hajj*

For a complete list of books in the series, please see the Columbia University Press website.

Feasting on History

Ethiopia and the Orientalists

JAMES DE LORENZI

Columbia

University

Press

New York

Columbia University Press
Publishers Since 1893
New York   Chichester, West Sussex
cup.columbia.edu

Copyright © 2025 Columbia University Press
All rights reserved

Library of Congress Cataloging-in-Publication Data
Names: De Lorenzi, James author
Title: Feasting on history : Ethiopia and the Orientalists / James De Lorenzi.
Other titles: Ethiopia and the Orientalists
Description: New York : Columbia University Press, [2025] |
Series: Columbia studies in international and global history |
   Includes bibliographical references and index.
Identifiers: LCCN 2024057441 | ISBN 9780231217750 hardback |
   ISBN 9780231217767 trade paperback | ISBN 9780231217774 ebook
Subjects: LCSH: Ethiopia—Relations—Italy | Italy—Relations—Ethiopia |
   Cerulli, Enrico | Heruy Walda Sellase, 1878-1938 | Ethiopia—Politics and
   government—20th century | Italy—Politics and government—20th century |
   Ethiopia—Intellectual life—20th century | Italy—Intellectual life—
   20th century | Ethiopia—Historiography | Italian East Africa
Classification: LCC DT382.5.I8 D45 2025 | DDC 963/.05—dc23/eng/20250328
LC record available at https://lccn.loc.gov/2024057441

Cover design: Milenda Nan Ok Lee
Cover image: *Tipografia "Corriere Impero" (edizione amarica)*. Biblioteca
Nazionale Centrale 'Vittorio Emanuele II' di Roma.

GPSR Authorized Representative: Easy Access System Europe,
Mustamäe tee 50, 10621 Tallinn, Estonia, gpsr.requests@easproject.com

Dedicated to Abebe Ambatchew

Contents

Acknowledgments ix

Introduction 1

Part I: Feasts of History
 1 The Power of Tradition 15
 2 Mysterious Magic 34
 3 Reading Philology in Addis Ababa 54

Part II: Imperial Andromeda
 4 Ferragosto 77
 5 Mäskäräm 94
 6 "Cerulli and His Ilk" 114

Part III: Years of Hardship
 7 The Chronicler of Asinara 141
 8 Survival in Shäwa 167
 9 Bath and Dhanaane 198

Part IV: Dead Reckoning

10 Case 7887   217

11 Field Operations   247

Conclusion   277

Glossary   287
Transliteration and Dates   291
List of Abbreviations   293
Notes   297
Bibliography   395
Index   435

Acknowledgments

This book has created many debts. I hope to repay them by following the generous example of those who helped me.

Innumerable colleagues shaped this project over the past decade. I am especially grateful to those who read some or all of what became this book, and I thank the following for their time and work: Ruth Iyob, Abebe Ambatchew, Matteo Salvadore, Shiferaw Bekele, Francesca Orsini, Alessandro Triulzi, Brian Yates, Shimelis Bonsa Gulema, Mary Gibson, Elleni Centime Zelleke, Lee Cassanelli, Xerxes Malki, Noelle Turtur, Nicolas Virtue, and Wen-Wei Lai. I was fortunate to receive valuable comments from two readers through Columbia University Press, who challenged me to sharpen, deepen, and restructure my arguments. I also learned much by discussing this project with a series of perceptive and critical audiences. In New York City, I thank the participants in the 2019 Ifriqiyya Colloquium at Columbia University, especially Mahmood Mamdani, Elleni Centime Zelleke, Shimelis Bonsa Gulema, Mamadou Diallo, and Manan Ahmed Asif. In New Delhi, I thank the participants in the 2017 SOAS-Raza Foundation MULOSIGE workshop, especially Sara Marzagora, Shiferaw Bekele, Uoldelul Chelati Dirar, Francesca Orsini, Karima Laachir, Kumkum Sangari, Khalid Zekri, and Sadhana Naithani. I began this project in earnest during a 2016 summer fellowship at the School for Advanced Research at Santa Fe, where I enjoyed many illuminating conversations with Hoda Bandeh-Ahmadi.

A large number of other colleagues shared insights in conversation, correspondence, and brief comments, often taking my research in new directions. More than a few shared useful documents. Among many, I especially thank Bairu Tafla, Christopher Clapham, Christopher Ehret, *abba* Daniel Assefa, Bertie Pearson, David Rifkind, Deresse Ayenachew Woldetsadik, Gail Hansberry, Ian Campbell, Nicola Camilleri, Donald Crummey, Fenta Tiruneh, Gebru Tareke, Getatchew Haile, Tim Carmichael, Herbert Lewis, Hiwot Teffera, Irma Taddia, Jakob Zollman, John Farago, Hugh Williamson, John Henry, Bereket Habte Selassie, Karin Spencer, Katrin Bromber, Claudia Launhardt, Lacey Feigh, Massimo Zaccaria, Abdi Ismail Samatar, Sydney Silverstein, Salome Gebre Egziabeher, Tewodros Abebe, and Elizabeth Wolde Giorgis. Looking back to graduate school, early conversations with Jonathan Steinberg, Teshale Tibebu, and Richard Pankhurst addressed questions that later proved central to this book.

The research underpinning this project was made possible by my research collaborators. They were willing to discuss family histories, share personal documents and photos, and consider my questions about topics that were often painful and complex. I could not have completed this book without the conversations and hospitality of Abebe Ambatchew, Terrefe Ras Work, Shimelis Yilma, Mulugeta Wodajo, *liqä kahenat* Qalä Heywät, Aklilu Habte, Levon Djerrahian, and Tadesse Ambatchew. I hope this book validates their trust.

My research was also facilitated by many archivist and librarian colleagues. In particular, I thank the staff of the Archivio Centrale dello Stato (Rome), the Archivio Storico del Ministero degli Affari Esteri (Rome), the Institute of Ethiopian Studies (Addis Ababa), the Evangeliska Fosterlands-Stiftelsen Arkiv (Uppsala), the United Nations Archives (New York City), the Brooklyn College Library (New York City), the Library of Congress (Washington, DC), the Hill Monastic Manuscript Library (Collegeville), and the Wolfsonian Library (Miami). My colleague Karen Okamoto of the John Jay College Library tenaciously located many hard-to-find interlibrary loan items. Funding for this research was provided by the Professional Staff Congress–CUNY, the American Philosophical Society, the School for Advanced Research, and the Office for the Advancement of Research at John Jay College.

Many other people supported this project in intangible ways. In Addis Ababa, I thank Munir Jemal and family, Levon Djerrahian, Terrefe Ras Work,

Yitateku Nega, and Hailu Gebrehiwot. In Ankober, I thank the communities of Qeddus Täklä Haymanot, Mädhané Aläm, and the Ras Work Memorial School. In Rome, I thank Alessandro Triulzi and Paola Splendore. In New York City, I thank Edward Paulino, Xerxes Malki, Barbara Josiah, Anissa Hélie, Hyunhee Park, Dehne Ambatchew, Dara Byrne, Musabika Nabiha, Esha Adnan, Daniel Melendez, Danny Farran, Asma Sajid, Fernando Aguilera, Sierra Stoneman-Bell, Anthony Matteo, Theresa Marchetta, Karen Rattan-Achong, and Chanel Nuñez. My extended family always provided support and encouragement in Toronto, Albuquerque, Gibsonia, and London. At home, my partner Jennifer Maloy and children Bruno and Albert are always sources of encouragement, affection, and joy, and they were committed to helping me find time for this work despite our busy lives. I could not have done it without you. My late father Albert is my example.

Three people shaped this book more than any other. Ermias Zemichael spent many hours reviewing, discussing, and correcting my translations, bringing to our conversations the rigor of an editor, the patience of a teacher, and the enthusiasm of a co-conspirator. Ruth Iyob encouraged me from beginning to end, through many queries, drafts, calls, and texts. I hope this book does justice to her steady mentorship and formidable critical sensibility. Finally, Abebe Ambatchew transformed the scope of this project. We met improbably, and after realizing we were neighbors in Queens, we spent many Sundays together in conversation, discussing history, current events, and his life and family. He graciously introduced me to people he thought could help my research, methodically investigated my questions, shared and explained illuminating family documents, and commented on my early drafts. He continuously challenged and redirected my thinking, and was supremely generous with his time, erudition, and wit. He did not live to see the completion of this book, but it is dedicated to his memory.

Feasting on History

Introduction

It was August 2, 1928, in the rainy season. The occasion was the signing of the Italo-Ethiopian Treaty of Friendship, the product of years of tense negotiation, and the setting was the Italian Legation of Addis Ababa, a rough neoclassical villa that radiated imperial influence across the Horn of Africa. Among the gathered elite were Crown Prince Täfäri Mäkonnen, an aristocratic reformer who would in two years become Emperor Haylä Sellasé; Minister of War Mulugéta Yeggäzu, an august veteran of the Battle of Adwa; Minister Plenipotentiary Giuliano Cora, a specialist in Ethiopian diplomacy; and physician Edoardo Borra, a key interlocutor in Italo-Ethiopian relations. The atmosphere was triumphant. While the accord was a major achievement, it had very nearly failed. Broadly, this was because it confronted the historic antagonism between the Ethiopians and their erstwhile colonizers, who viewed each other through their respective memories of the 1896 Italian defeat at Adwa. But this old dynamic also underpinned new conflicts. On one side, the outward-looking Täfäri Mäkonnen challenged a cohort of isolationist Ethiopian elites allied to the reigning Empress Zäwditu, and on the other, the détente-minded Cora confronted senior regime officials who aimed to destabilize Ethiopia by fomenting dynastic intrigue, seeking fascist victory through liberal failure. The negotiations were forced to navigate these interlocking tensions, and Täfäri Mäkonnen and Cora—the self-imagined progressives—emerged the victors.¹

Their success proved fleeting, as suggested by the discordant press coverage that summer. The normally effusive *Berhanenna sälam*, Ethiopia's state-run Amharic newspaper, contained nothing about the agreement, and observers among the Addis Ababa intelligentsia scarcely noted the occasion in their private annals.² Meanwhile, the bombastic *Italia coloniale* celebrated the effectiveness of Mussolini's foreign policy after years of African stalemate, while *Corriere della sera* lauded its decisive advance of the Italian colonial endeavor.³ Despite these accolades, saboteurs in the Roman ministries immediately undercut the treaty, and the following month, Täfäri Mäkonnen deflected a coup by *däjjazmach* Weqaw Berru, a partisan of Zäwditu and the conservative opposition.⁴ Within a decade, the eviscerated agreement became an emblem of failed internationalism. In 1935, on the eve of the Italian invasion of Ethiopia, Baron Pompeo Aloisi decried Haylä Sellasé's betrayal of the accord before the Genevan press corps, and the following year, the emperor condemned its bad faith in his historic address to the League of Nations. The entire affair was a sequel and harbinger of past and future conflicts.

A photo of the 1928 gathering reveals two additional figures present that day, standing discreetly in the second row (figure 0.1). One of these was *blatta* Heruy Wäldä Sellasé, the director of the Ministry of Foreign Affairs, an advisor to the crown prince, and a distinguished member of the Ethiopian literati. He was most recently the author of a synoptic institutional history of his country and the editor of a massive anthology of Ge'ez and Amharic poetry.⁵ The other figure was Enrico Cerulli, a Legation employee and budding Orientalist whose interests ranged from history, ethnology, and folklore to philology, bibliography, and Semitic and Cushitic linguistics. Both men were counselors to the political elite, experts in international affairs, and leaders in their intellectual fields, and for this reason they jointly supervised the delicate matter of the agreement's Amharic translation, hoping to avoid the linguistic duplicity that had provoked the Adwa debacle.⁶ According to Cora, it was Cerulli who produced most of the final text, both because of his attention to detail and because Heruy rejected the proposals of his own delegation.⁷ Amid the high politics of the day, the act of joint translation was an interlude of linguistic and intertextual erudition.

FIGURE 0.1 Signing ceremony of the Italo-Ethiopian Treaty of Friendship, Addis Ababa (1928).

The Addis Ababa meeting was a portent of Heruy and Cerulli's intertwined futures. In the decade after 1928, the political and military contest that engulfed their governments enlisted them as statesmen and engaged intellectuals, and in the process, they became adversaries on the international stage. They sparred in scholarly publications, waged a public war of words at the League of Nations, and ultimately faced each other as negotiators and finally foes on the colonial frontlines, where Cerulli supervised the counterinsurgency in Ethiopia as Heruy organized the anticolonial resistance in exile. At the apex of the colonial bureaucracy in Rome and Addis Ababa, Cerulli ultimately oversaw the detention of his adversary's family and the devastation of his ancestral home. After the liberation of Ethiopia in 1941, by which time Heruy was dead, their connection endured through a series of contentious legal, political, and intellectual confrontations with Cerulli's colonial past, in part spurred by Heruy's wartime demand for justice with respect to Italian atrocities in Ethiopia. Their meeting on the Legation steps was the first act in this extended engagement across the overlapping worlds of power and learning—across the political and epistemic regimes of empire. This sinuous history of expert struggle is the subject of this book.

Weaponizing Knowledge

This confrontation richly epitomizes the colonial politics of expertise. In the decades since Edward Said's influential studies of Orientalism, researchers in a range of fields have scrutinized the manifold links between state policy and academic research, challenging disciplinary self-definitions rooted in objectivity and scientific impartiality by pointing to the political dimensions of Western representations of the wider world.[8] Some have attacked Said's arguments, and especially his perceived methodological and analytic shortcomings.[9] Others have historicized the emergence, operation, and institutionalization of specific Orientalist schools: on the one hand, this has involved the examination of individual scholars, national traditions, and their distinctive representational politics;[10] on the other, it has led to an appreciation of Orientalism's early modern roots, most notably in the Vatican-sponsored fields of *philologia sacra* and Catholic Indology.[11] Still other researchers have considered the mediated nature of Western knowledge of the wider world, reconstructing the foundational contributions of African and Asian intellectuals to Western scholarship.[12] Most recently, a few have attacked the scope of Said's analysis, arguing that the core failings of the Orientalist project underpin most academic knowledge.[13] Parallel research has critically examined the history of anthropology and sociology,[14] and collectively, this work has deepened and complicated our understanding of the genealogy of Orientalism and its adjacent disciplines.

An emerging theme is the reception of academic knowledge within traditional domains of learning.[15] Recent scholarship has reconstructed contacts between Orientalists and intellectuals from the putative Orient, who occasionally visited European research centers and evaluated Western representations of their home societies. These nineteenth- and early twentieth-century encounters varied considerably. Some proved amicable and even dialectical in an intellectually generative sense, particularly with respect to those Muslim and Arab scholars who viewed Orientalist research as an instrument for furthering the Islamic sciences and Arabic literary revival.[16] Other contacts proved contentious and adversarial. Surveyed collectively, the anti-Orientalist critiques of learned interlopers like Jamal ad-Din al-Afghani, Rifa'a at-Tahtawi, and Ahmad Faris al-Shidyaq suggest several key themes. First, these scholars rejected the tyranny of philology, as Tarek El-Ariss puts it, defending exegetic and salvific traditions of textual analysis and contesting the heuristic supremacy of disenchanted secular humanist categories.[17] Second, they fused inherited analytic tools with new ideas culled from Western literature and philosophy, inaugurating the modern critical position conventionally associated with later generations of academics. Third, they decried institutional restrictions on the circulation of texts as patrimonial colonialism and commodified heritage. Finally, they attacked the linguistic skills of some of their Orientalist counterparts, contesting the rigor of a field that validated knowledge based on shaky foundations. Research into these traditionalist responses complements recent studies of heterodox modes of Orientalist inquiry. Exemplars of this countervailing tendency include Ignaz Goldziher, Louis Massignon, Jean-Mohammed Abdeljalil, and René Guénon, who rejected the secular study of Islam and embraced "anagogical meaning" and religious conversion as avenues to authentic understanding.[18] All these cases historicize the academic critique of Orientalism, introducing vernacular, traditionalist, and dissident positions beyond disciplinary conventions.

Parallel research has scrutinized the internationalization of expert power—a process that was similarly predicated on monopoly, exclusion, and conflict.[19] The institutional wellspring of this development was the Western academy, whose members worked in distinct national and disciplinary traditions as they contributed to their international fields. Until the postcolonial era, this was a realm that largely excluded African and Asian intellectuals, whether the latter worked in traditional domains of learning or bore credentials from modern universities. Beyond the academy were the intra- and extragovernmental forums of the League of Nations and United Nations, which further institutionalized expert power within the persona of the international specialist. Both bodies drew on professional experts through their bureaucracies and advisory groups, from the committees of the League and UN secretariats to the United Nations Educational, Scientific, and Cultural Organization (UNESCO) and the United Nations Human Rights Commission (UNHRC).[20] League and UN member states also employed experts in their delegations, and both bodies faced interventions by external actors whose advocacy hinged on professional claims of disinterested specialist arbitrage.[21] These developments routinized a new kind of expert power and authority legitimized as rational, technocratic, and supranational, though it was in fact intensely competitive, conflictual, and transactional.

This power and authority was intertwined with empire. This link is most evident in the instrumentalization of academic inquiry, from the anthropological and sociological works that shaped, validated, and critiqued late colonial policy to the area studies research that informed strategic planning during the Cold War and Global War on Terror.[22] International fascism developed a corollary framework of applied colonial science.[23] The now-considerable literature on these topics has reached varying conclusions about the nature, extent, and significance of this instrumentalization.[24] Within the international system, the colonial politics of expertise are manifest in the shared liberal imperial architecture of the League and United Nations,[25] most notably the League's Permanent Mandates Commission, which claimed to be liberalizing colonial rule through supranational management, and the UN Trusteeship Council,[26] which continued this supervised developmental project in a more technocratic and accountable form.[27] Both the League and the UN also addressed colonial questions in dialogue with outside experts and consultants: European academics intervened in League debates about trusteeship and settler power,[28] the National Association for the Advancement of Colored People (NAACP) advocated for the human rights of colonized peoples worldwide,[29] and African academics oversaw a collective effort to decolonize specialist research through the antiracist UNESCO General History of Africa project.[30] During an era in which the international system turned on the defense and dismantling of empire, it is unsurprising that experts routinely addressed imperial questions on the international stage, and that they often possessed colonial or anticolonial commitments.

This book unites these overlapping lines of inquiry through the framework of counterinsurgency. Moving beyond the intellectual history of Orientalism and the politics of cultural representation, it scrutinizes the bodily and epistemic violence perpetrated by producers of applied knowledge in militarized colonial situations.[31] Although counterinsurgency is typically understood as a strategic doctrine governing asymmetric and unconventional warfare, it is also fruitfully conceptualized as a late colonial repertoire predicated on mass surveillance, detention, and extrajudicial violence.[32] This distinctive politico-military framework of rule emerged alongside metropolitan militarized policing,[33] and proliferated over the twentieth century as counterinsurgencies and "emergencies" were declared across the imperial world—from the Philippines to Vietnam, Palestine, Malaysia, Algeria, Kenya, Malawi, and Zimbabwe.[34] While each of these cases reflected a distinctive interplay of local specificities and contingent imperial dynamics, they shared a governmentality predicated on population control, collective punishment, psychological warfare, intensive intelligence gathering, and racial theories of behavior. With respect to international law, their unabashed escalation of mass violence and dislocation was legitimized as a colonial exception to liberal norms, specifically with respect to the laws of war, universal human rights, and interstate relations.[35] This exceptionality rested on the premise that colonial counterinsurgencies were not armed conflicts but domestic emergencies, civil disturbances, or simply *événements*, since the designated enemy was not a conventional combatant but a racially inferior criminal or terrorist.[36]

In all these aspects, the counterinsurgent colonial state weaponized specialist knowledge.[37] As a theoretically rationalized, technocratic, and humane framework of colonial rule, its development coincided with the institutionalization of expert power, and its military, police, and civilian agents routinely mobilized academic research to the needs of military planning, colonial policy, and information warfare. In some cases, these agents were themselves knowledge producers. This deployed specialist work can be characterized as dual-use research, following David Price.[38] The linguistic surveys, local histories, press commentaries, development reports, and basic descriptive studies of Africa- and Asia-focused Orientalists, anthropologists, sociologists, and area specialists mapped human terrain that was vital to colonial rule, irrespective of the researchers' intentions with respect to the applied implications of their work. In the context of the panoptic surveillance and classificatory systems undergirding counterinsurgent colonial states, their fieldwork, publications, and command of language had potentially traumatic consequences for their research subjects.[39] Put simply, expertise frequently underpinned the exertion of the sovereign right to kill.[40]

This book offers a microhistorical case study of colonial and anticolonial expert conflict, one that unfolds on the frontlines of the Italian counterinsurgency in Ethiopia, across the evolving institutions of the international system, and within the interlinked intellectual arenas of Europe, Africa, the African diaspora, and the Third World. Bringing together intellectual, imperial, and international history, it offers a case study of the relationship between academic research, colonial rule, and structural genocide. Specifically, this book contends that Cerulli's long career epitomized the deep connections between imperial and expert power. He was a career agent of the Italian colonial state, and his scholarship exemplified the counterinsurgent power of dual-use research. He produced countless studies with practical utility for diplomacy, intelligence operations, military planning, and colonial administration, and he published overt and covert defenses of the colonial enterprise, even decades after its demise. In a striking institutional manifestation of these interlinked activities, his remit at the Ministry of Italian Africa in the 1930s included the Office of Political Affairs, which oversaw colonial policy and intelligence; the Scientific Section of the Research Office, which sponsored academic conferences and publications on colonial topics; and the interministerial management of the detention regime of Africa Orientale Italiana, which incarcerated and surveilled thousands of Ethiopians, Eritreans, and Somalis at remote sites across Italy and the Horn of Africa. In a host of settings, Cerulli used his academic training, linguistic skill, field experience, and intellectual prestige to shape colonial policy and speak for Ethiopia. He did so not as an engaged advocate or sympathetic interpreter of the "native," assuming the roles envisioned by his specialist contemporaries Michel Leiris, Georges Balandier, or Bronislaw Malinowski, but as an agent of the colonial endeavor dedicated to the explication of African deficiency and the repression of African dissent.[41] This dual orientation was the defining feature of his professional identity: he was a "proconsul and scholar," as his colleague Edward Ullendorff once put it.[42] Cerulli was an unrepentant paragon of empire and its duress.[43]

This book also reconstructs the Ethiopian critique of colonial knowledge. This counterattack was both intellectual and political, as befit Cerulli's dual roles, and it was advanced in multiple languages and institutional settings. It began in the years before the Italian invasion with the epistemic commentary of Heruy and other Ethiopian intellectuals, continued after the 1941 liberation with the legal and political denunciations of Aklilu Habtäwäld, Ethiopia's foreign minister and eventual prime minister, and ultimately concluded with the moral-intellectual charges of leading figures in the postcolonial African academy, most notably the Senegalese historian Cheikh Anta Diop. Though these arguments first emanated from Ethiopian civil society, they achieved their international apogee at the 1948 hearings of the United Nations War Crimes Commission (UNWCC), which endorsed the indictment of Cerulli for war crimes and crimes against humanity. This judgment provoked a series of explosive confrontations with his colonial past in the academic fields of Ethiopian and African studies, spanning international specialist congresses to the research institutions of postcolonial Ethiopia and the advisory commissions of UNESCO. This collective and sustained Ethiopian critique of Cerulli—and by extension, the expert-dominated international system that had repeatedly undermined Ethiopian sovereignty—was a pioneering African and Third World effort to decolonize the academy and international human rights.[44]

Structured Silences

The expert mobilized the power of speech. But this book is also about the valences of silence, and specifically the manifold ways the colonial archive and disciplinary knowledge can mute discordant conceptions of the past, as Michel-Rolph Trouillot put it.[45] Most enveloping are the ontological silences enforced by the Italian archives, which replicate the analytic categories of the colonial state by reducing Ethiopians and other Africans to the singular roles of loyal collaborators, dangerous intellectuals, exiled criminals, detained militants, and targeted insurgents. The shifting politics of the fascist regime conditioned these designations. But there are other silences beyond the colonial archive. The mutually reinforcing exonerative impulses of the international system and liberal academy with respect to colonial violence effaced the mass trauma preserved in Ethiopians' collective memory and historical record. The experts that populated these same spaces frequently silenced Ethiopians as advocates, authors, and researchers, converting them into informants and their work into primary sources stripped of intellectual rigor and creativity. At times, the experts themselves became mute. They adopted pseudonyms or anonymity when advancing illiberal, impolitic, and undisciplinary positions, and they occasionally retreated into secrecy when faced with critiques of bad faith. Ultimately, Heruy refused to address Cerulli, instead choosing to step into the shadows of their discursive relationship.[46] Meanwhile, the professional specialist field has largely ignored Cerulli's criminal past, such that today he is remembered as a distinguished scholar of the Horn of Africa and greater Mediterranean, and even as an exemplar of philological political innocence.[47] His involvement in colonial atrocities and unprecedented international legal sanction have been effaced from the historical record, in a specialist parallel to the structured silence that conditions the memory of colonialism in contemporary Italy.[48] This book attempts to explore these silences, filling the lacunae of the archives with oral testimony, vernacular historiography, and other materials. In this undertaking, I am indebted to my research collaborators, who showed me these silences, helped me begin to understand them, and pushed me to return to the archives with new questions to address them.

This book also maintains its own silences. It is not a systematic study of Cerulli's immense oeuvre, which remains foundational to multiple academic fields.[49] I have instead restricted my analysis to Cerulli's political career and its archival as well as academic record, rejecting the premise that these can be disentangled or isolated. A fuller evaluation of Cerulli's scholarship might complicate my analysis of his research politics. Another lacuna involves Cerulli's political and intellectual significance to communities in the Horn of Africa outside historic Shäwa. In particular, I have not examined his legacy among the Somali, Oromo, and Harari, or the peoples of southwest Ethiopia. This neglect is complicated by Cerulli's complex relationship to the discourses of ethnic grievance and minority rights advanced by some of these groups, both in the past and present. A systematic evaluation of this intellectual genealogy awaits further study, and my limited treatment of these topics is not a comment on the validity of these discourses. Instead, I have focused on events in Shäwa because of their centrality to the legal case against Cerulli. A final limitation of this book is its incomplete examination of the Ethiopian reception of Orientalism, which neither began nor ended with Heruy and his contemporaries.[50] Though their critique was chiefly addressed to early twentieth-century Ethiopian readers, it is also a valuable warning to present-day researchers.[51] It inspired this project.

Outline of Argument

Eleven chapters follow. Part I reconstructs the intellectual context of the 1928 Legation encounter. It examines the early biographies of Heruy and Cerulli, their antagonistic visions of Ethiopia as a sociohistorical subject, and their multilingual polemic across the divided fields of vernacular Ethiopian scholarship, on the one hand, and Italian Orientalist letters, on the other. The crux of this dispute was a series of claims and counterclaims about the nature of expertise, the constitution of historical knowledge of Ethiopia, the documentary regime that could best steward its textual patrimony, and the role of authorship in knowledge production. I argue that this debate and its ensuing elaboration in the Ethiopian public sphere reveal diverging conceptions of scholarship as a shared and culturally situated collaborative endeavor, on the one hand, and a competitive and commodified academic field, on the other. For Heruy, rigorous historical research was akin to a religious feast; for Cerulli, it was a positivist etic exercise. The remainder of this book applies these two models as theories of paradigms.[52]

Part II examines the intellectual history of the 1935–1936 Italo-Ethiopian crisis. Now at the vertices of state power, Heruy and Cerulli continued their earlier dispute through the international confrontation of their governments at the League of Nations. As the world watched, they and their proxies in Geneva engaged in a multistage memoranda war that situated the politico-diplomatic crisis in antagonistic models of modern Ethiopian history and ethnic politics, in the process translating vernacular and academic knowledge into the international languages of liberal imperialism, interventionist humanitarianism, race science, cultural relativism, and anticolonial liberation. Their public debate about African sovereignty, Italian fascism, and the global color line enlisted the nascent academic field of Ethiopian studies, provoking interventions by leading Italian Ethiopianists, their Ethiopian and Eritrean allies, and their Marxist and pan-Africanist antagonists. These events reified the international authority of the Africanist.

Part III scrutinizes the counterinsurgency in Africa Orientale Italiana, focusing on the experiences of a group of displaced Ethiopian intellectuals and their families. Juxtaposing the colonial archive with the oral history of trauma, it reconstructs the violence of the war of occupation across the Ethiopian highlands and Italian metropole.[53] The modalities of this routinized violence encompassed dislocation, detention, torture, hostage taking, sexual assault, and mass killing. Specifically, this section documents Cerulli's role as an architect, agent, and arbiter of the counterinsurgency in Ethiopia, first through his intelligence work at the Ministry of Italian Africa in Rome, and subsequently via his role as vice governor general and viceregal regent in Addis Ababa. In these senior regime positions, he applied his years of research to the evolving problems of militarized colonial rule, directly involving himself in events later classified as war crimes and crimes against humanity. These atrocities reached his former adversary Heruy, who negotiated with Cerulli and demanded justice from the international system even as his own family disappeared into detention and oblivion. Among the dead were his eldest son and infant granddaughter.

Part IV outlines the inconclusive reckoning with these years of hardship, across several intertwined trajectories through the era of decolonization. It first considers the Ethiopian government's nearly derailed UNWCC process, which after a series of transparently politicized judgments determined that Cerulli was a suspected war criminal. This decision was an unprecedented application of international law to specifically colonial crimes, notable in particular for its use of the emerging concept of genocide to describe European violence in Africa. It then examines the aftermath of these events on the international stage, culminating in Cerulli's public rejection of victor's justice, his own colonial guilt, and the concept of war crimes. This defiant auto-exoneration coincided with Cerulli's ascent to the apex of his professional stature in the international academy, which sanitized his fascist and colonial career. But this professional eminence soon collided with his past. Ethiopian intellectuals raised the issue of Cerulli's criminal acts in various international and Third World fora, from academic congresses and prize committees to the UN General Assembly and UNESCO, and it ultimately surfaced within his own scholarship, which used Heruy's writings to relitigate fascist-era debates about the morality of mass killing. In this, Cerulli sought absolution through the silence of the dead.

The conclusion recapitulates the argument in the context of alternative conceptions of expertise, juxtaposing Cerulli's political and intellectual choices with those of his American contemporary William Leo Hansberry.

PART I
Feasts of History

1
The Power of Tradition

The military hospital in Naples was an unlikely crucible of Orientalist fascination. Set on an escarpment above the Quartieri Spagnoli, it occupied the immense seventeenth-century complex known as Santissima Trinità delle Monache, which was for nearly two hundred years one of the largest and most imposing monasteries in the city. During the French occupation of 1806–1815, Joseph Bonaparte converted the building and its walled grounds into a military hospital, and after the 1815 Bourbon restoration, the complex retained this function while gradually falling into a state of disrepair. The hospital had become a palimpsest of state power (figure 1.1). By the early twentieth century, it served as a treatment center for veterans of Italy's colonial wars, and in 1914, many of its patients were Eritrean, Ethiopian, and Somali conscripts wounded in the ongoing invasion of Libya.

As some of these African *askaris* convalesced in the hospital wards and arcades, they were approached by a curious interlocutor: a sixteen-year-old Neapolitan boy who spoke Amharic, Oromo, Somali, and Maghrebi Arabic. Enrico Cerulli was then attending the University of Naples as well as the nearby Regio Istituto Orientale, the oldest institution of its kind in Europe, and in the recollection of his former professor Giorgio Levi Della Vida, the precocious student routinely visited the hospital to collect the veterans' testimony in "four or five languages."[1] His research collaborators

FIGURE 1.1 Ex-Military Hospital, Naples.

Source: Author's photo.

included Sängal Wärqenäh of Hamasén, a former colonial interpreter who taught Amharic and Tigrinya at the Istituto Orientale, as well as Agha Muhammad Sa'id of Wälläga and Loränsiyos Wäldä Iyäsus of Shäwa,[2] two injured soldiers whose knowledge of Oromo orature was so expansive that their testimony eventually filled a book.³ These interviews with displaced colonial veterans, or *mutilati*, began Cerulli's lifelong effort to document the historical cultures of the Horn of Africa, now localized through the circuits of empire and the bodily trauma of conquest. By 1919, when he decamped for Somalia, he had already published three academic articles based on his fieldwork in Naples.⁴

That same year, Heruy Wäldä Sellasé arrived in Washington. His path to the White House from the mountains of Shäwa was extraordinary. Educated at Enṭoṭṭo overlooking Addis Ababa, Heruy mastered several fields of Orthodox Christian learning as well as Amharic, Ge'ez, Arabic, French, and English, and by thirty, he was a key intermediary in his government's diplomatic engagement with the wider world. In 1911, he attended the coronation of George V in London, stopping afterward at the libraries of Oxford,⁵ and in 1919, he joined a delegation to the postwar settlement in Paris,⁶ supporting *käntiba* Gäbru Dästa and *däjjazmach* Naddäw Abba Wällo, whose fearsome nom de guerre was *abba* Mäbräq, or "Father of Lightning."⁷ In the French capital, the Ethiopians found themselves excluded from the negotiations, and their queries about the nascent League of Nations proved fruitless.⁸ Undaunted, they proceeded on to London, New York City, and Washington, where President Woodrow Wilson accepted their congratulations on the Allied victory.⁹ Newspapers across the country featured photos and accounts of the unprecedented summit.

The official fanfare was encouraging, but the mood changed when the group returned to New York City. They arrived amid the racialized violence of the "Red Summer," which saw vigilante and police attacks on Black communities across the country.¹⁰ After meeting the mayor, sailing the Hudson River, and visiting Coney Island, the Ethiopians' farewell dinner at the National Democratic Club was canceled when a member discovered the guests of honor were African.¹¹ The delegation instead proceeded to Harlem's Metropolitan Baptist Church, where they were enthusiastically received by the congregation.¹² Reverend W. W. Brown welcomed the guests on behalf of "black folk throughout America," and Heruy commended the audience for "the wonderful progress Africans have made in this country," urging them to always remember Ethiopia.¹³ Weeks later, W. E. B. Du Bois honored this supplication by featuring Heruy's photo in *The Crisis*, the NAACP monthly (figure 1.2).¹⁴ By then, the Ethiopians were returning home. As they crossed the Atlantic, Heruy surely reflected on the significance of

FIGURE 1.2 Heruy Wäldä Sellasé (*right*), New York City (1919).

his international odyssey.[15] The mission had taken him beyond his training as a *liq*, or church scholar, propelling him into a new role as a public intellectual, counselor to the political elite, and authority on the liberal world order. He had become a student of the modern predicament, and would dedicate the rest of his life to imagining Ethiopia's future beyond the Western-facing locus of empire.[16] In this, he refused to "pick crumbs like a beggar" from the banquet of the world, as he put it.[17] One aspect of his 1919 confrontation with the global color line proved especially instructive. That same year, Du Bois joined Ho Chi Minh and Faysal al-Hashemi in Paris seeking the Wilsonian promise of self-determination, only to discover that they too were denied their promised seat at the table.[18]

These were formative encounters. Cerulli and Heruy spent the next two decades as statesmen and engaged intellectuals, and this conjuncture shaped their research as well as their conceptions of knowledge and its production. For Cerulli, scholarship was an extractive etic enterprise through which alien cultural traditions could be rigorously documented, translated, and published, using secular disciplinary tools to comprehend and critique the African subject. In the process, the foreign expert became an interpreter of the inscrutable, and the exotic text a prestigious academic commodity. For Heruy, in contrast, scholarship was a salvific, dialogic, and culturally situated undertaking through which trained specialists elucidated socially meaningful problems using the evolved apparatus of tradition. The goal was service to Ethiopia and Ethiopians. Both writers translated the world and its texts, but in fundamentally different ways. For Cerulli, the pursuit of truth was a positivist competition;[19] for Heruy, it was a collective enterprise akin to a religious feast.

Taking this disjuncture as a starting point, the next three chapters explore the Ethiopian reception of Orientalism at the precise moment the latter generated its paradigmatic claims about the Ethiopian subject. Chapters 1 and 2 consider how Heruy and Cerulli developed new frameworks for understanding the Ethiopian past and future: Heruy elaborated a neotraditionalist historical imaginary rooted in preserved sovereignty and encompassing heritage, whereas Cerulli outlined a model of structured ethnic antagonism centered on the dialectic of "Abyssinian" colonizer and "Cushitic" subject. In the process, both reconceptualized the meaning of indigeneity. Chapter 3 reconstructs their multilingual dialogue concerning epistemic politics, which eventually spilled over into the Ethiopian public sphere. The central questions of this polemic involved the basis of specialist knowledge, the purpose of historical inquiry, the relationship between traditional scholarship and academic philology, and the documentary regime best suited to Ethiopia's textual patrimony. In juxtaposing generically disparate writings and spatially distant readers, these chapters explore the worldliness of texts, mapping the intertwined lives of Ethiopian texts in Europe and Orientalist texts in Ethiopia.[20] They consider how scholarship emerged from, circulated through, and intervened in specific institutional and sociocultural environments across Europe and the Horn of Africa, and additionally, how different publics envisioned these texts as cultural and political objects. These imbricated relationships expose the interplay between the cloistered and public lives of history, as Dipesh Chakrabarty terms it, documenting the dialogic pressure between specialist conclaves, the state, and wider domains of historical conversation.[21] This dynamic precisely anticipates the colonial and postcolonial politics of expertise.

Heruy Wäldä Sellasé is a singular figure in modern Ethiopian political and intellectual history.[22] He was born in 1878 near Märhabété, in the mountains of north Shäwa, and his parents Wäldä Sellasé and Wälättä Maryam christened him Gäbrä Mäsqäl. When he was still a child, his unlettered father helped prepare a feast at the nearby monastery of Dän Abbo, established by the local noblewoman and exiled former queen Bafäna Wäldä Mika'él. The abbot resented the presence of an illiterate commoner at the table, and his insults resolved Wäldä Sellasé to ensure his son would pursue a life of learning.[23] As Heruy later recalled, his father prayed, "If God gives me a son, I will send him away to the city for education, but I will not make him live in the countryside."[24] In fulfillment of this pledge, the young boy began a traditional church education at Dän Abbo, where he learned to read and write Amharic. With his father's guidance, he continued his studies at the nearby churches of Sellasé and Mädhané Aläm, where he mastered liturgical music and began advanced ecclesiastic training. After an intervening period of work as a farmer, deacon, and secretary in rural Shäwa, his thirst for learning finally brought him south to Enṭoṭṭo Qeddus Ragu'él.

Shrouded in clouds, the religious complex on Mount Enṭoṭṭo towers over Addis Ababa. The settlement was founded in the late nineteenth century by Emperor Menilek, who subjugated the local Oromo villages and established his imperial capital on the summit. His official biographer described this event as the fulfillment of a prophecy delivered to Emperor Lebnä Dengel nearly five hundred years before.[25] By the early twentieth century, the twin churches of Enṭoṭṭo Maryam and Enṭoṭṭo Qeddus Ragu'él had become preeminent centers of Orthodox Christian learning, supreme among the churches of Shäwa, and they trained many luminaries of the early-twentieth-century intellectual scene. The imperial family routinely hosted feasts at the sanctuaries, with the aid of a tram that linked the complex to the city below, and the widowed empress Ṭaytu Beṭul spent her final years in seclusion at the mountaintop.[26] Looking back, one alumnus described these years as the "golden age" of Enṭoṭṭo.[27] The settlement symbolized the power of tradition and the culture of power.

Heruy distinguished himself in this rarefied environment. Once established at Qeddus Ragu'él, he began advanced study with its *liqawent*, or church scholars, mastering Ge'ez as well as poetry and scriptural exegesis. His teachers included *mämher* Wäldä Giyorgis Habtä Maryam, a famed educator and expert on Gospel commentary who trained under *mämher* Wäldä Mika'él of Gondär.[28] While still a young man, the newcomer from

Märhabété undertook original translations of the Ge'ez scriptures and the Solomonid legal code,[29] and also studied English, French, and Arabic in the nearby capital, where he was hired as a translator by the British Foreign Bible Society (BFBS).[30] Among the *liqawent* of the mountaintop, his intellectual gifts were by this time judged so distinctive that he was rechristened Heruy, or "Precious," the name he maintained for the remainder of his life.

In 1908, the community introduced him to *neburä ed* Gäbrä Sellasé Wäldä Aregay, the head of Qeddus Ragu'él. He was among the most influential ecclesiastics in the country.[31] Born in Däbrä Berhan, he ascended through the church hierarchy to become a trusted advisor of Menilek, joining his military campaigns and serving from the 1870s as his court historian, or *ṣähafé te'ezaz*. Throughout this work of state, he remained a servant of the church, leading the religious community at Qeddus Ragu'él as well as that of Addis Aläm Maryam, near the summer palace west of Addis Ababa. In 1907, Menilek elevated Gäbrä Sellasé to the new office of minister of the pen, where he served as chief historian, managed the court secretaries, and supervised the first government press.[32] On meeting Heruy at Entoṭṭo, the new minister noted his intellect and brought him to the capital for an audience with Menilek.[33] The emperor commended the young man from Märhabété, and as a sign of confidence, Gäbrä Sellasé instructed Heruy to begin work on a printed anthology of Ge'ez poetry, the first of its kind.[34]

So it was that after years of church training, Heruy began a career in public service.[35] Shortly after his palace audience, he joined the 1911 delegation to the coronation of George V, serving as secretary and translator for the Shäwan aristocrat *däjjazmach* Kassa Haylu.[36] On their return, the latter's recommendation won Heruy the first of many government posts.[37] Over the next two decades, he served as chief director of the Addis Ababa municipality (1917–1921), chief judge of the extraterritorial court (1921–1925/1926), advisor of state (1925/1926–1929), and director of the Ministry of Foreign Affairs (1929–1931), along the way receiving the learned title *blatta*. Throughout this period, he led his government's engagement with the international system: he joined the 1919 delegation to Europe and the United States; served on *etégé* Mänän Asfaw's 1923 tour of the Levant; supported Täfäri Mäkonnen's 1924 mission to Europe; and attended the 1925 conference that established the Geneva Protocol. By this time, his name and photo routinely appeared in *A'emro* and *Berhanenna sälam*, the country's leading Amharic newspapers.[38] After Täfäri Mäkonnen's 1930 coronation as Emperor Haylä Sellasé, Heruy was promoted to foreign minister (1931–1939) and granted the learned title *blattén géta*, the highest state honor for scholars. Throughout these years, he and his wife Hamärä Eshäté lived in the capital with their six children.

It was during this period of professional ascent that Heruy produced the more than twenty books that secured his fame. By the mid-1920s, he had emerged as one of the most prolific and creative writers of his generation, both in terms of the scope of his intellectual interests and his dedication to the printed word. His greatest passion was historiography. He wrote dynastic histories, church histories, and intellectual histories, and he dabbled in book history and prosopography, or group history. He also produced the second Amharic novel, then considered an innovative genre of imaginative historical narration—literally, "history born from the heart."[39] As this last example suggests, much of his work elaborated the vernacular historical tradition in dialogue with Western literature and scholarship, in particular Ethiopia-focused historiography. His oeuvre was also distinctive in its popular and instructive purpose. Heruy wrote to edify the contemporary Ethiopian reader, and in this respect, his accessible and widely reprinted Amharic histories departed from the courtly and monastic traditions of manuscript Ge'ez historiography that had flourished over the preceding centuries.

Beyond history, Heruy was also a steward of the cultural patrimony. His first contributions to this endeavor were an Amharic digest of spiritual and moral instruction, which addressed his children as synecdoches of a young nation, and a monumental anthology of Ge'ez and Amharic poetry, which fulfilled the request of his former superior *ṣähafé te'ezaz* Gäbrä Sellasé.[40] In the mid-1920s, he also established a private press called Goha Ṣebah, or Light of Dawn, which aimed to uplift Ethiopian readers. In the estimation of his contemporary Mahtämä Sellasé Wäldä Mäsqäl, it supported "the fruit of learning, the progress of Western civilization, [and] the preparation of the scriptures," while additionally translating "books of learning written by the *liqawent* of foreign lands."[41] Goha Ṣebah rapidly became a leading institution of Ethiopian civil society, delivering Heruy's traditionalist syntheses alongside more eclectic works of Amharic literature, such as Ṗawlos Män Amäno's guide to the Holy Land and *aläqa* Zännäb's spiritual and philosophical reflections.[42] The press also supported a state-backed, *liqawent*-led initiative to produce new Amharic translations of the

Ge'ez Gospels and Acts of the Apostles, which appeared as bilingual Ge'ez and Amharic editions in an envisioned prelude to a complete Amharic Bible.[43] In an interconfessional twist, Heruy's press also printed individual editions of the rival and unsanctioned BFBS Amharic Gospels.[44]

A third pursuit was travel writing, a new genre of Amharic literature that fused Heruy's diplomatic and historical functions.[45] His first experiment was an account of *etégé* Mänan's 1923 visit to Egypt and Palestine, and over the next decade, he produced three more travelogues, all sumptuously illustrated.[46] These narrated Täfäri Mäkonnen's 1924 tour of the Levant and Europe,[47] his own 1931 journey to Japan,[48] and his 1934 travels in the Eastern Mediterranean.[49] He also wrote a practical guide for Ethiopian visitors to Europe filled with advice on passports, etiquette, and maritime travel; a moral and spiritual treatise that used travel and imaginative geography as instruments of self-discovery; and a novel that addressed the cultural dilemma of Ethiopians returned from Europe, set near his ancestral home in Märhabété.[50] As growing numbers of Ethiopians ventured abroad, and as local newspapers increasingly featured news of unfamiliar people and places, Heruy offered readers an authoritative armchair guide to the modern world, rendered in an accessible yet erudite vernacular voice.

Heruy used this representational project to address the challenges of modern Ethiopia. The intellectual creativity this entailed is exquisitely demonstrated by his lone account of Italy, a centerpiece of his 1924 European travelogue *Dästanna kebber*, or *Happiness and Honor*.[51] As historiography, this work is generically synthetic. On the one hand, it narrates Täfäri Mäkonnen's journey through Europe in the descriptive style of a vernacular chronicle, focusing on reportage, observed reality, and the chronological documentation of events. A photographer joined the group to visually commemorate this history. On the other hand, the work introduces macrohistorical and ethnological arguments through transcribed conversations and texts, interpolated references to scripture and literature, and explanations of unfamiliar beliefs, practices, and historical topics. In these respects, it resembles Heruy's other experiments with biographical and autobiographical travel writing, which were variant forms of instructive historiography. However, *Dästanna kebber* is distinguished by its unique concern with interrogating the Italo-Ethiopian relationship as an inchoate colonial situation, in all its complexity. Through the device of narrative juxtaposition, Heruy counterposes the predation of international diplomacy with the fortifying power of traditional knowledge. In the world of the text, his visit to Italy elucidated the politics of the Ethiopian present.

The trip itself was unprecedented. As the first overseas mission of a head of state, Täfäri Mäkonnen's 1924 tour was a milestone in Ethiopian statecraft.[52] For the crown prince and his reformist coterie, the mission instantiated a new foreign policy predicated on diplomatic and economic partnership, responding to the overtures that followed Ethiopia's 1923 admission to the League.[53] This internationalist turn was opposed by the reigning Empress Zäwditu, who led a conservative faction within the politico-imperial elite that endorsed isolationism and viewed the heir's departure from the country as potentially calamitous. In March 1924, these positions were evaluated by a conference of government ministers and advisors who endorsed the policy of the crown prince. Outmaneuvered, the empress publicly endorsed the tour alongside the most senior ecclesiastics in the country.[54] Ethiopia's would-be modern sovereign was poised to make his debut on the world stage.

His selected retinue was illustrious, albeit shaded by realpolitik.[55] The delegation included the aristocrats *le'ul ras* Seyyum Mängäsha of Tegray and *le'ul ras* Haylu Täklä Haymanot of Gojjam, among the most formidable challengers to Täfäri Mäkonnen's dynastic claim. They were joined by League delegate *ras* Naddäw Abba Wällo, the erstwhile head of the 1919 Washington embassy;[56] *däjjazmach* Haylä Sellasé Gugsa, the son-in-law of the crown prince; *däjjazmach* Mulugéta Yeggäzu, the future minister of war;[57] and *däjjazmach* Gäbrä Sellasé Baryagabber, an Adwa veteran who had briefly supported the Italian cause.[58] These politico-imperial elites were joined by the comparatively junior Heruy, who served as secretary and advisor to Täfäri Mäkonnen. The group was also accompanied by several minor notables, a team of interpreters, and a freight of gifts.

In April, the delegation left Addis Ababa for Djibouti. After two months visiting Palestine, Egypt, France, Belgium, and Sweden, they reached the Italian peninsula. They found its parliament in crisis. That April, Prime Minister Benito Mussolini and the National Fascist Party had triumphed in elections, winning by historic margins through a consensus-building accommodationist approach. In June, however, this victory was threatened when the socialist opposition leader Giacomo Matteotti denounced the legitimacy of the elections and was then kidnapped and murdered by fascist *squadristi*. The incompetence of Matteotti's killers quickly revealed that the execution had been condoned at the highest levels of the party, and likely by Mussolini. In the ensuing government crisis, popular support for the prime minister wavered until he consolidated his grip on power by outflanking the antifascist opposition, winning the Catholic Church, and placating liberals with an investigation into what he described as the act of militants. It was a critical moment in the history of fascism. In retrospect, these events are now viewed as inaugurating the shift toward regime dictatorship.[59]

The Ethiopians arrived at the apex of this crisis. On June 18, they reached Rome's Stazione Termini, where they were greeted by King Vittorio Emmanuele and an immense crowd.[60] Facing them across the piazza was the Dogali obelisk, the city's most prominent monument to Italian colonial martyrdom in Africa.[61] After stopping at the royal residence, they viewed a massive military parade and toured the cheering streets of the capital, a reception that foreshadowed the ensuing week of exhibitions, official visits, and champagne banquets. The itinerary included a stop at the Tomb of the Unknown Soldier, where Täfäri Mäkonnen genuflected at a monument to the Italian veterans of Adwa; an inspection of the industrial plants at nearby Terni, which included the largest armaments factory in the country; and a reception at the Palazzo della Consulta and its newly established colonial museum, home to a collection of artifacts from the Horn of Africa (figure 1.3).[62] At the last site, the Ethiopians were excitedly queried by a group of Italian Orientalists.[63] The delegation also viewed several military demonstrations, including a mechanized infantry parade at Centocelle airfield and a staged alpine operation near Lake Bracciano, northwest of Rome.[64] The latter demonstration was surely alarming: the terraced foothills, rolling plains, and verdant crater lakes of Lazio likely suggested the similar terrain encircling Addis Ababa, even if the peaks outside the Italian capital were less dramatic than their Shäwan counterparts. Finally, on June 24, the Ethiopians departed for La Spezia.[65] Years later, Heruy recalled the mass adoration of the Romans during the week and wondered, "When they think of this today, does it astonish them?"[66]

Narrating these events in *Dästanna kebber*, Heruy emphasized two episodes of metahistorical significance. The first was Täfäri Mäkonnen's June 19 summit with Mussolini at the Palazzo Chigi, which proved the only face-to-face meeting between the two heads of state.[67] It was an illuminating encounter. After initial exchanges of goodwill, the crown prince

FIGURE 1.3 Täfäri Mäkonnen and Benito Mussolini, Rome (1924).

advanced the Ethiopian claim on the Eritrean port of Assäb, countering a just-failed effort to obtain similar concessions in French Djibouti.[68] Mussolini replied that this proposal would be considered by Salvatore Contarini, head of the Office of Political Affairs at the Ministry of the Colonies. The latter was a conservative nationalist who had participated in the post-Adwa treaty negotiations, and as this punt suggests, the imperial dynamics of the negotiations now became transparent. Contarini conferred with diplomat Giuseppe Colli di Felizzano, a critic of the crown prince,[69] and then produced a draft treaty that guaranteed conditional access to Assäb in exchange for Italian commercial supremacy in Ethiopia.[70] In effect, the proposal outlined a protectorate relationship. Heruy presented an Amharic translation of the draft and informed readers that it was largely derided by the Ethiopian delegation.[71]

As this wariness suggests, the summit exposed Italy's barely concealed imperial designs. The proposal's grasping logic belied the week-long displays of monarchic and national fraternity, much like the Dogali obelisk that dominated the Ethiopians' arrival in Rome. Broadly, this was because the draft treaty exemplified the emerging framework of strategic bilateralism with respect to Italian policy toward Ethiopia. One year after the summit, Mussolini instructed Minister of the Colonies Pietro Lanza di Scalea—Contarini's supervisor—to prepare for the future destruction of the Ethiopian state, in the interim "chloroform[ing]" the crown prince and the Ethiopian elite with bad-faith negotiations.[72] Seen in the context of this development, the cooperative framework of the treaty was thus a potential instrument of informal imperial influence and cover for a planned invasion, anticipating the seemingly liberal mood of the 1927 Addis Ababa talks, the 1928 Treaty of Friendship, and contemporaneous shifts in Italian policy toward Yemen and Albania.[73] If Täfäri Mäkonnen aimed to publicly assert Ethiopian sovereignty and membership in the international system, Mussolini had instead suborned him into a position suggesting neocolonial subjecthood. It was precisely for this reason that he arrived late to the crown prince's welcome banquet, dismissively leaving the seat of honor vacant.[74]

But salvation awaited. In Heruy's narrative, the conference at the Palazzo Chigi was followed by a redemption rooted in the power of heritage. In the ensuing days, the Ethiopians visited the major Roman churches, finally proceeding to Saint Peter's Basilica for an audience with Pope Pius XI.[75] A fateful development then ensued. In Heruy's telling, the travelers now wearied of sightseeing, and they decided to rest in a quiet area within the walls of the Vatican.[76] They discovered they were outside Santo Stefano degli Abissini, the sixteenth-century diasporic monastery known to Ethiopians and Eritreans as Däbrä Qeddus Esṭifanos.[77] The building was a small church behind the basilica, and after five centuries of service as a residence for Ethiopian pilgrims, in 1919 it was transformed into the Pontifical Ethiopian College, a dedicated seminary for Catholic students from the Horn of Africa.[78] After relating this history to readers, Heruy explained that when Täfäri Mäkonnen and his companions entered Santo Stefano, they were greeted by a group of seven Ethiopian and Eritrean students. In the world of the text, a supposedly chance discovery produced a moment of profound metahistorical significance. The crown prince had followed the path blazed by centuries of intrepid Ethiopian faithful.

The residents received their guests with a celebration recalling a royal feast at Enṭoṭo. In its rich multilingualism, erudite historicality, and learned culture of praise, the meeting resembled a *liqawent* conclave in the heart of fascist Italy. The contrast with the patronizing colonial politics of the Palazzo Chigi is stark. Within the narrative, this dichotomy is textually manifest through a shift in register, from the terse descriptive reportage of foreign people and places in translation to an expansive Amharic, Tigrinya, and Ge'ez dialogue rooted in the vernacular historical imagination. Heruy describes the Santo Stefano encounter in such detail that it consumes nearly half of the chapter in which it appears, and as an episode of intra-Ethiopian and Eritrean dialogue, it is a unique moment in the narrative. For an instant, the reader glimpses the intellectual world of the *liqawent* as it might be represented in a Ge'ez chronicle.

The guests were first approached by Hagos Fessuh, an Ethiopian student from Agamé. He welcomed them with a Ge'ez- and Tigrinya-inflected Amharic speech that Heruy transcribed in full. Hagos first observed that "even though our land of Ethiopia has preserved its kingdom and Christianity, it has had no rest from the violence of its enemies. But the savior of the world has at all times given it children who have served it with honest hearts, and even if the enemies of Ethiopia have been strong, they have not been known to defeat it."[79] He then outlined the modern history of this perseverance. He described Emperor Yohannes's dual confrontation with the Sudanese Mahdists, or "the cruel enemy of faith," and the Italian colonizers, or "the cruel enemy of the kingdom," and suggested that his battlefield martyrdom made him "the pride of his country through a pendant of bullets."[80] Privation filled the land until Menilek delivered Ethiopia from its suffering, earning his moniker "Conquering Lion of Judah." The host then praised the guests. In his assessment, Täfäri Mäkonnen continued the achievements of his forbears: he was "the peaceful glory, the great pride, and the hope of Ethiopia," for which reason the progressive savior had secured his place in "the history of the sovereigns," encompassing "the wisdom of Solomon" through "the heroism of Yohannes" and "the patience and wisdom of Menilek."[81] Hagos added, "Ethiopia praises you, saying [in Ge'ez] 'I found what my heart wanted, like all the kingdoms of the world.'" For Heruy's readers, the contours of this triumphalist narrative were familiar: the divinely sanctioned struggle of the Solomonids was the fulcrum of Ethiopian historicity, and its narration required a deferential but learned vernacular historical voice.[82] Despite the unusual Roman setting, *abba* Hagos had proven himself a true *liq*.

Two more presentations followed. The first was delivered by an unnamed orator, who explained in Amharic that he and the other students had come to Rome to study and "benefit our land."⁸³ Life in Europe was difficult, which is why they had welcomed the news of Täfäri Mäkonnen's visit, despite the ostensibly accidental nature of the occasion. Next to speak was Zär'ay Soqwar, an Eritrean student from Akkälä Guzay. He recited a long Tigrinya praise poem on behalf of "Ethiopia's children, your brothers and servants who live in the city of Rome."⁸⁴ It too celebrated the achievements of Yohannes, Menilek, and Täfäri Mäkonnen, whose fulfillment of God's plan had secured the future of "the descendents of the ancestral Ge'ez speaking peoples,"⁸⁵ for which reason the latter now adorned the banquet halls of the land, from Adwa to Addis Ababa. This verse replicated the historical logic of Hagos's speech within the conventions of *massä* Tigrinya poetry.⁸⁶

The welcome was stirring. According to Heruy, the crown prince was moved by "these children of Ethiopia overcome with love for their country," and when the reception concluded, the delegation toured Santo Stefano. Heruy showed particular interest in its sepulcher, and translated its Ge'ez epitaphs into Amharic. These commemorated the monastery's past residents, among whom was *mämher* Täsfa Ṣeyon of Däbrä Libanos, a sixteenth-century monastic and curial advisor who published the *editio princeps* of the Ge'ez New Testament and was esteemed by later generations as a progenitor of the Ethiopian encounter with Europe.⁸⁷ Heruy concluded his account by reflecting on the achievements of the pilgrims and the historical significance of an Ethiopian space at the heart of global Catholicism. "To find Ethiopian monasteries in Jerusalem and Rome is a great point of pride for all the children of Ethiopia," he remarked, "and this [fact] explains why Ethiopian Christianity has endured since many earlier times."⁸⁸ Santo Stefano epitomized the nation's transcendent history.

As this observation suggests, Heruy framed this diasporic encounter as a symbolic commentary on the Ethiopian past and future. Like the reception itself, his intricate narration of the delegation's "discovery" of Santo Stefano outlined a historical trajectory of moral-political fulfillment. It confirmed the crown prince as the redeemer of Ethiopia, despite the danger revealed in the Palazzo Chigi and mountains of Lazio. If this fact is literally asserted within the text by the diasporic *liqawent*, it is also suggested by the plot and intertextual features of the encompassing chapter. The narrative structure of Täfäri Mäkonnen's pilgrimage from Rome to the Vatican replicates the historical logic outlined in the oration of Hagos Fessuh and the poem of Zär'ay Soqwar. All three are concerned with overcoming the colonial past, juxtaposing antecedent moments of trial with the liberatory promise of the crown prince. Heruy documents this transcendence of Ethiopia's "cruel enemies" through the sequence of three interpolated texts: the translated Italian treaty of Contarini, the Amharic excursus of Hagos Fessuh, and the Tigrinya verse of Zär'ay Soqwar. The peril of the first was resolved by the grandeur described in the second and third. For a close reader, the chapter thus offers an intricately composed lesson on the Italo-Ethiopian relationship—set in a little-known diasporic site, outlined in a resonant symbolic language, and oriented toward the transcendent greater meaning of the regime of history, as François Hartog terms it.[89] Unexpectedly, Rome revealed Ethiopia becoming itself.

At the same time, Heruy used the encounter to elaborate a neotraditionalist vision of the Ethiopian nation. Its organizing category is "the descendants of the ancestral Ge'ez speakers," or *behérä ag'azit*, a precise and erudite concept of Christian group identity that underpinned both Hagos Fessuh's speech and Zär'ay Soqwar's poem. Etymologically, this expression is derived from the Amharic, Tigrinya, and Ge'ez term for the ancient Ge'ez speakers of the northern highlands, *ag'azyan*, which is attested in Aksumite-era Greek and Sabaean epigraphy. In its ancient context, this term is believed to have meant "free-born or independent."[90] In conjunction with *behér*, the Amharic, Tigrinya, and Ge'ez word for land or people, the expression *behérä ag'azit* thus refers to the lineal descendants of that ancient unconquered population. It notably appears in the liturgy of Saint Yaréd, as the honorific *abunä* Sälama bestowed on the people of Ethiopia.[91] The expression is thus a traditionalist antecedent of "greater Ethiopia," a modern official nationalism that similarly evades ethno-religious difference and inequality.[92] If the learned northern concept of *behérä ag'azit* was likely unfamiliar to many of Heruy's readers, it was a vision of the past that endured. Decades later, the historian Gäbrä Iyäsus Abbay used it to describe a shared protonational ancestry derived from Aksum, and in the present day, it is occasionally used to invoke or contest the common heritage of Eritrean and Ethiopian Christians, especially with respect to Tegray.[93]

In *Dästanna kebber*, Heruy maps the modern contours of the *behérä ag'azit*, bringing the ancient demonym into the twentieth century. In his presentation, the Santo Stefano *liqawent* use the term to emphasize the kinship of Ethiopian and Eritrean Christians, pointing to a historical fraternity and shared heritage that transcended ethno-sectarian particularity and colonial partition. As an analytic category, *behérä ag'azit* deftly sidestepped the question of Italian rule in Eritrea, such that Heruy could call all the students "children of Ethiopia," and even note that some hailed from the *awraja* of Hamasén, describing the central Eritrean highlands as an Ethiopian—rather than Italian—province. The recurrence of Ge'ez in the reception was a linguistic confirmation of this kinship, as was the common intellectual world of hosts and guests. Whether Orthodox or Catholic, Ethiopian or Eritrean, all affirmed "the history of the sovereigns," imagining their collective history through the prism of Solomonid agency originating with Aksum. This was the binding power of tradition. Transcending contingencies of political, territorial, and religious partition, the concept of *behérä ag'azit* had an inherently anticolonial historical logic.

It also gestured to the wider world. The erudition of the students complemented the brilliance of the monastery's past residents, and Heruy's juxtaposition of these living and dead *liqawent* subtly commented on the nature of Ethiopian diasporic identity. During the early modern era of Täsfa Ṣeyon, this identity was imagined through the scriptural language of pilgrimage and displacement, or "uprootedness,"[94] drawing on the example of Israelite exile and return.[95] Heruy revised this understanding. By the early twentieth century, Ethiopian and Eritrean students were frequently venturing abroad for education, and this fact led many observers—African as well as European—to challenge their politics, faith, and cultural authenticity. Indeed, this issue figured in Heruy's 1933 novel *Addis aläm*, or *New World*, which explores the vicissitudes of a young Shäwan returned from Paris, where he had studied European "wisdom and learning."[96] Given this charged context, Heruy's Roman narrative can be read as a refutation of these derogatory heritage politics. Like Täsfa Ṣeyon and his compatriots, Hagos Fessuh and Zär'ay Soqwar were paragons of Ethiopian-ness abroad—even allowing for their Tigrinya accent, foreign training, and subtle *italianità*, or Italian-ness. This was key. In Heruy's view, the modern descendants of the ancestral Ge'ez speakers should embrace an expansive vision of Ethiopia's place in the world, rejecting the assimilative telos of Western tutelage as well as the naive prescription of cultural isolation. It was a collective gesture that echoed the diasporic solidarity he discovered in Harlem five years earlier. Ethiopians did not need crumbs from the international table. They deserved happiness and honor.

A decade after this Roman tour, Heruy built a home in Addis Ababa that evoked this cosmopolitan vision. On returning from his 1931 visit to Japan, he began construction of a grand family residence. The compound was situated in the patrician suburb of Gullälé, on the leafy foothills of Mount Enṭoṭṭo near the road north to Däbrä Libanos, Gojjam, and Tegray. Even in the context of the eclectic built environment of the burgeoning Ethiopian capital, there was no other building like the foreign minister's new home. The residence had style. In keeping with Heruy's eclectic cultural interests, the stately main building was planned by Japanese architects, who fused Japanese and Ethiopian design elements—most conspicuously topping octagonal towers that recall Enṭoṭṭo Qeddus Ragu'él with spires that suggest a pagoda (figure 1.4). The interior maintained this spirit. Approaching through eucalyptus trees and impressive gardens, the visitor first entered Heruy's private prayer room, a modest sanctuary of Orthodox Christian devotion. A main door then opened to a grand salon with high ceilings,

FIGURE 1.4 Heruy Wäldä Sellasé at home, Addis Ababa.

Source: Personal collection of author.

ornate wood floors, and mixed Ethiopian and European decor. Throughout were material hints of the English education of sons Sirak and Fäqqädä Sellasé and daughter Amsalä, who died suddenly in 1933.[97]

The encircling compound similarly reflected the foreign minister's many projects. To the rear of the house was a small building connected to Goha Ṣebah, Heruy's prolific private press. Another rear building housed his personal library of Ethiopian and foreign books, coupled with his prized Japanese sword. The grounds also featured a lion sanctuary and aviary, the latter left open so that birds could come and go at will.[98] The entire family moved to the compound just before the main home was completed in 1935, inhabiting it together for eight months.[99] In that short time, its grand salon became an effervescent hub of Addis Ababa society, with large conclaves of intellectuals holding discussions late into the night, served tea and coffee by Heruy's highly educated children.[100] A photo of the *blattén géta* on the exterior steps shows him decorously smiling with pride. Today, the compound is home to the Ethiopian Academy of Sciences.

2
Mysterious Magic

By 1935, Enrico Cerulli had become Italy's most powerful Africanist.[1] His ascent to this position was swift. Born in 1898 to a middle-class Neapolitan family, he inherited some of his inclinations from his father, a lawyer and civil servant who spoke Mandarin. As a teenager, he attended the city's Regio Istituto Orientale, or "L'Orientale," the oldest institution of its kind in Europe. Housed in the former Collegio dei Cinesi, a missionary training school, the Istituto Orientale was by the early twentieth century one of Italy's leading centers for African and Asian research, rivaling its institutional peers in Rome and Venice. After the 1911 invasion of Libya, it was subordinated to the Ministry of the Colonies and refocused on training aspiring state functionaries. With classrooms, specialist libraries, and a museum now dedicated to Italy's African colonies, the school became a counterpart to the British School of Oriental and African Studies and the French École Nationale de la France d'Outre-Mer.[2] Its faculty included the country's leading experts, and the language-focused curriculum included Arabic, Amharic, Tigrinya, Oromo, Somali, and Berber, with additional courses on colonial geography, history, law, and ethnology.[3]

Cerulli's teachers introduced him to the fullness of the Orientalist endeavor. One early influence was Giorgio Levi Della Vida, among the most distinguished Italian Semiticists of the twentieth century.[4] Born to a Venetian Jewish family, he attended the University of Rome and studied with Ignazio Guidi, the Arabic, Ge'ez, and Amharic specialist considered the modern founder of Italian Semitic studies.[5] Levi Della Vida's research encompassed Hebrew, Syriac, and Arabic literature as well as the broader premodern history of the Middle East and North Africa, and in 1913, he began teaching Arabic and Islamic studies in Naples, where he trained Cerulli. He left three years later, and in 1920, he assumed Guidi's chair in Rome, where he remained for the next decade. He occasionally taught Arabic at the Ministry of the Colonies, and briefly met Täfäri Mäkonnen and Heruy during their 1924 European tour.

Another mentor was Francesco Gallina. Born in Asti and an alumnus of Guidi's courses in Rome, Gallina taught Amharic in Naples for over three decades. Although he published little of his own scholarship, he facilitated the publication of Amharic and Tigrinya works by Ethiopian and Eritrean authors, and he eventually collaborated with Cerulli on a supplement to Guidi's Amharic-Italian dictionary, the standard reference of the era. Gallina's professional identity was instead rooted in the preparation of competent colonial officials and experts, in keeping with the institutional mission. Cerulli went so far as to attribute his teacher's thin publication record to nationalist altruism, suggesting Gallina had sacrificed "scientific glory" in order to train those who would continue Italy's "illustrious tradition of Ethiopian studies."[6]

A third influence was Carlo Alfonso Nallino, a Turin-born specialist in Arabic and Islamic studies.[7] His career spanned the Istituto Orientale, the University of Palermo, the Egyptian University in Cairo, and finally the University of Rome, where he remained for two decades. Cerulli described Nallino's L'Orientale lectures on Islamic topics as a uniquely fascinating component of his education, and the two remained lifelong colleagues.[8] Nallino eventually became an academic powerbroker: he established the Istituto per L'Oriente in Rome; edited the Orientalist section of the *Enciclopedia italiana*, or "Treccani"; and served as founding editor of *Oriente moderno*, the leading Italian publication on modern Asia, North Africa, and the Horn of Africa. He also advised the Ministry of the Colonies and represented the Ministry of Foreign Affairs. Despite this proximity to the state, he proved an occasional critic of Italian colonial policy.[9]

In addition to these Italian scholars, the institute also employed several African instructors, or *assistenti*.[10] They were tasked with explaining the languages and institutions of the Horn of Africa within the framework of colonial studies, from a social position of racial and diasporic precarity. The most famous of these instructors was Afäwärq Gäbrä Iyäsus, a leading Ethiopian intellectual of the era.[11] Born in Gondär, he served as Menilek's emissary to Italy, after which he studied in Turin and alerted a visiting Ethiopian delegation to the linguistic inconsistencies of the Treaty of Weçhalé, which eventually provoked the Battle of Adwa. After returning to Shäwa, where he painted murals at Enṭoṭṭo Maryam and Enṭoṭṭo Ragu'él, Afäwärq ventured to France and then again to Italy, where in 1902 he joined the Istituto Orientale. He taught Amharic there for a decade, and worked with Gallina to produce the language manuals and creative works that established his literary fame. These include an Amharic grammar for Italian students, the first Amharic novel, an Amharic biography of Menilek, and a satirical French-Amharic guide to Ethiopia.[12] In 1912, Afäwärq returned to the Horn of Africa and began a long career in government service.

His replacement was Sängal Wärqenäh.[13] Born near Adwa, he spent his youth in Eritrea and Italy, where he became so acculturated that one acquaintance described him as "less native and more Italian than one could believe."[14] After enlisting in the military, Sängal obtained Italian citizenship and returned to Eritrea, where he married an Italian and worked as an interpreter. By 1912, he was back in Italy, where he taught Amharic and Tigrinya at the Istituto Orientale for more than a decade, along the way serving in the First World War and publishing a Tigrinya poem about the conflict. It was during this period that he helped Cerulli interview wounded soldiers at the military hospital. Sängal was joined in Naples by his wife and three children, and his daughter Elena would go on to study with Gallina and obtain a degree from the University of Naples, where she wrote a thesis on Ethiopian perceptions of Adwa. She eventually replaced Gallina as the primary L'Orientale Amharic instructor, and she became a fixture in its halls and classrooms, conversing with instructors and pupils in their languages of study and starting a family with one alumnus.[15]

This unique intellectual milieu introduced Cerulli to the major vernaculars of the Horn of Africa, both as research subjects and languages of command.[16] He proved a student of distinction, well prepared to undertake the directive, classificatory, and persuasive work of empire. While completing a thesis in Somali customary law at the University of Naples, he studied Amharic, Arabic, Oromo, and Somali at the Istituto Orientale, with additional coursework on colonial subjects, including Islamic studies and ethnology. Methodologically, his L'Orientale training followed the nineteenth-century model of adisciplinary Semitic studies, elaborated in its Italian variant by Guidi. This approach emphasized language study, Islamic and Eastern Christian literature, and the translation of texts, with limited disciplinary preparation in philology, history, anthropology, sociology, or folklore. For this reason, its exponents occasionally offered philological and historical arguments that some later specialists have judged naïve,[17] and its anachronistic adisciplinarity was eventually exacerbated by the diversification of the historical discipline and the development of an Italian anthropological tradition in dialogue with the international field.

In 1917, Cerulli completed his academic training. He received a degree in jurisprudence from the University of Naples and a diploma in Amharic from the Istituto Orientale, with additional qualifications in classical and colloquial Arabic.[18] Around this time, the Ministry of the Colonies directed him to begin a Somalia-focused research project, some of which he published while still a teenager.[19] As these developments suggest, he was despite his youth already considered a notable colonial expert—a distinction compounded by the largely nonprofessional composition of the colonial bureaucracy at that time.[20] Yet this work was soon interrupted. In 1918, the director of the military hospital instructed him to enlist, and he served in the Italian auxiliary infantry in France, briefly returning to Campania for officer training. He was wounded in October, the penultimate month of the war, and then spent three months convalescing at the military hospital in Naples, his former research site. In 1919, he was released and immediately redeployed to Italian Somalia.[21]

The colony was then in a state of disarray. As the Italians fitfully expanded from the coast into the hinterland, the Somalis grappled with the upheavals of political partition, a smallpox epidemic, and the defeat of *sayyid* Muhammad Abdallah Hasan, a formidable religious leader and guerilla poet who led a two-decade movement to expel the European invaders.[22] The territory was at a political turning point. Cerulli reached the booming capital of Mogadishu alongside Prince Luigi Amedeo di Savoia-Aosta, the Duke of Abruzzi, an enterprising aristocrat who spent the next decade developing planned agricultural estates along the Shebelle River.[23] Four years later, they were joined by Cesare Maria De Vecchi, a Piedmontese *squadrista* and leader of the March on Rome, who as the colony's first fascist governor pursued a policy of aggressive consolidation and economic exploitation.²⁴ This turbulent expansion routinized forced labor, land expropriation, and racial humiliation, and along the way, the new governor replaced many veteran liberal-era Italian administrators with "inexperienced" juniors more inclined toward his radical direct rule agenda.²⁵ In De Vecchi's estimation, fascist colonialism would rapidly forge "a New Somalia," toppling every human and natural obstacle to the glory of the nation and regime. For the Somali people, this was an era of escalating violence and displacement.²⁶

Cerulli spent seven years in the colony. During his initial military deployment, he served at the Governo Generale in Mogadishu (1919–1920), and after his discharge, he joined the civilian bureaucracy (figure 2.1).²⁷ He served as resident of Balad (1920–1923), a village northeast of Mogadishu involved in the Villabruzzi agricultural scheme; director of the Office of Political Affairs at the Governo Generale in Mogadishu (1923); and resident of Baidoa (1923–1925), a town between the Shebelle and Jubba Rivers, then caught in the insurrection of *shaykh* Farag, a messianic former slave whose movement attracted subaltern Somali laborers and attacked Italian settlements.²⁸ Cerulli received glowing evaluations from De Vecchi, who judged him an "excellent" official.²⁹

In 1926, Cerulli was transferred to the Italian Legation in Addis Ababa.³⁰ He was now at the epicenter of Italo-Ethiopian diplomacy and intelligence in the Horn of Africa, and for the next five years, he served as advisor to ministers plenipotentiary Giuseppe Colli di Felizzano (1926), Giuliano Cora (1926–1930), and Gaetano Paternò di Manchi di Bilici (1930–1931). Their major initiatives included the negotiation of the 1928 Treaty of Friendship, the Lake Tana and Assäb-Dässé concessions, and the 1929–1930 British Italian Somalia border survey, which under Cerulli's supervision demarcated the strategically significant territorial boundary from the Somali coast to the Haud Plateau.³¹ Throughout this period, the Legation also coordinated intelligence and propaganda work within Ethiopia. This entailed the expansion of the provincial consular network as well as the covert cooptation of Ethiopian elites like *le'ul ras* Haylu Täklä Haymanot of Gondär and *le'ul ras* Gugsa Ar'aya of Tegray.³² Cerulli was repeatedly decorated and commended for his work in the Ethiopian capital.³³ In 1929, he joined the National Fascist Party and cofounded its Addis Ababa branch.³⁴

It was during these years that Cerulli forged his international specialist reputation. Broadly, his research surveyed modern Ethiopia and Somalia:

FIGURE 2.1 Governo Generale, Mogadishu (1920s).

Source: © Brooklyn College Library Special Collections.

he collected and translated Amharic, Oromo, and Somali songs, poems, and orature; published translations of Arabic and Amharic manuscripts and books; and wrote short regional histories and ethnographies, frequently related to his official posts. A central concern was the "Cushitic" people of the Horn of Africa. In Somalia, his publications in this area became paradigmatic. Most notably, he developed a model of Somali society centered on the supremacy of the agnatic clan group, beyond which individual actors had limited social identity.[35] This politicization of descent became foundational to the academic field of Somali studies.[36] His contributions to local Islamic history proved similarly enduring, particularly in terms of source translation and basic description. He outlined the development of Somalia's Islamic brotherhoods, and categorized their orientation toward the colonial state and the specter of Muhammad Abdallah Hasan,[37] whose career in his view exemplified the "tribal" orientation of "the Somali mind."[38] He also became embroiled in the efforts of coastal elites to buttress their socio-religious authority, realized through their efforts to provide Cerulli with genealogies asserting pious Hijazi origins.[39] This policy-facing scholarship broadly resembled the "bush research" framework of Francophone colonial sociology and ethnology, particularly to the extent that it obscured the colonial situation and administrative function of the researcher.[40] It was celebrated by De Vecchi,[41] and decades later, it was ensconced as basic ethnography within the Human Relations Area Files, a massive database of dual-use research funded by the United States government.[42]

After Cerulli relocated to Addis Ababa, this Somalia work underpinned his ensuing scholarship on the Oromo. Its defining and most heralded aspect was his 1927–1928 field research in western Ethiopia, which established his international reputation as well as his distinctive vision of modern Ethiopian ethnopolitics. The mission originated with Minister of the Colonies Luigi Federzoni, who sought to encourage private Italian investment in Ethiopia as part of a broader vision of national imperial commitment.[43] To this end, in 1927 Cora tasked Cerulli with investigating the lucrative mining concessions of western Wälläga.[44] This reconnaissance complimented two concurrent Italian expeditions the following year: Raimondo Franchetti's expedition across the Danakil Desert on the northeastern Ethiopian-Eritrean border, which surveyed its potential as an oil-producing region; and Luigi Amedeo's expedition along the Shebelle

River from eastern Ethiopia to Somalia, which mapped the Ogaden riverine system to support the export crop plantations at Villabruzzi.[45] Cerulli's field research thus contributed to a coordinated Italian survey of the geography, cultural environment, and political economy of the Ethiopian borderlands, furthering the "chloroform" policy of covert imperial development in the guise of political and economic rapprochement.

In November 1927, Cerulli's expedition left Addis Ababa. His companions included an interpreter and twelve Eritrean and Ethiopian *askari*s, some hailing from the regions that were their destination. The group advanced through southwest Shäwa to Jimma, a quasi-independent Oromo sultanate in the Omo-Gibe river basin. Cerulli spent several weeks in its capital and environs, during which time he met Sultan Abbaa Jifar II. The expedition then continued southwest to the former Gibe state of Gera, where Cerulli met *fitawrari* Dästa Damṭäw, the local proconsul and son-in-law of Täfäri Mäkonnen, and then onward to the former kingdom of Käffa (figure 2.2),

FIGURE 2.2 Enrico Cerulli in Käffa (1927/1928).

where he met governor *fitawrari* Birratu as well as *lej* Bäzabeñ, the scion of the deposed local dynasty. Returning to Jimma, the group next descended to the marchland entrepot of Goré, where Cerulli met governor *ras* Naddäw Abba Wällo, formerly of the Washington and Rome delegations.[46] After finally reaching western Wälläga, the group passed a week near Gambella on the Sudanese border and then returned to Shäwa via Bénishangul and Naqamtee. In the last of these, Cerulli met governor *däjjazmach* Haylä Maryam Gäbrä Egzi'abhér, heir to the coopted local dynasty. The expedition reached Addis Ababa in May, seven months after its departure.

The mission proved a professional triumph.[47] In 1929 and 1933, Cerulli published a major two-volume study entitled *Etiopia occidentale*, or *Western Ethiopia*, to immediate government and academic acclaim.[48] An extensively illustrated work of more than five hundred pages, it was dedicated to Gallina and published by the Ministry of the Colonies. It describes the expedition in two alternating registers. Some chapters narrate the journey as observed autobiography, embracing the literary conventions of fin-de-siècle expeditionary anthropology and travel writing.[49] In these, Cerulli relates the events and atmosphere of the field experience in an informal affective voice, outside the language of objective investigation. Other chapters interrupt this autobiographical narrative with detailed descriptions of encountered people and places, outlining the findings of his field interviews and documentary research in the positivist language of basic ethnography and Rankean historiography. In this duality of register, *Etiopia occidentale* integrates the genres of personal memoir and scholarly monograph that the era's ethnologists typically decoupled.[50]

Etiopia occidentale has three interlinked concerns. The first is the cultural variety and regional particularity of greater Oromiyya, especially with respect to the *gadaa* social system, guest-host relations, and Islamic history. This field description uses the framework of nonimmersive, informant-based ethnography to situate western Ethiopia within the broader Cushitic world, the subject of Cerulli's prior writings on Somalia and eastern Ethiopia.[51] A second theme is Menilek's historical subjugation of the region and the ensuing post-conquest ethnopolitical order, which Cerulli conceptualized as "Abyssinian military colonization," employing the Western demonym for the Orthodox Christians of northern Ethiopia and Eritrea. This was the first sophisticated and fieldwork-based study of this topic. A final theme is Italy's past and future relationship with

Ethiopia, manifest in Cerulli's preoccupation with earlier Italian explorers of the Horn of Africa and the local memory of their exploits.

This last theme underpinned Cerulli's imagined authorial identity. As he explained in the introduction, he envisioned his work as a singular continuation of the scientific project of nineteenth-century explorers like Giovanni Chiarini, Antonio Cecchi, and Vittorio Bottego. In this, he distinguished himself from the sentimental, amateurish, and derivative travelography of the era—to say nothing of armchair ethnography. Unlike most of his poorly informed contemporaries, Cerulli considered himself technically prepared "to observe and understand the life of the peoples whose lands he would pass through," and for this reason, he would contribute to the "most Italian tradition" of enlightened exploration that reached back to the medieval era. Like his heroic national forebears, his research transcended simple adventure through the work of rigorous scientific analysis, revealing Ethiopia's past and present complexity as well as the trajectory of its "future evolution."[52] His travelogue thus fused African history and ethnology within a world-historical vision of the Italo-Ethiopian relationship.

These concerns coalesce in what is arguably the narrative's most dramatic episode: Cerulli's encounter with Abbaa Jifar II, the last sovereign of Jimma. Once a powerful Oromo sultanate that dominated the prosperous Gibe region, Jimma became a tributary of the Ethiopian empire in the late nineteenth century through the campaigns of *negus* Täklä Haymanot of Gojjam and *ras* Gobäna Dachi of Shäwa.[53] In 1882, Abbaa Jifar submitted to Menilek, thereby obtaining a mediated sovereignty akin to protectorate status. Unlike the rest of western Ethiopia, the sultanate continued to be directly administered by an independent member of its ruling dynasty, and not an appointed regional governor.[54] In 1910, Abbaa Jifar strengthened his position through the marriage of his daughter Fatuma to *lej* Iyyasu, Menilek's grandson and heir,[55] and by the 1920s, he had transformed Jimma into a booming commercial hub and coffee exporter.[56] Along the way, it became a major center of Islamic learning, chiefly through the construction of religious schools and embrace of Muslim emigrants from across the Horn of Africa. These successes induced Täfäri Mäkonnen to undermine Jimma's autonomy, and in 1932, the elderly Abbaa Jifar finally abdicated, after which his realm became a directly administered imperial province.[57] So ended Jimma's half-century as a bulwark of Oromo political independence.[58]

In December 1927, Cerulli reached the sultanate.[59] It was then home to approximately three hundred thousand inhabitants, and the market and residential districts of its eponymous capital encircled the hilltop royal complex of Jiren, comprised of the palace, a reception hall, and a mosque.[60] Cerulli arrived in the company of a local named Muhammad Abbaa Digga, a courtier from Addis Ababa who the sultan had tasked with bringing the expedition to Jimma.[61] As the caravan approached the capital, Abbaa Digga announced that the sultan was ill, for which reason a military escort would bring the visitors into town.[62] This group led the expedition to the local Italian mission station, where they awaited news from Abbaa Jifar. In the world of the text, Cerulli used this delay to introduce readers to the history of the sultanate, surveying the events and personalities of its nineteenth-century subjugation and ensuing relations with the surrounding "Abyssinian" empire.

In a suggestive development, Cerulli himself now became a purveyor of this history. Days later, the escort returned to bring him to the palace. It now included three grandsons of Abbaa Jifar, who began to speak with Cerulli about the defunct Gibe kingdom of Guummaa, the birthplace of the sultan's mother and a favorite family topic. Cerulli informed his hosts that he had recently translated and published fragments of the history of Guummaa in his 1922 *Folk Literature of the Galla*.[63] This revelation electrified his interlocutors. Cerulli reported that "the young man from Guummaa [a maternal grandson] and the chiefs looked at me with amazement and incredulity, and the [two] sons of Abbaa Fita [the son of the sultan] urged me to let them see this extraordinary book. I limited myself to reading several passages [aloud], in the midst of the surprise and general attention. 'You should give the book to Abbaa Jifar,' the group of grandsons [respectfully] said to me in unison."[64] The narratives Cerulli transcribed in Naples were now poised to return to their subjects' living descendants.

Amid the excitement, the group ascended to the palace. Entering the sultan's chamber, the Italian judged his host an archetypal Oriental despot, "deformed" by confinement in his harem. "It seems incredible," he ventured, "that a man of indubitable intelligence and the head of a country so populous could be reduced to vegetate for years within a small space, surrounded by the company of his women and servants." Abbaa Jifar spoke first, querying Cerulli in Amharic about the religion of the Italian people.

Learning they were Catholic, the sultan quipped that they shared the faith of the Shäwans—a jab at the perceived influence of missionaries in Täfäri Mäkonnen's court. He then inquired about the Muslims in Cerulli's caravan, whereupon the latter replied that Italy had more Muslim subjects than Jimma. This revelation surprised Abbaa Jifar. The conversation now shifted from "official Amharic to confidential Arabic," as Cerulli put it, and the sultan revealed "he was very well informed about me and my journey," suggesting intelligence gleaned from Abbaa Digga. Reverting to Amharic, Abbaa Jifar now exclaimed, "I am very sorry if I was wrong with a few details of the welcome that I extended to you here in Jimma. You know that I am a poor Galla [Oromo] and I am not accustomed to dealing with those from foreign legations who live in the court of Shäwa, because I have been away from Shäwa for twenty years."[65] This last detail subtly flagged the sultan's ethnopolitical precarity, since Menilek had imprisoned Abbaa Jifar for a year during his last "visit" to Addis Ababa. In Cerulli's account, the sultan now developed this theme, informing him in Arabic, "I am a poor man, I am a poor man, my brother! I am a poor Galla . . . in need of the help of Allah the most high!" In the world of the text, Abbaa Jifaar was a helpless Oromo victim, and Cerulli his foreign sympathizer. As they parted, Abbaa Jifar grasped Cerulli's hand and asked him in Oromo if he had brought the history of Guumaa. He instructed the Italian to return, alone and with the book.

Days passed. In the meantime, Cerulli visited nearby Limmu, a former Gibe state that was now a directly administered Ethiopian province. Like Jimma, it figured prominently in his *Folk Literature*, and the fieldwork allowed comparison of the two locales. In its capital, Cerulli met governor *däjjazmach* Habtä Mika'él Yenadu, a Shäwan courtier of Menilek and seasoned frontier administrator, as well as his son *fitawrari* Dämissé, a modernizer who "passionately dreamed of a trip to Europe" beyond "the earthly paradise of his father's military camps."[66] He next proceeded to nearby Saqqa, where he recalled the local imprisonment of nineteenth-century explorers Antonio Cecchi and Giovanni Chiarini, and then interviewed an elder who remembered the Italians and the downfall of Limmu. Cerulli now related this history: the invasion of *ras* Wäldä Giyorgis Abboyé of Shäwa; the conversion from Islam to Christianity of dynastic heir *fitawrari* Gäbrä Sellasé, formerly Abbaa Bagiboo II; and the ensuing rule of *däjjazmach* Habtä Mika'él, a foreign autocrat whose soldiers—known to locals as *täkläñas*, or "the Implanted Ones"—crippled the land through tribute, such that the area's once fecund coffee plantations were now fallow.[67] In Cerulli's assessment, Limmu had become an oppressive feudal society, with Shäwan Christian settlers ruling Oromo Muslim natives. By way of illustration, he described the institutional modalities of ethnopolitical domination, including the imposed system of land tenure, the hierarchy of appointed *qäññazmach*s and *balabbat*s, and the intermarriage of settlers into local families. The Limmu fieldwork allowed Cerulli to offer readers a granular and historicized model of "Abyssinian military colonization," as he christened it.[68]

Past and present now collided in the world of the text. Returning to Jimma, Cerulli ascended to the palace to deliver his book to the sultan. He related the following:

> Abbaa Jifar greeted me with great courtesy and invited me to take a place on an enormous chair that he had brought in front of him. Then, after a brief exchange of greetings, he invited me to read the history of the kingdom of Guummaa to him, adding with a smile that his mother was a native of Guummaa, and for this reason, he could properly verify what I was about to say. And with another smile, he gestured to the line of his wives, the unusual audience that my reading was about to have. I began to read, and truly, no Westerner can boast of having had a similar audience for his own book in the Ethiopian highlands! The stories that I had collected ten years ago from our brave wounded *askari*s in the sad wards of the military hospitals, where the memories of a distant homeland gave a pronounced flavor of nostalgia to the accounts of these heroes, were now revived here in the court of Abbaa Jifar, in this chamber housing the *mooti* [hereditary ruler] and his women, as if a mysterious magic had restored life to the figures of the king, the warriors, [and] the Galla [Oromo] heroines that had been imprisoned for years in the motionless words of the book.[69]

This Malinowksian magic was the worldly power of documentary scholarship.[70] Cerulli's palace reading emerged from an improbable intertextual conjuncture: his hospital interviews in Naples allowed his fieldwork in Jimma to resurrect the Oromo tales of Abbaa Jifar's childhood, filtered through an intercultural chain of testimony and translation spanning time and place. As orature, these texts were transmitted from unknown nineteenth-century sources in western Oromiyya to the itinerant *askari* Loränsiyos Wäldä Iyäsus, whose imperfectly recalled versions were decades later preserved in print by Cerulli, who now read this recension aloud for his "unusual audience" (figure 2.3). In strangely-accented Oromo,[71] the unlikely Neapolitan bard recounted the saga of Guummaa's buffalo-eating dynastic founder Adam and the princess who tamed his supernatural powers; the tragedy of their ludic grandson Oncho, who filled a barrel with *tej* and drank himself to death; and the exploits of their great-grandson Gäwé, or Abbaa Balloo, who provoked a war with neighboring Jimma after serving its ambassadors donkey meat. These were the glorious maternal forebears of Abbaa Jifar.

According to Cerulli, the audience listened silently, only once breaking into exclaims at the climax of the founders' courtship tale. When he finished reading, he reported that the sultan leaped from his seat and "offered me a hand, holding it tightly between his own while saying to me, with no other preamble, 'You sir, are my brother!'" Abbaa Jifar then ordered those in the room to address Cerulli as "my brother" when communicating on his behalf. Momentarily interrupting this drama, Cerulli informed readers that he had subsequently discovered that Abbaa Jifar had once addressed a

FIGURE 2.3 Abbaa Jifar II and Genne Mingitti, Jimma (1927).

British consul as "my friend, but not my brother," thus confirming Cerulli's supposedly singular position in the sultan's imagination.[72] Cerulli's command of language had produced a literal gesture of Italo-Oromo fraternity, rooted in the sultan's appreciation of the Orientalist documentary enterprise. By performing an oral chronicle that celebrated the dynasties of Guummaa and Jimma, Cerulli proved himself to be a steward of Oromiyya's endangered historical traditions and the ally of its lone contemporary sovereign. He was, in short, the professional friend of the Oromo.[73]

Months later, this role revealed its ambiguities. The setting was Naqamtee, the historic capital of eastern Wälläga. Like Jimma and Limmu, it was a region that exemplified the complex history of Oromo political subjugation. After the 1881 invasion of *ras* Gobäna Dachi, Naqamtee was administered by *däjjazmach* Gäbrä Egzi'abhér, formerly Kumsaa Moroda, the submitted heir to the local Leeqaa Naqamtee dynasty. As governor, the *däjjazmach* used his imperial fealty to develop the local economy and consolidate his rebellious peripheries, even as his autonomy dwindled through the proliferation of Amhara garrisons across the province.[74] On his death in 1924, he was succeeded by his young son *däjjazmach* Habtä Maryam, an ambitious Francophone reformer who continued his father's projects under the watchful eye of his uncle *fitawrari* Oljira Moroda.[75]

In April 1928, Cerulli arrived in Naqamtee, on the expedition's return to Shäwa. In the world of the text, he paused to introduce the history of the region, situating its rulers within the larger history of Abyssinian colonialism, as he now routinely termed it. He outlined the nineteenth-century conflicts between Muslim and "pagan" Oromo, the saga of the Shäwan invasion and ensuing campaigns to the west, and the contrasting strategies of accommodation pursued by the converted Gäbrä Egzi'abhér of Naqamtee and the unconverted Abbaa Jifar of Jimma. With this context established, he then described his conference with *däjjazmach* Habtä Maryam, who he found "very attuned to the ideas of the Abyssinian modernizing faction." Though unmentioned in the text, the young governor was then collecting the historical traditions of Wälläga in an effort to realize his father's dream of printing a history of Oromiyya.[76] Given this shared interest, it is fitting that Cerulli again interrupted the narrative with a multichapter history of Naqamtee, possibly drawing on his conversations with the *däjjazmach*. He closed by relating his subsequent encounter with another local notable named Boshara Bidaru, whose exploits against the

Amhara invaders featured in *Folk Literature*. The Italian likened this final meeting to his earlier audiences with Abbaa Jifar—it was a chance to meet his research subjects.

Given this concern, it is striking that Cerulli ignored the town's most illustrious resident, the pioneering linguist and evangelical pastor Onesimos Näsib.[77] It was a curious snub, since *Folk Literature* included translated excerpts from Onesimos's 1894 Oromo reader, which Cerulli disparaged as "a strange little book ... the substance of which was until now unknown."[78] This was, in fact, a serious misrepresentation. At the time of Cerulli's transit through Naqamtee, Onesimos was an eminent church leader, Bible translator, and longtime client of Gäbrä Egzi'abhér and Habtä Maryam. Born near Goré, he had converted to Christianity in Eritrea, studied at a Lutheran seminary in Sweden, and then led the Evangeliska Fosterlands-Stiftelsen (EFS) mission among the Oromo of western Wälläga, with Menilek's blessing. In 1904, Onesimos relocated to Naqamtee, where Gäbrä Egzi'abhér granted him land even after the pastor was condemned for heresy by the Orthodox church.[79] With the governor's protection, Onesimos spent two decades developing the local evangelical congregations, and by the 1920s, the province boasted numerous schools, mission stations, and a hospital. Central to this ministry was the widespread use of Onesimos's "strange" reader. After Gäbrä Egzi'abhér's death, Habtä Maryam maintained his father's support for Onesimos and the EFS community, working closely with Täfäri Mäkonnen and Heruy in the capital.[80] When Onesimos died in 1931, a *Berhanenna sälam* obituary described the congregations of Wälläga singing his Oromo hymns in mourning.[81] He was, in short, Naqamtee's most famous adopted son.

Despite this fact, Cerulli made no mention of Onesimos in *Etiopia occidentale*. The omission is especially curious given the precise timing of the expedition's arrival in Naqamtee. Cerulli's visit coincided with the celebration of Fasika, or Orthodox Easter, and while he did not mention the Holy Week in his account, a glimpse of the occasion comes from the diary of local EFS missionary Olle Eriksson. According to the latter, the Easter vigil at Naqamtee Maryam church was attended by Swedish missionaries as well as *däjjazmach* Habtä Maryam, and the following day, Onesimos led the entire community in an interdenominational celebration, after which many of them attended a reception at the mission residence.[82] It was possibly the most important religious feast of the year. Cerulli said nothing about these events in his account of Naqamtee, and in a suggestive parallel, Eriksson made no mention of Cerulli in his diary, though he noted another European visitor during this same week. The situation is especially striking since the two men were likely acquainted through their years in Addis Ababa, even sharing an unusual facility for Ethiopian languages.[83] This double silence suggests that Cerulli avoided Onesimos and the local EFS community. In so doing, he missed the opportunity to consult the greatest living Oromo linguist and the coauthor of one of his translated texts.

East of town, events in the adjacent province of Gédo further complicated Cerulli's role as an interlocutor of Oromiyya. The province was then governed in absentia by *däjjazmach* Wäldä Gabr'él, an aged veteran of Menilek's army known by the terrible nom-de-guerre "Father of Satan."[84] When the caravan reached the province, they hastily established camp to shelter from a storm, and during the night, two muskets disappeared. After the expedition's *askari*s failed to locate the culprits, Cerulli instructed them to fetch a farmer mentioned by some passing merchants the previous day. When this individual was brought to the camp, he professed ignorance of the robbery. Cerulli admitted his innocence to the reader, but in the field, he demanded restitution from the farmer as the most eminent local. As onlookers gathered, Cerulli ordered his *askari*s to release the man and detain four notables from among the crowd. He now brandished a letter of safe passage from none other than Täfäri Mäkonnen, and instructed an *askari* to bring it to the nearest "Abyssinian chief," with the request that the latter come to Cerulli's aid. Days later, this stalemate ended with the arrival of *qäññazmach* Habtä Mika'él, a provincial judge who Cerulli described as an "Abyssinianized" Oromo. This official produced one of the missing muskets, offered another as compensation, and instructed Cerulli to free his detainees. The Italian acquiesced, happily noting that the substitute musket was marked with a dedication to Menilek.

But he soon faced another crisis. The caravan continued east, stopping to camp outside the eponymous provincial capital. The area disquieted Cerulli, since its residents came from the same Oromo lineage as the "brigands" just encountered near the Gibé River. During the night, the skittish *askari*s captured a passerby, confiscated his firearm, and tied him to a tree, and in the morning, Cerulli interrogated this unfortunate, who proved to be neither an Oromo nor a local resident but instead an Abyssinian traveler. Cerulli informed the man that he would be shot if he called for help, and then ordered the gathering onlookers to disperse. The camp was now on edge. The following day, the situation developed with the arrival of the governor's delegate *fitawrari* Faysa, who offered to bring the prisoner to the capital, or alternatively, render judgment in situ with Cerulli. The Italian opted for the latter, but when the two men formed an ad hoc tribunal, the *fitawrari* recognized the detainee as a government clerk just dispatched to the area from Addis Ababa. This individual explained that he had simply wandered into Cerulli's camp while drunk, which led the Ethiopian official to suggest a fine, "a bit of the whip," and a complaint to the governor. Satisfied with this resolution, Cerulli departed for the capital, leaving the hapless civil servant to his punishment.

These contrasting encounters in Jimma, Naqamtee, and Gédo reveal how Cerulli's relationship with Oromiyya was mediated through its powerbrokers. There were narrow limits to his professional friendship. Some of these were categorical: he interacted extensively with Oromo dynasts, religious leaders, and traditional elites, and additionally, with the Shäwan imperial governors and "Abyssinianized" Oromo who ruled the provinces of subjugated Oromiyya. His encounters with these figures anchor his narrated field experience, as exemplified by his accounts of his interactions with Sultan Abbaa Jifar, *däjjazmach* Habtä Mika'él Yenadu, and *däjjazmach* Habtä Maryam, whose Amharic, Arabic, and Oromo speech he presented to the reader in Italian translation. Yet Cerulli proved more imperious with the subalterns of Oromiyya, such that he arbitrarily detained six individuals and threatened to kill the clerk from Addis Ababa. These incidents demonstrate his willingness to mobilize the political and juridical institutions of the Ethiopian state, personally wielding the instruments of ethnopolitical domination—his central research concern—when the situation suggested it would be to his own advantage. In the years to come, he would decry these institutions as barbarous and despotic. His relationship to power was transactional.

This dimension of his field relationship illuminates his disregard for Onesimos Näsib. Was Cerulli's avoidance of his most influential research subject an intimation of discomfort with Oromo—and indeed Ethiopian—intellectuals who deviated from his models of expected African thought and behavior? Onesimos was neither a native informant from whom culturally authentic knowledge or texts could be collected, nor was he a modern African subject who conformed to a colonial schema of European tutelage and non-European deference. Instead, he was a foreign-educated organic intellectual dedicated to ethnic salvation, vernacular education, and the liberatory power of the printed word. He exemplified the religious modernism of the missionary encounter, an alternative locus of African-European dialogue that was despised by many Italian colonial officials.[85] How did Cerulli comprehend such a figure? Given his later comments about Ethiopian modernity, nationalism, and cultural alienation, it is tempting to interpret his silence about Onesimos as a reflection of unease with the latter's intellectual self-understanding. Perhaps it was unclear how Onesimos would respond to the agenda of a strident Italian expert. A shared respect for foreign scholarship underpinned Cerulli's described fraternity with Abbaa Jifar, who affirmed the former's documentary project of cultural salvage. Perhaps Cerulli instead saw Onesimos as a potentially hostile interlocutor, or even an intellectual competitor.[86]

Ultimately, Cerulli's *Etiopia occidentale* elaborated a new theorization of modern Ethiopia. Its analytic categories coalesced in the concept of Abyssinian military colonialism, a model of the Ethiopian social formation centered on the imperial dialectic of Abyssinian conqueror and Oromo subject. Cerulli's interviews and observations across Oromiyya reveal the complexity of this relationship through time and space, from the nineteenth-century campaigns of Menilek's "conquistadors" to the ensuing process of frontier settlement, ethnic intermarriage, and feudal subordination.[87] This modern colonial order fueled new ethnopolitical and center-periphery antagonisms. In some sites, it rested on coopted local elites, as in Jimma and Naqamtee; in others, it was directly imposed by *balabbat* and *täkläña* proconsuls, as in Limma and Gédo. Everywhere, it forged a hegemonic culture of "Abyssinianization," which encompassed the supposedly developing embrace of Orthodox Christianity, the Amharic language, and the modernizing state. Nearly everywhere, it was acutely despotic, as suggested by Cerulli's conflicts on the road in Wälläga. Crucially, this paradigm could not account for African agency outside the binary of ruler and ruled—a heuristic deficit epitomized by Cerulli's disregard of the most important Oromo intellectual of the era and the alternative vision of modern community he espoused. It did, however, enshrine Italy as the protector of the colonized "Cushitic" subject, as suggested by the fraternal gesture of the lone remaining Oromo sovereign. In the ensuing decade, this model transformed the international understanding of Ethiopia as a distinct African polity. It ultimately instrumentalized ethnic suffering and a pessimistic vision of modern Ethiopian history, power relations, and political economy, legitimizing international oversight and supposedly liberatory colonial interventions. Ethiopian exceptionalism would prove a curse.

Cerulli's fieldwork in western Ethiopia established his reputation as the leading Italian specialist on the modern Horn of Africa. It transformed his career. In April 1931, the Eritrean governor Riccardo Astuto informed the Ministry of the Colonies that Cerulli's "perfect understanding of Ethiopian people and matters" could advance the regime's effort to transform its Ethiopian policy along "more practical and effective lines," enlisting his expertise in the developing plans for a military invasion.[88] Minister Emilio De Bono agreed, and in June, he ordered Cerulli's transfer to the Ministry of the Colonies in Rome.[89] For the next six years, Cerulli served as director of the Office of Political Affairs at the Palazzo Chigi.[90] His office was one of three units dedicated to the Italian colonies in Africa, and his portfolio now included Eritrean and Somali policy, Ethiopian intelligence and counterintelligence, and colonial diplomacy. He reported directly to the minister of the colonies, initially De Bono (1929–1935) and then Mussolini (1935–1936), both supported by undersecretary Alessandro Lessona (1929–1936). This was a major promotion. Cerulli's years of education, research, and service won him a position at the apex of the colonial state, where he marshaled his training and experience to the needs of the institution expressly tasked with subjugating Ethiopia. He had become the regime's authoritative Africanist.

3
Reading Philology in Addis Ababa

Over two formative and intellectually ebullient decades, Heruy and Cerulli proposed new and enduring paradigms for understanding Ethiopia. In the process, it became a significant geography.[1] The emergence of this shared problematic is suggestive. By the 1920s, the interplay between Ethiopian and Western scholarship had become increasingly extensive, worldly, and dialogic. If this interface was not always dialectical, in the intellectually generative sense envisioned by Markus Keller and Javier Irigoyen-García with respect to early modern Orientalism, it was increasingly nuanced, critical, and synthetic.[2] This heightened imbrication of knowledge and texts is exemplified by the fact that Heruy and Cerulli began to address each other in print, in the process raising philosophical and methodological questions that were beyond the scope of their respective fields. This mutual scrutiny began in 1924, when Cerulli published translations from Heruy's 1917/1918 anthology of Amharic funeral dirges through a copy obtained from L'Orientale alumnus Afäwärq Gäbrä Iyäsus, now serving as *näggadras* in Dire Dawa.[3] Heruy was in Europe when the article appeared, but on his return to Ethiopia, he cited two of Cerulli's publications in his 1927/1928 catalog of Amharic and Ge'ez texts. Both were translations of his own work.[4]

These preliminaries complemented a more substantive commentary that began in 1926, when Cerulli penned the first of a series of articles on

Amharic print culture for the journal *Oriente moderno*.[5] Edited by his former professor Carlo Alfonso Nallino and published under the auspices of the Ministry of Foreign Affairs, the monthly was the leading Italian publication dedicated to the contemporary Maghreb, Middle East, and Horn of Africa.[6] Writing from his new Legation post in Addis Ababa, Cerulli informed readers that the development of printing in Ethiopia had fomented new forms of literary expression, which in his view documented the changing political currents in the country and the intellectual life of its urban elite. In his judgment, this dynamic was epitomized by Heruy's 1917/1918 book *Lä'abbat mättassäbiya lälej meker*, or *Reminder for Fathers, Advice for Children*.[7] Scrutinizing this treatise of spiritual and moral instruction, Cerulli suggested that it demonstrated how Western ideas were "badly superimposed" on inherited traditions in Ethiopia. More specifically, he ventured, its author exemplified "the mentality of the Abyssinians" in that "the contrast between the two civilizations [i.e., Ethiopian and Western] more or less known to him had produced in his spirit a strange, discouraging skepticism towards all the ideals of each civilization."[8] In other words, Heruy had become culturally alienated through his experiences in Paris, Rome, and New York City, and was consequently no longer authentically Ethiopian but instead "a Europeanized Abyssinian," as Cerulli put it.[9] The pure native had become a nihilistic *évolué*. If this diagnosis accorded with the colonial science of ethnopsychiatry,[10] it was not easily reconciled with the fact that Heruy imagined the work under review as an archive of the cultural patrimony. As he explained in its introduction, *Lä'abbat mättassäbiya* aimed to preserve what he had learned from his own father, "the books I have read," and "all the things I have heard over time from elders and learned people," thereby disseminating the moral teachings of the inherited tradition and true faith in an accessible printed form.[11] It was for this reason an odd proof of mental or cultural dislocation. Left unaddressed was the question of whether its Italian reviewer suffered from a similar psychological condition.

Over the next three years, Cerulli elaborated his argument that Heruy epitomized the predicament of Ethiopian—and especially Abyssinian—modernity. Months later, he penned another précis for *Oriente moderno* on a travel guide for Ethiopians in Europe, anonymously written by Heruy.[12] Cerulli suggested its author's effort "to lessen the harshness of the contacts of his fellow citizens with advanced Europe" typified "the Europeanizing movement" of the crown prince as well as the domestic antagonisms it engendered. The following year, he reviewed Heruy's *Dästanna kebber*, which in his view documented "the adaptation of Amharic to the expression of new concepts and ideas from European culture." By way of illustration, Cerulli translated two passages on church-state relations from the book's Italian chapter, curiously overlooking Heruy's narrative focus on the episodes at the Palazzo Chigi and the Vatican, and more obscurely, fixating on minor linguistic points while ignoring the distinctive multilingualism of the Santo Stefano encounter.[13] Finally, in 1928 Cerulli evaluated Heruy's anthology of Ge'ez and Amharic poetry, which reached nearly four hundred pages.[14] Commending the "ingeniousness" of its editor's system of organization, Cerulli translated several verses, including a messianic Amharic *qené* about Täfäri Mäkonnen's relationship with the West. The poems, he explained, enabled foreign readers to glimpse "the national character of modern Ethiopians." Throughout these discussions, Cerulli reduced Heruy to a historico-cultural synecdoche, diminishing his literary creativity and misrepresenting his neotraditionalist intellectual politics. The *blatta* and his oeuvre became exemplars of an atavistic African society that naively denied its need for European tutelage. In the process, Cerulli became a foreign critic of the native author.[15]

The following year, Heruy reversed the gaze. This development occurred in his 1929 book *Wazéma: bämagestu yä'ityopyan nägästat yätarik bä'al lämakebbär*, or *Vigil: Celebrating the Feast of History of the Ethiopian Kings on the Morrow* (figure 3.1).[16] Its evocative title suggested his ambitious purpose. As he explained in the introduction, *Wazéma* invoked the eve before the religious feast when the *liqawent* gathered together in solemn fellowship, in advance of the celebration with the congregation, which included "the king and the nobility, the soldiers, farmers, and merchants, and even the women and children."[17] In a similar fashion, Heruy envisioned his book as a joyous "feast of history" for the Ethiopian literati, who would savor it together like the *liqawent* at the vigil. Noting that he had already begun another monumental study of Ethiopia for a general audience, he proposed that the publication of this forthcoming work would be a "happy celebration" for all Ethiopians, learned and unlearned alike, as well as "all the writers and readers of history in the world."[18] In the interim, *Wazéma* served as a refined specialist prequel that metaphorically "proclaimed the grandeur of the [coming] feast," as lexicographer Kässaté Berhan Täsämma put it.[19] The

FIGURE 3.1 Frontispiece of *Wazéma*.

book was a revelatory history for the experts that looked to a transcendent Ethiopian future.[20]

Heruy's subject suited this rarefied audience. *Wazéma* offered a panoramic history of church and state, rooted in a genre-bending historiographic synthesis across 120 pages of text, supplemented by illustrations and chronological tables. Heruy structured his study institutionally, dividing it into four synchronic narratives. The first examined the history of Ethiopia's rulers from antiquity until the regency of Täfäri Mäkonnen, adopting the generic conventions of dynastic history, or *tarikä nägäst*. This discussion notably featured an account of the ancestral *ag'azyan* and their monarchs through Makedda, or the Queen of Sheba, who Heruy described as the lineal forebear of Menilek II.[21] A second narrative treated the Alexandrine Patriarchs, or *liqä pappasats*, who led the See of Saint Mark of which the Ethiopian Orthodox Church was a part, while a third addressed the Metropolitans of the Ethiopian Orthodox Church, widely known as *abuns*, who were until the twentieth-century Coptic ecclesiastics. A fourth and final section considered the abbots of Däbrä Libanos monastery, or *eçhägés*, who were at that time the highest-ranking Ethiopians in the Ethiopian Orthodox Church. This last section notably took a modern and quasi-secular approach to monastic history, and to a lesser extent, the history of ideas.

The introduction outlined a dialogic philosophy of history attuned to the era's developing representational politics. Heruy first explained the value of historical knowledge through the metaphor of material wealth. As he put it, a great lord must know the precise details of the riches in his "storehouse."[22] Failing this, he must at least know the general extent of his wealth, since absent either of these, he was akin to an animal that "only eats what it is given." In the same way, Heruy opined that Ethiopians should know the names and deeds of the past rulers of their country, or at least the broad contours of the latter's history, since in his view one who lacked this basic knowledge was akin to an infant who unthinkingly nursed from its mother. In short, the modern Ethiopian subject required a suitably developed historical consciousness. Heruy added that true historical wealth did not just encompass the great deeds of monarchs, nobles, and soldiers. It also included the achievements of men of faith and learning, whose endeavors ornamented the church and the kingdom. For this reason, his book synthesized dynastic and church history, documenting Ethiopia's full historical riches.[23]

He then turned to questions of historical method and epistemology. These were rarely addressed in vernacular historiography beyond prefatory supplications for divine guidance in the flawed human search for truth.[24] In a short notice after the introduction, Heruy considered the problems of his source material.[25] As with many of his other works, *Wazéma* was based on both European and Ethiopian sources, the latter consisting of histories, martyrologies, and hagiographies. In his view, these sources presented several interpretive issues. For one, they routinely differed on points of detail, especially with respect to precise chronology. To address this problem, Heruy explained that when he found discrepancies, his principle of source criticism was to follow the majority and disregard the exception, on occasion exercising his better judgment. He also refrained from offering conclusive dates when these could not be reliably ascertained. Sound research required analytic caution in the face of an imperfect historical record, even while allowing for the subjectivity of the historian.

A second interpretive issue involved the inadequacy of European scholarship on Ethiopia, a topic he was well qualified to address.[26] In his estimation, foreign studies of his country tended to be methodologically flawed, since their authors often mishandled their sources and fieldwork. This issue was leading to the intellectual malnourishment of Ethiopians. As he explained to readers:

> It has come to pass that many of the histories of Ethiopia are [now] written by people of foreign lands. Some of these men do not question the *liqawent*, but instead question every farmer and trader [they meet]. Everything that they hear they write as if it were true. And thus the *liqawent* of Ethiopia [must now] read these falsified books of history, and even if they do not accept them as true ... the people of other countries accept them as the true history of Ethiopia. ... In the future, when we write for them [and] investigate and expose these lies, all readers [i.e., both Ethiopians and foreigners] will undoubtedly be happy as well as wary [of such foreign works].[27]

The problem, in his view, was that foreign researchers were ignoring the authoritative local specialists, impoverishing the study of Ethiopia by divorcing it from the indigenous custodians of historical knowledge, the *liqawent*. As one of these tradition-based experts, Heruy wrote to expose and correct this error. Though his critique did not name Cerulli, he might have had the Italian writer in mind, especially since the first volume of the latter's folkloric and fieldwork-based *Etiopia occidentale* appeared that same year. Complicating this possibility, however, is the fact that Heruy also knew of Cerulli's translations of his own work,[28] one of which included a note of thanks to the *liqawent* who had helped the Italian with his translations.[29]

Target or not, Cerulli quickly responded to this critique in a review of *Wazéma*, published in *Oriente moderno* in 1932.[30] After contextualizing and summarizing the book, he turned to its critical introductory note. Though he commended Heruy's "correct and level-headed" diagnosis of foreign scholarship, which he had elsewhere affirmed,[31] he disputed Heruy's particular prescription for this historiographic problem. Rather than producing corrective studies that would expose foreign ineptitude, Cerulli instead urged learned Ethiopians to publish editions of the chronicles, hagiographies, and other manuscript works that were hidden from prying outsiders in remote church libraries. In his view, it was through this preliminary project of textual commodification and dissemination that Ethiopians could become "collaborators" in the academic study of their own history, abandoning the work of tradition-based exegesis to serve the needs of the international reader.[32] The underlying problem was not sloppy foreign research but the restricted access to Ethiopia's literary patrimony—one whose significance, Cerulli implied, Ethiopian intellectuals were at present ill-equipped to fully grasp. In short, Ethiopians should make their texts available to the real experts: the Western philologists.

Heruy had already rejected the premise of this position. This point is suggested by his 1917/1918 *Lä'abbat mättassäbiya*, the very publication that spurred Cerulli's inaugural commentary on Ethiopian print culture and cultural alienation. Addressed to Heruy's son Fäqqädä Sellasé, this short Amharic treatise unfolds as a monologue on the pursuit of a moral yet successful life, addressing problems that might be encountered in work, faith, and relationships. Broadly, Heruy situates the individual pursuit of the good in a specifically modern context, envisioning its realization within Ethiopia's ongoing struggle against its foreign enemies and the concomitant choice between defeatist spiritual asceticism, on the one hand, and fortifying outward-looking education, on the other. This distinct framing might have contributed to Cerulli's accusations of cultural nihilism.

In the book's fourth chapter, Heruy addressed the limitations of human knowledge and the nature of collective endeavors. He first observed, "Even if you are not able to study the entirety of what God has created on earth, investigate some small aspect of it."[33] The proper scope of individual understanding was thus limited. He then explained how such focused inquiry should ideally unfold: "Oh my child! Know that any human being, no matter how wise and knowledgeable, cannot depend on their own endeavors alone. Instead, everyone [should] remain steadfast in their respective endeavors, [since] they require one another [for their own success]. For this reason, respect all people; do not look down on people and criticize their efforts."[34] He illustrated his point with a series of professional examples, from the farmer and the merchant to the soldier and the priest, adding in conclusion that one should generally refrain from criticizing members of one's own field. Given the categorical nature of this judgment and his later comments in *Wazéma*, it is tempting to extend these admonitions to the profession of the historian. Two points seem inherent to Heruy's position. First, historians should work diligently but collaboratively in their chosen pursuit, striving to understand some particular aspect of the greater whole. Analytic restraint was a virtue, not a sign of intellectual deficiency. Second, scholarly collaboration should not be structured by hierarchies of expertise, as Cerulli had implied, since historians—and indeed all researchers—depend on intellectual community through their inevitable need to transcend the limitations of their individual capacity and skill. Critique hampered these necessary partnerships, weakening the sodality and proximity required by nonintrusive, feedback-based knowledge production.[35] Developing this point, Heruy would likely have suggested that the science envisioned by Cerulli was impossible without humility, mutual respect, and authentic collaboration.

The crux of this exchange was intellectual authority. Heruy and Cerulli each identified the foundation of Ethiopia-focused knowledge as a modified version of their respective fields and the individuals, methods, and institutions that comprised them. For Heruy, this knowledge could be obtained through the rigorous and collective elaboration of the inherited traditions of scholarship, drawing on Ethiopia's cultural patrimony and the insights of Western research—as exemplified by his own critical-dialogic approach to Ethiopian history. The Amharic language was both the medium and an aspect of this endeavor. Cerulli, in contrast, saw the academic disciplines as superior instruments for comprehending Ethiopia, even if the utility of their methodological tools was constrained by the practical challenges of fieldwork and translation. Implicit in these two positions is the distinction between emic and etic analysis. On the one hand, Heruy called for an interior and particular approach to the study of Ethiopia, and a holistic understanding of its traditional fields of learning, the ontologies these proposed, and the questions and perceived needs of Ethiopian readers. On the other,

Cerulli defended an exterior and general approach, one based on disciplinary tools, their ostensibly universal analytic categories, and a positivist research agenda rooted in the concerns of foreign specialists. The implications of these positions were clear. For Heruy and Cerulli alike, it was the trained members of their own fields—whether in Ethiopia or abroad, or via the manuscript or printed word—who were the real experts.

In 1933, these cloistered debates became public history. The forum for this development was *Berhanenna sälam*, the leading institution of Ethiopia's effervescent public sphere.[36] Established in 1924, the state-owned Amharic newspaper flourished under the direction of editors Gäbrä Krestos Täklä Haymanot and Mahtämä Wärq Eshäté, and by the 1930s, its production had expanded from Addis Abäba to Harär and Jimma, with a considerable number of international subscribers. Each Thursday, equestrian couriers delivered the latest issue to local readers, who shared, discussed, and occasionally responded to its contents. These varied considerably. If *Berhanenna sälam* consistently celebrated the grandeur of the monarchy, in keeping with the era's statist political culture, it was in other respects eclectic and even iconoclastic. Its pages included reports on Ethiopian and world affairs; editorial and reader commentaries on political, social, and religious controversies; popular histories of Ethiopian and non-Ethiopian topics; and profiles and obituaries of Ethiopian and foreign notables of diverse backgrounds. For many of its readers and employees, the newspaper epitomized the promise of the burgeoning culture of progress, especially with respect to the elaboration of a modern civic and national identity. It was the era's primary forum for the development of public opinion through circumscribed intellectual and intergroup debate.

In 1933, *Berhanenna sälam* featured a series of articles on Italian Orientalist scholarship that explored the epistemic politics of Ethiopia's relationship with the West. Its instigator was Tä'amrat Ammanu'él.[37] Born to a Jewish Bétä Esra'él family from Gondär, he had emigrated at a young age to Asmara, where he attended an EFS mission school and met the Polish Orientalist Jacques Faitlovitch. The latter was affiliated with the Alliance Israélite Universelle, an international Jewish organization dedicated to the education of non-European Jews, and in 1904, this connection brought Tä'amrat to Paris and then Florence, where he began rabbinical training and studied philology, literature, and Semitic languages at the University of Florence. Along the way, he moved in socialist circles and had a romantic relationship with anarchist Leda Rafanelli. By the early 1920s, Tä'amrat was back in Ethiopia, where he managed a Jewish school in Addis Ababa, worked with the Florentine Zionist Carlo Alberto Viterbo, and regularly contributed to *Berhanenna sälam*, notably translating a 1928 French syndicalist critique of Italian fascism. The controversy produced by this last effort created discord with Täfäri Mäkonnen and Faitlovitch, and ultimately led to the firing of the newspaper editor.[38] In 1930–1931, Tä'amrat traveled to New York City, where he attended Columbia University, visited a Black Israelite congregation in Harlem, and met the Garveyite rabbis Wentworth Arthur Matthew and Arnold Josiah Ford.[39] The latter was the magnetic leader of an Ethiopia-focused Black American settler movement, and shortly after meeting Tä'amrat in New York, he emigrated to Addis Ababa with several members of his congregation. The two remained in contact after Tä'amrat returned to the Ethiopian capital.[40]

Given this cosmopolitan background, Tä'amrat was supremely qualified to introduce the newspaper's readers to Italian Ethiopianist scholarship. He began this project by reviewing Carlo Conti Rossini's 1928 *Storia d'Etiopia* and Silvio Zanutto's 1932 *Bibliografia etiopica*,[41] after which he turned to Ignazio Guidi's 1932 *Storia della letteratura etiopica*. Guidi was then the dean of Italian Ethiopian studies, and his magnum opus was the first book-length academic survey of Ge'ez literature, with a special section dedicated to the Bétä Esra'él.[42] It was immediately acclaimed by specialists.[43] Tä'amrat quickly obtained a copy from Heruy,[44] and in April 1933, he began a serial overview of its contents for *Berhanenna sälam* that proved a sophisticated work of linguistic and intellectual translation.[45] In its first installment, Tä'amrat introduced readers to the field of academic philology. He explained that the European *liqawent* devoted their lives to research, and that they scrutinized the language, script, and material form of texts to determine their date of composition—although in his view, their judgments were not always as certain as they believed. He then introduced Guidi as among the foremost of these European *liqawent*, noting that the elderly professor was renowned for his Amharic-Italian dictionary, his translation of the Ge'ez *Fetha nägäst*, or *Law of Kings*, and his translations of Islamic and Eastern Christian Arabic literature. He was additionally "very polite and generous," an assessment that suggests some personal acquaintance.[46]

A dense summary followed. Adopting Guidi's periodization, Tä'amrat devoted the remainder of the article to the Aksumite epoch, and two subsequent articles to the fourteenth- and fifteenth-century reigns of emperors Amdä Ṣeyon and Zä'ra Ya'eqob.⁴⁷ These discussions encompassed broad topics like the literary culture of Aksum and the development of fidäl, as well as commentaries on specific texts, such as the Ethiopian Maccabees and the *Kebrä nägäst*, or *Glory of Kings*. Throughout, Tä'amrat emphasized the interplay between Greek, Syriac, Arabic, and Ge'ez literatures, the systematic delineation of which was among Guidi's most significant achievements. On occasion, he subtly modified the professor's characterizations.⁴⁸

Tä'amrat's author function shifted with the fourth installment in the series.⁴⁹ After resuming his literary history with the sixteenth-century conflict between the Solomonids and Sultanate of Adal, he interrupted the summary with an original essay on the *Mäṣhafä hatäta*, or *Book of Inquiry*.⁵⁰ This was a provocative intervention. The work in question was a Ge'ez treatise attributed to the seventeenth-century *däbtära* Zär'a Ya'eqob and his student Wäldä Heywät, who together outlined a rationalist philosophical system that was heretical in its account of human subjectivity and religious difference. In *Storia della letteratura etiopica*, Guidi introduced the *Mäṣhafä hatäta* as a unique text that did not fit "the conditions of the times and the Abyssinian psychology," and then noted that his student Conti Rossini had persuasively demonstrated that the text attributed to Zär'a Ya'eqob and Wäldä Heywät had in fact been forged by a nineteenth-century Italian Capuchin missionary named Giusto da Urbino, who devised both the iconoclastic Ge'ez text and the authorial personae of the two free-thinking *liqawent*.⁵¹

Conti Rossini's argument electrified the field of Ethiopian studies.⁵² In their fin-de-siècle editions of the text, philologists Enno Littmann and Boris Turayev emphasized the authentic and original nature of the *Mäṣhafä hatäta*, a position Conti Rossini challenged with linguistic, biographical, and intertextual evidence.⁵³ His revisionist argument won the specialists. In 1926, Cerulli gestured toward the debate in his inaugural *Oriente moderno* article on Amharic print culture, going so far as to suggest that the alienation of the "Europeanized" Heruy could be fruitfully contrasted with the case of the "Abyssinianized" Giusto da Urbino, and in 1933, he further affirmed Conti Rossini's assessment of authorial imposture by holding that the *Mäṣhafä hatäta* could not be Ethiopian since its contents were not "rigidly enclosed in schemas and forms handed down for centuries."⁵⁴ In short, the burden of dogmatic tradition constrained Ethiopian intellectuals from original philosophical or critical inquiry.

By this time, Littmann's Latin-Ge'ez edition of the *Mäṣḥafä hatäta* was circulating in Ethiopia. In the material context of local print culture, it was a rare printed Ge'ez book with foreign origins. One of its close readers was *aläqa* Dästa Täklä Wäld of Shäwa, a distinguished lexicologist, Däbrä Libanos alumnus, and *Berhanenna sälam* employee. The *aläqa* rejected Conti Rossini's arguments. In 1926, he informed a German correspondent that "[foreign] researchers say he [Zär'a Ya'eqob] is Italian . . . [and] that a *liq* like this cannot be found in Ethiopia, but it is known that he is completely Ethiopian from his book and manner of writing," even allowing for his heretical ideas.[55] A half-century later, *aläqa* Dästa developed this critique to address the domestication of Conti Rossini's arguments, acidly writing "some [Ethiopian] falsifiers who do not seek their country's glory say, 'but these philosophers are *liqawent* of foreign lands.'"[56]

This heated and multisited intellectual context underpinned Tä'amrat's essay in *Berhanenna sälam*, which introduced the Orientalist controversy to a mass Ethiopian audience. Tä'amrat began with the text. He explained that a manuscript copy of the *Mäṣḥafä hatäta* could be found in the Bibliothèque Nationale in Paris, and that it had been sent by Giusto da Urbino to the Franco-Irish adventurer Antoine d'Abbadie. Tä'amrat added that to his knowledge, its vorlage had "to this day" never been located, offering a deft Amharic translation of this descriptor of textual filiation.[57] He then outlined the life and thought of Zä'ra Ya'eqob, quoting from the text. He described the *liq*'s flight from Aksum during the reign of Susenyos, his ensuing time of reflection in the wilderness, and his later years of writing and teaching in Enfraz, a village on the eastern shore of Lake Tana. Summarizing Zä'ra Ya'eqob's ideas, Tä'amrat emphasized his conception of the fundamental unity of God, irrespective of the particular teachings of "Moses, Jesus, Muhammad, and other people who are not Christian," and noted the *däbtära*'s understanding of the antagonism between received knowledge and critical rational inquiry. He informed readers, "The main question of the book is [this]: if there is only one truth, [then] where did all this division come from?"[58]

With respect to the question of authorship, Tä'amrat sided with the Italians. He explained that two decades prior, he had personally read the *Mäṣḥafä hatäta* in Paris, and that "even before investigating what the *liqawent* of Europe had said about it, I realized just by evaluating how the book starts that its author could not be Ethiopian." He did not explain whether this assessment reflected the caliber of its Ge'ez or the arguments it contained. Yet he remained curious, and continued researching the issue on his return to Ethiopia. This only confirmed his original assessment: "Whenever I found a learned person, I did not fail to ask them about this book, but until the present I have not found one person who knew the book, the author, and [his] disciples." For this reason, Tä'amrat shared Guidi's doubts. He informed readers that the author was in reality "a *liq* called *padre* Giusto da Urbino," and referred the curious to Conti Rossini's articles. In the context of the era's public culture, Tä'amrat's essay was a sophisticated work of linguistic and intellectual mediation. He translated not only selections from the *Mäṣhafä hatäta*, but also the findings of the foreign scholarship devoted to it and the technical apparatus this literature deployed.

Four months later, this essay elicited a sharp riposte. Its author was *aläqa* Gäzahäñ Aflañ, a witty church scholar who seems to have made no other contributions to *Berhanenna sälam*.[59] In a glimpse of the diverse world of readers that now encompassed both the newspaper and the *Mäṣhafä hatäta*, the *aläqa* explained that Tä'amrat's arguments had generated considerable controversy in the months since their publication. He knew "many people had reservations" about the essay, but these skeptics had so far kept their views to themselves rather than sharing them with the newspaper's readers. This reticence had induced *aläqa* Gäzahäñ to present his own position on the controversy, so as to "help one another through truth and falsehood" as Ethiopians traversed the minefield of foreign commentary on their culture and history. His dialogic intervention-in-print aimed to disrupt the foreign and foreign-derived monologue on the authenticity of the *Mäṣhafä hatäta* and the study of Ge'ez literature, as a public and traditionalist rejection of the core assumptions of Orientalist philology.[60]

The *aläqa* first recapitulated the biography of Zä'ra Ya'eqob. This amounted to a statement of confidence in the truth claims of received tradition, implying that Tä'amrat had erred by neglecting the fullness of the text's biographical aspect. The *aläqa* then attacked Tä'amrat's research logic. In his view, the latter had not found any Ethiopians acquainted with Zä'ra Ya'eqob because of the flawed nature of his search: "If he [Tä'amrat] wanted to question [people], go to Aksum or query the *liqawent* of Aksum...

or go to Enfraz the land where he [Zä'ra Ya'eqob] lived and died ... [and] if in this place where he was buried no person who knew of him could be found, then that which he [Tä'amrat] stated could be said to be true. But he [only] asked laypeople who came to Addis Ababa for unrelated reasons, and who blather on aimlessly ... [and] it is just an old story to them."[61] Extending this argument to Wäldä Heywät and the town of Enfraz, aläqa Gäzahäñ added, "If one endeavors to know true history, go to the place where it happened and he [the researcher] will not miss the object." In short, proper investigation of the historicity of Zä'ra Ya'eqob and Wäldä Heywät—or indeed any topic—required consultation with the requisite authorities, in this case the knowledgeable locals far beyond the arrogant intellectual circles of Paris, Rome, and Addis Ababa. By extension, this argument suggested that philological analysis and close reading were in themselves inadequately certain avenues to historical truth. Context and extrinsic historical evidence underpinned sound textual understanding.

The aläqa next outlined a revisionist provenance for the known complete copy of the Mäṣhafä hatäta. He explained that after the accession of Menilek II, the emperor ordered the exhumation of the remains of his ancient namesake—Menilek I, the son of Makedda and Solomon—from a grave west of Aksum. The precise location of this tomb had been determined by Enno Littmann, who was then in Tegray with the 1906 Deutsche Aksum Expedition. According to aläqa Gäzahäñ, the professor dispatched an engineer from Germany to oversee the relocation, and after Menilek I's remains were re-interred in Aksum Ṣeyon church, Menilek II allowed Littmann to take a manuscript containing the Mäṣhafä hatäta from Aksum. It was this bequeathed text, the aläqa averred, that Littmann had published in his translated edition. This account of an Aksum manuscript obtained from Menilek—as distinct from the Paris manuscript originating with d'Abbadie—diverged from the provenance presented by Littmann himself.[62]

The aläqa finally critiqued the broader issue of Western intellectual arrogance. He first asked how a Catholic missionary could write such a book, sarcastically wondering "whether he was sent [to Ethiopia] to teach philosophy." He then considered the confounding role of temporal distance in the discernment of historical truth. Giusto da Urbino had died nearly two centuries after the text was said to have been written, and nearly eighty years separated the Capuchin's death from Conti Rossini's article. In the *aläqa*'s view, these long intervening periods precluded definitive judgments about the origins of the *Mäṣḥafä ḥatäta*. He explained with a complex intertextual analogy: the Book of Genesis contains an account of the destruction of Sodom and Gomorrah, which took place one and a half millennia before the birth of Christ, and much later, this same event was described in the *Mäṣḥafä arde'et*, or *Book of the Disciples*, an esoteric early Christian text.⁶³ Yet this parallel should not lead one to conclude that the two temporally remote texts were linked, or that they could be compared with respect to the accuracy of their depictions of an ancient event. Instead, he observed, "We understand which of the two is truthful, and we do not append it [i.e., the antecedent true one] to the later [less reliable] ones like [Guidi and Conti Rossini have done in] this other case."⁶⁴ His point, it would seem, was the necessity of acknowledging both the particularity of historical sources and the opacity of history itself—a suggestion of the limited nature of temporal perception described in 1 Corinthians 13:12.⁶⁵ Tä'amrat and the Orientalists were guilty of overconfident historical positivism, arrogating a certain truth known only to God. In a final flourish, the *aläqa* noted that some observers had similarly misattributed the Aksum obelisks to foreign creators, denying their Ethiopian origins.

Two weeks later, Tä'amrat replied to this attack.⁶⁶ The centerpiece of his rebuttal involved the stinging charge of methodological sloppiness, specifically with respect to the supremacy of in situ research. In a surprising development, Tä'amrat explained that over a decade prior, he had personally visited Enfraz—only thirty miles away from his own birthplace—to learn what its residents knew about "this book and its author." He likened the endeavor to "searching for dung where there was no cow." He had spoken with the "*balabbat*s and educated men" of the village, who listened as he introduced the controversy about the seventeenth-century philosopher from Enfraz. Tä'amrat reported that they rejected the very possibility of debating the truth claims of the text, saying, "Because there is no witness beyond the author [lit., the owner] and no creator beyond God, [then] according to the book, the people called Zär'a Ya'eqob and Wäldä Heywät are our own [i.e., from Enfraz]. If the text says that they authored it, then they are the authors, and it is not another who wrote it."⁶⁷ Tä'amrat rejected this logic, implying that the villagers' confidence was a symptom of local pride or their simplistic understanding of historical argumentation. He provocatively suggested that Guidi publish an Amharic translation of his "entire work," which would enable Ethiopian readers to judge "the evidence" for themselves through "a satisfactory investigation." In other words, the notables of Enfraz had revealed their limited intellectual horizons, as indicated by their conflation of the world within the text and its generative historical context.

Tä'amrat then addressed *aläqa* Gäzahäñ's alternative provenance. Recapitulating the consensus on Giusto da Urbino and d'Abbadie, he observed that the *aläqa* claimed to have "overturned the ideas of Guidi and his ilk, the [foreign] *liqawent*, and my own lowly words" by establishing that Littmann had obtained the manuscript directly in Aksum.[68] This was, Tä'amrat observed, "a blunder,"[69] which he demonstrated through a literature review. Citing Zanutto, he noted that Littmann had seen twelve of the more than one hundred manuscripts at Aksum Ṣeyon, and the *Mäṣḥafä hatäta* was not among them. Nor was it among the manuscripts in Littmann's personal collection, "today in Germany and the United States." The Swedish Orientalist Johannes Kolmodin had also visited Aksum Ṣeyon, and the lone codex he was shown did not include the controversial text. Finally, the published editions of Turayev and Littmann linked the manuscript to Giusto da Urbino, and not Menilek and the Aksum *liqawent*, as the *aläqa* contended. Tä'amrat thus concluded that "until evidence is found that exceeds what he [*aläqa* Gäzahäñ] has brought [in his essay], it is not possible to say that the author and *Mäṣḥafä hatäta* are Ethiopian."

But he then reconsidered the text in light of its worldly significance. Although it was likely forged, Tä'amrat supported its reprinting in a popular edition. For his imagined Ethiopian reader, the real value of the *Mäṣḥafä hatäta* came from the rich philosophical system it contained, and not its academic idealization as a historical source or cultural-linguistic exemplar. Its ideas and mode of expression mattered. As he explained:

> When the author gives advice, it is like a father or a relative, [and] the criticism is very slight. Leaving this aside, even if from time to time he spreads words of disagreement, it gives [the text] melody. He dismantles the thought that possessed him, [and] what he scatters he reassembles in a novel framework, refining his own ideas accordingly, matching, verifying, linking them like a chain, making them his own, bringing them forward, [and] the articulation has structure and form, beauty and complexion, and it has weightiness. If such an author says "I am Ethiopian,"

and they [i.e., the Orientalists] instead say "he is a *färänj* [foreigner],"
when those of us who have a love of country cry out in protest, we should
never be judged.[70]

As much as this peroration defended the intellectual rigor of the text and
the patriotism of *aläqa* Gäzahäñ, it also rejected the desocialized framework of academic philology. For Tä'amrat, the questions of authenticity
and authorial identity that preoccupied the Orientalists threatened to
impoverish the text's worldly value. He had accepted their position on
imposture after completing his own research, but this narrow point did
not efface the intellectual, literary, and spiritual significance of the work
for Ethiopian readers. It might have been written by a maverick Italian
friar, but its sophisticated Ge'ez apparatus of critical reasoning and its
iconoclastic philosophical approach to specifically Ethiopian problems
gave it a unique "weightiness,"[71] as he put it, and it was precisely for this
reason that he recommended the *Mäṣhafä hatäta* to the newspaper's readers. In so doing, Tä'amrat rejected the modern concept of singular and
prestige-based authorial identity, and instead endorsed an older model of
self-effaced authorship subsumed within a holistic transmitted canon.[72]
He spurned an academic philology dismissive of traditionalist reading,
and the premise of world literature mapped strictly through indigeneity.[73]
What ultimately mattered was the edifying and salvific truth of a text, not
the specific identity of the person who wrote it.

On one point, however, Tä'amrat and *aläqa* Gäzahäñ concurred. Like
Heruy, they both recognized the supremacy of situated knowledge. With
respect to the debate about the historicity of Zä'ra Ya'eqob and Wäldä
Heywät, they agreed that the testimony of relevant *liqawent* was a critical
component of historical inquiry, even if Tä'amrat remained unconvinced
after his Enfraz fieldwork. Conti Rossini had skipped this vital consultative step, which in the *Mäṣhafä hatäta* preoccupies Zä'ra Ya'eqob himself. In
private, Tä'amrat admitted that there was simply no other way to understand complex Ge'ez texts. In a contemporaneous letter to Faitlovitch, he
offered that serious translation and analysis could only proceed through
sustained dialogue with a *liq* who possessed the requisite linguistic mastery and exegetic training, and who could therefore help a reader understand the meaning of a text.[74] Noting that Guidi had such a partner in
his collaborator *mämher* Käflä Giyorgis of Santo Stefano, Tä'amrat then

lamented several issues related to his own Amharic translation of the Ge'ez Psalms, undertaken at Heruy's behest with the assistance of a certain *aläqa* Esṭifanos. The latter was deeply knowledgeable about Ge'ez and scriptural commentary, but their joint translation had been challenging. Tä'amrat believed the issues could be resolved through a salary that would formalize the *aläqa*'s role as a research collaborator. This was a reasonable request, he informed Faitlovitch, since he knew Cerulli spent "considerable sums" hiring *liqawent* to answer his questions, particularly with respect to topics about which he and other foreign specialists knew little. Indeed, Tä'amrat had so many Ge'ez-related questions for *aläqa* Esṭifanos that he could not keep track of all the latter's replies, despite their probity. Notwithstanding Tä'amrat's own linguistic competency and distinctive academic training, dialogue with a master of the tradition was the only way to proceed. When it came to rigorous scholarship, some matters were best left to the experts.

It was November 1927. The same week that Cerulli left Addis Ababa for Jimma, an incendiary essay appeared in *Berhanenna sälam*. Entitled "On the Use of the Word *habäsha*," its author was identified only as a "messenger" of the newspaper, ostensibly from Wälläga.[75] Announcing that he was "not a *liq*," the writer nonetheless displayed a wide knowledge of Ethiopian and European languages as well as a provocative critical sensibility. He lamented the fact that many of his peers had recently embraced the exonymic concept of Abyssinia through its Amharic false cognate *habäsha*. While the latter was a vernacular term derived from an Aksumite-era demonym for an ancient Red Sea population, he found its contemporary assumed equivalence with Abyssinia ill-considered.[76] As he informed readers, Abyssinia is "a derogatory term given to us by foreign historians, [and] we are taking on this epithet without understanding its meaning."[77] These foreigners, he explained, employed the term Abyssinia following the Arabic exonym *habash*, and both concepts implied an imagined process of Semitic and non-Semitic racial integration that was absent from the vernacular meaning of *habäsha*.[78] The slippage confused. "They are muddled and mixed up," he thundered, "but we are not mixed [people]."[79]

The "messenger" then suggested the implications of this conceptual borrowing for the distortion of Ethiopian identity. Demonstrating considerable linguistic dexterity, he reported that the Oromo elders of Wälläga had once called the wilderness *abäsha*, but in the present day, few still remembered this meaning of the term, and some Oromo youth had even adopted its Amharic counterpart *bäräha*. In his estimation, this was because "they pass all their time with the Amhara and have forgotten their own language," in a parallel to the emerging Abyssinia-*habäsha* equivalency. His point, it would seem, was that these linguistic shifts exemplified an ongoing process of cultural and intellectual dislocation, as documented by the asymmetric lexical interplay between Oromo, Amharic, Arabic, and European languages. This development encompassed both the modern process of "Abyssinianization" that Cerulli observed across Oromiyya as well as the broader racialization of Ethiopia and its history. The erudite "messenger" attacked this reimagination of self and other, castigating those who accepted the equation of language groups and biological races, and who mistranslated Ethiopian particularity into the impoverishing language of world-history.[80]

This timely critique suggests the growing influence of exogenous conceptions of Ethiopia within local intellectual life.[81] Like the commentary of Heruy, Tä'amrat, and *aläqa* Gäzahäñ, this anonymous essay illustrates the public repercussions of cloistered debates about the Ethiopian past and future. The Orientalist representation of Ethiopia was beginning to alter the language of lived experience, such that the ethnopolitically laden exonym Abyssinia was becoming naturalized within a new, hybrid framework of racial thought, literally displacing vernacular alternatives. One aspect of this domestication was the local circulation of foreign publications rooted in these categories, as suggested by the *Mäṣḥafä hatäta* debate in *Berhanenna sälam*. This development was perhaps epitomized by Conti Rossini's 1928 *Storia d'Etiopia*, which was read by many Italophone Ethiopians,[82] and which reconstructed the early history of the Horn of Africa through the framework of typological physical anthropology, tying "Abyssinians" to a hybrid "Ethiopian" racial type.[83] Another influential agent of this category domestication was Afäwärq Gäbrä Iyäsus, formerly of the Istituto Orientale. Now the *näggadras* of Dire Dawa (1921–1932) and chief judge of the extraterritorial court (1924–1932), Afäwärq had become a prominent voice in Ethiopian public life as well as a sophisticated translator of the Abyssinian paradigm.[84] This tendency was exemplified by the 1926 local edition of his novel *Lebb wälläd tarik*, or *History Born of the Heart*, which imagined Ethiopia through the chronotope of *habäsha* domination,[85] and additionally by his 1929 *Berhanenna sälam* essay on "The Middle Ages," which equated the inequalities of medieval Europe and modern Ethiopia in a Montesquieu-esque parallel to Cerulli's military colonial model.[86] These developments recast the supposedly distinctive complexities of Ethiopian history and ethnic difference into intellectual categories amenable to a global binary of White and non-White nations.[87] In this, they paralleled the ongoing Orientalist effort to explain the similarly exceptional peoples of the Maghreb.[88]

Heruy challenged this intellectual project. At the very moment the Orientalists reorganized Ethiopian history, literature, and society through the elaborated concept of Abyssinian hegemony, he instead reimagined modern national identity through the framework of the *ag'azyan* and encompassing ethnolinguistic ancestry. In the process, he elided social difference and inequality through a historicized redefinition of indigeneity. This vision suffuses his other historical works, which generally rejected the Abyssinian premise of racial mixing and ethnic antagonism, and instead proposed an idealized vision of primordial pan-Ethiopian-ness rooted in collective lineal descent from the ancient Ge'ez speakers and a concomitant shared heritage and preserved sovereignty. This neotraditionalist historical imaginary accounted for the modern disarticulation of the nation through empire and diaspora, and affirmed the stabilizing power of tradition and its defenders—the *liqawent*—in an era of dislocation and challenge. In this, his vision of the past buttressed the authority of the politico-imperial elite. Heruy was not the only Ethiopian writer in this period to reject the emerging Abyssinian paradigm. A distinct but broadly complementary vision of the Ethiopian past emerges in *aläqa* Tayyä Gäbrä Maryam's 1922 *Yä'ityopya hezb tarik*, or *History of the People of Ethiopia*, which critically engaged Orientalist scholarship while imagining Ethiopia as a fundamentally multiethnic polity of distinct groups with intertwined histories.[89] A variant of Heruy's vision features in Gäbrä Krestos Täklä Haymanot's 1924 *Aċher yä'aläm tarik bamareña*, or *Short History of the World in Amharic*, an instructive work that likewise imagined Ethiopia through the narrative of enduring Solomonid power, and which said little about the question of ethnic difference or inequality beyond sectarian conflict.[90] Broadly similar views can be found in countless *Berhanenna sälam* articles from the era.

These debates mattered. The developing intellectual armature of Ethiopian exceptionalism—specifically, the supposed racial distinctiveness of Abyssinia, its colonial relationship with its Cushitic neighbors, and its precise position within the national hierarchy of Africa and the modern world—reinscribed the global color line across the Horn of Africa through Orientalist and historicist tools. This act raised the question of sovereignty. In 1923, Ethiopia applied for admission to the League of Nations. In the Amharic letter of application to Secretary General Eric Drummond, Täfäri Mäkonnen explained that he wrote on behalf of "the state of Ethiopia,"[91] and the official French translation by his Ministry of Foreign Affairs employed similar language.[92] When the two documents reached Geneva, however, the secretary general rendered these expressions as "the Empire of Abyssinia," and then advanced the application to the Secretariat and General Assembly.[93] It was an ominous act of political forgetting.[94]

PART II
Imperial Andromeda

4
Ferragosto

Tässäma Eshäté was a renaissance man.[1] Born in southeast Shäwa to a family of troubadours, he was a canny entrepreneur and civil servant whose career spanned the reigns of Menilek, Iyyasu, Zäwditu, and finally Haylä Sellasé, who elevated him to the post of *näggadras* in the years before the Italian invasion. He was also an accomplished musician and poet. In his youth, he lived in Berlin, where in 1908 he signed a contract with Beka Records and produced seventeen records of Amharic praise songs, an achievement that ranks him among the first African recording artists. He subsequently became a celebrated master of Amharic poetry, especially the genre of crypt word and double-entendre verse called "wax and gold."[2] One of his couplets skewered the moral hypocrisy of the League of Nations:

> The leaders of [world] peace, Britain and France
> Let God not kill me before seeing the good they will do.[3]

The lines rely on a rich multilingual irony. As he elsewhere explained, the Amharic word *gud*, an interlingual homophone for "good," means unacceptable, strange, or shocking, in contrast to its English false friend. In this verse, these antagonistic meanings of *gud* and *good* expose the breach between the humanitarian veneer and realpolitik core of the League, here represented by its British and French agents.⁴ Tässäma offered Ethiopia as his proof. When read from an international position—that is, through the English meaning of *good*—the couplet appears to celebrate the achievements of these altruistic peacekeepers. But when read from an Ethiopian position—through the Amharic meaning of *gud*—this celebration mutates into a critique, since these "leaders of peace" ultimately abandoned Ethiopia to Italy, allowing an unlawful war of aggression that violated the most sacrosanct principles of Geneva. In the estimation of the *näggadras*, the liberal internationalists proved themselves more *gud* than *good*, despite their claims to the contrary. The self-appointed guardians were predators.

This deft poem illuminates the distinctive imperial and racial politics of the interwar international system. If the League was once considered a flawed instrument of interstate arbitration and an ineffective precursor to the United Nations, it is now seen as a crucible for the internationalization of empire and new forms of conditional sovereignty.⁵ Over its twenty-six-year existence, League bureaucrats and member states deployed humanitarian rationales for foreign intervention, developed models of statehood rooted in supranational trusteeship, adjudicated the legal claims of African and Asian colonial wards, and institutionalized the international authority of Western experts, technocrats, and nonstate actors.⁶ It even sought to manage material heritage.⁷ These developments reified a liberal world order predicated on a hierarchy of racialized sovereignty, a discourse of regulated modernization, and corresponding mechanisms of extra-European oversight, remediation, and intervention. This innovative imperial repertoire is exemplified by the League mandate system, a colonial arrangement comprised of trust territories, mandatory powers, and the supervisory Permanent Mandates Commission of the League Secretariat.⁸ Yet it also underpinned the dynamics of the League Council and General Assembly, as was demonstrated during the 1935–1936 Italo-Ethiopian crisis. For one tense year, the world watched as the struggle between Ethiopia—one of the League's two African member states—and Italy—its fascist would-be colonizer—exposed the antagonism between the League's collective security guarantee and the disposable sovereignty of its non-European members. It was precisely this tension that *näggadras* Tässäma attacked in verse.

As his poem suggests, the Italo-Ethiopian crisis transfixed an array of global publics.⁹ Many European liberals judged it a pivotal trial of internationalism. For British historian Arnold Toynbee, the conflict demonstrated that "if the world was not to be unified politically by a voluntary agreement," then it was "destined to have its inevitable unity imposed upon it by a violence armed with the full powers of the latest Western technique."[10] Others saw the showdown as an alarming crisis of empire: French colonial governor Hubert Deschamps believed it would destabilize the apportioned status quo, imperiling his own "kingdom of stones and sand" in Djibouti;[11] while American anthropologist Carleton Coon worried an Italian defeat would embolden anticolonial protest worldwide, weakening the global color line.[12] This revolutionary development was welcomed by Italian communist Palmiro Togliatti, who believed the regime's invasion of Ethiopia would trigger "open struggle between the imperialist world and the colonial people," unifying the Italian proletarian and the Ethiopian farmer.[13]

For observers throughout Africa and the Black Atlantic, however, the crisis was an outrage that demanded solidarity. Leading this effort in North America, William Leo Hansberry of Howard University mobilized public support for "one of the oldest civilizations in the world," noting that it had maintained its culture and independence despite repeated invasion.[14] In London, meanwhile, Jomo Kenyatta of the International African Friends of Ethiopia decried the moral irony of "the [fascist] violators of every recognized law and right" purporting to show Africans "the light of better days,"[15] while C. L. R. James informed the League of Coloured Peoples that the Europeans had shown "the Negro only too plainly that he has got nothing to expect from them but exploitation, either naked or wrapped in bluff."[16] Standing alone before the General Assembly in Geneva, Haitian League delegate Alfred Nemours warned the world that all states should fear "being somebody's Ethiopia one day."[17] For these activists, the crisis was a concentrated manifestation of the predicament of modern Africa.

These interventions paralleled Ethiopian arguments. Student Mäkonnen Haylé told NAACP readers that the dispute was no more than "an accusation of Ethiopia before the eyes of the world and a justification to wage war against her,"[18] while his compatriot Täsfay Zaphiro apprised Harlem audiences that Ethiopia refused to be "a pawn in the European game of territorial robbery."[19] Diplomatic secretary Emmanu'él Abraham judged the invasion simple vengeance, and in a Haitian echo, he informed London's Royal African Society that "it may be our turn today but, sure as fate, it will be the turn of other weak and backward nations tomorrow."[20] In Geneva, meanwhile, Ethiopia's League delegate *fitawrari* Täklä Hawaryat Täklä Maryam considered the crisis nothing more than a brutish "spectacle" unjustly forced on his government.[21] For all these observers, as for their constituencies and audiences worldwide, the international confrontation was a world-historical conjuncture, exposing the contingency of the imperial order and the exceptionality of African sovereignty. In this respect, the Ethiopian present anticipated the postcolonial future.[22]

Part II of this book explores the role of experts and specialist knowledge in these events, anatomizing their impact in Geneva as well as the sinews of expert communication that linked the League to audiences worldwide. Its chief focus is the role of intellectuals in enforcing and contesting Ethiopia's powerless sovereignty. Chapters 4 and 5 scrutinize the interventions of Cerulli and Heruy through their respective governments and proxies, setting their efforts against the backdrop of the evolving diplomatic negotiations and the rationalization of diplomacy in the international press. These intertwined developments coalesced in a memoranda war that marked the intellectual apex of the crisis in Geneva, which translated their clashing visions of the modern Ethiopian subject into the international languages of liberal imperialism, race science, cultural relativism, and anticolonial struggle. Chapter 6 examines the reverberations of these developments across the academic field of Ethiopian studies, which publicly debated the history and future of Ethiopian statehood. When viewed collectively, these dynamics document the internationalization of the authority of the Western Africanist, the weaponization of specialist research through the model of the dispassionate and objective expert, and the critique of imperial humanitarianism by Ethiopian intellectuals and their foreign allies.

By the summer of 1935, the duel between Italy and Ethiopia had dramatically escalated international tension. Four decades earlier, in the era of Adwa and the European partition of Africa, the failed Italian invasion of northern Ethiopia had been one of many colonial wars, distinctive in its outcome rather than its unilateral aggression and transparently imperial motives. In 1935, however, the imminent renewal of colonial war in the Horn of Africa threatened to destabilize the entire international order, and for this reason, the unfolding crisis was followed far beyond Rome and

Addis Ababa (figure 4.1). While diplomats negotiated in the corridors of Geneva, demonstrators filled the streets in London and Paris, Lagos and Tunis, and Calcutta, Kingston, and New York City. In the last of these, Mayor Fiorello La Guardia—a lukewarm antifascist descended from an Istrian Jewish family—presided over a massive Italian diaspora population as well as the most militantly internationalist segment of Black America,

FIGURE 4.1 John Heartfield, "Fascist Monument" (1936).

Source: © The Heartfield Community of Heirs/Artists Rights Society (ARS).

then neighbors in Harlem and Brooklyn.[23] For months, the city was consumed by demonstrations, boycotts, and street battles, culminating in a massive Harlem rally that attracted tens of thousands of Black and Italian American antifascists.[24]

This globalization of a regional dispute reflected the perceived supralocal significance of Ethiopian sovereignty. One issue involved the architecture of the Genevan system and its evolving concepts of statehood. As a League member state, Ethiopia's independence and territorial integrity were theoretically protected by the collective security articles of the League Covenant. These guarantees, however, were complicated by Ethiopia's admission to the League as a subordinate African member, within a category of racialized, unequal, and "burdened" member polities that also included Liberia, Haiti, and India, the last the only non-self-governing League member.[25] Ethiopia's monitored and provisional membership effectively entailed "mandation by other means," as Adom Getachew puts it, qualifying the theoretically-universal protections of the Covenant.[26] Would an international system predicated on the maintenance of imperial power mobilize to defend one of its African members from a European colonial aggressor? The very question revealed the political contingency of the rights of all member states, compounding the League's prior abandonment of China during the 1931–1932 Japanese invasion of Manchuria and portending its future inability to restrain Germany.[27] The Italian challenge to Ethiopian sovereignty was thus a referendum on the entire international system. As one Secretariat official observed, it proved "the most important and the most decisive chapter in the history of the League."[28]

A second dimension of the crisis involved the potent symbolism of Ethiopian independence. For observers in Africa, Black America, and much of the colonized world, the threat to the continent's oldest polity and the crude attacks on its modern ruler underscored the moral hypocrisy of liberal internationalism on the questions of racial equality and colonial rule. In this respect, the League's unjust treatment of Ethiopia compounded its prior discrimination against Haiti, which had been subjected to a United States military occupation, as well as Liberia, which had faced a demeaning international inquiry into labor practices widespread in the European colonies.[29] This pattern of open disregard for the sovereignty of Black states laid bare the liberal-fascist racial consensus at Geneva and spurred an unprecedented international Ethiopian solidarity movement. Its critique of the League's politico-moral legitimacy paralleled attacks by anticolonial activists elsewhere in the colonized world and within the international Left, and more broadly complemented Western liberal support for Ethiopia within the framework of Genevan multilateralism.[30] Arrayed against these defenders of Ethiopian freedom were White supremacists, fascist organizations of different national varieties, and much of the global Italian diaspora, from Melbourne to Toronto, Jersey City, and Buenos Aires.[31]

The precipitating cause of the crisis was a frontier incident at Wälwäl, a watering network in the Ogaden foothills near the Ethiopian border with Somalia. Claimed by the Majeerteen Somali clan, the site was used by migrating pastoralists from Ethiopia, British Somaliland, and Italian Somalia. In August of 1934, the Italians established an extraterritorial garrison at Wälwäl, and in October, this development led the Ethiopian and British governments to dispatch a joint commission to demarcate the now-contested border. When the commission and its military escort reached the area, they found it occupied by Italian colonial troops. In response, the Ethiopians marked an informal border and established themselves against it, but as the negotiations dragged for several weeks, a series of minor provocations heightened tensions until December 5, when an unclear event triggered an exchange of fire. The Italians immediately launched an airstrike into Ethiopian territory, and the Ethiopian-British group withdrew. Over the course of the ensuing fighting, more than thirty Somalis and one hundred Ethiopians died, including *fitawrari* Alämayyähu Goshu, a notable from Bägémder.[32]

This clash in the borderlands of the Horn of Africa revealed the willingness of European governments to circumvent the dispute resolution mechanisms of the League.[33] Over the next six months, as Haylä Sellasé and Foreign Minister Heruy demanded intervention from Geneva, Mussolini negotiated directly with the British and French governments, widely viewed as guarantors of the international system. This Italian evasion of the Council and Assembly was a violation of the League framework, especially since it excluded one of the aggrieved member states in an effort to satisfy another.[34] The talks induced French Prime Minister Pierre Laval to offer support for Italian expansion in the Horn of Africa in exchange for Franco-Italian border security, while British Foreign Secretary Samuel Hoare proposed awarding the Ogaden to Italy in exchange for Ethiopian access to the port of Zayla, which would be detached from British

Somaliland. By August, these covert intra-European negotiations led the British and French governments to propose a tripartite pseudomandate over Ethiopia as the price of European stability, an arrangement Mussolini rejected, as Italian mobilization massed thousands of metropolitan soldiers and African conscripts on Ethiopia's northern and eastern frontiers. Clearly, the fascist colonial dream would not be addressed by negotiated agreements. The national Adwa complex required invasive therapy.

Meanwhile, the Ethiopian government demanded international intervention. In truth, the emperor had little choice: Ethiopia's allies were few, its military was outnumbered by Italy's combined metropolitan and colonial forces, and its access to arms was constrained by an embargo imposed on its admission to the League.[35] Diplomacy was thus the only available tool. On December 18, immediately after the events at Wälwäl, Heruy alerted the League to the Italian aggression and requested bilateral arbitration per the League Covenant and 1928 Treaty of Friendship.[36] The Italian government instead demanded reparations. After a failed attempt to bring the question to the Council and two months of further negotiations, Heruy notified the League of the diplomatic impasse on March 16, the same day Adolf Hitler announced German rearmament. The Ethiopian government now requested intervention in response to an aggression against a member state.[37] But the procedural sparring continued, as rumors swirled about France's negotiations with Italy and abandonment of Ethiopia.

Finally, on May 25 the Council established an arbitration commission. It was comprised of two nominees from each side. Italy was represented by Luigi Aldrovandi Marescotti, an alumnus of the 1919 Paris conference, and Raffaele Montagna, an experienced arbiter and League Secretariat veteran, while Ethiopia was represented by Albert Geouffre de La Pradelle, a Sorbonne law professor, and Pittman Potter, a professor of international affairs at Geneva's Graduate Institute of International Studies. This panel was aided by an Italian-dominated secretariat, one of whose four members was Cerulli, now director of the Office of Political Affairs at the Ministry of the Colonies.[38] Over June and July, the commission met in Milan and the Hague to review documentary submissions and interview representatives of each government. This process stalled, however, when the Ethiopian representative Gaston Jèze, a Sorbonne law professor, asserted Ethiopian sovereignty over Wälwäl, whereupon his Italian counterpart Silvio Lessona, a professor at the University of Florence and brother of colonial undersecretary Alessandro Lessona, interjected that this point exceeded the commission's jurisdiction.[39] This dispute paralyzed the group until August 3, when the League Council endorsed the Italian position. The commission then reconvened in Paris with a fifth member, Nicolas Politis of Greece, and on September 3, it issued a no-fault decision on the question of the initiation of hostilities. This was a weak verdict that nonetheless partially vindicated Ethiopia in that it undermined the Italian reparations claim.

The ruling came one week before the sixteenth annual session of the League General Assembly. When the latter convened in Geneva's Palais Électoral, the months of delay ensured the Italians were prepared. In anticipation of the upcoming showdown and with the intention of swaying global opinion after the arbitral deflection, the Italian League delegation staged a public relations coup. It was led by Baron Pompeo Aloisi, a bombastic Roman patrician and seasoned League delegate; Riccardo Astuto, the influential governor of Eritrea; and Aldrovandi Marescotti, who had just returned from the arbitration in Paris. Cerulli served as their technical advisor.[40] On September 3, as the Wälwäl verdict was announced, Aloisi convened a press junket at the Hôtel des Bergues in Geneva, where he unveiled a six-hundred-page memorandum on the underlying causes of the crisis. The massive document critiqued the Ethiopian government, outlined the history of the Horn of Africa from an aggrieved Italian perspective, and relitigated the question of responsibility for the outbreak of hostilities, effectively offering a systematic presentation of the Italian *casus belli*. After Aloisi circulated Italian and French editions of the memorandum and fielded questions from journalists, he delivered the document to the Council along with a reference library for those who wished to learn more about Ethiopia.[41]

Clearly long in preparation and strategic in approach, the memorandum offered a sleek academic analysis of Ethiopian country conditions and Italo-Ethiopian relations, complete with citations of non-Italian specialists and a massive documentary appendix.[42] Its principal claim was that the Ethiopian government was an aggressive and barbaric failed state that had defaulted on the conditions of League membership, and that this breach justified Italian military intervention. This represented a major reversal of the Italian position. For months, Aloisi had raised procedural questions related to the arbitral process while preventing discussion of Italian mobilization, but with the memorandum in hand, he now openly called for intervention as a humanitarian enterprise only tangentially related to the border clash ten months prior.[43]

The memorandum outlined the Italian case. It began by asserting that Ethiopia had barred Italy from assuming its role as a favored economic partner. Rather than embracing the progressive spirit suggested by the 1924 Rome talks and 1928 Treaty of Friendship, its government had systematically obstructed Italian commerce and finance, orchestrated attacks on Italian consulates, citizens, and subjects, and fomented disorder on its borders with Italian Eritrea and Somalia. The clash at Wälwäl was thus one of many provocations. The memorandum claimed these aggressions violated the sovereignty of the Italian colonies in the Horn of Africa as well as the obligations established by the 1928 Treaty of Friendship, the 1908 Treaty on the Treatment of Foreigners, and the 1885 General Act of the Berlin Congress. They represented, moreover, a "menace" to Italian citizens and subjects in Eritrea and Somalia.

The memorandum attributed this "xenophobia" to underlying disorder in Ethiopia. It outlined the coups and countercoups that transpired during the reigns of Iyyasu, Zäwditu, and Haylä Sellasé, and claimed these intrigues were symptoms of the country's political instability and sociocultural backwardness. These deficiencies encompassed the "largely medieval structure" and "primitive administration" of the Ethiopian state as well as its broken legal system and discriminatory extraterritorial regime. More broadly, the memorandum asserted that the Ethiopian population was uneducated and trapped in "barbarous customs," while the economy was constrained by inadequate infrastructure and the widespread problem of slavery. Given this situation, the text advanced the historicist conclusion that "the Ethiopian state is an anachronism when contrasted with all the other parts of Africa, which, whether as independent states like South Africa and Egypt, or under the control of European powers, have long enjoyed the benefits of civilization and progress."[44]

The memorandum then contextualized this exceptionalist claim with a surprisingly granular ethnohistorical analysis. Looking beyond the terrain of interstate relations, it scrutinized Ethiopia's domestic sociopolitical order. It disputed the national basis of Haylä Sellasé's government by distinguishing between the "old Abyssinian state" and the "colonies" of the borderlands, which had been conquered in the nineteenth century by Menilek. Adopting the analytic framework elaborated by Cerulli, it explained that Abyssinia was a smaller "Semiticised" Christian society in the northern highlands with clear historic, geographic, and racial boundaries, and this kingdom had violently subdued the racially distinct and predominantly Muslim peoples of the south, west, and east.[45] In the process, Menilek ended the historic sovereignty of Käffa, Wälayta, Jimma, and Harär. Now subjugated by the Christian highlanders and their oppressive system of land tenure, which was itself "a form of slavery," these newly conquered subject peoples deserved liberation from the dominion of their Abyssinian masters, "their age-long enemy." In short, the bold claim was that Ethiopia—and not Italy—was the base colonial predator.

The memorandum's final sections addressed international law. Their principal concern was slavery, an issue that had long preoccupied League officials like Frederick Lugard, theorist of British indirect rule in Africa and a prominent member of the League Permanent Mandates Commission. Building on the League precedent of monitoring African labor practices to deflect from the autocratic labor regimes of European colonies, the memorandum argued that Ethiopia's provisional League membership hinged on the successful eradication of slavery, a condition Haylä Sellasé had breached. Slavery continued to flourish, which point the memorandum advanced through anecdotal evidence from Lugard. The discussion concluded with a lurid description of extrajudicial violence in Ethiopia, which purportedly demonstrated the primitive nature of local law. Like the rest of the memorandum, these arguments rested on a potent analytic synthesis: they deployed the specialist model of Abyssinian colonialism within the racially inflected language of liberal internationalism, with the goal of anatomizing, historicizing, and thereby resolving an exceptional case of continuing African sovereignty. In their attention to the pivotal questions of civilization and minority rights, the Italian arguments invoked earlier debates about humanitarian interventions in Haiti, Liberia, and the Ottoman Empire. This was the responsibility to protect, League-style.

The anonymous document emerged from a shadowy collaboration. Its architects were three veterans of the international system: League secretary general Joseph Avenol, an Italophilic French monarchist; Alberto Theodoli, the Italian chair of the Permanent Mandates Commission; and Raffaele Guariglia, an Ethiopia expert at the Italian Ministry of Foreign Affairs.[46] The last of these had joined Luigi Amedeo during the 1927 negotiations in Addis Ababa, and he subsequently participated in the regime debates concerning the "chloroform" policy and planned invasion.[47] By April 1935, Guariglia was tasked with interministerial coordination on Ethiopian affairs. In a transgression of the neutrality of the League Secretariat, Avenol and Theodoli met that June to discuss the technical grounds for expelling Ethiopia from Geneva, and Guariglia was directed to lead this undertaking as the arbitration and intra-European negotiations proceeded.[48] According to Guariglia, the plan was to demonstrate that the Ethiopian government had violated the 1928 Treaty of Friendship through its efforts to bring the dispute to the Assembly, and that it had more broadly defaulted on its provisional and process-dependent League membership. Avenol and Theodoli believed these accusations would isolate Ethiopia, win international support for Italy, and allow Britain and France to abandon Ethiopia while plausibly maintaining their commitment to collective security. Guariglia reported that he then helped "compile a detailed and annotated indictment of Ethiopia to present at Geneva," whereupon "the relevant ministerial offices [in Rome] dedicated themselves, with my collaboration, to drafting the voluminous memorandum."[49]

Guariglia's collaborators clearly included Cerulli. The latter was the leading Italian authority on the memorandum's subject matter, and specifically modern politics, ethnic history, and center-periphery relations in Ethiopia. All coalesced in his model of Abyssinian military colonialism, which underpinned the memorandum arguments. While stationed at the Addis Ababa Legation, he participated in the border disputes detailed in the document, and he was a leading expert on the geography and ethnopolitics of the Ogaden, developed through his fieldwork with Luigi Amedeo and the Somalia border commission. More immediately, the project also fell directly within his professional remit. As head of the Office of Political Affairs at the Ministry of the Colonies, Cerulli coordinated with the Ministry of Foreign Affairs—and thus his longtime colleague Guariglia—on matters of colonial diplomacy, and his office supervised the Ethiopian intelligence that underpinned the memorandum and its documentary appendix.[50] He additionally served in the Research Office at the Ministry of the Colonies, which undertook ministerial projects. All these roles exemplified the concept of applied expertise that defined the memorandum strategy. Perhaps most tellingly, Cerulli attended the August arbitral talks in Paris, and then two weeks later arrived in Geneva for Aloisi's release of the memorandum to the international press.⁵¹ Among the latter, it was whispered that Cerulli was the document's author.⁵²

This attribution is buttressed by his other covert interventions in the crisis. Months earlier, in March and July, Cerulli published a pair of provocative essays in *Nuova antologia*, Italy's most distinguished academic journal. They were titled "L'Etiopia di oggi," or "Ethiopia Today," and "Etiopia schiavista," or "Slavedriving Ethiopia."⁵³ If their subject matter was opportune, their timing was potentially compromising, since they appeared during his tenure on the Wälwäl arbitration secretariat. The essays were therefore attributed only to "Niliacus," though Cerulli was in fact their author.⁵⁴ This esoteric but richly symbolic pseudonym would appear to be a reference to Horapollo Niliacus of Alexandria, a fifth-century Neoplatonic philosopher who produced the lone received late-antique exegesis of the Egyptian hieroglyphs. An unknown later writer expanded and possibly translated Horapollo's text from Coptic into Greek, and in the sixteenth-century, a print edition of this work fueled a wide-ranging Egyptomania in the republic of letters, transforming early modern European conceptions of Egyptian culture.⁵⁵

Why did Cerulli adopt this cryptic pseudonym? In part, the decision surely reflected the regime's restrictive intellectual politics and escalating pressure on scholars to serve its domestic and foreign policy goals. Anonymity allowed Cerulli to satisfy these demands without tarnishing his international academic reputation.⁵⁶ But his chosen moniker also permits speculation about his self-imagined intellectual identity. One implication involves Horapollo's mediating function. Early modern humanists considered the Egyptian savant-in-translation an authoritative broker of a remote yet fascinating culture, and it was precisely this persona that Cerulli assumed in *Nuova antologia*. He was the translator of Ethiopia. Another possibility derives from the then-revisionist scholarship of French Egyptologist Jean Maspero, who suggested that Horapollo exemplified a fifth-century spirit of pagan Egyptian separatism with respect to Christian Byzantium. For Maspero, Horapollo defiantly attempted to document a fading historical, cultural, and religious patrimony that was under Hellenic Christian assault.⁵⁷ The resonance is striking. Maspero's vision of sectarian late-antique Egypt paralleled Cerulli's conception of modern Ethiopian ethnic politics, with both cases sharing the essentialist binary of Christian imperium and non-Christian subjugation. When seen in the context of Maspero's work, Cerulli's pseudonym can be plausibly interpreted as signaling his orientation as the self-appointed defender of the beleaguered "pagan" subject. He was the interpreter of Ethiopia and the champion of Abyssinia's victims.

Cerulli assumed the first role in "Etiopia di oggi," where he argued that Haylä Sellasé had fractured the country's institutional and sociocultural order. After introducing the Abyssinian colonial model, he contrasted its historic antagonism between *negus* and *ras* with the despotic power of the modern emperor. This autocracy developed, Cerulli argued, from Haylä Sellasé's political strategy as crown prince, when he used his domestic reforms and outward-looking foreign policy to undermine the position of Zäwditu, thereby establishing himself as Ethiopia's preeminent interlocutor with the West. It was an approach epitomized by the 1924 European tour and 1928 Treaty of Friendship. As emperor, Haylä Sellasé thus assumed a throne with diminished powers, from whence he nonetheless pursued a "traditional" centralizing project of eliminating regional rivals like *ras* Haylu Täklä Haymanot, *ras* Kassa Haylu, *ras* Seyyum Mängäsha, *ras* Gugsa Ar'aya, and *däjjazmach* Gäbrä Egzi'abhér.[58] This "silent struggle" further weakened the binding power of church and state, fueling chaos and mass discontent.

Cerulli next proposed that the sociocultural dimensions of this disorder were personified by the Young Ethiopians. Adopting a common exonym for the country's reformist intelligentsia, he suggested that these nationalists similarly undermined the cause of progress. Their "coryphes" were socially marginal and mission-educated civil servants whose positions derived not from merit but from basic European language skill, and they were "totally ignorant" of Ethiopian culture since "they learned what little they know about their homeland not from Ethiopian books but from error-strewn European tracts."[59] They were, moreover, equally unfamiliar with Western culture, which Cerulli purported to demonstrate by noting that the historian *aläqa* Tayyä Gäbrä Maryam had once described Homer and Herodotus as "professors."[60] This was an obscure proof: the Protestant *aläqa* was a traditional church scholar, grammarian, and *qené* expert who substantially diverged from Cerulli's Young Ethiopian profile, and more precisely, he offered this unusual designation in an erudite Amharic ethnohistory wherein he identified all foreign and domestic writers as *liqawent*, reserving the borrowed term *professor* for ancient and modern

Western scholars. Nonetheless, Cerulli proposed that this author and text demonstrated how "the strangest cultural confusionism [of the Young Ethiopians] perfectly corresponds to the genuine political hodgepodge [of the Ethiopian state]."[61] The country's modern intellectuals were alienated, sharing the nihilistic disorientation that Cerulli had already attributed to blattén géta Heruy.

A final discussion addressed xenophobia. Cerulli explained that the emperor and Young Ethiopians had developed the historic Abyssinian "diffidence" toward strangers into a collective hostility toward Europeans, even though, he brazenly added, "nobody in Europe thought even remotely of inserting themselves into the internal questions of Ethiopia."[62] Cerulli then anatomized this antipathy through texts. He first quoted a 1924 Amharic poem whose Young Ethiopian author—who "hid himself" behind a pseudonym—lamented with "boorish coarseness" that Ethiopia's enemies had encircled the country like "a lion's den," reducing its people to a "toilet for their urine."[63] In Cerulli's view, this hostile verse paralleled the public discourse of the emperor, who in 1934 reminded the nation that "among beasts and wild animals ... [when] another foreign beast comes to overwhelm them, they abandon the[ir] private quarrel, and reunited, they protect and defend themselves." For Cerulli, these texts documented a national tendency toward paranoid dehumanization, and it was this "mentality" that provoked the events at Wälwäl. In seeking to overcome Ethiopia's "ancestral medieval barbarism," the country's leaders had brought the country to a perilous modern crisis.

Four months later, Cerulli took up the ethnopolitical dimensions of this juncture in a second essay, "Etiopia schiavista," which historicized the case for Italian intervention. His principal focus was Menilek's nineteenth-century conquest of the borderlands. Cerulli began by quoting the emperor's correspondence with King Umberto of Italy, in which the Ethiopian ruler attacked the lackluster abolitionism of Isma'il Pasha of Egypt, and he then contrasted this critique with Menilek's involvement in the enslavement of the Wälayta during his campaigns in southern Ethiopia. These brutal methods, Cerulli suggested, typified Menilek's conquest of the Oromo, Sidama, and Somali, and he then offered an ethnohistory of the Horn of Africa that paralleled both the corresponding section of the memorandum and his own Etiopia occidentale. He contrasted the historic ethnic pluralism of Abyssinia, defined here as a highland Christian polity comprised of the

Amhara, Tigrayan, and Agäw peoples, with the more expansive ethnic heterogeneity of "the non-Abyssinian lands of the current Ethiopian empire," which encompassed various Cushitic, Nilotic, and Omotic speaking peoples as well as the former states of Käffa, Jimma, Gomma, and Harär. He then explained that Menilek's armies had conquered these independent polities "for the first time in Ethiopian history," transforming the territorial boundaries, economic foundation, and sociopolitical structure of the Solomonid kingdom. In the process, historic Abyssinia became the modern Ethiopian empire—secured by imported European firearms and the counsel of foreign advisors, and sustained at the expense of the subjugated peoples of the borderlands. In a vernacular glimpse of the latter's understanding of this process, Cerulli presented a defiant Oromo verse that assailed the Shäwan invaders, adapted from his 1922 *Folk Literature*.[64] A map visually depicted the ethnopolitical geography of this expansion, complementing a similar map in the memorandum.[65]

Cerulli next detailed the "barbaric destruction" of this conquest. He contrasted the mass violence and enslavement of Menilek's deputies in Wälayta and Käffa with the noble achievements of Italians in these same regions, listing the expeditions of Italian explorers into the borderlands—tactfully excluding his fieldwork in western Ethiopia, but including the mission of Luigi Amedeo in which he himself had served. He then rhetorically asked, "Will there be anyone in Europe who believes it appropriate to compare these glories and conquests of science and courage to the capture of slaves, the mutilations, the mass killings, [and] the blind destruction of men and riches that marked the expeditions of the Abyssinians in these same regions?"[66] With noble Italy and predatory Abyssinia—and more hazily, himself and Menilek—so juxtaposed, Cerulli closed the essay by outlining the treaty framework that accompanied the Italian penetration of the Horn of Africa, arguing that it offered a legal remedy to the persecuted minorities of Ethiopia. These agreements, he proposed, established Italy's "juridical, political, and human[itarian] right to realize its historic mission in East Africa."[67] In tandem with his earlier essay on modern Ethiopian political and cultural disorder, the article's anatomization of state violence and ethnic predation precisely anticipated the position his government advanced in Geneva, welding decades of textual translation, field research, and political surveillance to the project of demonstrating Ethiopian deficiency.

This undertaking was a point of pride for the regime. According to colonial undersecretary Alessandro Lessona, the memorandum was "the result of meticulous and formidable work," and it presented "the cause of Italy in its true and just light."[68] Mussolini approved, albeit cagily. In public, he dismissed the humanitarian and legal arguments for Italian intervention as ancillary rationalizations of a revolutionary colonial enterprise that was a demographic, strategic, and historical necessity,[69] but in private, he informed his ministerial council that the memorandum revealed "the Abyssinian problem in all of its brutal reality," adding that its arguments rested on the latest specialist research.[70] In Geneva, meanwhile, the Italian strategy proved sensational, and the memorandum's accusations were widely reported in the international press.[71] In the assessment of one Secretariat observer, the Italian gamble was "a clever and effective move" that overturned the expected political dynamic: "Ethiopia had come to the Council as an accuser: she suddenly found herself unexpectedly in the dock."[72] The international crisis was now at its zenith.

5
Mäskäräm

At the palace in Addis Ababa, the Italian memorandum produced alarm. Beyond its insults and relitigation of Wälwäl, the emperor was troubled by the argument that Ethiopia had breached the Covenant, since he had long believed League solidarity could preserve its sovereignty, even if this might require a quasi-mandatory arrangement.[1] A confident internationalism had underpinned his government's defensive strategy over the past ten months, and indeed his entire foreign policy since Ethiopia's 1923 application to the League. Aloisi's last-minute reversal of the Italian position was thus a shock, especially since it altered the terms of debate on the eve of the critical Assembly confrontation. While Heruy's Foreign Ministry coordinated the official reply in Addis Ababa, Ethiopia's League delegation organized an immediate counter in Geneva. Ultimately, their attack on the memorandum and its intellectual politics exposed the antagonism between the emerging model of institutionalized and dispassionate expert judgment, on the one hand, and the instrumentalization of Africanist knowledge by the international system, on the other.

Ethiopia's rebuttal was delivered by its League delegate, *fitawrari* Täklä Hawaryat Täklä Maryam.[2] Born near Däbrä Berhan to a family of ecclesiastics, Täklä Hawaryat pursued a church education in Harär, served at Adwa, and attended a military academy in Russia. After several years in Paris and

London, he returned to Ethiopia and began a turbulent career in government. During the reign of *lej* Iyyasu, he served alongside Heruy in the Addis Ababa municipality, and during the regency of the crown prince, he governed the eastern provinces of Jijiga and Chärchär, where he applied his reformist zeal to public administration. As a literary complement to his government service, he wrote a satirical drama that attacked the Ethiopian elite for its impoverished concept of modernization. Heruy was among its targets.[3] Täklä Hawaryat's fortunes turned in 1928 when he was imprisoned following a Bolshevik scare in Addis Ababa, but they reversed again three years later when Haylä Sellasé asked him to draft the 1931 constitution.[4] He was then appointed *bäjerond*, or chief treasurer, and additionally elevated to the rank of *fitawrari*.[5] As these developments suggest, Täklä Hawaryat was by this time a prominent figure in Ethiopian civil society: Heruy judged him destined for "important tasks,"[6] while Cerulli considered him "one of the interesting figures in the modernizing faction."[7] Fluent in English, French, and Russian, and outspoken on Ethiopian as well as European affairs, Täklä Hawaryat epitomized the era's cosmopolitan culture of progress and reform.

He was also a strident critic of internationalism. For this reason, he protested vigorously in 1933 when Haylä Sellasé appointed him League delegate and minister plenipotentiary in Paris and London.[8] In his autobiography, Täklä Hawaryat recalled telling a council of senior cabinet officials—among them Foreign Minister Heruy and Minister of War Mulugéta Yeggäzu—that the only worthy foreign policy was the pursuit of arms to reduce Italy's military advantage. In his view, all other security gains were illusory. He also disputed the utility of diplomatic negotiation, arguing, "It is not the time to go to foreign lands. It is not possible for the work of an emissary to be useful. An emissary just takes and conveys what has [already] been decided, and he is not able to do anything else. It is better [for me] to be here helping when the debate happens and the decision is reached. . . . I am really sad that you are making me leave the country to fulfill Heruy's will."[9] Years later, the *fitawrari* explained that these theoretical objections were compounded by the fact that his wife Sahlämaryam Negatu was pregnant. But as he confided to her at the time, he had no choice but to accept the emperor's decision, and they could only mitigate the situation by bringing their entire family to France, where their eldest son Germachäw was in school. After a final audience with Haylä Sellasé in Djibouti, they departed for Marseille.

Ethiopia's most important League delegate thus reached France reluctantly. He immediately busied himself with the overseas diplomatic staff. They included Täsfayé Tägäñ and Éfrém Täwäldä Mädhen, the respective secretaries of the French and British Legations, as well as Aklilu Habtäwäld, the Sorbonne-educated secretary to the League delegation, and Gaston Jèze, the latter's former law professor and the emperor's legal advisor.[10] The team worked closely with the Foreign Ministry staff in Addis Ababa. In addition to Heruy, the latter now included his son Sirak Heruy and son-in-law Yelma Gäbrä Kidan, as well as American advisors Everett Colson and John Spencer.[11] This group drafted ministerial correspondence in Amharic, translated these into French, and cabled the coded result to Paris and Geneva, where Täklä Hawaryat issued his replies.[12] Notable events of his first two years of diplomatic service include the signing of the 1933 Ethio-Swiss Treaty of Friendship, his participation in the 1933 World Economic Conference in London, and his attendance at the 1934 royal wedding at Westminster Abbey.[13]

The course of events soon vindicated Täklä Hawaryat's skepticism. In the hectic months after Wälwäl, he coordinated his government's effort to resolve the crisis through the machinery of the international system. In mid-January 1935, he joined the Council negotiations that postponed consideration of the dispute,[14] and when this delay yielded nothing, on March 17, he submitted his government's request for League intervention, as Heruy negotiated in Addis Ababa.[15] Two weeks later, on March 29, Täklä Hawaryat debated ministerial undersecretary Fulvio Suvich over the stalled arbitration and ongoing Italian mobilization, their fractious correspondence reaching the Council and Assembly.[16] After another month of delay, on May 11, he pushed the Council to address the Italian failure to nominate arbitrators, and eleven days later, on May 22, he dispatched a memorandum to the Council that outlined the Ethiopian position on Wälwäl, supported by eyewitness affidavits and official correspondence.[17]

By the summer, Täklä Hawaryat was installed at the Hôtel de Russie in Geneva and consumed by the arbitration process. The work was frenetic. While coordinating with the arbiters,[18] he clashed with Aloisi at the Council, urged the emperor to reject the rumors that he would accept mandation,[19] and challenged the Laval-Eden compromise.[20] On August 12, outrage spilled from his pen in a letter to the Council in which he decried the hypocrisy of resuming arbitration in Europe while Italy mobilized in

Africa. Noting the shortage of arms in Ethiopia and the unequal impact of the international embargos, he asked, "Will the Council assume responsibility, in the eyes of the world, for allowing preparations to continue unchecked for the massacre of a people which constitutes a menace to none?"[21] The situation then deteriorated further. On August 29, he testified at the final arbitration meetings in Paris, where he and his colleague Aklilu were queried on points of Amharic translation, apparently with Cerulli nearby.[22] Days later, the panel issued its decision, and Aloisi unveiled the Italian memorandum.

On September 4, Täklä Hawaryat joined Jèze for an extraordinary session of the Council. Convened at the Palais Wilson in Geneva, its chair was the Argentinian fascist Enrique Ruiz Guiñazú, and the agenda promised an examination of the Italo-Ethiopian dispute.[23] Anthony Eden of the British Foreign Ministry began by summarizing the summer intra-European talks, which had produced a humiliating proposal in which Ethiopia would be obliged to "collaborate" with Britain, France, and Italy while assenting to territorial adjustments, in violation of its juridical sovereignty. This effective mandate had been rejected by Italy. In response, Eden now pledged his government's commitment to collective security, noting that failure would undermine the League system. After Laval seconded Eden's position, Aloisi spoke. As the cameras of the assembled journalists twittered and flashed, the baron called the Council's attention to the now-circulated memorandum and explained that his government had refused the Franco-British scheme for the reasons described therein. These were, in his assessment, the persistent hostility of Ethiopia toward Italy, the ongoing border security threat posed by this antipathy, and the failure of Ethiopia to fulfill the requirements of League membership—a situation suggested by its government's use of foreign advisors like Jèze. He then revealed the implications of the Italian position. His government believed Ethiopia's admission to the League had been "a mistake made in good faith," and for this reason, it would no longer negotiate with its government.[24] The move affirmed the remedial understanding of Ethiopian statehood and the corresponding racial hierarchy of League membership.

Stunned, Jèze issued the Ethiopian reply. He and his colleagues welcomed the statements of Eden and Laval, but they were shocked by the "violent indictment" of Aloisi. The professor explained that the Ethiopian government would formally respond to the memorandum, leaving the immediate question of whether the Council should undertake to evaluate the domestic conditions of a member state. This possibility was, in his view, "an extremely dangerous precedent." He further noted that the arbitration commission had cleared Ethiopia of responsibility for the Wälwäl clash, which introduced a fundamental contradiction. The Italian mobilization was previously explained as a defensive measure necessitated by Ethiopian aggression, but those grounds for military action had just been invalidated. It was precisely for this reason, he concluded, that Italy had now shifted its rationale to the arguments presented in the memorandum, continuing a pattern of using misdirection and diplomatic delays to obtain planning and operational advantages.[25]

The following day, Jèze renewed the attack in the Council. With Täklä Hawaryat at his side, he demanded concrete action to prevent a war that seemed imminent. The memorandum had clearly been months in preparation, demonstrating the duplicity of Italy's participation in the arbitration process, and in his view, its seemingly academic arguments about Ethiopian barbarism were nothing but an effort to destroy the reputation of an adversary for crass political gain. In the face of this accusation of bad faith, Aloisi and the Italian delegation abruptly stood and left the chamber. For a moment, the room froze as all attempted to discern whether Italy had just signaled its resignation from the League.[26] Unfazed by the commotion, Jèze, meanwhile, issued a condemnatory ultimatum: "Do not let it be written in the annals of history that, as a result of intimidation, or by connivance or selfish indifference, the nations abandoned a small people the very existence of which is menaced."[27]

As the Italian delegation reentered the room, the Soviet representative Maxim Litvinov spoke in defense of Ethiopia. The Old Bolshevik and influential commissar of foreign affairs rejected the claim that its government had defaulted on League membership and thereby relinquished its due protections, and observed that the Italian government was requesting League neutrality in a conflict between member states. The situation recalled the destabilizing Sino-Japanese precedent, with the added risk of a wider European conflict. Turning to the fundamental issue, he flagged the antagonism between the egalitarian rhetoric of the League and the hierarchical conception of nation-states that underpinned the Italian position. In his view, discrimination against League members on the basis of "their internal regimes, the colour of their skin, their racial distinctions, or the stage of their civilizations" would be nothing less than a violation of the Covenant.[28] This stand was part of an international overture toward collective security that ultimately contributed to Litvinov's political decline at the Kremlin.[29] But he was the lone delegate to openly defend Ethiopia at the Council, and he did so representing an illiberal, antifascist, and anticolonial pariah state.[30] The meeting adjourned, and the following day, the members voted to establish a Committee of Five—comprised of Britain, France, Poland, Spain, and Turkey—to further examine the problem, since Italy's refusal to participate in Ethiopian motions had effectively paralyzed the Council.[31] The decision amounted to death by subcommittee. Throughout the spectacle, Täklä Hawaryat remained unfazed, sitting at a table before the guardians of the world order.[32]

It was in these bleak circumstances that he found an unlikely ally, the maverick French ethnologist Marcel Griaule.[33] A sinuous history united the two that week in Geneva. A First World War veteran, Griaule had attended the École Pratique des Hautes Études and École Nationale des Langues Orientales Vivantes, where he studied with Marcel Mauss and Marcel Cohen. The latter was an eminent Ethiopianist, and Griaule became entranced. He studied Amharic and Ge'ez, and befriended fellow student Agäññähu Engeda,[34] a Gondärine artist in Paris, as well as *abba* Jérôme Gäbrä Musé, an Eritrean exile in Nice.[35] On graduation, Griaule joined the Musée d'Éthnographie, became secretary general of the Société des Africanistes, and dabbled in exoticist avant-garde circles, notably collaborating with Georges Bataille and André Breton.[36] He increasingly espoused a dialogic and collaborative model of interdisciplinary anthropological research that diverged from the emerging Anglophone consensus around immersive participant observation, and he embraced imaginative literary experimentation as a mode of cultural representation precisely as the anthropological discipline asserted its scientific credentials.[37]

Though renowned for his research in Mali, Griaule began his career in Ethiopia. In 1928–1929, he conducted fieldwork in Gondär, where he enjoyed the patronage of *le'ul ras* Haylu Täklä Haymanot, an Italophilic rival of Täfäri Mäkonnen and alumnus of the 1924 European tour.[38] Griaule's ensuing publications included two specialist monographs as well as an ethnographic novel that described the experiences of a European researcher through the narrative voice of an Ethiopian *liq*.[39] Three years later, Griaule returned to the Horn of Africa with the famed Mission Dakar-Djibouti.

Sponsored by the Musée Nationale d'Histoire Naturelle and the Ministry of the Colonies, the mission was envisioned as a grand survey of Francophone Africa and a collection-building enterprise for metropolitan museums.[40] As its director, Griaule led a team that included the poet-chronicler Michel Leiris, an erstwhile acolyte of Breton, and the linguist-ethnologist Deborah Lifschitz, a fellow Cohen alumna. After traversing French West Africa, the team conducted five months of fieldwork in Ethiopia.[41] Among their concerns was the practice of *zar* spirit possession, which brought Griaule and Leiris into an intensive collaboration with *abba* Jérôme, now employed by Heruy at the Ministry of Foreign Affairs.[42] The team also amassed an immense corpus of tens of thousands of photographs, fieldnotes, and artifacts, including more than three hundred manuscripts, now at the Bibliothèque Nationale de France.[43] Many of these items were looted.[44]

This fact provoked a major conflict with the Ethiopian government. According to Leiris, the mission traversed northern Ethiopia in a series of colonial-tinged scandals. At the Sudanese border, they disputed their terms of entry with the Foreign Ministry, and after a clash with Ethiopian soldiers, Griaule complained to the French minister in Addis Ababa, Paul Verchère de Reffye, threatening to alert the League.[45] The team was nonetheless permitted to reach Gondär, where they stayed with Italian consul Raffaele Di Lauro. Their host was renowned as a cunning intelligence officer whose largesse, legal mind, preference for Ethiopian attire, and deep regional knowledge allowed him to coopt local powerbrokers and undermine the authority of the central government.[46] Unsurprisingly, this connection proved disquieting. Given Di Lauro's reputation, the recent murder of an Italian trader,[47] and Griaule's link to the now-arrested *le'ul ras* Haylu, rumors swirled about the sinister purpose of the mission.[48] Heruy dispatched *abba* Jérôme from the capital to monitor their activities, leading Leiris to wonder which badly behaved foreigners—the French or the Italians—Griaule's acquaintance had been ordered to surveil.

The situation then deteriorated through the team's quest for artifacts. After obtaining two frescoes from a local church, Griaule approached a senior ecclesiastic named *aläqa* Ṣägga with a scheme to substitute replicas for original paintings in another church.[49] The alarmed *aläqa* alerted the emperor as well as local *däjjazmach* Wänd Bäwässän Kassa,[50] the son of *le'ul ras* Kassa, but the unfazed French team proceeded to the building with an armed escort, hoping to replace the art "as if nothing had happened," as

Leiris later recalled. The *aläqa* was absent, and the villagers blocked their plan. The priest then banned the foreigners from the church, but Griaule later returned and had a physical altercation with its guards. Leiris called this "the most serious incident to date involving the mission."[51] As the locals decried the "unseemly" French visitors, Griaule publicly denounced the emperor, and the team was blocked from town.[52] They were then ordered to inventory their acquisitions and forward any disputed items to the capital.[53] In response, they frantically concealed "the most precious objects and compromising documents," disguising original paintings as copies, hiding items in false suitcase bottoms, and most egregiously, burning a *tabot*, or sacred tablet ark, that they had been accused of stealing.[54] This was an act of extreme sacrilege. The mission finally departed for the Eritrean border, where they abandoned the panicking *abba* Jérôme.[55]

The denouement of these patrimonial crimes was a confrontation between the French ethnologist and the Ethiopian emperor. In Addis Ababa, Griaule demanded an indemnity for the mission's perceived misfortunes, "payable in cash and in manuscripts and items." He was discouraged by Verchère de Reffye, who considered the mission's actions detrimental to French interests in Ethiopia.[56] Undeterred, Griaule pressed his case in an audience with Heruy, who requested documentation of the complaint before denouncing Griaule to the French minister.[57] Griaule then proceeded to Djibouti to confront Haylä Sellasé, who had just arrived in the colony from Aden. In the French port, Griaule first declined the emperor's dinner invitation and then visited him at his beachside residence. The reception was icy, and Griaule brazenly accused first *däjjazmach* Wänd Bäwässän and then Haylä Sellasé himself of responsibility for the team's hardships, as Leiris watched from a distance. Receiving only the promise of an investigation, the furious director could only return to France.[58]

Less than two years later, Täklä Hawaryat enlisted Griaule in the struggle at Geneva.[59] It was a partnership born of necessity. In July of 1935, Griaule arrived in the Swiss city amid the ongoing arbitration process, intending to cover the crisis for the international press.[60] Disgusted by the ineffectual culture of the League and journalistic misrepresentation of Ethiopia, he witnessed the drama of the commission's no-fault decision and Aloisi's subsequent delivery of the Italian memorandum. As Griaule later wrote, after the arbitral judgment, "Ethiopia smiled," but then it was "struck in the head by a two kilogram memorandum."[61] He quickly read the

Italian document, concluding that the text had been long in preparation and that the Ethiopians should have anticipated the procedural and public relations broadside it represented.

This assessment led him to contact Täklä Hawaryat during the extraordinary Council session. In a *Nadja*-esque coincidence, Griaule had met the Ethiopian delegate two years prior when they were passengers on the same boat from Djibouti to Marseille, but they did not speak given the dark circumstances of Griaule's departure from the country.[62] Both were in fact leaving the Horn of Africa in a mood of defeat, resenting the diktats of the emperor. In December 1934, immediately after Wälwäl, the two again crossed paths in Paris during an interview with a French journal: Täklä Hawaryat compared the border skirmish to the Italian invasion of Libya, while Griaule predicted the incident would lead to "a more serious and generalized crisis."[63] They were then denounced in the Italian press.[64] Now reunited in Geneva and apparently sharing a commitment to the Ethiopian cause, Griaule approached a suspicious Täklä Hawaryat in the halls of the Palais Wilson. The latter lamented the exclusive and transparently imperial culture of the League, saying "I am a stranger here. This world, this process, this diplomacy, [they] are unknown to me. I walk blindly and my only guide is my despairing love for my far away country."[65] Griaule then offered to respond to the Italian memorandum, and after the emperor approved this intervention by his erstwhile accuser, Griaule quickly completed a countermemorandum.[66] It was published months later in Ethiopia.[67]

Griaule's motives were complex. He clearly saw the rebuttal as a professional task he alone could fulfill. Not only was he a specialist whose publications and intellectual authority were cited in the Italian memorandum, but he was also already involved in the crisis through his journalism. He was a public-facing expert. If Cerulli had attempted to segregate his scholarship and political advocacy by anonymizing his contributions to the memorandum and *Nuova antologia*, Griaule instead reconciled these roles through a vision of engaged expertise. In a contemporaneous interview for the Parisian communist monthly *Regards*, he described himself as "a simple informant" who could provide "the fullest and most objective information on Ethiopia, which should be defended and protected against the web of slander that has been heaped upon it."[68] In short, he was protecting scientific truth as well as beleaguered Ethiopia—even if, as he told his interviewer, he had been received "coldly" during his last visit to the country.

However, this position was complicated by additional concerns. In his autobiographical account of these events, Griaule confessed to having acted because of "the abandonment of Ethiopia by most of those who live there or who have benefited from it," adding, "I found [them all] against me when I wanted to ask the government of Addis Ababa to repair the wrongs that had been caused to me in Gondär. If they hadn't been there, I am certain that the King of Kings [Haylä Sellasé] would have had another attitude."[69] His cryptic point, it would seem, was that the professional rivals who spurned him during his own trials had now abandoned Ethiopia, and thus his solidarity with its government and fidelity to truth had the additional value of countering these unnamed competitors. His intervention thus aided his position in his field. A third and more straightforward aspect of Griaule's involvement was suggested by Täklä Hawaryat's colleague Aklilu, who years later described the French ethnologist as "an effective purveyor of counter-propaganda," despite his scandalous behavior in Ethiopia.[70] For Aklilu, Griaule was less a disinterested expert than a useful ally, with politic non-Ethiopian origins and academic credentials.

If Griaule's stridency was destructive in Gondär, it proved valuable in Geneva. His memorandum methodically addressed the Italian arguments with countervailing analysis and evidence.[71] On the essential question of failed statehood, he began with "[the] disturbing fact that the question of the disorganization of the public authorities [in Ethiopia] should be taken up by the very people who have been attempting to undermine them for close ... [to] half a century." As evidence, he enumerated Italian intrigues within and around Ethiopia, offering that its porous borders resembled those of many African colonies.[72] He next rejected the memorandum's racial distinction between highlander and lowlander as well as the Abyssinian colonial paradigm that rested on these categories. Echoing the ethnocentric "Greater Ethiopia" historical narrative, Griaule instead argued that since the Oromo had settled the highlands during the medieval era, Menilek's expansion to the north was not colonialist but revanchist, in that the Abyssinians "possessed those regions centuries ago, and were driven out of them." For Griaule, the subjugation of the south and east involved similar complexities: Käffa had once been Christian, Jimma had remained a semiautonomous protectorate, and Harär had served as a staging ground for the sixteenth-century invasion of the Sultanate of Adal, whose military leader Ahmad Ibrahim al-Ghazi, or "Grañ," was the Muslim villain of the

Christian historical imaginary. This history undercut the lachrymose Italian arguments about Abyssinian colonial predation and perennial ethnic and/or sectarian suffering. In any event, Griaule reasoned, related African peoples had a stronger claim to rule their neighbors than a European conqueror, adding that "Abyssinian civilization will succeed better than any other among peoples like those of southern Ethiopia."[73]

Griaule then challenged the memorandum's charge of barbarism. He reviewed the country's "magnificent literature," noting the existence of Ge'ez translations of otherwise unattested ancient texts as well as the vast written culture of which they were a part. With respect to slavery, he observed that the current government—like emperors Téwodros, Yohannes, and Menilek—was undertaking important reforms, despite the roots of the practice in "Mosaic and Roman law, Islamic law, and the *Fetha nägäst*." He then described the distinctive features of kinship slavery in Ethiopia, adding that some emancipated slaves had reached the senior echelons of state power. In his view, the most distinguished of these was *fitawrari* Habtä Giyorgis, the former minister of war, who Griaule curiously judged "the foremost figure in the country, next to the heir to the throne."[74] Given these developments, he ventured that the eradication of slavery would "proceed in the best possible conditions if the Ethiopian empire remains mistress of its own destiny."[75]

Beyond these counterarguments, Griaule more broadly attacked the Italian memorandum's academic trappings. In his introduction, he decried its methodological shortcomings, which included basic errors of fact, careless use of sources, and tendentious historical analyses.[76] He explained these deficiencies by noting that the anonymous document had apparently circumvented the relevant Italian experts. He informed readers that:

> Italy has an Oriental Institute at Naples . . . [which] trains each year a large number of distinguished students interested in Ethiopian affairs. Their assistance would undoubtedly have given a scientific character to a work of this importance, and would have made it clearer and more convincing. They would have given considerable space to writers whose studies are authoritative in the matter. . . . Orientalists of all schools of thought will be surprised that the name of Enrico Cerulli, the best known linguist and philologist who has specialized in Ethiopian studies, is omitted from this document.[77]

This final reference is cryptic, especially given Cerulli's presence in the Italian delegation and the widespread gossip that he was behind the Italian memorandum, which Griaule elsewhere noted. Did Griaule mean to say that by eschewing Cerulli's expertise, the memorandum sacrificed academic rigor for the illusion of non-Italian impartiality? This implies a belief that objective experts like Cerulli would have rejected overtly partisan scholarship. Or, reading more closely, was Griaule's point that Cerulli had obviously contributed to the report, but was apparently reluctant to put his name on it because of its patently political and unscientific nature? Either way, the "omission" violated the rules of the field: the memorandum could not withstand informed scrutiny. It was bad scholarship.

In a parting volley, Griaule disputed the racial infrastructure of the Abyssinian colonial model. He closed with a map depicting the broad geographic distribution of the "Ethiopian" racial type across the Horn of Africa, encompassing nearly all the ethnic groups of Ethiopia as well as present-day Eritrea, Somalia, northern Kenya, and eastern Sudan. This represented the then-influential position of anthropologists Vincenzo Giuffrida-Ruggeri and Charles Seligman, which in its assertion of "Hamitic" regional uniformity challenged the concept of a racially distinct "Semitic" or "Semiticized" Abyssinia, as represented in the maps attached to the Italian memorandum and Cerulli's "Etiopia schiavista" article.[78] In a twist, Griaule had obtained his map from a voluminous 1932 article on Ethiopia in the *Enciclopedia italiana*, or "Treccani," a third of which had been written by Cerulli.[79] It was a learned jab only discernable to the cognoscenti.

Meanwhile, Täklä Hawaryat launched his own counterattack. Educated in both Ethiopian and European institutions and armed with a defiant critical sensibility, he was fluent in the liberal internationalist language of the Italian memorandum and acutely cognizant of the threat it posed. He grasped the dangers of weaponized scholarship. At one point during these pivotal weeks, he angrily informed Griaule that "Mussolini uses his experts dishonestly, like his missionaries and travelers," an assertion the French ethnologist could not wholly accept, even as he privately contemplated the extent to which Cerulli's actions validated Täklä Hawaryat's charge.[80] This issue induced the *fitawrari* to focus his rebuttal on the methodological problems of the Italian memorandum, leaving the task of its systematic refutation to his government and a future "international commission of inquiry."[81] His own countermemorandum instead offered an epistemic metacritique of the international representation of Ethiopia.

Täklä Hawaryat first suggested that the timing of the memorandum's delivery revealed its authors' bad faith. Despite their purported rigor, the urgent diplomatic conjuncture prevented the document's hundreds of pages of claims and evidence from receiving an appropriate evaluation. This fact indicated the memorandum's intellectual dishonesty. As he explained, its authors did not intend to educate the reader, but instead to "surprise" and "paralyze" the opponent, "taking advantage of his confusion and reducing him to silence, and then, profiting by the advantage thus unjustly gained, representing this silence as a confession."[82] In short, the anonymous Italian writers posed as scholars while evading debate or peer review. This deceptive intent was further demonstrated, in his view, by the fact that the memorandum reproduced over a hundred pages of material related to the Wälwäl arbitration, using a barrage of information to firehose an issue that had just been adjudicated.

Täklä Hawaryat then linked this bad faith to flawed methods. These involved standards of evidence as well as shoddy scholarship. An overarching issue was the logical fallacy of selective argumentation. As he explained: "From the scientific point of view, it is with regret that specialists find that in a country which possesses scholars of the first rank[,] it is not on their authority that the Italian memorandum is based but on the accounts of travelers and writers whose previous training provides no degree of accuracy, like the young woman traveler whom the Italian memorandum quotes side by side with the distinguished orientalist Conti Rossini. Facts are reported and figures given without the most elementary rules of observation being respected."[83] In other words, the seemingly academic arguments of the memorandum's authors were undermined by their poorly chosen and ignorant informants—the very issue Heruy had decried years before in *Wazéma*. Täklä Hawaryat developed this critique by noting factual errors that revealed the document's inadequate grounding in Ethiopian as well as Ethiopianist scholarship, Italian or otherwise. These included quantitative data arbitrarily derived from "sentimental travel literature" instead of reliable sources, geographic and chronological imprecisions, idiosyncratic and anachronistic accounts of Ethiopian history, and major errors of translation—a point that surprised Täklä Hawaryat given "the accurate knowledge of the Amharic language possessed by Italian science."[84] Despite appearances, the text failed to meet the standards of the academic field.[85]

Täklä Hawaryat coupled this methodological critique with provocative comparative analysis. One issue involved the composition of the Ethiopian nation, now a pressing international question. With respect to the collective identity of the diverse peoples within the territorial boundaries of contemporary Ethiopia, he observed that centuries of intermarriage between highland Christians and lowland Oromo had produced "a veritable nationality" that satisfied the definition of none other than Giuseppe Mazzini, the Italian nationalist icon. This fusion, in his view, entitled the Ethiopian nation "to claim the whole country as far as the sea," including Eritrea.[86] This was a shrewd reversal of the Abyssinian colonial argument and its underlying vision of primordial ethnic or racial antagonism. Täklä Hawaryat instead re-envisioned Ethiopian history through the prism of modern nationalism, irredentism, and regionalism, effectively equating the Solomonid dynasty to the similarly nationalized House of Savoy—and by extension, southern Italy and peripheral Ethiopia. Far from being an African anachronism, Ethiopia had undertaken its own Risorgimento through a modern ethnocultural synthesis.

A second comparison was abstract. In the penultimate section of his memorandum, Täklä Hawaryat attacked the hierarchical racial schema of the Italian document with anthropological tools. He took as his illustrative case the Ethiopian practice of execution by fire, which had featured prominently in both the Italian memorandum and Griaule's ethnographic novel.[87] Noting that incineration was the penalty for regicide or attempted regicide, "the greatest of crimes," Täklä Hawaryat wondered:

> When the supreme head of the State is concerned ... is it not natural that there should be extraordinary means of punishment with the object of discouraging further attempts of the same kind? And in practicing this intimidation by inflicting a punishment which must transcend all others, why should not account be taken of the degree of resistance either to suffering or to the idea of suffering opposed by the physical and moral temperament of the natives of the country? ... Cruelty which appears indispensable to the severity of the punishment assumes different forms in different times and places without the people of one time or of one place having the right to regard this difference as representing stages in

a hierarchy of culture when it is merely a case of psychological variations on the same plane of human conscience.... What opinion might be held of those [other countries] whose legislation provides for electrocution, [or] with regard to others whose laws provide for execution under the axe, or by hanging?[88]

The problem was interpretive and theoretical. Execution by fire was not a symptom of sociocultural and legal barbarism, as the Italian memorandum had claimed, but was instead a culturally-logical form of criminal deterrence, a practice attuned to a specific context. This was an antiexceptionalist position rooted in cultural relativism.

As Griaule and Täklä Hawaryat prepared these rebuttals, the Ethiopians unexpectedly met new allies from the Black Atlantic.[89] On September 9, four days after the decisive Assembly confrontation, Täklä Hawaryat and Éfrém Täwäldä Mädhen hosted an American delegation comprised of William Jones of the *Baltimore Afro-American* and Benjamin Careathers and James Ford of the Communist Party (CPUSA).[90] Building on Jones's recent mission to Liberia,[91] the group came to Geneva from the Seventh Comintern Congress in Moscow, where Ford had joined Palmiro Togliatti in denouncing the Italian attack on Ethiopia and urging international anticolonial unity.[92] Now in the Swiss city, the delegation visited the Ethiopians at the Hôtel de Russie.[93] Ford apprised Täklä Hawaryat of the widespread support for Ethiopia in Black America, which reflected "racial ties" as well as "the desire to aid a small nation whose independence and national and economic existence is threatened by ... so-called civilized nations."[94] The *fitawrari* lauded this solidarity, and then opined that the crisis was proving a decisive test of "the right of colored nations to independence." Put simply, Ethiopia's position would demonstrate the durability of non-White sovereignty worldwide.[95]

The discussion then turned to the racial politics of international antifascism in the context of the broader struggle against White supremacy. Months before, the NAACP had publicly reprimanded Litvinov for his seemingly tepid anticolonialism, and its monthly featured an article by George Padmore in which the latter denigrated the Popular Front as "a united front of white Europe against black Africa."[96] The charge, in short, was that the Soviet Union had sacrificed Ethiopian sovereignty in the hopes of obtaining a strategic alliance with the European colonial powers.

The ensuing solidarity debates were threatening to splinter the Harlem pro-Ethiopia movement between antifascist communists and anticolonial pan-Africanists, in the context of the unprecedented popular mobilization on Ethiopia's behalf.[97] Facing this CPUSA credibility crisis over the Kremlin position on Ethiopia, Ford pointedly asked his hosts to assess Litvinov's role at Geneva, and in reply, Éfrém and Täklä Hawaryat judged the commissar a "sincere" defender of their country. This was unsurprising given Litvinov's prominence in the diplomatic showdown of the previous week. The meeting then concluded, and detailed accounts of the Genevan summit were quickly published by the *Baltimore Afro-American* and Harlem division of the CPUSA.

During these same weeks, Täklä Hawaryat also met the Jamaican writer and activist Una Marson.[98] Like the Ethiopian delegate, her road to Geneva was sinuous. After beginning her literary career in Kingston, she relocated to London, where the city's intense racism pushed her toward Black internationalist politics. She became the secretary of the League of Coloured Peoples, Britain's largest race-focused civil rights organization, and worked with prominent activists like Harold Moody, Jomo Kenyatta, C. L. R. James, T. Ras Makonnen, and Paul Robeson. In 1934, she was the personal assistant to King Ofori Atta I of the Gold Coast colony during his visit to Britain, and in 1935, she attended the International Alliance of Women for Suffrage and Equal Citizenship conference in Istanbul. She was by this time the most prominent Black feminist in Britain, publishing widely on racial and colonial topics and staging radical theater productions. This stature induced the League Secretariat to invite her to attend the 1935 Assembly session in Geneva as a journalist liaison, and she spent three weeks touring the Secretariat offices and attending the September meetings.[99] At some point during this period, she approached Täklä Hawaryat and offered her services to his government, even volunteering to travel to Ethiopia. He instead invited her to join the staff of the Ethiopian Legation in London, now headed by the new minister plenipotentiary Wärqenäh Eshäté. Marson accepted, and after returning to Britain in October, she became its lead Anglophone secretary. Over the coming year, she would prove the closest Black internationalist ally of the Ethiopian government.

Meanwhile, the Ethiopians' official counter began on September 11, the Ethiopian New Year. For the first time, Täklä Hawaryat faced the General Assembly (figure 5.1).[100] At the morning plenary session, Hoare pledged

FIGURE 5.1 Täklä Hawaryat Täklä Maryam at the League of Nations (1935).

Source: © United Nations Archives Geneva.

Britain's commitment to collective security, an electrifying deception that led most observers to incorrectly believe the foreign secretary had announced an anti-Italian turn in British foreign policy.[101] For a moment, the mood in Geneva shifted. That afternoon, Täklä Hawaryat delivered a long address to the Assembly, with Legation secretary Éfrém at his side. He conveyed Ethiopia's respect for the League and its principles, which in his estimation accorded with the progressive and egalitarian spirit of his country, and with a tactful deference, he explained that his government would nonetheless accept the guidance of "sister nations which have reached a more advanced stage of civilization," provided that this tutelage involved "disinterested" collaboration and not forced imposition.

He then addressed the Italian memorandum. He offered that "we . . . who have been described as 'barbarians,' have given manifold proofs of our great toleration, our spirit of patience, and our sincere humility." In his view, this fact would shortly reveal whether the Covenant was "a tangible reality" or "dangerous illusion." He next considered the Italian arguments.

He provocatively noted that slavery was by no means an Ethiopian invention, adding the illiberal fillip that ancient slavery was surely preferable to the plight of modern humanity, theoretically free but "crushed... under the weight of the machine." He then argued that a new war of colonial conquest would not liberate but immiserate Ethiopia, which revealed the speciousness of the entire Italian position. In his view, the memorandum contained nothing but "mendacious documents" and "iniquitous denunciations" couched in humanitarian language. These attacks were "designed as it is to show the unworthiness of a sister nation which is guilty only of having faith in the guarantees of treaties and in the sanctity of pacts, but which refuses to condone ambitious designs under the cloak of justice. My nation does not fear the light: it desires the impartial demonstration of the truth. I therefore solemnly declare on its behalf, before all the nations here represented, that Ethiopia asks for the immediate dispatch of an international commission of inquiry to ascertain the truth of the complaints brought against her." Truth was being expertly concealed on the international stage, to Ethiopia's peril. It was an impassioned defense, but after Täklä Hawaryat took his seat, the assembled delegates studiously ignored the crisis for the remainder of the session. The silence was surreal, since as one representative publicly confessed, the dispute "preoccupies all our minds."[102] This concern reverberated that same day in Addis Ababa, where the emperor delivered a radio address that reviewed the events of the previous year, the injustice of Italian bellicosity on Ethiopia's borders, and "the rude and mendacious accusations" of the Italian memorandum.[103] Three days later, on September 14, Täklä Hawaryat formally submitted the two Ethiopian countermemoranda to the Council and Assembly.[104] For colonial undersecretary Lessona, these replies refuted "superficial facts" but not the essence of the Italian argument.[105]

Täklä Hawaryat's skepticism of foreign experts and the international system proved prescient. As the memoranda war unfolded, the Italians worked behind the scenes to strengthen their position in Geneva. Cerulli led this effort. On September 12, the day after Täklä Hawaryat's assembly address, he joined Aloisi for lunch with Secretary General Avenol, who was worried by Hoare's apparent reversal.[106] The Italians urged Avenol to accept the memorandum's race-based distinction between Semitic Abyssinia and the non-Semitic borderlands, rejecting the critiques of Griaule and Täklä Hawaryat. They also renewed the earlier call for an Italian mandate in

Ethiopia by explaining that the more recently conquered imperial peripheries could be easily transferred to Italy.[107] These geohistorical distinctions had underpinned the summer negotiations between Eden and Mussolini, though it is unclear how this new lobbying fit with Mussolini's past rejection of similar proposals. In any event, Avenol dismissed the scheme on the grounds that the territories in question were obtained prior to Ethiopia's League admission, but he accepted the larger point that its government had failed the requirements of League membership. This was unsurprising, since it was precisely what he had suggested to Theodoli and Guariglia months before. But Cerulli and Aloisi left the meeting knowing exactly where the secretary general stood at the critical juncture. This was significant because Avenol was informally participating in the Committee of Five.[108]

One week later, on September 18, the latter issued its preliminary decision. Claiming to have ignored the Italian and Ethiopian memoranda, the committee instead proposed an indefinite international administration of Ethiopia, with territorial adjustments between Italy and Ethiopia.[109] This was effectively a pseudo-mandate in which Italy would enjoy a position resembling a mandatory power. On September 22, Aloisi formally rejected this proposal, arguing that it ignored the memorandum arguments about Ethiopia's failed statehood and invalid League membership.[110] The following day, Täklä Hawaryat countered this rejection with his government's assent to the now moribund proposal, with the proviso that the particulars required further discussion.[111] But the negotiations were fruitless. On the early morning of October 3, Emilio De Bono ordered six divisions of Italian and Eritrean troops across the Märäb River, traversing the Ethiopian frontier and beginning the advance toward Adwa and imagined historical redemption. That same day, Heruy telegrammed Avenol to report the mass killing of civilians and the destruction of medical facilities in northern Tegray.[112]

One week later, on October 10, the Assembly convened for the year's penultimate plenary meeting. It was the first to address the now ongoing war between two member states. In the morning, Aloisi opened the session by attacking the Council's "extraordinary" procedural approach to the dispute, by which he meant its disregard of the Italian memorandum.[113] He then reviewed his government's contributions to the League over the preceding fifteen years, contrasted these with Ethiopia's alleged defaulted membership, and proposed that the Council's rejection of the Italian position had provoked the ongoing invasion, which was a response to the security threat posed by the Ethiopian mobilization. In this, he claimed, Italy was honoring "the real spirit" of Geneva, which through torturous logic made the war an undertaking to defend the Covenant.

After brief replies by the French, Swiss, and Soviet representatives, the day's most formidable counter was delivered by Haitian delegate Alfred Nemours.[114] An experienced statesman, diplomat, and army officer, he had nearly two decades of international experience, having twice served as his government's League delegate, and he was additionally a prolific historian, specializing in the military history of the Haitian Revolution.[115] Facing the Assembly on behalf of its other sovereign Black member state, Nemours denounced the hypocrisy of Ethiopia's provisional League membership, the denial of its collective security guarantee, and the premise of a colonial exception to international law. As he observed, "There are not two truths—one for Africa and the other Europe." The Covenant made no hierarchical distinction between member states or European and colonial wars, and assertions to the contrary were the unjust deceits of brutish and atavistic powers. It was Italy, not Ethiopia, that was barbaric. The invasion was a flagrant violation of international law, in his view, and the denial of this fact would legitimize and invite future wars of aggression rooted in claimed racial superiority. Undaunted by these ominous developments, Nemours urged international solidarity. He informed the Assembly that his speech would be followed by "millions of negroes and men of color" worldwide, and explained that "the Black republic of Haiti, realizing the gravity of the hour, is ready to shoulder its responsibilities" by volunteering its youth to the Ethiopian cause. He concluded by urging the chamber to remember that "one day we may [all] be somebody's Ethiopia."

That afternoon, Täklä Hawaryat publicly thanked Nemours.[116] It was his final speech to the Assembly.[117] Weeks later, he left Geneva, telling Griaule, "Everything is finished for us here. I must leave: my advice is indispensable over there, and I want to fight."[118] The conflict he predicted had finally arrived—the shrewd colonial gamble later judged Mussolini's political masterstroke.[119]

6

"Cerulli and His Ilk"

On October 30, Täklä Hawaryat arrived in Addis Ababa. The atmosphere in the capital was bracing. Over the previous months, *Berhanenna sälam* had reported on the confrontation in Geneva, complete with Amharic translations of the decisive Council and Assembly showdown, and it now featured a photograph of the returned League delegate and the news he would "spill his blood for his country."[1] Fittingly, the same issue of the newspaper also contained a final salvo in the international memoranda war. It was a scathing Amharic critique of foreign specialists that served as a warning for Ethiopian readers, appearing as a preface to a revisionist history of Italo-Ethiopian relations.[2] Its anonymous author noted the importance of scrutinizing the motivations of strangers, whatever their professed allegiance, and offered as a cautionary example the case of the Italian Orientalists. Surveying the coauthors of the Treccani article on Ethiopia that had just figured in the League memoranda debate, the essayist urged readers to remember that "Cerulli and his ilk" were "not born to us and are not related to us," but were in fact "employees of the Italian government" who endeavored "to know the history [of Ethiopia] . . . because they planned to seize our country."[3] In his or her view, this duplicity aided the regime's colonial project while imparting a distorting bias to Italian scholarship on Ethiopia, which was riddled with "impurities and lies." Alienated foreign research thus threatened freedom and corrupted truth, as had been just demonstrated on the international stage. One day, the essayist suggested, the Ethiopian *liqawent* would write a corrective true history of their country.

Who issued this attack on weaponized scholarship? Given the timing of the essay's publication and its unstated reference to the Treccani article, Täklä Hawaryat is a strong candidate, especially given his earlier comments to Marcel Griaule about the dishonesty of Mussolini's experts. By coincidence or design, the ex-delegate's photo appeared in the column adjacent to the critical article, next to its very first lines—perhaps he telegrammed the text to Addis Ababa before departing from Geneva. A second possibility is Tä'amrat Ammanu'él, another contributor to *Berhanenna sälam* who was deeply familiar with Italian Ethiopianist research. He had previously contributed an antifascist article to the newspaper, and was of course the author of its series on Ignazio Guidi, Silvio Zanutto, and Carlo Conti Rossini, though his treatment of these writers had been more celebratory than condemnatory. In an intriguing textual parallel, one of his earlier articles used the construction "Guidi and his ilk" to describe the collective shortcomings of Italian philologists.[4] Perhaps Tä'amrat now saw them in a new light. A third candidate is *blattén géta* Heruy. He was a longtime supervisor of the newspaper who was well acquainted with Cerulli's work, and he had just coordinated his government's response to the Italian memorandum. More specifically, the essay's defense of traditional authority and rhetoric of historical falsehood recalled his earlier comments in *Wazéma*.[5] But these attributions are ultimately speculative. Whoever its author, the piece laid bare the academy's inequitable representational politics and structural hostility toward "the impartial demonstration of the truth," as Täklä Hawaryat had put it in Geneva. Like the League guardians, the experts were dangerous.

This anonymous writer was doubly prescient. On the one hand, he or she recognized the distinctive contribution of Italian intellectuals to the fascist historical imaginary, a topic now judged central to understanding the distinctive mass culture of the regime.[6] On the other hand, the essayist's analysis of Italian Ethiopianist scholarship precisely anticipated later disciplinary critiques of Orientalism, anthropology, and sociology, which similarly anatomized the colonial politics and applied utility of academic research on non-Western societies. With respect to the Italian case, specialists have spent several decades historicizing the peninsula's Africanist scholarship, looking beyond national disciplinary historiography to assess the contributions of individual researchers to colonial administration, regime policy, and the creation of a metropolitan colonial culture.[7] This scholarship complicates exceptional models of fascist science, highlighting links between Italian, British, and French colonial studies that transcend the liberal-fascist divide, as epitomized by the transimperial 1938 Volta Congress in Rome.[8] Yet the central concern of this anonymous *Berhanenna sälam* essayist has remained largely unaddressed. What role did the field of Ethiopian studies play in the international crisis? How did the professional specialists respond to the public debate concerning Ethiopia's past and future?

The answers to these questions involve the intellectual context of the expert confrontation at the League, the variegated colonial and anticolonial politics of interwar Africanist research, and the reverberations of these within the Italian academy. By the 1930s, the regime and its ideologues had reimagined the nation's educational institutions as crucibles of a new fascist culture and professional-bureaucratic elite, and in pursuit of this goal, the Ministry of Education increasingly surveilled and intervened in the daily life of the universities and academic institutes.[9] The regime purged dissident faculty, required National Fascist Party membership for academic employment, and sanctioned *squadrista* intimidation of students and faculty. These trends intensified with the 1935 invasion of Ethiopia. Surveying Italian intellectual life in this repressive climate, Mario Isnenghi distinguishes between militant intellectuals, who were the creative elite of the party and state, and official intellectuals, who were the elaborators of fascist ideas and arguments in specific fields and institutional contexts.[10] This typology of accommodation usefully illuminates the situation of Italian academics during the second decade of the dictatorship. Allowing for notable exceptions like the philosopher and regime ideologue Giovanni Gentile, the Orientalist and overseas propagandist Giuseppe Tucci, or the exiled socialist historian Gaetano Salvemini, most researchers assumed positions resembling the official intellectual role.[11]

This cooptation restructured Italian colonial studies. Broadly speaking, the 1920s and 1930s witnessed tremendous growth in this applied field and its constituent disciplines, from history, linguistics, anthropology, and law to psychology, geography, and agricultural science. Institutional changes underpinned this development. The liberal-era universities and institutes that had educated and sustained generations of elite researchers were restructured to serve the aim of forging a national colonial culture and cadre of colonial functionaries.[12] They were joined by new regime entities dedicated to these same goals. The most prominent of these was the Istituto Coloniale Fascista (1928), which was the propaganda-focused successor to the Istituto Coloniale Italiano and the sponsor of courses, conferences, exhibitions, films, and two monthly periodicals, *Rivista coloniale* and *Oltremare*.[13] Its state counterpart was the Research Office at the Ministry of the Colonies, which maintained a massive library and published dual-use research, translated editions of foreign scholarship, and the journals *Rivista delle colonie italiane*, *Rassegna economica delle colonie*, and *Rassegna di studi etiopici*. Colonial research and propaganda were also coordinated through the Istituto per l'Oriente (1921), the Museo Coloniale Italiano (1923), the Centro di Studi Coloniali (1932), the Istituto Italiano per il Medio ed Estremo Oriente (1933), and African satellites of these metropolitan entities.[14] A series of state-backed international congresses (1931, 1934, 1937, and 1938) brokered dialogue between Italian and foreign researchers.[15]

This changing institutional environment paralleled developments within the intertwined disciplinary branches of the field. Academic anthropology entered a new phase as the older national traditions of ethnography and race-focused physical anthropology splintered into the distinct fields of peninsula-focused folklore, Africa-focused ethnology, and biological race science, all overlapping with the nascent interdiscipline of sociology.[16] These changes prefigured the development of a national tradition of cultural anthropology in dialogue with the international discipline. These emerging fields competed with the more venerable Orientalist domains of Islamic and Semitic studies, even as a new generation of linguists established innovative areas of research and responded to the practical needs of colonial rule and extra-European propaganda, from language pedagogy to jurisprudence, literature, religious studies, and contemporary history. Meanwhile, the new field of colonial psychiatry followed a similar path of growth and institutionalization,[17] while meteorology and agricultural science increasingly focused on the problems of colonial development, seeking to engineer and mobilize African biopower to serve the regime goal of national autarchy.[18]

This context transformed Italian Ethiopian studies. Its ranks now included amateur colonial officials as well as the country's most prominent specialists, and the border between the state and the academy was extremely porous. On either side, Italian Ethiopianists assumed the official intellectual role and published works with propagandistic and applied dimensions, avoiding professional silence by demonstrating overt or passive alignment with the regime's colonial and foreign policy goals in the Horn of Africa. This orientation did not necessitate acceptance of the fascist ideological apparatus in toto, since many Italian specialists—and in particular the senior generation of colonial experts—embraced a liberal-era and Guidi-esque vision of a classically inspired colonial enterprise that predated the National Fascist Party, but which broadly shared its nationalist values. Political engagement also did not require the wholesale corruption of scholarship. If some specialists produced academic and pseudo-academic works that transparently served the regime, others focused on a "pure" disciplinary research agenda while addressing obviously political topics in nonspecialist and nonacademic fora, in some cases behind the shield of anonymity. Still others produced dual-use scholarship. The pressure toward these forms of politico-intellectual accommodation intensified during the Italo-Ethiopian crisis, when Italian specialists were specifically tasked with anatomizing Ethiopians as national antagonists and prospective colonial subjects.[19] If a few specialists challenged this representational project, many more took up the work of the regime.[20] A handful even approached the militant intellectual ideal, as in the case of the physical anthropologist and regime ideologue Lidio Cipriani.[21]

Within the field of Ethiopian studies, this last possibility was exemplified by historian Carlo Conti Rossini.[22] Now ensconced at the University of Rome with more than one hundred publications to his name, he was among the most prominent specialists in the peninsula, and he mobilized his academic authority in service of the national colonial enterprise, most notably by producing nonspecialist works that purported to situate colonial affairs in their proper historical context.[23] If this was broadly achieved by his 1935 monograph on the Battle of Adwa, a narrative history of nineteenth-century Italo-Ethiopian diplomacy that imagined a redemptive colonial future,[24] it was more precisely realized by his two 1935 articles for *Nuova antologia*, published at the apex of the Italo-Ethiopian crisis. The first appeared in September, only days after Conti Rossini's name surfaced in the Geneva memoranda war, and its blunt title was "L'Etiopia è incapace di progresso civile," or "Ethiopia is Incapable of Civilized Progress."[25] The piece buttressed the Italian memorandum by challenging Ethiopia's fitness for League membership, focusing not on law and precedent but on race and culture. Wading into anthropological debates about racial typology, Conti Rossini first argued that "it is indisputable that Abyssinia is endowed with a civilization that is certainly extremely inferior to ours, but very superior to that of the surrounding regions." However, this intermediary position was complicated by the fact that Ethiopian civilization was frozen, lifeless, and shorn from its Semitic roots, a point he then illustrated through a grotesque cultural-historical survey. He described the ambiguities of the fidäl script, the deficiencies of Ge'ez literature, the obscurities of *qené* poetry, and the derivative nature of Ethiopian art, and then claimed these deficits were symptoms of underlying sociopolitical anarchy fostered by a weak state that was no more than "a federation of South Arabian colonies." There could be no autochthonous remedy for these ills, in his view, since the ruling Abyssinians were "Cushitic" inheritors of Semitic cultural gifts, and were thus incapable of endogenous civilizational development. As an illustration of this point, he noted the case of the *Mäṣhafä hatäta*, a "gem of Abyssinian literature" that had originated not with an Ethiopian philosopher but with an Italian missionary.

Conti Rossini then clarified the international implications of this analysis. In his view,

> Many centuries of history show us that Ethiopia was capable, at least to a certain degree, of receiving elements of civilization from without; but they show us also that she was sometimes unable to conserve them, [and] always [unable] to develop them and progress; as it was incapable of engendering its own evolutionary and civilizational movement... And, if from this long past one can turn to look to the future in order to foretell, one is forced to conclude that only a constant, wise, solid external intervention could lastingly correct and eliminate the contravening factors, drawing from the Abyssinian people the good qualities, today weighed down by the bad ones, to obtain from the country as much civilization as the rest of the world has the right to demand.[26]

In short, Ethiopia had been prematurely admitted to the ranks of the modern world, when it instead required colonial tutelage. If this exceptionalist conclusion complemented the arguments in Cerulli's articles and the Italian memorandum, it also countered the interpretive framework then being advanced by Griaule and Täklä Hawaryat. Whereas the latter attacked the historicist project of the racial, civilizational, and sociocultural ranking of Ethiopia from a relativist position informed by ethnological theory, Conti Rossini instead fused his deep specialist knowledge with the language of race science to defend the hierarchical conception of civilizations, the notion of primitiveness this entailed, and the centrality of the Hamitic hypothesis to understanding Ethiopian backwardness.

One month later, he continued the attack with philological weapons. The October issue of the journal featured a piece titled "Il fine di Re Teodoro in un documento abissino," or "The End of King Téwodros in an Abyssinian Document." Seemingly an example of the genre of source translation,[27] the article began with a potted biography of the nineteenth-century Ethiopian emperor, who Conti Rossini considered "among the most distinctive figures in Ethiopian history," a political reformer who succumbed to a syphilis-induced "bloodthirsty lunacy." He then sought to illuminate the life of Téwodros through the contemporaneous writings of *däbtära* Assäggahäñ, a Catholic savant from northern Shäwa who had corresponded with Antoine d'Abbadie.[28] A translated excerpt from one of these Amharic epistles followed, wherein Assäggahäñ narrated the downfall of the emperor in the vernacular historiographic style. The *däbtära* explained that Téwodros began his penultimate year with the sack of Gondär and Bägémder, where his forces destroyed local churches, massacred the population, and reduced the survivors to cannibalism. The following year, this carnage continued northward to the mountain redoubt of Mäqdäla, where the emperor parlayed with the British expedition until his final battle with the surrounding Oromo forces. After his suicide, the British looted the erstwhile looter, taking not only locks of his hair but also his wife and son, the contents of the treasury, and most of the immense royal library.

Conti Rossini closed the article by interpreting Assäggahäñ's text. He first observed that the Ethiopian masses had witnessed the "spectacle" of an invader whose technological capacity was previously unknown, and in consequence, they had abandoned their tyrannical ruler. Téwodros, however, was fettered by a "foolish blind pride" that prevented him from appreciating the superiority of his modern foe—in the same way, Conti Rossini added, that Ethiopian arrogance had isolated the country from the civilized world. This *däbtära*-mediated assessment amounted to historical revisionism. If Ethiopian intellectuals of the era typically judged

Téwodros a symbol of anticolonial defiance, Conti Rossini instead used the translated words of Assäggahän to recast the emperor as a deluded xenophobe and rapacious despot who used the state for his own aggrandizement, and whose subjects were liberated by foreign intervention. The implication was unmistakable. Téwodros was an autocratic purveyor of state-sanctioned barbarism, guilty of the same charges now being leveled at his successor Haylä Sellasé, whose regime would surely fall with equal speed.[29] For Conti Rossini, as for Cerulli, the reality of the Ethiopian present was revealed by its past.

If Conti Rossini openly marshaled his academic reputation to the colonial enterprise, other experts followed Cerulli by anonymizing their interventions in the international debate. The most significant of these was Martino Mario Moreno.[30] An academic prodigy, he published his first monograph while a teenager at the University of Genova, and then entered colonial administration: he worked alongside Conti Rossini in Tripolitania and Cyrenaica (1914–1920); joined the Ministry of the Colonies in Rome (1920–1929); became director general of political affairs in Eritrea (1929–1931), assuming a post once held by Conti Rossini; and finally moved to the Legation in Addis Ababa (1931–1934), where he replaced Cerulli. In the Ethiopian capital, he surveilled Ethiopian civil society while frequently interacting with Tä'amrat Ammanu'él, who mistakenly believed Moreno was Jewish.[31] By 1935, Moreno was back in Rome at the Ministry of the Colonies, where he supervised the Division of Economic Affairs and supported the Research Office, now working alongside Cerulli. By this time, he was an established specialist in Arabic, Amharic, Tigrinya, and Oromo literature, in addition to Islamic studies and Libyan Judaica. He envisioned himself not as an academic but a learned and humane colonial official, telling one colleague that he was but a scholar "in khakis."[32]

Given this distinctive outlook and career, Moreno was well-positioned to address the international crisis. He did so via an anonymous April 1935 contribution to *Nuova antologia*, entitled "Gli stranieri in Abissinia," or "Foreigners in Abyssinia."[33] The essay appeared one month after Cerulli's article on Ethiopian xenophobia. Continuing this theme, Moreno historicized the position of expatriates in the country. He began with an overview of European-Ethiopian contacts, noting that the Ethiopian openness of the early modern period had ended with the Jesuit proselytization during the reign of Emperor Susenyos, whose successors "severed . . . the bridge between Abyssinia and the West."[34] In the present day, he suggested, the memory of this history informed Ethiopian views of Europeans: for some, the latter were bearers of a superior culture; for others, they were dangerous strangers and future conquerors. He illustrated the second position by quoting Téwodros, who had pithily observed, "First the missionaries, then the merchants, and finally the soldiers."[35]

Moreno next scrutinized the status of foreigners in contemporary Ethiopia. He first sketched its legal system, which was in his view well suited to Ethiopians but "totally inapplicable" to Europeans, and then explained the provisions of the 1908 Klobukowski Treaty, which established a system of extraterritorial rights for resident foreigners resembling the capitulations imposed on the Ottoman Empire—though he added, "I must say this quietly because Abyssinians hate the word [capitulations]."[36] However, this treaty had proven insufficiently protective given the unreasonableness of Ethiopian judges, and foreigners were now fleeing the country. He attributed this exodus not to the innate hostility of the Ethiopian people or antipathy of the ruling elite, but instead to the provocations of nationalists who "fill their mouths with punctilious half-learned doctrines of sovereignty."[37] This judgment paralleled Cerulli's critique of the Young Ethiopians. Addressing these agitators, Moreno argued that Ethiopia's historic spirit of openness and record of foreign-led development would produce the best outcome for all. This was in his view the only possibility, for "if it lacks a guide, Ethiopia will march backward, believing itself to be going forward."[38]

Cerulli, Conti Rossini, and Moreno intervened in the crisis as academic specialists. Their efforts complemented other more popular deployments of expert knowledge. This approach was exemplified by Mario Pigli, a strident fascist journalist and party official who was by the 1930s the chief editor of *Azione coloniale*, the propaganda weekly of the Istituto Coloniale Fascista.[39] The author of numerous works on Italian foreign policy and colonial Africa, Pigli was a prolific commenter on Italian ambitions in Libya, Eritrea, and Ethiopia, most notably via a 1933 monograph on modern Italo-Ethiopian diplomacy and the Treaty of Weçhalé.[40] In September 1935, he published a short book entitled *La civiltà italiana e l'Etiopia*, or *Ethiopia and Italian Civilization*, under the bizarre pseudonym "Jihad," and then months later, he issued a revised English edition with a new title under his own name, which in turn enjoyed three subsequent editions.[41] Although not an

Ethiopianist by training or professional identity, Pigli's book synthesized the specialist research on pan-Mediterraneanism and the history of premodern Italo-Ethiopian relations, making esoteric Italian and Latin academic scholarship available in translation to a large international audience.[42] To this end, he cited leading Ethiopianists such as Cerulli, Conti Rossini, and Hiob Ludolf, and even discussed the sixteenth-century diasporic intermediary Täsfa Ṣeyon, who he considered an exemplar of Italo-Ethiopian fraternity. Accessible and extensively illustrated, Pigli's work adopted the trappings of academic rigor.

His argument was forceful and explicit. Buttressing the claims of the Italian memorandum as well as the *Nuova antologia* articles by Cerulli, Moreno, and Conti Rossini, Pigli argued that Italy was a uniquely constant and sincere protector of Ethiopia in its relations with the wider world. His book sketched the phases of this history: the late-medieval contacts between the Venetian Republic and the Solomonid kingdom, attested in Latin codices and Ethiopian art and architecture; the development of the early modern community of Ethiopian pilgrims in Rome, their impact on European learning, and the development of Catholic-Orthodox relations; and finally, the nineteenth-century exploration of Ethiopia by Italian missionaries and adventurers, the frustration of this scientific undertaking by Ethiopian rulers, and the ensuing contribution of Italian entrepreneurs, architects, and engineers to the development of the Horn of Africa. Rather uniquely for the moment, Pigli's narrative framed current events within the Mediterranean *longue durée*, which in his assessment demonstrated Italy's good faith and commitment to its long-frustrated civilizing mission in Ethiopia, now poised to resume via the colonial invasion.[43]

Another specialist contributed a series of anonymous articles to the popular monthly *Italia coloniale*. Over the course of 1934–1935, this publication featured ten pieces by "the Ethiopian," who the editors described as "a [male] researcher and observer who has lived ... in Ethiopia and Eritrea for nearly thirty years."[44] As they explained to readers, this distinctive background enabled him to offer a rigorous yet grounded analysis of the local situation, and his articles purported to reveal discomfiting realities concealed by Ethiopians and Ethiopianists alike. They addressed a range of topics, some relatively specialized: the features of Ethiopian painting; the persistence of slavery and its underlying causes; the ecclesiastic hierarchy of the Ethiopian Orthodox church; the history of the Ethiopian monarchy and its fundamentally despotic nature; the material conditions among the people of Tegray, in northern Ethiopia, as compared that of their ostensible kin across the border in colonial Eritrea; the history of Tegray and the neglect of its heritage by the Ethiopian state; and the biographies of Ethiopian notables, including *le'ul ras* Seyyum Mängäsha, *ras* Dästa Damṭäw, and *däjjazmach* Näsibu Zä'amanu'él. As these subjects suggest, "the Ethiopian" was largely concerned with the highland Christians of the north, and especially the Tigrinya-speaking peoples astride the colonial frontier.

Taken together, these articles broadly complement—and occasionally rehearse—the positions of the Italian memorandum. In the pages of *Italia coloniale*, "the Ethiopian" focused on the failings of the central institutions of highland Christian society: the church and state. After reviewing the situation of the fractious elite and impoverished farmers of Tegray, for example, he claimed that Menilek's subjugation of the north had led to "lands entirely destroyed" and "populations decimated and reduced to subjugation or total slavery." This spoliation was continued by Haylä Sellasé, for which reason it followed that the League had admitted as a member state a government that was nothing but "a true anachronism, organized and maintained by the barbaric lust for domination by the Amhara people."[45] As he elsewhere put it, Tegray was "a paradise" that was "governed by devils" camouflaged as civilized people.[46] He also attacked the Ethiopian church, arguing that its priests are "generally ignorant, scarcely knowing literature and little or nothing of the art of writing," while its monks "frequently intervene in political affairs siding with this or that chief, following convenience." After reviewing the internal politics of the Ethiopian Orthodox Church and its relationship with the Coptic See of Saint Mark, he queried, "What moral guide can the Abyssinian people find in an ecclesiastic hierarchy this chaotic and ignorant?"[47] Yet another article examined the Ethiopian martial tradition and contemporary army, suggesting these would be easily accommodated to a new colonial master.[48]

Who was "the Ethiopian"? Amid his racist diatribes are glimpses of an individual who grasped arcane topics like ecclesiastic and monastic nomenclature, vernacular historiography, and Semitic linguistics, adding to these political intelligence from Tegray and Addis Ababa. Some of his commentary suggests personal relationships with the Ethiopian elite. In one article, he offered observations on the Italian language competency of *däjjazmach* Näsibu, and in another, he recounted a conversation with an

Orthodox Christian priest in which the latter had related a parable about four naïve bulls who escaped the paddock only to be devoured by other animals, a supposed commentary on the enslaved's unpreparedness for freedom. Elsewhere, he made casual references to the insular world of Ethiopianist scholarship: he noted Enno Littmann's 1906 archaeological expedition; the impact of the sixteenth-century Venetian Nicolò Brancaleone on Ethiopian painting; the Meroitic, Egyptian, and Arab influence on Ethiopian architecture; and even Amharic and Tigrinya etymologies. These points suggest that "the Ethiopian" was likely a highly educated and long-serving member of the colonial administration in Eritrea, the Italian Legation in Addis Ababa, or the Italian consulates in Adwa or Gondär, with some Amharic or Tigrinya language fluency and an awareness of the arguments being prepared in the League memorandum.

An even more widely read pseudo-academic subterfuge emanated from the journalist Mario Missiroli, who wrote pseudonymously via the persona of "Professor" Giulio Cesare Baravelli of the University of Rome. Missiroli was hired by the regime to write a book entitled *L'ultimo baluardo della schiavitù: Abissinia*, or *The Last Bastion of Slavery: Abyssinia*, which was published in August of 1935, translated into more than five languages, and widely reprinted alongside the English edition of Pigli's work.[49] In it, "the Professor" claimed that Ethiopia had defaulted on the conditions of League membership: the central government controlled only the capital, with the rest of the country in chaotic disarray; the rule of law failed through bribery and excessive corporal punishments; foreigners and consular officials faced xenophobia and physical attacks; and enslavement remained widespread, extending into trade with the Arabian peninsula. He then rehearsed the Italian diplomatic grievances against Ethiopia, contrasting the bilateral treaty framework with the frustrated Italian concession schemes and the chronic border skirmishes with the Italian colonies, and he concluded by defending Italy's right to new colonies given the interwar growth of the British and French empires. The work was one of the most widely read texts on the question of Ethiopian barbarism.[50]

In several instances, "the Professor" anticipated the problematic of the Italian memorandum. This was particularly evident in his discussion of Griaule. Baravelli-Missiroli introduced the French ethnologist as "a scientist of unquestionable authority" with a "deep and unwavering love" for Ethiopia, and then offered Griaule's field experience in Gondär as proof of the Ethiopian government's xenophobia. He explained that grim Ethiopian realities had forced Griaule to document the horrors of execution by incineration in his ethnographic novel Les flambeurs d'hommes, or The Burners of Men, which figured in the Italian memorandum as well as the countermemoranda by Griaule and Täklä Hawaryat. The Professor added to this intertextual debate the claim that it was none other than Täfäri Mäkonnen himself who issued the order to light the flames in the episode in question, and further proposed that the crown prince had been opposed in his order of execution by Empress Zäwditu. Two months later, Baravelli-Missiroli's rebranding of Griaule's account perhaps inspired a cover feature in the Neapolitan weekly Mattino illustrato.[51]

Perhaps unexpectedly, a singularly multilingual intervention came from Afäwärq Gäbrä Iyäsus. Now the Ethiopian minister plenipotentiary in Rome, the näggadras and L'Orientale alumnus served as his government's representative in Italy during the international crisis, aided by his son Giovanni and abba Jérôme.[52] If Afäwärq's appointment to this post reflected his distinction as a leading Italophone intellectual, it was complicated by his past criticisms of the Ethiopian elite and rumored Italian sympathies. Even after his arrival in Rome, his perceived political ambiguity was such that he was obliged to publicly defend his patriotic credentials on the front page of Berhanenna sälam.[53] This stance was compromised in 1934, however, by the publication of his conversational Amharic textbook.[54] Ostensibly written decades earlier for his students in Naples, the work was now addressed to Italian travelers to Ethiopia, including the thousands of soldiers preparing to embark for the Horn of Africa. The manual introduced readers to practical vocabulary related to travel, commerce, faith, hygiene, warfare, and daily life, supplemented by imagined dialogues between an Italian and Ethiopian in facing Italian and Amharic text.

One of these addressed the timely question of Ethiopian despotism.[55] Afäwärq's position was suggested by its provocative bilingual title, "Tyranny and Barbarism."[56] The dialogue begins with an Italian interlocutor asking an Ethiopian about the kings of his country. Learning that Menilek is the current ruler, the Italian asks whether he is as despotic as he has heard. The Ethiopian replies that this is a lie, whereupon the Italian reviews the foreign allegations against Menilek and his "uncivilized" and "backward" state,[57] eliciting a response from the Ethiopian each time. To the accusation of leading military campaigns that "exterminated" the Oromo,[58] the

Ethiopian explains that this was a necessary aspect of Menilek's territorial expansion, and with respect to the practice of castrating prisoners of war, the Ethiopian concedes its incivility but then suggests that even if the emperor had banned the practice, his raucous militias would have disobeyed him.[59] He adds that perpetrators of this act could not be punished since this would require sanctioning the entire nation. When the Ethiopian next suggests that Menilek was at least better than his predecessors, the Italian replies that Europe has the greatest kings of all, since they exact no tribute and exist only as corpses, paintings, or individuals of no consequence. Facing this revolutionary idea, the Ethiopian finally concedes to the Italian and concludes that Menilek is "an abomination" and "filth" that makes one vomit.[60]

This dialogue is as distinctive as it is provocative. If its basic claims parallel the derogatory representations of Ethiopia then being made by Italian experts, the text uniquely articulates the Amharic lexical field related to Ethiopian deficiency, precisely identifying a vernacular form of the international language of condemnation. While some of Afäwärq's earlier publications addressed similar subjects, they did not employ this potent terminology.[61] Equally distinctive were his authorial politics: Afäwärq was the leading Italophone Ethiopian writer of his generation, and presumably an exemplary "Europeanized Abyssinian," as Cerulli had put it. Yet if this cosmopolitanism mired Heruy in fruitless nihilism, it enabled Afäwärq to offer an accessible yet erudite "native" articulation of the colonial language of ethnic suffering and humanitarian liberation. In this, Afäwärq anticipated the mediating author function Conti Rossini devised for *däbtära* Assäggahäñ: Afäwärq's dialogue similarly posed as authentic Ethiopian autocritique, offered in translation for Italian readers. This suggests the purpose of the work. Amid the flurry of popular Italian-Amharic textbooks issued on the eve of the invasion,[62] Afäwärq alone offered an authoritative guide to the colonial language of command. His manual was a practical handbook for dealing with Ethiopian subordinates, offering everyday models for issuing orders, correcting errors, and ensuring that all remained in their stations.[63]

A similar albeit less direct contribution to this project of cultural translation came from Elena Sengal. By the 1930s, she had replaced Gallina as the lead Amharic instructor at the Istituto Orientale in Naples, and was thus the most senior African academic in Italy. For this reason, she was like Afäwärq a prominent perceived exemplar of the assimilated modern African subject. This distinctive intellectual role bestowed a special significance to her 1935 article on "Favole e storielle abissine," or "Abyssinian Fables and Tales," which appeared in *Africa italiana*, the quarterly journal of the Società Africana d'Italia.[64] The piece offered Italian translations of more than sixty Amharic and Tigrinya folkloric texts. These were largely obtained from Gallina, she explained, but two were derived from Heruy's 1922/1923 prosopography of Ethiopia's notables, which was peppered with historical anecdotes.[65]

Broadly, Sengal's texts address the encounter of antagonistic types—hyenas and donkeys, rich men and paupers, soldiers and commanders, merchants and farmers, robbers and marks, and hosts and guests. Most of their subjects are nonspecific, but several feature named individuals, such as the comic anecdotes about the popular justice of Emperor Yohannes or the social iconoclasm of the ecclesiastic *aläqa* Käflä Giyorgis, both drawn from Heruy's book. Several texts gesture toward the discursive themes of Ethiopian deficiency, most notably the stories about the immolated and enslaved, the destructive role of Ethiopian kings, and the hypocrisy of the Ethiopian church and faithful, though these connections are subtle and unacknowledged. In orientation and timing, Sengal's article broadly complemented Afäwärq's Amharic textbook as a work of intellectual translation by a reliable "Europeanized" native, offering Italians a mediated glimpse of the Abyssinian mentality through its reflection in orature. In this, her folklore article paralleled Cerulli's investigation of Amharic print culture as a reflection of Abyssinian modernity.

Sengal's last text abandoned cultural exposition for political admonition. Continuing the theme of antagonistic encounter, she introduced the passage as "a final thought" distinct from the remainder of the article.[66] The text addresses the value of resentment,[67] and she speculatively attributed it to *aläqa* Zännäb, a nineteenth-century scholar who wrote a biography of Téwodros as well a work of moral reflections, published in 1924 by Heruy's Goha Ṣebah press.[68] Her text begins with the maxim "It is good to be resentful," which it then explains through a corporal analogy. The fingernails, toenails, and hair all resent the razor, but the last allows the others to grow and develop. Eyelashes, meanwhile, resent nothing, and for this reason remain forever the same. Given the timing of the publication, Sengal's metatextual framing, and the subject matter of the rest of the journal issue,⁶⁹ many readers would have surely understood this passage as an allegory for the Italian colonial project, here understood through the liberal guise of paternalistic tutelage rather than the fascist logic of national redemption through war. Read closely from this position, the passage suggests that mandatory or colonial rule in Africa was akin to the invigorating razor: if its imposition might involve momentary trauma, it was ultimately an instrument of historical progress, since it would broker a mutually beneficial relationship in which African submission facilitated future development. For Sengal, it would seem, this was the transaction refused by the Ethiopian government.

These Italian and African experts—whether actual, impostured, imagined, or perceived—instrumentalized specialist knowledge to serve the regime's representational politics. Their most authoritative academic critic was Marcel Cohen, Griaule's former teacher and the leading French Ethiopianist of his generation.⁷⁰ By the 1930s, Cohen was ensconced at the École Nationale des Langues Orientales Vivantes, where he was acclaimed for his work on Ethio-Semitic and Semitic linguistics as well as his groundbreaking studies of the Afroasiatic language family. A heterodox Marxist and member of the French Communist Party (PCF), he was also a close analyst of the social dimensions of language, anticipating the field of sociolinguistics, and he regularly published articles on these aspects of the French language in the PCF daily *Humanité*. He was also active in international Left organizations, from the Popular Front to the anti-imperial movement. His intellectual comrades included Marcel Mauss and Maurice Halbwachs, with whom he collaborated for Émile Durkheim's *Annales sociologiques*, as well as the detained Antonio Gramsci, who Cohen described as a role model with respect to their "shared task" of international revolutionary struggle.⁷¹

Given these credentials and commitments, Cohen was uniquely positioned to join the unfolding specialist showdown over Ethiopia. In the last months of 1935, he wrote a series of essays for *Humanité* that deployed historical materialist analysis to rebut the liberal and fascist attacks on Ethiopian sovereignty, ethnic relations, and League membership. The first appeared in September with the title "Genre de vie en Abyssinie," or "Way of Life in Abyssinia."⁷² In it, Cohen critiqued the chief claim of the Italian memorandum: Haylä Sellasé's government easily satisfied the League criteria for an effective government, as demonstrated by its functioning military, economy, administrative apparatus, and legal system. He added,

"It does these things like other governments, though it is autocratic and directed by an emperor." Ethiopia's admission to the League was thus no error. One month later, he continued the discussion with an assessment of Ethiopian ethnic politics entitled "Individu et société en Abyssinie," or "Individual and Society in Abyssinia."[73] It addressed the key question of the distinction between Abyssinians and the conquered subject peoples of the Ethiopian empire, complementing the arguments of Griaule and Täklä Hawaryat and disputing those of Cerulli and Conti Rossini. Cohen claimed these distinct groups had fused through "a progressive expansion, a slow appropriation and assimilation," starting with the ancient arrival of South Arabian immigrants, continuing through the development of the Solomonid polity and diffusion of Abyssinian culture through intermarriage and religious conversion, and culminating in Menilek's campaigns and establishment of the imperial capital in historic Oromiyya. Weeks later, Cohen delivered "Autorité et droit en Abyssinie," or "Authority and Law in Abyssinia," which anatomized Ethiopian feudalism.[74] Pointing to small landholding as the key distinction between the Ethiopian and European feudal modes of production, he observed that hereditary property rights in Ethiopia were mediated by state power, which was itself lineally insecure. Legal institutions reconciled the disputes of both, and consequently, "the ideas of law and the state dominate individuals in the highest places." In short, Ethiopian society was hyperlegal, not anarchic. As much as this model countered the arguments of Cerulli-Niliacus and the Italian détourneurs of Griaule's ethnographic novel, Cohen's elaboration of the Ethiopian mode of production also undermined exceptionalist arguments about Ethiopian society, anticipating a comparative problematic that would be more systematically explored by later generations of Ethiopian Marxists.[75]

These *Humanité* articles had an international sequel. In February 1936, Cohen published *L'Abyssinie doit rester indépendente*, or *Abyssinia Must Remain Independent*, a concise book that assailed the liberal presumptions and capitalist machinations of Genevan diplomacy.[76] It was sponsored by the Comité Internationale pour la Défense du Peuple Éthiopien et de la Paix, an organization whose leaders included the socialist politician—and grandson of Karl Marx—Jean Longuet, the British Abyssinia Association president Norman Angell, the exiled Italian antifascist journalist Luigi Campolonghi, the Martiniquan pan-Africanist Paulette Nardal, and the French feminist socialist Marguerite Martin.[77] Cohen's work methodically dismantled the

League response to Ethiopia, with documentary attachments that invoked the memoranda war of the previous autumn. His analysis was stark: the country's continued independence was "an embarrassment" to the European imperial powers, and this fact underpinned the Committee of Five's proposed mandatory scheme, which would have exposed Ethiopia "to the games, large and small, of colonialist capitalism." The proposed League oversight aimed to "perpetuate the order of white hegemony," with Ethiopia serving as "a guinea pig for the effort of a new type of imperialist colonization" akin to international trusteeship. If his *Humanité* essays rebutted the League arguments about failed statehood and civilizational deficiency, his publication for the Comité Internationale instead attacked the imperial and racial architecture of the liberal international order and its discursive superstructure of mandated progress and development.

A radically different defense of Ethiopia came from W. E. B. Du Bois. By the mid-1930s, the Atlanta University professor counted among the leading public intellectuals of the Black international. Nearing seventy, his stature had been secured by decades of leadership and journalism at the NAACP; his groundbreaking research on Africa, the African diaspora, and global White supremacy; and his distinctive and uncompromising vision of pan-African socialism. He had additionally established himself as a "leading champion" of Ethiopia in the United States through political activism and scholarship.[78] This interest is exemplified by his 1915 work *The Negro*, in which he advanced an iconoclastic account of the ancient Nile Valley as a coherent cultural zone originating with the pre-Aksumite societies of the Horn of Africa, an interpretation rejected in his day but now widely accepted. He subsequently developed this analysis in his 1939 *Black Folk Then and Now*, an Afrocentric world historical survey that attacked the prevailing Aryan interpretation of ancient Egypt, the exceptionalist narratives of ancient and modern Ethiopian history, and the analytic decoupling of Nilotic Africa from the rest of the continent.[79] This was a critique of the racial ontology undergirding the Orientalist imagination of Ethiopia. Yet despite the influence of Du Bois's Ethiopia-focused historiography in the Anglophone Black Atlantic, his work was ignored within the European-dominated and narrowly Semiticist academic field of Ethiopian studies. This marginalization replicated his position within his own discipline of sociology, whose founders similarly dismissed his pioneering contributions to the analysis of race.[80]

This Ethiopianist scholarship complemented Du Bois's contact with the Ethiopian government. After his indirect 1919 encounter with Heruy and the Ethiopian delegation, in 1921 he invited Ethiopian representatives to the Second Pan-African Congress,[81] and in 1930 he met *käntiba* Gäbru Dästa and Mälaku Bäyyan at the NAACP headquarters in New York City. The elderly diplomat and young student had come to meet a New York firm involved in a government project, and they took the opportunity to visit Du Bois in Greenwich Village. Elated by this overture, Du Bois quickly produced a white paper with comprehensive recommendations for the Ethiopian government, which appears to have shaped the latter's approach to foreign policy and economic development in the ensuing decade.[82] One year after this New York City meeting, Du Bois wrote directly to Haylä Sellasé to offer his service as an advisor, and over the next few years, he remained in regular contact with Mälaku, who obtained a medical degree from Howard University and cofounded its Ethiopian Research Council before returning to Ethiopia with his wife Dorothy Hadley, where he served with the Ethiopian Red Cross during the Italian invasion.[83] By then, Du Bois had left the NAACP and was using his pen and voice to mobilize thousands of Black Americans to the Ethiopian cause.[84]

These events were the intellectual and political context for his 1935 essay on the international crisis.[85] Originally titled "The Hands of Ethiopia" and written on the eve of the Italian invasion, Du Bois's essay outlined Ethiopia's role in African and world history since late antiquity, with a special focus on the modern imperial contest for the Horn of Africa. He celebrated Téwodros as an outward-looking ruler who correctly perceived the European threat, countering Conti Rossini's arguments in *Nuova antologia*,[86] and then related how Italy pursued its colonial ambitions through the "clumsy forgery" of the Treaty of Weçhalé and the invasion that culminated in Adwa.[87] For Du Bois, the latter was an epochal conjuncture: in tandem with the Mahdist rebellion in the Anglo-Egyptian Sudan, Ethiopia's victory at Adwa meant that "the headwaters of the Nile," the arena of the Red Sea, and "the path from the Cape-to-Cairo" were suddenly all "in the hands of black men," exposing Italian weakness to the world. Yet the "mutilated victory" of the First World War exacerbated Italian colonial grievances, fueling the fascist vision of redemptive Roman glory in Ethiopia. Du Bois juxtaposed these developments with the political ascent of Haylä Sellasé, who in his estimation inaugurated a pivot toward African liberation at the meridian of European empire. For Du Bois, this second epochal turning point was signaled by the emperor's embrace of the "Negro" concept of Ethiopia and not the "Semitic" alternative Abyssinia.

These dynamics underpinned the unfolding international crisis. For Du Bois, the imminent Italian invasion represented a third epochal conjuncture, in that the impact of League action or inaction and Italian victory or defeat would reverberate across the entire colonized world. Of this, he wrote:

> There will not only be the cost in debt, death, and hate, but the whole colored world—India, China, and Japan, Africa in Africa and America, and all the South Seas and Indian South America—all that vast mass of men who have felt the oppression and insults, the slavery and exploitation of white folk will say: "I told you so!" There is no faith in them even towards each other. They do not believe in Christianity and they will never voluntarily recognize the essential equality of human beings or surrender the idea of dominating the majority of men for their own selfish ends. Japan was right. The only path to freedom and equality is force and force to the utmost.[88]

In short, the Italian subjugation of Ethiopia would expose and undermine the imperial and racial logic underpinning the entire international order. Moreover, were the Ethiopians to successfully repel the Italians, this would "shake the centers of European imperialism" and break "the spell of Europe" over the colonized people of Africa and Asia, catalyzing movements of anticolonial liberation worldwide. The historic nature of this development is suggested by the scriptural and internationalist allusions in the title of Du Bois's article.

In October 1935, a modified version of this essay appeared in *Foreign Affairs*, a leading Washington policy journal.[89] Now retitled "Inter-Racial Implications of the Ethiopian Crisis: A Negro View," the essay was stripped of its sweeping Ethiocentric history of imperialism and more strictly focused on the potential international reverberations of Italian victory or defeat. Du Bois precisely and frankly stated the illiberal logic of the Italian arguments in Geneva:

Conquest and exploitation are brute facts of the present era, yet if they must come, is it better that they come from members of your own other races? To this question Italy is giving a terrible answer. Though the center of the Catholic Church and the home of the Renaissance of modern culture, she says flatly: We are going to subdue an inferior people not for their good but for ours. We are going to take Ethiopia just as we took Somaliland and as England took Kenya. We are going to reduce black men to the status of landless serfs. And we are going to do this because we have the power to do it, and because no white nation dare stop us and no colored nation can.[90]

He then explained the transparency of this predatory logic for colonial subjects in British East and West Africa, Francophone Africa, and the Anglophone Caribbean, and additionally, for Black Americans in the United States. Everywhere, the Italian invasion exposed the fundamentally exploitative essence of liberalism.

Of all the expert commentaries on the crisis, Du Bois's two intertwined essays most clearly explicated the racial and imperial architecture of the international system, the burdened nature of Ethiopia's position within that system, and the significance of the moment for the global color line. His structural analysis of these issues was singular. Du Bois's attack on Geneva's humanitarian imperialism and colonial conception of sovereignty complemented the arguments of Ethiopian intellectuals like Tässäma Eshäté and Täklä Hawaryat, as well as the positions of Griaule, Cohen, and Nemours. Ethiopia did not require foreign tutelage—it needed its due protections under international law. Yet Du Bois went further by situating his critique of disposable sovereignty within an expansive historical vision of worldwide anticolonial liberation, suggesting that Ethiopians could preserve their own freedom while catalyzing the collapse of the global imperial order.[91] This theorization of the power of pan-African and African-Asian solidarity in the face of the liberal-fascist colonial alliance rested on a categorical rejection of the premise of Ethiopian deficiency or racial subdivision, in which respect it subtly diverged from the Marxist critique of Cohen, who envisioned the Ethiopian social formation through the analytic category of Abyssinia and the prism of relative backwardness.[92] Griaule's analysis was compromised by a less materialist version of this same Eurocentric historicism. Ultimately, Du Bois was the lone—though denied—Ethiopianist to discern the world-historical implications of the crisis. He grasped its potential to reveal the deceit of liberalism's emancipatory promise. As a later generation of African historians would demonstrate, Du Bois correctly recognized the Italian invasion of Ethiopia as the twilight of colonial rule in Africa.[93]

Ultimately, the memoranda war rehearsed the League imperial project within the problematic of expertise. The fullness of this development was demonstrated by the 1935 International Congress of Orientalists, which convened at the apex of the diplomatic crisis.[94] Held at the University of Rome over five days in late September, and featuring audiences with Mussolini and Pope Pius XI, the conference united international specialists across Oriental studies, with sessions addressing Assyriology and Egyptology, the societies and languages of Africa and Asia, and the literatures of Judaism, Islam, and Eastern Christianity.[95] As an academic event, the congress affirmed the status of the Italian branch of the international field.[96] Its president was Indologist Emilio Pavolini, and its vice presidents included Berber specialist Francesco Beguinot and Tibetologist Giuseppe Tucci as well as Ethiopianists Cerulli, Conti Rossini, and Guidi. These coordinating scholars invited specialists from across the peninsula's universities and institutes, who presented alongside leading foreign researchers like Enno Littmann, Louis Massignon, Hamilton Gibb, Taha Hussein, and Shelomo Dov Gotein. Notably absent was Giorgio Levi Della Vida, then barred from the Italian academy because of his refusal to sign the fascist loyalty pledge, as well as his teacher Leone Caetani, a socialist historian of Islam then exiled to British Columbia.[97] Griaule, fully occupied in Geneva, also missed the event.

Despite the many Italians at the congress, there was only one specialist presentation on Ethiopia.[98] Lidio Cipriani offered a paper on African racial origins, scrutinized through the framework of the Hamitic hypothesis and typological physical anthropology.[99] In it, he developed Vincenzo Giuffrida-Ruggeri's revisionist arguments concerning the "Ethiopian" racial type, a supposedly ancient Hamitic population originating from an even earlier fusion of Semitic immigrants and Horn of Africa autochthons.[100] This concept had just figured in the memoranda debate and paralleled the racially hybrid understanding of Abyssinia, even as it diverged from Guidi's language-based reconstruction of proto-Semitic history.[101] In

Cipriani's congress paper, he proposed that this ancient "Ethiopian" race was once widely dispersed across the continent, only to become gradually diluted through mixture with various non-Hamitic African populations, which he deemed racially inferior. Following Giuffrida-Ruggeri, Cipriani held that the modern inhabitants of Ethiopia were "residues" of this ancient Hamitic—rather than Semitic—racial type, which point he asserted on the basis of the collection of skulls and skeletons at the National Anthropology Museum at the University of Florence.[102] He concluded by proclaiming that this racial identity made it a "biological absurdity" that Ethiopia would be able to join the modern world without colonial stewardship.[103]

This was an unusually public acknowledgment of the political implications of specialist research. If such transparent advocacy defined the engaged expert role at the League, it verged on professional impropriety in an ostensibly scientific academic setting—an implication provocatively suggested by the fact that Cipriani's paper was delivered in absentia.[104] This reputational issue likely explains the silence of the other Italian Ethiopianists at the congress, despite their productivity in the moment as official intellectuals. Even Guidi and Moreno, who had long affirmed the importance of marshaling academic inquiry to the national colonial project, did not present at the conference. On its final day, the Ethiopian government ordered the general mobilization.

These contradictions of expertise are suggested by the cryptic title of Griaule's 1936 account of the crisis, *La peau de l'ours*, or *The Skin of the Bear*. On one level, it invokes the French proverb "Don't sell the skin of the bear before it has been killed," suggesting that Italy's defamatory propaganda in Geneva was the precondition of a profitable colonial invasion.[105] Going further, the notion of a pelt-as-carcass also invokes the public fate of the exotic bears once imported to the Colosseum, where the ancient Romans watched as the animals slaughtered captives, or alternatively, were themselves butchered in staged hunts or contests. In this reading, Griaule's bearskin represents a trophy, recalling Ethiopia's fate in the international arena at the hands of modern Rome. It was the centerpiece of an imperial spectacle, precisely as Täklä Hawaryat lamented. A third possible referent is the bearskin headdress worn by the standard bearers of ancient Rome, or *signiferi*, with all the duality this role entailed. This martial metaphor suggests the deception of Ethiopia's specialist adversaries, for whom the external trappings of humanitarianism and dispassionate inquiry concealed the enduring reality of a conquering Caesar. In this reading, the bearskin invokes the Janus-faced power of modern experts, who monopolized the *signifer*'s mantle of scientific objectivity on the international stage, but who were in reality antagonists within an international struggle rooted in base realpolitik and military aggression. "Cerulli and his ilk" purported to represent Ethiopia to the world, when they were in reality the standard bearers of empire. This was regime Orientalism.

PART III
Years of Hardship

7
The Chronicler of Asinara

It was October 1935. Giuseppe Bottai stepped off a steamship in Massawa. A bombastic futurist and early Roman *squadrista*, by the 1930s he had become a leading fascist intellectual and theorist of revolutionary corporatism, and in January 1935, he was appointed governor of his hometown. He immediately began a wide-ranging effort to excavate the historical palimpsest entombed within Rome, including a major restoration of the Temple of Venus. But the colonial fervor of the ensuing months spurred him to abandon the intrigues of politics for the revitalizing battlefields of Africa, and he volunteered to serve in the Ethiopian campaign. Pietro Badoglio offered him command of an infantry battalion on the northern front. On April 1, across the Eritrean frontier at an old Italian fort near Mäqällä, the general informed Bottai that he would also be appointed governor of Addis Ababa, in which capacity Bottai would serve as the civilian counterpart to Viceroy Badoglio himself. It was a richly symbolic choice. As the latter explained, Bottai's nomination meant "the name of Rome will consecrate the victory."[1] The two imperial capitals would share a Blackshirt avant-garde mayor.

On the ensuing march south, Bottai surveyed the historic landscape of Wällo and Shäwa. In Dässé, he glimpsed the residence of *negus* Mika'él Ali, the father of *lej* Iyyasu, and he then surveilled Addis Ababa and its environs by airplane, spotting the palace of Haylä Sellasé in the city before circling to the mountaintop redoubt of Ankober, the former stronghold of Menilek. Days later, the Italians reached the Ethiopian capital. For Bottai, their arrival was a transcendent collective moment that reified the previously abstract colonial enterprise. "Our hands tremble," he wrote, as "they touch, after so much suffering, the purpose."[2] Inside the threateningly silent city, Badoglio's motorcade—which included just-arrived colonial undersecretary Alessandro Lessona—advanced to the old Italian Legation.[3] The rough villa represented, in Bottai's words, "a little intact world, this piece of Italy, around which all of Abyssinia is now Italian." This realization chilled him, for "the score has been settled." "The fifth of May," he exulted, "we will secure it in our flesh, this day, a fact of history, of place, of infinity."[4] The conquest represented both the culmination and negation of history: it was the awaited realization of an eternal fascist empire that would transform the nation and colony. But this revolutionary antihistoricist promise proved fleeting. Despite a flood of congratulatory telegrams, Bottai served as the acting governor of Addis Ababa and vice governor-general of Africa Orientale Italiana for less than three weeks, departing home with Badoglio at the end of May.[5]

Exactly five years later to the day, *blatta* Märse'é Hazän Wäldä Qirqos witnessed the emperor's triumphant return to Addis Ababa.[6] Originally from Jerru in northern Shäwa, he had pursued an ecclesiastic education before moving to the capital, where he worked as a palace clerk, newspaper editor, and Amharic teacher—all the while writing histories, publishing Ge'ez religious texts, and contributing articles to the local weeklies.[7] In 1934, he witnessed the explosive events at Wälwäl as secretary to the Anglo-Ethiopian Boundary Commission,[8] and after the Italian invasion, he spent the years of the colonial occupation with his family in the capital, watching as friends, teachers, and acquaintances disappeared into exile, detention, and oblivion.[9] In January 1941, news came that Haylä Sellasé had crossed the Sudanese border with a joint force of Ethiopian and British troops, and as the Royal Air Force covered the highlands with propaganda leaflets, the Italians faced successive defeats by the British East Africa Force and the Ethiopian anticolonial guerillas, or *arbäñas*. Finally, on April 6, the first liberators entered Addis Ababa.

The convoy of the restored emperor reached Shäwa that same month, as the fighting continued in Gondär.[10] Advancing south, they mourned the massacred monks at Däbrä Libanos, confronted the leading collaborators at Feché, and joyously greeted the religious communities of Mount Enṭoṭṭo. An immense procession then descended to Addis Ababa, as the local radio played the only surviving recording of the national anthem.[11] In a motorcade flanked by *arbäñas* and followed by Ethiopian, British, Sudanese, and South African troops, the emperor's convoy of exiles wound through the jubilant streets of the capital, as Märse'é Hazän and thousands of onlookers clapped, wept, ululated, and kissed the ground. It finally reached Menilek Palace in Arat Kilo—the precise location where Badoglio had announced the Italian conquest, and where an artist now displayed an image of the Lion of Judah disemboweling the Roman She-Wolf. On the palace steps, Haylä Sellasé addressed the multitude. Recounting the trials of the past five years, he explained that while Mussolini "believed that the land he declared conquered would be forever in his hands," he had profoundly underestimated "the fighting morale" of the patriots who toppled the colonial regime. The imperial infinite was a conceit. Gesturing to posterity, the emperor then reconsecrated May 5 as an annual commemoration of the anticolonial martyrs.[12] Describing this day of reunion and collective remembrance, *blatta* Märse'é wrote that the celebrants "met his majesty in a beautiful parade, showing their joy with boasts [of pride]."[13] The occasion was marred only by the gruesome public slaughter of the camels that had carried the liberators from the Sudanese border, on British orders.[14] Like the thousands of Italian soldiers and settlers who remained in the capital, it was a portent of the postcolonial future.

Taking its title from Märse'é Hazän's pithy characterization of the colonial era, part III of this book examines the traumatic events between these two epochal moments. Its focus is dual. It first considers the impact of colonial rule on a group of displaced Ethiopian intellectuals and their families, whose individual and collective experiences of detention, exile, loss, and survival unfolded within an enlarged imperial space that spanned the metropole, colony, and diaspora—from the Ministry of Italian Africa in Rome to the cities and villages of Shäwa, the concentration camps of Somalia and Italy, and the negotiating tables of Athens, Amsterdam, Geneva, and London. In fundamental ways, their experiences during these intervening "years of hardship" reflected the routinization of the colonial counterinsurgency in Ethiopia, both as an ongoing military and intelligence operation and as a framework for population control, ethno-social engineering, and political intimidation and punishment.[15] The structured violence of this endless war of occupation—which encompassed dislocation, torture, hostage-taking, sexual violence, and mass killing—represents the radicalization of the regime's metropolitan apparatus of repression through the colonial logic of the unbounded sovereignty to kill.[16] Fascist ideologues believed this violence would forge a disciplined Italian nation and obedient African subjects. Instead, colonial rule inflicted "ineffaceable" wounds, as Frantz Fanon later put it, descending into a generalized inhumanity whose racialized mental and physical trauma would take years to bind.[17] In the decade after liberation in 1941, the effort to bear witness to this collective suffering underpinned the Ethiopian campaign for justice at the United Nations War Crimes Commission.

With this postcolonial reckoning in mind, part III also scrutinizes Cerulli's actions during these years of hardship. As the seniormost expert of the Italian colonial state, Cerulli was a key agent of the Ethiopian counterinsurgency, and he played a critical role in its design and articulation in the metropole and colony. At the Ministry of Italian Africa in Rome, he oversaw the application of targeted deportation and surveilled confinement as tools of population control, intelligence gathering, and political bargaining, his imprimatur gilding this expert-supervised carceral regime as a supposedly enlightened, efficient, and humane alternative to the blunt military-based approach of mass killing.[18] This institutionalized detention-intelligence nexus exemplified colonial juridicality: it was arbitrary, legalistic, and intensely coercive, as exemplified by its reliance on concentration camps. After leaving the Ministry for Africa Orientale Italiana, Cerulli oversaw colonial administration, military operations, intelligence gathering, and propaganda work in the colony itself. As vice governor general, he was the public face of the regime in the urban centers, battlefields, and detention sites of the Horn of Africa, and he produced propaganda, field intelligence, and policy assessments that forcefully intervened in local politics and social relations. He recommended targeted killings. As viceregal regent, he temporarily occupied the seniormost position in the military command structure, and on at least one occasion, he assumed operational authority on the battlefield. Over these five years, Cerulli was directly and indirectly involved in events later classified as war crimes, crimes against humanity, and genocide. The next three chapters reconstruct their course and human impact, following the living memory of trauma into the colonial archive.

Dähné Wäldä Maryam was a survivor (figure 7.1).[19] Born in 1882, he was the scion of a distinguished family from Sälla Dengay, a mountain village in northern Shäwa.[20] His father worked at the imperial court in nearby Ankober, and as a young boy, Dähné studied at a local monastery until his father boldly introduced him to Emperor Menilek, who dispatched the fourteen-year-old to Addis Ababa to apprentice with *ṣähafé te'ezaz* Wäldä Mäsqäl Tariku at the newly established Ministry of the Pen. The newcomer quickly impressed the emperor, who within a short time selected him to be one of his personal secretaries, in which position Dähné served alongside Heruy under *ṣähafé te'ezaz* Gäbrä Sellasé Wäldä Aregay, Menilek's trusted advisor.[21] Abruptly thrust into a prominent role at the palace, the youngster was now tasked with documenting the emperor's ambitious project of state-led modernization. He monitored a host of government initiatives, from the development of plumbing, telephone lines, and paved urban roads to the establishment of a hospital and national mint,[22] and he eventually supervised Märha Ṭebäb, the scriptorium-cum-printing house that published the Amharic weekly *A'emro*, or *Intelligence*.[23] After Menilek died, Dahné became a critic of *lej* Iyyasu and advisor to Empress Zäwditu. By this time, he had earned the rank of *qäññazmach* as well as the unusual nom-de-guerre "*abba* Yelaq," or "Father of the Most Learned One,"[24] and he moved among the capital's intellectual elite, from the various palace historians to friend Märse'é Hazän and colleague Heruy.[25] His stature was such that in 1924, he delivered Zäwditu's official welcome on Täfäri Mäkonnen's return from Europe.[26] He married Taṭärä Wärq Sheberé, and they lived with their large family in Yeka, on the eastern outskirts of Addis Ababa. The empress was godmother to three of their children.

The fortunes of the *qäññazmach* turned, however, as the power of the crown prince deepened. In 1928, Dähné was accused of supporting the unsuccessful coup of *däjjazmach* Weqaw Berru, the head of the palace guards, which unfolded one month after the signing of the Treaty of Friendship. Though exonerated, Dähné became entangled in Täfäri Mäkonnen's power struggle with the empress, and the crown prince subjected him to house arrest followed by exile from the capital through a series of appointments to provincial government posts, most notably in Käffa and

FIGURE 7.1 Dähné Wäldä Maryam.

Source: Personal collection of author, courtesy Abebe Ambatchew.

Jimma.[27] His family remained in Addis Ababa. Dähné was temporarily rehabilitated in 1930, when the emperor ordered him to curate an exhibit for his coronation ceremony that same year, but he was again dismissed to the provinces when the proceedings concluded. His banishment was such that he was refused permission to join his family in mourning the death of their eldest daughter.[28]

These events were overtaken by the Italian invasion. Summoned from Jimma in 1935, Dähné was appointed advisor to *le'ul ras* Kassa Haylu, and that November, he accompanied the latter's army on the march north to Gondär and Mäqällä. After hasty stops at monastery libraries, the *qäññazmach* joined the turbulent campaign on the northern front. He survived an aerial bombardment and subsequently witnessed the Ethiopian counteroffensive in December, the decisive Italian victory at Tämbén in February 1936, and finally the disastrous Ethiopian defeat at Mayçhäw in March. The emperor and royal family left the country shortly thereafter. In the chaotic months that followed, Dähné returned to Shäwa and sought refuge at a family property outside Addis Ababa, where he coordinated with the simmering anticolonial resistance. This connection attracted the new Italian administration, which intercepted a letter to Dähné from *däjjazmach* Abärra Kassa—the son of his former commander—about a plan to recapture Addis Ababa.[29] With this damning intelligence in hand, Viceroy Rodolfo Graziani summoned the *qäññazmach* to the capital, where he was interrogated, forced to sign a letter of submission, and placed under surveillance.

On the morning of February 19, 1937, Dähné was ordered to appear at the former imperial palace in Seddest Kilo. The occasion was a ritual submission celebrating the birth of Vittorio Emmanuele, the Savoyard heir. As the viceroy, *abunä* Qérellos, and various dignitaries received the assembled crowd, two Eritrean colonial functionaries named Abreha Däboch and Mogäs Asgädom suddenly hurled grenades at the dais, wounding the two most senior Italian officials and several others. The shocking attack—now widely known by its Ethiopian date of Yekatit 12—had been coordinated by the emperor's government in exile, and aimed to spark a broader insurrection that would reveal Italy's weakness to the world.[30] Almost immediately, the Italians began firing indiscriminately into the crowd, and the capital descended into chaos. With the approval of the viceroy and Ministry of Italian Africa, Italian soldiers and settlers began a three-day campaign of looting, arson, sexual assault, and mass killing in Addis Ababa and its environs, summarily executing suspected conspirators, perceived enemies, and random civilians. It was the violent nadir of fascist colonialism, claiming the lives of approximately twenty thousand Ethiopian men, women, and children.³¹ Dähné was among the few survivors of the carnage on the palace steps. On March 6, he was abruptly arrested and deported to Italy, without a charge or hearing.³²

Eleven days later, he reached the desolate island of Asinara, off the northern coast of Sardinia. Once inhabited only by a population of feral albino donkeys, by the late nineteenth century the island had become a site of large-scale remote confinement, its lone village and rocky coasts remade into a modern penal colony.³³ In the liberal era, it served as an agricultural colony and internment camp for Austro-Hungarian prisoners of war,³⁴ and during the fascist period, it was reserved for political dissidents and colonial subjects, the latter chiefly Libyans deported to the metropole in a variation on the more common practice of intercolonial exile.³⁵ In the spring of 1937, the arrival of Dähné and more than two hundred Ethiopian detainees effectively transformed the island into an internment camp for "dangerous" or politically suspect Ethiopian colonial subjects, who were officially termed *confinati*, or "exiles."³⁶ Asinara was now the largest colonial carceral site in Italy, specifically dedicated to the detention and surveillance of African political prisoners. In this, it exemplified both the fascist system of extrajudicial internal exile, or *confino*, as well as the punitive model of the penal colony that culminated in the concentration camp.³⁷

The immediate situation of the Asinara detainees was dire.³⁸ Forcibly displaced from home, where their families remained in grave danger, the Ethiopians confronted an alien physical environment, a language barrier that constrained communication with Italian staff, and the daily challenges of medical crises, food shortages, population transfers, and racialized incarceration. A number of women in Dähné's group arrived pregnant and gave birth in detention. It was a situation of intense isolation, deprivation, and dehumanization, compounded by the psychological impact of their uncertain length of exile in the absence of criminal charges or adjudicated sentences. Years later, the writer Käbbädä Mika'él—whose uncle was detained on the island—recalled these realities in his poem "Prisoner of Asinara," which concluded with the acerbic line, "This new cruelty that made us like true savages, this new wickedness; this is what is called twentieth century progress."³⁹

Dähné confronted this adversity with the written word. Weeks after his arrival, he began a diary in which he recorded the struggles of the detainees, reassuming his ministerial role as the annalist of a displaced community in crisis. For the next three years, he carefully documented the lives of "the great and the small" on the island, as he termed them, paying particular attention to the fortunes of the royal family, the *mäkwannent*, the *liqawent*, and the intelligentsia. This large group included many prominent figures from the politico-imperial elite—from Princess Romanä Wärq Haylä Sellasé, the eldest daughter of the emperor, and *ras* Gäbrä Heywät Mika'él, the septuagenarian son of *negus* Mika'él Ali and elder brother of *lej* Iyyasu,⁴⁰ to a host of civil servants from the ministries and imperial council.⁴¹ Many were Dähné's former colleagues and superiors. Also among the detainees were Germachäw Täklä Hawaryat, the son of the former League of Nations delegate; Heruy's wife Hamärä Eshäté, their daughters Aṣädä Wäyn and Gännät Heruy, and their five grandchildren; and *käntiba* Gäbru Dästa, his wife Kassayé Eshäté, and their daughters Dästa, Gännät, and Yäwäbdar, the last the musician later renowned as *emmahoy* Ṣeggé Maryam.⁴² All these were joined by prominent *ulama* from Addis Ababa, Guragé, Harär, and Somalia, as well as several members of the Ethiopian Armenian community.⁴³ Collectively, the detainees represented a broad swathe of the Ethiopian elite, and together with their counterparts imprisoned elsewhere in Italy, Eritrea, and Somalia—such as *ras* Emru Haylä Sellasé, *ras* Gétachäw Abbatä, and *le'ul ras* Seyyum Mängäsha—they represented the most politically prominent survivors of the invasion and first year of colonial rule.⁴⁴ Some, like Heruy's multigenerational family, were nothing more than hostages.

For *qäññazmach* Dähné, the hardships of the camp compounded the trials of the colony. In his diary, he lingered on the grief following the death of *lej* Gédiyon Bäyyänä, the youngest child of Romäna Wärq, as well as the suffering of Haylé Wäldä Mäsqäl, the son of his former supervisor *ṣähafé te'ezaz* Wäldä Mäsqäl who succumbed to disease at a hospital in nearby Sassari.⁴⁵ Other challenges were constant. He lamented the difficulty of maintaining religious life in a foreign and oppressive environment: he recounted the efforts of *liqä liqawent* Gäbrä Ab to prepare a dignified community chapel, and he occasionally noted encounters with visiting Italian ecclesiastics.⁴⁶ Beyond the island, Dähné worried about events at home, in particular the seizure of family property, and he prepared a detailed outline of the inheritance laws of Shäwa that he hoped could serve returned detainees who faced challenges in reclaiming their patrimony.⁴⁷ He also closely followed international affairs via Italian newspapers and radio broadcasts.[48] In May 1938, for example, he noted Hitler's massively orchestrated seven-day tour of Italy, which purported to demonstrate fascist imperial achievement through a visit to the Aksum obelisk in Rome.[49]

One week after reaching Asinara, Dähné used his pen to confront the colonial state. Together with *ras* Gäbrä Heywät and thirty other detainees, he dispatched an Amharic letter to Mussolini in which he and the other signatories introduced themselves as "faithful Ethiopian subjects" of Italy.[50] Perhaps hoping their detention had been an error, they explained that they had been separated from their families despite their expressed loyalty to the viceroy and effort to "live peacefully under the Italian flag," and they rejected the outlook of those "few individuals" who sought to disrupt "the beginning of progress" and "the harmony between the [Italian] government and the people of Ethiopia."[51] For these reasons, they were alarmed by their suspected involvement in the Graziani attack, and requested a formal investigation. The entire document reflected a bleak but pragmatic calculus born of their precarious position. Far from home and with few options, the group could only invoke the reciprocity implied by the bargain of collaboration.[52] On March 24, they delivered this petition to Aldo Duce, the director of the Asinara medical clinic. Duce forwarded it to the Ministry of the Interior, which administered the camp, as well as the new Ministry of Italian Africa.[53]

One month later, Dähné met Cerulli. The latter now occupied the highest echelon of the colonial bureaucracy in Rome. In the two years since the showdown at Geneva and ensuing Italian invasion, the Ministry of Italian Africa had been renamed, enlarged, and restructured to administer the new colony of Africa Orientale Italiana, comprised of subjugated Ethiopia as well as the existing colonies of Eritrea and Somalia. Cerulli oversaw the Office of Political Affairs throughout this expansion, in coordination with the newly constituted colonial bureaucracy in the Horn of Africa, comprised of the central Governo Generale and five regional governates.[54] Beyond the broad formulation of colonial policy, his specific portfolio included colonial intelligence and counterintelligence; colonial diplomacy, including negotiations with the exiled emperor and management of international disputes involving Ethiopia; surveillance of the Ethiopian exile diaspora, particularly with respect to the royal family; foreign relations with the Italian colonies, including foreign consular activity within Ethiopia; and various economic development schemes, both parastatal and private. He also served in Lessona's ministerial cabinet, together with senior representatives of other branches of government. In 1936, he visited the colony immediately after the subjugation of Addis Ababa, where he attended public events in the company of prominent Italians as well as his interpreter, the artist Agäññähu Engeda.[55] The following year, in 1937, Cerulli allegedly participated in the ministerial coordination of the Yekatit 12 massacre.[56]

On April 9, Dähné's letter reached Lessona's cabinet. The response was swift. The Ministry immediately dispatched Cerulli to Asinara to gather intelligence on the detainees, with the aim of identifying conspirators in the Graziani plot as well as candidates for political cooptation. In the context of the violence in the capital and the searing insurrection across the highlands, this reconnaissance was critical, and Cerulli's language skills, knowledge of Ethiopian politics, and Legation experience made him a peerless candidate for the job.[57] On April 20, he left the capital for Asinara, accompanied by a telegram from Lessona that granted him sweeping authority at the camp.[58] After reaching the island, he spent several days engaged in an intensive and highly coordinated interrogation of the most prominent detainees.[59] He spoke with sixty prisoners, collected statements, and met the remaining two hundred detainees en masse, even as new arrivals continued to disembark from the Horn of Africa.[60] These encounters surely startled some of the Ethiopians. A few would have recognized Cerulli from his years in Addis Ababa, likely the only familiar Italian face at Asinara.[61]

He was joined on the island by his subordinate *basha* Asfeha Wäldä Mika'él, a complex and singular personality (figure 7.2).[62] A Catholic from Säganäyti in the Eritrean highlands, Asfeha had attended the Capuchin mission school in Kärän, where he learned Italian and distinguished himself at a young age through a chance encounter with the House of Savoy. In 1928, when Crown Prince Umberto stopped at the school during his tour of the colony, the fourteen-year-old Asfeha was selected to read a scriptural passage to the distinguished guests.[63] He provocatively chose Genesis 37, which recounts how Joseph was betrayed by his brothers and sold to a group of foreign merchants. The visitors were impressed by Asfeha's studious attitude and linguistic prowess, but after their departure, the school director confronted him about the reading. As Asfeha later recalled, he told the stunned official that he had selected the verse because of its

FIGURE 7.2 Asfeha Wäldä Mika'él.

Source: Personal collection of author.

political implications, saying, "We Eritreans were sold by *negus* Menilek to the Italians; but otherwise, we are Ethiopians."⁶⁴

Like many African students in the Italian colony, Asfeha used his education to pursue a career as a colonial functionary. From 1932–1934, he served as a translator for the colonial military command in Asmara, and after 1934, he worked at the Ministry of the Colonies in Rome, where he became Cerulli's subordinate in the Office of Political Affairs. He was thus one of the highest-ranking Africans in the colonial bureaucracy, and in 1937, it was this role that brought him to Asinara. On March 26, the Ministry dispatched Asfeha to work as an interpreter on the island,[65] and just over three weeks later, he joined Cerulli for the interrogations.[66]

This intelligence operation had major repercussions. On April 25, Cerulli sent Lessona a memorandum that systematically profiled the detainees and their apparent politics.[67] In the document, he began by noting the confusion that prevailed among the Ethiopians at Asinara, addressing the main theme of the March letter. In his view, their disorientation was understandable, in that the attack on Graziani appeared to be the work of a narrow group of "fanatical Young Ethiopians," possibly aided by "the ex-negus," the European exiles, and shadowy "elements of international organized subversion"—but not a broad swath of the Amhara or Shäwan elite, as some senior regime officials then believed. He added that most of these Young Ethiopians remained at large, though a few were now at Asinara. This was a countervailing assessment. In Cerulli's estimation, none of the prisoners themselves were directly implicated in the attack that had occasioned their detention, and many of them—like *qäññazmach* Dähné—had in fact submitted to the Italian government. Their politics were heterogeneous.

Cerulli then argued that this fact represented an expedient opportunity to eliminate the most defiant nationalists and engineer a new colonial elite. With respect to both the individuals he had interviewed and the broader collective, he suggested that "it is now in our interest to re-examine their situation politically, which I repeat is neither unique nor uniform, and reach a conclusive judgment of the condition of each of them so that the fate of each corresponds to their particular value to our discussions." In short, the arbitrary mass detention of the Ethiopian elite should be instrumentalized. To this end, he proceeded to categorize the detainees in terms of the policy aims of the colonial administration, listing the specific individuals who comprised each category and identifying the carceral measures that should be applied to each.

His typology began with the militant patriots. Cerulli termed these "our irreducible enemies," adopting the regime terminology for the most subversive Italian political prisoners.[68] In his assessment, a small subset of the detainees were unwavering anticolonialists—either actual or assumed members of the Young Ethiopian movement—toward whom "it is useless to adopt half measures."⁶⁹ They were dangerous as well as influential, and for this reason, he recommended their immediate removal from the general population on Asinara. He identified twenty members of this group, including Téwodros Wärqenäh, the eldest son of the London minister plenipotentiary Wärqenäh Eshäté, as well as Säyfu Mika'él, a colleague of Heruy and the uncle of Käbbädä Mika'él. He failed to appreciate, however, the militancy of Abäbäch Chärqosé, a formidable guerilla from Addis Ababa who had arrived at Asinara with the other detainees (figure 7.3).⁷⁰ Related to these "irreducibles," as Cerulli termed them, was a second group of Young Ethiopians who he considered "less directly compromised" by strident anticolonialism. In his view, these fourteen individuals— including Germachäw Täklä Hawaryat and *käntiba* Gäbru Dästa—should remain at Asinara under close surveillance. Whether militant or moderate, remote detention in Italy would isolate these individuals from the insurrection in Ethiopia.

Beyond these two dangerous groups, Cerulli identified six additional groups of more eclectic orientation. One was a cohort of five individuals who indicated that they wished to study in Italy, including Marqos Pawlos Män Amäno, the son of the former consul general of Palestine.⁷¹ Cerulli suggested sending these to an agrarian school on the peninsula, which would inoculate them from "the insidious propaganda of the political exiles" at Asinara and prepare them for potential membership in the colonial elite. A second group was comprised of seven "old chiefs of the Menilek era," including *ras* Gäbrä Heywät and *afä negus* Telahun Bähabté, who Cerulli viewed as conservative opponents of the emperor, the Young Ethiopians, and the reformist intelligentsia. He recommended transporting them to a more salubrious location on the mainland. A third category consisted of eight individuals who Cerulli believed could be coopted by the colonial state, and who for this reason should be relocated to the environs of Rome where they could be "surveilled and approached" so as to facilitate their reconciliation with the regime. This group of "recuperables," as Cerulli termed them, included *däjjazmach* Ayyaléw Berru, the former governor of Sämén, as well as Täsfayé Tägäñ, Cerulli's erstwhile League adversary.⁷² A fourth group consisted of Muslim *ulama*, some from regions recently subjugated by Menilek, and a fifth several dissident *liqawent*, who Cerulli suggested might be amenable to the new religious policies of the

FIGURE 7.3 Abäbäch Çhärqosé.

Source: © Institute of Ethiopian Studies.

colonial administration. He recommended the removal of both populations from Asinara.

A sixth and final category included the families of executed anticolonial leaders. These included the family of Romäna Wärq, the widow of *däjjazmach* Bäyyänä Märed, as well as the family of Abäbäch Abägaz, the widow of *däjjazmach* Wänd Bäwässän Kassa, Griaule's erstwhile adversary in Gondär.[73] Cerulli believed the privation of these aristocratic families did not create "favorable propaganda for us" among the other prisoners, and he specifically recommended the relocation of the princess and her sons to avoid "a useless spectacle of misery" on Asinara. He further recommended the relocation of several aristocratic detainees from the Tyrrhenian island of Ponza—including Emru Haylä Sellasé, the emperor's first cousin and acting regent until December 1936—to wherever the "irreducibles" would be isolated, since in his view the *ras* was the "recognized head of the Young Ethiopians." Cerulli concluded the report by stressing that none of the detainees should be returned to the Horn of Africa.[74]

This report was a sophisticated assessment of the colonial situation. Cutting against a simplistic model of collaboration and resistance widespread among regime powerbrokers, Cerulli rejected the notion of ethnicity, class, education, religion, and ritual submission as categorical markers of "native" affinity. He instead disaggregated the complex political factions of the Shäwan elite, challenging monolithic conceptions of Abyssinian or Ethiopian politics anchored to the emperor and exiled government. More specifically, he identified the potential utility of the *mäkwannent*, from the "old chiefs" to their juniors, as well as the foreign-educated intellectuals of subaltern origins, who numbered among his "recuperables" as well as "irreducibles." The colonial state could forge and mobilize this distinctive interclass alliance of opportunity. To this point, his conception of Ethiopian participation in the colonial administration involved an enlarged range of intermediary roles, from civil servants and translators to civil society defenders of Italian rule and commerce- and development-focused entrepreneurs. In all these respects, Cerulli's vision of a modern African colonial elite represented an eclectic, synthetic, and context-based variant of the British model of indirect rule and the French conception of conjunctive authority.[75] In the wake of the perceived treachery of African functionaries like Abreha Däboch and Mogäs Asgädom, the would-be assassins of Graziani, Cerulli's assessment of the importance of Ethiopian—and specifically Abyssinian—contributions to colonial rule was iconoclastic.[76]

This five-page memorandum established the framework for colonial detention until the collapse of Africa Orientale Italiana. It reimagined the metropolitan *confino* system of extrajudicial detention as an instrument of colonial counterinsurgency, outlining the operating policy toward Ethiopian detainees in Italy through an elaboration of the regime's existing distinction between "political" and "common" Italian detainees.[77] The day after Cerulli's report reached the Ministry, Lessona read it to Mussolini, who approved the proposed detainee placement protocol,[78] and in the months that followed, the Ministries of Italian Africa and the Interior implemented Cerulli's recommendations.[79] By late July, the latter informed Cerulli that the detainee transfers were unfolding with "maximum urgency."[80] The would-be students had departed for Palermo, and the additional detention sites had been identified:[81] the "irreducibles" would go to Longobucco, a remote town in La Sila, the snowy and pine-covered mountain range that divides western and eastern Calabria; the "old chiefs" would relocate to a monastery in Torre del Greco, between Herculaneum and Pompei at the foot of Mount Vesuvius in Campania; the women and children would move to the Institute of the Benedictine Sisters in Mercogliano, near Avellino in Campania; and the "recuperables" would settle in the ancient hilltop town of Tivoli in Lazio, just east of Rome. A month later, the relocations were nearly complete.[82] Almost half of the detainees were in transit or had left the island for other sites in Italy,[83] twelve had returned to Addis Ababa, and Romanä Wärq and her entourage had been sent to the Consolata Institute in Turin.[84] All the while, *qäññazmach* Dähné watched from Asinara, recording in his diary the sudden greetings and uncertain farewells of his friends, colleagues, and superiors.

As the relocations proceeded over the summer, a number of the detainees began writing to the Ministry, directly pleading their cases like the signatories of the March letter. Most of this correspondence was forwarded directly to Cerulli at the Office of Political Affairs, and today, the archive of this unit at the Ministry of Foreign Affairs contains hundreds of Amharic and Italian letters from Ethiopian *confinati*. Many of these were not state petitions but correspondence with friends and relations in Italy and the Horn of Africa, which were intercepted, reviewed, and censored by the Ministry. In some cases, these intercepted letters remained in Cerulli's office, buried in the archives with accompanying administrative documents; in others, a translation or executive summary was produced, and the original document was dispatched to its intended recipient.[85] Still other letters, however, reached the Office of Political Affairs because they were specifically addressed to Cerulli, Lessona, and other ministerial personalities. These documents offer a rare textual glimpse of the predicament of the Ethiopian detainees, their complex confrontations with the colonial state, and their individual relationships with the Orientalist director, who now became a powerful arbiter of detainee freedom, replicating the metropolitan model of pardon through direct appeal to Mussolini.[86] This archival record demonstrates that Cerulli not only devised the operating framework of colonial detention, but also that he deployed this system to coerce bargains from selected detainees by controlling their finances, family contacts, and access to the outside world. In this, Cerulli personified the colonial gatekeeper state.[87]

This power is most evident with the so-called recuperables, whose relocation to the environs of Rome was intended to facilitate exactly this dynamic.[88] A well-documented case is that of Berhanä Marqos Wäldä Ṣadeq, a Francophone Catholic from Harär.[89] Born to a family of state functionaries, he studied with the same Lazarist missionaries who tutored Täfäri Mäkonnen, and served as interpreter during the latter's 1923 trip to Aden.[90] He then began a government career that culminated in the posts of secretary general of the Ministry of Foreign Affairs, consul general of the Ethiopian Legation in Port Said, and chargé d'affaires of the Ethiopian Legation in Ankara.[91] Although he advised the emperor, he also maintained good relations with the Italian Legation in Addis Ababa,[92] and he was for this reason attacked by factions within the senior administration and reformist intelligentsia.[93] After the Italian invasion, Berhanä Marqos critiqued the emperor's departure from the country, and in late 1936, he accepted Italian sovereignty over Ethiopia, leaving Ankara to formally submit at the Italian Legation in Cairo. He was aided in this subterfuge by his cousin *blattén géta* Wäldä Maryam Ayyälä, who replaced Täklä Hawaryat as the Ethiopian minister in Paris, and additionally, by Angelo Giuseppe Roncalli, the apostolic delegate to Turkey who later became Pope John XXIII.[94] In the estimation of diplomats Aklilu Habtäwäld and John Spencer, the defections of the two cousins were among the most dramatic of the time, and were widely covered in the foreign press.[95] Graziani personally notified Cerulli of Berhanä Marqos's decision.[96]

Believing his position secure, the latter returned to Ethiopia in December 1936, accompanied by his brother-in-law Taddäsä Mäshäsha, the emperor's former secretary.⁹⁷ According to his relatives, this decision was a refusal of the comfort of exile.⁹⁸ Yet only months later, Berhanä Marqos was arrested in the aftermath of Yekatit 12 and deported to Asinara as "a precautionary measure."⁹⁹ In April, he met Cerulli. During his interrogation, he claimed, "Shäwa is no more difficult to govern than any other region of Ethiopia," despite recent events.¹⁰⁰ He explained that the restive province was ethnically heterogenous—including Amhara, Oromo, and Guragé—and the previous government had administered it directly, with no delegated authority or "feudatories" beyond village *capi* similar to those appointed by the Italians in Eritrea. Berhanä Marqos then proposed reconstituting political power along ethnic lines, an argument consonant with Cerulli's ethnopolitical vision of Abyssinian—and now Italian—colonial rule. Such a transformation might be slow, but Berhanä Marqos believed it necessary, since at present "the people do not know who to obey on daily basis."¹⁰¹ In short, his prescription for the chaos in Shäwa was the development of ethnically partitioned political authority and the cooptation of the Ethiopian elite. This was precisely the strategy Cerulli endorsed.

This shrewd assessment by a leading intellectual featured prominently in Cerulli's report to Mussolini and the Ministry. Unsurprisingly, Cerulli identified his interviewee as recuperable, and months later, Berhanä Marqos was transferred to Tivoli with the rest of this group. His situation then began to evolve, despite his continuing material hardship. On August 17, he coauthored a group letter to Lessona from his new home in Lazio in which he thanked the Ministry for the relocation, and the missive was forwarded to Cerulli.¹⁰² Nearly a year later, in July 1938, he was among the first detainees to return to Ethiopia, on Cerulli's specific recommendation and with the goal of demonstrating regime munificence to Italy's African subjects.¹⁰³ Berhanä Marqos then received a lucrative concession to operate a wholesale cotton and dry goods enterprise throughout Africa Orientale Italiana, apparently over the objections of some of the governors.¹⁰⁴

Broadly similar was the case of *däjjazmach* Ayyaléw Berru.¹⁰⁵ Born into an aristocratic northern family, he was a relative of *etégé* Ṭaytu and *le'ul ras* Kassa, and he served the former during the reign of Menilek. After the fall of Iyyasu, he became a stalwart of Täfäri Mäkonnen, and in 1930, he helped defeat *ras* Gugsa Wälé, the rebellious husband of Zäwditu.

This loyalty earned him the governorship of Sämén, but in the assessment of anthropologist Alberto Pollera, who wrote a profile of the *däjjazmach* on the eve of the Italian invasion, he remained a peripheral northern personality despite his ancestry and loyal service. It was perhaps for this reason that Ayyaléw contacted Gondär consul Raffaele Di Lauro and Eritrean governor Iacopo Gasparini, and during the invasion, Gasparini personally apprised Mussolini of the *däjjazmach*'s overtures.[106] Graziani then counted him among the most important of the coopted Ethiopian elite.[107] Yet after Yekatit 12, Ayyaléw was unexpectedly sent to Asinara, where he was interrogated by Cerulli. According to the latter, the *däjjazmach* shrewdly argued that Italian rule in Ethiopia required the support of the *mäkwannent*, and he compared the colonial state to "someone who had acquired beautiful land and a good plough, but who had liquidated the oxen without replacing them or obtaining other means of traction."[108] In Ayyaléw's view, powerful Ethiopian allies like himself had been doubly failed by the Italians. On the one hand, they were excluded from governance through their restriction to ineffective ceremonial roles, and on the other, they lived in peril because the state offered no protection from the vendettas of their rivals. His pragmatic implication was clear: the Ethiopian elite had little incentive to submit.[109]

Cerulli counted the *däjjazmach* among the recuperables, and the two remained in contact after his visit to Asinara. On June 8, Ayyaléw dispatched an Amharic letter to Cerulli in Rome.[110] Offering his respectful greetings, he explained that *basha* Asfeha had recently intervened in a financial dispute on Ayyaléw's behalf, obtaining for the *däjjazmach* an overdue stipend payment. Asfeha's role in this matter is intriguing, since he epitomized the role of the native intermediary envisioned by Cerulli, on the one hand, and the agent colonial subject suggested by Ayyaléw, on the other. In the summer relocations that followed, Ayyaléw was transferred to Tivoli, where he joined Berhanä Marqos in coauthoring the August 17 group letter to Lessona and Cerulli.[111] Months later, on December 9, the *däjjazmach* dispatched another letter to Cerulli, congratulating the Orientalist on his recent promotion, for which he and the Tivoli detainees "rejoiced."[112] The plaudits were unsurprising. Cerulli had already intervened twice in Ayyaléw's case, first in the financial dispute and then via the relocation, and this precedent surely suggested future possibilities given Cerulli's new position. The gambit worked. In 1938, Dähné reported that Ayyaléw returned to Ethiopia, and he later became one of the most prominent aristocratic supporters of Italian rule.[113]

Equally fruitful was the case of his acquaintance *däjjazmach* Amdé Ali.[114] Known by the evocative horse name *abba* Qeṭaw, or "Father of the Punisher," he was the grandson of *negus* Mika'él Ali and son of *däjjazmach* Ali Mika'él, and thus bore an august Wällo lineage spanning the Muslim-Christian and Amhara-Oromo divides.[115] He clashed with Haylä Sellasé and was imprisoned at the time of the Italian invasion. He then submitted to Graziani,[116] only to be deported to Italy in the spring of 1937 with his son *lej* Ali Amdé and brother *qäññazmach* Käbbädä Ali.[117] The three were sent to Naples, where the *däjjazmach* briefly met Cerulli, and this encounter led him to petition the Orientalist director. In October, he wrote to lament the brevity of their meeting, but added that he believed Cerulli's willingness to place him in Naples rather than Asinara reflected the latter's trust. He then asked Cerulli to transfer him to a location where the two could be in close proximity, and where his wife could be near her sister.[118] The Ministry acceded to this request, and transferred him to Tivoli and then Mercogliano.[119] The Office of Political Affairs explained the relocation by classifying the *däjjazmach* as recuperable, whatever Cerulli's initial assessment.[120]

Possibly encouraged, Amdé Ali next petitioned Cerulli for financial assistance. In December, he wrote to explain that he had not received compensation for his property in Dässé, then occupied by an Italian.[121] While others had received rent, he had not, and he lamented, "I alone find myself afflicted in squalid misery, aggravated by the fact that my children are also confined with me." He urged Cerulli to send the money. That same month, he wrote again to congratulate Cerulli on his promotion and decoration as Cavaliere di Gran Croce. Reminding the Italian of his unanswered letters, he added that he knew Cerulli followed the detainees' correspondence, and then recast his situation in moral terms. His conscience remained unimpeachable, but his initial relief for the "mercy" of being placed in Naples with his family was now diminished by his worsening material situation. In his view, this hardship was unrelated to the situation in Ethiopia, which led him to appeal to Cerulli's "noble heart." Succor came the following year, when the Ministry recommended his repatriation to Ethiopia, and he subsequently became a prominent member of the African colonial elite. Like Berhanä Marqos and Ayyaléw Berru, Amdé Ali convinced Cerulli of his political utility.

The apparent Italian sympathies of these detainees made them obvious candidates for a risky quid pro quo transaction: the coerced exchange of freedom for some form of political collaboration. In a few cases, though, Cerulli and his ministerial colleagues attempted to extend this same bargain to other less "recuperable" and more politically antagonistic detainees. This was the case with the aristocrat *däjjazmach* Tayyé Gullelaté of Shäwa.[122] Born in 1886, he was the great-grandson of *negus* Sahlä Sellasé, and as the only patrilineal male successor of his generation, he was the dynastic rival of his cousins Iyyasu, Zäwditu, and Täfäri Mäkonnen. For this reason, he was imprisoned for five years, later redeeming himself at the Battle of Sägälé, where Mika'él Ali and the partisans of Iyyasu were defeated. He then relocated to Addis Ababa, where he received the rank of *däjjazmach* and became a neighbor of *qäññazmach* Dähné.[123] After the Italian invasion, he led the armed resistance in Wälläga until his capture in December 1936, when he was deported to Ponza along with his cousin *ras* Emru.[124] The island was at that time a crowded penal colony for Italian political detainees.[125]

It was during this uncertain transit that Tayyé seems to have encountered Cerulli. According to fellow detainee Haddis Alämayyähu, the *däjjazmach* and his companions briefly stopped in Rome, where they stayed in a hotel and toured the capital in the company of an Italian chaperone. One morning, the group proceeded to the Ministry of Italian Africa, where an Eritrean interpreter and an Italian military officer brought them to "the Chief Director of Colonial Affairs."[126] Haddis was struck by his encounter with the latter individual, who he described as a young and slender academic who resembled Mussolini in bearing and appearance. The director listened silently with a furrowed brow as the group described their lodging and sightseeing, one of them replying in English to the translator's query in Amharic. Outraged, the director exclaimed, "You are prisoners, not tourists!" and admonished them for speaking a European language other than Italian in his presence.[127] The director dispatched them to Ponza the next day. In a surprising development, he suddenly arrived on the island months later, reaching the detainees' residence in the middle of the night. Now assuming a friendlier demeanor, the director attempted to convince *ras* Emru to submit in exchange for freedom and the restoration of his lost property. The offer came directly from Mussolini. Insulted, the *ras* refused to sit at the negotiation table, and the visitor left after an awkward silence, as the detainees watched in amusement.[128]

Months of chaos ensued. In April, Cerulli recommended transferring Tayyé to join "the old chiefs," despite his being only fifty years old,[129] and by May, he was on the island of Ischia in the Gulf of Naples, apparently facing an imminent move to Torre del Greco.[130] In October, however, he was returned to Ponza with *ras* Emru, where he reported having coordinated his personal affairs in Ethiopia through the assistance of an unnamed interpreter, possibly *basha* Asfeha.[131] This development suggests a possible acceptance of the proffered ministerial bargain. By November, the displaced *däjjazmach* had been relocated to Mercogliano with his family.[132] He was now in considerable financial hardship, which led him to request loans from the apparently better-situated *le'ul ras* Seyyum, *ras* Gétachäw, and *däjjazmach* Ayyaléw.[133]

At the end of 1937, Tayyé dispatched a flurry of correspondence to improve his standing. On December 16, he sent a letter of congratulations to Cerulli on his promotion, adding, "I hope that your distinctive competence will bring tranquility, peace, and enduring achievement in Ethiopia."[134] He then outlined his position. Since Cerulli understood his peaceful intentions, he explained, "I am available in the future to help you with my advice." In a linguistic flourish, he offered an Amharic proverb that illustrated the logic behind this proposal: "The good grass of the land is [only] pulled up by a native bull."[135] The following day, he dispatched a second letter to missionary Gaudenzio Barlassina in which he judged himself "a useful instrument for the powerful Italian government,"[136] and two days later, he sent a third missive to Pope Paul XI, in which he introduced himself as "Prince *däjjazmach* Tayyé" and requested a pardon and transfer to Rome.[137] The consequences of these epistolary negotiations are unclear.[138] According to fellow detainee Mahtämä Sellasé, Tayyé remained in Italy until after liberation.[139]

Also rebuffed was Berhanä Habtämika'él, an ill-fated civil servant from Addis Ababa.[140] In his own narration, he met Prince Luigi Amedeo during the latter's 1927 visit to the Ethiopian capital, and obtained his permission to study in Italy.[141] This connection introduced Berhanä to Afäwärq Gäbrä Iyäsus, Minister Cora, and the Italian Legation, but his educational plan was foiled when his visa was rejected by Täfäri Mäkonnen and Heruy, who were "always stubbornly opposed to the education of the children of the poor who were not their relatives," as he later put it. The crown prince then dismissed Berhanä from his post. Believing himself redeemed by the

Italian conquest, he worked as an interpreter and secretary at the Office of Political Affairs in Addis Ababa, only to find himself arrested after Yekatit 12 and transported to Asinara. He claimed to have met Cerulli during his April visit to the island, and it is possible the two were acquainted through their common circles in Addis Ababa, but Cerulli did not mention Berhanä in his report. It was a curious omission. The latter then wrote to the Orientalist director to explain that he had "loyally served the government" without fault, and wanted to study "the learning and progress of Rome" at an agricultural school.[142] When Cerulli did not reply, he penned another letter to Lessona that outlined these events and reasserted his request for education.

Surprisingly, Berhanä was then transferred to Longobucco with the irreducibles.[143] Did Cerulli and the Ministry perceive his past collaboration as duplicitous, more like Abreha Däboch and Mogäs Asgädom than the supposedly reliable *basha* Asfeha? Or was he a useful plant? Whatever the reason, Berhanä was now impoverished, indebted, and in declining health, and he began to clandestinely correspond with the Ministry to report on his fellow detainees.[144] In October, he wrote that he found himself among "elements that do not love the Italian government," and he wished to be transferred to a more suitably patriotic location where he could begin his studies.[145] To buttress his case, he described the anticolonial politics of four of his fellow detainees: *balambaras* Emmañu Yemär, the Anglophile son-in-law of Hakim Wärqenäh; Aramast Baghdassarian, an outspoken Ethiopian Armenian who mocked the regime in the streets of town; Bäqqälä Kiros, "an absolute anti-fascist" who dissected the newspapers for news of Ethiopia; and the latter's friend Germachäw Täklä Hawaryat, the son of the defiant League delegate. Berhanä advised the Ministry that these individuals might "corrupt the few that love the Italian government like a father and mother," adding that he would reveal more in a future letter. Cerulli received this intelligence on November 11, but Berhanä did not profit from his gambit. Four years later, in 1941, he remained at Longobucco, deep in debt to local shopkeepers due to unpaid remittances for his seized property in Ethiopia; and even in 1943, by which time the colony no longer existed, he continued writing frantically to the Ministry from the mountains of Calabria.[146] If his reports shaped the state's management of the other detainees, they failed to win him the education or freedom he desired. His six years in remote detention suggest that the senior government elite were more fruitful negotiators than their political and social subordinates, who ultimately had less to bargain with.

If these contacts were transactional, other detainees wrote Cerulli simply to request freedom. According to *qäññazmach* Dähné, this was the case with several authors of the March 1937 letter who remained at Asinara after the mass relocations that summer. On October 5, a few of these individuals decided to send another missive to Rome, at the suggestion of someone they described only as "the visitor."[147] To plan their effort, *ras* Gäbrä Heywät, *ṣähafé te'ezaz* Afäwärq Wäldä Maryam, *ligaba* Ṭassäw Walälu, and Täsfayé Tägäñ visited medical clinic director Aldo Duce, who Dähné termed "the judge" of the camp. The detainees presented their case plainly, saying, "It has been ten months since we came, we who came without committing any crime or even hearing of one.[148] When we came in the month of Mägabit [March], we wrote and sent a letter with words of supplication for mercy to the great government [of Italy]. Until now we have not received a reply. And now, [if] it is your will, pass to us the word of our salvation if you are able."[149] According to Dähné, who witnessed this exchange, Duce encouraged the plan. A few days later, on October 10, an evolved version of the group returned to the clinic, this time comprised of *ras* Gäbrä Heywät, *ṣähafé te'ezaz* Wäldä Mäsqäl, *fitawrari* Asfaw Manayé, *kantiba* Gäbru Desta, *blatta* Täsämma Däbalqé, and Täsfayé Tägäñ. They gave Duce an Amharic letter addressed to the Minister in which they introduced themselves as subjects of "the magnificent and powerful Italian government" who were exiled in Asinara.[150] Explaining that they had waited for a response since March, they again requested clemency, reaffirming their submission and pledging their loyalty should they return to Ethiopia.[151] The letter's logic doubled down on the desperate calculation behind the March effort. As agreed, Duce prepared an Italian translation and dispatched both versions to the Ministry of the Interior, which forwarded the correspondence to Cerulli.[152] The latter received a précis of the letter shortly thereafter, but he does not appear to have responded in any way.[153]

Cerulli's silence meant Dähné was trapped. For two more years, the chronicler of Asinara could only watch and write about events unfolding near and far. In his diary, he described the ascent of *däjjazmach* Haylä Sellasé Gugsa to the circumscribed apex of the African colonial elite, the repatriation of Ayyaléw Berru and Amdé Ali, the death of Pope Pius XI in Rome, the search for better clothing, the arrival of a rare Amharic newspaper from Addis Ababa, and the frigid mistral wind that pierced the island. His meticulous notebook, its pages neatly filled with twin columns of carefully dated annotations in red and black fidäl script, was an attempt to write something more than an annal of his own years of hardship. Its heterogeneous contents, largely invisible author, and rigorously traditionalist scribal aesthetic transcend Ngũgĩ wa Thiong'o's observation that the narration of prison life is "nothing more than an account of oppressive measures in varying degrees of intensity and one's individual or collective responses to them."[154] For Dähné, it was additionally a dutiful and suitably rigorous continuation of the collective historical record of the Ethiopian politico-religious elite: a narrative of exile by a trained specialist. Historiography was an act of testimonial defiance.

While the *qäññazmach* chronicled detention abroad, his family survived the violence at home. As the insurrection and counterinsurgency raged across Shäwa, his relatives sought refuge south of the capital, where the family owned land around Zeqwalla. They struggled to obtain basic necessities, cannily maneuvered to reclaim lost family property, and faced continuous harassment from the colonial authorities and their allies. While caring for their children, his sons, nephew, and mother-in-law supported the local *arbäña*s, and were repeatedly detained for their activities.[155] From time to time, Dähné dispatched letters to his family from the island concentration camp, which passed across the censors' desks in the Office of Political Affairs.[156] In March 1939, the *qäññazmach* noted the viceroy's arrival in Rome from Addis Ababa. It was his final diary entry. On May 23, he was suddenly returned home.

8
Survival in Shäwa

For *mämher* Ras Wärq Wäldä Mäsqäl (figure 8.1), the Italian advance to the capital augured peril.¹ It was time to leave. Born in the mountain village of Jerru, he left home as an adolescent to pursue an ecclesiastic education, and by twenty, he had mastered the fields of liturgy, religious music, poetry, and scriptural exegesis through a grueling course of study that concluded at Enṭoṭṭo Ragu'él, Heruy's alma mater.² This was a rare and distinguished attainment. Seemingly established in his calling, he married Askalä Maryam Gäbrä Giyorgis and became a priest at Enṭoṭṭo Maryam.³ A chance development then changed the course of his life: the opportunity to work at the newly established Täfäri Mäkonnen School in Addis Ababa, the glittering centerpiece of its namesake's project of state-led educational reform.⁴ Housed in the former compound of *lej* Iyyasu and envisioned as an academy for civil servants, the school epitomized the cosmopolitan intellectual foment of the era as well as the deepening influence of the crown prince. For these reasons, its Western-influenced curriculum alarmed the conservative elite, who feared it would encourage pupils to abandon the "ancient traditions" safeguarded by church education, as one critic put it.⁵ In 1924, these concerns induced school director Wärqenäh Eshäté to request an instructor from Enṭoṭṭo, and the community nominated Ras Wärq for the job. He thus became the first Ge'ez and Amharic teacher at the country's preeminent modern

FIGURE 8.1 Ras Wärq Wäldä Mäsqäl.

Source: Personal collection of author, courtesy Terrefe Ras Work.

educational institution, his presence signaling its fidelity to the cultural patrimony.[6] On opening day, Täfari Mäkonnen announced that the school would emancipate the nation by advancing knowledge of "foreign languages and wisdom" alongside "the holy books of our country and the faith of the only son of God," since the exclusive study of Western knowledge could only produce "a raft without an oarsman."[7] The *mämher* had accepted an immense responsibility.

Over the next decade, Ras Wärq became a distinctive figure in the capital's burgeoning intellectual scene. He was an august member of the *liqawent* moving within civil society. He taught hundreds of students, including many prominent politicians and intellectuals,[8] and he mixed with key figures in the urban intelligentsia, most notably British-educated school director Wärqenäh as well as fellow teachers Märse'é Hazän, a cousin from his hometown, and Éfrém Täwäldä Mädhen, later destined for the Foreign Ministry.[9] Ras Wärq also met the royal family, ministerial officials, and foreign dignitaries, all frequent visitors to the school.[10] The pioneering *mämher* was thus intertwined with the personalities and institutions that exemplified the era's public culture of progress. At the same time, he remained ensconced among the *liqawent* of Enṭoṭṭo Maryam and close to its head, *mäl'akä ṣähay* Zälläqä.¹¹ His mediation between established and emerging worlds of learning won the esteem of the crown prince and *etégé* Mänän, who granted him a home near the school.

All this crumbled with the Italian invasion. In October 1935, Ras Wärq and Askalä's eldest son Yohannes departed for the northern front, and after the defeat at Mayčhäw, he joined the guerilla struggle. In Addis Ababa, meanwhile, Askalä was pregnant with their third son, and the family decided to leave the capital with three of their children, seeking refuge in northeast Shäwa, Ras Wärq's ancestral home.¹² Their two eldest daughters remained behind. After the Italians took the capital in May, the colonial administration seized the Täfäri Mäkonnen School amid its mass expropriations of public and private property. The building was converted into an army barracks, and then enlarged and reconstituted as the Vittorio Emmanuele Reale Liceo-Ginnasio, now a secondary school for Italian settlers.¹³ By this time, many of its former Ethiopian teachers and pupils were wanted, detained, or in exile—among them Yohannes Ras Wärq, Abreha Däboch, and Fäqqadä Sellasé Heruy, the foreign minister's eldest son.

Ras Wärq and Askalä escaped to Ankober. A remote mountain-top redoubt one hundred miles northeast of Addis Ababa, the town is perched at an altitude of more than eight thousand feet, encircled by thick forests and cave-punctured cliffs. On a clear day, the vista from Ankober's heights reaches the foothills approaching Däbrä Berhan; in fog, the cloud cover is so dense that it can be difficult to see one hundred feet in any direction. It is locally known as the top of the world. This extreme location suggests why the town long served as the royal capital of Shäwa: it was the residence of *negus* Sahlä Sellasé, his heir *negus* Haylä Mäläkot, the latter's son Emperor Menilek, and finally *lej* Iyyasu. Haylä Sellasé's father was born nearby and raised in Menilek's court. This lineage imbued the town with an august symbolism, exemplified by Sahlä Sellasé's entombment in a local church.¹⁴ Years later, his grandson Menilek married *etégé* Ṭaytu in Ankober, built his palace on an imposing peak at its center, and installed within it the country's first telephone, scarcely a decade after its invention.¹⁵ In the estimation of *ṣähafé te'ezaz* Gäbrä Sellasé, the future emperor's grand residence and pious endowments in "the town of his fathers" epitomized the splendor of his reign.¹⁶ By 1886, when Menilek relocated to Addis Ababa,

Ankober was among the most important settlements in Shäwa, an imperial citadel and gateway to the wider world.[17] Haylä Sellasé reaffirmed this distinction through a 1934 royal visit to the town.[18] Bottai's triumphant aerial reconnaissance was no accident.

If Ankober symbolized power, it also exuded learning. One dimension was institutional. By the early twentieth century, the town maintained five churches and a large scriptorium attached to the old palace.[19] Together with the churches of the surrounding villages, the libraries of these institutions represented a major repository of Orthodox Christian learning, with the oldest Ge'ez codices dating to the fifteenth century.[20] According to local tradition, this corpus was but a remnant of an even more immense manuscript patrimony that had been plundered in the nineteenth century, when the army of Emperor Téwodros looted the town's churches and massacred its priests.[21] In the years that followed, the *liqawent* of Ankober remained fiercely devoted to the stewardship of their textual inheritance, concealing it from Marcel Cohen during his 1910–1911 visit,[22] but sharing it with Märse'é Hazän when he arrived decades later.[23]

A second dimension of Ankober's significance was the deluge of intellectuals who emerged from its traditional and mission schools. Like Ras Wärq, some of these were outward-looking church scholars, such as the famed Catholic historian *aläqa* Aṣmä Giyorgis,[24] a Latin- and Arabic-speaking emissary of Menilek who grasped the duplicity of the Treaty of Weçhalé; *mämher* Käflä Giyorgis, a theologian and lexicographer who taught Ge'ez at Santo Stefano in Rome and collaborated with Ignazio Guidi on an Amharic dictionary;[25] and *aläqa* Sahlé, the Catholic teacher and church leader who traveled to Rome and translated the Gospels of Matthew and John into Amharic.[26] Other notable Ankoberites were civil servants whose careers led to the capital and beyond. These included *blattén géta* Sahlé Ṣädalu, a polyglot who studied in Paris and became the minister of education;[27] *däjjazmach* Yeggäzu Bähabté, a veteran of the Ministries of Foreign Affairs and Finance;[28] Habtäwäld Wärqenäh, who served in Menilek's court alongside *qaññazmach* Dähné;[29] and Habtä Sellasé, who worked as a translator for the Italian Legation in Addis Ababa.[30] This accomplished diaspora further burnished Ankober's august reputation.

But colonial rule proved devastating. After Badoglio's lorries thundered into Addis Ababa, Ankober became a colonial administrative center and a hub of anticolonial insurrection. Though considerably reduced in population, the town held critical strategic significance for the Italians and *arbañas* alike, both because of its potent association with Menilek and because of its proximity to the road linking Asmara and Addis Ababa. For both sides, Ankober posed high stakes: a successful guerrilla campaign in the historic heartlands of Shäwa—just a day from the political and military center of Africa Orientale Italiana, and emanating from what Ruggero Tracchia called "the stronghold of the Shäwan-Amhara rulers"—threatened to undermine the already-fragile international legitimacy of the Italian colony.[31] It was precisely this logic that motivated the Yekatit 12 attack.

Acutely aware of these issues, Viceroy Graziani remade Ankober into an outpost of empire, incorporating it into the colony's growing network of military bases. The first step in this transformation was the construction of a colonial residence in Menilek's former palace, the strategic highpoint of the town. This position was fortified with an airfield and garrison of Italian officers and Eritrean *askari* in the nearby market town of Goräbéla, and together, the two settlements became the administrative center of the Ancoberino subsector of the northeast Shäwa sector. Though the town remained an arduous day-long journey from Däbrä Berhan, its exalted history and extreme location fueled the impression that its subjugation was an emblematic achievement of the Italian colonial enterprise.[32] Ankober epitomized the dream of the conquered highlands—the redemptive defeat of Menilek. For some Italians, it was a near-mystical site. Visiting in 1939, the writer and aesthete Curzio Malaparte was mesmerized by its natural splendor, informing readers of *Corriere della sera* that "the golden grass shines in the clear darkness" on the slopes of its "delicate and guileless blue mountains."[33]

But control of the guileless peaks proved impossible. As Ras Wärq ministered to the faithful in his new parish,[34] Governor Alessandro Pirzio Biroli installed *däjjazmach* Mätafäriya Mälkä Ṣédéq as the local *capo*. It was a shrewd political calculation. The elderly *däjjazmach* was a protégé and longtime functionary of Menilek, and his appointment suggested continuity with Ankober's storied past.[35] Yet despite such efforts at projected stability, rebellion burned outside town, and a host of guerrilla leaders found refuge in the rugged area between Ankober and Däbrä Berhan. The most renowned of these included *ras* Abäbä Arägay, who led the insurrection in north Shäwa and maintained a residence near Ankober; *lej* Haylä Maryam Mammo, the so-called first patriot who battered Badoglio's troops on their march through Shäwa;[36] *wäyzero* Lakälesh Bayyän, the formidable sniper known by her firing cry, "Strike him!";[37] and *fitawrari* Wändämeh Gäbrä Kidan, a sharpshooter who would only camp in close proximity to the enemy.[38] In Ankober itself, the preeminent *arbäña* leaders were *lej* Ayyälä Haylé and *wäyzero* Wäläla Wändeyyerad, a married duo whose family coordinated a large rebel network in the town and adjacent Goräbéla.[39] A local chant celebrated the *lej*'s sustenance through combat:

> Warrior at lunch, whistling triumphantly at dinner
> His shower [is] splattering blood
> Had his mother given birth to me, I would have [proudly] been his sister[40]

Ankober was also the adopted home of guerrilla-king Mäl'akä Şähay Iyyasu, the illegitimate son of *lej* Iyyasu who had been raised by the family of Täsämma Eshäté until ascending to the throne in 1937, and who reigned in secret until his death the following year.[41] These leaders and their followers fought the Italian and Eritrean battalions of the local garrison as well as Italian-allied irregulars, or *banda*, most notably the forces of *shaykh* Muhammad Sultan of Yefat.[42] Ankober escaped the war of conquest, but it was now engulfed by the violence of occupation.

It was in these dark circumstances that *wäyzero* Askalä gave birth to her third son. He was born in Ankober on March 11, 1936. By late spring, the fighting intensified as insurrection exploded in nearby Däbrä Berhan and Däbrä Sina. Finally, on June 7, the forces of *lej* Dästa ambushed an *askari* battalion from Ankober on the road outside town. The battalion retreated to the garrison, where the assault continued overnight with heavy losses.[43] In Tracchia's assessment, the highly coordinated ambush portended a major offensive. As reinforcements arrived, the general ordered airstrikes, Mussolini authorized the use of chemical weapons, and Graziani covered the countryside with propaganda leaflets.[44] One month later, on July 20, the forces of *däjjazmach* Asfaw, *däjjazmach* Mängäsha, and *balambaras* Bokkalä again attacked the garrison, this time threatening the entire town.[45] In response, Graziani ordered the strategic bombing of Ankober, to make an example of the rebellion's symbolic center. At sunrise the next day, a squadron of four planes from Dire Dawa launched a high-altitude assault that destroyed most of old Ankober, including Menilek's palace and three of the town's churches, including Mädhané Aläm cathedral.[46] Days later, the Italians retook the town in heavy fighting, looted Mädhané Aläm, and demolished the historic buildings that had survived the bombardment, including the remnants of Menilek's palace.[47] For a second time, Ankober was decimated by the invader.[48]

As the bombs plummeted, *wäyzero* Askalä fled the smoky inferno with her newborn son, eventually finding shelter in a remote cave outside of town. After the airstrikes and street battles ended, the residents returned to the rubble of Ankober, where it became clear to Ras Wärq and the other survivors that Askalä and her baby were missing. A search yielded nothing, whereupon the townspeople began to weep and ululate for the apparently lost mother and child. It was a calamity. When Askalä and her child emerged from her cave, ascended to the town, and discovered the mourners, she was greeted with joy by her relieved family. In recognition of God's deliverance of his loved ones from the carnage, Ras Wärq that day renamed the young boy Tärräfä, or "he survived."[49]

By the end of the next year, Cerulli oversaw the counterinsurgency in Ankober. His path from the ministries of Rome to the battlefields of Shäwa developed from Mussolini's dismissal of Graziani, one of the most dramatic events of the entire colonial era. The change was long in preparation. Viewed from Rome, Graziani's viceregal tenure had become a chaotic disaster: it was marred by unrelenting insurrection, sputtering economic development, and constant feuding between the viceroy and now-minister Lessona, who disputed the scope of viceregal authority as well as the details of colonial policy and military strategy.[50] The assassination attempt of February 1937, just six months after the destruction of Ankober, confirmed Graziani's ineffectiveness to Mussolini. In the months that followed, Lessona counseled the latter to replace the rough soldier with the more cultivated Prince Amedeo di Savoia, the Duke of Aosta, an educated aristocrat and military officer who Lessona believed would be a more effective colleague and head of state.[51] These entreaties prevailed on August 30, when the duke met Mussolini and presented the latter with an academic publication on his research expedition to southern Libya.[52] The audience so impressed the duce that he immediately informed d'Aosta of his intention to appoint him viceroy.[53] Several months later, on November 10, he dismissed Graziani.[54] The apparent triumph led Lessona to "leap with joy."[55]

Graziani was shocked. Officially, he accepted the decision with the decorum required by the chain of command, and he publicly congratulated the duke, with whom he had served in Libya.[56] But behind the scenes, he fought for his position. He first challenged Mussolini's logic. According to Edoardo Borra, who was d'Aosta's doctor and confidant, the marshal told the duce, "If the duke was experienced, as Mussolini asserted, he [Graziani] was more experienced."[57] When this argument failed, Graziani then tried to salvage his position atop the colonial military command, even proposing to serve as viceregal regent in the absence of d'Aosta.[58] Although he allowed these arrangements to be celebrated in the Addis Ababa press, he soon discovered that his continued role was opposed not only by Lessona but also by d'Aosta, who apparently considered him untrustworthy, heavy-handed, and unpopular.[59] In a striking parallel, the so-called *condottiero*'s predicament with respect to his patrician successor exemplified Machiavelli's object lesson about Cesare Borgia's punishment of his violent subordinate Ramiro d'Orco: the disgrace of the bad marshal improved the position of his replacement, the good duke.[60] Stripped of all duties in the Horn of Africa, Graziani's military command instead passed to Ugo Cavallero, an ex-senator and Libya and World War I veteran.[61] Graziani seemed finished. Privately, Mussolini quipped, "He fought well, but he has governed badly."[62]

Yet in a further intrigue, this power struggle also consumed Graziani's "sworn enemy" Lessona.[63] On November 22, just weeks after announcing d'Aosta's appointment, Mussolini summoned and dismissed the colonial minister. Officially, the duce told Lessona that the duke's royal lineage required an equally august ministerial counterpart—Mussolini himself.[64] Yet Lessona's replacement in fact proved to be the loyal militant Attilio Teruzzi, a *squadrista* and ex-governor of Cyrenaica who occupied the post in an acting capacity until October 1939, when he became minister.[65] Lessona later described Teruzzi's elevation as a personal betrayal, despite his claim to be ready to retire and his face-saving professorship at the University of Rome.[66] He was not the only senior official to fall alongside Graziani that November. Also dismissed were governors Alessandro Pirzio Biroli of Amhara, Vincenzo De Feo of Eritrea, and Ruggero Santini of Somalia, who were replaced by Ottorino Mezzetti, Giuseppe Daodice, and Francesco Caroselli, respectively. Within weeks, the shakeup was announced in the press.[67] It was fascism's most dramatic colonial *rimpasto-shumsher*.[68]

As the positions of his superiors crumbled, Cerulli stepped into the breach. According to Borra, Cerulli joined Lessona in counseling Mussolini, which won him the post of vice governor general—the second-most senior executive in the colony.⁶⁹ His accession to this position hinged on the selection of d'Aosta as viceroy. If the duke was a relative outsider to Africa Orientale Italiana, Cerulli's appointment would provide continuity with the Graziani administration, with which he had been closely involved, as well as a link between the Governo Generale in Addis Ababa and the Ministry in Rome, his former bureaucratic home. This argument proved persuasive, and Mussolini announced Cerulli's appointment on December 8, with Martino Mario Moreno taking over the ministerial Office of Political Affairs.⁷⁰ Caught up in this power struggle was *basha* Asfeha, who Cerulli selected as his personal advisor in the colony. Looking back on these events, Asfeha recalled that he told Cerulli he wished to remain in Italy to pursue advanced education, but his learned superior forbade this, saying, "Your administrative skill is enough for Ethiopia." Instead, Asfeha received the title of Cavaliere di Gran Croce from Mussolini at the Palazzo Venezia, after which he followed Cerulli back to the Horn of Africa.⁷¹

Collectively, the new rulers of Africa Orientale Italiana represented a pivot to expert rule. In addition to the veteran researcher-functionaries⁷² Cerulli, Moreno, and Caroselli, this shift was exemplified by the viceroy himself—a fellow intellectual "in khakis," as Moreno put it.⁷³ A cousin of King Vittorio Emmanuele and nephew of Prince Luigi Amedeo, the Anglophilic d'Aosta personified the ideal of the learned soldier: Lessona called him "a man of immense culture and lively intelligence," while Borra said he was a paragon of "humanity and progress."⁷⁴ After graduating from an English boarding school and the Nunziatella military academy, the duke volunteered in the First World War, toured Somalia and Congo, and then completed a degree in jurisprudence at the University of Palermo, with a thesis advancing liberal conclusions on colonial law and administration.⁷⁵ He next served in Libya and obtained the rank of general in the Regia Aeronautica, along the way publishing Africanist research and developing a reputation as a charismatic avatar of modern colonial martial virtue. This association only deepened on his appointment as viceroy. Despite Graziani's popularity, the Savoyard "prince of the Sahara" was greeted ecstatically by the press, and some colonial officials believed he would end the regime's most brutal excesses.⁷⁶ The specialists would solve the problems that had stymied the military conquerors.

In late December, d'Aosta and Cerulli reached Addis Ababa. They were greeted with a massive parade at the Jan Méda and acclaim in the streets of the capital.⁷⁷ The local press coverage was frenzied. Though its chief focus was the viceroy, Cerulli enjoyed an adulatory profile in *Corriere dell'impero*, the colony's bombastic multilingual newspaper.⁷⁸ As this reception suggests, he now assumed a more public role than ever before. By decree, the office of the vice governor general was invested with three functions: assisting the viceroy in managing the civil and military affairs of the colony, in part by assuming the role of viceregal regent in the viceroy's absence; supervising the Office of Political Affairs and the other directorates of the Governo Generale, which replicated the structure of the Ministry of Italian Africa;⁷⁹ and, after November 1938, overseeing the new governate of Shäwa, formerly the Addis Ababa special district, or *governatorato*.⁸⁰ The vice governor general was in this last capacity also one of the six colonial governors responsible for local administration, in which they enjoyed considerable autonomy and corresponded directly with the Ministry. Despite these neat jurisdictional divisions, the vice governor general thus occupied a fundamentally ambiguous and antagonistic position: he reported directly to both the viceroy and the minister. This structural tension only deepened the frequently intense personal rivalries that existed between the governors, the military command, the Governo Generale, and the Ministry.⁸¹

Cerulli's first months in the colony involved protocol and administrative reform. He joined the viceroy for official visits to the governates and directorate offices and broadly supported the public functions of the Governo Generale.⁸² In March, he met Cavallero and the governors for a multiday summit in the capital;⁸³ in April, he joined *abunä* Abreham to celebrate Ethiopian Orthodox Easter, and then welcomed Libyan governor Italo Balbo to Addis Ababa;⁸⁴ and in May, he presided over the public celebration of the third year of the empire, leading the immense parade in the viceregal retinue.⁸⁵ Less conspicuously, he supervised the staff of his cabinet and the Addis Ababa Office of Political Affairs, which now included *basha* Asfeha, *abba* Jérôme, and Afäwärq Gäbrä Iyäsus as well as former Asinara detainees *blatta* Ayyälä Gäbrä, *ṣähafé te'ezaz* Wäldä Mäsqäl Tariku, and Marqos Pawlos Män Amäno.⁸⁶ This office undertook several new initiatives, including the publication of the weekly newspaper *Yäqésar mängest mälektäña*, or *Messenger of Caesar's Government*, and the illustrated monthly *Yäroma berhan*, or *Light of Rome*.⁸⁷ These Amharic publications disrupted the Italophone monologue of the colonial situation, contriving a public vernacular voice of the Ethiopian subject that replicated the visual and editorial style of *Berhanenna sälam*.⁸⁸ They were edited by Wäldä Giyorgis Wäldä Yohannes, ex-director of the latter newspaper.⁸⁹

This work complemented Cerulli's coordination of a delegation of African colonial notables to Italy. Amid great press fanfare, this group of fifty spent several months in the spring of 1938 visiting sites across the peninsula, along the way meeting Mussolini in Rome and the detained recuperables in Tivoli.⁹⁰ Among its members were *sharifa* Alawiyya al-Mirghani, the daughter of a prominent Eritrean religious teacher who had become a pan-Islamic spokesperson for the Muslims of Africa Orientale Italiana,⁹¹ and Sultan Abbaa Joobir Abbaa Dula, the grandson of Sultan Abbaa Jifar of Jimma and now the leading *capo* of the Galla Sidama governate.⁹² Cerulli likely met Abbaa Joobir during his 1927 visit to his grandfather's court, and a decade later, this connection bore considerable political fruit. In newspaper interviews and an audience with Mussolini, Abbaa Joobir praised the regime as the "immortal" liberator of the enslaved Muslims of Ethiopia, to wide acclaim in the metropolitan and colonial press.⁹³ Similar accounts of Muslim emancipation were issued by *sharifa* Alawiyya, who was also interviewed and photographed alongside the duce.⁹⁴ Around this time, Cerulli resigned from the League's Committee of Experts on Slavery.⁹⁵

Behind the scenes, however, relations between d'Aosta and Cerulli strained. According to their colleague Borra, who worked at the Governo Generale, Cerulli was "an upright, reserved, and rigorous man" whose approach to administration is instantly recognizable as academic. In Borra's recollection, "When one spent time with him [Cerulli], one had the impression that he was jealous of his own time, and that he intended to devote himself exclusively to his office and to his favoured studies of ethnology and linguistics, avoiding the distractions of meetings with people unrelated to his work projects. He thus established around himself an almost insurmountable protective halo against random interference. In his office he formulated administrative measures on the basis of his own knowledge, almost never consulting with colleagues."⁹⁶ More strident was the critique of Hugh Stonehewer-Bird, the British consul in Addis Ababa. He informed the Foreign Office that "Cerulli's pomposity and bad manner and general unsuitability for his job are making him extremely unpopular with everyone from the Duke downwards. . . . He might have made a valuable adviser on native affairs, but his knowledge of the geography of Abyssinia and of native dialects is of little value in his present exalted position[,] for which he has none of the requisite qualities either of personality or experience.... He just cannot get past the barrier of his own self-importance."[97] Weeks later, Stonehewer-Bird further reported that "Nobody can get anything done," since Cerulli was the chosen agent of Rome and the National Fascist Party, and "everything has to go through his hands."[98] These negative views were shared by Alberto Denti di Pirajno, the viceroy's personal physician and chief of cabinet, who found Cerulli so obstructionist that he eventually sought a new position in Somalia.[99]

Division ensued. In practice, Cerulli rarely met with d'Aosta, and he regularly corresponded directly with the Ministry, acting unilaterally and without consulting the viceroy. In Borra's assessment, the latter initially accepted this dynamic, and recognizing Cerulli as a specialist with impressive language skills, he directed others to him when their questions involved his areas of expertise. But as the months passed, the viceroy developed an intelligence-based understanding of the colony that diverged from the bookish outlook of Cerulli, whose "respectable knowledge sometimes proved insufficient or less corresponding to new realities," in Borra's assessment.[100] Compounding this issue was the fact that Cerulli saw the duke as a symbolic figurehead selected because of his useful patrician background, and instead believed himself the de facto authority in the colony.[101] Denti di Pirajno considered this usurpation "a scandal," while Borra more delicately characterized the situation as a diarchy that replicated the relationship of Vittorio Emanuele and Mussolini.[102] These problems eventually produced a gulf between d'Aosta and Cerulli that devolved throughout the colonial bureaucracy, which became divided between the military partisans of the viceroy and the civilian "errand boys" of the Ministry, as one journalist put it.[103] Surveying the chaos, Stonehewer-Bird opined, "The machine fell to bits when Graziani left[,] and now instead of one machine working to an end ... we have a lot of little machines all working for their own little purposes[,] with Cerulli, an incompetent mechanic, tinkering with all of them."[104]

The unifying concern, however, was the counterinsurgency. As vice governor general, Cerulli first contributed to this undertaking through field intelligence. In February 1938, d'Aosta dispatched him to Gédo, a predominantly Oromo market town outside Naqamtee, astride the historic border of Wälläga and Shäwa. It was a familiar area: during Cerulli's 1927-1928 expedition to western Ethiopia, the environs of Gédo were the setting for his dramatic encounters with Oromo "brigands" and "Abyssinianized" local officials. Now, a decade later, his former research site was an important center in the Ambo-Gédo sector of the Galla Sidamo governate, home to approximately two thousand inhabitants as well as a vice resident, airfield, telegraph station, and National Fascist Party branch office.[105] Nearby Naqamtee and the mountains south of Gédo were also emerging hubs of guerilla activity, the western counterpart of the insurrection outside Ankober.[106] That January, the Governo Generale reported widespread brigandage in the region, with local informants describing planned attacks on submitted *capi*,[107] and the following month, the military command dispatched four Italian battalions to the area and unleashed a storm of ordinance on the hills around town.[108] Ettore Formento, who led an *askari* company in this campaign, described days chasing an ever-elusive enemy and nights glimpsing shadowy phantasms.[109] The war of occupation had reached Oromiyya.

This punishing operation spurred Cerulli's reconnaissance mission. In early February, he returned to Gédo, interviewed the local notables and Italian residents, and issued a detailed report for the viceroy, and on February 17, the latter telegrammed Cerulli's findings to the Ministry.[110] These were wide-ranging. In an echo of Asinara, Cerulli first observed that the *capi* of the Wälläga-Shäwa frontier remained "scared and disoriented." He had encouraged them to submit, and recommended that the local colonial resident cultivate or bribe these individuals while demonstrating Italian munificence through competent supervision of the local markets. He then turned to the ethnopolitical situation. Deploying his earlier fieldwork and the model of Abyssinian military colonialism, he explained that the local Oromo population "understood the iron discipline of the Shäwan conquistadors," and their subjugation would require more than evanescent rituals of submission. It would be necessary to "discipline them for a permanent arrangement in a new context." In his view, this feat of ethnosocial engineering could be achieved by mobilizing Oromo moiety and clan divisions as well as "the traditional rights . . . that had been for centuries the base of their lineage," thereby alienating the population from anti-Italian actors. Gesturing to an earlier chapter in his career, he added that a similar intervention had previously worked against rebellious Sufi brotherhoods in Somalia.[111] In short, the institutions of tradition should be manipulated to stabilize the colonial situation.

Cerulli then identified three prominent local guerillas. One was Gärräsu Duki, identified simply as "Cherarsù," an Oromo military officer from Wäliso who served on the northern front before joining the insurrection in western Shäwa. In Cerulli's assessment, he was "more a brigand than a political rebel," and his forces were in disarray.[112] More dangerous, in Cerulli's estimation, were the Shäwan irreducibles *däjjazmach* Zäwdé Asfaw Dargé and *blatta* Takkälä Wäldä Hawaryat. The first was an aristocrat and former regional governor, and the second a reformer and ex-ministerial director. Both were now guerrillas.[113] In 1936–1937, the *blatta* had led the insurrection in Oromiyya, operating out of Jimma and Limmu until relocating to Sudan. He was well known to Cerulli. In 1928, the two met during the latter's fieldwork in Käffa, where Takkälä had been appointed to the local administration.[114] At that time, Cerulli cryptically described him as "a real 'Young Ethiopian,'" and the two may have even posed for a photo.[115] Now noting that *blatta* Takkälä was near Gédo and surrounded by similarly "fanatical" Young Ethiopians, Cerulli recommended his immediate execution, along with his comrade *däjjazmach* Zäwdé. In a further echo of the past, he concluded the report by recommending the extinction of a "curious mentality" of xenophobia that he once again observed among the local Oromo. These were his first direct interventions in the colonial administration of his area of field research.

Four months later, he deepened his involvement in the war of occupation as viceregal regent. It proved a critical juncture. Over the previous two years, the colonial military command developed an inchoate counterinsurgency doctrine that fused the ostensible lessons of the Libyan campaigns with the political models of Eritrean and Somali colonial administration. Its chief features were the coordination of political and military operations; the embrace of racial theories of behavior; the use of terror, violence, and hostage-taking as instruments of coercion; the reliance on local irregulars and conscripts from Eritrea, Somalia, and Libya; the development of a garrison network that projected Italian military power into rural areas; and the heavy use of air power, encompassing reconnaissance, tactical strikes, and strategic bombing.[116] The goal was the eradication of *arbänä* units and their base of civilian support, and the metrics of success were the daily situation reports that enumerated the number of killed insurgents, submitted *capi*, and surrendered firearms. As viceroy, d'Aosta embraced this doctrine while abandoning Graziani's policy of direct rule—encapsulated by the slogan "no power to the *rases*"—for a more collaborative vision of native administration, as advocated by Cerulli and Moreno and in keeping with the evolving British and French models.¹¹⁷ His first proclamations even promised justice for the diverse peoples of the empire and respect for their distinctive cultures and faiths.¹¹⁸

But the counterinsurgency did not relent. By the spring of 1938, two highly coordinated campaigns were underway across Shäwa, focusing on the Ancoberino subsector in the Amhara governate and the Ambo-Gédo sector in the Galla Sidamo governate. These operations were striking in their intensity. In a clandestine letter from Sudan, Takkälä Wäldä Hawaryat told the exiled emperor, "The enemy arose [in March] like a mad person."¹¹⁹ By May, Cavallero believed the situation had neared a turning point, and in June, Teruzzi arrived in Addis Ababa to assess the situation.¹²⁰ Within days, he notified Mussolini of the discord between d'Aosta and Cerulli, which he attributed to the former's patrician aspect and the latter's abstruse outlook and brusque style.¹²¹ But in a twist, the duke returned to Italy that same week. Officially, the visit involved treatment for a lingering health issue,¹²² but rumors and telegrams from Rome suggested that d'Aosta was in fact attempting to remove Cerulli, possibly by eliminating his office.¹²³ Either way, the latter was temporarily installed as vicegeral regent. For the first time, a civilian expert directed both the colonial administration and the counterinsurgency. In Borra's estimation, the ensuing two-month regency concentrated power in Cerulli's hands, exacerbating his antagonism with the viceroy.¹²⁴

The month of June witnessed the near-total militarization of north Shäwa. Now under the administration of Amhara governor Ottorino Mezzetti and the sector military command of Pietro Maletti, the residents of Ankober and its neighboring valleys were caught in a punishing asymmetric war. Ras Wärq, Askalä, and their family had nowhere to hide. Cerulli's daily situation reports describe constant airstrikes on the town and its environs as well as continuous sweeping operations from Däbrä Berhan and Ankober, supported by reinforcements from Gojjam and the expanding local garrison network. The immediate military objective was the encirclement and defeat of guerillas *lej* Haylä Maryam Mammo and *ras* Abäbä Arägay, who were seeking to escape the heavily patrolled Ankober area for the comparative safety of Mänz or Arsi. Despite the confidence of Cavallero and Teruzzi, the military situation remained uncertain. On June 7, Cerulli triumphantly toured Däbrä Berhan, in keeping with the official mood, but the Italians and Eritrean *askaris* in Ankober were so tense that they fed the first morsel of each meal to chickens, hoping to discover if their food had been poisoned.[125] Their invisible adversaries were formidable.

Haylä Maryam Mammo was among the most renowned guerillas of northern Shäwa. An ex-farmer known as "*abba* Gofen," or "Father of the Crafty One," he had hounded the Italians during their advance to the capital, briefly operating out of Chacha, a hilltop village south of Däbrä Berhan.[126] After the conquest, he led a campaign across northern Shäwa, participated in the failed 1936 attack on Addis Ababa, and obtained a major 1937 victory at Morät with Abäbä Arägay, his comrade and occasional rival. This triumph led Tracchia to term both irreducibles.[127] In September, however, the two suffered heavy losses and retreated to Mänz,[128] then returning to fight around Ankober.[129] By the spring of 1938, Haylä Maryam's forces were reduced to approximately six hundred, and were caught in a vast Italian encirclement that stretched from Ankober to the Kässäm River. On June 6, the *lej* and his followers were entrenched at Sekkest, east of the road between Däbrä Berhan and Addis Ababa, when they were surprised by Maletti in command of six companies and an artillery battery. In the ensuing combat, one hundred *arbañas* were killed, including Haylä Maryam himself. Announcing the news to the Ministry, Cerulli called the defeated leader "our irreducible enemy[,] the cruel instigator of the rebellion of the other *capi*,"[130] later adding—somewhat misleadingly—that the *lej* had been "the true head of the revolt, more important than the same Abäbä Arägay who is dominated and guided by him, [and who is] responsible for the killing of seven of our officers."[131] The killing was a major development. Cerulli exultantly proclaimed it the "definitive unravelling" of the rebellion in Shäwa,[132] which was in his judgment now fueled by personalities rather than anticolonial politics.[133]

Meanwhile, Abäbä Arägay seemed within grasp. The most renowned of the Shäwan guerillas, he had joined the 1936 attack on the capital and then coordinated the following year with the guerilla-king Mäl'akä Şahay in Ankober. Now surrounded with Haylä Maryam in the Kässäm area, the *ras* and his followers sought escape to the west, as Maletti and Cavallero pursued. On June 9, three days after Haylä Maryam's death, Cerulli reported that Abäbä Arägay's forces were low on supplies and splintering in order to evade the Italian lines,[134] and the next day, several of these smaller units were defeated.¹³⁵ By the end of the week, Cerulli announced that the guerillas numbered just a few hundred, with more than six hundred killed and one thousand wounded. Moreover, intelligence indicated that Abäbä Arägay was isolated, which Cerulli attributed to the fact that "the death of Haylä Maryam Mammo has deprived him of his principal support [among the local population,] while his prestige has been completely destroyed among the rebels."¹³⁶ But the airstrikes, aerial reconnaissance, and sweeps in the ensuing weeks failed to deliver the intrepid *ras*—even as Cerulli covered the area with Amharic leaflets, delivering his personal order to the population to submit and surrender their arms.¹³⁷

This frenzied campaign eventually consumed Dan'él Abäbä, the adolescent son of the *ras*.¹³⁸ After informing his father that he wanted to join the armed struggle, the two were separated in their first combat, and the son was surrounded by a group of Somali conscripts. Before he could be killed, an Italian officer intervened and transported the wounded Dan'él to Däbrä Berhan. When Cerulli learned of this development, he drove to the detention site, retrieved the boy, and returned him to Addis Ababa, where Dan'él lived at the vice gubernatorial residence. He later recalled that Cerulli treated him "like a son."¹³⁹ When the youth recovered from his injuries, he was told he would be executed to punish his defiant father, but he was instead freed and dispatched to Ankober on a white horse, a symbolic gesture intended to indicate the awaited submission of the *ras*. The absent d'Aosta later considered these events a testament to Cerulli, and Borra agreed.¹⁴⁰ This judgment, however, ignores the context of the counterinsurgency's objectives and Cerulli's history of support for hostage-taking and instrumentalized detention. The regent might have been kind, but his ward was an asset.

As these events unfolded outside Ankober, a parallel campaign concluded near Gédo. In the time since Cerulli's February reconnaissance, more than six hundred guerillas had concentrated around Mount Jebat and besieged the road from Naqamtee to Addis Ababa, as the sector counterinsurgency proceeded under Francesco De Martini, a capable intelligence officer fluent in Arabic and Amharic.¹⁴¹ On June 9, Cerulli toured the area with Teruzzi and De Martini,¹⁴² and three days later, he dispatched a report to the Ministry. In his judgment, the campaign was nearly complete: over the past two weeks, De Martini had swept the region's forests and caves, with over thirty guerillas killed and more in flight, and the remaining belligerents were surrounded and being "lured from their usual hideouts." As local *capi* submitted en masse, the situation stabilized such that De Martini could be transferred to Ankober, and by June 12, Cerulli considered the area secure. He added that "political operations already well underway will be able to quickly complement the results of [the] military operations." The insights of his fieldwork could now be applied.

Within a month, Cerulli pronounced the Shäwan counterinsurgency a success. On June 18, he informed the Ministry that Gédo was pacified. There had been over 250 submissions during the past four months, although Gärräsu Duki, *däjjazmach* Zäwdé, and *blatta* Takkälä were not among them. However, the local administration had established eleven residences in Gédo-Ambo, and Cerulli commended De Martini for his careful and measured political work.[143] Just over two weeks later, and after repeated consultations with Teruzzi,[144] he further reported that greater Ankober was also secure and had been fortified with new garrisons, although Abäbä Arägay and his followers had escaped.[145] This indisputable failure aside, two thousand rebels had been killed in the Ankober operations, and on July 5, Cerulli optimistically announced that they "completely achieved their objective."[146]

But appearances misled. Three weeks later, Cerulli dispatched a confidential assessment to the ministerial cabinet, notably evading the still-absent d'Aosta. Commending the achievements of the military, he reported that the guerillas had been driven from Ankober, suffering heavy losses with only a few local units remaining. However, in contrast to Gédo, there had been no submissions by *capi*, a serious failing that Cerulli attributed to the widespread animosity toward Maletti and Tracchia. Though commendable soldiers, he suggested that the generals' past actions had created harmful memories among the Ankoberites that alienated the latter from the colonial state. This was likely a reference to Tracchia's 1936 execution of the surrendered Abärra and Asfawässän Kassa, the sons of *le'ul ras* Kassa Haylu—the great-grandson of *negus* Sahlä Sellasé—as well as Maletti's supervision of the 1937 mass killing at Däbrä Libanos monastery, undertaken in the aftermath of Yekatit 12. These brutalities stained Italian prestige. In a subtle political jab, Cerulli added that he had personally apprised d'Aosta of this reputational issue, and further, that he had ordered Maletti's replacement Ettore Galliani "to work with every means in order to win over the population." The military excesses of the past were hindering political progress in the present.

He then turned to the future. While Ankober and Gédo were now pacified, he believed "the final contest from the political perspective is now risked during these months of the rainy season." In his view, if Abäbä Arägay and the other routed guerillas failed to rewin the local population, then the insurrection would collapse, since an "old tradition" held that the Ankoberites were the supreme arbiters of Shäwan politics, and dereliction of this standard would reduce the guerillas to "brigands without hope." They would have no option but submission. Paradoxically, he then advocated a military solution to this political problem: "The problem [of the *arbänäs'* resurgence] will be above all of policing [counterinsurgency] and no longer political. For this reason, I repeat, we face the most serious test. And I am certain that if we continue with a firm hand (I repeat, firm) to maintain the situation everywhere, above all intervening with immediate energy and promptness at the weak points as soon as they manifest themselves in whichever part of the empire, [then] we will be able to say at the end of September that the domestic political situation has been definitively resolved."[147] In short, Cerulli believed Shäwa could be permanently subjugated if the summer operation was followed by a conclusive redemonstration of Italian military supremacy after the Ethiopian New Year. The people of Shäwa required the "firm hand," a euphemism for the deployment of violence and terror to create submissive African subjects. This was a racialized colonial elaboration of Mussolini's repressive approach to the undisciplined Italian nation, which in his judgment only understood the physical language of the *bastone*, or cudgel.[148] In Cerulli's assessment, strict adherence to this eminently fascist vision of ruthless and unwavering autocracy would end the war of occupation in Ethiopia. It was a total reversal of the paternalistic liberal model of negotiated native policy espoused by d'Aosta.[149]

The hardship of the firm hand scarred *mämher* Ras Wärq such that he rarely spoke of it.[150] His youngest son survived, but his eldest did not. In February 1937, the defection of *le'ul ras* Haylu Täklä Haymanot led the Italians to Yohannes Ras Wärq, who they placed under house arrest with a sister in Addis Ababa. After Yekatit 12, he was abruptly taken from the home and shot. Months later, Maletti and his soldiers slaughtered the residents of Däbrä Libanos, the *mämher*'s alma mater. Meanwhile, the counterinsurgency burned through Ankober and its environs. Several local priests and deacons were killed,[151] and a number of Ras Wärq's contemporaries were deported to Asinara, including *däjjazmach* Mätafäriya Mälkä Ṣédéq, *qäñ-ñazmach* Ṣägga Wärädä Wärq, Säyfu Mika'él, and Germé Cherfé.[152] Those who remained behind struggled to survive and protect the community: *ṣähafi* Habtäwäld Wärqenäh sheltered women and children in local caves, while teacher *mämmeré* Fesseha dutifully buried the dead.[153]

Facing this onslaught, Ras Wärq fought back. He safeguarded Ankober's material heritage by collecting its manuscripts, religious artifacts, and historical objects, which he concealed at remote locations in the wilderness outside of town.[154] Among these treasures was the wedding attire of Emperor Menilek and *etégé* Ṭaytu.[155] Also a protector was *wäyzero* Askalä, who spent many nights in the woods with infant Tärräfä as the fighting raged in the mountains. Meanwhile, Ras Wärq encouraged his other son Tiruneh, a French-speaking alumnus of the Täfäri Mäkonnen School, to work as a translator at the Goräbéla garrison, where he obtained intelligence on Italian operations that his father passed to the guerrillas. Tiruneh also used his position at the local magistrate to aid Ethiopian defendants, and in Ankober today, numerous families remember his role in saving their relatives from harm through his adept mistranslations before the court.[156]

The rains brought reprieve. In August, d'Aosta returned from Rome,[157] and the following month, Cerulli left for Italy. In part, his trip was professional. That October, he attended the massive Volta Congress on Africa in Rome, which featured eminent international experts Bronislaw Malinowski, Louis Massignon, and Hubert Lyautey as well as futurist Filippo Tommaso Marinetti and fascist hierarchs Lessona, Bottai, Balbo, and De Vecchi.[158] The gathering was the largest international colonial conference of the interwar era, and in the assessment of one Italian attendee, it was a conclusive demonstration of "the maturity and importance" of Italian African studies, in this respect a colonial sequel to the 1935 International Congress of Orientalists.[159] But according to Borra, Cerulli was also exhausted by the events of the summer, and the trip was a necessary period of recuperation.[160] He did not return from the sabbatical until November.[161]

In his absence, the duke reasserted his political supremacy in the colony, overturning Cerulli's summer power grab. This reascendance was evinced through the viceroy's role in the September celebration of Mäsqäl, the Feast of the True Cross. Building on Haylä Sellasé's reinvention of the feast as a public state pageant, and elaborating on its use in colonial Eritrea as a ritual assertion of indirect rule, the viceroy used Mäsqäl to publicly demonstrate his respect for the Christian faithful and confer neotraditionalist titles that affirmed the hierarchy of native authority. It was a politicoreligious invention of tradition that reified d'Aosta's collaborative model of paternalistic colonial administration, displaying and affirming the grandeur of the viceroy and his chosen African partners.[162] Borra called the feast "a visible triumphant test" of the duke's new approach.[163]

The ceremony rehearsed colonial power through the ritual language of faith. On September 27, the viceroy joined *ras* Haylu Täklä Haymanot, *abunä* Abreham, and *eçhägé* Yohannes to observe the feast.[164] After a parade and ceremonial bonfire at the Jan Méda, the celebrants proceeded to the viceregal residence in Seddest Kilo. Surrounded by luminaries of the Ethiopian church in the former imperial palace, the duke greeted the attendees and then solemnly bestowed titles on select honorees.[165] The first and most senior of these was *däjjazmach* Haylä Sellasé Gugsa, the preeminent aristocratic supporter of the colonial order, who received the rank of *ras*. Other honors went to civil servants from the directorate offices and governate administrations, including *basha* Asfeha, who received the rank of *fitawrari*.[166] At the ceremony's conclusion, d'Aosta thanked the honorees for their service to the cause of progress, and in the weeks that followed, the Amharic colonial press documented the promotions through photos, biographies of the awardees, and reflections on the history and significance of Mäsqäl.[167] On sabbatical in Italy, Cerulli had missed the big day.

Yet the ensuing months suggested another reversal of his political fortunes. In January 1939, he assumed the governorship of Shäwa through an expansion of the office of the vice governor general. Established two months prior, this new governate combined the former Addis Ababa special district, comprised of the capital and sectoral military commands of Däbrä Berhan, Ambo, and Mojjo,[168] with the capital-adjacent areas of the Amhara, Galla Sidamo, and Harär governates, including Ankober and Gédo.[169] The territory thus encompassed the most densely populated urban center of the colony, now heavily fortified with bunkers and barbed wire, its streets filled with lorries, tanks, and identification control posts.[170] In the press, the Shäwa governate was described as the home of the "most civilized and intelligent" Ethiopians, lending it a special significance to the colony.[171] As its governor, the vice governor general also supervised the governate military command, whose functions were fulfilled by the colonial military command in Addis Ababa. In this capacity, Cerulli was thus theoretically—

though by no means effectively—senior to Cavallero with respect to military operations in Shäwa. This was a rare instance of civilian supremacy, since the other colonial governors were military officers who worked in tandem with their counterparts in the governate military commands.

Cerulli assumed this new role amid deepening administrative tensions. Compounding his own rivalry with the viceroy was a growing rift between d'Aosta and Cavallero.[172] Over the previous year, the general had consulted with d'Aosta and Cerulli on operational matters until he judged the duke an inferior strategist.[173] As d'Aosta continued to negotiate with the elusive Abäbä Arägay, Cavallero suggested to Rome that the viceroy was proving inadequate to the task of pacifying the colony, particularly given his opposition to the use of chemical weapons. Teruzzi supported this critique,[174] and by January 1939, Mussolini was privately fuming about the viceroy's performance.[175] In February, these developments induced Cavallero to meet with Orlando Lorenzini—a taciturn Tuscan *alpino* and reputed former monk—to plan a major new offensive across northern Shäwa.[176] This campaign had multiple goals. In addition to a decisive victory against *ras* Abäbä that would end d'Aosta's undignified diplomatic follies, it would also transform the restive Shäwa governate into a secure operational hub for the colony, enabling redeployments from the Horn of Africa that could address the now-imminent war in Europe and North Africa.[177] Facing this arrogation of power by Cavallero, d'Aosta returned to Rome in March to confront Mussolini, perhaps pursuing Teruzzi.[178] In his absence, Cerulli again assumed the position of viceregal regent, in which capacity he oversaw Cavallero's counterinsurgency across Mänz, Däbrä Berhan, and Ankober. It proved to be one of the most brutal campaigns of the entire colonial era, notable for its widespread use of chemical weapons. In an evocative coincidence, guerilla historian Taddäsä Zäwäldé noted that the struggle at one point unfolded in a place called "the field of bitters."[179]

The Italian base of operations was Däbra Berhan. An important commercial and administrative center of nearly seventeen thousand residents, the town itself was also the seat of Lorenzini's newly established sector command of seven battalions and three irregular *bandas*, supplemented by a new hospital, residential headquarters, and Blackshirt militia barracks.[180] Construction was everywhere. The campaign aimed at the mountainous riverine network around the town, a rugged area stretching from Sälla Dengay in the north to Chacha in the south, with supporting operations across Mänz and Ankober. Significantly, the remote mountain passes between Jerru and Sälla Dengay offered escape north to Gojjam, which suggests why Cavallero and Lorenzini aimed to rapidly defeat the now-proximate Abäbä Arägay. In conversation, Lorenzini openly disdained his Ethiopian adversary. According to the journalist Malaparte, who was embedded with one of his battalions, the colonel described the *ras* as no more than an "official gangster" drunk on champagne and the adulation of foreign journalists, even boasting "this time I will give him a thrashing, Maremma-style."[181]

At that very moment, Abäbä Arägay and his followers were in Tägulät, a strategically significant mountain area north of Däbrä Berhan.[182] In early March, the *ras* met with the notables of Tägulät to discuss local issues and plan his future political and military operations.[183] The villagers hosted the guerilla leader and his followers with feasts and gifts so lavish that they resembled the hospitality shown in the royal palace itself, as Taddäsä Zäwäldé recalled. In an act of reciprocal generosity, Abäbä Arägay then expropriated the crops and property of the townspeople of nearby Däbrä Berhan who had become "embracers of the enemy," redistributing these spoils to the guerillas' supporters across Tägulät and Mänz.[184] The *ras*'s depth of support in the immediate environs of the capital was much stronger than the Italians realized.

On March 12, Lorenzini initiated the occupation of the foothills outside Däbrä Berhan. Three days later, Cavallero reached the town to oversee the campaign, and that same day, Cerulli arrived with *fitawrari* Asfeha.[185] The regent informed the Ministry that he had proceeded to Däbrä Berhan "to personally assess the situation." It was an unusual development. Officially, Cavallero reported that Cerulli's presence in the field would facilitate the coordination of the military and political aspects of the counterinsurgency, which in practice meant supplementing military victories with political submissions.[186] Cerulli, however, viewed his role differently. In a March 15 telegram to the Ministry, dispatched on his arrival in Däbrä Berhan, he outlined a distinctive vision of his own expansive politico-military command.[187] Reviewing the progress of a recent campaign in western Shäwa, he explained that military success in Kachama had been augmented by the colonial residents, who obtained the submission of the defeated guerilla leaders. Comparing this situation to a similarly coordinated effort near Mount Jebat, he then suggested that "the concept of local operations conducted by the same political-military authority that presides over the government of the region appears very fruitful." In other words, governors should manage the counterinsurgency in their territories as they see fit, in concert with the military leadership.[188] Reading this statement in the context of Cerulli's arrival in Däbrä Berhan that same day, he was clearly betting on himself. He hoped to oversee the capture of Abäbä Arägay in his own governate, in the absence of d'Aosta and despite the involvement of Cavallero.

Over the next few days, Cerulli dispatched a torrent of telegrams from Däbrä Berhan. On March 15, he announced that Lorenzini had engaged Abäbä Arägay's forces outside Sälla Dengay,[189] and the next day, he reported continued fighting in the nearby Gado Valley. He added that one of Lorenzini's columns—with Malaparte in tow—had killed over three hundred guerillas, with further casualties inflicted by airstrikes. In his view, "The blow that the rebellion received yesterday was extremely serious." The population appreciated its significance, he added, and the local *liqawent* were inviting the guerillas to surrender. Later that same day, he reported more engagements in upper Gado, with the heavy losses a sign of the "crumbling" insurrection in the area, as Lorenzini's soldiers pursued. The local *capi* were now collaborating, and one had even delivered a captured rebel patrol to Däbrä Berhan.[190] Asfeha later recalled that Cerulli interrogated such prisoners of war in town, and that he personally determined whether they should be dispatched to the military tribunal, where summary execution was the most common sentence.[191] Some of those killed were buried in a mass grave outside town.[192] On March 17, Cerulli corresponded directly with Lorenzini in the field, ordering him to remain in place near Däbrä Sina—rather than continuing his pursuit of the agile *ras*—so as to demonstrate the permanence of the occupation to locals.[193] Cerulli's actions and field reports in these critical days suggest a confidence in his own operational superiority. That very same week, d'Aosta met Mussolini in Rome and requested his subordinate's dismissal. The duce assented.[194]

Presumably unaware of this development, Cerulli dispatched an update on March 18 that outlined the ongoing "pursuit and elimination" of the guerillas.[195] Irregulars were sweeping the Gobäna Valley, and one battalion had fought Abäbä Arägay's followers in the streets of Däbrä Sina, killing ninety. After the *arbäña* Wända Mina fortified himself in caves near Çhaçha, the military command ordered an airstrike on the area "with every means." In the ensuing attack, the village of Chacha was entirely demolished, killing more than fifty and leaving only its Italian-built bridge intact.[196] Cerulli explained this devastating strike on Haylä Maryam Mammo's old stronghold in terms of the strategic necessity for decisive action, echoing his recommendation of the previous summer: "It remains essential at this time to act promptly wherever units of deserters may strive to regroup again, so as to arrive at submission or elimination." If the destruction of Chacha was the stick, the carrot, he explained, was the simultaneous liberation of twenty prisoners at Däbrä Berhan, which would "counter reports of the strictness of the government towards those who submit."[197] His firm hand would prevail.

That same day, Cerulli delivered a message to the rural population through an aerial propaganda leaflet. His Amharic ultimatum fluttered down on the mountain villages:

> People of northern Shäwa, the power of Italian arms has beaten, destroyed, or dispersed those groups that, deceived by the ambitious lies of certain *capi*, have tried to raid you peaceful populations[,] moving from gullies and ravines [they have] believed inaccessible. Tell the fugitives if they present themselves to our officials, immediately surrendering their arms, their lives will be spared. The mercy that leads us to grant pardon today does not want hesitation or negotiation. You have seen how in a few days all of the area has been organized. You have [colonial] residents at the principal centers of Däbrä Berhan, Bannaber, Ankober, M[ofer?]. You have your *capi* in every district. Obey! Calmly take up the work in your fields! You are resolutely protected and safeguarded by the power of Fascist Italy.[198]

The message exemplified the weaponized language of command.[199] Yet Cerulli's words were directed toward a devasted and unreceptive population. On a march north from Däbrä Berhan in these same days, the young noncommissioned officer Alessandro Boaglio found all the villages razed and burned to the ground, their inhabitants "dispersed to the mountains to inculcate a not wholly unjustified hatred for us."[200] Deeper in the mountains, his superior Piero Farello wrote in a diary that the area was "completely destroyed [and] deserted," and those few who remained were "terrorized" and "skeletal from hunger."[201] There was nobody to return to the harvest and protection of fascist power.

One day after writing this leaflet, Cerulli returned to Addis Ababa. As the local press relayed the drama of Shäwa-Amhara interregional football matches, Cerulli dispatched a ministerial summary of the campaign outside Däbrä Berhan.[202] Its successes were now clear: he estimated that of the two or three thousand guerillas active in north Shäwa, seven hundred had been killed, with at least as many wounded. The surviving guerillas had subdivided in an effort to escape the Italian encirclement. In a surreal juxtaposition, two days later he was the guest of honor at a gallery opening for the painter Rosida Cuoco, with whom he chatted amid her portraits of smiling Ethiopian children, pastoralists, and *askari* (figure 8.2).[203] The next day, he dispatched another update to the Ministry, this time in the dead of night.[204] The pursuit of Abäbä Arägay and his allies had now led deep into the mountains north of Sälla Dengay, approaching the upper tributaries of the Blue Nile. A number of rebel bands had been engaged in recent days, with heavy losses, and one leader named *fitawrari* Damṭäw had been killed. But Abäbä Arägay was proving as elusive as ever.

FIGURE 8.2 Rosida Cuoco and Enrico Cerulli, Addis Ababa (1939).

Source: © Brooklyn College Library Special Collections.

He was, in fact, already gone. On the pivotal day of March 15, *ras* Abäba, *lej* Gezachäw Haylé, Taddäsä Bälaynäh, and their followers were surprised by Lorenzini and several thousand soldiers at Fit Méda, near Sälla Dengay and the newly completed Mussolini Pass. Caught unexpectedly in the middle of postfeast deliberations, the guerillas' position seemed dire. Yet despite the supporting airstrikes and arriving Italian reinforcements, the surprised Ethiopians eventually managed to rout the Italian forces, "scattering them with machine gun fire like teff chaff," in the words of Taddäsä Zäwäldé.[205] After this pivotal victory, in which over eighty Italian soldiers were killed, Abäbä Arägay slipped through Lorenzini's lines and headed south to Bulga. The Italians had supremely overestimated their ability to capture the *ras* alive.

In the meantime, the campaign approached its horrific nadir. On March 26, amid the twentieth-anniversary celebrations of the first fascist rally,[206] Mussolini dispatched an unequivocal telegram to Cerulli:

> I read with great pleasure the final report on the action undertaken to break off the Shäwan rebellion. While I send my praises to the commanders and troops, I order that no respite be given to the fugitives and stragglers so that the operation is truly definitive and ensures, together with concurrent political action, the beginning of an era of order and absolute normalcy in this region. Also[,] in view of the European situation[,] the military action in Shäwa has considerable importance because it eliminates the hopes cultivated in Djibouti by the Abyssinian exiles and their all too obvious supporters. Once the Shäwa operation is completed and perfected, the Amhara rebellion must be eliminated.[207]

The following day, Cerulli replied that the operations in Mänz were proceeding with "maximum energy," in pursuit of the duce's decisive victory. The troops displayed commendable "tenacity and offensive spirit" and had surprised three hundred guerillas in the Mofer River gorge, killing more than one hundred and fifty. The standing order was to crush all newly formed *arbäña* units.[208] That same day, he dispatched an updated summary of casualties, estimating that over a thousand guerillas had been killed in the past two weeks—possibly half of the total number in the field.[209]

The worst was still to come. Nearly two weeks later, on April 8, Cavallero and Lorenzini met in the capital to discuss the campaign. Given Mussolini's diktat on colonial stability, Cavallero ordered the continued pursuit of the remaining guerillas and the systematic integration of the region's garrisons, particularly in the area of Zärrät in northern Mänz. He then reviewed this plan with Cerulli.[210] The next day, Gennaro Sora and his troops surrounded the guerilla *däjjazmach* Täshomä Shänquṭ and his followers at a cave near Zärrät. At dawn, the young Boaglio descended the cliff face into the cave to deploy mustard gas munitions, and over the next two days, between fifteen hundred and three thousand men, women, and children were killed. Most of those who survived the chemical weapons attack and escaped to the cave entrance were executed by Sora's waiting soldiers, sometimes in gruesome displays of torture and extreme violence that traumatized witnesses.[211] In this same three-day period, Lorenzini's forces launched additional chemical weapons attacks in Chimas and the Mofär gorge. In the assessment of historian Matteo Dominioni, the mass killing at Zärrät was the most brutal massacre of the entire colonial era because of its deliberate targeting of women, children, and the elderly, all obvious noncombatants. The site of the atrocity is remembered in Ethiopia today as "the Cave of the Rebel."[212] It is not far from Heruy's ancestral home.

This dark week in Shäwa coincided with the viceroy's return. He arrived in the capital on April 1,[213] and nearly two weeks later, Cavallero left for Rome in disgrace.[214] On April 13, just as the killings unfolded at Zärrät, Mussolini dismissed the general because of his failure to capture Abäbä Arägay—an unforgivable shortcoming given the goals outlined in his March 26 telegram to Cerulli.[215] In Addis Ababa, the departing Cavallero referred to the viceroy with obsequious deference, but in Rome, he reportedly insisted that d'Aosta "lacked the maturity to govern efficiently and rectify the situation."[216] He later insisted that his campaign had dealt a "mortal blow" to the insurrection, despite Abäbä Arägay's escape.[217] Teruzzi disagreed. Weeks later, he publicly acknowledged that colonial tranquility was marred by the irreducible units still active in Amhara and Shäwa, motivated by brigandage as well as foreign propaganda.[218] Privately, he attributed Cavallero's demotion to his incompetence and thirst for power, while d'Aosta blamed the general's heavy-handedness and Borra his rivalry with the viceroy.[219] Cavallero's eventual replacement, Luigi De Biase, accepted d'Aosta's unrestricted autonomy in military and political matters, lessening the administrative antagonism in the colony.[220]

Two weeks after Cavallero's fall, Cerulli was also dismissed.[221] On the now-symbolic May 5, Guglielmo Nasi became the vice governor general, and Cerulli assumed the latter's former position as governor of Harär. His successor as the viceroy's senior colonial expert proved to be Enrico De Leone, a d'Aosta client and academic specialist in Islamic law who had worked under Cerulli in the Shäwa governate administration, and who was now elevated to the position of deputy chief of the viceregal cabinet.[222] Officially, the mood was celebratory. Greeting the Blackshirts of his new governate, Cerulli announced they would together further "the maximum development of the fascist empire,"[223] while Nasi assured the notables of Harär that his successor was "not a new man, but rather a man who knows the customs and practices of these populations, who knows all the problems of this country, who knows your language, and who loves the native populations as I love them."[224] But the accolades concealed real discord.

Why was Cerulli demoted through this "changing of the guard," as it was described in the press?[225] The ire of d'Aosta was surely not the lone cause. If Cerulli's expertise won the esteem of Mussolini and Teruzzi, he had a poor reputation among the Italians of the colony, and in the Roman assessment, his substitution by Nasi—a personal friend of d'Aosta—was welcomed by many.[226] This point is suggested by the local press coverage of the change. Cerulli's negative reputation was no doubt fueled by his personal style, but it likely also reflected his perceived ineffectiveness as regent. Given Mussolini's response to Cavallero's operational failures, Cerulli's performance during his 1939 regency may have similarly undermined his standing, compounding his existing antagonism with d'Aosta. A glimpse of this possibility was suggested in the aftermath of the Däbrä Berhan campaign, when the embedded Malaparte confidently told a press colleague, "Now that Cerulli is gone, things will change."[227] This comment by Lorenzini's sycophantic chronicler suggests a perception among the military that Cerulli's decisions had contributed to the operational failure, possibly because his direct order for Lorenzini to remain in Däbrä Sina facilitated the escape of Abäbä Arägay.

A further indication of Cerulli's possible perceived ineffectiveness involves Mussolini's March 26 "no respite" telegram. In the conclusion to Cavallero's summary report on the 1939 campaign, which was something of an exculpatory defense given his failure to capture the *ras*, the general indicated that he had strictly followed Mussolini's directive to pursue the interlinked military and political operation until the governate was pacified, without interruption or a ceasefire. There is some evidence that Cerulli had endorsed a different strategy. On March 16, Cerulli dispatched a report to the Ministry that contains a possible intimation of his decisive vision of his own gubernatorial civil-military authority: it includes a line that appears to say, "I ordered a ceasefire," though this line of the telegram was deliberately obscured on its arrival in the Ministry.[228] Could it be that Cerulli paused the campaign at the precise moment Cavallero considered its critical point, just as Lorenzini neared Abäbä Arägay? And could this decision have figured in Mussolini's subsequent specific instruction to Cerulli to pursue the pacification of Shäwa without quarter? Cavallero's summary report included Cerulli's March 17 telegram restraining Lorenzini, but not Cerulli's censored "ceasefire" telegram. Absent additional evidence, these points are speculative.

Cerulli spent the remainder of the year overseeing the governorate of Harär. Beyond the thirteenth-century walls of its eponymous capital, one of the oldest centers of Islamic learning in the Horn of Africa, the territory encompassed the bustling railway town of Dire Dawa as well as the entire eastern borderlands, from the Awash River to the Somali frontier. Over the summer, Cerulli toured the governate, lingering in eastern Oromiyya and his former fieldwork sites along the Shebelle River. His official schedule was packed: it included meetings with local notables and party officials; inspections of the territory's cotton schemes, coffee markets, and cement factories; and trips to Addis Ababa for bimonthly summits with d'Aosta and the other governors.[229] He attempted to repair his fascist credentials by publicly assuring Stefano Mario Cutelli, a leading exponent of Nazi-inflected biological racial theory, that he would diligently follow "the racial problem for its particular significance and the importance that it assumes in the lands of the empire."[230] Cerulli delivered this pledge as the regime implemented expansive legislation involving racial prestige,[231] and as the militant anthropologist Lidio Cipriani traversed the colony conducting anthropometric studies of hundreds of African subjects,[232] and it was published in *Il diritto razzista*, the leading journal dedicated to the official Aryan-focused racial ideology. His comments were featured alongside similar statements by fascist intellectuals and regime officials, most notably the now militant anti-Semite Bottai and the Nazi legal scholar Hans Frank, the future governor general of Poland and architect of its genocidal concentration camps.²³³ But Cerulli's political rehabilitation proved impossible. Finally, in February of 1940, only ten months after his demotion, Cerulli returned to Rome, where he administered his governate in absentia until the collapse of Africa Orientale Italiana.²³⁴ The expert had been undone by the arrogance of power.

As the counterinsurgency ravaged communities across Shäwa, Ras Wärq's clandestine subterfuges in Ankober eventually caught the eye of the local authorities. The violence reached his own home. One night, a group of Eritrean *askari* suddenly arrived at the residence of Ras Wärq and Askalä, intending to conduct a surprise search. The first to enter the premises was an Eritrean soldier from Hamasén, who brandished a rifle at the small family. The defiant *mämher* rose from his bed and confronted the intruder, holding a crucifix before him and verbally daring the surprised *askari* to shoot the holy object. Stunned, the Eritrean retreated from the home without firing. He later revealed to his comrades that his hand had been stayed because he experienced a vision of Saint Täklä Haymanot, the founder of Däbrä Libanos, superimposed on the face of Ras Wärq.²³⁵ The *mämher* had been saved by a miracle foretold by his own name.

9
Bath and Dhanaane

Bath is a Georgian city on Roman foundations. Situated in the Cotswolds, its first-century thermal spa and Temple of Sulis Minerva lie beneath its modern center, which was developed in the eighteenth century as a resort for the London elite, later savaged by reluctant resident Jane Austen. In the nineteenth century, the city revived its Latin heritage through public monuments to its ancient emperors and governors, gesturing to the neoclassical culture of Victorian imperialism, but by the early twentieth century, its fortunes began to wane with the decline of the local tourism and manufacturing industries. Another reversal came in the 1930s, when the city was flooded with newcomers, initially displaced unemployed workers from Wales and northern England, and then after 1939, refugees from London and other English urban centers. The ancient imperial bridgehead of Aquae Sulis was now a wartime receiving area.[1]

Among these exiles was *blattén géta* Heruy. He reached Bath in August 1936, after an arduous and uncertain odyssey that consumed the previous year, stretching from Addis Ababa to Amsterdam, Jerusalem, Geneva, and London. He had visited Europe many times and spent his life confronting the political and intellectual challenges it posed for his country, but never had he made it his home. He now had little choice. His arrival in Bath was the culmination of a bitter international education. Over the past two decades, his experiences with the racist elite of New York City, the fraudulent diplomacy of Rome, and the liberal casuistry of Geneva had honed his already sharp understanding of imperial power. He had glimpsed its many aspects, and was now confined to its most ebullient metropole. Exile revealed the fullness of empire, as Edward Said put it.[2]

It was a long road to Bath. After the invasion in October 1935, the atmosphere in Addis Ababa was tense yet defiant. As the Italians took Aksum and Mäqällä, the capital braced for war. In November and December, the pages of *Berhanenna sälam* and *A'emro* featured bellicose anti-Italian poetry,[3] accounts of the royal family mobilizing the troops, statements of international solidarity from figures like Alfred Nemours,[4] and caustic illustrations of the "Second Judas" Haylä Sellasé Gugsa in an Italian uniform (figures 9.1 and 9.2).[5] Hearing distant gunfire outside Addis Ababa, Tä'amrat Ammanu'él recalled that "nobody [in the capital] knew what these shots in the air meant," though he later realized they were signals of terror.[6] The city descended into lawlessness. Throughout this uncertain period, Heruy led the Foreign Ministry as well as the ad hoc regency council, in the latter capacity joining *etégé* Mänän to direct the caretaker government while Haylä Sellasé oversaw the campaign on the northern front. As foreign minister, Heruy corresponded directly with the League of Nations,[7] and he brokered the Ethiopian rejection of the December Hoare-Laval proposal, which offered Ethiopia the port of Assäb in exchange for territorial and economic concessions to Italy.[8] By January, when the American John Spencer arrived in Addis Ababa to advise the Foreign Ministry, Heruy was totally consumed by his regency duties, leaving the daily work of diplomacy to son Sirak Heruy, son-in-law Yelma Gäbrä Kidan, and Täsfayé Tägäñ, supported by Zälläqä Negatu and Everett Colson, an American advisor to the emperor.[9] The foreign minister's coded telegrams streamed throughout the country.[10] In the streets of the capital, meanwhile, Edoardo Borra found his longtime acquaintance hostile, a sentiment he attributed to Heruy's "unjustified" Italophobia.[11] In Geneva, the League offered limited sanctions on nonstrategic Italian imports.

As airstrikes pummeled Addis Ababa and the situation on the frontiers worsened, the Italian government launched a series of disjointed overtures to the Ethiopian government that aimed to resolve the conflict outside the League. Their seriousness is uncertain. Many of these plans involved the creation of a pseudomandate, capitalizing on liberal European anxiety

FIGURE 9.1 "How all the men, women, and elders of Ethiopia cursed Haylä Sellasé [Gugsa] as the Second Judas," *Berhanenna sälam* (1935).

FIGURE 9.2 "How the *liqä pappasat*, the *eçhägé*, and all the priests prayed curses upon the Second Judas Haylä Sellasé [Gugsa]," *Berhanenna sälam* (1935).

about the strategic implications of the contemporaneous German occupation of the Rhineland.[12] On the Italian side, the overtures proceeded through the Ministry of the Colonies, the Ministry of Foreign Affairs, and the Military Information Service, under the direction of Aloisi, Suvich, Lessona, Guariglia, and Cerulli. On the Ethiopian side, they involved a series of purported and actual intermediaries of the emperor, including the Greek consul Adrien Zervos, the diplomat Afäwärq Gäbrä Iyäsus, and the Palestinian entrepreneur Shukri Jasir Bey, with varying degrees of supervision by Heruy and the Foreign Ministry. These Ethiopian representatives were surveilled by the Italian ministries and their formidable consular and military intelligence network.

By early 1936, Zervos had relocated to Athens, where he reportedly received constant telegrams from Paris and Addis Ababa.[13] In February, he met with Cerulli and Sirak for direct talks concerning peace terms.[14] Although the scope of these discussions is unclear, the Italian Ministry of Foreign Affairs reported that the emperor was wary of the British but had resolved to continue fighting,[15] while Cerulli later recalled that the Italian side abruptly terminated the talks on the grounds that a military victory seemed imminent.[16] Italian intelligence also revealed that Sirak had brought photographic evidence of the Italian use of chemical weapons, which he intended to disseminate in the European capitals.[17] Meanwhile, similarly fruitless negotiations unfolded with Jasir Bey in Athens and Afäwärq in Djibouti,[18] as Heruy and the emperor negotiated an alternative protectorate scheme with Britain.[19]

In March, these clandestine efforts culminated in direct talks between Heruy and Cerulli. The two were reunited in Amsterdam, possibly with Zervos and Sirak, who according to Italian intelligence intended to proceed to Europe from Athens.[20] The negotiations seem to have involved the emperor's role in a future Italian-controlled polity, but the details are now difficult to ascertain since the intercepted telegrams that describe the talks are presently missing from the archive where they were once preserved.[21] According to Spencer, Heruy supported negotiation amid the intensifying chemical weapon attacks and the rapid Italian advance towards Shäwa, believing territorial concessions preferable to the mass immiseration that would accompany an Ethiopian military defeat.[22] The following month, Cerulli informed Aloisi that the emperor had resolved to remain in Addis Ababa,[23] and he later characterized the Amsterdam talks as a failed effort towards "the finalization of a peace treaty."[24]

Ethiopia gained nothing from the green baize table.[25] After the April retreat from Mayçhäw, Heruy joined Haylä Sellasé in the council deliberations about leaving the country, and he was together with *blatta* Takkälä Wäldä Hawaryat among the dissenting minority who urged the emperor to stay.[26] On May 1, just before Badoglio and Bottai reached Addis Ababa, the emperor and royal family left for Djibouti. They were accompanied by the foreign minister and sons Sirak and Fäqqädä Sellasé, with wife Hamärä Eshäté and daughters Gännät, Aṣädä Wayn, and Laqäch remaining at the family home in Gullälé. A British cruiser brought the exiles to Palestine, where the emperor visited the holy places and the Ethiopian monastery of Däbrä Selṭan, and then on to Britain, with *etégé* Mänän and the children remaining in Jerusalem. At sea, the British secretly feared an Italian attack on the Ethiopians' ship.[27] On June 3, the exiles reached London's Waterloo station, where they were welcomed by huge crowds and a contingent of the city's pro-Ethiopia activists. Later that month, the emperor proceeded to Geneva, where he delivered his unprecedented Amharic address to the Assembly. As the chamber read its French translation, he castigated the Italian government, the perfidy of the Italian memorandum, and the violence of the colonial occupation, and again urged the League to grant the now-conquered Ethiopia its due protections under international law—a supplication he called "the saddest duty that has befallen an emperor."[28] He was joined in Geneva by Heruy and *ras* Kassa Haylu, as well as a diplomatic entourage that included *däjjazmach* Näsibu Zä'amanu'él, Wälda Giyorgis Wäldä Yohannes, Lorenzo Ta'ezaz, Éfrém Täwäldä Mädhen, and the newly hired Una Marson, who was now the London Legation's public relations deputy. After the Assembly voted to end sanctions against Italy, the exiles returned to Britain. In September, the emperor purchased Fairfield House, an Italianate manor in a western suburb of Bath. The home would serve as his base for the next four years.

The struggle from Fairfield House was both political and military. If the prospect of a diplomatic solution through the mechanisms of the international system had dimmed, the emperor and Heruy continued to contest Italian sovereignty in Ethiopia, both through the legal framework of the League and the propaganda work of their skeletal government in exile. To these ends, they solicited a memorandum on their post-May 5 League standing from Hersch Lauterpacht, the Polish professor of international law and future Nuremberg prosecutor who was then developing the concept of crimes against humanity.²⁹ This international legal challenge complemented their broader campaign of resistance from Britain, which encompassed public relations to counter Italian propaganda about the "ex-negus" and colony, diplomatic maneuvers to prevent the formal expulsion of Ethiopia from the League, and the coordination and support of the anticolonial insurrection at home.

They were aided in this work by a dedicated diplomatic team. The London Legation in Westminster was directed by Wärqenäh Eshäté and Wäldä Giyorgis Wäldä Yohannes, with the support of Sirak, Marson, and Emmanu'él Abraham. All worked under the close supervision of Heruy, who frequently shared their office due to the limited space.³⁰ Their daily work was onerous: Marson recalled that the Ethiopians received "thousands and thousands of letters" from their international supporters, and even more when the emperor was in London, and she added that "the entire correspondence of the Legation passed through the Minister's hands to me."³¹ A second embassy operated in Paris under the direction of Aklilu Habtäwäld and Éfrém Täwäldä Mädhen, who worked with Fairfield House, the London team, and the Jerusalem exiles.³² Mälaku Bäyyan, meanwhile, mobilized support among Black Americans in New York City, organizing a newspaper called *The Voice of Ethiopia* while coordinating with W. E. B. Du Bois, the Howard University-based Ethiopian Research Council, and the Harlem-based Ethiopian World Federation. By 1940, the federation boasted twenty-two branches, with outposts in Jamaica and Cuba.³³

On all these fronts, the Ethiopians were supported by a cohort of London-based African and Black Atlantic allies. These coalesced around the International African Friends of Ethiopia (IAFE), a radical counterpart to the more liberal and less stridently anticolonial League of Coloured Peoples, Marson's former employer. The IAFE was established in 1935 by C. L. R. James, Jomo Kenyatta, and Amy Ashwood Garvey, the last a Jamaican activist whose restaurant served as the organization's headquarters, and it quickly became one of Britain's leading Ethiopian advocacy groups.³⁴ In 1935, it organized large solidarity rallies where speakers linked antifascism to the global struggle against colonialism and racism, and in 1936, its members greeted the Ethiopian exiles on their arrival in London, later hosting a reception for the emperor. That same year, the IAFE ranks were joined by T. Ras Makonnen, a Guyanese-Ethiopian activist who had just arrived in London.³⁵ He knew Wärqenäh from the latter's 1927 visit to New

York City, and he soon assumed a leading role as an organizer, speaker, and journalist, sometimes coordinating with Emmanu'él Abraham. In Makonnen's assessment, the organization proved a critical hub for international solidarity with Ethiopia, and it received thousands of letters of support from correspondents across Africa, the Caribbean, and the United States. Despite this fact, the IAFE operated somewhat independently from the Ethiopian exiles, a situation Makonnen attributed to the emperor's wariness of its combative radical politics. At the same time, some socialists and communists challenged the organization's revolutionary credentials in light of its support for a monarch.

These Black internationalists worked alongside Ethiopia's other British allies. The most outspoken of these was Sylvia Pankhurst, the militant feminist, socialist, and antifascist who had cofounded the British Communist Party (CPB) and who now lead the Abyssinia Association, a League- and government-focused lobbying organization. She proved a formidable advocate: she publicly harangued the British government and League, occasionally advised the emperor and exiles, and organized massive rallies and street demonstrations, notably participating in the 1936 Battle of Cable Street, which brought hundreds of thousands of protestors to East London to confront the British Union of Fascists.[36] In May of that same year, she and her partner Silvio Corio, an exiled Italian anarchist, began coediting *New Times and Ethiopia News*, a weekly that featured articles by Ethiopian exiles and original reporting about events in the Italian colony, including detailed accounts of atrocities and the anticolonial resistance.[37] The newspaper was widely read in Britain as well as Anglophone West Africa and the Caribbean, and even appeared in Amharic translation for clandestine circulation in the Horn of Africa. Pankhurst was denounced for her advocacy by the British establishment and Italian press, but the emperor found her service to his country exceptional, and Du Bois judged her a "staunch and brave" friend of Ethiopia.[38]

Meanwhile, the exiles faced constant Italian surveillance. This operation was supervised by Cerulli's Office of Political Affairs at the Ministry of Italian Africa, which reviewed incoming consular intelligence and maintained dossiers on individual exiles, complementing its monitoring of Ethiopian detainees in Italy.[39] As a racialized intelligence instrument, this ministerial exile surveillance rested on colonial models of Ethiopian politics and society, and in this respect, it was an African counterpart to the formidable regime apparatus of Italian domestic and diaspora surveillance. One of its intelligence dossiers was dedicated to Heruy.⁴⁰ Its contents include the correspondence surrounding the foreign minister's attempt to contact his family in Ethiopia, which was personally managed by Cerulli.⁴¹ The file also features an anonymous profile of the foreign minister: it describes his career and family while offering assessments of his psychology, political orientation, and intellectual outlook, drawing on personal observations, Legation reports, and his Amharic publications. This combination of source material suggests that Cerulli was the dossier's likely author or coauthor.⁴² Among its claims were that Heruy was xenophobic, prone to dilatory obfuscation and inaction, and "infatuated with his own literary merits," though the anonymous ministerial writer judged him intellectually ungifted. The profile further suggested that despite the *blattén géta*'s fame as an astute interlocutor of the West, he was in reality an "Abyssinian of the old school" who had cunningly put aside "a decent stash" for his own security. In short, Heruy was not as he appeared.⁴³

Over time, the exiles and their allies waned. In September 1936, Marson returned to Jamaica, depressed and exhausted from the work of the previous year, and in October, the veteran diplomat *däjjazmach* Näsibu—also known as "*abba* Mauser" for his able command of the eastern front after the 1935 invasion—died of tuberculosis in Switzerland.⁴⁴ At the end of the year, Täsfayé Tägäñ returned to Ethiopia, where only months later he was transported to Asinara. Meanwhile, James severed his ties with the IAFE, chiefly over disputes concerning international sanctions and the organization's support for a "feudal" autocrat, and the organization gradually disintegrated.⁴⁵ Wärqenäh, now impecunious, privately requested permission to take his young children to India, triggering an extended dispute with the emperor.⁴⁶ Finally, in April 1938 the London Legation closed after the British government recognized Italian sovereignty over Ethiopia.⁴⁷ The remaining staff, now led by Wärqenäh, Emmanu'él, and Wäldä Giyorgis, continued their work in a private residence. In Bath, Heruy began writing the emperor's autobiography and spent his evenings educating the children at Fairfield House.⁴⁸ His efforts to contact his family seem to have been unsuccessful.⁴⁹

Events in Ethiopia made exile difficult to bear. As international diplomacy proved increasingly pointless, Heruy and the exiles began to coordinate with the guerilla leaders in Ethiopia, and the foreign minister played a key role in the 1937 plot to assassinate Graziani. He paid a heavy price. Among those killed in the aftermath of Yekatit 12 was his son Fäqqädä Sellasé, who was reportedly asked by his Italian interrogator, "Is it not your father who is creating trouble abroad? And now you have returned here to give us trouble?"[50] Years later, *fitawrari* Asfeha alleged that Cerulli's office had prepared a list of names for targeted killings.[51] Heruy immediately denounced these atrocities to the World Council of Churches, and then directly to Joseph Avenol and the League.[52] Meanwhile, the remainder of his family was dispatched to detention sites around Italy and the Horn of Africa. In a further blow, the colonial administration expropriated the family home in Gullälé, which it assigned to the Commando Aviazione and renamed Villa Magliocco, after a deceased Italian pilot.[53] In the process, most of the family's personal property was stolen, including Heruy's library, international medals, and Japanese sword. Even his car was burned.[54]

By April of 1938, Heruy was ill. The malady was a resurgence of a longstanding intestinal disease, compounded by kidney issues. It was perhaps related to the illness that had already taken the life of his young daughter Amsalä. When a period of bedrest failed to improve his condition, the emperor dispatched him to Bath's Royal United Hospital. After a month of treatment, he returned to Fairfield House, still unwell. He now passed his time in bed, reading the newspapers and following international affairs over a pivotal summer. As d'Aosta and Cerulli struggled to contain the insurrection in Shäwa, Hitler and Mussolini cemented the Axis alliance, while Britain and France reprised the strategy of appeasement in the developing Czechoslovak crisis. According to one of Heruy's companions from this period, when the foreign minister's illness progressed to the point where he became too weak to read, he asked those around him to dictate the news aloud, much to their amazement. On September 19, he died. That same day, the British and French governments announced their acquiescence to the German demand for the Sudetenland, setting the stage for the Munich conference.[55]

The funeral took place the following day at Locksbrook Cemetery, amid its Japanese cherry trees. A motorcade brought the emperor and *étégé* Mänän, the royal family, Sirak, and Wärqenäh,[56] who were greeted at the gravesite by more exiles and some of Heruy's international comrades. After the prayers of *abba* Haylä Maryam and *abba* Marqos, who had just arrived from Jerusalem,[57] Haylä Sellasé delivered the eulogy, his voice cracking:

This person, *blattén géta* Heruy Wäldä Sellasé, who you see receiving the tradition [of burial] of the children of Adam, was educated according to our country's system and is counted among the great *liqawent* of Ethiopia. Because he used his intelligence and tenacity as instruments for good work, he was selected to work in our government and obtained the rank of minister of foreign affairs. The books he published . . . reveal his great character. His knowledge of the church and of history made him famous and honored among the *liqawent* of the world. It is needless to recount the history of a person you know well. But if I remember the greatness of his career, I would like [also] to mention the time he devoted to doing honorable deeds, his desire to help the troubled people around him, his respect for justice and truth, and his burning love of country. . . . My servant and friend Heruy! As you leave [this world] after your completion of the work you have undertaken on behalf of your country, if I fail to say "you are great," your work would disprove my words.[58]

It was a rare public display of emotion. Days later, *The Times* featured a letter from Heruy's longtime colleague Daniel Sandford, a former advisor to the emperor. After reflecting on the *blattén géta*'s long career in government, Sandford noted his deep faith and love of family. Sandford believed the latter was the greatest burden of Heruy's exile: the pain of separation from his wife and children, and the grief over the death of his son Fäqqädä Sellasé. These were "calamities perhaps more devastating to him than to most," Sandford opined, and though Heruy "bore them with outward serenity and unflinching courage . . . his world had crumbled about him and the strain was too much for a constitution never very strong."[59] The foreign minister's last years were dark.

Sirak attended the funeral, but the rest of the family mourned in detention. Youngest daughter Laqäch grieved alone.[60] Her life after the invasion had been hard. In the tense autumn of 1935, she worked alongside *etégé* Mänän making bandages at the Association of Ethiopian Women while her husband Yelma supported Heruy at the Ministry. When the Italians neared the capital, she and her family hid in a sawmill west of the city.[61] After they returned to Addis Ababa, she used her English language skills to obtain a post at the British Embassy, thereby obtaining a measure of security. But in the wake of Yekatit 12 and her brother's execution, her family was abruptly deported to Asinara. The detainees included her husband, her mother Hamärä Eshäté, her two elder sisters Gännät and Aṣädä Wäyn, their husbands Täklämaryam Kassahun and Asfaw Gäbräyohannes, and their children Denqenäsh, Gétachäw, Menassé, Éfrém, and Germa.[62] In the Roman ministries, the family's detention was discussed at the cabinet level: Lessona warned the Ministry of the Interior that *lej* Yelma in particular required "special measures of vigilance," presumably because of his education and international experience.[63] In the aftermath of these deportations, Laqäch—now alone and several months pregnant—fled the violent chaos of the capital for Sululta, a small town north of Gullälé on the road to Däbrä Libanos. It was there that she was eventually discovered by *bandas*, who forced her onto a prisoner lorry.[64]

On June 28, Laqäch reached the notorious concentration camp at Dhanaane, a sweltering complex on a beach south of Mogadishu.[65] Built in 1935 to detain prisoners of war, by 1937 the camp had swelled to accommodate more than six thousand political prisoners, in the process becoming the largest carceral site in the Horn of Africa.[66] Like its Graziani-designed counterparts in Libya, the camp was predicated on isolation, terror, and mass punishment. Far from the temperate highlands, its disoriented Ethiopian detainees were crowded into tents and crude tin-roofed shelters in extreme humidity, forced to subsist on seawater and rotten food, and required to perform hard labor on roads and nearby plantations. Illness and disease were widespread, and public flogging, torture, and executions routine.[67] The location made escape almost impossible. Years later, former detainee and camp medical assistant Mika'él Täsämma estimated that these conditions yielded a mortality rate nearing 50 percent.[68] Even its director Eugenio Mazzucchetti admitted in his private diary, "What a disgrace! The camp and empire create a 'great' impression [of Italians]!"[69] In all these respects, Dhanaane represented the extension of colonial extrajuridicality to an entire subject population, who were stripped of all rights and reduced to a state of bare biological existence.[70] Typologically, it resembles an extermination camp.

The guards and *carabinieri* targeted Laqäch because of her parentage and support for the anticolonial insurrection (figure 9.3). She was frequently isolated from the other prisoners, and her food ration was restricted to a single daily serving of tea and bread. She believed this extreme deprivation was intended to punish and demoralize her father, widely thought to have orchestrated the Yekatit 12 attack.[71] In September, she gave birth to her

FIGURE 9.3 Laqäch Heruy at Dhanaane.

Source: Personal collection of author, courtesy Shimelis Yilma.

first child, a daughter who she named Estägizé'aw, or "For a While." Seven months later, on April 30, 1938, the baby died of starvation. She was taken from her mother by the camp guards and buried in the desert without a funeral, apparently as a visiting Italian medical team looked on.[72] Mazzucchetti, who saved a haunting photo of Laqäch and her child, recorded the tragedy in his diary, noting that the baby was the granddaughter of the "ex-minister of foreign affairs of the *negus*, *blatta* Heruy."[73] It was in these horrific circumstances that Laqäch learned of the death of her father.

By November of 1937, her mother and sisters had been transferred to Mercogliano with the children, with Laqäch's husband and brothers-in-law remaining at Asinara.[74] It took a year for the family to learn of her fate. Their efforts to this end were so extensive that their queries and petitions filled a large file at the ministerial Office of Political Affairs, which under Cerulli and then Moreno's direction surveilled the family and shared its translated correspondence with senior regime officials.[75] In January of 1938, Tullio Tamburini—the prefect of Avellino who supervised the

Mercogliano detainees—contacted the Ministry of Italian Africa and the Ministry of the Interior at the request of wäyzero Hamärä, who asked about Laqäch. The family believed she was still in Addis Ababa.[76] At the Ministry of Italian Africa, the correspondence was forwarded to the cabinet, which at this time included Mussolini, Teruzzi, and Moreno, and several weeks later, the latter two brought the matter to d'Aosta and Cerulli.[77] On March 8, the Governo Generale notified the Ministry of Laqäch's transfer to Dhanaane,[78] and the next week, Tamburini relayed this news to the family.[79] Almost simultaneously, a brief letter from Laqäch reached Yelma in Asinara, announcing that she was in Somalia.[80]

This alarming revelation began a multiyear campaign by her mother, husband, and sisters. Already engaged in a complex dispute with the colonial administration concerning the expropriated home in Gullälé, wäyzero Hamärä also began contacting senior figures at the Ministry about Laqäch.[81] On June 11, just over a month after the death of her granddaughter in Dhanaane and amid a mass release of prisoners from the camp, she asked Tamburini about the lack of letters from Laqäch, and one week later, she wrote directly to the Ministry to request her daughter's transfer to Mercogliano.[82] Two months later, Teruzzi himself informed Tamburini that the petition was denied.[83] Undeterred, on September 11 Hamärä inaugurated the Ethiopian New Year with a plaintive letter to the Ministry about the transfer. She observed that concern for a child naturally vexed "the heart of a mother," and then explained that her daughter had lost her own daughter in Dhanaane, where she was bereaved and alone. She again asked the Ministry to transfer Laqäch and Yelma to join their family in Mercogliano, and Aṣädä Wäyn wrote to Teruzzi with the same request.[84] Heruy died eight days later. Hearing nothing about Laqäch, the now-widowed Hamärä wrote a third letter to the Ministry on October 15, in which she referred to her earlier requests.[85] Teruzzi denied all the petitions, clearly piqued by the persistent mother and daughter.[86]

Without options, the family could only plead again. The letters grew longer. In March of 1939, a full year after she first learned of her sister's fate, Aṣädä Wäyn wrote a second time to the Ministry, this time in polished Italian, to request the transfer of her sister and brother-in-law. The letter was classified and apparently widely reviewed, but she does not appear to have received a response. A note added to her letter at the Ministry simply observed, "Already replied: no."[87] Two months later, in May, Yelma wrote directly to Mussolini to present his "small wish" for the transfer of his wife, whose hair had greyed from the sadness of loss. If her time of pardon was nearing, he asked that the state transfer Laqäch to Italy so they could be together.[88] Again, the ministerial notation was simply "no," and by the end of the month, Moreno relayed the denial to the family.[89] At the beginning of June, Hamärä once more petitioned the Ministry, this time appealing for mercy. She tactfully suggested that the previous decisions had perhaps been made without full knowledge of the situation, and asked that her isolated daughter be transferred to Mercogliano, or alternatively, pardoned and returned to Addis Ababa.[90] For reasons that are unclear, this letter provoked action. After a discussion at the Ministry, Yelma and his brother-in-law Asfaw Gäbräyohannes were transferred to Mercogliano, though Laqäch remained at Dhanaane. Despite the mass releases from the camp that year, she remained in Somalia until 1940, when she was finally reunited with Yelma in Addis Ababa.[91] The endless denials of clemency during her three years of detention suggest she was a hostage.

As the family issued this deluge of correspondence from Asinara and Mercogliano, Cerulli visited Dhanaane. It was an opportunity to survey the colonial extension of the detention system he had developed in Italy. He arrived on November 21, 1938, immediately after his sabbatical in Italy, and he was joined at the camp by fellow expert Francesco Saverio Caroselli, the governor of Somalia with whom he had served in the 1920s under Cesare Maria De Vecchi. Caroselli was a friend of Mazzuchetti, and the three dined together on a meal of berbere-stained injera prepared by the women of the camp. The director found the vice governor general to be "a man of few words, closed but courteous," though he queried Mazzucchetti extensively about Dhanaane and its prisoners.[92] After lunch, the group toured the complex. A staged photo of the occasion depicts a macabre *passeggiata*, as the three dignitaries ambled casually through a landscape of suffering, chatting in crisp uniforms.[93] Cerulli then delivered speeches in Amharic and Somali to the assembled prisoners, much to their astonishment, and spent the remainder of the afternoon meeting with individual prisoners in Mazzucchetti's office. One wonders if Cerulli reviewed the latter's collection of photos—if he saw the grim image of the detained Laqäch and the deceased granddaughter of the now-dead foreign minister. Over the past three years, he had surveilled and met nearly all of Heruy's family, even as they themselves were separated in detention and exile. In key respects, he had helped forge their collective years of hardship—pointlessly conferring with Sirak and Heruy in Athens and Amsterdam, orchestrating the counterinsurgency that ravaged Addis Ababa and the family's ancestral home in north Shäwa, overseeing their detention in Italy and the expropriation of their property, perpetuating the isolation of Laqäch in Somalia, and bureaucratically sanctioning the deaths of Fäqqädä Sellasé and Estägizé'aw.

Looking back on these years, *shambäl* Abdissa Aga decided to title his memoir *Bä'iṭalya bärähawoch*, or *In the Deserts of Italy*.[94] Born in western Wälläga, he had been a military officer, anticolonial leader, and expatriate detainee, first in Naples and then at a prisoner of war camp outside Palermo. After a long Italian exile, he eventually returned to Addis Ababa in 1946, via Dire Dawa and Harär. The title of his autobiography evokes the harsh physical setting of his unusual guerilla campaign in the Sicilian scrub, where after escaping from the camp during an Allied bombing he led a group of Yugoslav ex-prisoners in raiding their former detention site. But as a metaphor, Abdissa Aga's title also suggests the ontological imagination of the desert as an anticivilizational space, and more precisely, the imperial metropole and colony as sites of structured dehumanization. The wilderness was barbaric and inhospitable. In 1936, this very metaphor was invoked by Haylä Sellasé in his speech before the League Assembly, where he described the immiseration of Ethiopia through the technologies of colonial war as a cruel desertification, one that had brought the nation "close to extinction."[95] Years later, Käbbädä Mika'él suggested something similar in his poetic lament about near-barren Asinara and its annihilative modern savagery. For Martha Näsibu, the daughter of the exiled *däjjazmach* Näsibu Zä'amanu'él, the terrifying conditions of her childhood confinement in the Libyan desert seemed maddening and death-like, beyond human.[96]

These reflections anticipate Giorgio Agamben's vision of the concentration camp as an acutely modern instrument of inhumanity.[97] For Agamben, the camp is a locus of suffering that can only emerge when an encompassing state of extrajudicial and extramoral exception has been routinized for an entire population, removing all conventional limitations on human action. The exception becomes the rule. This devolution in the camp parallels the unending war of occupation in Ethiopia, which similarly realized fascism's revolutionary liberation from all legal and moral constraint.

In both sites, violence was directed categorically at perceived racial inferiors, with little individuation or adjudication. If the full scope of this colonial barbarism was epitomized by the horrific conditions in Dhanaane and its counterparts in Libya, where public executions, forced labor, and deliberate starvation were so widespread that the detainees adduced a new specificity to the Arabic word for *evil*,[98] it also accreted across the Ethiopian highlands through the continuous violence in the streets of Addis Ababa, the interrogation rooms of Däbrä Berhan, and the decimated mountain towns of Shäwa—from Ankober to Däbrä Libanos, Zärrät, Sälla Dengay, and Chacha. The brutality of the counterinsurgency was intertwined with the dehumanization of the camps, two aspects of a colonial total war in which all rights were suspended. In the decades to come, its survivors sought international recognition of these atrocities as war crimes, crimes against humanity, and genocide.

PART IV
Dead Reckoning

10
Case 7887

By September 1936, Una Marson (figure 10.1) was back in Kingston.[1] She had been undone by her experience at the Legation. In an interview, she admitted, "The position of Ethiopia is very heart-breaking and the tribulations of the Ethiopians have cracked me up."[2] With respect to the exiles, she added, "I do not know what will happen; nobody knows. The most tragic thing . . . [is] that the men who fled with the emperor to London left their wives and families at home." The hardship of displacement compounded the toll of war. A year later, she ruminated further on this suffering in *The Moth and the Star*, a volume of poems that addressed the trauma of solidarity. In "To Joe and Ben," she mourned her dead comrades Yoséf and Benyam Wärqenäh, the eldest sons of Wärqenäh Eshäté, the Ethiopian minister in London and former director of the Täfäri Mäkonnen School. Born in Addis Ababa and partially raised in Burma, the brothers grew up with the emperor's children, attended university in England, and then worked alongside Marson at the Legation until October 1935, when they returned to Ethiopia. Yoséf served in the British Ambulance Service until both joined the campaign of *ras* Emru Haylä Sellasé in Wälläga. After their capture in 1936, the two remained in Addis Ababa until Yekatit 12, when their mother urged them to leave the capital and join Abäbä Arägay in the mountains. They refused. Within weeks, they were arrested and shot.[3] The news reached London in April 1937, passing through Cerulli's office in Rome.[4]

FIGURE 10.1 Una Marson in London (1941).

Source: © BBC Photo Archive.

Marson was devastated. Writing in Jamaica, she reflected on the profound injustice of the killings. Likening the brothers to the Israelites David and Jonathan, she lamented that Yoséf and Benyam had returned from the diaspora and survived the invasion only to die together under "savagery's dark reign." Of this tragedy, she wrote

> Death met you,
> Called you by name,
> Not in the midst of battle,
> Not hewn down
> In heated blood
> But after hellish tortures
> You were murdered
> In cold blood
> As traitors
> To the land
> For which you died.[5]

For Marson, the killing of the brothers was a crime that assaulted their individual humanity. They were murdered not because of what they had done, but because of who they were: "gallant sons of Ethiopia" dedicated to the cause of national liberation. Their race and political principles marked them as traitors to the colonial project, even off the battlefield. Eight years later, this notion of targeted killing based on individual and group identity underpinned the concept of crimes against humanity in the Nuremberg Charter.[6]

In these same months, Heruy also confronted the criminality of Italy's dark reign. Amid the mass killings of Yekatit 12, the punishing counterinsurgency across Shäwa, and the large-scale detentions at Asinara and Dhanaane, the foreign minister wrote the League secretary general to describe the situation in Ethiopia, drawing on the reports reaching Fairfield House in Bath. In a March 1937 letter, he outlined the violations of international law that were unfolding in the colony, deploying the Hague Conventions, League Covenant, and Genevan language of civilization and barbarism to describe ongoing atrocities. The League arguments about Ethiopian deficiency and Italian supremacy were now reversed: the regime's humanitarian intervention was proving its inhumanity by violating the rights of its supposed beneficiaries.[7]

In Heruy's judgment, the unlawful invasion had begun a series of escalating criminal acts. "Those who died in battle," he suggested, "are luckier than those who are suffering from recurrent torture at the hands of the brutal enemy." Among the war crimes he identified were the execution of prisoners of war, including the emperor's sons-in-law *ras* Dästa Damṭäw and *däjjazmach* Bäyyänä Märed, as well as *le'ul ras* Kassa Haylu's surrendered sons *däjjazmach* Abärra Kassa, *däjjazmach* Wänd Bäwässän Kassa, and *däjjazmach* Asfawässän Kassa. Countless others had been similarly killed. Beyond the battlefields, Italy's crimes also included the extrajudicial killing of thousands of civilians in Addis Ababa, "on the orders and with the full knowledge of Italian authorities." In the estimation of the foreign minister, this was an organized effort "to carry out horrible acts of extermination" against noncombatants, as "a measure of revenge taken against innocent people." Among the dead was his eldest son Fäqqädä Sellasé, who had just been executed alongside Yoséf and Benyam Wärqenäh.

The violence was collective, systematic, and by design. Heruy therefore demanded that "a special commission be formed to investigate and report the brutal crimes that the government of Italy has perpetrated on Ethiopia."[8] This was a doubly groundbreaking maneuver. With respect to international law, the foreign minister's request prefigured the logic of the postwar International Military Tribunals and contemporary International Criminal Court: crimes against humanity by definition require international instruments of justice, since they transcend national boundaries and state sovereignty.[9] They are crimes in any context, irrespective of cause or domestic law. But Heruy's demand also anticipated the diplomatic revolution of decolonization. His escalation of the anticolonial struggle to the international front anticipated later African and Asian efforts to use the framework of human rights and the mechanisms of the international system to challenge the legitimacy of colonial violence and denied national self-determination.[10] There could be no legal exception for the crimes of empire.

Though Heruy's call was ignored in his own life, it began a complex historical reckoning that continued in the decades after his death.[11] In the process, Cerulli became a representative of fascist colonial guilt on the world stage. The next two chapters reconstruct this process by examining two synchronic confrontations with Cerulli's colonial past, advanced by the survivors and agents of empire across the fora of the international system, the evolving academic institutions of Ethiopia and Italy, and the emerging politico-intellectual centers of the Third World, from Accra to Bandung and Addis Ababa. The first and most public of these confrontations developed from the Ethiopian effort to investigate and indict Italian war criminals, an undertaking that culminated in the 1948 hearings of the United Nations War Crimes Commission. Cerulli's case was the final substantive ruling of the Commission after thousands of similar hearings on German and Japanese cases, and it represents a little-noticed precedent for the application of international law to specifically colonial crimes. The second trajectory of Cerulli's postcolonial reckoning unfolded within the academic fields of Ethiopian and African studies, which witnessed multiple attempts to exonerate and sanction the proconsul scholar. Although these contests of history and memory were inconclusive with respect to Cerulli's legal and professional accountability, they induced him to covertly relitigate the disputes of the colonial era in scholarship, and ultimately, to publicly attack the concept of war crimes and crimes against humanity. These distinct processes were intertwined manifestations of decolonization as a liberatory political, institutional, and intellectual project, and in this respect, the impunity Cerulli enjoyed after 1941 documents the structural durability of colonial power and knowledge in the postcolonial world. He was a paragon of unrepentant empire.

———

This reckoning began at the Paris Peace Conference of 1946, which aimed to establish the treaty framework for the postwar international settlement. In attendance were the Big Four—Britain, France, the United States, and the Soviet Union—as well as seventeen additional countries, Italy and Ethiopia included, and among the questions at hand were the disposition of the former Italian colonies, the possibility of Italian reparations to Ethiopia, and the future relationship between Ethiopia, Eritrea, and Somalia. For the Horn of Africa, the conference represented the first international confrontation of the former colonizer and colonized, then collectively grappling with the complex project of postwar political and economic reconstruction. In Italy, the negotiations followed the 1943 demise of the fascist regime through civil war and German occupation, the ensuing British-American Allied Military Government, and the first postwar general election of the new republic, in which the Christian Democrats triumphed under the leadership of Alcide De Gasperi. In Ethiopia, meanwhile, the restored government of Haylä Sellasé navigated the dismantling of the Occupied Enemy Territory Administration, the British wartime governance structure that managed the country as a neoprotectorate until 1944; the suppression of the Wäyyanä insurrection in Tegray, which challenged the legitimacy of the emperor in 1943; and the broad developmental reorientation toward the United States, inaugurated by the Lend-Lease mission of 1944. In Somalia and Eritrea, a host of new political parties debated the uncertain national future under the contested supervision of British military administrations, which remained in place until 1950 and 1952, respectively. Although war abruptly ruptured Italy's empire in the Horn of Africa, actual decolonization proved protracted and uncertain.

As much as the Paris negotiations were a crucible for the emerging fault lines of the Cold War, they also resumed the past struggles of the League. This was manifest in the arguments and personalities on display. The Italian delegation, led by Prime Minister De Gasperi and Geneva veteran

Antonio Meli Lupi di Soragna, was barred from formally participating in the proceedings, but De Gasperi delivered a fiery plenary speech in which he denounced the "punitive character" of the draft treaty.[12] His team advanced this position through lobbying, oral asides, and memoranda on the proposed treaty articles, many of which concerned Ethiopia and the other former Italian colonies. Building on the foreign policy vision of the wartime unity government,[13] the delegation argued that republican Italy should retain its prefascist "liberal" colonies—Eritrea, Somalia, and Libya— as compensation for its post-1943 contributions to the German defeat, and more broadly, that Italy was a humane colonizer which had advanced African development through economic investment and ethnic mediation.[14] Its interventions on these topics were coordinated by its colonial advisors. These included Cerulli, who now occupied the post of consigliere di stato, as well as ex-minister plenipotentiary Giuliano Cora and ex-colonial governor Riccardo Astuto.[15] Before and during the proceedings, these veteran experts conferred with other delegations and produced white papers defending the Italian colonial enterprise and the restoration of Italian rule in Libya, Eritrea, and Somalia.[16]

Their chief adversary was the Ethiopian delegation, led by now-acting Minister of Foreign Affairs Aklilu Habtäwäld. Freshly arrived from signing the United Nations Charter in San Francisco (figure 10.2), Aklilu was joined in Paris by a team of veteran Ethiopian diplomats.[17] Like the minister himself, many were alumni of Heruy's Foreign Ministry and the exiled government of the 1930s. They included *blatta* Éfrém Täwäldä Mädhen and Emmanu'él Abraham, both Marson's colleagues at the London Legation; *blattén géta* Lorenzo Ta'ezaz, formerly of the Ethiopian delegation in Geneva; and Täsfayé Tägäñ and John Spencer, the ministerial coauthors of the emperor's 1936 address to the League.[18] In Paris a decade later, the Ethiopians once again demanded justice and security from the international system, but this time, they held a critical swing vote. Under Aklilu's adept leadership, they used this advantage to advance the Ethiopian position at the conference—presenting the Ethiopian irredentist claims on Eritrea and Somalia, demanding reparations from the Italian government, and calling for the total exclusion of Italy from the Horn of Africa.[19] In this, they confronted not only the emerging narrative of Italian victimhood within a German-led Axis, but also the framework of the 1943 "Quebec Document,"

FIGURE 10.2 Éfrém Täwäldä Mädhen signing the United Nations Charter (1945).

Source: © United Nations Archives.

through which Allied leaders promised preferential treatment to Italy in a theoretically unconditional postwar settlement.[20] Aklilu came prepared, having spent months lobbying the Big Four and developing counters to the anticipated Italian positions.

For the Ethiopian delegation, the Italians' insistent distinction between the fascist and postfascist governments was absurd. With respect to the colonial project, there seemed little difference between the two, a fact that led De Gasperi into hypocrisy.[21] For Aklilu, this continuity was embodied by Cerulli's presence in the Italian delegation. The two had faced one another in Geneva when the former was permanent secretary to Ethiopia's League delegation,²² and more significantly, Aklilu's ministry was then preparing criminal charges against Cerulli via the newly established Ethiopian War Crimes Commission (EWCC).²³ The foreign minister was not the only delegation member acquainted with the ex-regent. Täsfayé met Cerulli in detention at Asinara, Emru Zälläqä encountered him in occupied Addis Ababa, and Lorenzo had just discovered his personal archive in liberated Harär.²⁴ In addition, Vice Foreign Minister Ambayé Wäldä Maryam and *blatta* Éfrém both served on the EWCC, in which role they were involved in preparing his indictment.²⁵ For these Ethiopians, Cerulli's presence in the Paris delegation was "symbolic evidence" of the new republic's link to the regime, as one observer put it.²⁶

Aklilu raised the issue in committee. The forum was the Economic Commission for Italy, tasked with establishing the framework for Italian reparations to Ethiopia and the other Italian-occupied territories. For weeks, Aklilu and De Gasperi sparred over reparations. The Ethiopians emphasized the trauma of mass killings and expropriated property that underpinned their government's monetary claim, which was in Aklilu's assessment already inadequate.²⁷ In September, he informed the subcommittee that:

> It is impossible to describe the demoralising effects . . . of being hunted down and destroyed day after day, year after year, of having the entire countryside sprayed from the air with poison gas, of witnessing the destruction of churches and their replacement by posts with machine-guns, of having children impressed into organizations of *balilla* [fascist youth groups], to be taught a new fascist civilization. These are injuries which are irreparable and cannot be compensated.²⁸

In response, De Gasperi argued the Ethiopians had overstated their loss of life and disregarded the value of colonial development.²⁹ In other words, the meridian of Italian imperialism had been more beneficial than destructive, if the balance sheet of war crimes and capital investments was properly calculated. To support this position, Cerulli and Cora issued a memorandum documenting Italian achievements in Africa, developed in consultation with the British Foreign Office.³⁰ The unstated crux of this argument was that Italian colonial rule was broadly comparable to its British and French counterparts, despite the occasional fascist excesses. The civilizing mission had succeeded.³¹

Facing this appeal to imperial solidarity at a moment of resurgent colonial settlement and investment, Aklilu offered a history lesson.[32] In October, he informed the subcommittee that De Gasperi aimed "to avert the just retribution of a criminal aggression, not through atonement but by disavowing responsibility for and denying the actions of the fascist government."[33] This ahistoricism was immoral as well as absurd, which Aklilu illustrated by noting Cerulli's presence in the chamber. He explained that the Italian delegation included "a certain individual who was chief of the political section of the Fascist Ministry of Italian Colonies from 1932 to 1937 and who was rewarded for his fascist record by being made [Vice] Governor [General] of Italian East Africa in 1937. His term as Governor coincided with the period of the worst fascist atrocities in Ethiopia." To dispel any uncertainty, Aklilu then outlined some of these atrocities in detail, introducing evidence from the ongoing investigatory work of the EWCC. The Italian delegation had "studiously avoided" these events in its sanitized colonial balance sheet, and thus brazenly misrepresented the recent past. In the face of this denunciation, Cerulli immediately left the chamber.[34] This dramatic and public confrontation began a decades-long rivalry between the two men, against the backdrop of the broader international confrontation between the colonial and anticolonial powers.

As these events unfolded in Paris, Cerulli faced domestic scrutiny via the Italian High Commission for Sanctions Against Fascism. Established in 1944 after the Allied liberation of Rome, the Commission was a national investigatory body that aimed to prosecute the fascist elite and remove regime functionaries from public institutions.[35] Though hampered by intrapersonal vendettas and attacked as inadequate by the political left, the Commission conducted a sprawling multiyear review of military, ministerial, university, and local government personnel, wielding the power to terminate employment, dissolve pension rights, and initiate criminal prosecutions.[36] While this inquiry produced several high-profile trials, the sanction process was ultimately narrow. The Commission considered hundreds of thousands of cases, but it issued less than two thousand sentences. This already limited purge was further attenuated by the 1946 general amnesty offered by the minister of justice and Italian Communist Party (PCI) leader Palmiro Togliatti, which further emasculated the sanction process through pardons in the name of national reconciliation and transitional justice. The antifascist purge was less a political revolution than a calibrated reckoning that protected state continuity.[37]

In October of 1944, the Commission took up Cerulli's case.[38] Together with Martino Mario Moreno and other senior functionaries of the Ministry of Italian Africa,[39] Cerulli was accused of supporting the regime through his colonial service.[40] He was specifically charged with collaborating with the Repubblica Sociale Italiana (RSI), the German puppet state that ruled most of northern Italy between 1943 and 1945 from the Lake Garda town of Salò, from whence it fought a civil war against antifascist partisans while pursuing the systematic extermination of Italian Jews.[41] The charge was an accusation of treason, since the Commission resolved the problem of identifying fascists and ascribing guilt in a postfascist society by equating extreme fascist criminality with RSI/German collaboration, as distinct from support for the preceding twenty-year dictatorship.[42] The case against Cerulli and the other senior ministry officials unfolded shortly after the September 1944 trial and execution of Roman RSI police chief Pietro Caruso, the first Italian trial of its kind, as well as the first trials of Vichy collaborators in Paris, liberated that August.[43] In addition to the charge of collaborating with a foreign and illegitimate government, Cerulli was also accused of active participation in fascist politics during his tenure as vice governor general and governor of Harär, in which roles he was alleged to have tolerated unspecified abuses in the colonies. These interlinked charges rested on the premise that he was a senior regime agent, distinct from the broader mass of bureaucratic functionaries and technicians.

The case against Cerulli hinged on his conduct in Africa Orientale Italiana and German-occupied Rome. It was based on two anonymous affidavits submitted to the Commission, supplemented by the testimony of several ministerial employees.[44] With respect to events in the colony, the affidavits alleged that Cerulli had been a client of Attilio Teruzzi, the *squadrista* ex-minister of Italian Africa who was now an RSI loyalist and prominent exemplar of fascist guilt.[45] Cerulli's connection to this corrupt regime hierarch, it was claimed, had protected him from the antipathy of Viceroy Amedeo d'Aosta, who was popularly imagined as a moderating force. It was further alleged that Cerulli had created "a myth of [his own] intellectual hyper-superiority" that secured his influence in Rome and Addis Ababa, such that he was personally responsible for "the majority of the political errors of our embarrassing Ethiopian activity, on the highest directive of the madman from Predappio [Mussolini]." He was finally accused of having lived in Africa like "a nabob." With respect to German-occupied Rome, the affidavits alleged that Cerulli had collaborated with the RSI after September 8, 1943, when the city descended into civil war and extreme material scarcity. He was specifically accused of facilitating the relocation of ministerial personnel and property to the new seat of government at Salò, for which reason RSI undersecretary and Ethiopia veteran Francesco Maria Barracu had allegedly allowed him to live in relative comfort on a ministerial pension until he was dismissed for health reasons.

Cerulli vigorously disputed these charges.[46] In his view, the affidavits were "fantasies." With respect to the accusation of RSI collaboration, he minimized his role in creating the list of ministerial employees destined for Salò, and he detailed his efforts to preserve the ministerial archives and library, which he claimed to have personally secured at private locations in Rome while sending "useless" material to the north, where the RSI did not reconstitute a colonial ministry. He more unevenly addressed the charges related to his career in Africa. With respect to his proximity to the regime elite, he claimed to have clashed with the militant hierarch Cesare Maria De Vecchi in Somalia, and he disputed the suggestion of any discord with d'Aosta in Ethiopia, quoting as evidence his amicable personal correspondence with the viceroy and his eventual recall by Teruzzi.

He then addressed his expert role. He proposed that his oeuvre challenged the racial politics of the regime, and that he had "never written a single word in support of fascism," even perfunctorily. He instead considered himself an agent of a liberal and collaborative colonial policy in the context of the fascist program of racialized violence—what he had once termed "the firm hand." This orientation distinguished him from his anonymous accusers:

> With respect to the assertion of the accuser that my career is due to the understanding "of four trifles about the Abyssinian people, [who are] barely superior to apes," I will limit myself to saying that it is precisely this mentality . . . to which we largely owe the total failure that fascism brought to our colonies. . . . All of my own work, in the scientific field as well as the practical one, [was] dedicated to the study of African populations in their own history, culture, and institutions, [and] was constantly

aimed at demolishing this vulgar prejudice, [itself] culturally hasty and politically pernicious. And one can see with what elegance of phrase the anonymous accuser adopts the very worn-out slogan of racist colonialism; on one side the chosen people and on the other the dominated population, not human beings but "barely superior to apes."[47]

This defence rested on the premise that his apolitical expert identity maintained his independence and distance from the crimes of the regime—despite his senior positions in Rome, Addis Ababa, and Harär, his personal contacts with Mussolini, Lessona, and Teruzzi, and his policy papers, situation reports, and propaganda leaflets.[48] He was not an accomplice to fascism, but an advocate for Ethiopia and a servant of the Italian state. This self-understanding explains his detailed account of his protection of the colonial archive, as well as his silence about the question of colonial atrocities. His defence invoked a potential postfascist colonial understanding rooted in liberal politics and national—rather than fascist—continuity.

On February 26, the Commission issued its decision.[49] Secretary Francesco Curcio, the president of Italy's highest appellate court, found insufficient evidence to demonstrate that Cerulli had contributed to the regime beyond the designated administrative responsibilities of his offices: his function was to implement the policies established by the minister. With respect to events in Rome, Curcio ruled that contrary to the affidavits, Cerulli had worked within the scope of his office to keep the ministerial archive and library from Salò, and that he had transmitted transfer orders to ministerial personnel without enforcing them. The secretary's decision was challenged by the other two members of the Commission, Ambassador Sidney Prina Ricotti and veteran Somalia functionary Luigi Bruno Santangelo, who voted against Curcio and upheld the charges against Cerulli. The deferral to Curcio's minority position may reflect the fact that at one point during the proceedings, Cerulli threatened to list and even call as witnesses for his defence a group of unnamed senior figures in "the parties of democracy" and the Italian judicial system.[50] Perhaps the secretary sought to avoid this potentially compromising development, which suggested complexities that had recently marred other prominent cases.[51] Either way, the Commission process ultimately fixated on Italian concepts of guilt and colonial morality, leaving unaddressed the question of Cerulli's involvement in Ethiopian crimes.

This second issue produced a more damning sanction four years later at the hearings of the United Nations War Crimes Commission (UNWCC). Established by the Allies in 1943 to facilitate the prosecution of Axis war criminals, the UNWCC was an advisory international body that conducted pretrial investigations of alleged human rights violations, in anticipation of future trials by national and international tribunals.[52] It was in this respect distinct from the contemporary International Criminal Court, whose full judicial function is intended to complement rather than aid the domestic prosecutorial powers of states. The Commission was comprised of representatives appointed by the Allied member states, supported by a small international secretariat of legal experts, and it was for most of its existence chaired by Lord Robert Wright, a British High Court judge.[53] Though the Commission pioneered a multilateral model of international criminal justice rooted in intergovernmental prosecutorial coordination, it was vulnerable to political instrumentalization and legal inconsistency rooted in the inherent problems of victors' justice,[54] an issue broadly manifest in British-American attempts to constrain the UNWCC in service of foreign policy objectives.[55] This political interventionism was particularly apparent with respect to Italian war criminals, since Britain and the United States jointly oversaw the Allied Military Government that administered Italy until 1945, and were for this reason able to enforce or deny extradition requests for Italian citizens.

The consequence of this instrumentalization was the marginalization of Ethiopia, the only African state with standing before the Commission. The latter's deliberations on Italian war crimes in Ethiopia were prolonged, contentious, and marked by the overt intrusion of colonial racism and diplomatic expediency, and they frequently rehearsed in microcosm the underlying political dynamics of the emerging Cold War order. Specifically, the minutes of the UNWCC sessions at Lansdowne House in West London document the contours of the divide between the United States and Great Britain, on the one hand, and the states that would eventually coalesce around the Bandung principles of anticolonialism and nonalignment, on the other. Of the latter, the most significant allies of Ethiopia were India and Yugoslavia. The Soviet Union boycotted the Commission because of the British-American rejection of its demand that the Soviet federated republics be granted membership at parity with the British colonies and dominions.[56] At bottom, the conflict of these groups over the so-called "Abyssinian Question" centered on British attempts to scuttle Ethiopian claims through gatekeeping and jurisdictional politics that were transparently self-interested and neocolonial, drawing on earlier discourses about Ethiopian exceptionalism and African sovereignty to limit the scope of the nascent international human rights regime.[57] In response, Ethiopia and its allies asserted the universality of these rights in the context of an international system still predicated on empire.[58] In all these respects, the UNWCC reprised the imperial dynamics of the League and Paris Conference.

This clash over Ethiopia unfolded against the backdrop of the Commission's prior dismissal of Yugoslavia. As a non-armistice power and UNWCC member, Yugoslavia pressured Britain to facilitate the prosecution of Italian citizens for crimes in the Italian-occupied Balkans, of whom the most notorious were generals Mario Roatta, the ex-army chief of staff, and Alessandro Pirzio Biroli, the ex-Amhara governor.[59] After 1944, its government began demanding extraditions. The British Foreign Office viewed these efforts warily because of their potential implications for Pietro Badoglio, the former commander of the northern Ethiopian campaign and head of Italy's first postfascist wartime government. In their estimation, Badoglio was a shifty but vital partner in the construction of a Western-allied and non-communist postwar Italian republic. This Whitehall view, to which the Truman administration deferred, complemented the position of the new Italian government, which sought to reserve the right to try accused Italian war criminals as part of its reassertion of sovereignty and domestic legal reckoning with fascism.[60]

In 1945, Radomir Zivkovic, the outspoken Yugoslav representative on the Commission, raised the issue of Italian atrocities in the Balkans. The following year, increasingly frustrated by British-American stonewalling on the matter, Zivkovic convinced Robert Craigie, the influential British representative and former assistant undersecretary of state at the Foreign Office, to accept a reduced list of twenty-two Italian accused war criminals. This list was then further diminished by the secretariat to seven names, but the Foreign Office objected even to this number on the grounds that support for any Yugoslav cases whatsoever would weaken the British-American position in Italy. In October of that year, the Allied Military Government was instructed to reject Yugoslav extradition requests and direct the Yugoslav government to submit such requests directly to Italy. The result of this punt to a transitional government opposed to extradition was the predictable failure to extradite any accused Italian citizens.[61]

This Yugoslav deflection paralleled the developing Ethiopian predicament. In October 1943, Ethiopia was quietly excluded from the Commission's founding meeting by the British Foreign Office, possibly with the support of the US State Department. This was both because of the aforementioned Badoglio issue, and additionally because the Commission's Whitehall architects viewed it as a fundamentally European institution, despite its Chinese and Indian members. In November of that year, the Foreign Office position was exposed when activist Sylvia Pankhurst began to publicize Ethiopia's exclusion from the Commission.[62] In response to parliamentary queries related to Pankhurst's advocacy, the Foreign Office claimed that it had contacted the Ethiopian government about the UNWCC but received no reply, and further, that the Italo-Ethiopian conflict was beyond the Commission's remit because it predated the Second World War, though Chinese ambassador Wellington Koo had specifically raised the question of pre-1939 jurisdiction at the founding conference.[63] This situation became more compromising in July of 1945, when *blatta* Ayyälä Gäbrä, an ex-Asinara detainee who was now the London Legation representative, attempted to contact the Commission directly on behalf of Ethiopia, a founding UN member state and Allied power.[64] Months later, representative Zivkovic then rebuked the Commission for ruling that Italy, a non-UN member state and defeated Axis power, could submit war crimes charges against German citizens.[65] The inconsistency was telling: the UNWCC was excluding Ethiopia and Yugoslavia to protect compromised Italian powerbrokers central to British-American planning.

The following year, the Commission began formal deliberations on the Ethiopian issue. In July, Acting Vice Foreign Minister Ambayé Wäldä Maryam notified the UN Secretariat that the Ethiopian government had formed a national war crimes commission, and asked the UNWCC to recognize his government's right to prosecute Italian citizens.[66] At the same time, the British House of Commons witnessed an embarrassing exchange concerning the Commission's jurisdiction over Italian activities in Ethiopia, when Minister of Foreign Affairs Philip Noel-Baker—formerly a supporter of Ethiopia at the League—was obliged to publicly outline the unsavory Foreign Office position on Ethiopian exclusion.[67] On June 19, the UNWCC for the first time addressed the question of Ethiopian jurisdiction.

Chair Wright noted that the Commission had been specifically advised "not to be too anxious to curtail its jurisdiction or to take too narrow a view of its powers,"[68] and the matter was referred to Committee III, which provided legal analysis.

The subcommittee deliberations introduced several thorny questions. In a preliminary white paper, the Committee III secretary and legal counsel Egon Schwelb noted that the question of antebellum jurisdiction had been previously introduced by Ambassador Koo, and that consequently, the Commission had no "express limitation" to crimes committed between 1939 and 1945. In his view, however, this latitude was complicated by the de facto consensus on the end of the Italo-Ethiopian conflict in 1936, represented by the international recognition of Ethiopia's annexation and not the emperor's rejection of surrendered sovereignty.[69] At a subcommittee meeting on July 30, Craigie noted that his government had previously discouraged Ethiopian submissions on jurisdictional grounds, and then argued that the Chinese and Ethiopian cases were distinct because the East Asian conflict was a single, uninterrupted war that began in 1931 and concluded in 1945, while in Ethiopia "no sequence of events connected the two [wars]." This was, he added, also the Foreign Office position. In response, the Yugoslav representative Lazar Marković asserted that the Ethiopians would reject Craigie's reasoning because they saw the entire colonial occupation as a single war, and Herbert Mayr-Harting, the committee's Czechoslovak chair, added that they would view a negative decision as motivated by expediency rather than principle. Despite these objections, the subcommittee ruled that the UNWCC remit was limited to the Second World War, and further, that the latter had no "direct connection" to the Italian invasion of Ethiopia.[70] They returned their decision to the Commission, which adopted it on July 31.[71] This represented a very narrow reading of the issues raised in the Committee III debate.

Six months later, this situation was complicated by Vice Foreign Minister Ambayé. In a December 31 letter to the Commission, he explained that the EWCC had prepared cases against Badoglio and Graziani for war crimes and crimes against humanity, and that additional cases were nearly complete. This letter was accompanied by his earlier July correspondence with the UNWCC concerning the EWCC, which the UN Secretariat had for unclear reasons not forwarded to the Commission.[72] On receiving Ambayé's December letter, Committee III legal analyst Jerzy Litawski issued a white paper that identified two new conflicts: first, between the Ethiopian understanding of the situation and the Commission's July ruling; and second, between the logic of that ruling and the subsequent draft of the Paris Peace Treaty, which stipulated that it ended a war that began in 1935—a point specifically obtained by Foreign Minister Aklilu.[73] After a January 30, 1947 subcommittee meeting aired these discrepancies,[74] Litawski prepared two more reports. Though he continued to endorse the now anachronistic position that the two conflicts were distinct, he granted that the post-treaty situation put Ethiopia in a unique position with respect to the UNWCC. It was now the lone Allied power and treaty signatory that would not have the Commission's investigatory support and potential prima facie judgment when pursuing Axis war criminals.[75]

These developments led to a heated debate on March 12. On one side, the Yugoslav representative Zivkovic and the Polish representative Marian Muzkat forcefully argued the Ethiopian case.[76] Muzkat attacked the Commission's previous decision by noting that the 1945 London Agreement, which established the framework for the Nuremberg International Military Tribunal, specifically held that all the conflicts involving the Axis powers were part of a single war, and additionally, that the 1942 British-Ethiopian Agreement acknowledged that the Ethiopian government had never recognized its loss of sovereignty. He concluded by observing that in his view, "refusal to accept Ethiopian charges might be understood as discrimination against one of the Allied nations."

Zivkovic then pursued. He observed that the Commission's previous assertion of limited jurisdiction was based on a factual error, since it had already accepted antebellum cases related to the Japanese invasion of Manchuria in 1931. He next sharpened Muzkat's point: "The Ethiopian war [was not] an isolated case. It was within the general plan of conspiracy by the Axis Powers, and if the victim government thought that crimes were perpetrated—and they all knew horrible atrocities had been committed— if Ethiopia applied to the Commission . . . he did not see what could be the grounds[,] either legal or judicial, for refusing such a request." Craigie, clearly stung by these critiques, replied that whatever their merits, the Commission had nearly completed its work, and there was now insufficient time to consider Ethiopian cases—even though it was he himself who had delayed them until the final hour. In his estimation, the situation necessitated "a practical point of view," and the Ethiopians could still obtain justice directly from Italy. This was a convoluted, dishonest, and obviously self-serving reasoning that rehearsed the realpolitik of the earlier Yugoslav debate. After an initial vote on the matter failed, Wright instructed the representatives to consult with their respective governments.[77] At the following meeting on March 26, the members again voted to reject jurisdiction over Italian crimes in Ethiopia.[78]

This rebuke further mobilized the Ethiopians. On August 12, *blatta* Éfrém wrote to the UNWCC to request permission for a representative of his government to attend its next meeting in Westminster, stressing the inconsistency of the Commission's vote with respect to the now-signed peace treaty, the London Agreement, and its consideration of pre-1939 Chinese cases. These were precisely the points that Muzkat and Zivkovic had raised six months earlier.[79] On September 24, the Ethiopians pressed the issue by sending Baron Erik Leijonhufvud, the Swedish chair of the EWCC and advocate general of the Ethiopian government, to address the Commission at Lansdowne House.[80] The meeting proved a critical juncture. After Wright raised a host of objections to hearing Ethiopian cases, including his own ignorance of Ethiopian law and the misleading statement that "Ethiopia had never tried to be admitted as a member of the Commission," the representatives voted to allow Leijonhufvud's presentation.

The baron delivered. He reiterated the now-familiar points that the peace treaty specifically established the link between the Italian invasion and the Second World War, and that Ethiopian resistance to the Italians had not ceased until liberation, despite the hardship this entailed. The unceasing counterinsurgency was the proof. He then explained that in the emperor's view, the Commission was discriminating against Ethiopia by permitting Chinese but not Ethiopian cases. Leijonhufvud observed that this prejudice was part of a familiar and disturbing pattern: Ethiopia had been previously denied justice by the League in Geneva, and the Commission was now poised to repeat that injustice again in London. Compounding the situation was the fact that the Ethiopians had an especially pressing need for the Commission's legal and investigative apparatus. As he explained to the group, "The shortage of staff in this field as well as in the whole Ethiopian administration was due to the Italian policy of exterminating all educated Ethiopians. 'Your education is your crime,' was how an Italian officer put it to an Ethiopian prisoner." In short, the violence of the crimes hindered their effective prosecution.[81]

The presentation electrified the Commission. Despite the baron's points about attenuated prosecutorial capacity, Wright immediately returned to the argument that the treaty offered sufficient redress for Ethiopians, adding that he did not understand why the cases had been delayed. Craigie, obviously bothered by the accusations of discrimination, then claimed the previous refusal had been strictly procedural. But the two quickly lost the room. Milivoje Zimonjic, the Yugoslav representative, launched an extended defence of the Ethiopian position, adding the new point that it was "contrary to the purpose" of the Commission to acknowledge the existence of war criminals but leave them unpunished, and further, that it would be "an injustice to refuse the requests of the Ethiopian government simply because that small and unarmed people could not withstand the aggression of its powerful enemy" until 1939. He was seconded by the Indian representative Niharendu Dutt-Majumdar, a lawyer and founding member of the Bolshevik Party of India who had been absent during the previous Ethiopia discussions.[82] Dutt-Majumdar recast the legal and procedural arguments in historical and moral terms. He warned the group about taking "steps which might give the impression, perhaps not to the world of today but to the world of tomorrow, that a smaller power did not receive the help, advice, and guidance of all the big powers." He then explained that procedural issues were irrelevant when faced with the prospect of obtaining justice for heinous crimes. In his view, "Technical points could always be found for or against a thing, but they were dealing here with cases of crimes against humanity which did not admit of 'for or against,' women and children who suffered and lost their lives were not going to be satisfied with a legal 'for or against.' For such women and children the pain of hurt was still there and it was for them that they were asking that justice be done." He urged the group to "think very deeply about the request of Ethiopia." The Polish representative, Stanislaw Piotrowski, then introduced the jarring fact that the European Allies had brought thousands of cases before the Commission, while the Ethiopians were requesting only ten. Thus it "could gain much by doing very little."[83]

These were serious critiques of the Commission's past decisions. The discussion then moved to the critical question of whether Ethiopia had, in fact, been invited to the founding conference of the UNWCC. Litawski, the secretariat legal advisor, tried to evade by reporting that there had been "no objection" to Ethiopia joining, but that the latter's government had either ignored or not received an invitation from the Foreign Office. Piotrowski then plainly stated that no invitation had been sent. Wright and Craigie now became defensive: the former pled ignorance on the matter despite his earlier fixation on the consequences of this point, while the latter speculated that there had been no invitation because Ethiopia "did not take part in the war which began in 1939." Marcel De Baer, the Belgian representative, then interjected that he had been at the founding meeting, and Ethiopia had not been "represented" there. These were important revelations. What could not be stated by the British and American representatives was that the 1943 conference coincided with the moment of Badoglio's peak significance in the Foreign Office and State Department plans for a separate peace with Italy and a non-communist postwar government, and additionally, with a Foreign Office aspiration to transform Britain's wartime administration of Ethiopia into a more durable colonial relationship.[84] These objectives underpinned Ethiopia's original exclusion and current predicament at the Commission.

This increasingly compromising tangent led Wright to intervene as chair. He reframed his objection to focus on the primitive inadequacy of "Abyssinian law," echoing earlier League debates about the supposedly backward and barbaric nature of Ethiopian justice. He then made the contorted argument that the six months that had elapsed since the previous decision on Ethiopia strengthened the point that the Commission was too near the end of its work to consider new cases. He boldly asked whether the members would postpone the matter, a motion Craigie supported, and suggested a reply to Ethiopia indicating that "they did not feel in a position at the moment to give any immediate answer." Piotrowski then pounced: "The Ethiopian Government's first request to the Commission had been made in July 1946, and since then until now they had been given no answer—it was not right—the first request was before July 1946 . . . Ten cases were very few, but if the Commission was going to allow them to be presented . . . they should do so right away." Sensing the changed atmosphere, Wright adjourned the discussion to give the members time to consult with their governments, interjecting at the last moment that "he strongly resented . . . any suggestion that there was any discrimination."[85] This deferral was conveyed to the Ethiopian government the next day, which prompted Leijonhufvud and *blatta* Éfrém to contact Wright with further documentation, including confirmation that the Ethiopians had first contacted the Commission in 1945[86] and a preliminary list of charges and accused war criminals.[87] Just over a month later, on October 29, the Commission met again, and without discussion immediately voted on Ethiopian jurisdiction. This time, the majority supported the Ethiopian request. Only Australia, Belgium, France, and the Netherlands voted against, with the United States and China abstaining.[88]

In February, the charge files arrived. As Mogadishu recovered from settler-nationalist street fights and Asmara faced an international inquiry into its political future, Committee I considered Cerulli's case.[89] It convened on March 4. Craigie served as chair, with Wright, Zivkovic, E. Zeman (Czechoslovakia), and Jacob Aars Rynning (Norway) as the voting members, and Leijonhufvud joined the group as Ethiopia's delegate.[90] Cerulli stood accused by the Ethiopian government of "complicity in systematic terrorism," and was specifically charged with nine counts of war crimes and crimes against humanity in the UNWCC framework.[91] These included complicity in mass killings, the use of chemical weapons, the detention and torture of civilians, the confiscation and destruction of property, and the "denationalization" of the Amhara.[92] The last of these was a precursor concept to genocide, understood by the Commission as a charge for senior policymakers that encompassed mass violence and displacement as well as linguistic and religious repression, "the extermination of the intellectual class," and "attempts to disintegrate a nation by abusing regional differences."[93] Cerulli was additionally charged with domestic crimes under the Ethiopian Penal Code of 1930, drawing on its revised provisions for extraordinary cases. These charges included crimes against property, specifically theft, robbery with violence, and burning of property, as well as crimes against persons, specifically serious injury, forcible seizure of persons and forced employment, and murder. The last of these was a capital offense.[94]

The case against Cerulli hinged on the parallel case against ex-minister Alessandro Lessona, who was until 1937 his immediate superior at the Ministry of Italian Africa. The committee had already ruled Lessona was a suspected war criminal in tandem with its earlier judgment against Rodolfo Graziani.[95] As Leijonhufvud explained, Lessona was in his ministerial capacity organizationally responsible for what transpired in Ethiopia, and he had elected not to restrain Graziani—his theoretical subordinate—during the Yekatit 12 mass killings. It was in part for this reason that

Mussolini fired Lessona in 1937, when the former wished to move away from Graziani's failures. Leijonhufvud argued that this same logic of organizational culpability applied to Cerulli. As director of the Office of Political Affairs in Lessona's ministry until 1937, Cerulli occupied the senior post in the unit responsible for overseeing colonial policy, administration, and intelligence. Given this expansive portfolio, the Ethiopian government took the position that Cerulli knew of and therefore shared in the ministerial responsibility for Graziani's crimes.[96] Moreover, Cerulli was directly responsible for crimes in Ethiopia that transpired during his tenure as vice governor general, during which time he occupied the second-highest post in the colonial bureaucracy. Surveying Cerulli's approach to colonial policy, Leijonhufvud later asserted that he was "an advocate of the hard, if not the hardest, school."[97]

Yet the case nearly foundered in the committee. The documentary evidence in Cerulli's file was not specific to his particular charges, and for this reason, the members found it insufficient to demonstrate his influence on the course of events. Craigie had initially made this same assessment of the evidence against Lessona. However, Leijonhufvud revealed that the Ethiopian government had just completed an interrogation of Cerulli's personal interpreter, and that an affidavit containing "conclusive evidence" from the latter would arrive shortly. He therefore requested that Cerulli's case be adjourned pending the delivery of this document, or at least that the committee designate Cerulli a witness to war crimes given his seniority in the colonial administration and near-certain knowledge of atrocities.[98] But the group was now erroneously informed that Cerulli was then employed by the UN Secretariat, which required the committee to contact the latter to determine whether it had materials related to his case. In the interim, the members were opposed to even provisionally listing Cerulli as a witness. Facing these complexities, the committee adjourned the case with the proviso that it would be reopened should the promised affidavit arrive prior to the dissolution of the UNWCC, now only weeks away.[99]

A few days later, Craigie outlined the situation at the Foreign Office. In a summary of their departmental conversation, his colleague Francis Brown explained that it was Leijonhufvud who had raised Cerulli's supposed Secretariat connection, a confusion possibly related to the latter's denunciation in Paris two years earlier. However, Brown disputed the likelihood of such a link. In his view, it was improbable that the Secretariat would employ an Italian citizen since Italy was not then a UN member state, and the UN records in his office did not list Cerulli as an employee. He added that Cerulli was in fact then serving as an advisor to the Italian ambassador in London. This was a remarkable revelation, since it suggested that during the recent Commission deliberations at Lansdowne House, Cerulli had been working only steps away at the Italian embassy north of Berkeley Square. Reviewing the political implications of the case, Brown suggested, "We want to avoid a row with the Italians; at the same time[,] I think Cerulli is such a poisonous character that it would be no bad thing if we had some definite grounds on which to say to the Italians that he is a bad man to choose as their colonial advisor. His being placed on the list of witnesses might well provide such grounds." His colleagues at the Foreign Office endorsed this judgment, one adding, "I think it would be an excellent thing. He [Cerulli] has done a great deal of harm."[100] After coordinating with Craigie and George Alexander Ledingham, the British secretary general of the UNWCC, Brown contacted the UN Secretariat, which confirmed that Cerulli was not in its employ. He then notified the Commission of this point, adding that his government did not object to Cerulli's name appearing on the international register of war criminals.[101] With this penultimate procedural hurdle cleared, on March 19 Leijonhufvud submitted a memorandum to the Commission that reviewed these developments and recapitulated the case against Cerulli.[102]

Less than a week later, the promised affidavit arrived from Addis Ababa. It contained the succinct but damning testimony of *fitawrari* Asfeha Wäldämika'él, Cerulli's longtime subordinate in Rome and Addis Ababa. In a surprising development, Asfeha had emerged relatively unscathed by his years of colonial service. After liberation, he was commended by Haylä Sellasé for his clandestine work within the colonial bureaucracy on behalf of Ethiopian detainees, and his supporters went so far as to call for his decoration as a member of the anticolonial resistance.[103] His defence was the double game. Now in the emperor's trust, the *fitawrari* retained his colonial-era title and worked under minister Aklilu at the Ministry of Foreign Affairs, where he supported the Unionist cause, served as the secretary general of Tegray province, and contributed to the work of the EWCC.[104] If some former collaborators like Haylä Sellasé Gugsa, Afäwärq Gäbrä Iyäsus, and Abbaa Joobir faced public trials and remote confinement,[105] Asfeha instead obtained postcolonial redemption through his acts of covert resistance and demonstrable utility to the restored imperial government.[106]

This last point is indicated by his role in the case against Cerulli. He had closely observed the latter in both the metropole and colony, and was among the most highly ranked Africans in the colonial administration, possibly junior only to *afä qésar* Afäwärq. This distinctive position lent special significance to Asfeha's March 25 affidavit, which detailed Cerulli's activities at the apex of his powers.[107] Asfeha alleged that in Rome, Cerulli's expertise and ministerial influence were such that he enjoyed "the complete confidence and constant personal access of Mussolini and Lessona, who invariably followed his advice on Ethiopian questions." He reported that he had personally seen the order produced by Cerulli's office that the Young Ethiopians should be "liquidated" during the occupation of Addis Ababa, and that "Cerulli's position in Rome during the Graziani massacre was so influential that he could have limited the terror, but he chose to not intervene." Asfeha thus alleged that Cerulli was involved in the killing of Fäqqädä Sellasé Heruy, Yohannes Ras Wärq, and Yoséf and Benyam Wärqenäh, among thousands more. Asfeha added that Cerulli personally interrogated Ethiopian detainees and assessed their "degree of danger to Italian interests." In Ethiopia, he alleged that Cerulli had "clear authority" over his nominal superior d'Aosta, but had failed to act when news of atrocities came to his attention, and most damningly, that Cerulli had assumed command in the field during the Däbrä Berhan counterinsurgency. Comparing his former superior to other senior colonial officials, both military and civilian, Asfeha's assessment in the affidavit was unequivocal: "My opinion, based on the words and actions of Cerulli, is that he approved of the violent policies of Graziani." More broadly, he asserted that "the so-called moderation of the terror" during the d'Aosta-Cerulli years was in fact limited only to subjugated urban centers, with atrocities continuing in areas of rural insurrection.[108] As documented in part III of this book, most of these claims are corroborated by the archival record.

Asfeha's testimony complemented other documents in the charge file related to Cerulli's tenure in Africa Orientale Italiana. The most significant of these was an affidavit from former guerilla *däjjazmach* Täshomä Shänquṭ, who described the 1939 mass killing at Zärrät at the end of Cerulli's second tenure as viceregal regent. The affidavit documented the use of chemical weapons against several thousand men, women, and children in the cave, as well as the mass execution of survivors, including members of the *däjjazmach*'s own family. Returning to the cave after liberation, he reported that he had found hundreds of severed heads and other human remains, which he buried at a nearby church named Qeddus Giyorgis. In all, he estimated that the Italians had killed more than twelve hundred people at Zärrät.[109] Also included in Cerulli's charge file was a 1938 letter from *aläqa* Haylu of Däbrä Tabor, originally published in the *League of Nations Official Journal*.[110] In it, *aläqa* Haylu described atrocities that took place in the Amhara governate during Cerulli's first tenure as viceregal regent. These included two mass killings at Männa Mäkätäwa on July 14 and July 21; a mass killing of church worshippers in Aja Fasilädas on August 9; a mass killing of priests and notables in Ebnat on an unspecified date during this period; and a mass killing at Däbrä Tabor on an unspecified date during this period. The letter also documented acts of torture and violence that occurred during some of these massacres, as well as the burning of more than thirty churches. It is unclear whether the *aläqa* Haylu letter and the Täshomä Shänquṭ affidavit were included in Cerulli's charge file because of their connection to his 1938 and 1939 regencies, and further, whether the committee members realized that Cerulli occupied the seniormost position in the colony when some of these events took place.

On March 31, Committee I used Asfeha's affidavit to reevaluate the prima facie case against Cerulli. It ruled he was a suspected war criminal, issuing an "S" listing for complicity in systematic terrorism.[111] The judgment represented the final substantive decision of the Commission, after hearing tens of thousands of similar cases, and it was additionally an extremely rare instance of a ruling based solely on pre-1939 war crimes.[112] In May, Cerulli's name was added to the UNWCC's final list of war criminals, which was a formal notice that he should be taken into custody in anticipation of prosecution.[113] But Cold War realpolitik soon intervened. On November 23, the Ethiopian government relayed the Commission's decisions on the ten Italian cases to the Big Four governments, but then explained that it would only proceed with the apprehension and trial of Badoglio and Graziani, the most high-profile of the accused, and was abandoning the other eight cases in the interest of "the early re-establishment of peaceful and friendly relations" with Italy.[114] The latter's emergence as a founding member of NATO surely informed this calculation. Nonetheless, that same year, the Commission's official history noted that the call to investigate Axis war crimes was first issued by the Ethiopian government through Heruy's March 1937 letter to the League.[115] Over a decade later, and at the final hour, the foreign minister's demand for justice had been honored.

The following year, this international sanction was invoked at the UN General Assembly in Lake Success, a woody postwar suburb of New York City. The setting was the April and May 1949 meetings of the First Committee, which considered whether the former Italian colonies should be apportioned via the Bevin-Sforza plan, a controversial British-Italian proposal that aimed to award parts of Eritrea to Ethiopia in exchange for French, British, and Italian trusteeships in Libya and Somalia. Minister Aklilu led the Ethiopian delegation in its challenge to this baldly neocolonial arrangement, which was defeated in the General Assembly through an Afro-Asian bloc vote widely perceived as a rebuke to the European colonial powers.[116] Although Italy was not yet a UN member state, Foreign Minister Carlo Sforza participated in the deliberations in a consultative role, with Cerulli at his side as an advisor (figure 10.3).

FIGURE 10.3 Enrico Cerulli at the United Nations (1950).

Source: © United Nations Archives.

New York reprised Paris. On April 11, Aklilu held his tongue as Sforza advanced the argument for Italy's continued presence in Africa, but he reached his limit when the minister claimed "the Italian republic could not be held responsible for the deeds of the fascist regime," and that the expulsion of Italians from Eritrea "would be an act of racial discrimination."[117] Outraged, Aklilu replied that the League had previously watched as Italy invaded Ethiopia, and that his government would not permit Italian colonies on its borders again. He then followed with his coup de grace. He called the committee's attention to "the presence on the Italian delegation of a man who had been [Vice] Governor [General] of Ethiopia in 1937 when the Ethiopian population had been gassed and massacred. It was shocking to find that man, who had been on the list of war criminals, in the Italian delegation."[118] Aklilu's riposte again exposed the hypocrisy of the Italian government's renunciation of responsibility for the fascist past. It had its coda ten days later, when on April 21 Somali Youth League representative and future Prime Minister Abdullahi Issa told the committee that "Signor Cerulli . . . prior to the conquest of Ethiopia, had been one of the high administrative officials in Somaliland[,] and he was well known for his part in having framed discriminatory laws such as the *colonia* system."[119] In the midst of the era's heated Ethiopian-Somali nationalist rivalry and related struggle for the Ogaden, the joint denunciation of Cerulli at Lake Success was a brief moment of anticolonial solidarity—if allowing for a little one-upmanship. The dramatic exchange was widely reported in the international press,[120] and in Addis Ababa, it received a front page feature in the state-run Amharic weekly *Addis zämän*, or *New Era*.[121] Months later, further controversy erupted at the UN when Italy nominated accused war criminal Guglielmo Nasi to serve as governor of its Somalia trusteeship, triggering a public debate within Italy about the legality of colonial violence.[122] These international showdowns over Italian colonial impunity eventually informed Aklilu's fiery speech at the 1955 Asian-African Conference in Bandung, where he attacked the persistence of colonial racism and its connection to the structural inequities of the League and UN.[123]

Despite these episodes, Cerulli ultimately avoided prosecution. In this, his fate resembled the vast majority of the individuals whose names appeared on the international register of war criminals, Italian or otherwise. Badoglio spent his final years as a free private citizen, briefly barred from serving in the senate until this decision was reversed by the Italian supreme court. Graziani was incarcerated for his RSI service before receiving an amnesty, after which he and his rival Lessona became leading figures in the Movimento Sociale Italiana (MSI), the country's leading neofascist political party. Graziani served as its honorary president and Lessona as a one-term MSI senator. All three ex-colonials spent their later years writing exculpatory histories and autobiographies, along the way becoming influential figures in the articulation of far-right narratives of national defeat and betrayal.[124] These developments epitomized the fundamentally ambiguous relationship between the Italian republic and its fascist and colonial past. There was no Italian Nuremburg.

In 1958, Cerulli addressed this historical reckoning in a special issue of the Italian journal *Ulisse*, which retrospectively assessed European imperialism in "the twilight of colonialism." Appearing amid the British departure from Eritrea and Ethiopia (1952 and 1955), the Bandung Conference (1955), the independence of Sudan, Morocco, Tunisia, and Ghana (1956 and 1957), and the broader renegotiation of political sovereignty across Africa and Asia, the issue featured contributions by a host of European experts and ex-colonial officials, including Lanfranco Ricci, Enrico De Leone, Claude Bourdet, Basil Davidson, and Joseph Needham. It opened with a piece by Cerulli entitled "The End of Colonialism."[125] In it, he offered a coolly realist appraisal of the colonial enterprise: he equated colonialism with modernity, reaffirmed the premise of superior and backward civilizations, and argued in Nietzschean terms that Europe conquered Africa simply because it could. This was a rejection of the politics of national liberation. He then reflected on the morality of colonial violence in a section entitled "The Crimes of the Europeans." For readers, the phrase likely evoked the ongoing controversies concerning torture, mass detentions, and extrajudicial killing in British Kenya and French Algeria, which exposed the contradictions between late colonial violence, the liberal narrative of empire, and the postwar framework of universal human rights.[126] In Cerulli's assessment, the crux of the problem of colonial violence was

> not the question of the one or another particular way in which these "atrocities"—as they say—were committed; but [instead] the fundamental question: is it legitimate to use force to impose one's dominion on a foreign people? If the answer is yes—if, that is, one accepts the formulation of Niccolò Machiavelli that states cannot be governed through Lord's

Prayers—[then] the excesses and atrocities will no longer be in proportion to moral principles, but to the opportunities of particular situations. And to justify them is a vulgar act of political skill. If instead one does not accept [this view], and instead one judges the use of force for the subjugation of people to be immoral, [then] it is not the degree of intensity of this force that can render it an "atrocity," or instead, a justified measure of rule.[127]

In other words, colonial violence—and more precisely, Italian criminality in Ethiopia—was morally indistinguishable from the violence of warfare in general, and this violence was either justifiable categorically or not at all. Put simply, if he was a war criminal, so was everyone else. This was an open rejection of the premise of war crimes and crimes against humanity that underpinned the UNWCC judgment against him. For Cerulli, the indictment was nothing but arbitrary and hypocritical victor's justice, the product of a contingent historical outcome rather than moral principle or impartial legal argument. He returned to this theme in the article's conclusion, which offered a quotation from Senegalese philosopher Léopold Sédar Senghor in which the latter envisioned decolonization as liberation from the alienating colonial psychologies of superiority and inferiority, gesturing toward the just-published study of Tunisian writer Albert Memmi.[128] Given Cerulli's critique of the distinctiveness of European criminality, on the one hand, and Senghor's argument that postcolonial reconciliation should transcend the inherited mentalities of empire, on the other, Cerulli's implication—it would seem—was that the work of the UNWCC was intellectually retrograde as well as politically vulgar. The judgment was simple retribution: the lambs had attacked the birds of prey.[129]

If Cerulli was haunted by the colonial past, *fitawrari* Asfeha transcended it. His testimony for the Commission began a long period of professional success, most notably through his appointment as the chief executive of Eritrea (1955–1959) during the Ethiopian-Eritrean federal period (1952–1962).[130] For his service, he was subsequently promoted to the rank of *däjjazmach* and granted the distinguished title of *bitwäddäd*, or "the beloved of the emperor."[131] In Akkälä Guzay, his birthplace in the former Italian colony of Eritrea, a popular Tigrinya song celebrated the possibility of a local boy achieving such an exalted station.[132] Yet his spectacular ascent to the highest echelons of postliberation government provoked resentment among a few of his contemporaries, who felt that his colonial service was a stain he could never fully expunge. In his later years, he was attacked by some former anticolonial patriots, who pejoratively called him a *banda*, or collaborator, despite his reported attempts to moderate Italian ferocity. A few of his critics even disparaged him with a condemnatory Amharic couplet:

> The translator of Nasi, the awardee of Mussolini
> The duke of Aosta's *fitawrari*, the main advisor of Cerulli[133]

For these detractors, who had followed the bitter path of the guerilla like Abäbä Arägay, Haylä Maryam Mammo, and Täkkälä Wäldä Hawaryat, Asfeha was forever tainted by his proximity to the regime's criminal colonial elite. In this respect, the verse offered a postcolonial version of the adage, "Tell me the company you keep, and I'll tell you who you are," which appropriately exists in near-identical Italian and Amharic versions.[134] Though the couplet's intended target was the redeemed subordinate *bitwäddäd* Asfeha, its logic was more suited to his unrepentant superior Cerulli, who found himself in damning company before the UNWCC.

11
Field Operations

On September 21, 1947, Heruy returned to Addis Ababa. A plane brought his body to Ledäta Airport, in what is now Ṭor Hayloch, and the following day, a crowd assembled on the airfield. Among those gathered were Hamärä Eshäté, her surviving children, and a throng of students, ecclesiastics, and government officials. A hearse brought the foreign minister through the city, followed by hundreds of automobiles. According to one observer, it was among the biggest funeral motorcades in Ethiopian history. Their destination was Qeddest Sellasé cathedral, the newly constructed burial site for the nation's anticolonial martyrs, where the emperor and royal family were waiting. Inside the church, Haylä Sellasé escorted the casket to the altar, where *abunä* Yesehaq led the burial rite. When it finished, Heruy's son-in-law Täklämaryam Kassahun addressed the congregants. He thanked the emperor for honoring his wartime promise to return the foreign minister to Ethiopia, which meant the family could finally mourn together at home. Next to speak was Abäbä Arägay, now the minister of war and acting prime minister. Looking back on their shared struggle, the former guerilla commended Heruy's "exceptional loyalty" to Ethiopia and personal service to the exiled emperor, a patriotism that buttressed his peerless intellectual achievements. Addressing his former comrade, the *ras* proclaimed, "You never ceased to serve your country, even until the end of your life. . . . Future generations will respect and remember it." In a gesture to this posterity, he announced that the National Library Reading Room would be dedicated to Heruy.¹ In the local press, the repatriation and funeral were feature stories, and one newspaper offered an elegy that addressed the foreign minister's contribution to Ethiopia's intellectual awakening, likening his death in exile to a lost mirror of self-understanding.² As a public ritual of commemoration, the reinterment at Qeddest Sellasé was saturated with references to the collective trauma of the years of hardship. It affirmed the cathedral as a postcolonial memory site, securing Heruy's position in the national historical imagination while elaborating the official narrative of unified anticolonial resistance and heroic exile defiance.³ Two days later, the baron made his decisive presentation at Lansdowne House.

Heruy's repatriation coincided with Cerulli's ascent to the apex of his academic power. Undaunted by the ruling of the UNWCC, the inquiry of the High Commission for Sanctions Against Fascism, and the public denunciations on the international stage, he began a period of intense scholarly production. His principal focus was the literary sinews of the premodern Mediterranean, and especially the cultural interface between Western and Eastern Christendom.⁴ He completed a study of Ethiopian Orthodox Marian texts and their relationship to other Christian literatures (1943);⁵ a two-volume documentary study of the Ethiopian diaspora in the Levant (1943 and 1947);⁶ and an edition of a translated medieval Castilian-Arabic eschatological text that informed Dante's *Divine Comedy* (1949).⁷ During this same period, he served as vice president and then president of the Istituto Orientale in Naples,⁸ and after 1948, as editor of the Ge'ez section of the Corpus Scriptorum Christianorum Orientalium publication series, in which role he oversaw more than thirty translated editions. The next decade saw more major publications: his survey of Ge'ez and Amharic literature (1956);⁹ his three-volume collected writings on Somali history, ethnography, and linguistics (1957, 1959, and 1964);¹⁰ and finally his two volumes of translated Ethiopian Orthodox doctrinal polemics (1958 and 1960).¹¹ Though he lacked a university position, he had by this time attracted wider international attention through his influential Dante scholarship. This development is suggested by a 1954 appreciation for the UNESCO journal *Diogenes*, in which his colleague Francesco Gabrieli proposed that Cerulli's Mediterranean research exemplified not only a Braudel-esque "international medieval culture" but also the vibrant intellectual cosmopolitanism espoused by the journal's publisher.[12] The disjuncture between this assessment and the UNWCC judgment is jarring.

A corresponding myopia defined the academic field of Ethiopian studies, which sought to evade the question of Cerulli's colonial past. In 1959, one year after his defiant *Ulisse* article, the complexities of this ahistoricism suffused the first International Conference of Ethiopian Studies (ICES), remembered today as the founding professional event of the field.[13] Convened over three days in April at the Accademia Nazionale dei Lincei in Rome, its organizer was none other than Cerulli, who invited a cohort of nearly forty international specialists on Ethiopia and the Horn of Africa. The setting was suggestive. The Accademia, Italy's oldest and most distinguished learned society, is located in the Palazzo Corsini, an eighteenth-century compound on the verdant slope of the Janiculum, one mile from Santo Stefano and three miles from Cerulli's residence in Parioli.[14] Like this august venue, the conference reflected its organizer's vision of the field as a philologically inflected branch of Semitic studies, continuing the research paradigm developed by Ignazio Guidi. Nearly all the presenters were European, and with respect to the disciplines, the majority of the contributions focused on philology, literature, linguistics, and premodern history, with a pronounced thematic concentration on Christianity, Semitic languages, and Ethiopia's Middle Eastern heritage. In these respects, the conference paralleled Cerulli's own research agenda and forcefully reasserted the field's Orientalist lineage, as distinct from the alternative model of interdisciplinary African studies.[15] This aspect addressed ongoing debates about the future of area studies in postcolonial Italy.[16]

If the Rome conference was groundbreaking, it was also haunted by the past. As in the realm of international diplomacy, this was most overtly apparent in the participants themselves. Over one-third of the invitees were Italian, and many had played direct roles in the colonial enterprise. In addition to Cerulli, these ex-functionaries included Martino Mario Moreno, Cerulli's longtime colleague from the Addis Ababa Legation and the Ministry of the Colonies; Lanfranco Ricci, a student of Carlo Conti Rossini who subsequently served under Cerulli as a resident in the Shäwa governate;[17] Antonio Mordini, an ethnologist and archaeologist who joined Amedeo d'Aosta's research expedition in Libya, and who subsequently served under Cerulli as director of archaeological and ethnographic services in Addis Ababa;[18] and Felice Ostini, a lawyer, veteran of the colonial administration in Eritrea, and leader of the fractious Italo-Eritrean settler lobby.[19] Also in attendance was the once-exiled Giorgio Levi Della Vida, just retired from the University of Rome.

These Italians were joined by a small number of Ethiopian and Eritrean participants. The most prominent of these was Ambassador Germachäw Täklä Hawaryat, son of former League delegate *fitawrari* Täklä Hawaryat.[20] Germachäw had met Cerulli two decades prior when the latter visited Asinara, where he deemed the young detainee an "irreducible" and exiled him to Longobucco.[21] Another prominent Ethiopian attendee was Aklilu Habté (figure 11.1), who had just obtained a doctorate from Ohio State University and attended the proceedings on behalf of the newly established University College of Addis Ababa.[22] These two were joined by several visitors from the Ethiopian embassy and Pontifical Ethiopian College.[23] Also summoned was the unsettling specter of Heruy himself, whose *Wazéma* was cited by the Eritrean novelist, Catholic priest, and civil servant Gäbrä Iyäsus Haylu. The latter's presentation on a nineteenth-century Christological text from Däbrä Libanos was the lone Ethiopian or Eritrean paper published in the conference proceedings.[24]

FIGURE 11.1 Aklilu Habté at the International Conference of Ethiopian Studies, Rome (1959).

The event itself was framed by the politics of memory and historical representation. This context was signaled by the inaugural addresses, which obliquely referenced the colonial past through calls for rapprochement through collective inquiry. Ambassador Germachäw opened the conference with a brief welcome in French. After paying homage to the assembled scholars, he noted that while all could appreciate the "purely intellectual" aim of the occasion, the Ethiopians were especially pleased to see "the desire of the Italian intellect to give its contribution to the development of Ethiopian civilization," which knew how "to resist all attempts at denegation."[25] For this reason, he assured the attendees—Italian and non-Italian alike—that their research would enjoy the full support of his government. After this greeting, Cerulli delivered a keynote on ancient Ethiopia and the enduring intra-Mediterranean links between the Horn of Africa and the Middle East. He concluded this safely premodern presentation with the anodyne suggestion that the conference would help the world "appreciate and love Ethiopia in its past and prosperous future," in fulfillment of the Aksumite royal credo that one's work should always better the land.[26] In distinct but complementary ways, Germachäw and Cerulli politely gestured toward Senghorian postcolonial transcendence.

However, Marcel Cohen used his closing address to recommend a more assertive historical therapy. A staunch partisan of Ethiopia during the international crisis and colonial occupation, the septuagenarian Marxist was now an eminent public intellectual and academic specialist, just retired after nearly four decades at the École Nationale des Langues Orientales Vivantes.[27] In an earlier presentation on the development of Ethiopian linguistics, he had noted the colonial service of Cerulli and Moreno, an obvious point for most in the room.[28] He now returned to the topic of the colonial past, in what proved to be the conference's most explicit commentary on how the attendees should remember events in which some had been antagonists. Cohen acknowledged Cerulli's role as the architect of the Accademia meeting, for which the latter received "hearty applause" from the audience. He then provocatively observed that their work had "affirmed the peace between peoples" through "the deliberate forgetting of past conflicts," a conscious ahistoricism manifest "in our spirit and through our actions."[29] In his view, this development was demonstrated by the fact that the Ethiopian scholars had interacted "amiably" with their European counterparts. This was a bold assessment. Eleven years after the UNWCC decision, and a decade after the denunciation at Lake Success, the founding event of the field of Ethiopian studies attempted to rehabilitate Cerulli—"our venerated Maestro," as one presenter put it.[30] In this, the conference paralleled the exonerative logic of Cerulli's essay in *Ulisse* the previous year.

For the Ethiopians in Rome, the prescribed amnesia was an affront. This sentiment was suggested by Aklilu Habté in the lone Amharic presentation included in the proceedings, a formal greeting from the University College addressed to Cerulli.[31] Aklilu began by explaining that while the conference was taking place in English, French, Italian, and German, he nonetheless wished to speak in Amharic, since the event was devoted to Ethiopia and because he knew many in the audience would understand him. He commended the Accademia for convening the first academic conference devoted to his country, and additionally thanked the Italian government for supporting this undertaking "in spirit and idea." Turning to "the distinguished *liqawent*" in the audience, he observed that they served Ethiopia through their scholarship: if some of their predecessors had claimed his nation was backward or deficient, the present group had in his view worked to correct this error. There was surely shifting in seats. In a gesture to Heruy, Aklilu explained that this corrective function reflected the fact that the gathered specialists "pursued certain truth through the scientific method," unlike those who "came and asked the ideas of one or two people" or simply wrote from afar. Nonetheless, bad scholarship persisted. Despite the advances in international travel and education, some unscientific foreign writers still "distanced themselves from the truth, stripped themselves of the truth, or showed themselves to be ignorant of the changes [underway] in Ethiopia." This was, in his view, a "great error."[32] He concluded with the hope that his country would establish an institution like the Accademia to hold future specialist congresses.

Aklilu's careful words hinted at past conflicts. Read closely, his comments outlined the dangers of instrumentalized scholarship, from his opening attack on the denigration of Ethiopia to his more subtle celebration of rigor, his critique of shoddy foreign research, and his call for equitable Ethiopian participation in the academic field. Three decades before, these very points had figured in the multilingual sparring of Heruy and Cerulli, and they had reemerged in the 1935 memoranda debate and corresponding specialist commentary. As a protagonist in these episodes, Cerulli was almost obliged to address this history in his reply to Aklilu. Speaking in Italian, he thanked the latter for his appreciation of the conference and affirmed the proposal to convene future academic events in Ethiopia. He then directly addressed the issue of Ethiopian participation in the field. He offered his wish for "the young researchers [and] children of Ethiopia to acquire the methods of modern science, not abandoning but rather more and more exploiting the ancient traditions of their country in history, literature, and law. In this way the structure of modern Ethiopia will be established on a solid foundation, and the children of Ethiopia will be able to continue to make important contributions to the understanding of their own country."[33] This was a subtle revision of the racialized intellectual politics he had expressed decades earlier. Cerulli's evolved position now suggested a more liberal imagination of African agency, broadly adapted to the political independence of the postcolonial era. It was time for Ethiopians to join the ranks of the academic specialists.

In the audience and stairwells of the Palazzo (figure 11.2), the Ethiopians were dubious. Looking back on his first academic conference, Aklilu recalls that "a bit of nationalism" informed the views of some of the Ethiopian attendees.[34] Among themselves, they privately discussed the untrustworthiness of the European researchers, despite the official mood of cooperation. Many believed the foreigners still viewed Ethiopians as inferior and in need of tutelage, and that some even harbored a lingering desire to subjugate Africans, politically or otherwise. A particular point of concern was the role of the Italian state in sponsoring the conference. Aklilu was gracious in his formal remarks, but he remembers that he and the other Ethiopians "listened carefully to what was being said about Ethiopia, and who was saying it." On the latter point, many of the Ethiopians in Rome were apprised of Cerulli's colonial past. Although Aklilu had not followed the drama at the UNWCC, he knew Cerulli was a former colonial governor who "took advantage of this opportunity to collect manuscripts and other things," and he discussed these facts with the other Ethiopians at the conference. The gulf between these private judgments and the official accolades was considerable.

It was for all these reasons that Aklilu remained wary of simplistic notions of postcolonial reconciliation through "deliberate forgetting." This sentiment was likely shared by Ambassador Germachäw, whose decorous opening remarks masked a subtle warning for those who might yet seek to weaponize research, recalling his father's arguments in Geneva.

FIGURE 11.2 Interior of Accademia dei Lincei, Rome.

Source: Author's photo.

According to Aklilu, a similar skepticism prevailed among some of the other attendees:

> I remember that there were people at the conference trying to make Ethiopians change their minds about the Italians. But in my estimation, there was [also] a group of people, including some Ethiopians, who discussed how Ethiopia's heritage had been spoiled and how the Italians were responsible for it. This [history] was contrary to the spirit of the first conference of Ethiopian studies. Although there were not many Ethiopians with academic inclinations or the ability to offer an evaluation of the conference, the fact that the Italians took the initiative made Ethiopians suspicious of whether it was positive or meaningful.[35]

For Aklilu and these other critics, Ethiopian and non-Ethiopian alike, the continued prominence of Cerulli and other colonial actors in the academic field raised fundamental questions about the value and purpose of the knowledge it produced. This epistemic problem was compounded by the stolen material heritage that still remained in Italian institutions. For Aklilu, his experiences in Rome provoked further research on Cerulli. He eventually reached the conclusion that the latter was "a slick individual" with "the attitude of a colonial master," and "an educated, dangerous colonialist." The conference was not their last encounter.

That same week, another Roman event suggested the disjuncture between ICES and the ascendant politico-intellectual currents across Africa. This was the Second Congress of Negro Writers and Artists, convened at the Campidoglio one mile from the Accademia.[36] Sponsored by the Parisian journal *Présence africaine* and featuring a host of participants from Africa, the Caribbean, and North America, the congress addressed the revolutionary cultural politics of pan-African and Third World liberation.[37] The attendees included *Présence africaine* editor Alioune Diop and historian Cheikh Anta Diop, both from Senegal; psychologist Frantz Fanon, writer Édouard Glissant, and poet Aimé Césaire, all from Martinique; and current and future heads of state Sekou Touré of Guinea, Léopold Sédar Senghor of Senegal, and Eric Williams of Trinidad and Tobago. Also present was Mäshäsha Haylé, an advisor to the Ethiopian embassy in Paris.[38] Many of these had just attended the 1958 All African Peoples Conference in Accra, where they joined Kwame Nkrumah of Ghana, Patrice Lumumba of Congo, and George

Padmore of Trinidad and Tobago to chart a radical vision of pan-African political independence. Now in Rome, Alioune Diop used his opening speech to urge attendees to "free the mental disciplines and the arts from those shackles with which the demands of Western hegemony have compromised their universal application."[39] Over the ensuing days, the participants took up this critical-dialogic challenge in various fields, from archaeology to art, theology, sociology, and politics.[40] If decolonization required emancipation from impoverishing structures of thought, then culture would be the terrain of an anticolonial war of position.

Central to this project was the liberation of African historiography.[41] Among several presentations on this topic, Cheikh Anta Diop outlined the unity of African antiquity, Fanon discussed the role of history in national culture, and Césaire urged artists and writers to reclaim history from the Eurocentric periodization of colonial rule. With respect to the historical discipline, Nigerian historians Modilim Achufusi and Saburi Biobaku examined the responsibilities of African academics toward national education and patrimonial stewardship, jointly offering an explicitly anticolonial and Africanized vision of the historical profession. Achufusi outlined the continued impact of "imperialist ideologies" on historiography, urging African historians to "vigorously respond to these deformations of facts."[42] By way of example, he denounced ex-colonial governor Hubert Deschamps for claiming independence would fuel ethnopolitical chaos, rebutting this position with a survey of destructive European interventions in Africa. Biobaku, meanwhile, argued that while the craft of the African historian was theoretically no different from that of any other, he or she was uniquely burdened with dismantling pejorative Western narratives and developing new research methods suited to the continent's oral traditions.[43] These critiques were subsequently developed in an incendiary disciplinary manifesto for the congress proceedings.[44] Historical production was a vital aspect of self-determination beyond political sovereignty.

The dissonance between the two meetings was telling. Broadly speaking, the congress's radical antiracism, commitment to pan-African liberation, and culturally situated vision of Africa-focused knowledge production repudiated the intellectual conservatism and liberal colonial apologetics of ICES. The congress demanded a decisive break with the dominant institutional and epistemic frameworks of Africanist knowledge, in service of African nations and their diasporas.[45] The shackles of the existing academy were the problem. To this point, Achufusi's critique of Deschamps attacked the crux of Cerulli's world-historical arguments in *Ulisse*: colonial rule was a history of despotism and violence, not the culminating extension of a progressive and developmental modernity. As Fanon would write two years later, its legitimacy rested only on "the force of bayonets."[46] For this reason, decolonization required clear-eyed historiographic critique, not exculpatory ahistorical amnesia. In advancing this position, the congress rejected the future politics of ICES: the first embraced the liberatory power of intellectual rupture; the second affirmed the value of expert continuity.

Months later, these developments framed Cerulli's first public comments on the postcolonial future of the Horn of Africa. In a radio program on "The Changing Face of Africa" for the national broadcaster Radiotelevisione Italiana (RAI), Cerulli addressed the trajectories of Italo-African relations in the context of decolonization and the Cold War. His commentary subsequently appeared in the Italian journal *Africa*, published by the Istituto Italiano per l'Africa (IIA).[47] His concern was the "menacing crisis" that faced the continent. Returning again to the theme of Senghorian transcendence, he first argued that the economic development of independent Africa would require Africans and Europeans to embrace a truly reciprocal relationship, without mistrust on the part of Africans or paternalism on the part of Europeans. He then suggested that Italy, as the most geographically central Mediterranean nation-state, was spatially and historically suited to mediate between Europe, Africa, and Asia, adding that its relatively recent national unification gave it a particular sympathy for African liberation movements. Only months before, IIA secretary general Mario Dorato had celebrated a similarly nationalist Mediterraneanism in his welcome to the Congress of Negro Writers and Artists, and he developed this theme in his own contribution to the RAI program.[48] Similar ideas animated the contemporaneous French vision of a postcolonial Eurafrique.[49]

Moving on from this context, Cerulli turned to the Horn of Africa. In the case of Somalia, he argued that the soon-to-end Italian administration of its UN trusteeship (1950–1960) would facilitate future economic collaboration between the two countries, especially since Somalia's Italian-led industries were essential to its post-trust economy. This was a liberal rejection of the emerging concept of underdevelopment. With respect to Ethiopia, which had just reestablished bilateral relations with Italy, Cerulli noted with approval the resumption of cultural and economic cooperation between the two countries, and then offered ICES as a signpost to the future. In his assessment, the conference offered "beautiful evidence of the new contribution that scientific studies of Africa can now expect from Africans themselves," and he added that the dialogue "between researchers from Ethiopia and other various countries of the world concluded with a truly affectionate demonstration of friendly collaboration between Ethiopia and Italy in the field of high culture, reviving the centuries old tradition of Italian Ethiopian studies that dates back to the Renaissance."[50] This was a convoluted reading of the situation. Either unaware or dismissive of the Ethiopians' ambivalence about the proceedings and criticism of his specific role therein, and still defiantly contemptuous of the Ethiopian government's "mistrustful" legal case against him, Cerulli instead focused on Cohen's exculpatory ahistorical peroration at the Accademia, on the one hand, and the perceived parallels between ICES and Tridentine Santo Stefano, on the other. As much as this was a sweeping recuperation of the legacy of early modern intercultural and ecumenical Mediterranean dialogue, it was also an implicit repudiation of the models of liberatory scholarship and intellectual self-determination advanced at the Congress of Negro Writers and Artists. It is likely for this reason that Cerulli ignored the congress in his RAI discussion, despite his Senghorian mood. If his analogy with Santo Stefano was esoteric, his larger point was clear. In the postcolonial era, Italo-Ethiopian relations should follow the example of the experts.[51]

Cerulli sought reconciliation, and Rome erasure. In Ethiopia, however, the memory of his past was very much alive. The uncertainty of his future relationship with the country was suggested at the First International Congress of Africanists, convened in 1962 at the newly rechristened University of Ghana in Accra. Aklilu Habté served on the conference steering committee, and he recalls that the Accra congress built on the developing links between Ethiopia and other newly independent African states, complementing the 1963 selection of Addis Ababa as headquarters of the Organization of African Unity (OAU). For this reason, the Ethiopian delegation to the Accra congress was carefully selected.[52] The event was hosted by President and University Chancellor Kwame Nkrumah, whose inaugural keynote called for African regeneration through mental emancipation, and the meeting proved an opportunity for Aklilu to meet leading figures of the African and pan-Africanist political and intellectual elite, in a sequel to the earlier Congresses of Negro Writers and Artists.[53] Cerulli joined him in Accra. In a welcome address, historian Kenneth Onwuka Dike singled out the Italian for special recognition, greeting him personally alongside attendees Alioune Diop, Amadou Hampâté Bâ, and the elderly W. E. B. Du Bois, who had just moved to Ghana from the United States.[54] The audience also included leading members of the international Africanist academy, including J. F. Ade Ajayi, Joseph Ki-Zerbo, Bethwell Ogot, Georges Balandier, Jean Rouche, Conor Cruise O'Brien, and Melville Herskovits.[55] Also present was Rome congress alumnus Modilim Achifusi, who had developed his 1959 vision of African historical self-determination by obtaining a motion to establish the Congress of Africanists at the 1960 International Congress of Orientalists in Moscow.

Despite Cerulli's official reception in Accra, he did not present alongside the other specialists. In Aklilu's recollection, Cerulli spent the week studiously avoiding contact with the Ethiopian delegation, which included several members of Aklilu Habtäwäld's Foreign Ministry as well as expatriate historian Richard Pankhurst—the son of Sylvia Pankhurst and an occasional critic of Cerulli and correspondent with Du Bois. In conversations with other attendees, Aklilu Habté noted a consensus that some of the Europeans continued to harbor colonial mentalities, revealed through their disparaging statements about the trajectory of postcolonial African development.[56] It was a perception shared by some of the era's younger North American and European specialists, who recall a pronounced generational, political, and disciplinary divide between Cerulli and the emerging cohort of area studies–based historians and social scientists.[57] These academic fissures compounded the politico-intellectual gulf between the two Rome conferences. Cerulli endorsed a tutelary, dehistoricized, and ostensibly apolitical model of Africanist expertise at the precise moment that continental and diasporic scholars embraced an emancipatory, therapeutic, and pan-Africanist vision of engaged knowledge production—even as the newly institutionalized field of African area studies largely rejected this radical commitment.[58]

Four years after Accra, Cerulli's position in Ethiopian studies produced a major controversy in Addis Ababa. The setting was the Haile Selassie Prize Trust.[59] Founded in 1963 alongside the Institute of Ethiopian Studies (IES), the country's preeminent research institution, the Prize Trust was envisioned as a Nobel foundation for independent Africa that would encourage Ethiopian achievement, on the one hand, and forge pan-African cultural ties, on the other. It was thus an intellectual counterpart to the Addis Ababa-headquartered OAU. The Prize Trust offered fellowships and scholarships to promising Ethiopian students and also made annual awards in eight areas: agriculture, education, industry, humanitarianism, fine arts, Amharic literature, Ethiopian studies, and African studies. Two of these prizes were reserved for Ethiopians (Amharic literature and fine arts), whereas two more recognized non-Ethiopians (Ethiopian studies and African studies).[60] Nominations for specific prizes could be made by individuals or the award subcommittees, which were comprised of Ethiopian academics. These decisions were approved by the board of trustees, which then advanced candidates to the emperor, who presented the awards but otherwise had no formal role in the selection process. This structure was designed to ensure rigor and prevent lobbying.

The board chairperson was now-ṣähafé te'ezaz and Prime Minister Aklilu Habtäwäld, Cerulli's longtime adversary on the international stage. The Prize Trust awards remained relatively uncontroversial during the tenure of director Abebe Ambatchew (1963–1966), the grandson of qäññazmach Dähné Wäldä Maryam and recipient of a doctorate from Ohio State University. In these early years, the international award subcommittee repeatedly considered Cerulli's candidacy but declined to nominate him on the merits, even though many at the Prize Trust knew of his colonial career.[61] Looking back, Abebe recalls that this decision to refrain from recognizing Cerulli reflected the subcommittee's paramount concern for the African impact of a candidate's scholarship, a criterion manifest in their nominations of more broadly influential activist-intellectuals like philosopher-statesman Léopold Sédar Senghor, Howard professor William Leo Hansberry, and radical journalist Basil Davidson.[62] During Abebe's tenure, the inaugural prize for Ethiopian studies was awarded to Marcel Cohen (1964), and the subsequent award to linguist Wolf Leslau (1965).[63]

Things changed during the tenure of Abebe's successor Berhanou Abebe (1966–1967). In 1966, the subcommittee for Ethiopian studies nominated Cerulli for its annual prize,[64] and Aklilu rejected the nomination in his capacity as a trustee.[65] The award instead went to botanist Rodolfo Pichi Sermolli, a decision some perceived as demonstrating the absence of categorical opposition to an Italian awardee, even one with a colonial pedigree.[66] This reversal was an unprecedented instance of procedural drama at the Prize Trust, and Aklilu's supporters leaked the affair to the public, despite the confidential nature of the nomination process.[67] If the facts of Cerulli's colonial career were by this time common knowledge among Ethiopian academics,[68] the denial of the award still generated criticism among some foreign specialists. Most notably, linguist Edward Ullendorff later called Cerulli's rejection "a glaring omission" in the history of the Prize Trust.[69] In this, Ullendorff failed to grasp the central issue. Aklilu's intervention in the nomination process and the subsequent rejection of Cerulli's candidacy asserted the impossibility of separating the two sides of the latter's career, rejecting the alienated premise of intellectual rehabilitation without accountability or justice. The achievements of the scholar and the crimes of the proconsul could not be isolated.

That same year, Cerulli also found himself persona non grata at the third International Conference of Ethiopian Studies, convened in April at the IES on the campus of Haile Selassie University. The first event in the academic field where the attendees were predominantly Ethiopian, the occasion fulfilled Aklilu Habté's vision of a specialist academic conference hosted in the country. It coincided with the Liberation Jubilee, a year-long national commemoration of the twenty-fifth anniversary of the end of colonial rule. Featuring international experts as well as traditional scholars, with a separate Amharic salon specifically reserved for the latter, the conference keynote was delivered by Leslau, recipient of the 1965 Prize Trust award for Ethiopian studies. The colonial past was omnipresent. Most concretely, the IES occupied the former imperial palace, which meant that the proceedings unfolded on the site of the 1928 treaty negotiations as well as the 1937 Yekatit 12 attack and mass killing. Many of the attendees had lived through these events. In addition to Haylä Sellasé himself, these included Mahtämä Sellasé Wäldä Mäsqäl, an ex-Asinara detainee, former employee of the Addis Ababa Office of Political Affairs, and the recipient of the 1965 Prize Trust award for Amharic literature,[70] as well as Terrefe Ras Work, the Ankober-born son of *mämher* Ras Wärq, a graduate of New York's Rensselaer Polytechnic Institute, and a pioneer of fidäl telecommunications. The Italian attendees included linguist Luigi Fusella, who had conducted research in Africa Orientale Italiana with Cerulli's assistance,[71] as well as historian Carlo Giglio, who was a lukewarm colonial apologist then engaged in an extended polemic with historian Sven Rubenson concerning the Treaty of Weçhalé.[72]

Cerulli's absence was palpable. According to Rita Pankhurst, the conference organizers recognized the political implications of inviting him to Addis Ababa, and specifically obtained permission to do so from University President Kassa Wäldä Maryam, who was married to Princess Säblä Dästa, the daughter of famed anticolonial martyr *ras* Dästa Damṭäw. Cerulli reportedly declined to attend, citing his poor health, and instead submitted a paper to the proceedings in absentia.[73] Others, however, recall that Cerulli had been permanently barred from entering the country.[74] Further complicating his potential attendance was the fact that the EWCC had charged him with crimes under the Ethiopian Civil Code in addition to the UNWCC framework, and as a result, he would have faced potential arrest on arrival in Addis Ababa. Whatever the specifics, Cerulli's absence—like the imminent scandal at the Prize Trust—suggested that he now faced an uncertain welcome in Ethiopia.[75]

The predicament was subtly suggested by one of the conference presentations. This was Salome Gebre Egziabeher's multilingual paper on the anticolonial insurrection of Abäbä Arägay and Abärra Kassa, the first contribution to colonial historiography at ICES.[76] Using Amharic autobiographies, oral histories, and the war crimes publications of the Ethiopian government, she reconstructed the guerilla struggle in Shäwa across the Graziani and d'Aosta administrations, and translated Ethiopian correspondence with colonial officials. Along the way, she described the mass killing of Yekatit 12 and the careers of Haylä Maryam Mammo, Täkkälä Wäldä Hawaryat, and Zäwdé Asfaw Dargé—Cerulli's adversaries in the 1938 Ankober and Gédo counterinsurgency. Salome's presentation boldly interrupted the prevailing silence about colonial history among the academic specialists, drawing on official and collective memory in Ethiopia to challenge the deliberate forgetting prescribed in Rome. Her intervention amid the Liberation Jubilee highlighted the widening chasm between conclave and public historiography: if the academics of the first demanded ahistorical amnesia, the popular writers of the second were intensely focused on documenting the colonial era—most notably through the national culture of annual patriot remembrance and the booming genre of ex-guerilla autobiography. To this public historical end, Salome published a greatly expanded version of her conference paper in the monthly *Ethiopian Observer*, now featuring regional narratives of the resistance, lists of the patriots involved in each of these, and a discussion of the role of women in the anticolonial struggle.[77]

Meanwhile, Cerulli remained undaunted. In the coming decade, he served as vice president and then president of the Accademia dei Lincei, and in 1972, he convened the delayed fourth ICES at the Palazzo Corsini in Rome. This time, the conference included an official delegation of Ethiopian academics, one of whom recalls a favorable response to Cerulli as well as private discussions of his ban from Ethiopia.[78] Not invited were any exponents of the North American area studies and social science paradigms, and this exclusion produced a competing specialist conference the following year, convened at Michigan State University.[79] That same year, Cerulli did not participate in the 1973 third International Congress of Africanists in Addis Ababa, which was rocked by political controversies related to South African apartheid and clashing liberal and socialist visions of decolonization. Nor did he participate in the effort to institutionalize Somali studies through the creation of a dedicated professional organization, though one participant in this undertaking recalls that Cerulli's reputation as a Somalia specialist was in this period untarnished by his colonial past.[80] Yet as Cerulli continued to dominate Ethiopian studies and publish at an astonishing pace, he occasionally used his research to re-wage the battles of the colonial era, despite the pacific, positivist, and forward-looking mood of the Rome conference. Unlike Senghor and Cohen, he could neither transcend nor forget.

This orientation structured Cerulli's seminal history of Däbrä Libanos, a monastery north of Addis Ababa in his former governate of Shäwa. Founded in the fourteenth century by Saint Täklä Haymanot, Däbrä Libanos is a leading center of church learning in Ethiopia, and until the mid-twentieth century, its abbot, or *eç̣hägé*, was the de facto domestic head of the Ethiopian Orthodox Church, second only to the Coptic Metropolitan, or *abun*, appointed by the Alexandrian See of Saint Mark. For the Ethiopian faithful, it is a sacred and even miraculous place. During the colonial era, however, the Italians viewed the monastery as a wellspring of insurrection. In 1935, *eç̣hägé* Gäbrä Giyorgis Wäldä Ṣadeq of Märhabété—the future Patriarch Baselyos—joined Haylä Sellasé on the northern front, and then supported the anticolonial resistance from exile in Jerusalem.[81] In 1936, the monastery's acting head *abunä* Pétros similarly refused to submit to the Italians, and that July, he was publicly executed in Addis Ababa, after which he was succeeded by the more accommodating *eç̣hägé* Yohannes of Sämén.[82] The following year, these acts of monastic defiance and repression had their sequel during the events of Yekatit 12. In the carnage after the attempted assassination of Graziani, the enraged viceroy linked the plot to Däbrä Libanos, and three months later, Pietro Maletti and nine lorries of soldiers arrived at the monastery, where they executed approximately two thousand men and boys, burying them in mass graves near and far.[83] More than three hundred survivors and bereaved relatives were then transferred to the concentration camp at Dhanaane, and most of the monastery's sacred and royal objects were looted.

The following year saw attempted recuperation and official rapprochement. The new d'Aosta-Cerulli administration repaired the monastery and dispatched two hundred and fifty monks and priests to Däbrä Libanos from Harär and Jimma, in an effort to reconstitute its religious community.[84] That April, d'Aosta and Cerulli celebrated Orthodox Easter in Addis Ababa with *abunä* Abreham, an ecclesiastic from Gojjam who had been installed as an autocephalous Ethiopian metropolitan,[85] and in October, the viceroy visited the monastery for a tour with *eçhägé* Yohannes.[86] During this same period, the latter reportedly claimed that the monastery had now entered a new phase that "befits its happy and beautiful history."[87] When *abunä* Abreham died the following year, Yohannes became the metropolitan, and he was succeeded at Däbrä Libanos by *eçhägé* Yesehaq of Wällo, who had spent two years in detention in Italy.[88] The funeral, nominations, and Mäsqäl celebration that marked these transitions were extensively covered in the colonial press, and by 1940, the situation had evolved such that the colonial monthly *Yäroma berhan* featured an Amharic account of the monastery's feast of Saint Täklä Haymanot.[89] But the violent past was not long concealed. In 1941, the exiled *eçhägé* Gäbrä Giyorgis joined the emperor on his triumphant return to Addis Ababa, and the two stopped en route to pray at Däbrä Libanos and mourn its dead. Over the next seven years, the Ethiopian government then documented the mass killing as part of its UNWCC process. The atrocity had by this time become part of the collective memory of colonial rule. A glimpse of this is suggested by church poet *mämher* Géṭu Täsämma, who in 1948 lamented:

> O Däbrä Libanos, whose greatness has no equal
> There is nothing that resembles it or equates it in deeds
> And the earth that has dried is moist with the blood of the martyrs[90]

The trauma at Däbrä Libanos was singular. In contemporary Ethiopia and Italy, the atrocities at the monastery are remembered as among the most heinous crimes of the colonial era.[91]

In the mid-1940s, only a few years after the mass killing, Cerulli completed a major history of Däbrä Libanos.[92] Barred from Ethiopia, he made extensive use of Heruy's *Wazéma*, which was partially based on the latter's research at the monastery in the 1920s. Cerulli's tripartite study of Däbrä Libanos in the journal *Orientalia* effectively translated Heruy's vernacular history of the monastery into the international language of the historical discipline, converting an original work of research into an explicated primary source. The most overt manifestation of this category transformation is the fact that Cerulli used a Ge'ez poem Heruy discovered in the Däbrä Libanos scriptorium as the organizing device of his own study. Cerulli began his chronologically ordered biographies of the monastery's abbots with the relevant stanza from Heruy's poem. But the two histories of Däbrä Libanos were also intertwined in more subtle and complex ways. Though Cerulli emulated Heruy's prosopographical approach, focusing on the abbots rather than the institution of the monastery or the historical traditions of its inhabitants, he ignored some of Heruy's more significant contributions. These include his précis of *aläqa* Tayyä Gäbrä Maryam's now-lost etymology of the term *eçhägé* as well as his assertion that *eçhägé* Enbaqom was originally from Yemen, a point subsequently debated by Cerulli and other specialists.[93] On occasion, Cerulli closely followed Heruy's discussions, as exemplified by their parallel treatments of *eçhägé* Fileppos. At other times, Cerulli examined figures Heruy had ignored, such as *eçhägé*s Yohannes Käma and Endreyas.[94]

If Cerulli revisited the subjects of *Wazéma*, he also attempted to address developments in the years since its publication. In this, he failed abysmally and by design, since he ignored the three most significant events in the modern history of Däbrä Libanos: the exile of *eçhägé* Gäbrä Giyorgis, the execution of *abunä* Ṗeṭros, and the massacre of the monastic community. Though he devoted nearly ninety pages to the complexities of premodern politics and obscure interpretive questions suggested by close readings of abbot hagiographies, he allotted only two sentences to the comparatively well-documented events of the colonial period, in which he himself had played a direct role.[95] This is despite the fact that he was more informed about the recent history of the monastery than any other foreign specialist, given his ministerial surveillance work, vice gubernatorial experience, and personal acquaintance with the now-dead *abunä* Abreham. His ministerial office had even supervised the 1937–1938 detention of *echägé* Yesehaq in Rome. What motivated Cerulli's studied omission of these events? One explanation is that his narrative was a deliberate erasure of colonial violence in what came to be the definitive academic history of the monastery, countering the contemporaneous Ethiopian attempts to investigate, document, and commemorate the mass killing. Another explanation reflects his imminent war crimes indictment. His study of Däbrä Libanos appeared just as the UNWCC began its deliberations about Ethiopia, and a more truthful and complete history, at that particular moment, would have had potential implications for his individual guilt or innocence. Whatever his motives, his scholarship exonerated him through its silences.

This was not the last time that Cerulli used Heruy's scholarship to sanitize Italian atrocities in Ethiopia. A second salvo in this historical battle appeared in his 1956 *Storia della letteratura etiopica*, a spiritual successor to Guidi's 1932 work of the same name. Cerulli's wide-ranging study traced the development of Ge'ez and Amharic literature since antiquity, with a final chapter surveying the new genres of fiction, poetry, and historiography that emerged in the modern era. It features a comparative discussion of the works of Heruy and Afäwärq Gäbrä Iyäsus. The latter had just died in remote confinement near Jiren after a trial and commuted death sentence, and for Cerulli, this development perhaps suggested the possibility of definitive retrospection.[96] Reassuming the role of literary critic, he compared the achievements of the two writers. After celebrating the oeuvre of his erstwhile colleague Afäwärq, Cerulli offered a more equivocal assessment of his former adversary: "[Heruy has], literarily, a different figure than that of his contemporary Afäwärq. Much less heated in enthusiasm[,] and perhaps for this reason less brilliant, Heruy instead has greater freedom of thought and more rigorous logical power," yielding "less artistically striking results" despite his closer ties to traditional culture.[97] The jargon is enigmatic and the claims beyond the conventional scope of historical analysis, but Cerulli seems to be damning Heruy with faint aesthetic praise. The foreign minister wrote the second Amharic novel, edited a monumental anthology of Ge'ez and Amharic poetry, pioneered a host of new literary genres, and played a critical role in the development of the modern Amharic language—such that he is frequently considered a founder of Amharic literature—yet Cerulli's definitive assessment of Heruy's literary achievements rests on a facile interpretation of style. In a striking parallel, a similarly disparaging literary juxtaposition appears in the 1930s intelligence dossiers produced by Cerulli's office at the Ministry of Italian Africa. In these, Afäwärq was judged "the first literatus of his country," with "a deep knowledge of his own language," which "he loves to flaunt . . . in a style that is pretentious and full of uncommon words," such that the anonymous analyst likened him to the seventeenth-century Jesuit writer Daniello Bartoli.[98] Heruy, in contrast, was instead diminished as "one of the few literati that Abyssinia possesses," with "a simple, sober, [and] Anglicized style . . . attuned to puerile concepts."[99]

Chinua Achebe termed this colonialist criticism.[100] One could argue that Cerulli's 1956 analysis was simply an idiosyncratic take on a complex writer, or even a spirited critique of a former political antagonist, as the 1930s dossiers suggest. But his analysis is complicated by the translated text that accompanies his comments in *Storia della letteratura etiopica*. As an example of Heruy's considerable oeuvre, Cerulli translated a short historical passage from his 1927 *Goha ṣebah*, or *Light of Dawn*, which addresses the interference of Ethiopia's monastic orders in the political life of the Christian kingdom. Specifically, the excerpt describes the tendency of monks to use false prophecies to influence rulers and obtain temporal reward, intervening in worldly affairs in apparent violation of their ascetic and spiritual ideals. The chosen text is provocative. On the one hand, it nicely exemplifies Heruy's capacity for iconoclastic secular historical analysis, particularly in juxtaposition to the more traditionalist and deferential approach to monastic history he employed in works like *Wazéma*. On the other hand, when the passage is considered alongside Cerulli's comments about Heruy's inferior brilliance, it suggests a categorical suspicion of Ethiopia's traditionalist intellectuals, many of whom had struggled to survive the colonial war of occupation. Cerulli's point, it would seem, is that *liqawent* such as these were not noble scholars or aloof men of faith.

This speculative reading deepens when the passage is situated within the memory politics of Däbrä Libanos. After all, this was possibly the specific monastery about which Cerulli was most knowledgeable, and whose modern history he had already distorted in *Orientalia*. Could Cerulli have selected this particular passage from *Goha ṣebah* because Heruy's words indirectly supported the colonial-era assessment of the subversive politics of Däbrä Libanos? Seen in this light, the text parallels Conti Rossini's 1935 article for *Nuova antologia*, wherein the translated words of *däbtära* Assäggahäñ seemingly confirmed Italian claims of Ethiopian barbarism. In much the same way, Cerulli's translation of Heruy's passage on monastic politicking tacitly supported the view of figures like Graziani, who had once called Däbrä Libanos "a nest of murderers going by the name of monks," and who openly maintained this position in his 1948 autobiography.[101] If the monastery's modern residents had become embroiled in political activity during the colonial occupation, then they were simply following a path blazed by some of their forebears. They were clandestine combatants who had provoked military reprisals, and were thus not wholly innocent. This would be an overwrought interpretation of Cerulli's discussion were it not for his misleading history of Däbrä Libanos and his combative defense of colonial violence in *Ulisse*. Read collectively, these works suggest that Cerulli was not just writing history—he was trapped in it. His attempts at apologia and auto-absolution through historiography were an individuated counterpart to broader exonerative tendencies in postfascist and postcolonial Italian society.[102] With respect to the recent past, at least, his historical imaginary remained constrained by the reductive ontology of counterinsurgency.

In a paradox, however, Cerulli was eventually admitted into the most unlikely professional guild of the postcolonial era. This was the international team of scholars behind the monumental *UNESCO General History of Africa*.[103] The project had its genesis at the UNESCO-backed 1962 Accra Congress of Africanists, which identified the urgency of a collaborative intervention to rectify the colonial distortions of Africa's history, address the educational needs of independent African states, and meet the documentary challenge of preserving the continent's threatened archives and oral patrimony. The goal was a work that emphasized African perspectives. This antiracist effort would counter the concurrently developed *UNESCO History of Mankind*, which said relatively little about Africa, and the *Cambridge History of Africa*, which was a specialist reference work largely written by non-Africans.[104] In all these respects, the Accra proposal affirmed the historical agenda of the 1959 Congress of Negro Writers and Artists as well as the intellectual promise of Du Bois's unrealized Africana encyclopedia.[105] The new project was subsequently supported by the OAU and UNESCO, which convened the Committee of Scientific Experts on the General History of

Africa, chaired by Nigerian historian Kenneth Onwuka Dike. This committee began its work at a 1966 conference in Abidjan, Côte d'Ivoire, which established the periodization, scope, and themes of the planned survey.[106] A second 1969 meeting in Paris developed this framework, recommending that African historians predominate on the steering committee and among the authors.[107]

These sessions set the stage for the 1970 planning conference in Addis Ababa, hosted by Ethiopia's UNESCO National Commission. Established in 1960, the commission's first director was Abebe Ambatchew (figure 11.3), the grandson of *qäññazmach* Dähné and former director of the Prize Trust. His colleagues included eminent historian Täklä Ṣadeq Mekwuriya, an ex-student of *mähmher* Ras Wärq and a former Dhanaane detainee, as well as academic Haylä Mika'él Mäsgänna, Ethiopia's deputy at the UNESCO headquarters in Paris. In tandem with the relevant ministries, Abebe oversaw a range of UNESCO-sponsored and publicly funded initiatives. These

FIGURE 11.3 Abebe Ambatchew (*right*) at UNESCO General Conference, Paris (1968).

Source: Personal collection of author, courtesy Abebe Ambatchew.

included the development of Ethiopia-focused research through direct funding and sponsored conferences; the award of fellowships for Ethiopian students to study at foreign institutions; the restoration of heritage sites; and finally, the manuscript preservation project that eventually became the Ethiopian Manuscript Microfilm Library (EMML), a repository of tens of thousands of Ge'ez, Amharic, Tigrinya, and Arabic manuscripts copied from the country's church libraries, private collections, and state archives.[108] These projects integrated Ethiopia's intellectual and educational institutions into the international architecture of expert-led heritage management and its corresponding documentary regime.

Abebe's team sponsored the 1970 Committee of Experts meeting in collaboration with Aklilu Habté, now the president of Haile Selassie University.[109] At its first session, the attendees appointed Aklilu to chair the committee's steering bureau. This group included some of the most prominent African historians of the era, including Cheikh Anta Diop (Senegal), Bethwell Ogot (Kenya), J. F. Ajayi (Nigeria), Joseph Ki-Zerbo (Burkina Faso), and Amadou Hampâté Bâ (Mali). They were joined by a local delegation of specialists that included Richard Pankhurst, Sven Rubenson, Sergew Hable Selassie, Taddesse Tamrat, Muuse Galaal, Vinigi Grottanelli,[110] and Eike Haberland.[111] The team spent four days developing the eight-volume plan for the envisioned *General History*, pausing for audiences with the emperor and OAU secretary general.[112] They also elaborated what came to be the defining features of the project: first, a continental category of analysis that dismantled the territorial partitions of colonial and disciplinary knowledge, particularly with respect to North Africa and the Nile Valley; second, an explicit emphasis on African agency and knowledge, especially the inherited oral tradition; third, a revisionist periodization of decolonization, such that it began—pace Du Bois—with the 1935 Italian invasion of Ethiopia; fourth, a preference for African and African diaspora editors and authors, in an effort to address the structural inequities in the field; and fifth, a plan for two distinct editions, including an academic reference edition and an abridged popular edition, to be translated into multiple African languages.[113]

Over the ensuing decade, this vision was brought to fruition by the bureau and the newly established scientific committee. They conducted annual progress reviews through meetings at academic institutions across Africa, with one extraordinary session in Port-au-Prince, Haiti. After finalizing the authors and text of the volumes on prehistory (vol. I), antiquity (vol. II), and the colonial era (vol. VII), the group turned to the planned volume on the seventh to eleventh centuries (vol. III), edited by Mohammed El Fasi of the University of al-Qarawiyyin in Fez and Ivan Hrbek of the Oriental Institute in Prague. At the 1972 meeting in Butare, Rwanda, the bureau examined the editors' proposed structure and partial author list, and in an important intervention, asserted the unilateral right of the committee to judge the merits of nominated authors.[114] The following year, the full committee then met in Lusaka, Zambia, to review the editors' final list of prospective authors.

The chapter on Ethiopia and the Muslim world was assigned to Cerulli.[115] It is tempting to associate this nomination with Hrbek, given his similar disciplinary background and assumption of the de facto lead editorial role for the volume.[116] The two had even crossed paths at the 1962 Accra congress.[117] Looking back on these events, Aklilu recalls that Cerulli's nomination triggered an intense debate within the committee. A group of Francophone African historians led by the influential Cheikh Anta Diop raised the issue of Cerulli's record as a colonial administrator, and then argued that this fact disqualified him from inclusion in the *General History*. It was a critique Diop had previously made in the case of a similarly compromised Francophone scholar involved in the project, possibly the pied noir sociologist and UNESCO veteran Jacques Berque, who spent decades in Algerian and Moroccan colonial administration, but understood himself as an iconoclastic "mutineer within the colonial system."[118] Facing this effective internationalization of the earlier Prize Trust debate, Aklilu sought to mediate as bureau chair. In his recollection, he told the group, "We should not be like our colonial masters; we should show to them that we can forgive, and each person should be judged on their merits."[119] His position eventually won the room, and the members approved Cerulli's nomination while adopting a series of new resolutions that aimed "to associate the largest possible number of young African research workers with the project."[120]

Fifteen years later, in 1988, Cerulli's contribution to the *General History* finally appeared in print.[121] Now blind and over ninety years old, he died on September 19 that same year. It was the fiftieth anniversary of Heruy's death, to the exact day. Cerulli's final publication followed a chapter by Täklä Ṣadeq Mäkwuriya that surveyed the political, religious, and literary history of the Horn of Africa after the decline of Aksum.[122] The volume thus proved a textual reunion of sorts: the inspector of the Dhanaane concentration camp published alongside one of its former detainees, with the latter even including a generous citation of the former.[123] Seen in the long term, and perhaps outside the political and institutional pressures of the international academy, the decision of the Lusaka group to accept Cerulli as a *General History* author can be interpreted as a radical act of intellectual inclusion and testimonial justice,[124] made in full awareness of his dark past, as Aklilu later put it. The assembled scholars proved themselves singularly devoted to the rigorous collective pursuit of precise and undistorted historical truth, in dialogue with the continent's historical patrimony and in service of the future education of its citizens, translated into its many vernaculars. This undertaking welcomed all who could aid it. Their collective effort was, in short, a feast of history.

This fitful half-century reckoning illuminates the distinctiveness of colonial guilt. As these events unfolded on the international stage, Hannah Arendt reassessed the nature of guilt, responsibility, and judgment in the aftermath of the Holocaust. Initially questioning the meaning of German guilt in a society where the distinction between criminality and noncriminality had withered,[125] she subsequently attacked the concept of collective guilt.[126] In her view, there was a fundamental distinction between collective responsibility, which is a political question derived from what has been done in the name of a group, and individual guilt, which is a legal and moral question concerning the actions of a specific person. An individual might be responsible for crimes that he or she did not commit, but which were committed by a state or organization claiming to represent that individual, but such an individual could not be considered guilty of these crimes. Guilt, unlike responsibility, requires direct participation. With respect to postwar Germany, Arendt observed that those accused of genocide and crimes against humanity often elided this distinction between collective responsibility and individual guilt.[127] As she explained, "the cry 'we are all guilty' that at first hearing sounded so very noble and tempting has actually only served to exculpate to a considerable degree those who actually were guilty. Where all are guilty, nobody is. Guilt, unlike responsibility, always singles out; it is strictly personal. It refers to an act, not to intentions or potentialities."[128] Collective guilt was a shield for perpetrators.

Arendt's analysis illuminates Cerulli's postcolonial defiance. In a German echo, Cerulli argued in *Ulisse* that all modern actors were complicit in war crimes, in that they shared the Clausewitzian view that warfare was a legitimate political instrument. So envisioned, guilt appeared almost universal, and responsibility meaningless. This was a misdirection. The Ethiopian government and UNWCC had considered his personal complicity in specific war crimes and crimes against humanity, and the precise nature of his actions and inaction in Rome, Asinara, Addis Ababa, and Däbrä Berhan underpinned the case and ruling against him. The question of his individual guilt or innocence with respect to these events involved not his membership in a national collective that included all Italians, but instead his membership in the regime's colonial elite and his agency within this coordinating group. This same issue underpinned his domestic antifascist sanction process. Cerulli was in fact one of the lone surviving senior officials from the early d'Aosta administration: the duke had succumbed to disease in 1942 while detained at a British prison camp in Kenya; Ugo Cavallero had committed suicide in 1943 after refusing the RSI military command; Pietro Maletti had died in 1940 during the Italian invasion of Egypt; and Orlando Lorenzini had died in 1941 at the Battle of Kärän in Eritrea. There were few others to hold accountable for the atrocities perpetrated during the counterinsurgency of 1938–1939, during which time Cerulli twice held command responsibility as viceregal regent.[129] His universalization of guilt concealed these facts.

Yet Cerulli's concern with the crimes of others correctly highlighted the selective nature of the justice dispensed by the UNWCC. The regime's atrocities in Ethiopia categorically resembled the mass violence of the Allied bombing of Germany and Italy as well as the then-ongoing counterinsurgent colonial emergencies in Algeria and Kenya, and this kinship demonstrates the extent to which postwar international law was conditioned by the politics of victors' justice. This very point was made in 1948 by Radhabinod Pal, the dissenting Indian judge on the International Military Tribunal for the Far East: comparing the realities of European and Japanese imperialism in Asia, Pal pithily observed, "Only a lost war is a crime."[130] Though the Commission represented a groundbreaking international legal effort to address indisputably horrific events, its restriction to the crimes of the vanquished and its sometimes arbitrary treatment of these betrayed its universalist ideals.

Complicating this situation, however, is the fact that it was Cerulli and the other accused Italian war criminals—and not the Ethiopian survivors and bereaved—who benefited from the selective discretion of the UNWCC. Over the course of its five years of activity, the Commission consistently favored Italy at Ethiopia's expense for reasons of political expediency: the Ethiopian government was preemptively excluded from the founding conference where the UNWCC mandate was developed; its cases were repeatedly delayed and then restricted by procedural moves and inconsistent rulings, such that Cerulli's case was only resolved at the final meeting of the relevant committee; and it was ultimately obliged to abandon most of its cases for extralegal reasons of Cold War diplomacy. Finally, and perhaps most significantly, Cerulli evaded trial in Italy or extradition to Ethiopia, and instead enjoyed a long and distinguished political and academic career, such that he encountered Aklilu Habtäwäld at the UN General Assembly, Germachäw Täklä Hawaryat at the Accademia dei Lincei, and Nkrumah, Césaire, Diop, and Du Bois at the Accra Congress of Africanists. His Commission process and ensuing impunity epitomize the persisting coloniality of the international system. In his bold *Ulisse* critique, Cerulli denounced the instrumentalized justice that protected him.

It was for precisely this reason that the Ethiopians called the Commission discriminatory, echoing earlier criticisms of the League. The prolonged debates at Lansdowne House on the question of Ethiopian jurisdiction revealed not only the overt intrusion of Cold War realpolitik, but also the patently colonial mentality of powerbrokers like Wright and Craigie, both products of an interwar order that rested on the League framework of liberal imperialism, humanitarian interventionism, and the racialized concept of mandatory tutelage. This same mentality informed the UN founders and the postfascist Italian delegations to the Paris Peace Conference and UN General Assembly. If the Britons at the UNWCC rejected the accusations of prejudice by the Ethiopian team, their record as represented in the minutes of the Commission undermines their defense, as does their consistent opposition to their critics. When the process is viewed from an Ethiopian perspective, it suggests that the Commission had an "Africa problem" that anticipates contemporary perceptions of the International Criminal Court. Critics of the latter argue that its arbitrary dispensation of justice rests on a pessimistic view of African legal institutions, an imperial impulse couched in the language of humanitarianism, and a conception of Africans as wards rather than rights-bearing citizens. Similar problems clearly plagued the only African state to appear before the UNWCC.[131]

These neocolonial politics secured Cerulli's postcolonial fortunes. In the years after 1941, his international academic reputation hinged on his arrested legal process, his exculpatory liberal posture, and the structured domestic silence surrounding the Italian colonial past. This conjuncture foreclosed a fuller or more consequential reckoning, diminishing the impact of his denunciations on the international stage and his effective exclusion from the Ethiopian academy. As a result, he became a dominant figure in his specialist field even as he remained an indicted war criminal. This was the exceptionality of colonial guilt, which hindered the Third World project of grappling with historical violence and imagining a future free from trauma. The complexity of this memory problematic explains Cerulli's uneven reception within the African academy, from Accra to the Prize Trust and UNESCO, even as many non-African academics confidently believed him innocent or exonerated, despite the unambiguous UNWCC decision. For the latter group, he had nothing to confess or atone for; he had no personal guilt or need for fear. This collective myopia authorized his enduring refusal to bear witness.[132]

Conclusion

In the summer of 1964, William Leo Hansberry arrived in Addis Ababa. The visit crowned a lifetime of activism and research.[1] Born in Mississippi, he studied anthropology and archaeology at Harvard on the suggestion of his mentor W. E. B. Du Bois, and in 1922, he joined the faculty of Howard University, where he became a pioneering historian of African antiquity.[2] His chief interest was Ethiopia, and specifically the impact of Aksum, Kush, and Nubia on ancient Egypt, and over the next decade, he developed a new academic paradigm for understanding the African past. His goal was pan-African intellectual and political liberation. Through interdisciplinary teaching and research, he sought to challenge the distortions of racist scholarship and reconstruct the full grandeur of African history, thereby advancing the position of people of African descent worldwide.[3] In 1934, he deepened this commitment by establishing the Ethiopia Research Council, an advocacy organization focused on enhancing Black American awareness of Ethiopian affairs.[4] His colleagues at the Council included political scientist Ralph Bunche as well as Ethiopian students Mälaku Bäyyan, who attended Howard after meeting Du Bois, and Täsfay Zaphiro, who later supported Heruy, Wärqenäh Eshäté, and Una Marson at the London Legation.[5] During the Italo-Ethiopian crisis, the Council became the leading pro-Ethiopia organization in North America, as Zaphiro traveled throughout the United States meeting Black leaders and publicizing Ethiopia's struggle.[6] Hansberry coordinated its lobbying and public relations campaigns with the exiled government, proving so effective that the Italian foreign minister eventually complained to an American diplomat about the Howard professor and his "propaganda."[7]

Ethiopia's subjugation took Hansberry abroad. In 1937, he began a sabbatical at Oxford, where he pursued graduate study of Ethiopian-Nubian contacts in antiquity. His former Harvard professor Earnest Hooton attributed Hansberry's lack of an advanced degree to the fact that the latter's expertise in his area of specialization was unrivaled in North America. Although Hansberry's doctoral plans were scuttled by an unsupportive supervisor, he briefly worked with anthropologists Alfred Radcliffe-Brown and Edward Evans-Pritchard, and he additionally crossed paths with Jomo Kenyatta, then at the London School of Economics and leading the International African Friends of Ethiopia. At one point during his English sojourn, Hansberry visited the exiles in Bath, where the emperor promised to support his research with manuscripts from his personal library.[8] It was a pivotal moment. If Hansberry's professional standing and emancipatory vision of African studies were denied by the international Africanist academy, his deep learning, commitment to education, and public solidarity with Ethiopia won the esteem of the exiled emperor. Perhaps Hansberry chatted with Heruy about their shared interest in history.

Ensconced at Howard after the liberation of Ethiopia, Hansberry maintained his professional commitment to Africa and Africans. In 1953, he won a Fulbright fellowship to visit fourteen countries on the continent, with stops at archaeological sites in Ethiopia as well as Egypt and Sudan, and on his return, he received a grant from the Ethiopian government through now-ambassador Emru Zälläqä.[9] That same year, he cofounded the Africa-America Institute, dedicated to supporting African students in the United States.[10] His influence as a diasporic educator and mentor was by this time peerless. He continued to collaborate with Du Bois on the latter's Africana encyclopedia, and he trained, advised, and hosted countless African students in Washington. Some of these became prominent academics and political leaders, from J. F. Ade Ajayi and Kenneth Onwuka Dike to Nnamdi Azikiwe, Kwame Nkrumah, and Julius Nyerere. Others were the children of his former pupils, like Malaku "Chips" Bayen Jr., a jazz musician who managed Charlie Parker.[11] Despite this wide influence, Hansberry remained a relatively marginal figure within the Howard faculty and institutionalized area studies.¹² International recognition of his achievements finally came in 1964, when he was selected for the inaugural Haile Selassie Prize Trust award for African studies.

The nomination came from Mulugeta Wodajo. Like Hansberry, his life reflected the preceding years of struggle. He had spent his infancy in Gullälé alongside the family of Heruy, a longtime colleague of his father *näggadras* Wodajo Ali.¹³ After the Italian invasion, his parents and siblings were deported to Asinara, where Cerulli judged his father an irreducible.¹⁴ This decision transferred the *näggadras* to remote Longobucco, where he died of an unknown illness, separated from his family. He was forty-two years old.¹⁵ After liberation, his son Mulugeta attended Täfäri Mäkonnen School and then Columbia University. New York City radicalized Mulugeta's intellectual world, introducing him to the leading minds of the Black international. He led the African Students Association, visited Du Bois in Brooklyn Heights, and befriended Malcolm X in Harlem.¹⁶ Of the last, he recalls, "I was fascinated by what he said, and how he said it." The two discussed politics over lunches near Columbia, and joined each other in the streets to protest the 1960 Sharpeville Massacre.¹⁷ While in Washington for a meeting of Ethiopian students, Mulugeta seized the chance to visit Hansberry, who he knew through his study of Black history.¹⁸ The professor impressed him with his erudition and dignified commitment to "the African cause." After Mulugeta received his doctorate and returned to Ethiopia in 1963, he joined the university faculty and chaired the Prize Trust subcommittee for African studies.¹⁹ It was in this capacity that he nominated the Howard professor for the inaugural award.

One year after Du Bois died, Leo and Myrtle Hansberry arrived in Addis Ababa to receive the honor. The decision surprised many of the European academics at Haile Selassie University, who were largely unfamiliar with his work.²⁰ Yet as former Prize Trust director Abebe Ambatchew recalls, the criteria of the African studies committee transcended pure scholarship, and it was precisely for this reason that Hansberry—renowned as an activist-educator in African and African diaspora circles, but largely unknown in the specialist field of Ethiopian studies—was selected for the award. In Abebe's assessment, the decision was ultimately a question of "impact." The committee selected Hansberry because of his forceful advocacy at the Ethiopian Research Council and commitment to educating African students. In the local press, the trustees described him as a "torch bearer" who "opened the eyes of his fellow Americans to . . . the vast and still uncharted world of African history," and who inspired "the present leaders of Africa and through them the peoples of Africa."[21] Prize Trust historian Bärihun Käbbädä similarly characterized the professor as a *liq* who was "peerless with respect to education about African civilizations."[22] Generations of students credited him with inculcating "a new way of looking at Africa and the world, and themselves," as Maghan Keita observes.[23] Hansberry's lifelong solidarity made him a model expert.

In the Ethiopian capital, Hansberry was reunited with the emperor, who greeted him warmly in a private audience.[24] His achievements were celebrated in the local press, and at the award ceremony (figure C.1), he accepted his medal alongside writer Käbbädä Mika'él, artist Afäwärq Täklé, and the elderly Marcel Cohen, recipient of the inaugural prize for Ethiopian studies. The Howard professor thanked the Prize Trust for honoring his efforts to correct "longstanding misconceptions about Africa's place in world history and world affairs," and then delivered a lecture at Haile

FIGURE C.1 William Leo Hansberry (*third from left*), Addis Ababa (1964).

Selassie University, well-received by its students and faculty.[25] The occasion celebrated a career dedicated to Africa-focused activism, education, and research, and ultimately, the rigorous pursuit of a fuller interpretation of history that served humanity as well as truth. Looking back, daughter Gail Hansberry remembers that the award was an extremely significant moment for her father.[26] He died the following year. Five years later, the 1970 Addis Ababa meeting of the UNESCO Committee of Experts for the General History of Africa proved an impromptu international memorial for Hansberry.[27] Many of the attendees commended Abebe Ambatchew for the Prize Trust decision to recognize the Howard professor, warmly recalling the support they themselves had personally received from him.[28] Their UNESCO work would continue his vision of a unified understanding of the African past. It was a worthy tribute to an intellectual once called "the prophet without honor."[29]

In radically different ways, Hansberry and Cerulli were among the world's most influential Ethiopia experts. Yet they were political antagonists, not intellectual competitors in the academic sense envisioned by Pierre Bourdieu. They were trained in adjacent fields, as exemplified by their common connection to Harvard and Hooton, but their conceptions of the nature and purpose of Africa-focused knowledge were diametrically opposed. This disjuncture is exemplified by their clashing visions of the Ethiopian past. Like Hansberry, Cerulli was chiefly concerned with Ethiopia's ancient and "medieval" history, but he saw these as extensions of Near Eastern Christendom and the greater Mediterranean, and not fountainheads of African influence in the premodern world. Their study advanced specialist knowledge and provided intellectual armature to the colonial project, even after its political demise. For Hansberry, in contrast, ancient Ethiopia and the Nile Valley were the key to recovering Africa's misconstrued world-historical role, and the goal of the engaged researcher was the public dissemination of this emancipatory knowledge. Their conceptions of modern Ethiopia were equally discordant. Cerulli articulated a historicist and primordialist model of the Horn of Africa predicated on Abyssinian predation, perennial ethnic suffering, and the liberatory potential of Western modernity. This framework of African deficiency underpinned his commitment to empire and its tutelary epistemology. Hansberry, in contrast, understood Ethiopian society as a complex sociocultural aggregate, and linked contemporary Ethiopian suffering to the injustice of European imperialism and the discriminatory politics of the global color line. African salvation required diasporic succor, and as Ethiopians beckoned to the world, he was among the few foreign specialists who responded.[30] The disjuncture of Cerulli and Hansberry's respective choices as experts is encapsulated by their fates at the Prize Trust—the one denied, the other affirmed. These decisions suggest the moral judgment of history.[31]

Today, Heruy Wäldä Sellasé is remembered as a singular figure in Ethiopian intellectual and political history. Radio and television programs celebrate his life and contributions to Amharic literature, his books are assigned in Ethiopian high schools and universities, and reprinted editions of his histories and essays can be found in bookstores throughout the country. His manuscript writings, including a previously unpublished travel diary and a once-lost general history of Ethiopia, have recently been published for the first time. Few of his works are available in translation. As a historical actor, he is widely considered an iconic figure in the modern struggle to preserve Ethiopian sovereignty, even if this role is complicated by his lifelong proximity to the autocratic emperor and enduring commitment to the "Greater Ethiopia" nationalist project. Critics view his literary achievements as marred by these politics. But his historical prominence is indisputable. In 2023, his grave was relocated to a public monument outside Qeddus Sellasé church in Addis Ababa, where a plaque now depicts him in a cloak studded with medals. Meanwhile, his former residence in Gullälé today houses the Ethiopian Academy of Sciences, the leading research organization in the country. Its restored buildings and grounds are dedicated to a library, press, and artist residency program, and it hosts academic symposia, public workshops, and cultural events. Although most of the family property was looted during the Italian invasion, the private prayer room of the foreign minister has become a small museum of books and personal items. Contemporary Ethiopian intellectual and creative achievement literally draws on his material legacy.

The memory of Cerulli is more starkly divided. His immense personal library can today be found at the Biblioteca Apostolica Vaticana, encompassing at least three hundred Ethiopian manuscripts and more than two thousand printed volumes. Tens of thousands of archival documents related to his colonial career are preserved at the Archivio Centrale dello Stato, the Archivio Storico del Ministero dell'Africa Italiana, the Biblioteca

Apostolica Vaticana, and private archives in Ethiopia. With respect to his professional identity, the specialist field of Ethiopian studies has publicly tended toward selective amnesia and even intellectual apotheosis. In this, it has rejected the condemnation of the Prize Trust for the exoneration of the original ICES. This tendency is exemplified by Cerulli's entry in the *Encyclopaedia Aethiopica*, the standard specialist reference work. It celebrates his scholarship and Africa-related diplomacy, describes him as a "refugee" from fascism, and says nothing about his status as an indicted war criminal.[32] More broadly, specialists routinely cite Cerulli's scholarship and intellectual achievements, such that he has been torturously proposed as an exemplar of "counter-orientalism."[33] This institutionalized myopia replicates Cerulli's own position on his colonial biography, reifying and perpetuating the sanitized liberal academic image he crafted in the postcolonial era. Many in the field are invested in its false innocence.[34] In contrast to this prevailing silence are those dissenting and often Ethiopian voices who view Cerulli as a mediocre philologist, a naive ethnographer, a manuscript thief, an unprosecuted war criminal, or simply a despicable person. This disjuncture of memory—reflecting the divergent vistas of Rome and Addis Ababa—suggests the contemporary reverberations of the colonial politics of expertise.

Specialists need a better approach to the Cerulli aporia. An instructive comparison is Martin Heidegger. While the latter's involvement with National Socialism has long been acknowledged as a disquieting biographical detail, the 2014 publication of his anti-Semitic "Black Notebooks" compelled many specialists to reevaluate his philosophical system, disrupting the banal convention of acknowledging that a brilliant thinker might occasionally countenance abhorrent ideas or individuals.[35] In the assessment of Peter Trawny, the elaborate racism of Heidegger's once-private writings obliges specialists to systematically assess the "contamination" of his entire philosophy, rereading it in light of his previously unknown theorizations of world Judaism and Jewish annihilation. This collective reappraisal poses new research questions. To what extent do these anti-Semitic themes infiltrate Heidegger's published philosophical work?[36] How far beyond specific topics or problems does the intellectual contamination extend, and what remains untouched? And is it possible to fully disentangle the good and valuable from the bad and compromised? The goal, for some at least, is not exoneration or condemnation, but instead deeper and more nuanced understanding. More generally, Heidegger's anti-Semitic thinking challenges all those who engage with his work to remain "alert to its traces even where no overt marker exists."[37]

This situation offers a useful heuristic for understanding Cerulli and his scholarship. This book has not argued that his entire oeuvre is contaminated by colonial and/or fascist arguments, which in their categorical precision are distinct from the general epistemic problems of Orientalism. Instead, I have identified specific examples of weaponized scholarship, from dual-use research that informed diplomacy and policymaking to antecedent and retrospective legitimations of colonial violence in which Cerulli was directly and indirectly involved. These works are compromised by their historical politics. In the most extreme cases, they use academic tools to morally and legally exculpate their author from criminal charges, misrepresenting history through bad scholarship. The artful silences this requires suggest intellectual dishonesty, especially given Cerulli's characteristic concern for the precise detail of the historical event. These examples suggest that the remainder of Cerulli's oeuvre should be handled with care, beyond perfunctory footnotes about his complex biography. Specialists should remain attuned to the fact that Cerulli harbored the persistent colonial mentality he decried in *Ulisse*, and that this mentality informed his scholarship. Albert Memmi termed this "rot."[38] Cerulli was unrepentant, an outraged hostile witness. This is not an abstract position. Heidegger was a philosopher of little significance to the Third Reich. Cerulli rationalized and recommended killing people.

The ambiguity of academic specialists on this point stands in stark contrast with the definitive judgment of international law. The UNWCC decision to validate the Ethiopian indictment of Cerulli established an important but little-noticed legal precedent. His case was an extremely early instance of the successful application of human rights law to specifically colonial crimes. Unlike the German and Japanese war criminals identified by the Commission and subsequently tried by International Military Tribunals, Cerulli was exclusively charged with war crimes and crimes against humanity that took place in Ethiopia before the Second World War. These were strictly colonial crimes. This was a critical point, as suggested by the prolonged UNWCC jurisdictional debates about "the

Abyssinian Question." Cerulli's case involved not conventional interstate warfare but a colonial counterinsurgency fundamentally akin to its counterparts elsewhere in Africa and Asia. Nonetheless, the Commission proceeded to judge the actions of a European proconsul in Africa through the emerging legal framework of genocide, momentarily actualizing the universal implications of Raphael Lemkin's concept of group extermination.[39] For a brief instant, there was no legal or moral colonial exception. The potentially wide-ranging implications of this situation surely informed the sustained British hostility to the international adjudication of the Ethiopian cases, as parallel debates about the legality of colonial violence developed within Italy. Cerulli, meanwhile, rejected the premise of this position. In this, he resembles the German concentration camp guard imagined by Jorge Luis Borges, who remained permanently incapable of empathy with those he harmed.[40]

Within the framework of restorative justice, such intransigence prevents redress, recovery, and rehabilitation through truth-telling.[41] Evaluating the reparations claim for Germany's colonial genocide in Namibia, activist Nandiuasora Mazeingo observes, "When you have committed atrocities, you must atone by restoring your humanity and listening."[42] This very point preoccupied Aklilu Habtäwäld for the entire postliberation era, particularly with respect to his longtime adversary Cerulli. In 1946, Aklilu told the delegates to the Paris Peace Conference, "The moral burden resting upon Italy is of her own creation, and the sooner she recognizes it, the sooner she will cleanse herself. This moral burden is far greater than my ability to express and far greater than is possible to conceive for those who unlike the members of this conference have not experienced the horrors of war on their territories."[43] Though listening in the room that day, Cerulli refused this moral burden. In the judgment of one participant in these events, he remained forever like a deep-sea fish: "luminous but blind."[44] Another participant recalls that Cerulli's lack of contrition became Aklilu's decades-long fixation, as the ex-regent reached the apex of his intellectual eminence. For the foreign minister, Cerulli's defiant silence with respect to the moral burden of his past was an indication of damaged humanity. He evaded legal accountability as well as a potentially restorative reckoning of victim and perpetrator.

FIGURE C.2 Rebuilding Mädhané Aläm Church, Ankober (2020).

Source: Author's photo.

Glossary

(Amharic, Tigrinya, and Ge'ez, unless otherwise noted)

abba: Religious honorific, or general term of respect, lit. "father"
abbaa: Title of office holder or owner (Oromo)
abéto: Title or term of address for someone of importance
abun(ä): Honorific for Metropolitan of Ethiopian Orthodox Church, lit. "Our father"
afä negus: Chief justice
afä qésar: Colonial chief justice, lit. "mouth of Caesar"
agär gäzhi: Colonial governor
aläqa: Ecclesiastic title, or honorific denoting learning
arbäña: Anticolonial guerrilla, lit. "patriot"
aṣé: Term of address for emperor
askari: Colonial conscript (Amharic, Tigrinya, Italian, Arabic)
ato: Term of address for men, "Mr."
azmach: Title, usually for military leader
bäjerond: Chief treasurer
balabbat: Regional official or landowner, especially in recently subjugated territories
balambaras: Imperial title of sixth rank, lit. "head of the mountain/settlement"
banda: Colonial irregular from Ethiopia, Eritrea, or Somalia (It.); also a pejorative term for African colonial collaborator (Am.)
basha: Minor imperial and colonial title
bitwäddäd: Title, "the beloved of the emperor"
blatta: Learned title, second rank
blattén géta: Learned title, first rank

capo: Chief or leader, used widely by Italians to refer to African notables irrespective of regional, ethnic, or religious context (It.)
däbtära: Unordained clergy, scribe
däjjazmach: Imperial title of second rank, lit. "commander of the gate"
eçhägé: Abbot of Däbrä Libanos
emmahoy: Term of address for a nun
endärasé: Deputy, representative
etégé: Title of the emperor's spouse, as distinct from ruling empress
färänj: European or White foreigner, lit. "Frank"
fitawrari: Imperial title of third rank, lit. "commander of the vanguard"
governato(rato): Colonial province or district (It.)
grazmach: Imperial title of fifth rank, lit. "commander of the left"
haji: Honorific used in various Islamic contexts (Ar.)
imam: Title of leadership, used in various Islamic contexts (Ar.)
käntiba: Mayor
lej: Title for a young male noble
le'ul: Term of address for a prince, "highness"
le'ul ras: Hereditary prince of the blood
ligaba: Court official responsible for ceremonies
liq/liqawent: Church scholar(s)
liqä kahenat: Head of a church or parish, archpriest
liqä liqawent: "Head of the scholars"
liqä pappasat: Patriarch
mäkwannent: Nobility
mäl'akä ṣähay: Title of authority at Enṭoṭṭo Maryam
mälkäñña: Local official, community representative
mämher: Teacher
mär'ed azmach: Title of the ruler of Shäwa
mooti: Hereditary ruler (Or.)
musé: Term of address for foreigners, derived from "monsieur"
näggadras: Market/customs official
neburä ed: Senior ecclesiastic of Aksum Ṣeyon or Addis Aläm Maryam
negest: Queen
negus: King
negusä nägäst: Emperor, lit. "king of kings"
qadi: Judge or specialist in Islamic law (Ar.)
qäññazmach: Imperial title of fourth rank, lit. "commander of the right"
qés: Priest
ras: Imperial title of first rank, lit. "head"
ṣähafé te'ezaz: Court historian, later minister of the pen
ṣähafi: Secretary
sayyid: Honorific used in various Islamic contexts (Ar.)

shambäl: Military leader, equivalent to captain
sharif(a): Honorific for a descendent of the Prophet Muhammad (Ar.)
shaykh: Leader, used in various Islamic contexts (Ar.)
squadrista: Fascist activist and streetfighter (It.)
ulama: Muslim scholars (Ar.)
wäyzäro: Term of address for women, "Mrs."

Transliteration and Dates

Transliteration from Amharic, Tigrinya, and Ge'ez follows the *Journal of Ethiopian Studies* (Wright) system, simplified to reduce diacritics. Transliteration from Arabic follows the *International Journal of Middle East Studies* system. In cases where a toponym has a widely accepted English orthography, I use the latter.

All dates are given in the Gregorian calendar except in direct quotations and bibliographic references. In these instances, the use of the Ethiopian/Eritrean calendar is indicated by the abbreviation AM, for *amätä meherät*, or "Year of Grace." The Ethiopian/Eritrean calendar is seven or eight years behind the Gregorian calendar.

Abbreviations

Archives and Documents

ACS FG	Archivio Centrale dello Stato, Fondo Rodolfo Graziani
ACS MAI AGP	Archivio Centrale dello Stato, Fondi del Ministero dell'Africa Italiana, Direzione Generale Affari Generali e Personale
ASMAI	Archivio Storico del Ministero dell'Africa Italiana
ASMAI AP	Fondo Direzione Generale Affari Politici del Ministero dell'Africa Italiana
ASMAI GS	Archivio Segreto del Gabinetto del Ministro dell'Africa Italiana
BAV	Biblioteca Apostolica Vaticana
BCSC	Brooklyn College Library, Special Collections
BNF	Bibliothèque Nationale de France
CAB	Cabinet Office Records, National Archives (UK)
EFSA	Evangeliska Fosterlands-Stiftelsen Arkiv
EMML	Ethiopian Manuscript Microfilm Library, Saint John's University
FO	Foreign Office Records, National Archives (UK)
HRAF	Human Relations Area Files
IES	Institute of Ethiopian Studies, Manuscript Section

LNA	League of Nations Archives
LNDP	League of Nations Documents and Publications
UMAL	University of Massachusetts Amherst Libraries, Special Collections and University Archives
UNA	United Nations Archives
UNESCOA	United Nations Educational, Scientific, and Cultural Organization Archives
UN ORTSGA	Official Records of the Third Session of the United Nations General Assembly
UNWCC	United Nations Archives, Fonds United Nations War Crimes Commission

Academic Journals and Reference Works

AAAPSS	*Annals of the American Academy of Political and Social Science*
AAE	*Archivio per l'antropologia e l'etnologia*
AFLF	*Annali della facoltà di lettere e filosofia*
AHR	*American Historical Review*
AJS	*American Journal of Sociology*
ARSS	*Actes de la recherche en sciences sociales*
ASR	*African Studies Review*
BIFAO	*Bulletin de l'Institut français d'archéologie orientale*
BJMH	*British Journal for Military History*
BSAI	*Bolletino della società africana d'Italia*
BSOAS	*Bulletin of the School of Oriental and African Studies*
CEA	*Cahiers d'études africaines*
CEH	*Contemporary European History*
CIS	*Cahiers internationaux de sociologie*
CLF	*Criminal Law Forum*
CSSH	*Comparative Studies in Society and History*
EA	*Encyclopaedia Aethiopica*
EHR	*English Historical Review*
EIT	*Enciclopedia italiana di scienza, lettere ed arti* (Treccani)
EI1	*Encyclopaedia of Islam*, 1st edition
EI2	*Encyclopaedia of Islam*, 2nd edition
EJIL	*European Journal of International Law*

EJIR	European Journal of International Relations
GLFP	Georgetown Law Faculty Publications
HAR	History of Anthropology Review
IIJPS	Interventions: International Journal of Postcolonial Studies
IJAHS	International Journal of African Historical Studies
IJES	International Journal of Ethiopian Studies
IRSH	International Review of Social History
JAAH	Journal of African American History
JACS	Journal of African Cultural Studies
JAH	Journal of African History
JALHC	Journal of Afroasiatic Languages, History, and Culture
JAOS	Journal of the American Oriental Society
JBS	Journal of Black Studies
JCH	Journal of Contemporary History
JEMH	Journal of Early Modern History
JEPP	Journal of European Public Policy
JES	Journal of Ethiopian Studies
JGR	Journal of Genocide Research
JHIL	Journal of the History of International Law
JICH	Journal of Imperial and Commonwealth History
JMAS	Journal of Modern African Studies
JMIS	Journal of Modern Italian Studies
JMS	Journal of Mediterranean Studies
JNH	Journal of Negro History
JRAS	Journal of the Royal African Society
JSS	Journal of Semitic Studies
JWH	Journal of World History
JWL	Journal of World Literature
LNJ	League of Nations Journal
MFO	Mélanges de la faculté orientale
NAMSL	Nouvelles archives des missions scientifiques et littéraires
NEAS	Northeast African Studies
NJAS	Nordic Journal of African Studies
NRS	Nuova rivista storica
OPIIC	Occasional Publications of the India International Center
PBA	Proceedings of the British Academy
PJCP	Puncta: Journal of Critical Phenomenology

PSAS	*Proceedings of the Seminar for Arabian Studies*
RHMC	*Revue d'histoire moderne et contemporaine*
RISI	*Rivista italiana di storia internazionale*
RRAL	*Rendiconti della Reale Accademia dei Lincei*
RSE	*Rassegna di studi etiopici*
RSO	*Rivista degli studi orientali*
RSPI	*Rivista di studi politici internazionali*
TWQ	*Third World Quarterly*
UTLJ	*University of Toronto Law Journal*

Notes

Introduction

1. For recollections, see Giuliano Cora, "Il trattato italo-etiopico del 1928," *RSPI* 15, no. 2 (1948): 205–226; Enrico Cerulli, "Giuliano Cora e l'Etiopia," *RSPI* 36, no. 1 (1969): 18–24; and Haylä Sellasé, *My Life and Ethiopia's Progress, Volume 1: 1892-1937*, trans. Edward Ullendorff (New York: Oxford University Press, 1976), 145–151. More generally, see Giuseppe Vedovato, *Gli accordi italo-etiopici dell'agosto 1928* (Florence: Poligrafico Toscano, 1956).
2. Cf. Märse'é Hazän Wäldä Qirqos, የሐያኛው ክፍለ ዘመን መባቻ፡ የመጀ ታሪክ ትዝታዬ ካየሁትና ከሰማሁት 1896-1922 (አዲስ አበባ፡ አዲስ አበባ ዩኒቨርሲቲ ፕሬስ, 1999 ዓም), 344–345; IES Ms. 1996, the diary of *aläqa* Kenfé; and "ስለ ቅዱስ ጊዮርጊስ በዓል አከባበር," ብርሃንና ሰላም, February 7, 1929.
3. Giuseppe Borghetti, "Il trattato italo-abissino," *Italia coloniale* 5, no. 9 (1928): 175–176; and Roberto Cantalupo, "La politica del regime con l'Impero etiopico," *Corriere della sera*, August 7, 1928.
4. Giuliano Cora, "Un diplomatico durante l'era fascista," *Storia e politica* 5 (1966): 92; Vedovato, *Accordi*, 157–163; Asfa-Wossen Asserate, *King of Kings: The Triumph and Tragedy of Emperor Haile Selassie I of Ethiopia* (London: Haus, 2015), 69–72; and Fantahun Ayele, "The Life of *däǧǧač abba* Wəqaw Bərru: Some Notes on Sirak's Manuscript (Addis Ababa, Institute of Ethiopian Studies, Ms 400)," *Africa* 3, no. 2 (2021): 19–34.
5. Heruy Wäldä Sellasé, ዋዜማ፡ በማግሥቱ የኢትዮጵያን ነገሥታት የታሪክ በዓል ለማክበር (አዲስ አበባ፡ ጎሐ ጽባሕ, 1921 ዓም); and መጽሐፈ ቅኔ፣ ዘደዎምት ወደጋርት ሊቃውንቲሃ ወማዕምራኒሃ ለኢትዮጵያ (አዲስ አበባ፡ 1918 ዓም).

6. The 1889 Treaty of Weçhalé provoked war between Italy and Ethiopia after differences between the Italian and Amharic versions were discovered: Sven Rubenson, "The Protectorate Paragraph of the Wiçhalē Treaty," *JAH* 5, no. 2 (1964): 243–283.
7. Cora, "Il trattato italo-etiopico," 213–214; and Vedovato, *Accordi*, 96.
8. Edward Said, *Orientalism* (New York: Vintage, 1977). The literature is now immense. For overviews, see Wael Hallaq, *Restating Orientalism: A Critique of Modern Knowledge* (New York: Columbia University Press, 2018); and Edmund Burke III and David Prochaska, eds., *Genealogies of Orientalism: History, Theory, Politics* (Lincoln: University of Nebraska Press, 2009).
9. Daniel Varisco, *Reading Orientalism: Said and the Unsaid* (Seattle: University of Washington Press, 2007).
10. Case studies include Henning Trüper, *Orientalism, Philology, and the Illegibility of the Modern World* (London: Bloomsbury Academic, 2020); Peter Gran, *The Persistence of Orientalism: Anglo-American Historians and Modern Egypt* (Syracuse, NY: Syracuse University Press, 2020); Aamir Mufti, *Forget English! Orientalisms and World Literature* (Cambridge, MA: Harvard University Press, 2016); Zachary Lockman, *Field Notes: The Making of Middle East Studies in the United States* (Stanford, CA: Stanford University Press, 2016); Alain Messaoudi, *Les arabisants et la France coloniale 1780–1930* (Lyon, France: ENS Éditions, 2015); Edmund Burke III, *The Ethnographic State: France and the Invention of Moroccan Islam* (Berkeley: University of California Press, 2014); Alfrid Bustanov, *Soviet Orientalism and the Creation of Central Asian Nations* (New York: Routledge, 2014); Karla Mallette, *European Modernity and the Arab Mediterranean: Toward a New Philology and a Counter-Orientalism* (Philadelphia: University of Pennsylvania Press, 2010); Suzanne Marchand, *German Orientalism in the Age of Empire: Religion, Race, and Scholarship* (New York: Cambridge University Press, 2009); and Reynaldo Ileto, *Knowing America's Colony: A Hundred Years from the Philippine War* (Manoa: University of Hawai'i at Manoa, 1999).
11. Marcus Keller and Javier Irigoyen-García, eds., *The Dialectics of Orientalism in Early Modern Europe* (New York: Palgrave Macmillan, 2018); Sanjay Subrahmanyam, *Europe's India: Words, People, Empires, 1500–1800* (Cambridge, MA: Harvard University Press, 2017); Charles Burnett, Alastair Hamilton, and Jan Loop, eds., *The Teaching and Learning of Arabic in Early Modern Europe* (Leiden, Netherlands: Brill, 2017); Urs App, *The Birth of Orientalism* (Philadelphia: University of Pennsylvania Press, 2010); Robert Wilkinson, *Orientalism, Aramaic, and Kabbalah in the Catholic Reformation: The First Printing of the Syriac New Testament* (Leiden, Netherlands: Brill, 2007); and Alastair Hamilton, *The Copts and the West, 1439–1822: The European Discovery of the Egyptian Church* (New York: Oxford University Press, 2006). On *philologia sacra* and Catholic Orientalism, see Daniel Stolzenberg, "Les 'langues orientales' et les racines de l'orientalisme académique: une enquête préliminaire," *Dix-septième siècle* 268 (2015): 409–426; and Zoltán Biedermann, "Querying the Origins of Orientalism: Recent Approaches to the History of Representations," *Ler História*, 74 (2019): 261–275.
12. In particular, see Sadhana Naithani, *In Quest of Indian Folktales: Pandit Ram Gharib Chaube and William Crooke* (Bloomington: Indiana University Press, 2006); and

Shahid Amin, "The Marginal Jotter: Scribe Chaube and the Making of the Great Linguistic Survey of India c. 1890–1920," *OPIIC* 27 (2011): 1–17. See also Matteo Salvadore, James De Lorenzi, and Deresse Ayenachew Woldetsadik, *The Many Lives of Täsfa Ṣeyon: An Ethiopian Intellectual in Early Modern Rome* (New York: Cambridge University Press, 2024); Aurélien Girard, "Was an Eastern Scholar Necessarily a Cultural Broker in Early Modern Europe? Faustus Naironus (1628–1711), the Christian East, and Oriental Studies," *PBA* 225 (2019): 240–263; John-Paul Ghobrial, "The Life and Hard Times of Solomon Negri," in *Arabic in Early Modern Europe*, ed. Burnett, Hamilton, and Loop, 310–331; and John-Paul Ghobrial, "The Archive of Orientalism and Its Keepers: Re-Imagining the Histories of Arabic Manuscripts in Early Modern Europe," *Past and Present* 230, supplement 11 (2016): 90–111.

13. Hallaq, *Restating Orientalism*; and Mufti, *Forget English!* See also George Steinmetz, *The Colonial Origins of Modern Social Thought: French Sociology and the Overseas Empire* (Princeton, NJ: Princeton University Press, 2023).
14. For surveys, see Christine Laurière and André Mary, eds., *Ethnologues en situations coloniales* (Paris: Carnets de Bérose, 2019); and Helen Tilley and Robert Gordon, eds., *Ordering Africa: Anthropology, European Imperialism, and the Politics of Knowledge* (Manchester, UK: Manchester University Press, 2007). On predisciplinary forms of ethnographic description, see Frederico Delgado Rosa and Han Vermeulen, eds., *Ethnographers Before Malinowski: Pioneers of Anthropological Fieldwork 1870–1922* (New York: Berghahn, 2022); and Han Vermeulen, *Before Boas: The Genesis of Ethnography and Ethnology in the German Enlightenment* (Lincoln: University of Nebraska Press, 2015). On sociology, see George Steinmetz, ed., *Sociology and Empire: The Imperial Entanglements of a Discipline* (Durham, NC: Duke University Press, 2013).
15. Susannah Heschel and Umar Ryad, eds., *The Muslim Reception of European Orientalism: Reversing the Gaze* (New York: Routledge, 2018); François Pouillon and Jean-Claude Vatin, eds., *Après l'orientalisme: L'Orient créé par l'Orient* (Paris: Karthala, 2011); and Ronen Raz, "The Transparent Mirror: Arab Intellectuals and Orientalism, 1798–1950" (PhD diss., Princeton University, 1997).
16. Said Hassan and Abdullah Omran, "The Reception of the Brill Encyclopedia of Islam: An Egyptian Debate on the Credibility of Orientalism (1930–1950)," in *Reception of Orientalism*, ed. Heschel and Ryad, 61–79; and Umar Ryad, "'An Oriental Orientalist': Aḥmad Zakī Pasha (1868–1934), Egyptian Statesman and Philologist in the Colonial Age," *Philological Encounters* 3 (2018): 129–166.
17. Tarek El-Ariss, "On Cooks and Crooks: Aḥmad Fāris al-Shidyāq and the Orientalists in England and France (1840s–1850s)," in *Reception of Orientalism*, ed. Heschel and Ryad, 14–18.
18. Katalin Franciska Rac, "Arabic Literature for the Colonizer and Colonized: Ignaz Golziher and Hungary's Eastern Politics (1878–1918)," in *Reception of Orientalism*, ed. Heschel and Ryad, 80–102; Susannah Heschel, "Orientalist Triangulations: Jewish Scholarship on Islam as a Response to Christian Europe," in *Reception of Orientalism*, ed. Heschel and Ryad, 147–167; Mehdi Sajid, "A Muslim Convert to Christianity as an Orientalist in Europe: The Case of the Moroccan Franciscan Jean-Mohammed

Abdeljalil (1904–1979)," in *Reception of Orientalism*, ed. Heschel and Ryad, 209–232; and Hallaq, *Restating Orientalism*, 138–178.

19. David Kennedy, *A World of Struggle: How Power, Law, and Expertise Shape Global Political Economy* (Princeton, NJ: Princeton University Press, 2016). See also Timothy Mitchell, *Rule of Experts: Egypt, Techno-Politics, Modernity* (Berkeley: University of California Press, 2002); and Christina Boswell, "The Political Functions of Expert Knowledge: Knowledge and Legitimation in European Union Immigration Policy," *JEPP* 15, no. 4 (2008): 471–488.

20. Keith David Watenpaugh, *Bread from Stones: The Middle East and the Making of Modern Humanitarianism* (Berkeley: University of California Press, 2015); Poul Duedahl, "Selling Mankind: UNESCO and the Invention of Global History, 1945–1976," *JWH* 22, no. 1 (2011): 101–133; and Roger Normand and Sarah Zaidi, *Human Rights at the UN: The Political History of Universal Justice* (Bloomington: Indiana University Press, 2008).

21. Mark Lewis, *The Birth of the New Justice: The Internationalization of Crime and Punishment, 1919–1950* (New York: Oxford University Press, 2014), esp. 78–121; and Berit Bliesemann de Guevara, ed., "Knowledge Production in Conflict: The International Crisis Group," special issue, *TWQ* 35, no. 4 (2013).

22. David Price, *Cold War Anthropology: The CIA, the Pentagon, and the Growth of Dual Use Anthropology* (Durham, NC: Duke University Press, 2016); Montgomery McFate and Janice Laurence, eds., *Social Science Goes to War: The Human Terrain System in Iraq and Afghanistan* (New York: Oxford University Press, 2015); Robert Albro et al., *Anthropologists and the Securityscape: Ethics, Practice, and Professional Identity* (Walnut Creek, CA: Left Coast Press, 2012); and Laura McNamara and Robert Rubinstein, eds., *Dangerous Liaisons: Anthropologists and the National Security State* (Santa Fe, NM: School for Advanced Research Press, 2011).

23. Florian Wagner, *Colonial Internationalism and the Governmentality of Empire, 1893–1982* (New York: Cambridge University Press, 2022); and Tiago Saraiva, *Fascist Pigs: Technoscientific Organisms and the History of Fascism* (Cambridge, MA: MIT Press, 2016).

24. Cf. Talal Asad, "From the History of Colonial Anthropology to the Anthropology of Western Hegemony," in *Colonial Situations: Essays on the Contextualization of Ethnographic Knowledge*, ed. George Stocking (Madison: University of Wisconsin Press, 1991), 314–324; and Herbert Lewis, *In Defense of Anthropology: An Investigation of the Critique of Anthropology* (New Brunswick, NJ: Transaction, 2013).

25. Adom Getachew, *Worldmaking After Empire: The Rise and Fall of Self-Determination* (Princeton, NJ: Princeton University Press, 2019); Mark Mazower, *No Enchanted Palace: The End of Empire and the Ideological Origins of the United Nations* (Princeton, NJ: Princeton University Press, 2009); and Antony Anghie, *Imperialism, Sovereignty, and the Making of International Law* (New York: Cambridge University Press, 2004).

26. Sean Andrew Wempe, *Revenants of the German Empire: Colonial Germans, Imperialism, and the League of Nations* (New York: Oxford University Press, 2019); and Susan Pederson, *The Guardians: The League of Nations and the Crisis of Empire* (New York: Oxford University Press, 2015).

27. Jessica Lynne Pearson, "Defending Empire at the United Nations: The Politics of International Colonial Oversight in the Era of Decolonisation," *JICH* 45, no. 3 (2017):

525–549; and Neta Crawford, "Decolonization Through Trusteeship: The Legacy of Ralph Bunche," in *Trustee for the Human Community: Ralph J. Bunche, the United Nations, and the Decolonization of Africa*, ed. Robert Hill and Edmond Keller (Athens: Ohio University Press, 2010), 93–115.

28. Freddy Foks, "Bronislaw Malinowski, 'Indirect Rule,' and the Colonial Politics of Functionalist Anthropology, ca. 1925–1940," *CSSH* 60, no. 1 (2018): 35–57; and Mark Lamont, "Malinowski and the 'Native Question,'" in *Anthropologists and Their Traditions Across National Borders*, ed. Regna Darnell and Frederick Gleach (Lincoln: University of Nebraska Press, 2008), 69–110. See also Miguel Bandeira Jerónimo, "'Imperial Internationalisms' in the 1920s: The Shaping of Colonial Affairs at the League of Nations," *JICH* 48, no. 5 (2020): 866–891.

29. Carol Anderson, *Bourgeois Radicals: The NAACP and the Struggle for Colonial Liberation, 1941-1960* (New York: Cambridge University Press, 2014). See also Edgardo Krebs, "Popularizing Anthropology, Combatting Racism: Alfred Métraux at the UNESCO Courier," in *The History of UNESCO: Global Actions and Impacts*, ed. Poul Duedahl (New York: Palgrave, 2016), 29–48; and Michelle Brattain, "Race, Racism, and Antiracism: UNESCO and the Politics of Presenting Science," *AHR* 112, no. 5 (2007): 1386–1413.

30. Chloé Maurel, "L'Histoire générale de l'Afrique de l'UNESCO: Un projet de coopération intellectuelle transnationale d'esprit afro-centré (1964-1999)," *CEA* 3, no. 215 (2014): 715–737; and more broadly, Mamadou Diouf, *L'Afrique dans le temps du monde* (Sète, France: Ròt-Bòt-Krik, 2023).

31. In this, the present work follows Anouar Abdel-Malek, "Orientalism in Crisis," *Diogenes* 11, no. 44 (1963): 103–140.

32. In particular, see Laleh Khalili, *Time in the Shadows: Confinement in Counterinsurgencies* (Stanford, CA: Stanford University Press, 2013). On imperial repertoires, see Jane Burbank and Fred Cooper, *Empires in World History: Power and the Politics of Difference* (Princeton, NJ: Princeton University Press, 2010).

33. Julian Go, *Policing Empires: Militarization, Race, and the Imperial Boomerang in Britain and the US* (New York: Oxford University Press, 2024).

34. Thijs Brocades Zaalberg and Bart Luttikhuis, eds., *Empire's Violent End: Comparing Dutch, British, and French Wars of Decolonization, 1945-1962* (Ithaca, NY: Cornell University Press, 2022).

35. Darryl Li, "From Exception to Empire: Sovereignty, Carceral Circulation, and the 'Global War on Terror,'" in *Ethnographies of U.S. Empire*, ed. Carole McGranahan and John Collins (Durham, NC: Duke University Press, 2018), 456–475; and Fabian Klose, *Human Rights in the Shadow of Colonial Violence: The Wars of Independence in Kenya and Algeria*, trans. Dona Geyer (Philadelphia: University of Pennsylvania Press, 2013), 92–137.

36. Jacob Dlamini, *The Terrorist Album: Apartheid's Insurgents, Collaborators, and the Security Police* (Cambridge, MA: Harvard University Press, 2020).

37. Vicente Rafael, *Motherless Tongues: The Insurgency of Language Amid Wars of Translation* (Durham, NC: Duke University Press, 2016); Martin Thomas, *Empires of Intelligence: Security Services and Colonial Disorder After 1919* (Berkeley: University of California

Press, 2008); and Ranajit Guha, "The Prose of Counter-Insurgency," in *Selected Subaltern Studies*, ed. Ranajit Guha and Gayatri Chakravorty Spivak (New York: Oxford University Press, 1988), 45–86.
38. Price, *Cold War Anthropology*, xiv–xx.
39. For a key statement, see Delmos Jones, "Social Responsibility and the Belief in Basic Research: An Example from Thailand," *Current Anthropology* 12 (1971): 347–350.
40. Achille Mbembe, *Necropolitics*, trans. Steven Corcoran (Durham, NC: Duke University Press, 2019).
41. Benoît de L'Estoile, "Enquêter en 'situation coloniale': Politique de la population, gouvernementalité modernisatrice et 'sociologie engagée' en Afrique équatoriale française," *CEA* 228 (2017): 863–919; Jean Copans, "Leiris et Balandier face à la situation coloniale des années 1950. Entre dévoilements socio-politiques et redéfinitions disciplinaires," *Raison présente* 199 (2016): 61–73; Steinmetz, *Colonial Origins*, 271–314; Foks, "Malinowski"; and Lamont, "Malinowski."
42. Edward Ullendorff, review of *Somalia. Scritti vari editi ed inediti. I.*, by Enrico Cerulli, *BSOAS* 21, no. 2 (1958): 431.
43. Anna Laura Stoler, *Duress: Imperial Durabilities in Our Times* (Durham, NC: Duke University Press, 2016).
44. Cf. Abdullahi Ahmed An-Naim, *Decolonizing Human Rights* (New York: Cambridge University Press, 2021); Steven Jensen, *The Making of International Human Rights: The 1960s, Decolonization, and the Reconstruction of Global Values* (New York: Cambridge University Press, 2016); Roland Burke, *Decolonization and the Evolution of International Human Rights* (Philadelphia: University of Pennsylvania Press, 2010); and Samuel Moyn, *The Last Utopia: Human Rights in History* (Cambridge, MA: Harvard University Press, 2010).
45. Michel-Rolph Trouillot, *Silencing the Past: Power and the Production of History* (Boston: Beacon, 2015).
46. I thank Manan Ahmed for calling my attention to this point.
47. Mallette, *European Modernity*, 158.
48. I thank Alessandro Triulzi for suggesting this phrasing.
49. On the colonial politics of Cerulli's post-1941 Mediterranean scholarship, see Andrea Celli, *Dante and the Mediterranean Comedy: From Muslim Spain to Post-Colonial Italy* (Cham, Germany: Palgrave, 2022), 27–74.
50. With respect to Ethiopian intellectual history, it complements the recent academic interest in the work of Asräs Yänésäw: Messay Kebede, "Return to the Source: Asres Yenesew and the West," *Diogenes* 59, nos. 3–4 (2014): 60–71; and Teshale Tibebu, "Modernity, Eurocentrism, and Radical Politics in Ethiopia, 1961–1991," *African Identities* 6, no. 4 (2008): 345–371.
51. Serawit Debele, "The Politics of 'Queer Reading' an Ethiopian Saint and Discovering Precolonial Queer Africans," *JACS* 34, no. 1 (2022): 98–110; and Yirga Gelaw Woldeyes, "Colonial Rewriting of African History: Misinterpretations and Distortions in Belcher and Kleiner's *Life and Struggles of Walatta Petros*," *JALHC* 9, no. 2 (2020): 133–216.

52. On this approach, see Hallaq, *Restating Orientalism*. For the application of tradition-based scholarship as social theory, see Syed Farid Alatas, *Applying Ibn Khaldūn: The Recovery of a Lost Tradition in Sociology* (New York: Routledge, 2014); and for a parallel analysis, Delmos Jones, "Towards a Native Anthropology," *Human Organization* 29, no. 4 (1970): 251–259.
53. Michael Ebner, *Ordinary Violence in Mussolini's Italy* (New York: Cambridge University Press, 2011); and Mimmo Franzinelli, *Squadristi. Protagonisti e tecniche della violenza fascista 1919-1922* (Milan: Mondadori, 2003). For a comparative theorization, see Robert Paxton, *The Anatomy of Fascism* (New York: Knopf, 2004), 148–171.

1. The Power of Tradition

1. Giorgio Levi Della Vida, "Omaggio ad Enrico Cerulli," *Oriente moderno* 43, nos. 10/12 (1963): 795.
2. On Loränsiyos Wäldä Iyäsus, see Enrico Cerulli, *Folk Literature of the Galla of Southern Abyssinia* (Cambridge, MA: African Department of the Peabody Museum of Harvard University, 1922), 14, and passim; his "La seconda spedizione Bottego nei racconti galla," *BSAI* 36 (1917): 25; and Alessandro Triulzi, "Africani in Italia: La memoria e l'archivio," *Meridione* 2 (2010): 30–50. On Sängal Wärqenäh, see Giuseppe Puglisi, *Chi e'? dell' Eritrea 1952. Dizionario biografico con una cronologia* (Asmara: Agenzia Regina, 1952), 273; and Renato Paoli, *Nella colonia Eritrea* (Milan: Treves, 1908), 67–68. A fourth and less significant collaborator was *lej* Haylä Maryam Gugsa Dargé, the grandson of *ras* Dargé Sahlä Sellasé: see Cerulli, *Folk Literature*, 13; Heruy Wäldä Sellasé, የሕይወት ታሪክ *(Biographie)* በኋላ ዘመን ለሚነሡ ልጆች ማስታወቂያ (አዲስ አበባ: ተፈሪ መኰንን ማተሚያ ቤት, 1915 ዓም), 86; and Bairu Tafla, "Ras Dargé Sahlä-Sellasé, c 1827–1900," *JES* 13, no. 2 (1975): 17–35.
3. Cerulli, *Folk Literature*. For an assessment, see Desalegn Seyum, "E. Cerulli's *Folk Literature of the Galla of Southern Abyssinia*: A Critical Evaluation," (Master's thesis, Addis Ababa University, 1985); and more broadly, Tesfaye Tolessa, "A History of Oromo Literature and Identity Issues, c. 1840–1991" (PhD diss., Addis Ababa University, 2019).
4. Enrico Cerulli, "L'Islam nei regni galla indipendenti," *BSAI* 35 (1916): 113–119; "La poesia popolare amarica," *BSAI* 35 (1916): 172–178; and "La seconda spedizione Bottego."
5. Heruy Wäldä Sellasé, የኢትዮጵያ ልዑካን ቡድን በአውሮጳና መካከለኛው ምሥራቅ (1903 ዓም) (አዲስ አበባ: የኢትዮጵያ አካዳሚ ፕሬስ, 2009 ዓም), with a note about his passage through Naples on 232; and በኢትዮጵያ የሚገኙ የመጻሕፍት ቁጥር (አዲስ አበባ: 1904 ዓም), unpaginated introduction.
6. There were at least two other delegations: on the Franco-Belgian delegation and Italian delegation, see Märse'é Hazän Wäldä Qirqos, የዘመን ታሪክ ትዝታዬ ካየሁትና ከሰማሁት (አዲስ አበባ: አዲስ አበባ ዩኒቨርሲቲ ፕሬስ, 1999 ዓም), 220; but cf. Gäbrä Egzi'abhér Elyas, *Prowess, Piety, and Politics: The Chronicle of Abeto Iyasu and Empress Zewditu of Ethiopia,*

1909-1930, trans. Reidulf Molvaer (Cologne, Germany: Rüdiger Köppe Verlag, 1994), 397, which also lists a German delegation. For the context of these missions, see Massimo Zaccaria, "La lunga strada verso Ginevra. L'Etiopia e la Conferenza della Pace di Parigi," *RISI* 2, no. 1 (2019): 31–54; Jakob Zollmann, "Ethiopia, International Law and the First World War: Considerations of Neutrality and Foreign Policy by the European Powers, 1840–1919," in *The First World War from Tripoli to Addis Ababa (1911–1924)*, ed. Shiferaw Bekele et al. (Addis Ababa: Centre français des études éthiopiennes, 2018), https://books.openedition.org/cfee/1311?lang=en; and William Shack, "Ethiopia and Afro-Americans: Some Historical Notes, 1920–1970," *Phylon* 35, no. 2 (1974): 142–155.

7. Mahtämä Sellasé Wäldä Mäsqäl, "የኢትዮጵያ ባህል ጥናት፤ ቼ በለው፤" *JES* 7, no. 2 (1969): 245. In the teknonymic culture of horse naming, the perceived qualities of the subject are ascribed to his horse, who becomes the progeny of the subject.

8. "Une Mission Abyssine a Paris," *Le Temps*, May 20, 1919; "The Horizon," *The Crisis* 18, no. 5 (1919): 259; letter from Polk to Wilson, dated July 8, 1919, in *The Papers of Woodrow Wilson*, ed. Arthur Link and David Hirst (Princeton, NJ: Princeton University Press, 1989), 61:406; and British Foreign Office report on "Abyssinia and the League," dated August 14, 1919, LNA.

9. "The King and Ethiopia: Abyssinian Mission at the Palace," *The Times*, June 13, 1919; "Abyssinian Mission Here on Mauretania to Congratulate America on Victory," *New York Times*, July 6, 1919; "Greet Abyssinian Mission: State Department Officials Receive Delegation Sent to the President," *New York Times*, July 8, 1919; and letter from Polk to Wilson, dated July 8, 1919, and letter from Long to Tumulty, dated July 12, 1919, both in *Papers of Woodrow Wilson*, ed. Link and Hirst, 61:406, 470–474.

10. David Levering Lewis, *W. E. B. Du Bois: A Biography* (New York: Holt, 2009), 1:579–580, and 2:17–19.

11. "Abyssinians Visit City," *New York Sun*, August 1, 1919; "Club Bars Heir to Abyssinian Throne: National Democratic Organization Cancels Dinner After Learning Guests Are Black," *New York Times*, August 4, 1919; and "Black Ban Put on Abyssinians: Envoys from Emperor Are Deprived of Peace Feast in Democratic Club," *New York Sun*, August 4, 1919.

12. For accounts, see Roi Ottley, *New World A-Coming: Inside Black America* (New York: Houghton Mifflin, 1943), 106–107; *The Friends of Ethiopia in America* (New York: 1935), 4; and "Abyssinian Heir Ends Visit Here," *New York Times*, August 5, 1919. On this meeting, see Nadia Nurhussein, *Black Land: Imperial Ethiopianism and African America* (Princeton, NJ: Princeton University Press, 2019), 4, 8, 146; and Joseph Harris, *African-American Reactions to War in Ethiopia, 1936-1941* (Baton Rouge: Louisiana State University Press, 1994), 4–6.

13. *Friends of Ethiopia*, 4.

14. "The Horizon," *The Crisis* 8, no. 5 (1919): 258–259. Du Bois attempted to contact the delegation, but later asserted that his first "direct communication" with Ethiopia came in 1930: letter from Du Bois to Ellis, dated July 8, 1919; letter from Du Bois to

1. THE POWER OF TRADITION 305

Gäbru Dästa, dated May 26, 1921; and memorandum by Du Bois for Mälaku Bäyyan and Gäbru Dästa, dated August 14, 1930, all in Du Bois Papers, UMAL.
15. "Abyssinian Heir Ends Visit Here," *New York Times*, August 5, 1919.
16. Hamid Dabashi, *Reversing the Colonial Gaze: Persian Travelers Abroad* (New York: Cambridge University Press, 2020), 9.
17. Heruy Wäldä Sellasé, ወዳጄ ልቤና ሌሎችም (አዲስ አበባ: አዲስ አበባ ዩኒቨርሲቲ ፕሬስ, 2000 ዓም), 33: "ያ ወዳጄ ልቤም ከእኔ ጋር ነበረና ወጥተን እንሒድ እንጂ ለማኝ ይመሰል ፍርፋሪ ስንለቅም ልናድር ነውን አለኝ፡፡"
18. Marilyn Lake and Henry Reynolds, *Drawing the Global Colour Line: White Men's Countries and the International Challenge of Racial Equality* (New York: Cambridge University Press, 2008), 284–309; and Erez Manela, *The Wilsonian Moment: Self-Determination and the International Origins of Anticolonial Nationalism* (New York: Oxford University Press, 2007).
19. For Pierre Bourdieu, "The scientific field owes its main characteristics to the fact that the producers generally have no other possible clients than their direct competitors." See his "Le champ scientifique," *ARSS* 2, nos. 2–3 (1976): 88–104.
20. Francesca Orsini and Laetitia Zecchini, "The Locations of (World) Literature: Perspectives from Africa and South Asia," *JWL* 4, no. 1 (2019): 1–12; and Aamir Mufti, *Forget English! Orientalisms and World Literature* (Cambridge, MA: Harvard University Press, 2016), 99–146. See also Donald McKenzie, *Bibliography and the Sociology of Texts* (New York: Cambridge University Press, 2004).
21. On the distinction between conclave and public history, see Dipesh Chakrabarty, *The Calling of History: Sir Jadunath Sarkar and His Empire of Truth* (Chicago: University of Chicago Press, 2015).
22. For biographies, see Sännayt Täklämaryam, "ብላቴን ጌታ ኅሩይ ወልደ ሥላሴ ማን ነበሩ?" in Heruy Wäldä Sellasé, የኢትዮጵያ ታሪክ፡ ከንግሥት ሳባ እስከ ታላቁ የአድዋ ድል (አዲስ አበባ: ሥናይት ተከለማርያም, 2006), 16–23; Bahru Zewde, *Pioneers of Change in Ethiopia: The Reformist Intellectuals of the Early Twentieth Century* (Athens: Ohio University Press, 2002), 70–73; and James De Lorenzi, *Guardians of the Tradition: Historians and Historical Writing in Ethiopia and Eritrea* (Rochester, NY: University of Rochester Press, 2015), 94–113.
23. Sännayt Täklämaryam, "ኅሩይ ወልደ ሥላሴ," 10.
24. Heruy Wäldä Sellasé, የሕይወት ታሪክ, 67: "አምላኪ ልጅ የሰጠኝ እንደሆን ለትምህርት ወደ ከተማ አስደዋለሁ እንጂ በባላገር አላኖረውም፡፡"
25. Gäbrä Sellasé Wäldä Aregay, ታሪክ ዘመን ዘዳግማዊ ምኔልክ ንጉሠ ነገሥት ዘኢትዮጵያ (አዲስ አበባ: አርቲስቲክ ማተሚያ ቤት, 1959 ዓም), 96–97.
26. Märse'é Hazän Wäldä Qirqos, unpublished manuscript, 4; and Heruy Wäldä Sellasé, የሕይወት ታሪክ, 98.
27. Märse'é Hazän Wäldä Qirqos, *Of What I Saw and Heard: The Last Years of Emperor Menelik II and the Brief Rule of Iyassu*, trans. Hailu Habtu (Addis Ababa: Centre Français des Études Éthiopiennes, 2004), 15.
28. Heruy Wäldä Sellasé, የሕይወት ታሪክ, 73; and Märse'é Hazän Wäldä Qirqos, unpublished manuscript, 181, 189.

29. Adrien Zervos, *L'empire d'Éthiopie: Le miroir de l'Éthiopie moderne, 1906–1935* (Alexandria: Imprimerie de l'École professionnelle des frères, 1936), 118.
30. Gustav Arén, *Envoys of the Gospel in Ethiopia: In the Steps of the Evangelical Pioneers, 1898–1936* (Stockholm: EFS Förlaget, 1999), 122–126.
31. Mahtämä Sellasé Wäldä Mäsqäl, "ቼ በለው," 283; Heruy Wäldä Sellasé, የሕይወት ታሪክ, 91; and Bairu Tafla, "Three Portraits: Ato Aṣmä Giyorgis, Ras Gobäna Dači and Ṣähafé Tezaz Gäbrä Selassé," *JES* 5, no. 2 (1967): 133–138.
32. Mahtämä Sellasé Wäldä Mäsqäl, ዝክረ ነገር (አዲስ አበባ፡ አርቲስቲክ ማተሚያ ቤት, 1962 ዓም), 646; and Märse'é Hazän Wäldä Qirqos, unpublished manuscript, 397–398.
33. Sännayt Täklämaryam, "ንሩይ ወልደ ሥላሴ," 11: "ብሩህ ምሁርነት"
34. Heruy Wäldä Sellasé, ed., መጽሐፈ ቅኔ፣ ዘቀደምት ወደኃርት ሊቃውንቲሃ ወመዕምራኒሃ ለኢትዮጵያ (አዲስ አበባ፡ 1918 ዓም), unpaginated Ge'ez introduction. A third collaborator on this project was *aläqa* Haylä Sellasé of Addis Ababa: Bairu Tafla, "Three Portraits," 136.
35. This chronology is based on "ከቡር ብላቴን ጌታ ኀሩይ ስለ ሹመት," ብርሃንና ሰላም, April 23, 1931; and Zervos, *Éthiopie*, 118.
36. Heruy Wäldä Sellasé, የኢትዮጵያ ልዑካን ቡድን በአውሮጳና መካከሎኛው ምሥራቅ; and የመጻሕፍት ቆጥር, unpaginated introduction.
37. Asfa-Wossen Asserate, "The Emperor's Closest Friend: The Life and Work of Blattengeta Herouy," presentation at Freedom in the City, Bath, UK, September 20, 2021.
38. Heruy Wäldä Sellasé, "ይድረስ ለብርሃንና ሰላም ዲሬክተር," ብርሃንና ሰላም, August 15, 1925.
39. "ልብ ወለድ ታሪክ"
40. Heruy Wäldä Sellasé, ለአባት መታሰቢያ ለልጅ ምክር (አዲስ አበባ፡ 1910 ዓም); and መጽሐፈ ቅኔ.
41. Mahtämä Sellasé Wäldä Mäsqäl, ዝክረ ነገር, 684–685.
42. P̣awlos Män Amäno, የኢየሩሳሌምና የቅዱሳት ቦታዎች ታሪክ (አዲስ አበባ፡ ነሀ ጽባሕ, 1925); and [*aläqa*] Zännäb, መጽሐፈ ጨዋታ (አዲስ አበባ፡ ነሀ ጽባህ, 1924 ዓም).
43. Heruy Wäldä Sellasé, ed., መጽሐፍ ቅዳሴ (አዲስ አበባ፡ ኃይለ ሥላሴ ንጉሠ ነገሥት ዘኢትዮጵያ ማተሚያ ቤት, 1922 ዓም). This envisioned edition was completed after liberation: Bärihun Käbbädä, የእኔ ኃይለሥላሴ ታሪክ (አዲስ አበባ፡ አርቲስቲክ ማተሚያ ቤት, 1993 ዓም), 317–324.
44. Stephen Wright, *Ethiopian Incunabula* (Addis Ababa: Commercial Printing Press, 1967), 58–59.
45. De Lorenzi, *Guardians of the Tradition*, 94–113.
46. Heruy Wäldä Sellasé, የልዕልት ወይዘሮ መነን መንገድ በኢየሩሳሌምና በምስር (አዲስ አበባ፡ ተፈሪ መኮንን ማተሚያ ቤት, 1915 ዓም).
47. Heruy Wäldä Sellasé, ደስታና ክብር የኢትዮጵያ መንግሥት አልጋ ወራሽና እንደራሴ ልዑል ተፈሪ መኮንን ወደ አውሮፓ ሲሄዱና ሲመለሱ የመንዳቸው አኳኋን (አዲስ አበባ፡ ተፈሪ መኮንን ማተሚያ ቤት, 1916 ዓም).
48. Heruy Wäldä Sellasé, ማኅደረ ብርሃን ሀገረ ጃፓን (አዲስ አበባ፡ ነሀ ጽባሕ, 1924 ዓም).
49. Heruy Wäldä Sellasé, በዕድሜ መሰንበት ሁሉን ለማየት (አዲስ አበባ፡ ነሀ ጽባሕ, 1926 ዓም).
50. Heruy Wäldä Sellasé, ስለ አውሮጳ መንገድ የምክር ቃል (አዲስ አበባ፡ ተፈሪ መኮንን ማተሚያ ቤት, 1916 ዓም); ወዳጄ ልቤ; and አዲስ አለም፡ የቀኖችና የደግ አድራጎቶች መኖሪያ (አዲስ አበባ፡ ነሀ ጽባሕ, 1925 ዓም).
51. Heruy Wäldä Sellasé, ደስታና ክብር, 64–79. An earlier but only recently published account is Heruy Wäldä Sellasé, የኢትዮጵያ ልዑካን ቡድን በአውሮጳና መካከሎኛው ምሥራቅ, 197–234.
52. On the tour, see Asfa-Wossen Asserate, *King of Kings: The Triumph and Tragedy of Emperor Haile Selassie I of Ethiopia* (London: Haus, 2015), 52–61; and Boris Monin,

"The Visit of Rās Tafari in Europe (1924): Between Hopes of Independence and Colonial Realities," *Annales d'Éthiopie* 28 (2013): 383–389.
53. Heruy Wäldä Sellasé, ደስታና ክብር, 1–7.
54. Märse'é Hazän Wäldä Qirqos, unpublished manuscript, 232–233; and Gäbrä Egzi'abhér Elyas, *Zewditu*, 427–429.
55. For the full list, see Heruy Wäldä Sellasé, ደስታና ክብር, 6.
56. List of delegates and members of delegations, dated September 5, 1924, LNA.
57. One observer said his many decorations made him resemble "an angel ascending on wings." See Gäbrä Egzi'abhér Elyas, *Zewditu*, 295: "መልአክ ይመስሉ የረበበ በክንፉ"
58. Mahtämä Sellasé Wäldä Mäsqäl, "ቼ በለው፦" 282–283.
59. Mauro Canali, *The Matteotti Murder and Mussolini: The Anatomy of a Fascist Crime*, trans. Ann Pichey (Palgrave: New York, 2024); and Richard Bosworth, *Mussolini* (London: Bloomsbury, 2002), 194–216.
60. "Il reggente dell'Etiopia, Ras Tafari, ricevuto dal Re, dal Governo e dal popolo," *Giornale d'Italia*, June 19, 1924.
61. Arthur Weststeijn, "Egyptian Memorials in Modern Rome: The Dogali Obelisk and the Altar of the Fallen Fascists," in *The Iseum Campense from the Roman Empire to the Modern Age*, ed. Miguel John Versluys, Kristine Bülow Clausen, and Giuseppina Capriotti Vittozzi (Rome: Edizioni Quasar, 2018), 331–347; and Silvano Fallocco and Carlo Boumis, *Roma coloniale* (Rome: Commari Edizioni, 2022), 25–28.
62. "L'arrivo di Ras Tafari a Roma," *Corriere della sera*, June 19, 1924; and "Ricevimento alla Consulta per ras Tafari, una manovra d'artiglieria a Bracciano," *Corriere della sera*, June 24, 1924.
63. "Con Ras Tafari alla Consulta," *Giornale d'Italia*, June 24, 1924. The interlocutors included Carlo Conti Rossini and Giorgio Levi Della Vida. On the museum, see Beatrice Falcucci, "Bringing the Empire to the Provinces: Colonial Museums and Colonial Knowledge in Fascist Italy," *CFV* 3, no. 10 (2021): 113–146.
64. "Ras Tafari a un'esercitazione militare, la visita al Papa in Vaticano," *Corriere della sera*, June 22, 1924; and "Ricevimento alla Consulta per ras Tafari, una manovra d'artiglieria a Bracciano," *Corriere della sera*, June 24, 1924.
65. "Ras Tafari sulla 'Duillio' a Spezia, assiste a tiri di grossi calibri," *Corriere della sera*, June 25, 1924.
66. Haylä Sellasé [with Heruy Wäldä Sellasé], ሕይወትና የኢትዮጵያ እርምጃ (አዲስ አበባ፡ ብርሃንና ሰላም, 1965 ዓም), 76: "ዛሬ ይህን ሲያስቡት እንዴት ይገርማቸው ይሆን?" See also Ladislas Farago, *Abyssinia on the Eve* (London: Putnam, 1935), 126–127.
67. Heruy Wäldä Sellasé, ደስታና ክብር, 86–88; and "Ras Tafari a Terni, a Palazzo Chigi ed al Campidoglio," *Corriere della sera*, June 20, 1924.
68. For a comment on this point with respect to the negotiations, see Amedeo Giannini, "Riassunto della situazione," *Oriente moderno* 4, no. 7 (1924): 430.
69. Giuliano Cora, "Giuseppe Colli di Felizzano," *RSPI* 10, no. 4 (1943): 449. In the press, Colli di Felizzano opined that Täfäri Mäkonnen's visit was more of a "courtesy" than a political mission: "Le ragioni del viaggio di Ras Tafari in Europa," *Corriere della sera*, May 18, 1924.

308   1. THE POWER OF TRADITION

70. Heruy Wäldä Sellasé, ደስታና ክብር, 67–68.
71. The lone dissenter was *le'ul ras* Haylu, who reportedly said, "If there is value to this, let's welcome [it]." See Heruy Wäldä Sellasé, ደስታና ክብር, 68: "ጥቅም የምናገኝበት እንደሆነ እንቀበል"
72. Angelo Del Boca, *Gli italiani in Africa Orientale: II. La conquista dell'impero* (Milan: Mondadori, 1999), 70. See also Giuseppe Vedovato, *Gli accordi italo-etiopici dell'agosto 1928* (Florence: Poligrafico Toscano, 1956), 8–16.
73. On the 1927 talks, see Alberto Cauli, "At Ras Tafari Makonnen's Court: The 1927 Italian Diplomatic Mission to Ethiopia and Its Colonial Implications," in *Reflections on Leadership and Institutions in Africa*, ed. Kenneth Kalu and Toyin Falola (London: Rowan and Littlefield, 2020), 95–112; and on the parallel approach to Yemen, see Nir Arielli, *Fascist Italy and the Middle East 1933-40* (New York: Palgrave Macmillan, 2010), 20–26.
74. Luigi Federzoni, *Italia di ieri per la storia di domani* (Milan: Mondadori, 1967), 256.
75. "Le giornate romane di Ras Tafari," *Giornale d'Italia*, June 22, 1924.
76. Heruy Wäldä Sellasé, ደስታና ክብር, 71–75.
77. Lit., "The Mount of Saint Stephen," employing the Ge'ez monastic nomenclature.
78. Mauro da Leonessa, *Santo Stefano Maggiore degli Abissini e le relazioni romano-etiopiche* (Vatican City: Tipografia Poliglotta Vaticana, 1929), 299–300.
79. "ኢትዮጵያ አገራችን ምንም በመንግሥትና በክርስቲያንነት ጸንታ ብትኖር ከጠላቶች ሁከት አላረፈችም። ነገር ግን መድኃኔ ዓለም በየዚው በቅን ልብ የሚያለግሉ ልጆች ይሰግልና የኢትዮጵያ ጠላት ምንም ቢበረታ ድል አድርጋት አያውቀም።"
80. "አረር ማተብ"
81. "የልዑላን ታሪክ"
82. For Heruy's version of this narrative, see his የኢትዮጵያ ታሪክ. More generally, see Sara Marzagora, "History in Twentieth-Century Ethiopia: The 'Great Tradition' and the Counter-Histories of National Failure," *JAH* 28, no. 3 (2017): 425–444; Alemseged Abbay, "The Trans-Mareb Past in the Present," *JMAS* 35, no. 2 (1997): 321–334; and Bahru Zewde, *Pioneers of Change*, 141–158.
83. "የኤውሮጳ አገር አምሮን ንፋሱም ተመችቶን አይደለም።"
84. He was killed during the colonial occupation: Ian Campbell, *The Addis Ababa Massacre: Italy's National Shame* (New York: Oxford University Press, 2017), 385.
85. "ብሔረ አግአዚት," discussed below.
86. Solomon Şehayä, ማሰን መልቀስን ቀዳሞት (አስመራ: ቤተ ማሕተም ፍራንቼስካና, 2012). I thank Ruth Iyob for explaining this connection.
87. Heruy Wäldä Sellasé, ደስታና ክብር, 75. The inscriptions transcribed are the same as those presented in Marius Chaîne, "Un monastère éthiopien a Rome au XV et XVI siècle, Santo Stefano dei Mori," *MFO* V (1911): 27–32.
88. Heruy Wäldä Sellasé, ደስታና ክብር, 75: "በኢየሩሳሌምና ብሮምያ የኢትዮጵያ ገዳም መገኘት ለኢትዮጵያ ልጆች ሁሉ ታላቅ መመኪያ ነው። ይኸውም የኢትዮጵያ ክርስቲያንነት ከብዙ ዘመን በፊት የቆየ መሆኑን ያስረዳል።"
89. François Hartog, "Time, History and the Writing of History: The *Order* of Time," *KVHAA Konferenser* 37 (1996): 95–113.
90. Fesseha Giyorgis, *Storia d'Etiopia*, trans. Yaqob Beyene (Naples: Istituto Universitario Orientale, 1987), 170; and Manfred Kropp, "Abreha's Names and Titles: CIH 541, 4-Reconsidered," *PSAS* 21 (1991): 138–139.

91. Fesseha Giyorgis, *Storia d'Etiopia*, 173, where he notes that the term is a point of pride for the *liqawent* of Ethiopia. I thank Bairu Tafla for calling my attention to this reference. For another discussion of the term, see Gäbrä Mika'él Germu's comments on the ancient names of Ethiopia: EMML 1473, 23v–24r.
92. This is a place-based communal identification predicated on dynastic preservation: Benedict Anderson, *Imagined Communities: Reflections on the Origins and Spread of Nationalism* (New York: Verso, 1983), 159.
93. Gäbrä Iyäsus Abbay, መሠረት ዓሉት ሕዝቢ መረብ ምላሽ ብጅንጀ ትግርኛ ዝተዳለወ (አስመራ፡ ኮከብ ጽባሕ, 1954 ዓም), 3–6.
94. "ፈላሲ."
95. Matteo Salvadore, James De Lorenzi, and Deresse Ayenachew Woldetsadik, *The Many Lives of Täsfa Ṣeyon: An Ethiopian Intellectual in Early Modern Rome* (New York: Cambridge University Press, 2024).
96. Heruy Wäldä Sellasé, አዲስ ዓለም, 1–3.
97. "ስለ ወይዘሮ አምሳለ ጉዱይ ዕረፍት," ብርሃንና ሰላም, May 18, 1933.
98. Interview with Shimelis Yilma, January 26, 2021.
99. Interview with Hiwot Teffera, January 21, 2020; and Farago, *Abyssinia on the Eve*, 118–129.
100. Interview with Shimelis Yilma, January 26, 2021. One daughter attended a mission school in Addis Ababa, another graduated from a boarding school in Switzerland, and a third attended school in England. Their two sons graduated from Oxford and Cambridge.

2. Mysterious Magic

1. Extensive documentation of Cerulli's biography can be found in ACS MAI AGP Fascicoli del personale, fasc. 6625, bust. 335. Published biographies include Lanfranco Ricci, "Ricordo di Enrico Cerulli," *RSE* 32 (1990): 5–44; Lanfranco Ricci, "Enrico Cerulli e l'Istituto per l'Oriente," *Oriente moderno* 9, no. 70 (1990): 1–6; Andrea Celli, *Dante and the Mediterranean Comedy: From Muslim Spain to Post-Colonial Italy* (Cham, Germany: Palgrave, 2022), 27–89; and Karla Mallette, *European Modernity and the Arab Mediterranean: Toward a New Philology and a Counter-Orientalism* (Philadelphia: University of Pennsylvania Press, 2010), 132–161.
2. Ian Brown, *The School of Oriental and African Studies: Imperial Training and the Expansion of Learning* (Cambridge: Cambridge University Press, 2016); and Armelle Enders, "L'école nationale de la France d'Outre-Mer et la formation des administrateurs coloniaux," *RHMC* 40, no. 2 (1993): 272–288.
3. Nicola Nicolini, *L'Istituto orientale di Napoli. Origine e statuti* (Rome: Edizioni Universitarie, 1942), 161–162.
4. Giorgio Levi Della Vida, *Fantasmi ritrovati* (Venice: Pozza, 1966); Bruna Soravia, "Il percorso politico di Giorgio Levi Della Vida, dall'impresa libica al rifiuto del giuramento, 1911–1931," *Rivista di storia* 10, no. 2 (2021): 175–194; and Mario Liverani, "Giorgio Levi Della Vida e il suo contributo agli studi africanisti," *Africa* 23, no. 2 (1968): 222–224.

5. Gianfrancesco Lusini, "Ignazio Guidi, Martino Mario Moreno, Enrico Cerulli: studiosi dell'Etiopia," *RSE* ser. 3, 1 (2017): 163–174; and Bruna Soravia, "Ascesa e declino dell'orientalismo scientifico in Italia," in *Il mondo visto dall'Italia*, ed. Agostino Giovagnoli and Giorgio Del Zanna (Milan: Guerini, 2005), 271–286, which compares Guidi to Antoine Silvestre de Sacy.
6. Enrico Cerulli, "Francesco Gallina," *RSE* 2, no. 3 (1942): 348. See also Giorgio Levi Della Vida, "Omaggio ad Enrico Cerulli," *Oriente moderno* 43, nos. 10/12 (1963): 795n4; and Elena Sengal, "In Memoria di Francesco Gallina (1861–1942)," *Oriente moderno* 22, no. 7 (1942): 301–302.
7. Bruna Soravia, "Carlo Alfonso Nallino (1872–1938). Lineamenti di una biografia intellettuale," *Studi magrebini*, n.s. 8 (2010): 9–24; Francesco Gabrieli, *Orientalisti del novecento* (Rome: Istituto per l'Oriente "Nallino," 1993), 3–13; and Giorgio Levi Della Vida, "Carlo Alfonso Nallino (1872–1938)," *Oriente moderno* 18, no. 9 (1938): 459–478.
8. Enrico Cerulli, "Ricordo di Carlo Alfonso Nallino," *Levante* 20 (1973): 7–10.
9. Federico Cresti, "Il professore e il generale: La polemica tra Carlo Alfonso Nallino e Rodolfo Graziani sulla Senussia e su altre questioni libiche," *Studi storici* 45, no. 4 (2004): 1113–1149.
10. Nicolini, *Istituto orientale*, 139.
11. Alain Rouaud, *Afä-wärq 1868-1947: Un intellectuel éthiopien témoin de son temps* (Paris: Éditions CNRS, 1991).
12. Afäwärq Gäbrä Iyäsus, ኢትዮጵያ። *Grammatica della lingua amarica: metodo pratico per l'insegnamento* (Rome: Tipografia della Reale Accademia dei Lincei, 1905); ልብ ወለድ ታሪክ (ሮማ: 1900 ዓም); ዳግማዊ አጤ ምኒልክ (ሮማ: 1901 ዓም); and ኢትዮጵያ። *Guide du voyageur en Abyssinie* (Rome: De Luigi, 1908).
13. Nicola Camilleri, "How a Colonial Subject Became an Italian Citizen: The Life and Naturalization of Sengal Workneh Between Colonial Eritrea and Italy (1882–1929)," in *Languages of Discrimination and Racism in Twentieth-Century Italy: History, Legacies and Practices*, ed. Marcella Simoni and Davide Lombardo (New York: Palgrave Macmillan, 2022), 27–46; and Uoldelul Chelati Dirar, "Writing WWI with African Gazes: The Great War Through the Writing of Tigrinya Speaking Expatriates," in *The First World War from Tripoli to Addis Ababa (1911-1924)*, ed. Shiferaw Bekele et al. (Addis Ababa: Centre Français des Études Éthiopiennes, 2018), https://books.openedition.org/cfee/1379?lang=en. His appointment concerned Afäwärq: letter from Afäwärq Gäbrä Iyäsus to Gallina, dated May 14, 1915, in Alain Rouaud, "Quelques lettres et documents concernant Afä-Wärq (2)," *Annales d'Ethiopie* 19 (2003): 194–195.
14. Renato Paoli, *Nella colonia Eritrea* (Milan: Treves, 1908), 67.
15. "Un lutto italo-etiopico: Illeni," *Voce dell'africa*, November 16, 1962; and Luigi Fusella and Joseph Tubiana, "Souvenirs d'Elena Sengal," *Pount* 12 (2018): 27–35.
16. On this distinction, see Bernard Cohn, *Colonialism and Its Forms of Knowledge: The British in India* (Princeton, NJ: Princeton University Press, 1996), 16–56.
17. Paolo Marrassini, "Problems in Critical Edition and the State of Ethiopian Philology," *JES* 42, nos. 1/2 (2009): 25–68; Alessandro Bausi, "Philology, research in," in *EA* 4:142–144; and more generally, Richard Bulliet, "Orientalism and Medieval Islamic

Studies," in *The Past and Future of Medieval Studies*, ed. John Van Engen (Notre Dame, IN: University of Notre Dame Press, 1994), 94–104. Marrassini broadly judges the philological methods of Ethiopian studies adisciplinary, in that specialists in this period were "basically untouched by the development of the philological disciplines in Classical and Romance philology." See Marrassini, "Ethiopian Philology," 37. Bausi notes the important exception of Ge'ez Biblical studies, which were in this period distinct from the rest of the field in their methodological sophistication: Bausi, "Philology," 142.

18. "Prospetto Biografico," ACS MAI AGP Fascicoli del personale, fasc. 6625, bust. 335.
19. Curriculum vitae, ACS MAI AGP Commissione di Primo Grado per l'Epurazione, bust. 370; and list of publications, 1916–1923, ACS MAI AGP Fascicoli del personale, fasc. 6625, bust. 335.
20. Nicola Labanca, "L'amministrazione coloniale fascista: Stato, politica e società," in *Il regime fascista: Storia e storiografia*, ed. Angelo Del Boca, Massimo Legnani, and Mario Rossi (Bari: Laterza, 1995), 364–365.
21. Regio Esercito Italiano service records, undated, ACS MAI AGP Fascicoli del personale, fasc. 6625, bust. 335.
22. Said Samatar, *Oral Poetry and Somali Nationalism: The Case of Sayyid Maḥammad 'Abdille Ḥasan* (Cambridge: Cambridge University Press, 1982).
23. For a biography, see Alberto Cauli, "Italian Pioneers: Colonial Propaganda and Geographic Exploration" (PhD diss., University of Auckland, 2019), 47–136.
24. For an account, see Cesare Maria De Vecchi, *Orizzonti d'impero: Cinque anni in Somalia* (Milan: Mondadori, 1935).
25. "L'opera del governatore De Vecchi in Somalia," *Giornale d'Italia*, August 3, 1924.
26. Abdi Ismail Samatar, *Africa's First Democrats: Somalia's Aden A. Osman and Abdirazak H. Hussen* (Bloomington: Indiana University Press, 2016), 19–26.
27. Regio Esercito Italiano service records and Ministry of the Colonies service records, both undated and in ACS MAI AGP Fascicoli del personale, fasc. 6625, bust. 335.
28. De Vecchi, *Orrizzonti d'Impero*, 40–46. On the functions of the resident, see Cesare Marinucci and Tomaso Columbano, *Il governo dei territori oltremare* (Rome: Istituto Poligrafico dello Stato, 1963), 305–307; and on *shaykh* Farag, see Mohamed Haji Mukhtar, *Historical Dictionary of Somalia, New Edition* (Lanham, MD: Scarecrow, 2003), 207–209. For Cerulli's account of the movement, see his *Somalia. Scritti vari editi ed inediti* (Rome: Poligrafico dello Stato, 1964), 3:166–168.
29. Annual evaluation of Cerulli by De Vecchi, dated 1926, and telegram from De Vecchi to Ministry of the Colonies, dated January 17, 1924, both in ACS MAI AGP Fascicoli del personale, fasc. 6625, bust. 335.
30. Ministry of the Colonies service records, undated, ACS MAI AGP Fascicoli del personale, fasc. 6625, bust. 335.
31. Enrico Cerulli et al., "The Anglo-Italian Somaliland Boundary," *Geographical Journal* 78, no. 2 (1931): 102–125; and ASMAI pos. 89/4.
32. The link between the Legation's formal amity and covert subversion was obvious to both sides: Giuliano Cora, "Un diplomatico durante l'era fascista," *Storia e politica*

312   2. MYSTERIOUS MAGIC

5 (1966): 92–93; and Haylä Sellasé, *My Life and Ethiopia's Progress, Volume 1: 1892–1937*, trans. Edward Ullendorff (New York: Oxford University Press, 1976), 156–157.

33. Ministry of the Colonies service records, undated, ACS MAI AGP Fascicoli del personale, fasc. 6625, bust. 335.
34. "Scheda Personale," MAI AGP Commissione di Primo Grado per l'Epurazione, bust. 370; and "I nuovi governatori," *Corriere della sera*, December 8, 1937.
35. Cerulli, *Somalia*, 3:48–95; but see also his "Somaliland," in *EI1*, 4:483–488.
36. This analysis informed British anthropologist Ioan Lewis, whose structural-functionalist model of clan structure became widely influential in Somali studies, and which is now critiqued: cf. Ioan Lewis, *A Modern History of the Somali: Nation and State in the Horn of Africa* (Boulder, CO: Westview, 1965), with discussions of Cerulli on 270–279; Abdi Ismail Samatar, *Framing Somalia: Beyond Africa's Merchants of Misery* (Lawrenceville, NJ: Red Sea Press, 2022), 25–50; and Lidwien Kapteijns, "I. M. Lewis and Somali Clanship: A Critique," *NEAS* 11, no. 1 (2004–2010): 1–23.
37. In Cerulli's assessment, Muhammad Abdallah Hasan and his movement of "true banditry" epitomized the analytic category of "bad" Hijazi-connected Muslim, as distinct from the "good" cooptable Muslim.
38. Enrico Cerulli, "Muḥammad b. ʿAbd Allāh Ḥassān al-Mahdī," in *EI1*, 3:667–668.
39. Scott Reese, *Renewers of the Age: Holy Men and Social Discourse in Colonial Benaadir* (Leiden, Netherlands: Brill, 2008), 65–69.
40. George Steinmetz, *The Colonial Origins of Modern Social Thought: French Sociology and the Overseas Empire* (Princeton, NJ: Princeton University Press, 2023), 199–206. See also Martin Thomas, *Empires of Intelligence: Security Services and Colonial Disorder After 1919* (Berkeley: University of California Press, 2008), 45–72.
41. De Vecchi, *Orizzonti d'impero*, 369. In annual evaluations, De Vecchi praised Cerulli's linguistic and historical understanding: annual evaluation of Cerulli by De Vecchi, dated 1926, ACS MAI AGP Fascicoli del personale, fasc. 6625, bust. 335.
42. Among many, see Enrico Cerulli, "Observations on the Moslem Movement in Somalia," HRAF ms. 1–45 [originally 1–36]. On this program, see David Price, *Cold War Anthropology: The CIA, the Pentagon, and the Growth of Dual Use Anthropology* (Durham, NC: Duke University Press, 2016), 248–276; and "Counterinsurgency and the M-VICO System: Human Relations Area Files and Anthropology's Dual-Use Legacy," *Anthropology Today* 28, no. 1 (2012): 16–20.
43. Noelle Turtur, "Making Fascist Empire Work: Italian Enterprises, Labor, and Organized-Community in Occupied Ethiopia, 1896–1943" (PhD diss., Columbia University, 2022), 79–80; and Alessandro Rosselli, "Appunti sul colonialismo fascista. Venti mesi di azione coloniale (1926) di Luigi Federzoni," *JMS* 26 (2017): 89–98.
44. Enrico Cerulli, *Etiopia occidentale (dallo Scioa alla frontiera del Sudan)* (Rome: Sindacato Italiano Arti Grafiche, 1929 and 1933), 1:10.
45. The official accounts are Raimondo Franchetti, *Nella Dancàlia etiopica, spedizione italiana 1928-29* (Milan: Mondadori, 1930); and Luigi Amedeo di Savoia-Aosta, *La esplorazione dello Uabi-Uebi Scebeli dalle sue sorgenti nella Etiopia meridionale alla Somalia Italiana (1928–29)* (Milan: Mondadori, 1932). Cerulli joined the latter expedition

as an ethnological expert, at the duke's request: telegram from Cora to Guariglia, dated May 15, 1928, ACS MAI AGP Fascicoli del personale, fasc. 6625, bust. 335. For Ethiopian accounts, see "ስለ ልዑል ዳክ ዶዛብሩዝ መታሰቢያ," ብርሃንና ሰላም, April 6, 1933; and Haylä Sellasé, *My Life*, 1:149–150. On this initiative, see Angelo Matteo Caglioti, "Meterological Imperialism: Climate Science, Environment, and Empire in Liberal and Fascist Italy (1870–1940)" (PhD diss., University of California at Berkeley, 2017), 171–173; and Cauli, "Italian Pioneers," 127–133.

46. He died one year after this meeting: "ስለ ከቡር ራስ ናደው ዕረፍት," ብርሃንና ሰላም, November 21, 1929.

47. While still in transit, Cerulli penned a ministerial white paper on the Wälläga mining industry, and months later, he published a preliminary summary of his findings in *Oriente moderno*. The monograph text was written in 1928. See Turtur, "Making Fascist Empire," 63–64; Cerulli, "Notizia preliminare dei risultati scientifici del mio viaggio nell'Etiopia occidentale," *Oriente moderno* 8, no. 7 (1928): 325–328; and Cerulli, *Etiopia occidentale*, 1:18n1.

48. Telegram from Cora to Ministry of the Colonies, dated May 22, 1928, and telegram from Federzoni to Cerulli, dated March 1928, both in ACS MAI AGP Fascicoli del personale, fasc. 6625, bust. 335; and Carlo Alfonso Nallino, "I principali risultati del viaggio di Enrico Cerulli nell'Etiopia occidentale nel 1927–1928," *Oriente moderno* 13, no. 8 (1933): 430–436, which describes Cerulli as "vastly superior to that of all the other Italian explorers in Africa." For a local review, see Comte de Guényveau, "Revue Littéraire," *Courrier d'Éthiopie*, October 20, 1933.

49. Martin Thomas and Amanda Harris, "Anthropology and the Expeditionary Imaginary," in *Expeditionary Anthropology: Teamwork, Travel, and "The Science of Man,"* ed. Thomas and Harris (New York: Berghahn, 2018), 1–36.

50. Vincent Debaene, *Far Afield: French Anthropology Between Science and Literature*, trans. Justin Izzo (Chicago: University of Chicago Press, 2014).

51. On predisciplinary ethnography, see Frederico Delgado Rosa and Han Vermeulen, "Other Argonauts: Chapters in the History of Pre-Malinowskian Ethnography," in *Ethnographers Before Malinowski: Pioneers of Anthropological Fieldwork, 1870–1922*, ed. Delgado Rosa and Vermeulen (New York: Berghahn, 2002), 1–46. In Italy, this was a period when culture-focused disciplinary anthropology was relatively undeveloped. Some attribute this situation to Italy's lack of colonies in comparison to other European countries, while others observe that Italy's colonies were home to societies with written literatures that lent themselves to philological—rather than anthropological—analysis. Cf. Enzo Vinicio Alliegro, *Antropologia italiana: storia e storiografia, 1869–1975* (Florence: SEID, 2011), 209–211; Mariano Pavanello, "Vinigi L. Grottanelli a cento anni dalla nascita," *L'uomo* 1/2 (2012): 7–32; and William Shack, "Social Science Research in Ethiopia: Retrospect and Prospect," in *Proceedings of the Seventh International Conference of Ethiopian Studies, University of Lund, 26–29 April, 1982*, ed. Sven Rubenson (Addis Ababa: Institute of Ethiopian Studies, 1984): 411–417.

52. Cerulli, *Etiopia occidentale*, 1:7–9.

53. On Jimma, see Tesema Ta'a, *The Political Economy of an African Society in Transformation: The Case of Macca Oromo (Ethiopia)* (Wiesbaden: Harrasowitz Verlag, 2006); Guluma Gemeda, "Land, Agriculture, and Society in the Gibe Region: Southwestern Ethiopia, c. 1850-1974" (PhD diss., Michigan State University, 1996); and Herbert Lewis, *Jimma Abba Jifar: An Oromo Monarchy, 1830-1932* (Lawrenceville, NJ: Red Sea Press, 2001). More broadly, see Brian Yates, *The Other Abyssinians: The Northern Oromo and the Creation of Modern Ethiopia, 1855-1913* (Rochester, NY: University of Rochester Press, 2020); and Mohammed Hassan, *The Oromo of Ethiopia: A History, 1570-1860* (New York: Cambridge University Press, 1990).
54. There were six such regions, but Jimma alone maintained a formal embassy in Addis Ababa.
55. On the marriage, see Zuzanna Augustyniak, "Lïj Iyasu's Marriages as a Reflection of His Domestic Policy," in *The Life and Times of Lïj Iyasu of Ethiopia: New Insights*, ed. Éloi Ficquet and Wolbert Smidt (Berlin: Lit Verlag, 2018), 39–47; and more generally, Heran Sereke Brhan, "Building Bridges, Drying Bad Blood: Elite Marriages, Politics, and Ethnicity in 19th and 20th Century Imperial Ethiopia" (PhD diss., Michigan State University, 2002), 91–160.
56. Guluma Gemeda, "The Rise of Coffee and the Demise of Colonial Autonomy: The Oromo Kingdom of Jimma and Political Centralization in Ethiopia," *NEAS* 9, no. 3 (2002): 51–74.
57. "ላገርና ለሕዝብ የተደረገ ርኅራኄ," ብርሃንና ሰላም, April 12, 1932. This article describes Abbaa Jifar as the *balabbat* of Jimma. See also Cerulli's anonymous comments on the abdication in "Etiopia," *Oriente moderno* 12, no. 6 (1932): 305.
58. In a revealing disjuncture, two years later *Berhanenna sälam* featured an article about the celebration of Haylä Sellasé's birthday in Jimma, but did not acknowledge the death of Abbaa Jifar the following month: "ጃንሆይ ቀዳማዊ ኃይለ ሥላሴ ከተማ የጃንሆይ ቀዳማዊ ኃይለ ሥላሴ የልደት በዓል አከባበር," ብርሃንና ሰላም, August 23, 1934. On Abbaa Jifar's death, see Adrien Zervos, *L'empire d'Éthiopie: Le miroir de l'Éthiopie moderne, 1906-1935* (Alexandria: Imprimerie de l'École professionnelle des frères, 1936), 341-343.
59. Yonas Seifu and Jan Záhořík, "Jimma Town: Foundation and Early Growth from ca. 1830-1936," *Ethnologia Actualis* 17, no. 2 (2017): 46–63; and Lewis, *Oromo Monarchy*, 68–73.
60. Estimates based on Zervos, *Éthiopie*, 337; and *Guida dell'Africa Orientale Italiana* (Milan: Officine Fotolitografiche, 1938), 523.
61. Cerulli, *Etiopia occidentale*, 1:18–19, 95.
62. Unexpectedly, this escort was comprised of mercenaries from Gojjam, whose leader described Italy as a "great country" north of Tegray. Abbaa Digga then added that Europe was a hot and unhealthy place, which explained why the French were so enthralled by Djibouti: Cerulli, *Etiopia occidentale*, 1:66–68.
63. Cerulli, *Folk Literature*, 148–162 ["The Oral Chronicle of the Kingdom of Gúmā"]. Cerulli attributed the disappearance of this tradition to the fact that the chronicle's subjects were the rivals of the now dominant Amhara elite.
64. Cerulli, *Etiopia occidentale*, 1:108: "Il giovanotto di Guma ed i capi mi guardano meravigliati ed increduli, ed i figli di Abba Fità mi pregano di far loro vedere

questo libro straordinario. Io mi limito a leggerne qualche periodo tra l'attenzione generale e la sorpresa. 'Bisogna che lei dia il libro ad Abba Gifar!' mi dice in coro il gruppo dei nipoti."

65. Cerulli, *Etiopia occidentale*, 1:111: "Mi scusi tanto se io ho sbagliato in qualche particolare delle accoglienze che le ho fatto qui nel Gimma. Lei sa che sono un povero Galla e non sono abituato a trattare con quelli delle Legazioni estere, che vivono alla corte dello Scioa, perchè io manco ormai dallo Scioa da venti anni."

66. Cerulli, *Etiopia occidentale*, 2:118; and more generally, Mahtämä Sellasé Wäldä Mäsqäl, "የኢትዮጵያ ባህል ጥናት፡ ቼ በለው," *JES* 7, no. 2 (1969): 211.

67. On these events, see Guluma Gemeda, "Land, Agriculture, and Society," esp. 197–199; and Bairu Tafla, "Two of the Last Provincial Kings of Ethiopia," *JES* 11, no. 1 (1973): 50–55.

68. Cerulli, *Etiopia occidentale*, 1:133–140, and also his discussion of Käffa in 1:203–208. For earlier comments on the feudal nature of Abyssinian society, see his "La poesia popolare amarica," *BSAI* 35 (1916): 172–174.

69. Cerulli, *Etiopia occidentale*, 1:144: "Abba Gifar mi saluta con grande cordialità e mi invita a prender posto in un enorme seggiolone che ha fatto porre innanzi a lui. Poi, dopo un breve scambio di saluti, mi invita senz'altro a leggergli la storia del regno di Guma, aggiungendo con un sorriso che sua madre era nativa di Guma e perciò egli può ben controllare quello che sto per dire; e con un altro sorriso mi accenna alla fila delle sue donne, pubblico non comune che la mia lettura sta per avere. Comincio a leggere; e veramente nessun occidentale può vantare di aver avuto per un suo libro un pubblico simile sull'altopiano etiopico! I racconti, che dieci anni fa io avevo raccolto dai nostri bravi ascari feriti nelle tristi corsie degli ospedali militari, dove i ricordi della patria lontana davano un così forte sapore di nostalgia ai discorsi di quei valorosi, ora rivivono qui alla corte di Abba Gifar in questo salone che ospita il *motì* e le sue donne come se veramente una misteriosa magia abbia rimesso nel movimento della vita le figure di Re, di guerrieri, di eroine Galla che le parole fermate per anni nel libro hanno tenuto prigioniere."

70. The phrase suggests Bronislaw Malinowski's 1922 characterization of the ethnographic method: George Stocking, *The Ethnographer's Magic and Other Essays in the History of Anthropology* (Madison: University of Wisconsin Press, 1992), 12–59.

71. Desalegn Seyum, "Folk Literature," 13–25.

72. This was possibly George Howland, who met Abbaa Jifar in late 1928 or early 1929 during a survey of Jimma's potential as a tea producing region: George Howland, "Tea in Abyssinia," *Courrier d'Éthiopie*, April 26, 1929.

73. On this, see Jomo Kenyatta, *Facing Mount Kenya* (New York: Vintage, 1962), xviii.

74. Alessandro Triulzi, "Neḳemte and Addis Ababa: Dilemmas of Provincial Rule," in *The Southern Marches of Imperial Ethiopia: Essays in History and Social Anthropology*, ed. Donald Donham and Wendy James (Athens: Ohio University Press, 2002), 51–68. On the *däjjazmach*, see Heruy Wäldä Sellasé, የሕይወት ታሪክ (*Biographie*) በኋላ ዘመን ለሚነሡ ልጆች ማስታወቂያ (አዲስ አበባ፡ ተፈሪ መኰንን ማተሚያ ቤት, 1915 ዓም), 92; and Bairu Tafla, "Four Ethiopian Biographies: Däjjazmač Gärmamé, Däjjazmač Gäbrä-Egzi'abehér Moroda,

Däjjazmač Balča and Käntiba Gäbru Dästa," *JES* 7, no. 2 (1969): 11–13. According to Cerulli, Loränsiyos served in his army: Cerulli, *Folk Literature*, 14, with song from Kumsaa Moroda on 57.

75. "ስለ ከቡር ፊታውራሪ አልጂራ አረፍት," ብርሃንና ሰላም, January 28, 1932.
76. Letter from Gäbrä Egzi'abhér to Täfäri Mäkonnen, dated Tahsas 19, 1916 AM, and letter from Habtä Maryam to Haylä Sellasé, dated Ṭeqemt 24, 1926 AM, both in የወላጋ የታሪክ ሰነዶች h1880ዎቹ እስከ 1920ዎቹ (አ.አ..አ.), ed. Tesemma Ta'a and Alessandro Triulzi (አዲስ አበባ: አዲስ አበባ ዩኒቨርሲቲ ፕሬስ, 1999 ዓም), 162, 209–210.
77. On his life and legacy, see Tasgaraa Hirphoo, *Abbaa Gammachiis (Oneesimos Nasib)*, trans. Magarsaa Guutaa (Hermannsburg, Germany: 1999); Gustav Arén, *Envoys of the Gospel in Ethiopia: In the Steps of the Evangelical Pioneers, 1898-1936* (Stockholm: EFS Förlaget, 1999), 287–340; and Mekuria Bulcha, "Onesimos Nasib's Pioneering Contributions to Oromo Writing," *NJAS* 4, no. 1 (1995): 36–59.
78. Onesimos Näsib and Astér Ganno, ጀልቀብ ቢርሲሳ እንከ መጫፈ ዱቢሱ ቢርሲሱን አፋን ኦሮሞት (ሙንኩሎ: 1894); and Cerulli, *Folk Literature*, 15. For a critique, see Fride Hylander, "Onesimus Nesib: Some Remarks on Cerulli's 'The Folk-Literature of the Galla,'" *JES* 7, no. 2 (1969): 79–87. The author was the son of EFS missionary Nils Hylander, who collaborated with Onesimos Näsib and Astér Ganno.
79. On this relationship, see Emmanu'él Abraham, *Reminiscences of My Life* (Trenton, NJ: Africa World Press, 2010), 4–7.
80. Tasgaraa Hirphoo, *Abbaa Gammachiis*, 67–99; and Arén, *Envoys of the Gospel*, 311–319. For Heruy's approving comments, see Heruy Wäldä Sellasé, የሕይወት ታሪክ, 53.
81. Edossa Gammachiis, "ስለ አቶ ኦኔሲሞስ ነሲብ አረፍት," ብርሃንና ሰላም, November 12, 1931.
82. Entry dated April 15, 1928, Olle Eriksson diary (1928–1930), Gustav Arén Collection, EFSA.
83. Eriksson was notably one of the few European contributors to *Berhanenna sälam*: Olle Eriksson, "ስለ ብርሃን," ብርሃንና ሰላም, March 11, 1926.
84. Mahtämä Sellasé Wäldä Mäsqäl, "ቼ በለው," 266; Heruy Wäldä Sellasé, የሕይወት ታሪክ, 71; and Cerulli, *Etiopia occidentale*, 2:160.
85. Heather Sharkey, ed., *Cultural Conversions: Unexpected Consequences of Christian Missionary Encounters in the Middle East, Africa, and South Asia* (Syracuse, NY: Syracuse University Press, 2013); and Peter van der Veer, ed., *Conversion to Modernities: The Globalization of Christianity* (New York: Routledge, 1996).
86. This possibility is further suggested by his affiliation with the EFS, which the Italians viewed as hostile to the colonial project, and which they eventually suppressed: Arén, *Envoys of the Gospel*, 454–505; and Karl Johan Lundström and Ezra Gebremedhin, *Kenisha: The Roots and Development of the Evangelical Church of Eritrea, 1866-1935* (Trenton, NJ: Red Sea Press, 2011).
87. Cerulli, *Etiopia occidentale*, 1:19.
88. Telegram from Astuto to Ministry of the Colonies, dated April 1, 1931, ACS MAI AGP Fascicoli del personale, fasc. 6625, bust. 335. On the state of this planning in 1931–1932, in which Astuto played an important role, see John Gooch, *Mussolini and His Generals: The Armed Forces and Fascist Foreign Policy, 1922-1940* (New York: Cambridge University Press, 2007), 239–241.

89. Telegram from De Bono to Ministry of Foreign Affairs, dated June 6, 1931, ACS MAI AGP Fascicoli del personale, fasc. 6625, bust. 335.
90. He also served as director of the Office of Civilian Affairs and Services for an indeterminate period before joining the Office of Political Affairs.

3. Reading Philology in Addis Ababa

1. Karima Laachir, Sara Marzagora, and Francesa Orsini, "Significant Geographies in Lieu of World Literature," *JWL* 3 (2018): 290–310.
2. Marcus Keller and Javier Irigoyen-García, "Introduction: The Dialectics of Early Modern Orientalism," in *The Dialectics of Orientalism in Early Modern Europe*, ed. Keller and Irigoyen-García (London: Palgrave: 2018), 1–16. On this intellectual history, see Derek Peterson and Giacomo Macola, eds., *Recasting the Past: History Writing and Political Work in Modern Africa* (Athens: Ohio University, 2009); and on the Ethiopian case, see Bairu Tafla, "A Turning Point in Ethiopian Historiography from Within," in *Die äthiopischen Studien im 20. Jahrhundert*, ed. Rainer Maria Voigt (Aachen, Germany: Shaker Verlag, 2003), 159–182; and James De Lorenzi, *Guardians of the Tradition: Historians and Historical Writing in Ethiopia and Eritrea* (Rochester, NY: University of Rochester Press, 2015), 1–12.
3. Enrico Cerulli, "Una raccolta amarica di canti funebri," *RSO* 10, no. 2/4 (1923–1925): 265–280. The original work is Heruy Wäldä Sellasé, የልቅሶ ዜማ ግጥም፡ ምስጢሩ ከመጻሕፍት ጋራ የተሰማማ (አዲስ አበባ፡ 1910 ዓም).
4. Heruy Wäldä Sellasé, በኢትዮጵያ የሚገኙ በግዕዝና በአማርኛ ቋንቋ የተጻፉ የመጻሕፍት ካታሎግ (አዲስ አበባ፡ ተፈሪ መኮንን ማተሚያ ቤት, 1920 ዓም), 23. The referred works are likely Cerulli's "Canti popolari amarici," *RRAL* V, 25 (1916): 563–658, described as "ያማርኛ ዘፈን"; and his "Canti funebri," described as "የለቅሶ ዜማ ትርጉም." These contain excerpts from Heruy's መጽሐፈ ቅኔ and የልቅሶ ዜማ ግጥም.
5. Enrico Cerulli, "Nuove idee nell'Etiopia e nuova letteratura amarica," *Oriente moderno* 6, no. 3 (1926): 167–173.
6. Federico Cresti, "Il professore e il generale: La polemica tra Carlo Alfonso Nallino e Rodolfo Graziani sulla Senussia e su altre questioni libiche," *Studi storici* 45, no. 4 (2004): 1116n13.
7. Heruy Wäldä Sellasé, ለልጅ ምክር ለአባት መታሰቢያ (አዲስ አበባ፡ ብራና ማተሚያ ቤት, 1997 ዓም).
8. Cerulli, "Nuove idee," 168.
9. Cerulli, "Nuove idee," 173n2.
10. On the Italian fields of ethnopsychiatry and race psychiatry, see Marianna Scarfone, "Italian Colonial Psychiatry: Outlines of a Discipline, and Practical Achievements in Libya and the Horn of Africa," *History of Psychiatry* 27, no. 4 (2016): 389–405. More generally, see Dane Kennedy, "Minds in Crisis: Medical-Moral Theories of Disorder in the Late Colonial World," in *Anxieties, Fear, and Panic in Colonial Settings: Empires on the Verge of a Nervous Breakdown*, ed. Harald Fischer-Tiné (Cham, Germany: Palgrave-Macmillan, 2016), 27–48.

11. Heruy Wäldä Sellasé, ለልጅ ምክር, 3-4: "ከመጻሕፍት ያገበሁትንና ከሸማግሌዎችም ከወቂያችም ሰዎች በየዜው የሰማሁትን ነገር ሁሉ"
12. Enrico Cerulli, "Notizie varie," *Oriente moderno* 6, no. 10 (1926): 557. For Heruy's claim to authorship of this work, see his ካታሎግ, 26.
13. Enrico Cerulli, "Notizie varie," *Oriente moderno* 7, no. 7 (1927): 353-357.
14. Enrico Cerulli, "Pubblicazioni recenti dei musulmani e dei cristiani dell'Etiopia," *Oriente moderno* 8, no. 9 (1928): 429-432. That same year, Cerulli published translated excerpts from this work: "Inni della chiesa abissina," *RSO* 12 (1929-1930): 361-407. See also the further translations in "Canti burleschi di studenti delle scuole abissine," *RSO* 13, no. 4 (1933): 342-350.
15. On this relationship, see Chinua Achebe, "Colonialist Criticism," in *Hopes and Impediments: Selected Essays 1965-1987* (New York: Penguin, 1988), 68-90; and Ngũgĩ wa Thiong'o, *Moving the Centre: The Struggle for Cultural Freedoms* (New York: James Currey, 1993), 100-105.
16. Heruy Wäldä Sellasé, ዋዜማ። በማግሥቱ የኢትዮጵያን ነፃሥታት የታሪክ በዓል ለማክበር (አዲስ አበባ፡ ጎሐ ጽባሕ, 1921 ዓም).
17. Heruy Wäldä Sellasé, ዋዜማ, 1.
18. It would appear that he is referring to a work that was then entitled የኢትዮጵያ ነፃሥታት ታሪክ, which he also noted in his 1928 bibliography of his own writings. This is presumably the major history of Ethiopia that he finished in 1935: Heruy Wäldä Sellasé, የኢትዮጵያ ታሪክ። ከንግሥተ ሳባ እስከ ታላቁ የአድዋ ድል (አዲስ አበባ፡ ሥዓይት ተከላማርያም, 2006), with note about completion on 26-27. The 1928 bibliography also identifies a second work with the title የኢትዮጵያ ነፃሥታትና ጸጻሳት፣ የአጨጌዎችም ቁጥር, which presumably became ዋዜማ: see Heruy Wäldä Sellasé, ካታሎግ, 26.
19. Kässaté Berhan Täsämma, መዝገበ ቃላት (አዲስ አበባ፡ 2008), 947. He notes that the word refers to both the vigil gathering and the work of preparing the text of the liturgy for the feast.
20. In this, Heruy suggested his work fulfilled the fifteenth-century wish of Emperor Zär'a Ya'eqob for a historical feast that would nourish future generations through the achievements of the ancestors: Heruy Wäldä Sellasé, ዋዜማ, 2.
21. Heruy Wäldä Sellasé, ዋዜማ, 12-14.
22. "ግምጃ ቤት"
23. Heruy Wäldä Sellasé, ዋዜማ, 2-3.
24. De Lorenzi, *Guardians of the Tradition*, 25-27.
25. Heruy Wäldä Sellasé, ዋዜማ, 5.
26. For his correspondence with German Orientalist Eugen Mittwoch, see Edward Ullendorff, "Some Early Amharic Letters," *BSOAS* 35, no. 2 (1972): 232-243; and on his encounter with the American physical anthropologist Carleton Coon, see the latter's *Measuring Ethiopia and Flight into Arabia* (London: Jonathan Cape, 1936), 55-57. For an Ethiopian assessment of foreign perceptions of Heruy's scholarship at this time, see Gäbrä Egzi'abhér Elyas, *Prowess, Piety, and Politics: The Chronicle of Abeto Iyasu and Empress Zewditu of Ethiopia, 1909-1930*, trans. Reidulf Molvaer (Cologne, Germany: Rüdiger Köppe Verlag, 1994), 525-526.

27. Heruy Wäldä Sellasé, ዋዜማ, 5: "ይልቁንም የኢትዮጵያን ታሪክ ከጻፉት ሰዎች ብዙዎቹ የውጭ አገር ሰዎች ስለሆኑ ከነዚሁ አንዳንዱ ከኢትዮጵያ ሊቃውንት ሳይጠይቁ ከየባላጉሩና ከየነጋዴው እየጠየቀ የሰሙትን ሁሉ እውነት እያደረጉ ጽፈውታል። ይህንም የመሰለውን በሐሰት የተጻፈውን የታሪክ መጽሐፍ የሚያነቡ የኢትዮጵያ ሊቃውንት ምንም እውነት ነው ብለው ባይቀበሉት እንኳ የኢትዮጵያን ታሪክ የማያውቁ የውጭ አገር ሰዎች እውነት ነው ብለው መቀበላቸው አይቀርምና ወደ ፊት ነገሩን አጣርተን ስሕተቱንም ገልጠን በምንጽፍላቸው ጊዜ አንባቢዎች ሁሉ ሳይጠነቀቁበትና ደስ ሳይላቸው አይቀርም።"
28. Heruy Wäldä Sellasé, ካታሎግ, 23.
29. This was his "Inni abissini," in which he thanked *aläqa* Haylä Sellasé, *däbtära* Täklä Giyorgis, and *aläqa* Gäbrä Heywät, all from Addis Ababa, as well as *aläqa* Gäbrä Maryam from Tegray. Cerulli was also colleagues with *aläqa* Kenfé, originally from Gojjam, who was then employed at the Italian Legation. For a discussion of *aläqa* Kenfé, see IES Ms. 1996.
30. Enrico Cerulli, "Nuovi libri pubblicati in Etiopia," *Oriente moderno* 12, no. 3 (1932): 170–175.
31. Enrico Cerulli, review of *Genti di Somalia*, by Giuseppe Caniglia, *Oriente moderno* 2, no. 8 (1923): 510–511.
32. Cerulli, "Nuovi libri," 174. On this distinction, see Sheldon Pollock, "Philology in Three Dimensions," *Postmedieval* 5, no. 4 (2014): 398–413.
33. Heruy Wäldä Sellasé, ለልጅ ምክር, 14: "ልጄ ሆይ፤ አግዚአብሐር በምድር ላይ የፈጠረውን ፍጥረት በሙሉ ባይሆን እንደ ተቻለህ መጠን በጥቂቱ መርምር።"
34. Heruy Wäldä Sellasé, ለልጅ ምክር, 15: "ልጄ ሆይ፤ ሰው ምንም ብልህና ዐዋቂ ቢሆን በሩሱ ሥራ ብቻ ራሱን ችሎ እንዳይኖር ዕወቅ፤ ነገር ግን ሁሉም በየስራው ጸንቶ እርስ በርሱ ይፋላለጋል። ስለዚህ ሰውን ሁሉ እከብረሀ ኑር እንጂ ሰውን አትናቅ፤ ስራውንም አትንቀፍ።"
35. Pierre Bourdieu, "Understanding," in *The Weight of the World: Social Suffering in Contemporary Society* (Stanford, CA: Stanford University Press, 1993), 610–611.
36. On this newspaper, see የብርሃንና ሰላም ቀ.ጋ.ሥ. ማተሚያ ቤት የወርቅ ኢዮቤልዩ 1914–1964 [ዓም] (አዲስ አበባ: ብርሃንና ሰላም, 1971); Bahru Zewde, *Pioneers of Change in Ethiopia: The Reformist Intellectuals of the Early Twentieth Century* (Athens: Ohio University Press, 2002), 188–194; and De Lorenzi, *Guardians of the Tradition*, 37–49.
37. Emanuela Trevisan Semi, *Taamrat Emmanuel: An Ethiopian Jewish Intellectual, Between Colonized and Colonizers*, trans. Jill Goldsmith (New York: Centro Primo Levi, 2016); and Brook Abdu, "Taamrat Emmanuel in Post-Italian Ethiopia," presentation at Ethiopian Jews Under Fascist Rule, New York City, October 23, 2014.
38. De Lorenzi, *Guardians of the Tradition*, 46–47.
39. Jacob Dorman, *Chosen People: The Rise of American Black Israelite Religions* (New York: Oxford University Press, 2013), 138–139; Joseph Harris, *African-American Reactions to War in Ethiopia, 1936-1941* (Baton Rouge: Louisiana State University Press, 1994), 12–13; and Trevisan Semi, *Taamrat Emmanuel*, 89–90.
40. Letter from Tä'amrat Ammanu'él to Faitlovitch, dated June 12, 1936, in *L'epistolario di Taamrat Emmanuel. Un intelletuale ebreo d'Etiopia nella prima metà del XX secolo*, ed. Emanuela Trevisan Semi (Turin: Harmattan, 2000), 219–220. On Ford's time in Ethiopia, see Dorman, *Chosen People*, 139–147.

41. Tä'amrat Ammanu'él, "ከቡር ዶክቶር ኮንቲ ሮሲኒ ስለ ጸፉት የኢትዮጵያ ታሪክ," ብርሃንና ሰላም, October 7, 1929; "ከቡር ኮንቲ ሮሲኒ ስለ ጸፉት የኢትዮጵያ ታሪክ," ብርሃንና ሰላም, October 14, 1929; and "ዜናሆሙ ለመጻሕፍት," ብርሃንና ሰላም, April 6, 1933. On Zanutto, see Ettore Rossi, "Silvio Zanutto (n. 1870–1946)," Oriente moderno 26, nos. 1/6 (1946): 55–57.
42. Ignazio Guidi, Storia della letteratura etiopica (Rome: Istituto per l'Oriente, 1932).
43. See Enrico Cerulli, review of Storia della letteratura etiopica, by Ignazio Guidi, Oriente moderno 13, no. 2 (1933): 111–112; and Giorgio Levi Della Vida, "L'opera orientalistica di Ignazio Guidi," Oriente moderno 15, no. 5 (1935): 246. Cerulli and Levi Della Vida relate the drama of the title of Guidi's work, altered by the publisher from "Brief History" to "History." Tä'amrat gestured to this change by noting the original title of Guidi's work ("አጭር ታሪክ") in his own article.
44. Letter from Tä'amrat Ammanu'él to Faitlovitch, dated December 10, 1932, in Epistolario di Taamrat Emmanuel, ed. Trevisan Semi, 153–154.
45. Tä'amrat Ammanu'él, "ዜናሆሙ ለመጻሕፍት፥ ጉዊዲ," ብርሃንና ሰላም, April 13, 1933.
46. "እጅግ ትሑትና ሰው አፍቃሪ"
47. Tä'amrat Ammanu'él, "ዜናሆሙ ለመጻሕፍት (ጉዊዲ አጭር) የግእዝ መጻሕፍት ታሪክ ዓምደ ጽዮን (ፈተኛው ታናሽ ክፍል)," ብርሃንና ሰላም, April 20, 1933; and "የ132 ገጽ ተከታይ ሁለተኛ ታናሽ ክፍል፡ ዘርአ ያዕቆብ," ብርሃንና ሰላም, May 18, 1933.
48. When describing the persistence of pre-Christian beliefs in Ethiopia, for example, he noted that the same situation persisted in "the developed countries," or "በሠለጠኑት አገሮች," for Guidi's geographic "Occident." He also offered "የጥንቆላንና የመሰግላን ፍቅር," or "the love of witchcraft and sorcery," for Guidi's "superstitious customs and beliefs." Cf. Tä'amrat Ammanu'él, "ዘርአ ያዕቆብ," ብርሃንና ሰላም, May 18, 1933; and Guidi, Storia, 52–53.
49. Tä'amrat Ammanu'él, "የ162 ገጽ ተከታይ ሦስተኛ ታናሽ ክፍል," ብርሃንና ሰላም, June 1, 1933.
50. Tä'amrat Ammanu'él, "ሐተታ ዘርአ ያዕቆብ ሐተታ ወልደ ሕይወት," ብርሃንና ሰላም, June 1, 1933.
51. Guidi, Storia, 77.
52. Specialists remain divided about the authorship of this text. For an elaboration and defence of Conti Rossini's arguments, see Anaïs Wion, "L'histoire d'un vrai faux traité philosophique (Ḥatatā Zar'a Yā'eqob et Ḥatatā Walda Ḥeywat)," Afriques, online "Debates and Readings" supplement (2013), https://journals.openedition.org/afriques/1063?lang=en. For a critique and argument that Giusto da Urbino modified the work of an Ethiopian däbtära, see Getatchew Haile, "The Discourse of Wärqe Commonly Known as Ḥatäta zä-Zär'a Ya'eqob," in Ethiopian Studies in Honour of Amha Asfaw (New York: Getatchew Haile, 2017), 51–71.
53. Carlo Conti Rossini, "Lo Ḥatatā Zar'a Yā'qob e il padre Giusto da Urbino," RRAL 29, no. 5 (1920): 213–223. See also his earlier comments in Fonti storiche etiopiche per il secolo xix. I, Vicende dell'Etiopia e delle missioni cattoliche ai tempi di Ras Ali, Deggiac Ubié e Re Teodoro secondo un documento abissino (Rome: Tipografia della R. Accademia dei Lincei, 1916).
54. Enrico Cerulli, "Giusto da Urbino," in EIT, https://www.treccani.it/enciclopedia/giusto-da-urbino_%28Enciclopedia-Italiana%29/. See also his Storia della letteratura etiopica (Milan: Nuova Accademia, 1956), 245–246.

55. Edward Ullendorff, "Some Further Material from the Eugen Mittwoch 'Nachlass,'" *BSOAS* 53, no. 1 (1990): 66: "ሮማዊ ነው የሚሉትም መርማሪዎች። እንዲህ ያለ ሊቅ በኢትዮጵያ አይገኝም በማለት ነው እንጂ እርሱ ግን ፍጹም ኢትዮጵያዊ እንደሆነ ካጸፋና [አጸጻፍ] ከመጽሐፉ ይታወቃል።"
56. Dästa Täklä Wäld, *ዐዲስ ያማርኛ መዝገበ ቃላት*። በካህናትና በሀገር ሰብ ቋንቋ (አዲስ አበባ፦ አርቲስቲክ ማተሚያ ቤት, 1970), 528: "ያገራችን ክቡር የማይፈልጡ እንዳንድ ሐሰተኞች ሰዎች ግን እነዚህን ፈላስፎች የውጭ አገር ሊቃውንት ናቸው ይላሉ።"
57. "ጭገራታ," or "source," but with additional meaning of "sprout," perhaps evoking stemma. In Ethiopian scribal and philological practice, the technical Amharic term is አብነት, meaning "original" or "exemplar": Mersha Alehegne, "Towards a Glossary of Ethiopian Manuscript Culture and Practice," *Aethiopica* 14 (2011): 147.
58. "የመጽሐፉ አይነተኛ ጥያቄ እውነት እንዲት ስትሆን ከምን መባ ይህ ሁሉ መለያየት ነው።"
59. Gäzahäñ Afläñ, "*መጽሐፈ ሐተታ የኢትዮጵያውያን ድርሰት መሆኑን ማረጃ*," ብርሃንና ሰላም, October 19, 1933.
60. On the links between *Berhanenna sälam* writers and readers, see Elizabeth Wolde Giorgis, *Modernist Art in Ethiopia* (Athens: Ohio University Press, 2019), 46–57.
61. "አጠያየቅ ማላት አኩሰም [አክሱም] ሄደው ወይም ከአኩሰም ሊቃውንት አቀፊ ቢያጡ ወይም እንፍራዝ ቢሄዱና የነበረበትን አገርና ሙቶ የተቀበረበትን ቦታ የሚያውቁ ሰው ቢጠፋ አውነትም እንዳለት ያስናቸው ነበር እርሳቸው ግን ባዲስ አበባ ለጨኸትና ለሌላ ጉዳይ ከመጣ ከማንም ሰው ቢጠይቁ የጊዮርጊስ ሰላምታ ለማርያም ምንም ነው እንደሚሉት ተረት ሁሶባቸዋል።"
62. Enno Littmann, ed. *Philosophi abessini* (Paris: Republic, 1904), 1.
63. Enno Littmann, "Arde'et: The Magic Book of the Disciples," *JAOS* 25 (1904): 1–48, specifically 15–18 and 36–39; Kässaté Berhan Täsämma, *መዝገበ ቃላት*, 719; and Dästa Täklä Wäld, *መዝገበ ቃላት*, 1136.
64. "ጀቱን ብንመለከተው እውነተኛው ማን እንድሆን እንረዳው አለን እንጂ ለሑላኞቹ እናጣብቅባቸውም የነዚሁም እንደዚሁ ነው።"
65. "ዛሬስ በመስተዋት በድንግዝግዝ እንደምናይ ነን," or "And now, it is as if we see through a blurred glass."
66. Tä'amrat Ammanu'él, "*ስለ ዘርአ ያዕቆብ ሐተታ*," ብርሃንና ሰላም, November 9, 1933.
67. "ከባለቤት ወዲያ መስካሮ ከግዚአብሔር ወዲያ ፈጣሪ የለምና በመጽሐፉ ዘርአ ያዕቆብና ወልደ ሕይወት የባልን ሰዎች ነን [የ]ደረስነው የሚል ቃል ከተገኘበት እነሱ ናቸው እንጂ ሌላ ሰውም አይደለ [አይደለም] የጸፋው ብለው ትተውታል።"
68. "የኔን የደካማውን ንግግር የሊቃውንቱን የነሀዊዲ አሳባ ገልብጬዋለሁ ሲሉ የዘርአ ያዕቆብን ሐተታ ፕሮፌሶር ሊጥማን ከአክሱሞች ተቀበለው ነው ያሳተሙት በማለታቸው ካልሆን ስሕተት ደርሰዋል።"
69. "ካልሆን ስሕተት"
70. "ደራሲው እንደ አባት እንደ ዘመድ ምክር ሲሰጥ የሚነቅፈው ነገር በጣም ጥቂት ነው። ይህን ተወት አድርጎ ስንኳ አልፎ አልፎ ቃላ ምጽጹን ሲነብት ለንግግሩ ላዩ አለው። የሚጠዋተውን አሳባ አፍርስ፥ በቶ እንደገና ከውኖ ሰብስቦ በሌላ መሠረት አንድ የገዛ አሳቡን እያራሪ እያሳማሜ፥ አየረጋገጠ እንደ ስንያለት [ስንስለት] አያያዘ ድርብና እንግብ አድርጎ ሲያመቼው አነጋሩ ቅርጹ መልጮ ውብትና ደም ግብት፥ ከርጽርት ጋራ የመላበት ነው። እንዲህ ያለውን ደራሲ፥ ኢትዮጵያዊ ነኝ አያለ ፈረንጅ ነው ሲሉብን ያገር ፍቅር ያለብን ሰዎች አሪ ብነል ፈጽም አይፈረዴብንም።"
71. "ብርታት"; alternatively, "depth" or "strength"
72. Michel Foucault, "What Is an Author?," in *Textual Strategies*, ed. Josué Harari (Ithaca, NY: Cornell University Press, 1979), 141–160.

73. Pollock, "Philology," 402–407; and Aamir Mufti, *Forget English! Orientalisms and World Literature* (Cambridge, MA: Harvard University Press, 2016), 1–55.
74. Letter from Tä'amrat Ammanu'él to Faitlovitch, dated December 10, 1932, in *Epistolario di Taamrat Emmanuel*, ed. Trevisan Semi, 153–154.
75. "ሐበሻ ስለ ተባለው ቃል," ብርሃንና ሰላም, November 24, 1927.
76. On the Amharic term, see Kässaté Berhan Täsämma, መዝገበ ቃላት, 58; and Dästa Täklä Wäld, መዝገበ ቃላት, 521–22; and more generally, Wolbert Smidt, "The Term Ḥabäša: An Ancient Ethnonym of the 'Abyssinian' Highlanders and Its Interpretations and Connotations," in *Multidisciplinary Views on the Horn of Africa: Festschrift in Honour of Rainer Voigt's 70th Birthday*, ed. Hatem Elliesie (Cologne, Germany: Rüdiger Köppe Verlag, 2014), 37–71. The cognation with Abyssinia was and remains common: for a contemporary statement, see Ignazio Guidi, *Vocabolario amarico-italiano* (Rome: Casa Editrice Italiana, 1901), 7.
77. "እኛም ይህ ቃል ከምን እንደ ተገኘ ትርጓሜውስ ምን እንደሆነ ሳንረዳው ጠላት ያወጣልንን የቅጽል ስም ተሸክመናል።"
78. Edward Ullendorff et al., "Ḥabash, Ḥabasha," in *EI2*, 3:2–8; and Rainer Voigt, "Abyssinia," in *EA*, 1:59–65.
79. "ስለዚህ ቃሉ በዞቶ ተዘርቆባቸውና ተደባልቆባቸው ይሆናል እንጂ እኛ ድብልቆች አይደለንም።"
80. On such translations, see Ranajit Guha, *History at the Limit of World-History* (New York: Columbia University Press, 2002); and Dipesh Chakrabarty, *Provincializing Europe: Postcolonial Thought and Historical Difference* (Princeton, NJ: Princeton University Press, 2000). For parallel cases, see Manan Ahmed Asif, *The Loss of Hindustan: The Invention of India* (Cambridge, MA: Harvard University Press, 2020); and Cemil Aydin, *The Idea of the Muslim World: A Global Intellectual History* (Cambridge, MA: Harvard University Press, 2017).
81. Lacy Feigh, "Abyssinia to Ethiopia: Slavery, Race, and the Transition from Empire to Nation, 1855–1974" (PhD diss., University of Pennsylvania, 2022); Brian Yates, "Ethiopian Categories, British Definitions: British Discovery of Ethiopian Identities from the Nineteenth Century to the First Decade of the Twentieth Century," *NEAS* 18, nos. 1–2 (2018): 231–269; and more broadly, Jonathon Glassman, "Towards a Comparative History of Racial Thought in Africa: Historicism, Barbarism, and Autochthony," *CSSH*, 63, no. 1 (2021): 72–98.
82. This influence is suggested by Tä'amrat's review, which addressed the etymology of *habäša*: Tä'amrat Ammanu'él, "ከቡር ዶክቶር ኮንቲ ሮሲኒ ስለ ጻፉት የኢትዮጵያ ታሪክ," ብርሃንና ሰላም, October 7, 1929. For a discussion of Conti Rossini's concurrent influence on the Eritrean historian Gäbrä Mika'él Germu, see De Lorenzi, *Guardians of the Tradition*, 91–92.
83. Carlo Conti Rossini, *Storia d'Etiopia* (Milan: Lucini, 1928), 69–70.
84. Alain Rouaud, *Afä-wärq 1868–1947: Un intellectuel éthiopien témoin de son temps* (Paris: Éditions CNRS, 1991), 140–155.
85. For a discussion, see Feigh, "Abyssinia to Ethiopia," 147–197. This novel was originally published in Rome in 1909, but its first Ethiopian edition appeared in 1926, printed in Dire Dawa.

86. Afäwärq Gäbrä Iyäsus, "መዳዉ ኤቢ," ብርሃንና ሰላም, July 25, 1929; and for a discussion, Bahru Zewde, *Pioneers of Change*, 120–121.
87. Marilyn Lake and Henry Reynolds, *Drawing the Global Colour Line: White Men's Countries and the International Challenge of Racial Equality* (New York: Cambridge University Press, 2008).
88. Abdelmajid Hannoum, *The Invention of the Maghreb: Between Africa and the Middle East* (New York: Cambridge University Press, 2021).
89. Tayyä Gäbrä Maryam, የኢትዮጵያ ሕዝብ ታሪክ ባጭር ቃል የወጣ (አስመራ፡ ሚሲአን ሱኤድዋ ማተሚያ, 1914 ዓም), which uses the term *ag'azyan*, but not *habäsha*.
90. Gäbrä Krestos Täklä Haymanot, አጭር የዓለም ታሪክ ባማርኛ (አዲስ አበባ፡ ተፈሪ መኮንን ማተሚያ ቤት, 1917 ዓም), 94–107.
91. Amharic letter from Täfäri Mäkonnen to Drummond, dated Nähasé 6, 1915 AM, Dossier Concerning Representation of Abyssinia (Ethiopia) at the Fourth Assembly, LNA: "የኢትዮጵያ መንግሥት" and "በኢትዮጵያ ንግሥተ ነገሥታት ዘውዲቱ ስም"
92. French letter from Täfäri Mäkonnen to Drummond, trans. Sahlé Şädalu, undated, Dossier Concerning Representation of Abyssinia (Ethiopia) at the Fourth Assembly, LNA.
93. "Request for Admission to the League of Nations from the Empire of Abyssinia, Translation," dated September 6, 1923, Dossier Concerning Representation of Abyssinia (Ethiopia) at the Fourth Assembly, LNA.
94. Ahmed Asif, *Loss of Hindustan*, 4–5.

4. Ferragosto

1. This biography is based on Tässäma Eshäté, ስምና ወርቁ (አዲስ አበባ፡ 1985 ዓም), 1–44; "የነጋድራስ ተሰማ እሽቴ አጭር የሕይወት ታሪክ," አዲስ ዘመን, Hedar 12, 1964; and Taddele Yidnekatchew, "Negadras Tessema the Witty Poet: Renderings of a Grandson," *IESB* 21/22 (2000): 18–24.
2. For his collected works, see Tässäma Eshäté, ስምና ወርቁ; and for early poems, see Tässäma Eshäté, "ስለ ደጃዝማች መኮሪ ገርማሜ ሞት," and "ኢጣልያ በግፍ ስለ መነሣቷ," ብርሃንና ሰላም, May 26, 1932, and November 21, 1935.
3. Tässäma Eshäté, ስምና ወርቁ, 92: "የሰላም አለቆች እንግሊዝ ፈረንሳይ[፤] አምላክ አይግደለኝ የናንተን ጉድ ሳላይ[።]"
4. Tässäma Eshäté, ስምና ወርቁ, 176.
5. Susan Pederson, "An International Regime in an Age of Empire," *AHR* 124, no. 5 (2019): 1676–1680; Sean Andrew Wempe, "A League to Preserve Empires: Understanding the Mandates System and Avenues for Further Scholarly Inquiry," *AHR* 124, no. 5 (2019): 1723–1731; and Susan Pederson, "Back to the League of Nations," *AHR* 112, no. 4 (2007): 1091–1117.
6. Adom Getachew, *Worldmaking After Empire: The Rise and Fall of Self-Determination* (Princeton, NJ: Princeton University Press, 2019); Sean Andrew Wempe, *Revenants of the German Empire: Colonial Germans, Imperialism, and the League of Nations* (New York:

Oxford University Press, 2019); Susan Pederson, *The Guardians: The League of Nations and the Crisis of Empire* (New York: Oxford University Press, 2015); and Keith David Watenpaugh, *Bread from Stones: The Middle East and the Making of Modern Humanitarianism* (Berkeley: University of California Press, 2015).

7. Billie Melman, *Empires of Antiquities: Modernity and the Rediscovery of the Ancient Near East, 1914-1950* (New York: Oxford University Press, 2020).
8. Pederson, *The Guardians*.
9. Valeska Huber and Jürgen Osterhammel, "Introduction: Global Publics," in *Global Publics: Their Power and Their Limits, 1870-1990*, ed. Huber and Osterhammel (London: Oxford University Press, 2020), 1–60.
10. Arnold Toynbee, *Survey of International Affairs 1935* (London: Oxford University Press, 1936), 2:7.
11. Hubert Deschamps, "Griaule, Mandel et l'Ethiopie," *JES* 4, no. 1 (1966): 72.
12. Carleton Coon, "A Realist Looks at Ethiopia," *Atlantic Monthly* (September 1935): 314.
13. Palmiro Togliatti [Comrade Ercoli], "The Preparations for Imperialist War and the Tasks of the Communist International," in *VII Congress of the Communist International* (Moscow: Foreign Languages Publishing House, 1939), 386–451.
14. Joseph Harris, *African-American Reactions to War in Ethiopia, 1936-1941* (Baton Rouge: Louisiana State University Press, 1994), 20.
15. Jomo Kenyatta, "Hands off Abyssinia!," *Labour Monthly* 17, no. 9 (1935): 532–536.
16. C. L. R. James, "Abyssinia and the Imperialists," *The Keys* 3, no. 3 (1936): 32–33.
17. Alfred Nemours, *Craignons d'être un jour l'Éthiopie de quelqu'un* (Port-au-Prince, Haiti: Imprimerie du Collège Vertières, 1945), 26.
18. Mäkonnen Haylé, "Last Gobble of Africa," *The Crisis* (March 1935): 70–71, 90.
19. Transcript of radio broadcast of Tesfay Zäphiro, dated January 3, 1936, ASMAI AP cart. 15.
20. Emmanu'él Abraham and Luigi Villari, "Abyssinia and Italy," *JRAS* 34, no. 137 (1935): 377.
21. Marcel Griaule, *La peau de l'ours* (Paris: Gallimard, 1936), 179.
22. Musab Younis, *On the Scale of the World: The Formation of Black Anticolonial Thought* (Berkeley: University of California Press, 2022), 128–155.
23. For the Ethiopian side of this mobilization, see Fikru Negash Gebrekidan, *Bond Without Blood: A History of Ethiopian and New World Black Relations, 1896-1991* (Lawrenceville, NJ: Africa World Press, 2015). On Black internationalism and the African diaspora, see Nadia Nurhussein, *Black Land: Imperial Ethiopianism and African America* (Princeton, NJ: Princeton University Press, 2019); Imaobong Umoren, *Race Women Internationalists: Activist-Intellectuals and Global Freedom Struggles* (Berkeley: University of California Press, 2018); Marc Matera, *Black London: The Imperial Metropolis and Decolonization in the Twentieth Century* (Berkeley: University of California Press, 2015); Minkah Makalani, *In the Cause of Freedom: Radical Black Internationalism from Harlem to London, 1917-1939* (Chapel Hill: University of North Carolina Press, 2013); Jennifer Anne Boittin, *Colonial Metropolis: The Urban Grounds of Anti-Imperialism and Feminism in Interwar Paris* (Lincoln: University of Nebraska Press, 2010); William

Scott, *The Sons of Sheba's Race: African-Americans and the Italo-Ethiopian War, 1935-1941* (Bloomington: Indiana University Press, 1993); and Harris, *African American Reactions*. The situation in Anglophone West Africa is described in S. K. B. Asante, *Pan-African Protest: West Africa and the Italo-Ethiopian Crisis, 1934-1941* (London: Longman, 1977). On the Italian diaspora response, see Chiara Grilli, "Making of the Italian American Colonizer: Colonialism, Race, and the Italo-Ethiopian War," *IIJPS* 23, no. 4 (2021): 526-543; and Fiorello Ventresco, "Italian-Americans and the Ethiopian Crisis," *Italian Americana* 6, no. 1 (1980): 4-27.

24. "White and Negro Join Peace Rally," *New York Times*, August 4, 1935.
25. Adom Getachew, *Worldmaking After Empire*, 18-21. See also Megan Donaldson, "The League of Nations, Ethiopia, and the Making of States," *Humanity* 11, no. 1 (2020): 6-31.
26. Adom Getachew, *Worldmaking After Empire*, 58.
27. Zara Steiner, *The Triumph of the Dark: European International History, 1933-1939* (New York: Oxford University Press, 2011), 100-161; and Thomas Burkman, *Japan and the League of Nations: Empire and the World Order, 1914-1938* (Honolulu: University of Hawai'i Press, 2007).
28. Francis Walters, *A History of the League of Nations* (New York: Oxford University Press, 1952), 623.
29. Harrison Ola Akingbade, "The Liberian Problem of Forced Labor, 1926-1940," *Africa* 52, no. 2 (1997): 261-273.
30. Arlena Buelli, "The Hands Off Ethiopia Campaign: Racial Solidarities and Intercolonial Antifascism in South Asia (1935-36)," *JGH* 18, no. 1 (2023): 47-67; and Richard Pankhurst, "The Short-Lived Newspaper *Abyssinia* (1935-1936): A Memory of the League of Nations," in *Varia Aethiopica in Memory of Sevir B. Chernetsov (1943-2005)*, ed. Denis Nosnitsin (Piscataway, NJ: Gorgias, 2009), 257-264.
31. Gianfranco Cresciani, *Fascism, Anti-Fascism, and Italians in Australia, 1922-1945* (Canberra: Australian National University Press, 1980); Federico Finchelstein, *Transatlantic Fascism: Ideology, Violence, and the Sacred in Argentina and Italy, 1919-1945* (Chapel Hill, NC: Duke University Press, 2010); Grilli, "Italian American Colonizer"; and Ventresco, "Italian-Americans." In Toronto's large Italian community, the Friulano anarchist Attilio "Art" Bortolotti led clashes with local fascists and regime propagandists: Olga Zorzi Pugliese, "Antifascisti friulani in Canada nel periodo interbellico, con la trascrizione dell'intervista inedita rilasciata ad Angelo Principe dall'anarchico Attilio Bortolotti," *Metodi e ricerche* 32, no. 2 (2013): 133-183.
32. On Alämayyähu Goshu, see Mahtämä Sellasé Wäldä Mäsqäl, "የኢትዮጵያ ባሕል ጥናት፡ ቼ በለው," *JES* 7, no. 2 (1969): 270. For an early Ethiopian account, see "በኢጣሊያና በኢትዮጵያ መካከል ያልያል ላይ የሆነ ድንገተኛ አደጋ," ብርሃንና ሰላም, January 3, 1935.
33. On these dynamics, see Bruce Strang, ed., *Collision of Empires: Italy's Invasion of Ethiopia and Its International Impact* (Surrey, UK: Ashgate, 2013); George Baer, *Test Case: Italy, Ethiopia, and the League of Nations* (Stanford, CA: Hoover Institution Press, 1976); and Steiner, *Triumph of the Dark*, 100-166.
34. Walters, *History of the League*, 638.

35. Harold Marcus, "The Embargo on Arms Sales to Ethiopia," *IJAHS* 16, no. 2 (1983): 263–279.
36. "Telegram, dated December 18th, 1934, from the Abyssinian Government to the Secretary General," *LNJ* (February 1935): 249; and "Letter, dated January 15th, 1935, from the Abyssinian Government to the Secretary-General, and Memorandum concerning the incidents at Walwal between November 23rd and December 5th, 1934," *LNJ* (February 1935): 252–274.
37. "Communication from the Ethiopian Government," dated March 19, 1935, C.126.M.64.1935.VII, LNDP.
38. Pittman Potter, *The Wal Wal Arbitration* (Washington, DC: Carnegie Institute, 1938), 11–12.
39. Alessandro Lessona, *Verso l'impero. Memorie per la storia politica del conflitto italo-etiopico* (Florence: Sansoni, 1939), 130.
40. Letter from Mussolini to Avenol, dated September 2, 1935, League of Nations Secretariat Registry Files, LNA.
41. "Letter, dated September 5th, 1935, from the Representative of Italy to the Secretary-General," *LNJ* (November 1935): 1585–1586.
42. "Memorandum by the Italian Government on the Situation in Ethiopia: I. Report," dated September 11, 1935, C.340.M.171.1935VII; and "Memorandum by the Italian Government on the Situation in Ethiopia: II. Documents," dated September 28, 1935, C.340(A).M.171(A).1935VII, both in LNDP.
43. Walters, *History of the League*, 641–642.
44. "Memorandum," 38.
45. In the official French translation, this phase was instead given as "Les Ethiopiens sont un peuple sémitique," though Abyssinia was used elsewhere in the discussion: annotated French translation of Italian memorandum, dated September 1935, Ethiopian-Italian Relations, Correspondence with the Italian Government, LNA.
46. On Avenol, see James Barros, *Betrayal from Within: Joseph Avenol, Secretary-General of the League of Nations, 1933-1940* (New Haven, CT: Yale University Press, 1969); on Theodoli, see Elisabetta Tollardo, *Fascist Italy and the League of Nations, 1922-1935* (New York: Palgrave, 2016), 159–213; and on Guariglia, see Raffaele Guariglia, *Ricordi 1922-1946* (Naples: Edizione Scientifiche Italiane, 1950).
47. Guariglia, *Ricordi*, 54–59.
48. Guariglia, *Ricordi*, 241–242; and Barros, *Betrayal from Within*, 77–79.
49. Guariglia, *Ricordi*, 243.
50. A 1938 entry on Cerulli in the *Enciclopedia italiana* noted that he participated in nearly all of the diplomatic and political preparations for the invasion: "Enrico Cerulli," in *EIT*, https://www.treccani.it/enciclopedia/enrico-cerulli_%28Enciclopedia-Italiana%29/.
51. "La conférence a trois est réunie," *Journal de Genève*, August 17, 1935; and "La delegazione italiana all'assemblea ginevrina," *Corriere della sera*, September 3, 1935.
52. Griaule, *Peau de l'ours*, 100–101.
53. Enrico Cerulli [Niliacus], "L'Etiopia di oggi," *Nuova antologia* 1511 (1935): 43–53; and "Etiopia schiavista," *Nuova antologia* 1520 (1935): 161–169.

54. The attribution comes from Lanfranco Ricci and Gianfrancesco Lusini: Lanfranco Ricci and Gianfrancesco Lusini, "Enrico Cerulli [con Bibliografia]," *RSE* 32 (1988): 27, though they only note the second Niliacus article.
55. On Horapollo, see Mark Wildish, "Hieroglyphic Semantics in Late Antiquity" (PhD diss., Durham University, 2013), 29–40; and Stewart Karren, "Horapollon," in *The Coptic Encyclopedia*, ed. Aziz Suryal Atiya (New York: Macmillan, 1991), 4:1255–1256. On his influence, see Anthony Grafton, "Foreword," in *The Hieroglyphics of Horapollo*, trans. George Boas (Princeton, NJ: Princeton University Press, 1993), xi–xxi.
56. His contributions to *Oriente moderno* in this period were similarly anonymous.
57. Jean Maspero, "Horapollon et la fin du paganisme égyptien," *BIFAO* 11 (1914): 163–195.
58. Cerulli, "Etiopia di oggi," 46–47. This argument parallels the analysis in "Memorandum," 36–37.
59. Cerulli, "Etiopia di oggi," 50.
60. The reference is not given, but for the passage in question, see Tayyä Gäbrä Maryam, የኢትዮጵያ ሕዝብ ታሪh, 2.
61. Cerulli, "Etiopia di oggi," 51.
62. Cerulli, "Etiopia di oggi," 51.
63. Cerulli, "Etiopia di oggi," 52.
64. Cerulli, "Etiopia schiavista," 166; and Enrico Cerulli, *Folk Literature of the Galla of Southern Abyssinia* (Cambridge, MA: African Department of the Peabody Museum of Harvard University, 1922), 80.
65. Cerulli, "Etiopia schiavista," 163; and "Memorandum," unpaginated backmatter.
66. Cerulli, "Etiopia schiavista," 168: "Ci sarà qualcuno in Europa che creda conveniente il contrapporre a queste glorie ed a queste conquiste della scienza e dell'ardimento le catture di schiavi, le mutilazioni, le uccisioni in massa, la cieca distruzione di uomini e di ricchezze che hanno contrassegnato le spedizioni degli Abissini nelle stesse regioni?"
67. Cerulli, "Etiopia schiavista," 169.
68. Lessona, *Verso l'impero*, 141.
69. "Il 'dato' irrefutabile," *Opera omnia di Benito Mussolini*, ed. Edoardo and Duilio Susmel (Florence: La Fenice, 1959), 27:110–111.
70. "364 Riunione del Consiglio dei Ministri," *Benito Mussolini*, ed. Susmel, 27:115.
71. "Quatre Septembre," *Journal de Genève*, September 4, 1935; and "First Day at Geneva," *The Times*, September 5, 1935.
72. Walters, *History of the League*, 644; but cf. Guariglia, *Ricordi*, 259.

5. Mäskäräm

1. John Spencer, *Ethiopia at Bay: A Personal Account of the Haile Selassie Years* (Algonac, MI: Reference Publications, 1984), 25n5.
2. On his life, see Bahru Zewde, *Pioneers of Change in Ethiopia: The Reformist Intellectuals of the Early Twentieth Century* (Athens: Ohio University Press, 2002), 57–64; and Täklä

Hawaryat Täklä Maryam, አቶባዮግራፊ *(የሕይወቴ ታሪክ)* (አዲስ አበባ፡ አዲስ አበባ ዩኒቨርሲቲ ፕሬስ, 1998 ዓም).

3. Elizabeth Wolde Giorgis, *Modernist Art in Ethiopia* (Athens: Ohio University Press, 2019), 58–59; Lealem Berhanu Terega and Mahlet Solomon, "Religious, Political and Cultural Influences on the First Ethiopian Playwright, Teklehawariat Teklemariam and His Play 'Fabula: Yawreoch Commedia,'" *JACS* 26, no. 3 (2014): 276–286; and Lanfranco Ricci, "La 'komidiyā' di Takla Hawāryāt," in *Proceedings of the Ninth International Congress of Ethiopian Studies, Moscow, August 26–29, 1986*, ed. Anatoly Andreevich Gromyko (Moscow: Nauka Publishers, 1989), 193–203.
4. Mahtämä Sellasé Wäldä Mäsqäl, ዝክረ ነገር (አዲስ አበባ፡ አርቲስቲክ ማተሚያ ቤት, 1962 ዓም), 800–834.
5. "ሹም ሽር," ብርሃንና ሰላም, September 17, 1931.
6. Heruy Wäldä Sellasé, የሕይወት ታሪክ *(Biographie)* በኋላ ዘመን ለሚነሡ ልጆች ማስታወቂያ (አዲስ አበባ፡ ተፈሪ መኮንን ማተሚያ ቤት, 1915 ዓም), 31–32.
7. Enrico Cerulli, "Rassegna periodica di pubblicazioni in lingue etiopiche fatte in Etiopia. I," *Oriente moderno* 13 (1933): 61. See also his "Nuovo ministro d'Etiopia a Parigi," *Oriente moderno* 13 (1933): 108.
8. "ሹም ሽር," ብርሃንና ሰላም, January 12, 1933.
9. Täklä Hawaryat Täklä Maryam, የሕይወቴ ታሪክ, 415–417: "ጊዜው ወደ ውጭ አገር የምሄድበት አይደለም። በመልከተኛነት የምሠራው ጠቃሚ ሊሆን አይችልም። መልከተኛ የተቆረጠውን ሐሳብ እየተቀበለ አቀላይ ይሆናል እንጂ ሌላ ምንም ማድረግ አይችልም። አዚሁ ሆኜ ሐሳብ ለመቅረጥ ክርክር ሲደረግ ብረዳ ይሻላል። እባከዎ፣ አገልግሎቴ ጠቃሚ እንዲሆን ያድርጉ፡ የጎሩይን ፈቃድ አደረስ ብለው፣ ታገር እንድወጣ በማድረግም በጣም አዝናለሁ።"
10. Aklilu Habtäwäld, የአክሊሉ ማስታወሻ *Aklilu Remembers* (አዲስ አበባ፡ አዲስ አበባ ዩኒቨርሲቲ ፕሬስ, 2010), 119–120.
11. Adrien Zervos, *L'empire d'Éthiopie: Le miroir de l'Éthiopie moderne, 1906-1935* (Alexandria: Imprimerie de l'École professionnelle des frères, 1936), 117; interview with Shimelis Yilma, January 26, 2021; Spencer, *Ethiopia*, 14–21; and Costantino Paleologos, *Tafari & Ci.* (Trieste: Delfino, 1938), 204–205.
12. Spencer, *Ethiopia*, 20–21; and Marcel Griaule, *La peau de l'ours* (Paris: Gallimard, 1936), 70–71.
13. Täklä Hawaryat Täklä Maryam, የሕይወቴ ታሪክ, 417–419; "Un traité de commerce et d'amitié a été signé entre l'Éthiopie et la Suisse," *Courrier d'Éthiopie*, June 23, 1933; "Etiopia," *Oriente moderno* 13 (1933): 428–429; and "The Economic Conference," *The Times*, June 8, 1933.
14. Francis Walters, *A History of the League of Nations* (New York: Oxford University Press, 1952), 629–631.
15. "Communication from the Ethiopian Government," dated March 18, 1935, C.126.M.64.1935.VII, LNDP; and Marse'é Hazän Wäldä Qirqos, ቀዳማዊ ኃይለ ሥላሴ 1922–1927 (አዲስ አበባ፡ አዲስ አበባ ዩኒቨርሲቲ ፕሬስ, 2009 ዓም), 207.
16. "Communication from the Italian Government: Observations of the Italian Government," dated March 22, 1935, C.132.M.69.1935.VII; and "Communication from the Abyssinian Government," dated April 1, 1935, C.148.M.78.1935.VII, both in LNDP.

On a parallel development involving Ethiopian overtures to Egypt, see Nir Arielli, *Fascist Italy and Middle East 1933-40* (New York: Palgrave Macmillan, 2010), 54.
17. "Dispute Between Ethiopia and Italy, Request by the Ethiopian Government: Memorandum," dated June 12, 1935, C.230(1).M.114(1).1935.VII, LNDP.
18. Letter from Täklä Hawaryat to Potter, dated June 18, 1935, in Pittman Potter, *The Wal Wal Arbitration* (Washington, DC: Carnegie Institute, 1938), 38.
19. "La séance privée," *Journal de Genève*, August 2, 1935.
20. "Laborieuse discussion du compromis Laval-Eden," *Journal de Genève*, August 4, 1935; and "Le ministre d'Éthiopie chez M. Laval," *Gazette de Lausanne*, August 12, 1935.
21. "Request by the Ethiopian Government: Note by the Secretary General," dated August 14, 1935, C.312.M.164.1935.VII, LNDP.
22. The transcript of Täklä Hawaryat's testimony can be found in Potter, *Wal Wal*, 167–169. Cerulli's role is suggested by the reference to an Italian translator who was apparently close at hand, and additionally by a newspaper article that describes his presence in the Italian arbitral delegation: Potter, *Wal Wal*, 166–167; and "Le conflit italo-éthiopien," *Journal de Genève*, August 17, 1935.
23. *LNJ*, November 1935, 1133–1134. On Ruiz Guiñazú's politics, see Federico Finchelstein, *Transatlantic Fascism: Ideology, Violence, and the Sacred in Argentina and Italy, 1919–1945* (Chapel Hill, NC: Duke University Press, 2010), 208–209n54.
24. "First Meeting (Private then Public)," *LNJ* (November 1935): 1137.
25. "First Meeting," 1137–1139.
26. "Un grave incident," *Journal de Genève*, September 7, 1935.
27. "Second Meeting (Public)," *LNJ* (November 1935): 1141.
28. "Second Meeting," 1141–1142.
29. Hugh Phillips, *Between the Revolution and the West: A Political Biography of Maxim M. Litvinov* (Boulder, CO: Westview, 1992), 155–166; and Zara Steiner, *The Triumph of the Dark: European International History, 1933–1939* (New York: Oxford University Press, 2011), 134–135.
30. Walters later celebrated his principled and "clear-sighted" understanding of the implications of the crisis: Walters, *History of League*, 712–713.
31. "Third Meeting (Private then Public)," *LNJ* (November 1935): 1144–1145.
32. Griaule, *Peau de l'ours*, 67.
33. For biographies, see Isabelle Fiemeyer, *Marcel Griaule, citoyen dogon* (Paris: Actes Sud, 2004); and Éric Jolly, "Marcel Griaule, ethnologue: La construction d'une discipline (1925–1956)," *Journal des africanistes* 71, no. 1 (2001): 149–190.
34. Fiemeyer, *Griaule*, 25–27. On Agäññähu Engeda, see Elizabeth Wolde Giorgis, *Modernist Art in Ethiopia*, 63–66; and on his connection to Cerulli, see Bälätä Gäbré, የጉዞ ትዝታ (አዲስ አበባ: ቼምበር ማተሚያ ቤት, 2004 ዓም), 100.
35. For *abba* Jérome's account of his education and escape from Eritrea, see Gäbrä Mädhen Gäbrä Musé [*abba* Jérome], "Souvenirs d'Erythrée," in *Guirlande pour Abba Jérôme: travaux offerts à Abba Jérôme Gabra Musé par ses élèves et ses amis*, ed. Joseph Tubiana (Paris: Mois en Afrique, 1983), 7–46. On his diplomatic career, see Berhanou

Abebe, "Quelques notes sur le rôle d'abba Jérôme Gabra-Muse dans la diplomatie éthiopienne de l'entre-deux guerres," in *Proceedings of the Eighth International Conference of Ethiopian Studies*, ed. Taddese Beyene (Addis Ababa: Institute of Ethiopian Studies, 1989), 299–313.

36. Fiemeyer, *Griaule*, 32–33.
37. For all these reasons, his legacy is complex: he is seen variously as a disciplinary founder, an exemplar of ethnographic surrealism, and an influential but methodologically flawed fieldworker. For assessments, see Walter E. A. van Beek et al., "Dogon Restudied: A Field Evaluation of the Work of Marcel Griaule [and Comments and Replies]," *Current Anthropology* 32, no. 2 (1991): 139–167; and Geneviève Calame-Griaule, "On the Dogon Restudied," *Current Anthropology* 32, no. 5 (1991): 575–577. On Griaule's "ethnographic surrealism," see James Clifford, *The Predicament of Culture: Twentieth-Century Ethnography, Literature, and Art* (Cambridge, MA: Harvard University Press, 1988), 55–91; and on his ethnological-literary method, see Vincent Debaene, *Far Afield: French Anthropology Between Science and Literature*, trans. Justin Izzo (Chicago: University of Chicago Press, 2014), esp. 151–172.
38. Heruy Wäldä Sellasé, የሕይወት ታሪክ, 43–44; and Mahtämä Sellasé Wäldä Mäsqäl, "የኢትዮጵያ ባሕል ጥናት፡፡ ቼ በለው፣" *JES* 7, no. 2 (1969): 243.
39. The last of these is Marcel Griaule, *Les flambeurs d'hommes* (Paris: Calmann-Lévy, 1934).
40. Fiemeyer, *Griaule*, 34–44; Alice Conklin, *In the Museum of Man: Race, Anthropology, and Empire in France, 1850–1950* (Ithaca, NY: Cornell University Press, 2013), 199–219, 292–301; and Jacques Bureau, *Marcel Cohen et ses successeurs, ou Cent ans d'études éthiopiennes en France* (Addis Ababa: Maison des Études Éthiopiennes, 1997).
41. Fiemeyer, *Griaule*, 31–44; and Bureau, *Cohen*, 11–15.
42. For Heruy's notice of *abba* Jérôme's writings in this period, see his በኢትዮጵያ የሚገኙ በግዕዝና ባማሪኛ ቋንቋ የተጻፉ የመጻሕፍት ካታሎግ (አዲስ አበባ፡ ተፈሪ መኮንን ማተሚያ ቤት, 1920 ዓም), 23.
43. Collection Marcel Griaule, BNF.
44. Thus Éric Jolly terms Griaule's expeditions in this period "scientific raids": Jolly, "Griaule," 159.
45. Michel Leiris, *Phantom Africa*, trans. Brent Hayes Edwards (Chicago: University of Chicago Press, 2017), 349, 368, 370.
46. Täklä Ṣadeq Mäkwuriya, የኢትዮጵያ ታሪክ፡፡ ከአጼ ቴዎድሮስ እስከ ቀዳማዊ ኃይለ ሥላሴ (አዲስ አበባ፡ አርቲስቲክ ማተሚያ ቤት, 1946 ዓም), 142–144; and more generally, Raffaele Di Lauro, *Come abbiamo difeso l'impero* (Rome: Casa L'Editrice Arnia, 1949), and *Tre anni a Gondar* (Milan: Mondadori, 1936), with discussion of Griaule on 92–100 of the latter.
47. This was Alfredo Peluso: Di Lauro, *Tre anni*, 84–91. The consulate was also attacked in November 1934, in what was later perceived as a prelude to Wälwäl: see "L'Incidente Italo-Abissino," *Italia coloniale* XI, no. 11 (1934): 167; and "Necessità di una chiarificazione," *Italia coloniale* XI, no. 12 (1934): 177.
48. Leiris, *Phantom Africa*, 415, 439.
49. Broadly, see Éric Jolly and Marianne Lemaire, eds., *Cahier Dakar-Djibouti* (Meurcourt: Éditions les Cahiers, 2015), 733–777. See also Di Lauro, *Tre anni*, 98–99.
50. Leiris, *Phantom Africa*, 501; and Mahtämä Sellasé, "ቼ በለው፣" 268.

5. MÄSKÄRÄM   331

51. Leiris, *Phantom Africa*, 610.
52. Leiris, *Phantom Africa*, 616.
53. Leiris, *Phantom Africa*, 634.
54. Leiris, *Phantom Africa*, 629, 634–639, 647.
55. Leiris, *Phantom Africa*, 661–662.
56. Leiris, *Phantom Africa*, 685, 688.
57. Leiris, *Phantom Africa*, 691, 697. Later that same year, Heruy expelled the American physical anthropologist Carleton Coon from the country for breaching the terms of his research agreement with the Ethiopian government: see James De Lorenzi, *Guardians of the Tradition: Historians and Historical Writing in Ethiopia and Eritrea* (Rochester, NY: University of Rochester Press, 2015), 132–137.
58. Leiris, *Phantom Africa*, 697. Months later, the similarly defiant Henri de Monfreid was expelled from the country: "ከአገር ማስወጣት፣" ብርሃንና ሰላም, May 11, 1933.
59. For recollections, see Aklilu Habtäwald, የአክሊሉ ማስታወሻ, 122–123; and Griaule, *Peau de l'ours*. See also Olivier Chambard, "Marcel Griaule, un ethnologue français et le conflit italo-éthiopien," *Journal des africanistes* 54, no. 2 (1984): 101–106; and Conklin, *Museum of Man*, 294–308.
60. See his "La future campagne d'Abyssinie," *Journal de Genève*, August 4, 1935; and "Concessions abyssines sous conditions," *Journal de Genève*, August 14, 1935.
61. Griaule, *Peau de l'ours*, 51–52: "Un mémoire de deux kilogrammes lui est asséné sur la tête et tout est à recommencer."
62. Griaule, *Peau de l'ours*, 32; and "Departs," *Courrier d'Éthiopie*, February 17, 1933. Täklä Hawaryat did not mention this point in his account of the journey: የሕይወቴ ታሪኽ, 418–19.
63. *Nouvelle dépêche*, December 11, 1934.
64. "La incomprensione di certi ambienti coloniali francesi," *Italia coloniale* XII, no. 12 (1934): 188.
65. Griaule, *Peau de l'ours*, 70: "Je suis un étranger ici. Ce monde, cette procédure, cette diplomatie me sont inconnus. Je marche en aveugle et mon seul guide est mon amour désespéré pour mon pays qui est bien loin."
66. The exact dating of Griaule's document is somewhat uncertain. The League records indicate that Täklä Hawaryat sent it to the secretary general on September 4, but that the latter transmitted it to the Council on September 14. The evidence in other sources suggests that this first date was a typographic error and that the memorandum was submitted to both the secretary general and the Council on the same day, September 14.
67. "Le document Marcel Griaule," *Courrier d'Éthiopie*, December 17, 1935.
68. "L'Italie vaincra-t-elle le peuple éthiopien?," *Regards*, October 17, 1935.
69. Griaule, *Peau de l'ours*, 83: "L'une des raisons qui me font accepter de répondre au Mémoire italien est bien l'abandon de l'Ethiopie par la plupart de ceux qui en vivent ou qui en ont tiré un bénéfice quelconque. Tous ces gens, je les ai trouvés contre moi quand j'ai voulu demander au gouvernement d'Addis Ababa réparation des torts qu'on m'avait causé à Gondar. S'ils n'avaient pas été là, je suis certain que le Roi des Rois aurait eu une autre attitude."

70. Aklilu Habtäwäld, የአክሊሉ ማስታወሻ, 122–123.
71. "Comments by M. Marcel Griaule on Some of the Questions Dealt With in the Italian Government's Memorandum on the Situation in Ethiopia," dated September 4, 1935, C.357.M.182.1935.VII, LNDP.
72. "Comments by Marcel Griaule," 4.
73. "Comments by Marcel Griaule," 7–8.
74. "Comments by Marcel Griaule," 13.
75. "Comments by Marcel Griaule," 14.
76. "Comments by Marcel Griaule," 2–3.
77. "Comments by Marcel Griaule," 2.
78. Vincenzo Giuffrida-Ruggeri, "Nuovi studi sull'antropologia dell'Africa orientale: etnologia e antropometria delle popolazioni eritreo-somale-abissine e delle regioni vicine," *AAE* XLV (1915): 123–179; and Charles Seligman, *Races of Africa* (London: Thornton Butterworth, 1930), 114–126.
79. "Map Annexed to Document C.357.M.182.1935.VII: Distribution of Ethiopian Type According to Giuffrida-Ruggeri," *LNJ* (November 1935): 1595; and Enrico Cerulli et al., "Etiopia," in *EIT*, https://www.treccani.it/enciclopedia/etiopia_(Enciclopedia-Italiana)/, with the map on page 485 of the print edition.
80. Griaule, *Peau de l'ours*, 100–101.
81. "Preliminary Observations on the Italian Memorandum Submitted to the Council of the League of Nations by the Ethiopian Delegation Accredited to the League," dated September 14, 1935, C.358.M.183.1935VII, LNDP.
82. "Preliminary Observations," 2.
83. "Preliminary Observations," 3.
84. "Preliminary Observations," 4.
85. He later revealed that one of the photographs in the appendix to the memorandum had been so misconstrued by the authors that its creator formally protested to Aloisi, the Ethiopian delegation, and the League Council: "Preliminary Observations," 6; and "Annex," *LNJ* (November 1935): 1586–1587.
86. "Preliminary Observations," 4.
87. This topic emerged via Griaule's account of this practice in his *Les flambeurs d'hommes*: for discussions, see Berhanou Abebe, "*Les Flambeurs d'Hommes*. Interrogations croisées sur une réalité devenue mythe," *Annales d'Éthiopie* 20 (2004): 13–22; and Vincent Debaene, "Les 'Chroniques éthiopiennes' de Marcel Griaule," *Gradhiva* 6 (2007): 86–103.
88. "Preliminary Observations," 7–8.
89. While in Paris that July, Täklä Hawaryat also met Willis Huggins, a Harlem activist, historian, and cofounder of the Friends of Ethiopia organization. Huggins had previously met the 1919 Ethiopian delegation in New York. On these contacts, see *The Friends of Ethiopia in America* (New York: 1935), 4–6.
90. For accounts, see James W. Ford, "An Interview with Tecle Hawariate, Ethiopian Ambassador," in *The Communists and the Struggle for Negro Liberation* (New York: Harlem Division of the Communist Party, n.d.), 29–33; and William Jones, "Ethiopian

Delegate Tells Afro How America Can Help," *Baltimore Afro-American*, September 28, 1935.
91. Letter from Murphy to Du Bois, dated January 19, 1934, Du Bois Papers, UMAL.
92. James W. Ford, "The Struggle for Peace and the Independence of Ethiopia," in *Struggle for Negro Liberation*, 41–47. See also Jones, "Ethiopia has 50–50 Chance to Win," *Baltimore Afro-American*, September 14, 1935; and Harry Haywood, *A Black Communist in the Freedom Struggle*, ed. Gwendolyn Midlo Hall (Minneapolis: University of Minnesota Press, 2012), 216–217.
93. Ford, "Interview with Tecle Hawariate," 29.
94. Ford, "Interview with Tecle Hawariate," 30.
95. Jones, "How America Can Help."
96. Mark Naison, *Communists in Harlem During the Depression* (New York: Grove, 1984), 156–157.
97. Nadia Nurhussein, *Black Land: Imperial Ethiopianism and African America* (Princeton, NJ: Princeton University Press, 2019), 144–168; and Joseph Harris, *African-American Reactions to War in Ethiopia, 1936–1941* (Baton Rouge: Louisiana State University Press, 1994), 34–62.
98. Lisa Tomlinson, *Una Marson* (Kingston, Jamaica: University of the West Indies Press, 2019); Delia Jarrett-Macauley, *The Life of Una Marson, 1905–1965* (Manchester, UK: Manchester University Press, 1998); and Imaobong Umoren, *Race Women Internationalists: Activist-Intellectuals and Global Freedom Struggles* (Berkeley: University of California Press, 2018).
99. "Circulaire interne. Collaborateurs temporaires. Rapport pour 1935," dated December 1935, League of Nations Secretariat Internal Circulars, LNA. On this role, see Emil Eiby Seidenfaden, "The League of Nations' Collaboration with an 'International Public,' 1919–1939," *CEH* 31, no. 3 (2022): 368–380.
100. "Fourth Plenary Meeting," *LNJ*, special supplement 138 (1935): 49–51.
101. George Baer, *The Coming of the Italian-Ethiopian War* (Cambridge, MA: Harvard University Press, 1967), 327–331.
102. "Fourth Plenary Meeting," 57.
103. Haylä Sellasé, *My Life and Ethiopia's Progress, Volume 1: 1892–1937*, trans. Edward Ullendorff (New York: Oxford University Press, 1976), 221–225.
104. "Preliminary Observations"; and "Comments by Marcel Griaule."
105. Alessandro Lessona, *Verso l'impero. Memorie per la storia politica del conflitto italo-etiopico* (Florence: Sansoni, 1939), 150.
106. Pompeo Aloisi, *Journal (25 Juillet 1932–14 Juin 1936)*, trans. Maurice Vaussard (Paris: Plon, 1957), 304; and Luigi Villari, *Storia diplomatica del conflitto italo-etiopico* (Bologna: Zanichelli, 1943), 133–134.
107. Alberto Sbacchi, "Italian Mandate or Protectorate over Ethiopia in 1935–1936," *RSPI* 42, no. 4 (1975): 559–592; and Richard Bosworth, *Mussolini* (London: Bloomsbury, 2002), 302–303.
108. James Barros, *Betrayal from Within: Joseph Avenol, Secretary-General of the League of Nations, 1933–1940* (New Haven, CT: Yale University Press, 1969), 94–95.

334   5. MÄSKÄRÄM

109. "Text of the Note Handed by the Chairman of Five to the Ethiopian and Italian Representatives on September 18th," dated September 21, 1935, C.375.M.189.1935.VII, LNDP.
110. "Summary of the Oral Observations of the Delegate of Italy," dated September 22, 1935, C.379.M.191.1935.VII, LNDP.
111. "Reply of the Ethiopian Government to the Suggestions and Communications of the Committee of Five," dated September 23, 1935, C.378.M.190.1935.VII, 2, LNDP.
112. "Note by the Secretary General," dated October 4, 1935, C.409.M.205.1935.VII, LNDP.
113. Statement by Pompeo Aloisi, verbatim record of the Sixteenth Ordinary Session of the Assembly of the League of Nations, October 10, 1935 [Morning session], LNA.
114. Statement by Alfred Nemours, verbatim record of the Sixteenth Ordinary Session of the Assembly of the League of Nations, October 10, 1935 [Morning session], LNA.
115. For a biography and bibliography, see Alfred Nemours, *Craignons d'etre un jour l'Éthiopie de quelqu'un* (Port-au-Prince, Haiti: Imprimerie du Collège Vertières, 1945), 3–8. Nemours's research was celebrated by C. L. R. James, *The Black Jacobins: Toussaint L'Ouverture and the San Domingo Revolution* (New York: Vintage, 1989), 382.
116. Statement by Täklä Hawaryat, verbatim record of the Sixteenth Ordinary Session of the Assembly of the League of Nations, October 10, 1935 [Afternoon session], LNA.
117. This break is described in Spencer, *Ethiopia*, 37n1; and Griaule, *Peau de l'ours*, 179–181. He was replaced by *blattén géta* Wäldä Maryam Ayyäla, who eventually sided with the Italians: Aklilu Habtäwäld, የአክሊሉ ማስታወሻ, 126–130.
118. Griaule, *Peau de l'ours*, 179. After his return to Ethiopia, he joined Heruy and *ras* Mulugéta Yeggäzu in opposing the emperor's exile from the country, a view that ultimately led to a breach with Haylä Sellasé: for accounts, see Henri de Monfreid, *L'Avion noir* (Paris: Bernard Grasset, 1936), 43–45; and additionally, George Steer, *Caesar in Abyssinia* (London: Hodder and Stoughton, 1936), 364, with Täklä Hawaryat possibly the third unknown dissenter.
119. Renzo De Felice, *Mussolini il Duce: I. Gli anni del consenso 1929–1936* (Turin: Einaudi, 1974), 642.

6. "Cerulli and His Ilk"

1. "የከተማ ወሬ," ብርሃንና ሰላም, October 31, 1935.
2. "መቅድም," ብርሃንና ሰላም, October 31, 1935.
3. "እነ ቸሩሊ," or alternatively, "these Cerullis." The author also names the following coauthors of the Treccani article on Ethiopia: Nello Puccioni, Ignazio Guidi, Carlo Conti Rossini, Agostino Gaibi, Attilio Mori, and Giuseppe Stefanini.
4. See chapter 3.
5. Two years later, he employed similar language in the emperor's autobiography: Haylä Sellasé, *My Life and Ethiopia's Progress, Volume 1: 1892–1937*, trans. Edward Ullendorff (New York: Oxford University Press, 1976), 3. On Heruy's role in the

authorship of this work, see Richard Pankhurst, "Haile Sellasie's Autobiography and an Unpublished Draft," *NEAS* 3, no. 3 (1996): 102n1.

6. Claudio Fogu, *The Historic Imaginary: Politics of History in Fascist Italy* (Toronto: University of Toronto Press, 2003); and Ruth Ben-Ghiat, *Fascist Modernities: Italy, 1922–1945* (Berkeley: University of California Press, 2001).

7. Most notably, Barbara Sòrgoni and Gianni Dore: see Barbara Sòrgoni, *Etnografia e colonialismo. L'Eritrea e l'Etiopia di Alberto Pollera (1873–1939)* (Turin: Bollati Boringhieri, 2001); Sòrgoni, *Parole e corpi. Antropologia, discorso giuridico e politiche sessuali interrazziali nella colonia Eritrea (1890–1941)* (Naples: Liguori, 1998); Sòrgoni, "Pratiche antropologiche nel clima dell'impero," in *L'Impero fascista. Italia ed Etiopia (1935–1941)*, ed. Riccardo Bottoni (Bologna: Il Mulino, 2008), 411–423; Gianni Dore, "Scienze sociali, colonialismo e fascismo. La missione al lago Tana (1937)," *Lares* 87, nos. 2–3 (2021): 409–432; Dore, "Carlo Conti Rossini in Eritrea tra ricerca scientifica e prassi coloniale (1899–1903)," in *Linguistic, Oriental and Ethiopian Studies in Memory of Paolo Marrassini*, ed. Alessandro Bausi, Alessandro Gori, and Giuseppe Lusini (Wiesbaden: Harrassowitz, 2014), 221–242; Dore, "Identity and Contemporary Representations: The Heritage of Alberto Pollera's Monograph, *I Baria e i Kunama*," *NEAS* 10, no. 3 (2003): 71–99; Dore, "Ideologia coloniale e senso comune etnografico nella mostra delle terre italiane d'oltremare," in *L'Africa in vetrina: storie di musei e di esposizioni coloniali in Italia*, ed. Nicola Labanca (Treviso: Pagus, 1992), 47–65; Dore, "Antropologia e colonialismo italiano nell'epoca fascista: il razzismo biologico di Lidio Cipriani," *AFLF*, n.s. 2, no. 39 (1981): 285–313; and Dore, "Antropologia e colonialismo italiano. Rassegna di studi di questo dopoguerra," *La ricerca folklorica* 1 (1980): 129–132. See also Fabiana Dimpflmeier, ed., "Antropologia italiana e fascismo: Ripensare la storia degli studi demoetnoantropologici," special issue, *Lares* 87, nos. 2–3 (2021).

8. Emanuel Rota, "'We Will Never Leave.' The Reale Accademia d'Italia and the Invention of a Fascist Africanism," *Fascism* 2, no. 2 (2013): 161–182.

9. Ruth Ben-Ghiat, "Italian Universities Under Fascism," in *Universities Under Dictatorship*, ed. John Connelly and Michael Grüttner (University Park, PA: Penn State University Press, 2005), 45–74.

10. Mario Isnenghi, *Intellettuali militanti e intellettuali funzionari. Appunti sulla cultura fascista* (Turin: Einaudi, 1979).

11. On this academic accommodation, see Dino Piovan, "Ancient Historians and Fascism: How to React Intellectually to Totalitarianism (or Not)," in *Brill's Companion to the Classics, Fascist Italy and Nazi Germany*, ed. Helen Roche and Kyriako Demetriou (Leiden, Netherlands: Brill, 2017), 82–105; Joshua Arthurs, *Excavating Modernity: The Roman Past in Fascist Italy* (Ithaca, NY: Cornell University Press, 2012); Margherita Angelini, "Clio Among the Camicie Nere: Italian Historians and Their Allegiances to Fascism," in *In the Society of Fascists: Acclamation, Acquiescence, and Agency in Mussolini's Italy*, ed. Giulia Albanese and Roberta Pergher (New York: Palgrave, 2012), 211–231; Massimo Mastrogregori, "Sulla 'collaborazione' degli storici italiani durante il fascismo," *Belfagor* 61, no. 2 (2006): 151–168; and Renzo De Felice, "Gli storici italiani

nel periodo fascista," in *Federico Chabod e la "nuova storiografia" italiana del primo al secondo dopoguerra, 1919–1950*, ed. Brunello Vigezzi (Milan: Jaca Book, 1984), 559–630.
12. Valeria Deplano, *L'Africa in casa: Propaganda e cultura coloniale nell'Italia fascista* (Milan: Mondadori, 2015); and Carlo Giglio, "Le discipline africanistiche orientalistiche e coloniali nelle Università italiane," *Africa* 15, no. 3 (1960): 107–120.
13. Deplano, *Africa in casa*, 44–50, 82–90.
14. Deplano, *Africa in casa*, 50–52; and for a contemporary survey, Angelo Piccioli, *La nuova Italia d'oltremare* (Milan: Mondadori, 1933), 2:1717–1757.
15. Giampaolo Calchi Novati, "Studi e politica ai convegni coloniali del primo e del secondo dopoguerra," *Il Politico* 55, no. 3 (1990): 487–514; and Rota, "'We Will Never Leave.'"
16. Enzo Vinicio Alliegro, *Antropologia italiana: storia e storiografia, 1869–1975* (Florence: SEID, 2011), 145–311; and Marco Santoro, "Empire for the Poor: Imperial Dreams and the Quest for an Italian Sociology, 1870s–1950s," in *Sociology and Empire: The Imperial Entanglements of a Discipline*, ed. George Steinmetz (Durham, NC: Duke University Press, 2013), 106–165.
17. Marianna Scarfone, "Italian Colonial Psychiatry: Outlines of a Discipline, and Practical Achievements in Libya and the Horn of Africa," *History of Psychiatry* 27, no. 4 (2016): 389–405.
18. Michele Sollai, "How to Feed an Empire? Agrarian Science, Indigenous Farming, and Wheat Autarky in Italian-Occupied Ethiopia, 1937–1941," *Agricultural History* 95, no. 3 (2022): 379–416; Angelo Matteo Caglioti, "Meteorological Imperialism: Climate Science, Environment, and Empire in Liberal and Fascist Italy (1870–1940)" (PhD diss., University of California at Berkeley, 2017), 155–210; and Tiago Saraiva, *Fascist Pigs: Technoscientific Organisms and the History of Fascism* (Cambridge, MA: MIT Press, 2016), 143–155.
19. On this context, see Gino Satta, "L'ultimo baluardo della schiavitù. La 'barbarie abissina' nella propaganda per la guerra d'Etiopia," in *Variazioni africane: saggi di antropologia e storia*, ed. Fabio Viti (Modena: Fiorino, 2016), 67–93. See also Amalia Ribi Forclaz, *Humanitarian Imperialism: The Politics of Anti-Slavery Activism, 1880–1940* (New York: Oxford University Press, 2015), 139–170; Jean Allain, "Slavery and the League of Nations: Ethiopia as a Civilized Nation," *JHIL* 8 (2006): 213–244; Richard Pankhurst, "Pro- and Anti-Ethiopian Pamphleteering in Britain During the Italian Fascist Occupation (1935–41)," *IJES* 1, no. 1 (2003): 153–176; and Luigi Goglia, "Propaganda italiana a sostegno della guerra contro l'Etiopia svolta in Gran Bretagna nel 1935–36," *Storia contemporanea* 15, no. 5 (1984): 845–906.
20. Most prominently, Cerulli's teacher Levi Della Vida signed 1925 manifesto of antifascist intellectuals, refused the 1931 fascist loyalty oath, and subsequently went into exile.
21. Dore, "Cipriani"; and Sòrgoni, "Pratiche antropologiche," 421–423.
22. Lanfranco Ricci, "Conti Rossini, Carlo," in *EA*, 1:791–792.
23. "Lo storiografo dell'Etiopia," *Italia coloniale* 6, no. 8 (1929): 143–145.

24. Carlo Conti Rossini, *Italia ed Etiopia dal trattato d'Uccialli alla battaglia di Adua* (Rome: Istituto per L'Oriente, 1935).
25. Carlo Conti Rossini, "L'Etiopia è incapace di progresso civile," *Nuova antologia* 1524 (1935): 171-177.
26. Conti Rossini, "Progresso," 177: "Molti secoli di storia ci mostrano che l'Etiopia fu, almeno in certa misura, capace di accogliere elementi di civiltà dal di fuori; ma ci mostrano altresì che incapace essa fu talvolta di conservarli, sempre di svilupparli e di progredire, come incapace fu d'imprimersi un proprio movimento d'evoluzione e di civiltà ... E, se dal lungo passato può volgersi lo sguardo all'avvenire per trarne auspicî, si è indotti a pensare che soltanto un costante, savio, solido intervento esteriore potrebbe durevolmente correggere ed eliminare i fattori contrari, trarre dal popolo abissino le buone qualità, oggi gravate dalle cattive, ottenere dal paese quanto la civiltà nel resto del mondo ha diritto di esigervi."
27. Carlo Conti Rossini, "La fine di Re Teodoro in un documento abissino," *Nuova antologia* 1526 (1935): 453-458.
28. Conti Rossini had previously published *däbtära* Assäggahäñ's letters in the original Amharic: Carlo Conti Rossini, "Epistolario del debterà Aseggachègn di Uadlà," *RRAL* 6, no. 1 (1925): 449-490.
29. If the article left this link implicit, it was forcefully asserted in a September issue of the weekly *Mattino illustrato*, which featured a cover image of an enslaved Ethiopian adapted from a photograph in the Italian memorandum, and an article entitled "King Téwodros[,] the 'Hyena' of Abyssinia." See *Mattino illustrato*, September 30, 1935.
30. Lanfranco Ricci, "Martino Mario Moreno," *RSE* 20 (1964): 3-11.
31. Martino Mario Moreno, review of Heruy Wäldä Sellasé, *Mahdärä berhan, hagärä japan*, *Oriente moderno* 13, no. 5 (1933): 279-280; and letters from Tä'amrat Ammanu'él to Faitlovitch, dated September 8 and November 3, 1933, in Emanuela Trevisan Semi, ed., *L'Epistolario di Taamrat Emmanuel. Un intelletuale ebreo d'Etiopia nella prima metà del XX secolo* (Turin: Harmattan, 2000), 173, 188.
32. Ricci, "Moreno," 7.
33. Martino Mario Moreno [XXX], "Gli stranieri in Abissinia," *Nuova antologia* 1514 (1935): 443-464; with attribution from Francesco Castro, "Scritti di Martino Mario Moreno," *RSE* 20 (1964): 13.
34. Moreno, "Stranieri," 555.
35. Moreno, "Stranieri," 555.
36. Moreno, "Stranieri," 559.
37. Moreno, "Stranieri," 565: "Si riempiono la bocca con puntigliose teorie imparaticce di sovranità."
38. Moreno, "Stranieri," 565.
39. Deplano, *Africa in casa*, 80-81.
40. Mario Pigli, *L'Etiopia moderna nelle sue relazioni internazionali 1859-1931* (Padua: Antonio Milani, 1933). He also wrote articles on colonial topics for *Corriere della sera*,

and subsequently worked in Harär: Emanuele Ertola, *In terra d'Africa: Gli italiani che colonizzarono l'impero* (Bari: Laterza, 2017), 176–177.

41. Mario Pigli [Gihâd], *La civiltà italiana e l'Etiopia* (Rome: Tipografia Editrice Italiana, 1935); and Mario Pigli, *Italian Civilization in Ethiopia* (London: Dante Alighieri Society, 1936).
42. Camillo Pellizzi's preface to the English edition made this explicit: Pigli, *Italian Civilization*, 5. Decades later, Cerulli termed the work "a political-historical popularization": Cerulli, review of *Ethiopian Itineraries circa 1400-1524*, ed. O. G. S. Crawford, *Orientalia* 28, no. 4 (1959): 391n5.
43. Pigli, *Civiltà italiana*, 55.
44. "La schiavitù e la favola in Abissinia," *Italia coloniale* 12, no. 3 (1935): 36–37.
45. "Togliamo la maschera civile all'Etiopia," *Italia coloniale* 12, no. 4 (1935): 49–50.
46. "Il Tigrai sotto il millenario despotismo etiopico era un paradiso governato da diavoli," *Italia coloniale* 12, no. 10 (1935): 148–149.
47. "Che cosa è in realtà il clero etiopico," *Italia coloniale* 12, no. 12 (1935): 148–149.
48. "Che cosa è il soldato etiopico?," *Italia coloniale* 12, no. 5 (1935): 74–75.
49. Mario Missiroli [Giulio Cesare Baravelli], *L'ultimo baluardo della schiavitù: L'Abissinia* (Rome: Novissima, 1935); and Satta, "Schiavitù," 79–81.
50. Pankhurst, "Pro- and Anti-Ethiopian Pamphleteering," 169.
51. *Mattino illustrato*, October 28, 1935.
52. Alain Rouaud, *Afä-wärq 1868-1947: Un intellectuel éthiopien témoin de son temps* (Paris: Éditions CNRS, 1991), 155–158.
53. Afäwärq Gäbrä Iyäsus, "እውነትን መግለጫ፣ ሐሰቶቾችን መግለጫ," ብርሃንና ሰላም, July 20, 1933.
54. Afäwärq Gäbrä Iyäsus, *Manuale di conversazione italiano-amarico con la pronuncia figurata* (Rome: Tipografia Poliglotta Vaticana, 1934), which gives this as the third edition. The dating of the earlier editions is unclear. Albert Gérard gives the date of the first edition as 1905, while in the 1934 edition, Afäwärq states that the work was originally written in Napoli in 1917/1918, though he was in fact in Asmara at that time: see Albert Gérard, "Amharic Creative Literature: The Early Phase," *JES* 6, no. 2 (1968): 56; and Afäwärq Gäbrä Iyäsus, *Manuale*, unpaginated Amharic preface. At the time of publication, Conti Rossini judged the 1934 edition to be an updated version of Afäwärq's 1908 French-Amharic ኢትዮጵያ፡ *Guide du voyageur*, though the two works differ considerably: Carlo Conti Rossini, "Bibliografia etiopica (1927–giugno 1936)," *Aevum* 10, no. 4 (1936): 567n689. The 1934 *Manuale* is sufficiently distinct from Afäwärq's other publications that it is best seen as an original work rather than a re-edition. For a discussion of his works on the Amharic language, see Rouaud, *Afä-wärq*, 129, 225–233.
55. Afäwärq Gäbrä Iyäsus, *Manuale*, 117–119.
56. "ጥቅና ኣረመኒት" and "Tirannia e barbarismo."
57. "ኣገራችሁ ገና ኣልሰለጠነም" and "vostro paese è ancora indietro."
58. "ጋላውን ፈጀት" and "ha sterminato i galla."
59. "ፋሞ"
60. "እርኩስ ነገር ነው ያስታውካል" and "una schifezza che fa vomitare."

61. The closest antecedents would seem to be the French-Amharic dialogues "Les souverains d'Ethiopie" and "L'Empereur d'Ethiopie actuel," both in Afäwärq Gäbrä Iyäsus, ኢ.ትዮጵያ። *Guide du voyageur en Abyssinie* (Rome: De Luigi, 1908), 213–224.
62. Conti Rossini identifies at least eight such works, in addition to specialist publications such as the 1935 edition of Guidi's dictionary: Conti Rossini, "Bibliografia," 566–567.
63. In these respects, it parallels other dialogue-based colonial language manuals: Bernard Cohn, *Colonialism and Its Forms of Knowledge: The British in India* (Princeton, NJ: Princeton University Press, 1996), 39–45.
64. Elena Sengal, "Favole e storielle abissine," *Africa italiana* 53, nos. 1–13 (1935): 124–151.
65. Elena Sengal, "Favole e storielle abissine," 125; and Heruy Wäldä Sellasé, የሕይወት ታሪክ *(Biographie)* በኋላ ዘመን ለሚነሙ ልጆች ማስታወቂያ (አዲስ አበባ፡ ተፈሪ መኮንን ማተሚያ ቤት, 1915 ዓም), 64, 82–83.
66. Elena Sengal, "Favole e storielle abissine," 151.
67. "Invidioso"
68. Zännäb [*aläqa*], መጽሐፈ ጨዋታ (አዲስ አበባ፡ ጎሀ ጽባህ, 1924 ዓም). Cerulli possessed a manuscript copy of this work: Cerulli Et. Ms. 112, BAV.
69. In particular, Henri de Monfreid, "Abissinia," *Africa italiana* 53, nos. 1–13 (1935): 66–84, which critiqued Haylä Sellasé and Ethiopian society.
70. Stefan Strelcyn, "Marcel Cohen," *BSOAS* 38, no. 3 (1975): 615–622; and Jacques Bureau, *Marcel Cohen et ses successeurs, ou Cent ans d'études éthiopiennes en France* (Addis Ababa: Maison des Études Éthiopiennes, 1997), 4–8.
71. Marcel Fournier, *Marcel Mauss: A Biography*, trans. Jane Marie Todd (Princeton, NJ: Princeton University Press, 2006), 297; and *Antonio Gramsci: Témoignages* (Paris: Entente Internationale pour la Défense du Droit, de la Liberté et de la Paix en Italie, 1938), unpaginated remembrance by Cohen.
72. Marcel Cohen, "Genre de vie en Abyssinie," *Humanité*, September 26, 1935.
73. Marcel Cohen, "Individu et société en Abyssinie," *Humanité*, October 31, 1935.
74. Marcel Cohen, "Autorité et droit en Abyssinie," *Humanité*, November 19, 1935.
75. Bahru Zewde, *The Quest for Socialist Ethiopia: The Ethiopian Student Movement, c. 1960–1974* (New York: James Currey, 2014).
76. Marcel Cohen, *L'Abyssinie doit rester indépendente* (Paris: Bureau d'Éditions, 1936).
77. On this organization, see Imaobong Umoren, *Race Women Internationalists: Activist-Intellectuals and Global Freedom Struggles* (Berkeley: University of California Press, 2018), 40–43; and Jennifer Anne Boittin, *Colonial Metropolis: The Urban Grounds of Anti-Imperialism and Feminism in Interwar Paris* (Lincoln: University of Nebraska Press, 2010), 161–166.
78. On Du Bois and Ethiopia, see Fikru Negash Gebrekidan, "Pan-Africanist in the Court: W. E. B. Du Bois and His Vision of Ethiopian Internationalism," in *Routledge Handbook of Pan-Africanism*, ed. Reiland Rabaka (New York: Routledge, 2020), 273–288; Wayne Rose, "W. E. B. Du Bois: Ethiopia and Pan-Africanism," *JBS* 50, no. 3 (2019): 251–272; and Fikru Negash Gebrekidan, "Ethiopia in Black Studies from W. E. B. Du Bois to Henry Louis Gates, Jr.," *NEAS* 15, no. 1 (2015): 1–34. On his roles at the Peace

Conference and Pan-African Congress, see David Levering Lewis, *W. E. B. Du Bois: A Biography* (New York: Holt, 2009), 1:535–580; and Clarence Contee, "Du Bois, the NAACP, and the Pan-African Congress of 1919," *JNH* 57, no. 1 (1972): 13–28.
79. Fikru Negash Gebrekidan, "Ethiopia"; and Lewis, *Du Bois*, 1:635–638.
80. Aldon Morris, *The Scholar Denied: W. E. B. Du Bois and the Birth of Modern Sociology* (Berkeley: University of California Press, 2015).
81. Letter from Du Bois to Gäbru Dästa, dated May 26, 1921, Du Bois Papers, UMAL.
82. Memorandum by Du Bois for Mälaku Bäyyan and Gäbru Dästa, dated August 14, 1930, Du Bois Papers, UMAL. For a discussion, see Fikru Negash Gebrekidan, "Pan-Africanist," 275–276.
83. On Mälaku Bäyyän, see Bahru Zewde, *Pioneers of Change in Ethiopia: The Reformist Intellectuals of the Early Twentieth Century* (Athens: Ohio University Press, 2002), 134–135; and William Scott, "Black Nationalism and the Italo-Ethiopian Conflict 1934–1936," *JNH* 63, no. 2 (1978): 127–128. For his service during the invasion, when he survived a hospital bombing, see "Communication from the Ethiopian Government," dated December 9, 1935, C.474.M.250.1935.VII, LNDP. On Mälaku's death in 1940, Du Bois eulogized him as "an Ambassador of Pan Africanism in a singularly happy sense." See "As the Crow Flies," dated June 1, 1940, Du Bois Papers, UMAL.
84. Du Bois had ceded the editorship of *The Crisis* to his NAACP colleague Roy Wilkins, who featured numerous articles on Ethiopia over 1935: in addition to the previously cited Mäkonnen Haylé, "Last Gobble of Africa," *The Crisis*, March 1935; see J. A. Rogers, "Italy Over Abyssinia," *The Crisis*, February 1935; George Padmore, "Ethiopia and World Politics," *The Crisis*, May 1935; and Reuben S. Young, "Ethiopia Awakens," *The Crisis*, October 1935.
85. W. E. B. Du Bois, "The Hands of Ethiopia," Du Bois Papers, UMAL.
86. Five years later, Du Bois described the Napier expedition as an event "so fateful for all my people." See his *Dusk of Dawn* (New York: Oxford University Press, 2007), 4.
87. Du Bois, "Hands of Ethiopia," 11.
88. Du Bois, "Hands of Ethiopia," 20–21.
89. W. E. B. Du Bois, "Inter-Racial Implications of the Ethiopian Crisis: A Negro View," *Foreign Affairs* 14, no. 1 (1935): 82–92.
90. Du Bois, "Implications," 89.
91. Rose, "Du Bois," 267.
92. This same analytic predicament constrained later Marxist analysis of Ethiopian feudalism: for a discussion, see Teshale Tibebu, "Modernity, Eurocentrism, and Radical Politics in Ethiopia, 1961–1991," *African Identities* 6, no. 4 (2008): 345–371.
93. This was the periodization later adopted by the *UNESCO General History of Africa*, as discussed in chapter 11.
94. *Atti del XIX congresso internazionale degli orientalisti, Roma 23–29 settembre 1935-XIII* (Rome: Tipografia del Senato, 1938).
95. "Cronistoria del congresso," in *Congresso internazionale degli orientalisti*, 2, 26–27; and "La visita degli orientalisti del congresso internazionale," *Africa italiana* 53, no. 4 (1935): 195–196.

96. The popular press acclaimed the gathering as proof of Italian national achievement: "Il Congresso internazionale degli orientalisti sarà inaugurato domani a Roma," *Corriere della sera*, September 22, 1935. See also Maria Nallino, "Il XIX Congresso internazionale degli orientalisti," *Oriente moderno* 16, no. 2 (1936): 97–110.
97. On their relationship, see Valeria Fiorani Piacentini, "Tra oriente e occidente: una galleria di profili della storiografia arabo-islamica italiana," *Studi storici* 50, no. 4 (2009): 965–981.
98. Cf. Giovanni Galbiati, "Notizia sui manoscritti etiopici della Biblioteca Ambrosiana," in *Congresso internazionale degli orientalisti*, 619–625.
99. Lidio Cipriani, "Il significato degli etiopici nell'antropologia africana," in *Congresso internazionale degli orientalisti*, 155–162.
100. Vincenzo Giuffrida-Ruggeri, "Nuovi studi sull'antropologia dell'Africa orientale: etnologia e antropometria delle popolazioni eritreo-somale-abissine e delle regioni vicine," *AAE* XLV (1915): 123–179.
101. Ignazio Guidi, *Della sede primitiva dei popoli semitici*, ed. Mario Liverani (Rome: Bardi Edizioni, 2015).
102. Cipriani, "Etiopici," 161.
103. On Cipriani's development of this argument, see Sòrgoni, "Pratiche antropologiche," 421–423.
104. Cipriani, "Etiopici," 155n2. Two months later, as the invasion proceeded, Cipriani reprised the main themes of his congress paper in an article for a leading regime monthly: Lidio Cipriani, "Il passato e l'avvenire degli etiopici secondo l'antropologia," *Gerarchia* 15 (1935): 916–919.
105. "Il ne faut pas vendre la peau de l'ours avant de l'avoir tué."

7. The Chronicler of Asinara

1. Giuseppe Bottai, *Quaderno affricano* (Florence: Giunti, 2016), 137.
2. Bottai, *Quaderno affricano*, 159; and additionally, his reflection on these lines in "Cinque Maggio," *Etiopia* 3, no. 6 (1939): 10–12. More generally, see Giordano Bruno Guerri, *Giuseppe Bottai* (Milan: Mondadori, 1996), 575–590.
3. Alessandro Lessona, *Verso l'impero. Memorie per la storia politica del conflitto italo-etiopico* (Florence: Sansoni, 1939), 221.
4. Bottai, *Quaderni affricani*, 207–209.
5. The telegrams are contained in ASMAI Gabinetto Ordinario, pos. 28/204.
6. For biographies, see Sergew Hable Selassie, "Two Leading Ethiopian Writers," *JSS* 25, no. 1 (1980): 88–93; and Märse'é Hazän Wäldä Qirqos, የኢትዮጵያና የአንግሊዝ ሶማሊላንድ የወሰን መካለል ታሪክ (አዲስ አበባ፡ አዲስ አበባ ዩኒቨርሲቲ ፕሬስ, 2007 ዓም), 341–343.
7. Among many contributions, see "ስለ አአምሮና ብርሃንና ሰላም," *ብርሃንና ሰላም*, September 29, 1927.
8. Märse'é Hazän Wäldä Qirqos, የወሰን መካለል ታሪክ; and ቀዳማዊ ኃይለ ሥላሴ 1922-1927 (አዲስ አበባ፡ አዲስ አበባ ዩኒቨርሲቲ ፕሬስ, 2009 ዓም), 206–210.

9. Interview with Abebe Ambatchew, March 13, 2019.
10. The journey is recounted in Haylä Sellasé, *My Life and Ethiopia's Progress: Haile Selassie I King of Kings of Ethiopia. Vol. 2, Addis Abeba, 1966 E.C.*, trans. Ezekiel Gebissa et al. (East Lansing: Michigan State University Press, 1994), 159–166; and George Steer, *Sealed and Delivered: A Book on the Abyssinian Campaign* (London: Hodder and Stoughton, 1942), 185–220.
11. Steer, *Sealed and Delivered*, 204.
12. Haylä Sellasé, *My Life*, 2:160–161.
13. EMML 3754, 105: "ሰልፋቸውን ኣሳምረው በፉከራ ደስታቸውን እየገለጡ ከግርማዊነታቸው ተገኛኙ።" This manuscript history relates the events of the emperor's arrival in Shäwa within a biography of *däjjazmach* Täshomä Shänquṭ. See also Märse'é Hazän Wäldä Qirqos, የአምስቱ የመከራ ዓመታት አጭር ታሪክ (አዲስ አበባ፡ ብርሃንና ሰላም ማተሚያ ቤት, 1947 ዓም), 102–106.
14. Haylä Sellasé, *My Life*, 2:161.
15. On this framing, see Laleh Khalili, *Time in the Shadows: Confinement in Counterinsurgencies* (Stanford, CA: Stanford University Press, 2013). On the Italian counterinsurgency in the Horn of Africa, see Nicolas Virtue, "Royal Army, Fascist Empire: The Regio Esercito on Occupation Duty, 1936–1943" (PhD diss., Western University, 2016); Nicolas Virtue, "Technology and Terror in Fascist Italy's Counterinsurgency Operations: Ethiopia and Yugoslavia, 1936–1943," in *Fascist Warfare, 1922–1945: Aggression, Occupation, Annihilation*, ed. Miguel Alonso, Alan Kramer, and Javier Rodrigo (New York: Palgrave, 2019), 143–168; and Federica Saini Fasanotti, *Vincere! The Italian Royal Army's Counterinsurgency Operations in Africa, 1922–1940* (Annapolis, MD: Naval Institute Press, 2020), which closely replicates Italian colonial and military perspectives. On Libya, see Nir Arielli, "Colonial Soldiers in Italian Counterinsurgency Operations in Libya, 1922–1932," *BJMH* 1, no. 2 (2015): 47–66.
16. Achille Mbembe, *Necropolitics*, trans. Steven Corcoran (Durham, NC: Duke University Press, 2019), esp. 66–92. On the centrality of violence to the regime, see Michael Ebner, *Ordinary Violence in Mussolini's Italy* (New York: Cambridge University Press, 2011); and on fascist colonial violence, see Matteo Dominioni, *Lo sfascio dell'impero. Gli italiani in Etiopia, 1936–1941* (Bari: Laterza, 2019); and Ali Abdullatif Ahmida, *Genocide in Libya: Shar, A Hidden Colonial History* (New York: Routledge, 2021).
17. Frantz Fanon, *The Wretched of the Earth*, trans. Constance Farrington (New York: Grove, 1968), 249.
18. Khalili, *Time in the Shadows*, 11–43.
19. This biography is based on Dähné Wäldä Maryam, የሕይወት ታሪክ [unpublished Amharic diary]; የተከበሩ ቀኛዝማች ደህኔ ወልደ ማርያም የሕይወት ታሪክ ባጭሩ (አዲስ አበባ: 1956); and Abebe Ambatchew, *His Share of the Universe* (Abebe Ambatchew, 2014). I gratefully thank Abebe Ambatchew for sharing and discussing these materials with me. See also Mahtämä Sellasé Wäldä Mäsqäl, "የኢትዮጵያ ባህል ጥናት። ቼ በለው," *JES* 7, no. 2 (1969): 274.
20. At the time, the most notable resident was *abunä* Mattéwos, who hosted Menilek in the town: Gäbrä Sellasé Wäldä Aregay, ታሪክ ዘመን ዘዳግማዊ ምኔልክ ንጉሠ ነገሥት ዘኢትዮጵያ (አዲስ አበባ: አርቲስቲክ ማተሚያ ቤት, 1959 ዓም), 174–175.

21. Dähné Wäldä Maryam, የሕይወት ታሪክ ባጭሩ, 6, which lists his title as *endärasé*, or deputy.
22. Märse'é Hazän Wäldä Qirqos, የሐያኛው ክፍለ ዘመን መባቻ፡፡ የዘመን ታሪክ ትዝታዬ ካየሁትና ከሰማሁት 1896-1922 (አዲስ አበባ፡ አዲስ አበባ ዩኒቨርሲቲ ፕሬስ, 1999 ዓም), 39-40.
23. Dähné Wäldä Maryam, የሕይወት ታሪክ ባጭሩ, 6-7.
24. This is a distinctive horse name in that it refers to erudition, and not military or administrative skill. Although he was an intellectual, *qäññazmach* Dähné likely qualified for a horse name because of his involvement in the Battle of Sägalé. I thank Shiferaw Bekele for calling my attention to this point.
25. Märse'é Hazän was godfather to two of Dähné's children, and he mentions him repeatedly in his የሐያኛው ክፍል ዘመን መባቻ and ቀዳማዊ ኃይለ ሥላሴ. See also Heruy Wäldä Sellasé, ደስታና ክብር የኢትዮጵያ መንግሥት አልጋ ወራሽና እንደራሴ ልዑል ተፈሪ መኮንን ወደ አውሮፓ ሲሄዱና ሲመለሱ የመንገዳቸው አኳኋን (አዲስ አበባ፡ ተፈሪ መኮንን ማተሚያ ቤት, 1916 ዓም), 127; and Gäbrä Egzi'abhér Elyas, *Prowess, Piety, and Politics: The Chronicle of Abeto Iyasu and Empress Zewditu of Ethiopia, 1909-1930*, trans. Reidulf Molvaer (Cologne, Germany: Rüdiger Köppe Verlag, 1994), 445.
26. Heruy Wäldä Sellasé, ደስታና ክብር, 127.
27. Dähné Wäldä Maryam, የሕይወት ታሪክ ባጭሩ, 7-11; and Adrien Zervos, *L'empire d'Éthiopie: Le miroir de l'Éthiopie moderne, 1906-1935* (Alexandria: Imprimerie de l'École professionnelle des frères, 1936), 339.
28. Abebe Ambatchew, *Share of the Universe*.
29. Abebe Ambatchew, *Share of the Universe*.
30. Ian Campbell, *The Plot to Kill Graziani: The Attempted Assassination of Mussolini's Viceroy* (Addis Ababa: Addis Ababa University Press, 2010).
31. Ian Campbell, *The Addis Ababa Massacre: Italy's National Shame* (New York: Oxford University Press, 2017).
32. Dähné Wäldä Maryam, የሕይወት ታሪክ, 72.
33. On the distinction between the penal colony and the Foucauldian prison, see Mary Gibson and Ilaria Poerio, "Modern Europe, 1750-1950," in *A Global History of Convicts and Penal Colonies*, ed. Clare Anderson (London: Bloomsbury Academic, 2018), 337-370.
34. Franca Mele, "L'Asinara e le colonie penali in Sardegna: un'isola penitenziaria?," in *Le colonie penali nell'Europa dell'Ottocento*, ed. Mario Da Passano (Rome: Carocci, 2004), 189-213.
35. Francesca Di Pasquale, "The Other at Home: Deportation and Transportation of Libyans to Italy During the Colonial Era (1911-1943)," *IRSH* 63 (2018): 211-231; and more generally, Ahmida, *Genocide in Libya*. Before the establishment of Africa Orientale Italiana, Eritrean and Somali colonial subjects were typically imprisoned at locations in the Horn of Africa, most notably Nokra in the Dahlak archipelago.
36. On the Asinara detainees, see Paolo Borruso, *L'Africa al confino: la deportazione etiopica in Italia (1937-39)* (Rome: Lacaita, 2003); Giuseppe Ferraro, "I deportati dall'impero. Gli etiopi confinati in Italia durante il regime fascista," *NRS* 100, no. 1 (2016): 243-265; and Alberto Sbacchi, *Legacy of Bitterness: Ethiopia and Fascist Italy*,

1935-1941 (Trenton, NJ: Red Sea Press, 1995), 123–163. The Longobucco detainees are discussed in Giuseppe Ferraro, "From the Mountains of Africa to Italy: The Experience of Ethiopian Deportees Confined in Longobucco (Calabria) in the Period 1937–1943," *Annales d'Éthiopie* 31 (2016–2017): 293–319. For another case of metropolitan exile, see Sarah Ann Frank, *Hostages of Empire: Colonial Prisoners of War in Vichy France* (Lincoln: University of Nebraska Press, 2021).

37. On *confino*, see Ilaria Poerio, *A scuola di dissenso. Storie di resistenza al confino di polizia (1926-1943)* (Rome: Carocci, 2016); and Ebner, *Ordinary Violence*, 103–138. On the evolution of the concentration camp, see Gibson and Poerio, "Modern Europe."

38. Letter from the inspector general of public health, dated March 20, 1937, ASMAI AP cart. 83, fasc. 245.

39. Käbbädä Mika'él, "የአዚናራ አስረኛ," የዕውቀት ብልጭታ (አዲስ አበባ: አርቲስቲክ ማተሚያ ቤት, 1956 ዓም), 132–136, here 136: "እኛን ያደረገን ልክ እንደ አረመኔ[፤] ይኸ አዲስ ከፋት ይህ አዲስ ጭካኔ[፤] የሃኛው መቶ ይባላል ሥልጣኔ[፡]" The rhyme scheme juxtaposes "progress" with "savages" and "cruelty."

40. Mahtämä Sellasé Wäldä Mäsqäl, "ጄ በለው," 281.

41. This group included *ṣähafé te'ezaz* Wäldä Mäsqäl Tariku and *ṣähafé te'ezaz* Afä Wärq Wäldä Maryam, both Dähné's erstwhile superiors at the Ministry of the Pen; *afä negus* Aṭnaf Sägäd Wäldä Ṣadeq and *afä negus* Ṭilahun Bahabté, both of the imperial council; *ligaba* Ṭassäw Wallälu, the majordomo of the imperial court; *liqä liqawent* Gäbrä Ab, the head of Bä'ata Maryam Church in Addis Ababa; *blattén géta* Sahlé Ṣädalu, the minister of education and former League delegate; Täsfayé Tägäñ, the director general at the Ministry of Foreign Affairs; and Yelma Gäbrä Kidan, an employee at the Ministry of Foreign Affairs and Heruy's son-in-law.

42. "Elenco generale dei confinati etiopici nel regno," and "Elenco dei confinati etiopici a Mercogliano, bambini," both in ASMAI pos. 181/54; letter from Yelma Gäbrä Kidan, dated May 11, 1939, ASMAI AP cart. 83, fasc. 245; interview with Shimelis Yilma, January 26, 2021; and Mahtämä Sellasé Wäldä Mäsqäl, ዕጹብ ድንቅ (አዲስ አበባ: ነጻነት ማተሚያ ቤት, 1943 ዓም), 69, 71.

43. This group included *shaykh* Mähammäd Shaffi Mussa, *shaykh* Shoré, *qadi* Ahmed, *qadi* Jammi, and *haji* Bedasso Abdullah.

44. The two months following their departure (April and May 1937) were among the most violent periods of the entire occupation, culminating in the mass killings in Addis Ababa and Däbrä Libanos: see Campbell, *Addis Ababa Massacre* and *The Massacre of Debre Libanos, Ethiopia 1937: The Story of One of Fascism's Most Shocking Atrocities* (Addis Ababa: Addis Ababa University Press, 2014).

45. Dähné Wäldä Maryam, *የሕይወት ታሪክ*, 73, 80; and "Elenco generale dei confinati etiopici nel regno," and telegram from Ministry of Interior to Ministry of Italian Africa, dated April 15, 1937, both in ASMAI pos. 181/54.

46. "ጸሎት ቤት"

47. Dähné Wäldä Maryam, *የሕይወት ታሪክ*, 74–78; and on the issue of detainee property, see Ferraro, "Deportati," 256–258.

7. THE CHRONICLER OF ASINARA

48. This limited access to media was a privilege that reflected the elite and political—as opposed to criminal—status of the Ethiopian detainees within the *confino* system. I thank Mary Gibson for calling my attention to this point.
49. Although it did not lead to a formal diplomatic agreement, this visit produced the concession of South Tyrol to Italy and fueled an increasing German orientation in Italian fascist culture. On the visit, see Paul Baxa, "Capturing the Fascist Moment: Hitler's Visit to Italy in 1938 and the Radicalization of Fascist Italy," *JCH* 42, no. 2 (2007): 227–242.
50. Letter from Ethiopian detainees to Mussolini, dated March 24, 1937, ASMAI pos. 181/54: "የኢትዮጵያ ታማኝ ዜጎች"
51. The Italian translation differs from the Amharic original on this phrase, substituting "the good start of Roman civilization" for the Amharic "the work of progress that has been started," or "በተጀመረው የሥልጣኔ ሥራ."
52. On this bargain, see Benjamin Lawrance, Emily Lynn Osborn, and Richard Roberts, eds., *Intermediaries, Interpreters, and Clerks: African Employees in the Making of Colonial Africa* (Madison: University of Wisconsin Press, 2006).
53. Letter from Minister of Interior to Ministry of Italian Africa, dated March 31, 1937, ASMAI pos. 181/54. For Duce's appointment, see *Ministero dell'interno, Bollettino ufficiale del personale* 47, nos. 1–2 (1938): 357.
54. On these developments, see Chiara Giorgi, *L'Africa come corriera: Funzioni e funzionari del colonialismo italiano* (Rome: Carocci, 2012), 94–100; and Cesare Marinucci and Tomaso Columbano, *Il governo dei territori oltremare* (Rome: Istituto Poligrafico dello Stato, 1963), 133–194.
55. Bäläṭä Gäbré, የጉዞ ትዝታ (አዲስ አበባ፡ ቺምበር ማተሚያ ቤት, 2004 ዓም), 101. The author describes the funeral of his brother Mogäsé Gäbré, where Agäññahu served as Cerulli's translator and chaperone. Years later, the artist told the author that he met Cerulli during his time in Paris, and later helped him study Ge'ez.
56. For a discussion of this allegation, see chapter 10.
57. That same week, he led a section at the Congress of Colonial Studies in Florence, where he praised the academic wing of the National Fascist Party: "Il Congresso di studi coloniali," *Corriere della sera*, April 16, 1937.
58. Telegram from Ministry of Italian Africa to the Ministry of the Interior, dated April 20, 1937, ASMAI AP cart. 83, fasc. 245.
59. Telegram from Lessona to Ministry of Interior, dated May 1, 1937; telegram from Minister of the Colonies to Minister of the Interior, dated April 15, 1937; telegram from Graziani to Ministry of Italian Africa, dated April 12, 1937; and telegram from Graziani to Ministry of Italian Africa, dated April 24, 1937, all in ASMAI AP pos. 83/245.
60. Report from Cerulli, dated April 25, 1937, ASMAI AP cart. 83, fasc. 245.
61. It is possible that Dähné himself recognized Cerulli through his participation in the Crown Council during the 1928 treaty negotiations.
62. This biographical sketch is based on Zäwdé Rätta, በቀዳማዊ ኃይለ ሥላሴ ዘመነ መንግሥት የኤርትራ ጉዳይ 1941–1963 (አንድ አውሮፓውያን አቆጣጠር) (አዲስ አበባ፡ ሻማ ቡክስ, 2006), 460–465,

which contains Asfeha's own account of these years; and Giuseppe Puglisi, *Chi è? dell' Eritrea 1952. Dizionario biografico con una cronologia* (Asmara: Agenzia Regina, 1952), 26.

63. On the visit, see "Il Principe Ereditario a Cheren," *Corriere della sera*, February 18, 1928; "Umberto di Savoia in Eritrea," *Italia coloniale* 5, no. 4 (1928): 66–68; and "Diario del viaggio," *Italia coloniale* 5, no. 5 (1928): 84–88, with picture of school on 86.

64. Zäwdé Rätta, የኤርትራ ጉዳይ, 460: "እኛ ኤርትራውያኖች ንጉሥ ምኔልክ ሰጣልያን ሸጠውን ነው እንጂ፤ ኢትዮጵያውያን ነን።"

65. Letter from Lessona to Ministry of the Interior, dated March 26, 1937, ASMAI AP cart. 83, fasc. 245. Asfeha is identified as "basciai Asfaba Uoldenchiel," a misspelling of his name in Tigrinya.

66. A third visitor in this same period was Gaudenzio Barlassina, the superior general of the Consolata Mission, who visited again later that same year: report from Barlassina, dated April 17, 1937, and telegram from Lessona to Ministry of Interior, dated August 1937, both in ASMAI AP cart. 83, fasc. 245. On Barlassina, see Lucia Ceci, "Chiesa e questione coloniale: guerra e missione nell'impresa d'Etiopia," *Italia contemporanea* 233 (2003): 617–636; and Alberto Sbacchi, "The Archives of the Consolata Mission and the Formation of the Italian Empire, 1913–1943," *History in Africa* 25 (1998): 319–340. On Barlassina's relationship with Cerulli, see Cerulli, *Etiopia occidentale (dallo Scioa alla frontiera del Sudan)* (Rome: Sindacato Italiano Arti Grafiche, 1929 and 1933), 1:11, 18. A fourth visitor was Massimo Grisolia, the director general of the Office of Public Health at the Ministry of the Interior, who reviewed the medical conditions of the detainees: report by Grisolia to Ministry of Interior, dated May 1, 1937, ASMAI AP cart. 83, fasc. 245.

67. Report by Cerulli for the Ministry of Italian Africa, dated April 25, 1937, ASMAI AP cart. 83, fasc. 245.

68. Ebner, *Ordinary Violence*, 74, 76, 88, 120.

69. On this somewhat misleading exonym, see Bahru Zewde, "The Ethiopian Intelligentsia and the Italo-Ethiopian War, 1935–1941," *IJAHS* 26, no. 2 (1993): 271–295.

70. She was later transferred to Mercogliano, where she corresponded with the Ministry. See Amharic letter from Abäbäch Chärqosé to Minister, undated, and Amharic letter from Abäbäch Chärqosé to Mussolini, dated September 21, 1937, both in ASMAI pos. 181/54; and Mahtämä Sellasé Wäldä Mäsqäl, ዕጹብ ድንቅ, 87.

71. Pawlos Män Amäno died just a few years prior: see Marqos Pawlos Män Amäno, "የቶ ጸሎሎስ መን አመኖ የሕይወት ታሪክ," ብርሃንና ሰላም, March 5, 1934, which contains a poem by Marqos about his father.

72. According to colleague Spencer, the last of these was compelled to submit after being abandoned by the emperor: John Spencer, *Ethiopia at Bay: A Personal Account of the Haile Selassie Years* (Algonac, MI: Reference Publications, 1984), 81.

73. Another family identified for special attention was that of Denqenäsh Täfäri, the wife of *qäññazmach* Bezabeh Sellasé and niece of *le'ul ras* Kassa. See list of detainees submitted by Ministry of Interior, dated April 16, 1937, ASMAI pos. 181/54.

74. One week earlier, Barlassina submitted a short memorandum that echoed these findings: report by Barlassina for Ministry of Italian Africa, dated April 17, 1937, ASMAI AP cart. 83, fasc. 245.
75. Mahmood Mamdani, *Citizen and Subject: Contemporary Africa and the Legacy of Late Colonialism* (Princeton, NJ: Princeton University Press, 1996); and Alice Conklin, *A Mission to Civilize: The Republican Idea of Empire in France and West Africa, 1895-1930* (Stanford, CA: Stanford University Press, 1997). On the development of Italian native policy, see Nicola Labanca, *L'Oltremare. Storia dell'espansione coloniale italiana* (Bologna: Mulino, 2002), 309-368; and Alberto Sbacchi, *Ethiopia Under Mussolini: Fascism and the Colonial Experience* (London: Zed, 1985), 41-118.
76. Another prominent case of "collaboration as resistance" was that of Zär'ay Därräs, the Eritrean interpreter who worked with the detainees in Rome, and who in 1938 made a public demonstration at the Lion of Judah monument in the Italian capital: Matteo Salvadore, "Zär'ay Därräs," in *EA*, 5:151-152.
77. Ebner, *Ordinary Violence*, 108-109. In the late 1930s, these two populations were often separated so as to isolate "nonpolitical" detainees from the influence of antifascists and communists.
78. Handwritten comment by Lessona, dated April 26, 1937, on report by Cerulli for Ministry of Italian Africa, dated April 25, 1937, ASMAI AP cart. 83, fasc. 245. This level of personal attention to detail typified Mussolini's relationship with the regime's detention and surveillance apparatus: Ebner, *Ordinary Violence*, 13.
79. Memorandum from Lessona to Ministry of the Interior, dated May 11, 1937, ASMAI pos. 181/54.
80. Notes for Cerulli, dated July 27, 1937, ASMAI pos. 181/54.
81. This use of mainland exile paralleled the regime's developing approach to "ordinary" nonpolitical Italian prisoners, who—unlike the Ethiopians—were sent to rural locations in southern Italy because they were deemed less subversive than antifascists or communists. See Ebner, *Ordinary Violence*, 131-135.
82. Report on placement of Ethiopian detainees, dated August 26, 1937, ASMAI AP cart. 83, fasc. 245.
83. Of the 317 Ethiopian detainees in Italy by August, 144 were at other sites, including Mercogliano (53), Longobucco (28), Torre del Greco (15), Tivoli (11), and Palermo (5), and interpreters were stationed at some of these locations (*fitawrari* Fesseha Gäbräkidané in Mercogliano, and *balambaras* Däboch Bahta in Tivoli). Ethiopians thus accounted for approximately 15 percent of the total number of detainees in Italy in 1938: Ebner, *Ordinary Violence*, 135; and report on placement of Ethiopian detainees, dated August 26, 1937, and list of colonial subjects in Italy, dated November 28, 1938, both in ASMAI AP cart. 83, fasc. 245.
84. Barlassina was involved in the Turin relocation: Sbacchi, "Consolata Mission," 334. The reasons for the return are unclear, given Cerulli's recommendation that they stay.
85. For examples, see the many "Notes for the Director" in ASMAI pos. 181/54.
86. Ebner, *Ordinary Violence*, 1-22, 139-165.

87. On this, see Frederick Cooper, *Africa Since 1940: The Past of the Present* (New York: Cambridge University Press, 2002); and Jean-François Bayart, *The State in Africa: Politics of the Belly* (New York: Longman, 1993). With respect to Cerulli's relationship with detainees, this situation is contra Karla Mallette, *European Modernity and the Arab Mediterranean: Toward a New Philology and a Counter-Orientalism* (Philadelphia: University of Pennsylvania Press, 2010), 266n29, which cites without evidence his "efforts to expose and correct injustices against Ethiopians," following Sbacchi.
88. Report from Ministry of Italian Africa to the Ministry of the Interior, dated May 11, 1937, ASMAI pos. 181/54. This document states that this location would allow them to remain in contact with the Ministry.
89. ASMAI AP cart. 83, fasc. 245, which contains the extensive Office of Political Affairs file on Berhanä Marqos. For biographies, see Mickaël Bethe Selassié, *La jeune Éthiopie: Un haut-fonctionnaire éthiopien Berhanä-Marqos Wäldä-Tsadeq (1892-1943)* (Paris: Harmattan, 2004); and Zervos, *Éthiopie*, 120.
90. Afäwärq Gäbrä Iyäsus, የኢትዮጵያ መንግሥት አልጋ ወራሽና እንደራሴ ልዑል ተፈሪ መኮንን የአደን መንገዳቸው አኳኋን (አዲስ አበባ፡ ተፈሪ መኮንን ማተሚያ ቤት, 1918 ዓም).
91. Telegram from Moreno, dated December 4, 1936, ASMAI AP cart. 83, fasc. 245. He was replaced by Sirak Heruy: Zervos, *Éthiopie*, 117.
92. Telegram to Moreno, dated November 8, 1939, ASMAI AP cart. 83, fasc. 245.
93. Telegram from Ministry of Foreign Affairs to the Ministry of the Colonies, dated December 10, 1936, ASMAI AP cart. 83, fasc. 245.
94. Telegram from Moreno, dated December 4, 1936, telegram from the Ministry of Foreign Affairs, undated, and letter from Roncalli, dated August 25, 1936, all in ASMAI AP cart. 83, fasc. 245. According to these documents, Wäldä Maryam was then at the Consolata Mission in Rome.
95. Spencer, *Ethiopia at Bay*, 80–81; and Aklilu Habtäwäld, የአክሊሉ ማስታወሻ *Aklilu Remembers* (አዲስ አበባ፡ አዲስ አበባ ዩኒቨርሲቲ ፕሬስ, 2010), 126–131.
96. Telegram from Graziani with note to Cerulli, dated November 28, 1936, ASMAI AP cart. 83, fasc. 245.
97. Telegram from Moreno, dated December 4, 1936, ASMAI AP cart. 83, fasc. 245. Taddäsä had contacted the Italians through Borra: for a detailed discussion, see Edoardo Borra, *Prologo di un conflitto: Colloqui col segretario del Negus (Dicembre 1934-Ottobre 1935)* (Milan: Paoline, 1965), passim. He was executed after Yekatit 12.
98. Mickaël Bethe Selassié, *La jeune Éthiopie*, 131.
99. Telegram from Office of Political Affairs to Office of Economic and Financial Affairs, undated, ASMAI AP cart. 83, fasc. 245.
100. The two may have already been acquainted through their shared link to the Italian Legation in the Ethiopian capital.
101. Notes appended to report by Cerulli, dated April 25, 1937, ASMAI AP cart. 83, fasc. 245.
102. Amharic group letter, dated Nähasé 17, 1929 AM, ASMAI pos. 181/54. The other signatories were *liqä liqawent* Gäbrä Ab, *blattén géta* Sahlé Ṣädalu, Berhanu Marqos,

Mäkonnen Wässäné, *blatta* Feqre Sellasé Kätämma, *däjjazmach* Ali Gwangul, and *fitawrari* Gédéwon Gwangul.
103. Telegram from Teruzzi, dated June 23, 1938, and telegram from Office of Political Affairs, dated July 6, 1938, both in ASMAI AP cart. 83, fasc. 245.
104. Telegram from Office of Political Affairs to Office of Economic and Financial Affairs, undated, and telegram from Office of Economic and Financial Affairs to Office of Political Affairs, dated October 29, 1939, both in ASMAI AP cart. 83, fasc. 245.
105. Mahtämä Sellasé Wäldä Mäsqäl, "ቼ በለው," 253–254; "ስለ ከቡር ደጃዝማች አያሌው ብሩ ሽልማትና ወዳጋራቸው መገባት," ብርሃንና ሰላም, December 15, 1932; and A. P. [Alberto Pollera], "Un fedele che non ha fatto gran fortuna: Degiacc Aialieu Burru," *Italia coloniale* 12, no. 10 (September 1935): 130–131.
106. Telegram from Badoglio to Mussolini, dated February 7, 1936, ASMAI AP cart. 15.
107. Raffaele Di Lauro, *Tre anni a Gondar* (Milan: Mondadori, 1936), 136–141; Luigi Goglia, "Un aspetto dell'azione politica italiana durante la campagna d'Etiopia 1935–36: la missione del senatore Jacopo Gasparini nell'Amhara," *Storia contemporanea* VIII (1977): 791–822; and Rodolfo Graziani, *Una vita per l'Italia* (Milan: Mursia, 1986), 63. His submission was reported in the metropolitan press: "Aialeu Burrù rende omaggio a Graziani," *Corriere della sera*, August 14, 1936; and "La devozione di Aialeu Burrù all'Italia," *Corriere della sera*, August 15, 1936.
108. Notes appended to report by Cerulli, dated April 25, 1937, ASMAI AP cart. 83, fasc. 245.
109. This was a general problem of colonial counterinsurgency: Alfred McCoy, *Policing America's Empire: The United States, the Philippines, and the Rise of the Surveillance State* (Madison: University of Wisconsin Press, 2009), 6.
110. Amharic letter from Ayyaléw Berru to Cerulli, dated Genbot 30, 1929 AM, ASMAI pos. 181/54.
111. Amharic group letter, dated Nähasé 17, 1929 AM, ASMAI pos. 181/54.
112. Amharic group letter to Cerulli, dated December 9, 1937, 841, ASMAI pos. 181/54. The other signatories include *blatta* Feqré Sellasé Kätämma, *däjjazmach* Ali Gwangul, *fitawrari* Gédéwon Gwangul, *blattén géta* Sahlé Ṣädalu, Mulatua[?] Belayneh, Berhanä Marqos, *däjjazmach* Mäkonnen Wässäné, *däjjazmach* Täsfa Tukku, and *liqä liqawent* Gäbrä Ab.
113. Photograph with Amharic caption, የቄሣር መንግሥት መልከተኛ, December 18, 1938. He died only a few years after his return to Ethiopia: Mahtämä Sellasé Wäldä Mäsqäl, "ቼ በለው," 254.
114. Their connection is documented in Amharic letter from Ayyaléw Berru, dated October 10, 1937, ASMAI pos. 181/54.
115. Mahtämä Sellasé Wäldä Mäsqäl, "ቼ በለው," 246.
116. Telegram from Graziani to Lessona, with note to Cerulli, dated July 7, 1936, ASMAI pos. 181/47.
117. Telegram from Ministry of Italian Africa to the Ministry of the Interior, dated May 11, 1937, ASMAI pos. 181/54.
118. Amharic letter from Amdé Ali to Cerulli, dated October 10, 1937, ASMAI pos. 181/54.

119. List of Ethiopian detainees in Italy, undated, ASMAI pos. 181/54.
120. Memorandum from Office of Political Affairs to Office of Governor General, dated July 9, 1938, ASMAI AP cart. 83, fasc. 245.
121. Amharic letter from Amdé Ali to Cerulli, dated December 26, 1937, ASMAI pos. 181/54. On this situation, see Pier Marcello Masotti, *Ricordi d'Etiopia di un funzionario coloniale* (Milan: Pan, 1981), 81–82. According to Amdé Ali, the Italian was named Cibelli.
122. Mahtämä Sellasé Wäldä Mäsqäl, "ቼ በለው," 237; and Heruy Wäldä Sellasé, የሕይወት ታሪክ *(Biographie)* በኋላ ዘመን ለሚነሡ ልጆች ማስታወቂያ (አዲስ አበባ: ተፈሪ መኮንን ማተሚያ ቤት, 1915 ዓም), 37.
123. Interview with Abebe Ambatchew, December 10, 2018.
124. This special action was distinct from the mass detention of Ethiopians in Italy the following year. On the deportation, see list of arrived detainees, with note about Tayyé Gullelaté at bottom, undated, ASMAI pos. 181/54. These two were eventually joined in Ponza by Haddis Alämayyähu: for his detailed account, see Haddis Alämayyähu, ትዝታ (አዲስ አበባ: ማንኩሳ ማተሚያ ቤት, 2013 ዓም), 204–222. See also their letters in ASMAI pos. 181/54.
125. Ebner, *Ordinary Violence*, 120–125.
126. "የቅኝ ግዛቶች ጉዳይ ሚኒስቴር 'ዋና ዳሬክተር'," for "Chief Director of the Ministry of Colonial Affairs," a title that does not exist. Since both "director" and "minister" have obvious Amharic cognates, it seems unlikely that Haddis Alämayyähu would have confused them. He identified this director as "Doctor Micelli," a name that does not correspond to any senior ministerial officials. It therefore seems likely that the individual in question was in fact Cerulli, though this identification is speculative. The supporting evidence is the phonetic similarity of the two names, Cerulli's subsequent contacts with *däjjazmach* Tayyé, and this individual's ministerial title, physical description, academic credentials, and Eritrean interpreter. The comparison with Mussolini may have referenced the fact that both men were bald. Against this identification is the fact that Haddis Alämayyähu likely knew of Cerulli at the time of writing, and he did not mention that the individual in question spoke Amharic, which he did note when describing his interaction with another multilingual Italian. For the episode, see Haddis Alämayyähu, ትዝታ, 213–214, with the discussion of the Amharic skill of "Signor Marciano," presumably Amedeo Marciano, on 195.
127. Haddis observed that this imperious attitude was typical of those Italians who had worked in the colonies. The image of detention as a "holiday" sometimes proved contentious for regime officials, with militants arguing that the sites and conditions of detention were insufficiently punitive: Ebner, *Ordinary Violence*, 116.
128. Haddis Alämayyähu, ትዝታ, 217–221.
129. Report by Cerulli, dated April 25, 1937, ASMAI AP cart. 83, fasc. 245.
130. Ministry of Italian Africa to the Ministry of Interior, dated May 11, 1937, ASMAI pos. 181/54.
131. Memorandum by Senise for the Ministry of Italian Africa, dated October 11, 1937, ASMAI pos. 181/54.

132. List of Ethiopian detainees at Mercogliano, undated, ASMAI pos. 181/54.
133. Letters from Tayyé Gulelaté, dated April 8, 1938, ASMAI pos. 181/54.
134. Letter from Tayyé Gulelaté, dated December 16, 1937, ASMAI pos. 181/54.
135. The saying would appear to be a variant of "ያገሩን ሰርዶ ባገሩ በሬ."
136. Amharic letter from Tayyé Gulelaté to Barlassina, dated December 17, 1937, ASMAI pos. 181/54: "ለኃያሉ ለኢጣልያን መንግሥት ዋና ታማኝ መሳሪ [መሳርያ]", varying somewhat from the ministerial translation "un ottimo strumento per il Governo Italiano."
137. Letter from Tayyé Gulelaté to Pope Pius XI, dated December 19, 1937, ASMAI pos. 181/54.
138. Prememoria for the undersecretary of state, dated January 4, 1938, and letter from Ministry of Italian Africa to Barlassina, dated February 3, 1938, both in ASMAI pos. 181/54.
139. Mahtämä Sellasé Wäldä Mäsqäl, "ቼ በለው," 237.
140. Cf. Ferraro, "Ethiopian Deportees," 309, which mistakes his title as *ras*.
141. Letter from Berhanä Habtämika'él to Lessona, dated July 1, 1937, ASMAI pos. 181/54.
142. "የሮማ ትምህርት እና ሥልጣኔ"
143. Specifically, he was one of eight additional "irreducibles" beyond the twenty identified by Cerulli, who the latter had originally designated moderate Young Ethiopians who should remain at Asinara: "Sistemazione confinati etiopici nel regno," dated August 26, 1937, ASMAI AP cart. 83, fasc. 245. According to Haddis Alämayyähu, who arrived from Ponza via Lipari, the Longobucco detainees included *däjjazmach* Mängäsha Webé, *balambaras* Emañu Yemär, *grazmach* Lägässä Gäbré Näbbäru, *musé* Abraham and his family, Germachaw Täklä Hawaryat, Téwodros Wärqenäh, Kossrof Boghossian, Abäbä Gäbräṣadeq, Samu'él Gäbrä Yäsus, Berhé Keflum, and Berhanä Habtämika'él: Haddis Alämayyähu, ትዝታ, 230–231.
144. The regime also surveilled nondetained colonial subjects and citizens of African origins, much as it did the metropolitan and diasporic Italian population more broadly. For example, in 1938 the interministerial surveillance of African subjects residing in Italy led to the arrest and deportation of Habtämaryam Gareh, an Eritrean language instructor at the Istituto Orientale in Naples who ran afoul of the new laws protecting White racial prestige by allowing himself to be photographed in the act of giving money to an Italian street musician. This crime compounded a prior incident in Jerusalem, where he had reportedly defamed Italy on the occasion of Haylä Sellasé's arrival in the city. His L'Orientale employment despite this suspicious history led to the additional scrutiny of his sponsor Elena Sengal, who was then an Amharic instructor at the same institution. On these events, see telegram from Ministry of the Interior to Office of Political Affairs, Ministry of Italian Africa, dated March 28, 1938, and telegram from Senise to Ministry of Italian Africa, dated February 16, 1938, both in ASMAI AP cart. 83, fasc. 245.
145. Letter from Berhanä Habtämika'él to Lessona, with note about Cerulli's review at top, dated October 2, 1937, ASMAI pos. 181/54.
146. Ferraro, "Ethiopian Deportees," 305–308.

147. The same group also wrote a letter that July: notes for director, dated December 1937, ASMAI pos. 181/54.
148. "ጥፋት"
149. Dähné Wäldä Maryam, የሕይወት ታሪክ, 80: "የአዚናራውን ዳኛ ዶክቶር ዱቼን ኤራስ ጎብረሆት[ጎብረሕይወት]ና ጸሐፌ ትእዛዝ አፈወርቅ ሊጋባ ጣሰው አቶ ተስፋዬ ተገኝ እሚስሩበት ቢሮ ሄደው ከመጣን ፯ ወር ሆነን የመጣነው ባልሰራን ባልሰማን ጥፋት ነው እንደመጣንም በመጋቢት ወር ወደ ታላቁ መንግሥት የምሕረት የልመና ቃል ወረቀት ጽፈን ልከን ነበር እስካሁን መልስ አላገኘንም አሁንም ፈቃድዎ ሁኖ የምሕረት ቃል ሊያሰፉልን ይቻልዎ እንድሆን ብለው·"
150. "የገናናውና የሃያሉ የኢጣሊያ መንግሥት"
151. Amharic and Italian group letters, dated October 5, 1937, ASMAI pos. 181/54.
152. Memorandum by Ministry of the Interior for the Ministry of Italian Africa, dated October 15, 1937, ASMAI pos. 181/54.
153. Notes for director, dated December 1937, ASMAI pos. 181/54.
154. Ngũgĩ wa Thiong'o, *Detained: A Writer's Prison Diary* (New York: Heinemann, 1981), 100.
155. Abebe Ambatchew, *Share of the Universe*, 93–104.
156. Memorandum by Ministry of Interior for Ministry of Italian Africa, dated October 12, 1937, with receipt of Office of Political Affairs stamped on page 1, and note about letter from "cagnazmac Dehnie Uoldemariam" on page 2, ASMAI pos. 181/54.

8. Survival in Shäwa

1. This biography is based on Terrefe Ras Warq, የአንጥቦሩ ሰው· ቢጀኔቫ (አዲስ አበባ፡ 2011 ዓም); "ራስ ወርቅ ወልደመስቀል የመጀመሪያው የተፈሪ መኮንን ትምህርት ቤት መምህር," አዲስ ዘመን, undated obituary [October 1963?]; and interview with Terrefe Ras Warq, January 21, 2020. I thank *ato* Terrefe for sharing and discussing these materials with me.
2. "ራስ ወርቅ ወልደመስቀል." He also studied at Denbaro Maryam, Qundi Qeddus Giyorgis, Däbrä Libanos, and Shenkurt Mika'él.
3. Terrefe Ras Warq, የአንጥቦሩ ሰው·, 9–11.
4. የተፈሪ መኮንን ትምህርት ቤት አጭር ታሪክ (አዲስ አበባ፡ ብርሃንና ሰላም ማተሚያ ቤት, n.d.); and Bahru Zewde, *Pioneers of Change in Ethiopia: The Reformist Intellectuals of the Early Twentieth Century* (Athens: Ohio University Press, 2002), 24–26.
5. Gäbrä Egzi'abhér Elyas, *Prowess, Piety, and Politics: The Chronicle of Abeto Iyasu and Empress Zewditu of Ethiopia, 1909-1930*, trans. Reidulf Molvaer (Cologne, Germany: Rüdiger Köppe Verlag, 1994), 459.
6. "ራስ ወርቅ ወልደመስቀል"; Märse'é Hazän Wäldä Qirqos, የሐያኛው ክፍለ ዘመን መባቻ፡ የዘመን ታሪክ ትዝታዬ ካየሁትና ከሰማሁት 1896–1922 (አዲስ አበባ፡ አዲስ አበባ ዩኒቨርሲቲ ፕሬስ, 1999 ዓም), 282; and interview with Terrefe Ras Warq, January 21, 2020.
7. "ልዑል የኢትዮጵያ መንግሥት አልጋ ወራሽ ለኢትዮጵያ ይህን የተማሪ ቤት በገንዘባቸው ሠርተው በረከት ሲያቀርቡ ከዚህ ቀጥሎ ያለውን በጉባኤ ተናገሩ፣" ብርሃንና ሰላም, May 7, 1925.
8. These included Aklilu Habtäwald, Akkala Wärq Habtäwald, Mengistu Neway, Täklä Ṣadeq Mekwuriya, Emmanu'él Abraham, and Emru Zälläqä.

9. Another colleague was Ambachäw Dähné, the Francophone son of *qäññazmach* Dähné.
10. የተፈሪ መኰንን ትምህርት ቤት አጭር ታሪክ, 5–15. One notable foreign visitor was Prince Luigi Amedeo, who toured the school in 1927: "ስለ ልሁል ዱክ ዮዘብሩሲስ አቀባበል መሰናዳት," ብርሃንና ሰላም, May 19, 1927.
11. Märse'é Hazän Wäldä Qirqos, የሕያዉ ክፍለ ዘመን መባቻ, 388; and interview with Terrefe Ras Warq, January 21, 2020.
12. His paternal great grandfather *aläqa* Wäldä Sellasé had been the first priest at Qeddus Täklä Haymanot, one of Ankober's oldest churches: Terrefe Ras Wärq, የአንኮበሩ ሰው, 8.
13. የተፈሪ መኰንን ትምህርት ቤት አጭር ታሪክ, 15; *Guida dell'Africa Orientale Italiana* (Milan: Officine Fotolitografiche, 1938), 488; and Ertola Emanuele, "L'impero immaginario: i coloni italiani in Etiopia, 1936–1941" (PhD diss., Università degli studi di Firenze, 2014), 92.
14. This was Qeddus Mik'aél.
15. Gäbrä Sellasé Wäldä Aregay, ታሪክ ዘመን ዘዳግማዊ ምኔልክ ንጉሥ ነገሥት ዘኢትዮጵያ (አዲስ አበባ: አርቲስቲክ ማተሚያ ቤት, 1959 ዓም), 293.
16. Gäbrä Sellasé Wäldä Aregay, ዳግማዊ ምኔልክ, 194.
17. For decades, the town maintained the old *gebbi* in anticipation of the emperor's return. Some among the *liqawent* attributed the famines of the 1890s to the emperor's departure: Wolfgang Weissleder, "The Political Ecology of Amhara Domination" (PhD diss., University of Chicago, 1965), 31–32.
18. "ግርማዊ ቀዳማዊ አጼ ኃይለ ሥላሴ የደብረ ብርሃንንና የአንኮበርን የአባቶታቸውን ከተሞች መጎብኘት," አአምር, January 13, 1934.
19. The churches were Qeddus Giyorgis, Qeddus Maryam, Qeddus Mik'aél, Qeddus Täklä Haymanot, and Mädhané Aläm.
20. EMML 3071; see also EMML 2426 and EMML 2464. For a discussion, see Wondwosen Admasu Woldehana, "A Catalogue of Some Manuscripts in Ankobär Mädhane Aläm Church Museum" (Master's thesis, Addis Ababa University, 2011); and Rita Pankhurst, "In Quest of Ankobar's Church Libraries," in *New Trends in Ethiopian Studies: Papers of the Twelfth International Conference in Ethiopian Studies, 5-10 September 1994*, ed. Harold Marcus (Lawrenceville, NJ: Red Sea Press, 1994), 198–216.
21. For this reason, it is alleged that much of the immense royal library of Mäqdälä—looted by the Napier Expedition in 1868 and now chiefly at the British Library—originated in Ankober. See Gäbrä Sellasé Wäldä Aregay, ዳግማዊ ምኔልክ, 53–54; and Rita Pankhurst, "The Library of Emperor Tewodros II at Mäqdäla (Magdala)," *BSOAS* 36, no. 1 (1973): 30.
22. Marcel Cohen, "Rapport sur une mission linguistique en Abyssinie (1910–1911)," *NAMSL*, n.s. 6 (1912): 35. This eminence with respect to Orthodox Christian scholarship had its Islamic counterpart in the nearby town Araf Lebbé, a center of Islamic learning a short distance from Aliyu Amba, the predominantly Muslim market town southeast of Ankober.

23. Märse'é Hazän Wäldä Qirqos, "በአንኮበር ከተማ የሸዋን ነገሥታት መቃብር መኅብናት፣" EMML 3764. See also his ቀዳማዊ ኃይለ ሥላሴ 1922–1927 (አዲስ አበባ፡ አዲስ አበባ ዩኒቨርሲቲ ፕሬስ, 2009 ዓም), 170–171.
24. Bairu Tafla, "Three Portraits: Ato Aṣmä Giyorgis, Ras Gobäna Dači and Ṣähafé Tezaz Gäbrä Selassé," *JES* 5, no. 2 (1967): 141.
25. Ewa Wolk and Denis Nosnitsin, "Kəflä Giyorgis," in *EA*, 3:370–371; and Ignazio Guidi, *Vocabolario amarico-italiano* (Rome: Casa Editrice Italiana, 1901), viii.
26. Heruy Wäldä Sellasé, የሕይወት ታሪክ *(Biographie)* በኋላ ዘመን ለሚነሡ ልጆች ማስታወቂያ (አዲስ አበባ፡ ተፈሪ መኮንን ማተሚያ ቤት, 1915 ዓም), 19.
27. Adrien Zervos, *L'empire d'Éthiopie: Le miroir de l'Éthiopie moderne, 1906–1935* (Alexandria: Imprimerie de l'École professionnelle des frères, 1936), 223; and Shiferaw Bekele, "Śahle Ṣädalu," in *EA*, 4:467–468.
28. Mahtämä Sellasé Wäldä Mäsqäl, "የኢትዮጵያ ባህል ጥናት፡፡ ቼ በለው፣" *JES* 7, no. 2 (1969): 273.
29. Interview with *liqä kahnat* Qalä Heywät, January 25, 2020.
30. Cohen, *Rapport*, 37.
31. Report by Tracchia on operations in Shäwa, dated February 26, 1937, ASMAI pos. 181/39.
32. *Guida*, 407.
33. "Passaggio di armati per le alte terre dell'Uoranà," *Corriere della sera*, October 19, 1939.
34. Terrefe Ras Warq, የአንኮበሩ ሰው, 8. His parish of Afar Baynä Täklä Haymanot was at that time an important center of church learning: Pankhurst, "Ankobar," 216n33.
35. He was later detained at Asinara and then killed in battle with Abäbä Arägay in 1929 AM: Mahtämä Sellasé Wäldä Mäsqäl, "ቼ በለው፣" 217; and interview with *liqä kahnat* Qalä Heywät, January 25, 2020. In Ras Wärq's hometown of Jerru, west of *qäññazmach* Dähné's hometown of Sälla Dengay, Pirzio Biroli appointed *däjjazmach* Mäshasha Täwänd Bälay—another longtime servant of Menilek from Ankober—to a similar post. The latter was later deported to Asinara, where he met Dähné. He provided the latter with a historical manuscript from Ankober that the *qäññazmach* copied in his diary: see Dähné Wäldä Maryam, የሕይወት ታሪክ.
36. Taddäsä Zäwäldé, ቀሪን ገረመው፣ የአርበኞች ታሪክ (አዲስ አበባ፡ ብርሃንና ሰላም ማተሚያ ቤት, 1960 ዓም), 19–58; and Mahtämä Sellasé Wäldä Mäsqäl, "ቼ በለው፣" 240.
37. "በለው!" See Tsehai Berhane Silassie, "Women Guerilla Fighters," *NEAS* 1, no. 3 (1979–1980): 78–80.
38. Weissleder, "Political Ecology," 337–339.
39. Taddäsä Zäwäldé, ቀሪን ገረመው, 278–282.
40. Taddäsä Zäwäldé, ቀሪን ገረመው, 281: "ገለሌ ምሳው ፉጨት እራቴ[፤] መለቃቂያው ደም [መ]ራጨቴ[፤] እናቱ ወልዳኛ በሆንኩኝ እ[ህ]ቴ[።]"
41. Taddäsä Zäwäldé, ቀሪን ገረመው, 146; and Gäbrä Egzi'abhér Elyas, *Zewditu*, 571–575. This coronation was supported by Abäbä Arägay but not Haylä Maryam Mammo.
42. Ahmed Hassen Omer, "Italian Local Politics in Northern Shäwa and Its Consquences 1936–1941," *JES* 28, no. 2 (1995): 3–5.
43. Report by Tracchia on operations in Shäwa, dated February 26, 1937, ASMAI pos. 181/39.

44. Matteo Dominioni, *Lo sfascio dell'impero. Gli italiani in Etiopia, 1936–1941* (Bari: Laterza, 2019), 138–140.
45. Report by Tracchia on operations in Shäwa, dated February 26, 1937, ASMAI pos. 181/39; Taddäsä Zäwäldé, ቀዳን ገረመው, 281–282; and Dominioni, *Sfascio dell'impero*, 144–145.
46. Roberto Gentilli, *Guerra aerea sull'Etiopia, 1935–1939* (Florence: Edizioni Aeronautiche Italiane, 1992), 111–112, 212–213; and Terrefe Ras Warq, የአንኮቡፉ ሰው, 6, 19.
47. Report by Tracchia on operations in Shäwa, dated February 26, 1937, ASMAI pos. 181/39; interview with *liqä kahnat* Qalä Ḥeywät, January 25, 2020; and Sergew Hable Selassie, አማርኛ የቤተ ክርስቲያን መዝገበ ቃላት (አዲስ አበባ: 1988), 1:39.
48. After the destruction of old Ankober, some of the remaining population resettled just below Goräbéla: Weissleder, "Political Ecology," 27.
49. A local poet commemorated these events with the couplet: "ያየ ከእሳት ቃጠሎ የተረፈ የዳነ[፤] ዛሬ በሰራው የብዙዎቹን አፍ አስከደነ", or "The one who once was spared and survived the fire / The work that he did today [has] caused many mouths to close [in astonishment]." See Terrefe Ras Work, የአንኮቡፉ ሰው, 16.
50. On the rivalry between the two, see Angelo Del Boca, *Gli italiani in Africa Orientale: III. La caduta dell'impero* (Milan: Mondadori, 1992), 86–106; and Alberto Sbacchi, *Ethiopia Under Mussolini: Fascism and the Colonial Experience* (London: Zed, 1985), 48–54.
51. Alessandro Lessona, *Memorie* (Florence: Sansoni, 1958), 315–320; and *Un ministro di Mussolini racconta* (Rome: Edizioni Nazionali, 1973), 167–173.
52. In its conclusion, the duke ventured that his research complemented the military operations of that year in that it "conquered [Fezzan] for science." See Amedeo di Savoia-Aosta, *Studi africani* (Bologna: Zanichelli, 1942), 91. The expedition also included L'Orientale linguist Francesco Beguinot as well as anthropologists Lidio Cipriani and Antonio Mordini.
53. Edoardo Borra, *Amedeo di Savoia: terzo duca d'Aosta e viceré d'Etiopia* (Milan: Mursia, 1985), 66.
54. Borra, *Amedeo*, 67.
55. Lessona, *Racconta*, 168. According to Graziani, Afäwärq Gäbrä Iyäsus, then serving as the *afä qésar* in Addis Ababa, wrote that the elation over the viceroy's dismissal was shared by the *arbäña*s in the mountains: Rodolfo Graziani, *Una vita per l'Italia* (Milan: Mursia, 1986), 84. The referent text is unclear.
56. "Uno scambio di telegrammi tra il Duca d'Aosta e Graziani," *Corriere della sera*, November 25, 1937. See also Graziani, *Una vita*, 84–86.
57. Borra, *Amedeo*, 68.
58. Telegram from Graziani to Ministry of Italian Africa, dated December 9, 1937, ASMAI GS, cart. 249.
59. Borra, *Amedeo*, 71; and Lessona, *Memorie*, 316.
60. Niccolò Machiavelli, *The Prince*, trans. Daniel Donno (New York: Bantam, 1981), 31–32.
61. John Gooch, *Mussolini and His Generals: The Armed Forces and Fascist Foreign Policy, 1922–1940* (New York: Cambridge University Press, 2007), 70–80.
62. Galeazzo Ciano, *Ciano's Hidden Diary: 1937–1938*, trans. Andreas Mayor (New York: Dutton, 1953), 81.

63. It was a development anticipated by Starace and Ciano, but not by Lessona: Ciano, *Hidden Diary*, 19.
64. Lessona, *Memorie*, 340–342. This development was furthered by his parallel feud with Emilio De Bono, the original commander of the invasion's northern front: Richard Bosworth, *Mussolini* (London: Bloomsbury, 2002), 322–323.
65. "Cambio della guardia nelle alte gerarchie," *Corriere della sera*, November 1, 1939; and Cesare Marinucci and Tomaso Columbano, *Il governo dei territori oltremare* (Rome: Istituto Poligrafico dello Stato, 1963), 413. On Teruzzi, see Victoria De Grazia, *The Perfect Fascist: A Story of Love, Power, and Morality in Mussolini's Italy* (Cambridge, MA: Harvard University Press, 2020).
66. Lessona, *Memorie*, 342. Ciano found him sad, but added that Teruzzi was judged "loyal but mediocre . . . in fact more loyal than mediocre." See Ciano, *Hidden Diary*, 34.
67. "Mussolini assume il Dicastero dell'Africa Italiana," *Corriere della sera*, November 21, 1937.
68. "Administrative reshuffling."
69. Borra, *Amedeo*, 68.
70. "I nuovi governatori," *Corriere della sera*, December 8, 1937; and "La nomina del nuovo Vice Governatore Generale dell'A.O.I. e dei Governatori dell'Eritrea e della Somalia," *Corriere dell'impero*, December 8, 1937.
71. Zäwdé Rätta, በቀዳማዊ ኃይለ ሥላሴ ዘመነ መንግሥት የኤርትራ ጉዳይ 1941–1963 (እንደ አውሮፓውያን አቆጣጠር) (አዲስ አበባ: ሻማ ቡክስ, 2006), 460–461.
72. On this role and the development of "totalitarian research," see Gianni Dore, "Scienze sociali, colonialismo e fascismo. La missione al lago Tana (1937)," *Lares* 87, nos. 2–3 (2021): 416–417.
73. A fourth expert was Enrico De Leone, who had obtained degrees in Islamic law and colonial jurisprudence from the University of Rome and the University of Padua, studied further at the University of Algiers and the Institute des Hautes Études Marocaines in Rabat, and then joined the colonial administration in Libya. He arrived in Ethiopia in February 1938, where he served in the viceroy's office: telegram from d'Aosta to Balbo, dated February 2, 1938, Enrico De Leone Papers, BCHC.
74. Lessona, *Memorie*, 315; and Borra, *Amedeo*, 6. Ciano more ambiguously found him "sympathetic" but "rather bewildered": Ciano, *Hidden Diary*, 40.
75. Amedeo di Savoia-Aosta, *Studi africani*, 1–32.
76. Lino Calabrò, *Intermezzo africano: Ricordi di un residente di governo in Etiopia (1937-1941)* (Rome: Bonacci, 1988), 43; and Pier Marcello Masotti, *Ricordi d'Etiopia di un funzionario coloniale* (Milan: Pan, 1981), 124–125.
77. "Il Duca d'Aosta a Addis Abeba," *Corriere della sera*, December 27, 1937.
78. "S.E. Enrico Cerulli Vice Governatore Generale dell'A.O.I.," *Corriere dell'impero*, December 26, 1937. See also "ልዑል ዱካ ዳኦስታ ከናፖሊ ባሕር ጠረፍ በመርከብ ሁነው ሲነሡ የሕዝቡ አልልታና ደስታ," *Corriere dell'impero*, December 19, 1937; and "Il Vice Re Amedeo di Savoia-Aosta raccogliera' oggi il trionfale omaggio e il giubilante saluto di Addis Abeba," *Corriere dell'impero*, December 26, 1937. The slogan of the newspaper,

emblazoned on the masthead, was "Roma doma," or "Rome subdues." On the newspaper, see Emanuele Ertola, *In terra d'Africa: Gli italiani che colonizzarono l'impero* (Bari: Laterza, 2017), 178–179.
79. "Regio decreto-legge 1 giugno 1936-XIV, n. 1019: Ordinamento e amminstrazione dell'Africa Orientale Italiana," *Gazzetta ufficiale* 77, no. 136 (1936): 1912–1917.
80. "Regio decreto-legge 11 novembre 1938-XVII, n. 1857, Istituzione del Governo dello Scioa," *Gazzetta ufficiale* 79, no. 287 (1938): 5179–5180.
81. On these, see Alberto Sbacchi, "I governatori coloniali italiani in Etiopia: gelosie e rivalità nel periodo 1936–1940," *Storia contemporanea* 8, no. 1 (1977): 835–877.
82. "La riunione dei Federali dell'A.O.I.," *Corriere dell'impero*, December 31, 1937; "Il duca d'Aosta ispezione improvvisamente," *Corriere dell'impero*, January 23, 1938; "Il Duca d'Aosta visita ad Oletta," *Corriere dell'impero*, January 30, 1938; "S.A.R. Il duca d'Aosta in visita ufficiale a Gimma," *Corriere dell'impero*, February 24, 1938; "Le visite di Amedeo di Savoia nei territori dell'Impero," *Corriere dell'impero*, March 5, 1938, with photo of d'Aosta and Cerulli; "L'ispezione del Vicerè ai territori del sud-ovest," *Corriere dell'impero*, March 22, 1938; and "Feste accoglienze di Mogadiscio al Principe Amedeo di Savoia-Aosta," *Corriere dell'impero*, March 31, 1938.
83. "Il Vice Re preside la riunione dei Governatori," *Corriere dell'impero*, March 6, 1938, with photo of the group on the front page of the March 8 issue.
84. "Il Sabato Santo etiopico," *Corriere dell'impero*, April 24, 1938, with photo in the following April 26 issue; and "Il Maresciallo Balbo entusiasticamente accolto dai fascisti e dalle genti di Addis Abeba," *Corriere dell'impero*, April 28, 1938.
85. "Annuale dell'impero ad Addis Ababa," *Corriere dell'impero*, May 10, 1938.
86. Other employees of this office included Emru Zälläqä, Yilma Deressa, Befekadu Wäldä Mika'él, and *fitawrari* Kidane Maryam Haylé: Emru Zälläqä, *A Journey: Memoirs* (North Charleston, NC: Createspace, 2016), 45; and Mickaël Bethe Selassié, *La jeune Éthiopie: Un haut-fonctionnaire éthiopien Berhanä-Marqos Wäldä-Tsadeq (1892-1943)* (Paris: Harmattan, 2004), 140–141.
87. Cerulli closely supervised the newspapers of the colony, in one instance retracting an issue because of its coverage of the viceroy: see telegram from Cerulli to Ministry of Italian Africa, dated April 20, 1938, ASMAI pos. 181/44-46.
88. On the colonial monologue, see Frantz Fanon, *A Dying Colonialism*, trans. Haakon Chevalier (New York: Grove, 1994), 95. On the history of these publications, see "የቁዛር መንግሥት መልክተኛ ጋዜጣና የሮማ ብርሃን የተባለው በወር በወሩ የሚመጣው እንደምን እንደሚታተሙ ጥቂት ማስረጃ," *የሮማ ብርሃን*, February 11, 1940; and "ሁላተኛ ዓመት," *የቁዛር መንግሥት መልክተኛ*, March 12, 1939.
89. Mickaël Bethe Selassié, *La jeune Éthiopie*, 140.
90. On the planning of this sequel to the 1924 Täfäri Mäkonnen visit and the 1925 jubilee delegations, see the extensive correspondence in ASMAI pos. 181/54; and Paolo Borruso, ed., *Il mito infranto: la fine del "sogno africano" negli appunti e nelle immagini di Massimo Borruso, funzionario coloniale in Etiopia (1937-46)* (Manduria: Lacaita, 1997), 38–40.
91. "Il Duce riceve 50 notabili della Libia e dell'Africa Orientale," *Corriere della sera*, May 12, 1938; and Borruso, *Mito infranto*, 41–42. More generally, see Silvia Bruzzi, *Islam*

and *Gender in Colonial Northeast Africa: Sittī 'Alawiyya, the Uncrowned Queen* (Leiden, Netherlands: Brill, 2018), 189–193.

92. "Il Balabbat del Gimma è giunto a Roma," *Corriere della sera*, April 2, 1938.
93. "L'omaggio al Duce del Balabbat del Gimma," *Corriere della sera*, April 10, 1938; "La gratitudine dei musulmani al Governo d'Italia," *Corriere della sera*, April 15, 1938; and "La riconoscenza dei musulmani d'Etiopia verso l'Italia fascista," *Corriere dell'impero*, April 20, 1938. See also Mussolini's reply: "Risposta al Sultano del Gimma," in *Opera omnia di Benito Mussolini*, ed. Edoardo Susmel and Duilio Susmel (Florence: La Fenice, 1959), 29:83.
94. Bruzzi, *Islam and Gender*, 190.
95. Letter from Cerulli to Avenol, dated January 11, 1938, and "Resignation of Italian Subjects Appointed by the Council to Membership of League Committees," dated January 22, 1938, both in C.41.1938, Mandates Slavery, LNA.
96. Borra, *Amedeo*, 81: "Frequentandolo, si aveva l'impressione che fosse geloso del proprio tempo e intendesse dedicarlo esclusivamente all'ufficio e ai suoi studi prediletti di etnologia e di linguistica, evitando le distrazioni degli incontri con persone estranee ai suoi progetti di lavoro. Si era cosí costituito un alone protettivo quasi invalicabile da inframmettenze occasionali. In ufficio formulava provvedimenti amministrativi basandosi sulle proprie cognizioni, quasi mai si consultava con i colleghi."
97. Letter from Stonehewer-Bird to Foreign Office, dated March 1, 1938, FO 371/22021.
98. Telegram from Stonehewer-Bird to Foreign Office, dated March 29, 1938, FO 371/22021.
99. Letters from Stonehewer-Bird to Foreign Office, dated February 28 and April 8, 1938, both in FO 371/22021.
100. Borra, *Amedeo*, 83.
101. Sbacchi, "Governatori," 866–867. Stonehewer-Bird speculated, "Perhaps the Duce's idea was that he himself would run Abyssinia through Cerulli with the Duca d'Aosta as a puppet Viceroy."
102. Letter from Stonehewer-Bird to Foreign Office, dated April 8, 1938, FO 371/22021; and Borra, *Amedeo*, 82. More broadly, see Alessandro Pes, "An Empire for a Kingdom: Monarchy and Fascism in the Italian Colonies," in *Crowns and Colonies: European Monarchies and Overseas Empires*, ed. Robert Aldrich and Cindy McCreery (Manchester, UK: Manchester University Press, 2016), 245–261.
103. Berretta, *Amedeo*, 91–92: "gallopini." These ministerial allies were widely disparaged by the colonial military as the "Swiss Navy," in the recollection of Alessandro Boaglio, who describes them strolling the Piassa neighborhood with their Italian wives: see his *Plotone chimico: Cronache abissine di una generazione scomoda*, ed. Giovanni Boaglio and Matteo Dominioni (Milan: Mimesis, 2010), 91.
104. Letter from Stonehewer-Bird to Foreign Office, dated April 8, 1938, FO 371/22021.
105. On these episodes, see chapter 2. On Gédo in 1938, see *Guida*, 499; and "Fascio di Ghedò," *Corriere dell'impero*, October 24, 1937.
106. On colonial Naqamtee, see Tesemma Ta'a and Alessandro Triulzi, eds., የወለጋ የታሪክ ሰነዶች ከ1880ዎቹ እስከ 1920ዎቹ (እ.ኢ.ኢ.) (አዲስ አበባ: አዲስ አበባ ዩኒቨርሲቲ ፕሬስ, 1999 ዓም), 308–322.

107. Telegram from d'Aosta to Ministry of Italian Africa, dated February 9, 1938; and telegram from d'Aosta to Ministry of Italian Africa, dated February 15, 1938, both in ASMAI pos. 181/41.
108. Gentilli, *Guerra aerea*, 164–165.
109. Ettore Formento, *Kai bandera: Etiopia 1936-1941, una banda irregolare* (Milan: Mursia, 2000).
110. Telegram from d'Aosta to Ministry of Italian Africa, dated February 17, 1938, ASMAI pos. 181/41.
111. For example, see Enrico Cerulli, "Note sul movimento musulmano nella Somalia," *RSO* 10, no. 1 (1923): 1–36.
112. The following year, Gärräsu Duki was involved in the killing of Sebastiano Castagna, an engineer and long-time resident of Ethiopia who had worked for Menilek and Täfäri Mäkonnen and subsequently served as a negotiator for Graziani. For some Ethiopians, his nefarious intentions were suggested by the Amharic meaning of his name, *qästaña*, or "the one with the bow." On his life and death, see Edoardo Borra, *Prologo di un conflitto: Colloqui col segretario del Negus (Dicembre 1934-Ottobre 1935)* (Milan: Paoline, 1965), 213–223; and Taddäsä Zäwäldé, ቀሪን ገረመው, 104–105. On Gärräsu Duki, see Taddäsä Zäwäldé, ቀሪን ገረመው, 398; Formento, *Kai bandera*, 144–184; and Tabor Wami, አባ ቦሩ (1897–1958 E.C.) (የደጃዝማች ገረሱ ዱኪና የሌሎች አርበኞች ታሪክ) (አዲስ አበባ: 1986 ዓም).
113. Heywät Hadaru, ያቺ ቀን ተረሳች ከትምህርት ቤት ወደ ቆንስላ ሥራ (አዲስ አበባ: ብርሃንና ሰላም ማተሚያ ቤት, 1967 ዓም); Zervos, *Éthiopie*, 107; and Bahru Zewde, "The Ethiopian Intelligentsia and the Italo-Ethiopian War, 1935–1941," *IJAHS* 26, no. 2 (1993): 283. In 1937, Ruggero Tracchia described *däjjazmach* Zäwdé as an irreducible: report by Tracchia on operations in Shäwa, dated February 22, 1937, ASMAI pos. 181/39.
114. "የምሥራች," ብርሃንና ሰላም, April 19, 1928.
115. Enrico Cerulli, *Etiopia occidentale (dallo Scioa alla frontiera del Sudan)* (Rome: Sindacato Italiano Arti Grafiche, 1929 and 1933), 1:227–231, and unpaginated photo between 236–237, reproduced earlier as figure 2.2. The photo depicts Cerulli at the Gojeb River with local notables, a group described in the narrative as including Takkälä Wäldä Hawaryat. The helmet and clothing of the figure standing to the immediate left of Cerulli in the photo suggest someone like the *blatta*.
116. Nicolas Virtue, "Royal Army, Fascist Empire: The Regio Esercito on Occupation Duty, 1936–1943" (PhD diss., Western University, 2016); and Federica Saini Fasanotti, *Vincere! The Italian Royal Army's Counterinsurgency Operations in Africa, 1922-1940* (Annapolis, MD: Naval Institute Press, 2020).
117. On this policy shift, see Dominioni, *Sfascio dell'impero*, 70–74; and Sbacchi, *Ethiopia*, 133–135.
118. Borra, *Amedeo*, 73.
119. Haylä Sellasé, *My Life and Ethiopia's Progress: Haile Selassie I King of Kings of Ethiopia. Vol. 2, Addis Abeba, 1966 E.C.*, trans. Ezekiel Gebissa et al. (East Lansing: Michigan State University Press, 1994), 86. From France, the pilot-turned-Ethiopianist Griaule attempted to coordinate an April relief operation for the *arbañas* via Hubert

Deschamps, the governor of Djibouti: Hubert Deschamps, "Griaule, Mandel et l'Ethiopie," *JES* 4, no. 1 (1966): 71–73.

120. "Il sottosegretario per l'Africa Italiana giunge oggi ad Addis Abeba," *Corriere dell'impero*, June 1, 1938.

121. Borra, *Amedeo*, 83–84. This assessment was likely conditioned by the fact that Teruzzi and Cerulli were then sparring over the African delegation to Italy: see their correspondence in ASMAI pos. 181/44-46.

122. "Il Vice Re si reca in Italia per una breve vacanza," *Corriere dell'impero*, June 5, 1938; Borra, *Amedeo*, 129–130; and Ciano, *Hidden Diary*, 130.

123. Letter from Stonehewer-Bird to Foreign Office, dated April 5, 1938, FO 371/22021; and correspondence between Teruzzi and Meregazzi in ASMAI GS, cart. 251.

124. Borra, *Amedeo*, 83.

125. "S. E. Teruzzi inaugura la galleria del Passo Mussolini," *Corriere dell'impero*, June 7, 1938; and interview with *liqä kahnat* Qalä Heywät, January 25, 2020.

126. A praise song of the era celebrated his shrewdness: "ሴቶች ተሰብሰቡ ኑ ጠላ ቅመሱ[፤] እንደገፍን እናት እንድትጠነስሱ[፤] ፋሺስት ተሰብስቦ ሲጫወት ገበጣ[፤] ያባገፍን አሽከር ጆምአፍራሹ መጣ[።]" or "Women, come and gather! Taste the *ṭälla* [teff beer]! So you will brew *ṭälla* like the mother of Gofen / When the fascists were gathered playing cribbage [*gäbäṭa*] / The soldier[s] of *abba* Gofen came and ambushed them." See Taddäsä Zäwäldé, ቀሪን ገረመው, 19–130, with praise song on 40; and also Salome Gebre Egziabeher, "The Ethiopian Patriots 1936–1941," *Ethiopian Observer* 12, no. 2 (1969): 76–77.

127. Report from Tracchia on operations in Shäwa, dated February 22, 1937, ASMAI pos. 181/39.

128. Telegram from Graziani to Ministry of Italian Africa, dated September 6, 1937, and report on operations in Däbrä Berhan sector from September 1937 to July 1938, undated, both in ASMAI pos. 181/39-40.

129. Report on operations in Däbrä Berhan sector from September 1937 to July 1938, undated, ASMAI pos. 181/39-40.

130. Telegram from Cerulli to Ministry of Italian Africa, dated June 9, 1938 [morning], ASMAI pos. 181/41.

131. Telegram from Cerulli to Ministry of Italian Africa, part I, dated June 13, 1938, ASMAI pos. 181/41.

132. Telegram from Cerulli to Ministry of Italian Africa, part II, dated June 13, 1938, ASMAI pos. 181/41.

133. Telegram from Cerulli to Ministry of Italian Africa, dated May 20, 1938, ASMAI GS cart. 251.

134. Telegram from Cerulli to Ministry of Italian Africa, dated June 9, 1938 [morning], ASMAI pos. 181/41.

135. Telegram from Cerulli to Ministry of Italian Africa, dated June 10, 1938, ASMAI pos. 181/41. The killed leaders were *fitawrari* Habtä Sellasé and *qäññazmach* Zälläqä.

136. Telegram from Cerulli to Ministry of Italian Africa, part II, dated June 13, 1938, ASMAI pos. 181/41.

137. Telegram from Cerulli to Ministry of Italian Africa, dated June 19, 1938, ASMAI pos. 181/41.

138. The exact timing of this episode is uncertain, but Borra's testimony suggests it took place during Cerulli's 1938 regency. He provides two key details: first, the viceroy was away when Cerulli took Dan'él as his ward; and second, the original detention site, Däbrä Berhan, was very far from where Dan'él was captured. Since the campaign involving Abäbä Arägay during Cerulli's 1939 regency took place in the mountains around Däbrä Berhan, it thus seems more likely that the 1938 Kässäm operation and not the 1939 Däbrän Berhan operation led to Dan'él's capture. This dating is also suggested by Dan'él's testimony, in which he states he joined his father in the campaign near the end of 1937 and was captured in his first battle. For the accounts, see Borra, *Amedeo*, 85; and Angelo Del Boca, *The Ethiopian War, 1935-1941*, trans. P. D. Cummins (Chicago: University of Chicago Press, 1969), 243–244; and on Dan'él Abäbä, see Mahtämä Sellasé Wäldä Mäsqäl, "ቼ በለው፣" 278.
139. Del Boca, *Ethiopian War*, 244.
140. Borra, *Amedeo*, 85.
141. Report on operations in Ambo-Gédo sector, August 1937–July 1938, undated, ASMAI pos. 181/39-40.
142. "Il Generale Teruzzi ad Oletta, Addis Alem, Gaggi, ed Ambò," *Corriere dell'impero*, June 10, 1938.
143. Telegram from Cerulli to Ministry of Italian Africa, dated June 18, 1938, ASMAI pos. 181/41.
144. "Giornate di fervida attività del Sottosegretario per l'A.I.," *Corriere dell'impero*, June 28, 1938.
145. Telegram from Cerulli to Ministry of Italian Africa, dated July 2, 1938, ASMAI pos. 181/41.
146. Telegram from Cerulli to Ministry of Italian Africa, dated July 5, 1938, ASMAI pos. 181/41.
147. Telegram from Cerulli to Ministry of Italian Africa, dated July 27, 1938, ASMAI pos. 181/41: "Comunque il problema sarà soltanto di polizia e non più politico. Perciò ripeto siamo alla prova più grave. Ed io sono sicuro se continuiamo con mano ferma (ripeto ferma) a tener dovunque situazione, sopratutto intervenendo con immediata energia e tempestività nei punti deboli appena si manifestino in qualunque regione Impero, potremo dire a fine settembre di aver definitivamente risolto la situazione politica interna."
148. Michael Ebner, *Ordinary Violence in Mussolini's Italy* (New York: Cambridge University Press, 2011), 13–14.
149. In the coming months, Cavallero had similarly optimistic assessments of the insurrection: in September, he told Ciano that the rebellion could be "liquidate[d]" by Christmas: Ciano, *Hidden Diary*, 152. In November, however, Stonehewer-Bird informed the British Foreign Office that the Ankober area remained outside "the full control" of the Italians: "Memorandum Respecting the Present Situation in Ethiopia," dated November 1, 1938, CAB 24/281, NAUK.
150. Interview with Terrefe Ras Warq, January 21, 2020.
151. Sergew Hable Selassie, አማርኛ የቤተ ክርስቲያን መዝገብ ቃላት, 38–41.
152. List of Ethiopian detainees, dated November 10, 1937, ASMAI pos. 181/54.

153. Interview with *liqä kahnat* Qalä Heywät; and EMML 3982, 2r, an Ankober manuscript that contains a marginal note by *mämmeré* Fesseha.
154. Terrefe Ras Warq, የአንከቡሩ ሰው, 9.
155. Interview with Terrefe Ras Warq, January 21, 2020. Also destroyed during this same period was the nearby library of *aläqa* Aṣmä Giyorgis, which contained his unpublished writings: Bairu, "Three Portraits," 142.
156. Terrefe Ras Warq, የአንከቡሩ ሰው, 10.
157. Telegram from d'Aosta to Ministry of Italian Africa, dated August 11, 1938, ASMAI pos. 181/41. On his activities in Italy, see "Il Vicerè d'Etiopia sbarcato ieri a Napoli," *Corriere della sera*, June 14, 1938; and "Il Duca d'Aosta riferisce al Duce sulla situazione e i problemi dell'Impero," *Corriere dell'impero*, June 26, 1938.
158. Florian Wagner, *Colonial Internationalism and the Governmentality of Empire, 1893–1982* (New York: Cambridge University Press, 2022), 257–280; and Emanuel Rota, "'We Will Never Leave.' The Reale Accademia d'Italia and the Invention of a Fascist Africanism," *Fascism* 2, no. 2 (2013): 161–182.
159. *Annali dell'Africa Italiana* 1, nos. 3–4 (1938): 1251.
160. Borra, *Amedeo*, 82–83.
161. In late November, the visiting Kenyan settler Katherine Fannin found Francesco Canero Medici serving as the acting vice governor general and was told the absent Cerulli was "difficult" and "a 'Rome appointment.'" See "Mrs. C. Fannin's Journey through Italian East Africa," dated December 20, 1938, FO 371/22030/4677.
162. On Haylä Sellasé's approach to to Mäsqäl, see "የመስቀል በዓል," ብርሃንና ሰላም, October 1, 1931; and Martha Nasibù, *Memorie di una principessa etiope* (Vicenza: Neri Pozza, 2005), 75–77; and on its role in colonial Eritrea, see James De Lorenzi, *Guardians of the Tradition: Historians and Historical Writing in Ethiopia and Eritrea* (Rochester, NY: University of Rochester Press, 2015), 71–72. On colonial ritual, see Terence Ranger, "The Invention of Tradition in Colonial Africa," in *The Invention of Tradition*, ed. Eric Hobsbawm and Terence Ranger (Cambridge: Cambridge University Press, 1983), 211–262; and also his "The Invention of Tradition Revisited: The Case of Colonial Africa," in *Inventions and Boundaries: Historical and Anthropological Approaches to the Study of Ethnicity and Nationalism*, ed. Preban Kaarsholm and Jan Hultin (Roskilde, Denmark: Roskilde University, 1994), 5–50.
163. Borra, *Amedeo*, 133. The viceroy similarly coopted the Muslim celebration of Eid al-Fitr: "La fine del Ramadan celebrata a Addis Abeba," *Corriere della sera*, November 26, 1938.
164. "ስለ አጼ መስቀል በዓል አከባበር," የቄሣር መንግሥት መልከተኛ, September 25, 1938; "ሹመት," የቄሣር መንግሥት መልከተኛ, October 2, 1938; and "Il Vicerè assiste alla seconda festa del 'Mascal,'" *Corriere della sera*, September 28, 1938.
165. This was Piero Franca, the director of the Office of Political Affairs.
166. "ለመስቀል በዓል የተሸሙ ሰዎች," የቄሣር መንግሥት መልከተኛ, October 9, 1938. In 1940, he received another award: "ክፍተኛ የሆነ የማዕርግ ሽልማት," የርማ ብርሃን, November 11, 1940.
167. In the years to come, several Asinara detainees would be similarly honored at the feast. In 1939, recuperables *däjjazmach* Ayyaléw Berru and *däjjazmach* Amdé Ali were elevated to the rank of *ras*, alongside *abba* Weqaw Berru; and in 1940,

balambaras Mahtämä Sellasé Wäldä Mäsqäl was recognized alongside the former irreducible *däjjazmach* Zäwdé Asfaw Dargé. See "አስይ መስቀል ጠባ አስይ መስከረም ጠባ," የሮማ ብርሃን, September 27, 1939; "ከፍተኛ የሆነ የማዕርግ ሽልማት," የሮማ ብርሃን, November 11, 1940; "የመስቀል በዓል አከባበር," የቄሣር መንግሥት መልከተኛ, September 29, 1940; Fantahun Ayele, "The Life of *däǧǧač abba* Wəqaw Bərru: Some Notes on Sirak's Manuscript (Addis Ababa, Institute of Ethiopian Studies, Ms 400)," *Africa* 3, no. 2 (2021): 33; Alberto Sbacchi, "Italy and the Treatment of the Ethiopian Aristocracy, 1937–1940," *IJAHS* 10, no. 2 (1977): 22; and Borra, *Amedeo*, 133. Some of these developments were foreshadowed in 1938, when one local newspaper featured a group photo of *däjjazmach* Ayyaléw Berru, *däjjazmach* Makonnen Wässäné, *ṣahafé te'ezaz* Wäldä Mäsqäl, *balambaras* Mahtämä Sellasé, and their families: የቄሣር መንግሥት መልከተኛ, December 11, 1938.

168. "Esame delle questioni relative all'assetto dei territori dell'impero," undated [early 1938?], ASMAI pos. 181/47; and *Gazzetta ufficiale* n. 136 (June 13, 1936): 1912.
169. *Gazzetta ufficiale*, n. 287 (December 17, 1938): 5179–5180.
170. For an account of militarized Addis Ababa, see "Mrs. C. Fannin's Journey Through Italian East Africa," dated December 20, 1938, FO 371/22030/4677.
171. "Il governo dello Scioa," *Corriere dell'impero*, May 9, 1939.
172. In December 1938, Teruzzi found relations between Cerulli and d'Aosta somewhat improved: Sbacchi, "Governatori coloniali," 869.
173. Borra, *Amedeo*, 89. He attributed this to the duke's air force background. Cerulli's army background seems to have been unappreciated.
174. Borra, *Amedeo*, 92–94.
175. Galeazzo Ciano, *Diario* (Milan: Rizzoli, 1946), 1:11.
176. Ugo Cavallero, *Gli avvenimenti militari nell'impero: dal 13 gennaio 1939–XVII al 14 aprile 1939–XVII* (Addis Ababa: 1940). On Lorenzini, see Curzio Malaparte, "In guerra muiono i migliori," in *Viaggio in Etiopia e altri scritti africani*, ed. Enzo Laforgia (Bagno a Ripoli: Passigli, 2019), 164–171; and "የኩሎኔሎ ሎረንዚኒ ታሪኪ," የሮማ ብርሃን, February 1940.
177. Cavallero, *Avvenimenti*, 1:10–11, 13, 53–54; report for Mussolini on military situation at the end of January 1939, undated, ASMAI pos. 181/43; and more generally, Gooch, *Mussolini and His Generals*, 397–399.
178. D'Aosta's last situation report appears to be his telegram to the Ministry of Italian Africa, dated March 8, 1939, ASMAI pos. 181/41. He reached Rome on March 11: "Il Vice Re d'Etiopia giunto a Roma," *Corriere dell'impero*, March 11, 1939. On Teruzzi's departure, see "የኢጣልያ አፍሪካ ምክትል ሚኒስትር ወደ ኢጣልያ ለመመለስ ምጽዋ ላይ በመርከብ ተሳፈሩ," የቄሣር መንግሥት መልከተኛ, February 12, 1939.
179. Tadässä Zäwäldé, *ቀሪን ገረመው*, 155.
180. *Guida*, 406; Cavallero, *Avvenimenti*, 1:56, and 2:198–199; "Il Generale Passerone a Dessiè, dopo le ispezioni a Scianò, Debra Berhan e Debra Sina," *Corriere dell'impero*, March 10, 1939; and "Il governo dello Scioa," *Corriere dell'impero*, May 5, 1939.
181. Malaparte, *Viaggio in Etiopia*, 141.
182. It was coincidentally the birthplace of the protagonist of Heruy's novel: አዲስ አለም፡ የቅኖችና የደግ አድራጊዎች መሪያ (አዲስ አበባ፡ ጎሀ ጽባሕ, 1925 ዓም), 1 [fidäl pagination].
183. Tadässä Zäwäldé, *ቀሪን ገረመው*, 148–165.

184. Tadässä Zäwäldé, ቀሪን ገራሙው, 155: "የጠላት ግብረ አበሮች"
185. Telegram from Cerulli to d'Aosta, dated March 13, 1939, ASMAI pos. 81/41. Cerulli worked with Lorenzini in the Ancoberino counterinsurgency during his 1938 regency.
186. Cavallero, *Avvenimenti*, 1:67.
187. Telegram from Cerulli to Ministry of Italian Africa, dated March 15, 1939, ASMAI pos. 181/41.
188. Teruzzi appears to have reached similar conclusions in January: report by Teruzzi for Mussolini, undated, ASMAI pos. 181/43.
189. Telegram from Cerulli to d'Aosta and Ministry of Italian Africa, dated March 15, 1939, ASMAI pos. 181/41.
190. Telegram from Cerulli to d'Aosta and Ministry of Italian Africa, dated March 16, 1939, ASMAI pos. 181/41.
191. "Dr. Cerulli and Ethiopia," *Ethiopian Herald*, April 18, 1949.
192. Correspondence with Deresse Ayenachew Woldetsadik, February 6, 2024.
193. "Marconigramma" from Cerulli to Lorenzini, dated March 17, 1939, in Cavallero, *Avvenimenti*, 2:306–307.
194. "Il Vicerè d'Etiopia a colloquio col Duce," *Corriere della sera*, March 17, 1939; "I problemi sulla difesa e la valorizzazione dell'Impero illustrati al Duce dal Vice Re d'Etiopia," *Corriere dell'impero*, March 17, 1939; Borra, *Amedeo*, 85; and Sbacchi, "Governatori coloniali," 869.
195. Telegram from Cerulli to d'Aosta and Ministry of Italian Africa, dated March 18, 1939, ASMAI pos. 181/41.
196. Community interviews in Çhaçha and Çhaçha Maryam, January 24, 2020.
197. Telegram from Cerulli to d'Aosta and Ministry of Italian Africa, dated March 18, 1939, ASMAI pos. 181/41.
198. Telegram from Cerulli to d'Aosta and Ministry of Italian Africa, dated March 18, 1939, ASMAI pos. 181/41: "Popolazioni dello Scioa settentrionale, la potenza delle armi Italiane ha battuto, distrutto o disperso quei gruppi i quali, ingannati dalle ambiziose menzogne di alcuni capi, avevano tentato di razziare voi pacifiche popolazioni muovendo dai burroni ed anfratti creduti inaccessibili. Dite ai fuggiaschi che si presentino ai nostri ufficiali consegnano immediatamente le armi, avranno la vita salva. La clemenza che ci spinge ad accordare oggi il perdono, non vuole però indugi nè trattative. Avete visto come in pochi giorni tutto il paese è stato organizzato. Avete a Debre Brehan, a Bannaber, ad Ancober, a M (manca) centri principali i residenti. Avete in ogni distretto i vostri capi. Ubbidite! Riprendete tranquilli il lavoro nei vostri campi! Siete sicuramente protetti e garantiti dalla forza dell'Italia Fascista."
199. Vicente Rafael, *Motherless Tongues: The Insurgency of Language Amid Wars of Translation* (Durham, NC: Duke University Press, 2016), 120–146.
200. Boaglio, *Plotone chimico*, 100, 106.
201. Piero Farello, "Le bande irregolari indigene a caccia di partigiani in Etiopia," *Studi piacentini* 11, no. 1 (1992): 149, 155.

8. SURVIVAL IN SHÄWA   365

202. "Marconigramma" from Cerulli to Ministry of Italian Africa, dated March 19, 1939, in Cavallero, *Avvenimenti*, 2:198–200. The football coverage appears in *Corriere dell'impero* as well as its illustrated supplement *Lunedi dell'impero*.
203. "Mostra Personale della pittrice Rosida Gaione-Cuoco" with accompanying photos, in Rosida Cuoco Papers, BCSC; and "Il Vice Governatore Generale inaugura la mostra della pittrice Rosida Gaione-Cuoco," *Corriere dell'impero*, March 21, 1939. For an earlier show, see "L'apertura della mostra," *Corriere della Somalia*, April 6, 1932. Cuoco was a painter and photographer who was likely the most prominent settler artist in the colony. She was married to Luigi Gaione, a military officer previously stationed in Somalia.
204. Telegram from Cerulli to d'Aosta and Ministry of Italian Africa, dated March 22, 1939 [2:00AM], ASMAI pos. 181/41. Cerulli sent four situation reports to Rome this day.
205. Taddäsä Zäwäldé, ቀሪን ገሪሞው, 158–161: "እንደጤፍ አበቅ [አብቅ] በሞተረየስ ጥይት እያራገቡ"
206. "L'odierna celebrazione del Ventennale del Fascismo," *Corriere dell'impero*, March 26, 1939.
207. "Marconigramma" from Mussolini to Cerulli, dated April 8, 1939, in Cavallero, *Avvenimenti*, 2:201: "Con vivo compiacimento ho preso visione del rapporto conclusive sull'azione svolta per troncare ribellione Scioa. Mentre mando mio elogio at commandanti et truppe, ordino che nessuna tregua sia data a fuggiaschi et sbandati in modo che operazione sia veramente definitiva e assicuri, insieme con la simultanea azione politica, inizio epoca ordine et assoluta normalità in quella zona. Anche in vista situazione europea azione militare Scioa ha notevole importanza perchè elimina speranze cultivate a Gibuti dai fuorusciti abissini e dai loro ormai sin troppo palesi sostenitori. Ultimata et perfezionata operazione Scioa, bisogna eliminare ribellione Amara."
208. Telegram from Cerulli to d'Aosta and Ministry of Italian Africa, dated March 27, 1939, ASMAI pos. 181/41.
209. "Marconigramma" from Cerulli to Ministry of Italian Africa, dated March 27, 1939, in Cavallero, *Avvenimenti*, 2:399.
210. Minutes of Cavallero-Lorenzini-Cerulli meeting, dated April 8, 1939, in Cavallero, *Avvenimenti*, 2:203–204.
211. Reflecting on the torture and mass killing at Zärrät—through mustard gas, firing squad, and bludgeoning—Boaglio later wrote, "Innumerable other episodes crowd my mind remembering these bloody hours, episodes of cruelty, ferocity, infinite wickedness, and also of heroism—not on our side, unfortunately, but the heroism of the poor, miserable, persecuted natives." See Boaglio, *Plotone chimico*, 117. On these events, see Dominioni, *Sfascio dell'impero*, 205–214.
212. "አሞጻኛ ዋሻ"
213. See *Corriere dell'impero*, April 1–3, 1939. His first field report to the Ministry appears to be telegram from d'Aosta to Ministry of Italian Africa, dated April 3, 1939, ASMAI pos. 181/41.
214. Dominioni, *Sfascio dell'impero*, 215–217.

215. "S.A.R. il Vice Re assume il Comando Superiore diretto delle Forze Armate dell'A.O.I.," *Corriere dell'impero*, April 14, 1939.
216. Cavallero, *Avvenimenti*, 1:130; and Borra, *Amedeo*, 91.
217. Cavallero, *Avvenimenti*, 1:92.
218. "I problemi e le realizzazioni dell'Impero nel discorso di S.E. Teruzzi alla Camera dei Fasci e delle Corporazioni," *Corriere dell'impero*, May 12, 1939.
219. Borra, *Amedeo*, 90–91; and Sbacchi, "Governatori coloniali," 870–871. Borra's assessment is supported by the extent to which Cavallero remained in Mussolini's favor: see Ciano, *Diario*, 1:130; and Gooch, *Mussolini's Generals*, 460–461.
220. Dominioni, *Sfascio dell'impero*, 216–217.
221. Curiously, the first announcement in the local press appears to be "Cronaca di Harar," *Corriere dell'impero*, April 26, 1939. In this same period, Tommaso Columbano was dispatched from the Ministry of Italian Africa to serve as the new secretary general of the Shäwa governate: "Il Segretario Generale del Governo dello Scioa," *Corriere dell'impero*, April 1, 1939. Columbano later cowrote the official history of the colonial administration.
222. The viceroy personally requested De Leone's transfer from Libya. In early 1939, De Leone implemented and supervised a new course for colonial officials in Addis Ababa, focused on Ethiopian languages and Islamic and Orthodox Christian law: curriculum vitae of Enrico De Leone, De Leone Papers, BCSC; and Borra, *Amedeo*, 98–99.
223. "Cronaca di Harar," *Corriere dell'impero*, April 26, 1939.
224. "Capi e notabili portano a S.E. Nasi il saluto e l'augurio delle genti del Harar," *Corriere dell'impero*, April 28, 1939.
225. "Cambio della guardia nelle alte cariche dell'impero," *Etiopia* 3, no. 5 (1939): unpaginated front matter.
226. Sbacchi, "Governatori coloniali," 871. On Nasi and d'Aosta's relationship, see "Mrs. C. Fannin's Journey Through Italian East Africa," dated December 20, 1938, FO 371/22030/4677.
227. Letter from Malaparte to Borelli, dated April 25, 1938, in Malaparte, *Viaggio in Etiopia*, 307.
228. Telegram from Cerulli to d'Aosta and Ministry of Italian Africa, dated March 16, 1939, ASMAI pos. 181/41.
229. "S.E. Cerulli in visita ai centri del territorio," *Corriere dell'impero*, May 17, 1939; "Il Governatore del Harar ad Adama e nella zona del Mingiar," *Corriere dell'impero*, May 23, 1939; "Il Governatore del Harar visita gli impianti industriali di Dire Daua," *Corriere dell'impero*, May 24, 1939; "Il Governatore del Harar nella regione del Cercer," *Corriere dell'impero*, May 30, 1939; and "L'arrivo in Addis Abeba dei Governatori dell'A.O.I.," *Corriere dell'impero*, December 12, 1939.
230. *Diritto razzista* 2, nos. 5–6 (1940): 233, with additional list of supporters in appendix, 15.
231. *Diritto razzista* 2, nos. 5–6 (1940): 299–301.

232. "Il Galla e Sidama nei risultati della Missione Cipriani," *Corriere dell'impero*, December 29, 1939.
233. On Frank, see Phillipe Sands, *East West Street: On the Origins of "Genocide" and "Crimes Against Humanity"* (New York: Vintage, 2017).
234. Marinucci and Columbano, *Governo dei territori oltremare*, 427.
235. Terrefe Ras Warq, የአንከበሩ ሰው, 16; and interview with Terrefe Ras Warq, January 21, 2020.

9. Bath and Dhanaane

1. Graham Davis and Penny Bonsall, *A History of Bath: Image and Reality* (Lancaster, UK: Carnegie, 2006), 247–274.
2. Edward Said, *Culture and Imperialism* (New York: Vintage, 1994), xxvii.
3. Tässäma Eshäté, "ኢጣልያ በግፍ ስለ መነሳቷ," ብርሃንና ሰላም, November 21, 1935.
4. "የሐይቲ ሬፑብሊክ መንግሥት መልእክተኛ," ብርሃንና ሰላም, November 14, 1935.
5. ብርሃንና ሰላም, December 5, 1935.
6. Letter from Tä'amrat Ammanu'él to Faitlovitch, dated May 14, 1936, in Emanuela Trevisan Semi, ed., *L'epistolario di Taamrat Emmanuel. Un intelletuale ebreo d'Etiopia nella prima metà del XX secolo* (Turin: Harmattan, 2000), 208.
7. Telegram from Heruy Wäldä Sellasé to Avenol, dated December 2, 1935, C.467.M.245.1935.VII; telegram from Heruy Wäldä Sellasé to Avenol, dated December 7, 1935, C.474.M.250.1935.VII; and telegram from Heruy Wäldä Sellasé to Avenol, dated December 24, 1935, C.502.M.271.1935.VII, all in LNDP.
8. Haylä Sellasé, *My Life and Ethiopia's Progress, Volume 1: 1892–1937*, trans. Edward Ullendorff (New York: Oxford University Press, 1976), 251–257; and George Steer, *Caesar in Abyssinia* (London: Hodder and Stoughton, 1936), 208–209, 214–216. More generally, see Zara Steiner, *The Triumph of the Dark: European International History, 1933–1939* (New York: Oxford University Press, 2011), 122–130; and George Baer, *Test Case: Italy, Ethiopia, and the League of Nations* (Stanford, CA: Hoover Institution Press, 1976), 121–155.
9. On Colson, see "E.A. Colson Dies; ex-Ethiopian Aide," *New York Times*, February 24, 1937.
10. Telegrams from Heruy Wäldä Sellasé to Haylä Sellasé, dated January 5, 1936, and January 6, 1936, both in ACS FG bust. 20.
11. Edoardo Borra, *Prologo di un conflitto: Colloqui col segretario del Negus (Dicembre 1934–Ottobre 1935)* (Milan: Paoline, 1965), 173–174.
12. Avenol, for example, supported the talks: James Barros, *Betrayal from Within: Joseph Avenol, Secretary-General of the League of Nations, 1933–1940* (New Haven, CT: Yale University Press, 1969), 106–107.
13. Telegram from Ministry of Foreign Affairs to Ministry of the Colonies, dated March 7, 1936, ASMAI AP cart. 15.

14. Pompeo Aloisi, *Journal (25 Juillet 1932-14 Juin 1936)*, trans. Maurice Vaussard (Paris: Plon, 1957), 352-353; and John Spencer, *Ethiopia at Bay: A Personal Account of the Haile Selassie Years* (Algonac, MI: Reference Publications, 1984), 53. On Zervos's relationship with Cerulli, see Enrico Cerulli, *Etiopia occidentale (dallo Scioa alla frontiera del Sudan)* (Rome: Sindacato Italiano Arti Grafiche, 1929 and 1933), 1:11.
15. Telegram from Ministry of Foreign Affairs to Ministry of the Colonies, dated February 24, 1936, ASMAI AP cart. 15.
16. Promemoria by Cerulli, undated, ACS MAI AGP Commissione di Primo Grado per l'Epurazione, bust. 370.
17. Telegram from Ministry of Foreign Affairs to League delegation, dated February 11, 1936, ASMAI AP cart. 15. On this plan, see Aklilu Habtäwäld, የአክሊሉ ማስታወሻ *Aklilu Remembers* (አዲስ አበባ፡ አዲስ አበባ ዩኒቨርሲቲ ፕሬስ, 2010), 21.
18. On these, see Franco Bandini, *Gli italiani in Africa: storia delle guerre coloniali 1882-1943* (Milan: Longanesi, 1971), 350-366; Alain Rouaud, "Les contacts secrets italo-éthiopiens du printemps 1936 d'après les archives françaises," *Africa* 37, no. 4 (1982): 400-411; and Alberto Sbacchi, "Italian Mandate or Protectorate over Ethiopia in 1935-1936," *RSPI* 42, no. 4 (1975): 577-578. Born in Bethlehem and acquainted with the Ethiopian community in Jerusalem, Jasir Bey alleged that he was connected to Minister of War Mulugéta Yeggäzu, *abunä* Qérellos, and the emperor himself, and on these grounds he obtained a contract from the Italian government to undertake negotiations with Ethiopia: Bandini, *Italiani in Africa*, 532n3 and 533n6. The Djibouti talks tangentially involved Amedeo Marciano, the Fiat representative in Addis Ababa who subsequently supervised Berhanä Habtämika'él at the Office of Political Affairs in Addis Ababa: Rouaud, "Contacts secrets," 406; and correspondence related to Berhanä Habtämika'él in ASMAI pos. 181/54.
19. Telegram from Ministry of Foreign Affairs to Ministry of the Colonies, dated April 20, 1936, ASMAI AP cart. 15.
20. Report by Morin for the Ministry of War, February 7, 1936, ASMAI AP cart. 15.
21. These intercepted telegrams were previously located by historian Alberto Sbacchi, who was given special access to ASMAI in the 1970s and 1980s: Sbacchi, *Ethiopia Under Mussolini: Fascism and the Colonial Experience* (London: Zed, 1985), 27, 30-31n6. However, as of this writing, I have been unable to locate the specific telegrams discussed by Sbacchi, since their cited file is missing and they are not among the intercepted telegrams preserved elsewhere in ASMAI and ACS.
22. Spencer, *Ethiopia at Bay*, 56-57.
23. Aloisi, *Journal*, 366.
24. Giuseppe Puglisi, *Chi è? dell' Eritrea 1952. Dizionario biografico con una cronologia* (Asmara: Agenzia Regina, 1952), 77.
25. Frantz Fanon, *The Wretched of the Earth*, trans. Constance Farrington (New York: Grove, 1968), 61-62.
26. Steer, *Caesar*, 363-364; and Spencer, *Ethiopia at Bay*, 62.
27. Telegram from Italian ambassador in London to the Ministry of the Colonies, dated May 28, 1936, ASMAI AP cart. 15.

28. Haylä Sellasé, *My Life*, 1:312.
29. Elihu Lauterpacht, *The Life of Hersch Lauterpacht* (New York: Cambridge University Press, 2010), 79–80.
30. Emmanu'él Abraham, *Reminiscences of My Life* (Trenton, NJ: Africa World Press, 2010), 34.
31. "Racial Feelings," *The Gleaner*, July 17, 1937.
32. Aklilu Habtäwäld, የአክሊሉ ማስታወሻ, 131–135. On the exile community in Jerusalem, see Tä'amrat Yeggäzu, የስደት መታሰቢያ። ጠላት ኢትዮጵያን በወረረ ዘመን፤ ወደ ኢየሩሳሌም ስደት (አዲስ አበባ፡ ብርሃንና ሰላም ማተሚያ ቤት, 1944 ዓም).
33. Fikru Negash Gebrekidan, "Race, Gender, and Pageantry: The Ups and Downs of an African American Woman in Imperial Ethiopia," *NEAS* 21, no. 2 (2021): 265–300; Brett Shadle, "The Unity of Black People and the Redemption of Ethiopia: The Ethiopian World Federation and a New Black Nationalism, 1936–1940," *IJAHS* 54, no. 2 (2021): 193–215; and Joseph Harris, *African-American Reactions to War in Ethiopia, 1936–1941* (Baton Rouge: Louisiana State University Press, 1994), 120–141.
34. Minkah Makalani, *In the Cause of Freedom: Radical Black Internationalism from Harlem to London, 1917–1939* (Chapel Hill: University of North Carolina Press, 2013), 199–207; and Marc Matera, *Black London: The Imperial Metropolis and Decolonization in the Twentieth Century* (Berkeley: University of California Press, 2015), 62–73.
35. T. Ras Makonnen, *Pan-Africanism from Within, as Recorded and Edited by Kenneth King* (New York: Oxford University Press, 1973).
36. Rachel Holmes, *Sylvia Pankhurst: Natural Born Rebel* (London: Bloomsbury, 2020); and Richard Pankhurst and Ian Bullock, eds., *Sylvia Pankhurst from Artist to Anti-Fascist* (New York: Palgrave Macmillan, 1992).
37. Richard Pankhurst, "Sylvia and *New Times and Ethiopia News*," in *Sylvia Pankhurst*, ed. Pankhurst and Bullock, 149–191.
38. Haylä Sellasé, *My Life and Ethiopia's Progress: Haile Selassie I King of Kings of Ethiopia. Vol. 2, Addis Abeba, 1966 E.C.*, trans. Ezekiel Gebissa et al. (East Lansing: Michigan State University Press, 1994), 7; and Du Bois draft memorial, undated [1960?], Du Bois Papers, UMAL.
39. These dossiers can be found in ASMAI AP cart. 79. Among the other monitored exiles were princes Asfa Wässän and Mäkonnen Haylä Sellasé, *ras* Haylu Täklä Haymanot, *ras* Kassa Haylu, Wärqenäh Eshäté, Mäkonnen Endalkachäw, Lorenzo Ta'ezaz, and Mälaku Bäyyan. A separate file was maintained for the "The Ethiopian Association," and another for Afäwärq Gäbrä Iyäsus, though it seems to predate his period of diplomatic service in Italy and subsequent colonial collaboration.
40. File titled "Blattenghieta Herui," ASMAI AP cart. 79.
41. See the July–November 1936 correspondence between the Office of Political Affairs and Governo Generale in the file titled "Blattenghieta Herui," ASMAI AP cart. 79.
42. See also the profile of Afäwärq Gäbrä Iyäsus, which presents details about his L'Orientale period, in the file titled "Negadras Afeuorch," ASMAI AP cart. 79.
43. Jacob Dlamini, *The Terrorist Album: Apartheid's Insurgents, Collaborators, and the Security Police* (Cambridge, MA: Harvard University Press, 2020), 13–18.

44. "Jamaican Girl Who Was Personal Secretary to Haile Sellasie," *The Gleaner*, September 25, 1936; and Martha Nasibù, *Memorie di una principessa etiope* (Vicenza: Neri Pozza, 2005), 130, 136–140.
45. Makalani, *Cause of Freedom*, 209.
46. Peter Garretson, *A Victorian Gentleman and Ethiopian Nationalist: The Life and Times of Hakim Wärqenäh, Dr. Charles Martin* (Suffolk, UK: James Currey, 2012), 240–242.
47. Emmanu'él Abraham, *Reminiscences of My Life*, 30; and Garretson, *Victorian Gentleman*, 239.
48. Asfa-Wossen Asserate, "The Emperor's Closest Friend: The Life and Work of Blattengeta Herouy," presentation at Freedom in the City, Bath, UK, September 20, 2021.
49. Correspondence in file titled "Blattenghieta Herui," ASMAI AP cart. 79.
50. Haylä Sellasé, *My Life*, 2:81.
51. See chapter 10.
52. Haylä Sellasé, *My Life*, 2:25–27, 33–35.
53. Letter from Governo Generale to Office of Political Affairs, dated May 28, 1938, and letter from Teruzzi to Hamärä Eshäté, dated July 30, 1938, both in ASMAI pos. 83/245.
54. Interview with Shimelis Yilma, January 26, 2021. The seizure led to an extended struggle between Hamärä Eshäté, the Ministry, and the d'Aosta-Cerulli administration, which held that the family's claim to the property was illegitimate.
55. Steiner, *Triumph of the Dark*, 610–613.
56. See Märse'é Hazän Wäldä Qirqos, የአምስቱ የመከራ ዓመታት አጭር ታሪክ (አዲስ አበባ፡ ብርሃንና ሰላም ማተሚያ ቤት, 1947 ዓም), 69–71, which draws on the testimony of someone who was present during this period; and "Haile Selassie Loses His Closest Friend," *Bath Weekly Chronicle and Herald*, September 24, 1938, which is an eyewitness account of the burial.
57. Haylä Sellasé, *My Life*, 2:39.
58. Märse'é Hazän Wäldä Qirqos, የመከራ ዓመታት, 70–71: "እሁን የአዳምን ልጆች ወግ ሲቀበል የምታዩት ብላቴን ጌታ ኅሩይ ወልደ ሥላሴ ባገራችን ሥርዓት በመልካም ያደገ ከኢትዮጵያም ከፍ ካሉት ሊቃውንት የሚቆጠረው ነው። ብልሀቱንና ትጋቱን ለመልካም ሥራ የሚያገለግሉ መሳሪያዎች ሰለደረጋቸው በመንግሥታችን ሥራ ለመመረጥና ወደታላቁም የውጭ ጉዳይ ሚኒስትርነት ማዕረግ ለመድረስ በቃ፤ በየጊዜውም የጸፋቸው ከፍተኛ ባሕርዩን የሚገልጹ፤ መጻሕፍቶች ይልቁንም በቤተ ክህነትና በታሪክ እውቀት በአለም ሊቃውንት ዘንድ የታወቀና የተከበረ አደረጉት። ለምታወቁት ሰው ከታሪኩ ከዚህ የበለጠ ልንነግራችሁ የሚያስፈልግ አልመሰለንም፤ በአጭሩ ከጠባዩ ትልቅነት የሚሰማኝን ለመናገር ሳስብ ጊዜውን ሁሉ ቀም ነገር በሥሥራት ማሳለፉ፤ ከራሱ ይልቅ የተቸገሩትን ሰዎች ለመርዳት መጣሩ፤ እውነትን ፍርድንም ማክበሩና በአገር ፍቅር መቃጠሉ ትዝ ይለኛል። አገልጋይና ወዳጁ ኅሩይ! በተቻለህ ስለህገርህ ሥራውን በሚገባ ፈጽመህ በምትሰናበትበት ጊዜ ታላቅ ነህ ሳልልህ ብቀር ሥራዎችህ ቀድመውኝ ይናገሩሉ።"
59. "Blattengeta Herouy," *The Times*, September 23, 1938. See also "Ethiopian Foreign Minister Dead," *Voice of Ethiopia*, September 24, 1938; and Christine Sandford, *Ethiopia Under Hailé Selassié* (London: Dent and Sons, 1946), 98–105.
60. This biography reflects my conversations with Shimelis Yilma, the son of Laqäch Heruy. I thank *ato* Shimelis for discussing his family history and sharing documents with me.

61. Interview with Shimelis Yilma, January 26, 2021; Yaréd Gäbrä Mika'él, ግርማዊት እቴጌ መነን (አዲስ አበባ፡ አርቲስቲክ ማተሚያ ቤት, 1950 ዓም), 31; and telegram from Graziani to Lessona, dated August 21, 1936, ASMAI AP pos. 79.
62. "Elenco generale dei confinati etiopici nel regno," and "Elenco dei confinati etiopici a Mercogliano, bambini," both in ASMAI pos. 181/54; letter from Yelma Gäbrä Kidan, dated May 11, 1939, ASMAI AP cart. 83, fasc. 245; and interview with Shimelis Yilma, January 26, 2021.
63. List of individuals by Ministry of the Interior for Lessona, dated April 16, 1937, ASMAI pos. 181/54. Given this notice and the fact that Yelma was the liaison with British East Africa as well as the ministerial lead on European trade, it is curious that he did not appear in Cerulli's list of irreducibles.
64. Interview with Shimelis Yilma, January 26, 2021; and Märse'é Hazän Wäldä Qirqos, የመከራ ዓመታት, 54. On Graziani's use of covered lorries to conceal detentions, see Alberto Sbacchi, "Italy and the Treatment of the Ethiopian Aristocracy, 1937–1940," *IJAHS* 10, no. 2 (1977): 216.
65. For the date of her arrival, see letter from Laqäch Heruy to Yelma Gäbrä Kidan, dated February 1938, ASMAI pos. 181/54. On Dhanaane, see Angelo Del Boca, "Un lager del fascismo: Danane," *Studi piacentini* 1, no. 1 (1987): 59–70; Mariana De Carlo, "Colonial Internment Camps in Africa Orientale Italiana: The Case of Dhanaane (Somalia)," in *Themes in Modern African History and Culture: Festschrift for Tekeste Negash*, ed. Lars Berge and Irma Taddia (Padova: Libreria Universitaria, 2013), 193–208; and Matteo Dominioni, "Le fotografie di Danane nel contesto dell'immagine coloniale," *Studi piacentini*, no. 36 (2004): 213–226.
66. Sbacchi, "Aristocracy," 216.
67. De Carlo, "Camps," 200–202.
68. *Documents on Italian War Crimes Submitted to the United Nations War Crimes Commission by the Imperial Ethiopian Government* (Addis Ababa: Ministry of Justice, 1949), 1:69.
69. Eugenio Mazzucchetti, *Diario somalo di Eugenio Mazzucchetti*, ed. Guido Votano (2002), 171.
70. Giorgio Agamben, *Means Without End: Notes on Politics*, trans. Vincenzo Binetti and Cesare Casarino (Minneapolis: University of Minnesota Press, 2000), 37–38.
71. Interview with Shimelis Yilma, January 26, 2021.
72. Interview with Shimelis Yilma, January 26, 2021.
73. Mazzucchetti, *Diario*, 68, though the name of the child is mistaken. This was one of the few non-Italian deaths he recorded by name. For another example, see the case of would-be escapee Bäkkälä Ali: Mazzucchetti, *Diario*, 157.
74. General list of detainees in the kingdom, undated, ASMAI pos. 181/54.
75. This file can be found in ASMAI AP cart. 83, fasc. 245, with the title "Hameré Iscetié, Mercogliano."
76. Letter from Tamburini to Ministry of Italian Africa and Ministry of Interior, dated January 4, 1938, and letter from Tamburini to Ministry of Italian Africa, dated January 21, 1938, both in ASMAI AP cart. 83, fasc. 245.
77. Letter from Teruzzi to d'Aosta, dated February 4, 1938, ASMAI AP cart. 83, fasc. 245.

78. Letter from Governo Generale and Office of Political Affairs to Ministry of Italian Africa, dated March 28, 1938, ASMAI AP cart. 83, fasc. 245. Specifically, the decree was number 481, dated June 7, 1937.
79. Letter from Moreno to Tamburini, dated March 16, 1938, ASMAI AP cart. 83, fasc. 245.
80. Letter from Laqäch Heruy to Yelma Gäbräkidan, undated [February or March 1938], ASMAI pos. 181/54. Someone replied almost immediately, but the censored letter is not in the file: telegram from Teruzzi to Caroselli, dated March 11, 1938, ASMAI pos. 181/54.
81. This same file contains the family's extensive ministerial correspondence about the home, as well as the related ministerial correspondence with the Addis Ababa Office of Political Affairs.
82. Letter from Tamburini to Ministry of Italian Africa, dated June 11, 1938, ASMAI AP cart. 83, fasc. 245. On the releases, see "Il Viaggio di Teruzzi in A.O.," *Corriere della sera*, June 10, 1938.
83. Letter from Teruzzi to Tamburini, dated August 11, 1938, ASMAI AP cart. 83, fasc. 245.
84. Letter from Hamärä Eshäté to Ministry of Italian Africa, dated September 11, 1938, and letter from Aṣädä Wäyn Heruy to Teruzzi, dated September 12, 1938, both in ASMAI AP cart. 83, fasc. 245.
85. Letter from Hamärä Eshäté to Ministry of Italian Africa, dated 5 Ṭeqemt, 1931 AM, ASMAI AP cart. 83, fasc. 245. Unlike her other correspondence, this letter was not translated into Italian.
86. Letter from Teruzzi to Tamburini, dated October 22, 1938, ASMAI AP cart. 83, fasc. 245.
87. Letter from Aṣädä Wäyn Heruy to Ministry of Italian Africa, dated March 17, 1939, ASMAI cart. 83, fasc. 245.
88. Letter from Yelma Gäbräkidan to Ministry of Italian Africa, dated May 11, 1939, ASMAI AP cart. 83, fasc. 245.
89. Letter from Teruzzi to prefect of Sassari, dated May 30, 1939, ASMAI AP cart. 83, fasc. 245.
90. Letter from Hamärä Eshäté to Ministry of Italian Africa, dated June 1, 1939, ASMAI AP cart. 83, fasc. 245.
91. Interview with Shimelis Yilma, January 26, 2021.
92. Mazzucchetti, *Diario*, 86–87.
93. "Comando del campo di Danane," photograph, *I campi fascisti*, accessed November 22, 2024, https://campifascisti.it/scheda_img_full.php?id_img=48.
94. Abdissa Aga, በአጣልያ በረሃዎች (አዲስ አበባ: 1968).
95. Haylä Sellasé, *My Life*, 1:301.
96. Martha Nasibù, *Memorie*, 162–171.
97. Agamben, *Means Without End*, 37–45.
98. Ali Abdullatif Ahmida, *Genocide in Libya: Shar, A Hidden Colonial History* (New York: Routledge, 2021), 95.

10. Case 7887

1. Delia Jarrett-Macauley, *The Life of Una Marson, 1905-1965* (Manchester, UK: Manchester University Press, 1998), 104-105.
2. "Jamaican Girl Who Was Personal Secretary to Haile Selassie," *Daily Gleaner*, September 25, 1936.
3. Peter Garretson, *A Victorian Gentleman and Ethiopian Nationalist: The Life and Times of Hakim Wärqenäh, Dr. Charles Martin* (Suffolk, UK: James Currey, 2012), 246-250.
4. Correspondence in file titled "Dr. Martin," ASMAI AP, cart. 79. Their mother Qäṣälä Tullu did not learn of their death until the summer: Garretson, *Victorian Gentleman*, 250.
5. Una Marson, *The Moth and the Star* (Kingston, Jamaica: 1937), 81-83. The poem parallels David's lament for Saul and Jonathan in 2 Samuel 1:19-27.
6. It was subsequently enshrined as international law through the 1948 Genocide Convention and 1998 Rome Statute. On these developments, see Phillipe Sands, *East West Street: On the Origins of "Genocide" and "Crimes Against Humanity"* (New York: Vintage, 2017); Dan Plesch, *Human Rights After Hitler: The Lost History of Prosecuting Axis War Crimes* (Washington, DC: Georgetown University Press, 2017), esp. 158-177; and Ana Filipa Vrdoljak, "Human Rights and Genocide: The Work of Lauterpacht and Lemkin in Modern International Law," *EJIL* 20, no. 4 (2010): 1163-1194.
7. Abdullahi Ahmed An-Naim, *Decolonizing Human Rights* (New York: Cambridge University Press, 2021), xii.
8. Haylä Sellasé, *My Life and Ethiopia's Progress: Haile Selassie I King of Kings of Ethiopia. Vol. 2, Addis Abeba, 1966 E.C.*, trans. Ezekiel Gebissa et al. (East Lansing: Michigan State University Press, 1994), 33-35.
9. Hannah Arendt, *Eichmann in Jerusalem* (New York: Viking, 1963), 269.
10. Matthew Connelly, *A Diplomatic Revolution: Algeria's Fight for Independence and the Origins of the Post-Cold War Era* (New York: Oxford University Press, 2002).
11. Specifically, a confidential 1936 report concluded that while Italy and Ethiopia were both signatories to the conventions on the laws of war, and while there was credible evidence of Italian use of chemical weapons in Ethiopia, the League itself had no "special powers" for adjudicating alleged violations of the laws of war. It proposed that such cases should be resolved through an inquiry agreed on by the belligerents. See report by Committee of Jurists, dated April 10, 1936, confidential documents submitted to the Committee of Thirteen, LNA.
12. Transcript of the 11th Plenary Meeting, dated August 10, 1946, plenary session verbatim records, Fonds AG-033 International Paris Peace Conference (1946), UNA.
13. Claudio Pavone, *A Civil War: A History of the Italian Resistance*, trans. Peter Levy (London: Verso, 2013), 246-249.
14. Observations by the Italian delegation, dated August 26, 1946, General Commission documents, Fonds AG-033 International Paris Peace Conference (1946), UNA. More generally, see Gianluigi Rossi, *L'Africa italiana verso l'independenza (1941-1949)* (Milan: Giuffrè, 1980), 243-275; and Antonio Varsori, *L'Italia nelle relazioni internazionali dal 1943 al 1992* (Rome: Laterza, 1998), 27-42.

15. Career record of service for Enrico Cerulli, undated, and "Consigliere di Stato Dr. Enrico Cerulli," dated January 17, 1947, both in ACS MAI AGP Fascicoli del personale, f. 6625, bust. 335.
16. Giuseppe Brusasca, *Il ministero degli affari esteri al servizio del popolo italiano (1943-1949)* (Rome: Ministero degli Affari Esteri, 1949), 127–130; and Rossi, *Africa italiana*, 248–249.
17. The San Francisco delegation was comprised of Mäkonnen Endalkachäw, Aklilu Habtäwäld, Ambayé Wäldä Maryam, Éfrém Täwäldä Mädhen, Emmanu'él Abraham, Menassé Lämma, and Gétahun Tässäma: letter from Haylä Sellasé, dated March 29, 1945, Credentials-Ethiopia, Fonds United Nations Conference on International Organization (1945), UNA.
18. On the Ethiopian delegation, see Aklilu Habtäwäld, የአክሊሉ ማስታወሻ *Aklilu Remembers* (አዲስ አበባ፡ አዲስ አበባ ዩኒቨርሲቲ ፕሬስ, 2010), 39–46, 157–165; John Spencer, *Ethiopia at Bay: A Personal Account of the Haile Selassie Years* (Algonac, MI: Reference Publications, 1984), 159–184; and Norman Bentwich, *My 77 Years: An Account of My Life and Times, 1883-1960* (Philadelphia, PA: Jewish Publication Society of America, 1961), 241–242.
19. US Department of State, *Foreign Relations of the United States 1946* (Washington, DC: United States Government Printing Office, 1970), 3:95–97; and Aklilu Habtäwäld, የአክሊሉ ማስታወሻ, 42–43, 161–162.
20. Filippo Focardi, "Italy's Amnesia over War Guilt: the 'Evil Germans' Alibi," *Mediterranean Quarterly* 25, no. 4 (2014): 4–26.
21. At one point, *blattén géta* Lorenzo informed the conference, "The New Italy which claims to have broken with the past . . . does not hesitate to invoke rights" derived from the fascist regime and empire: transcript of the 14th Plenary Meeting, dated August 13, 1946, plenary session verbatim records, Fonds AG-033 International Paris Peace Conference (1946), UNA.
22. Aklilu Habtäwäld, የአክሊሉ ማስታወሻ, 9–13, 119–124.
23. Letter from Ambayé Wäldä Maryam to UNWCC, dated July 22, 1946, UNWCC Files, I/76.
24. Report from Cerulli to the Ministry of Italian Africa, dated April 25, 1937, ASMAI AP cart. 83, fasc. 245; Emru Zälläqä, *A Journey: Memoirs* (North Charleston, NC: Createspace, 2016), 36, 72–76; and George Steer, *Sealed and Delivered: A Book on the Abyssinian Campaign* (London: Hodder and Stoughton, 1942), 195. This personal archive was subsequently relocated to Addis Ababa, where it is now preserved at the Institute of Ethiopian Studies and in private collections: interview with Ian Campbell, January 19, 2020.
25. Also present was activist Sylvia Pankhurst, who recognized Cerulli in the delegation and circulated pamphlets on Italian war crimes in Ethiopia in response to the Italian white papers: Richard Pankhurst, "Sylvia and *New Times and Ethiopia News*," in *Sylvia Pankhurst from Artist to Anti-Fascist*, ed. Ian Bullock and Richard Pankhurst (New York: Palgrave Macmillan, 1992), 184.
26. Transcript of the 13th Plenary Meeting, dated August 12, 1946, plenary session verbatim records, Fonds AG-033 International Paris Peace Conference (1946), UNA.

They were likely unaware that Cerulli's official status as the Italian governor of Harär had only ended months before: Ministry of Italian Africa decree, dated June 16, 1946, ACS MAI AGP Fascicoli del personale, f. 6625, bust. 335.

27. Memorandum by the Ethiopian delegation, dated September 6, 1946, Economic Commission for Italy documents, Fonds AG-033 International Paris Peace Conference (1946), UNA. The claim was nearly two hundred million pounds sterling.
28. Statement by the Ethiopian delegation, dated September 9, 1946, Economic Commission for Italy documents, Fonds AG-033 International Paris Peace Conference (1946), UNA.
29. Statement by the Ethiopian delegation, undated [October 1946?], Economic Commission for Italy documents, Fonds AG-033 International Paris Peace Conference (1946), UNA.
30. This was *Memorandum on the Italian Colonies* (1945), which featured discussions drawing on Cerulli's expertise on 15–16 (an ethnographic analysis of Eritrea) and 17–19 (an overview of colonial policy in Somalia). It was followed by *Additional Notes to the Memorandum on the Italian Territories in Africa* (1946). On these Foreign Office meetings, see Rossi, *Africa italiana*, 155–157.
31. On the role of scientists in promoting this exculpatory "developmental" image, see Angelo Matteo Caglioti, "Meteorological Imperialism: Climate Science, Environment, and Empire in Liberal and Fascist Italy (1870–1940)" (PhD diss., University of California at Berkeley, 2017), 211–214.
32. John Hargreaves, *Decolonization in Africa* (New York: Routledge, 1996).
33. Statement by the Ethiopian delegation, undated [October 1946?], Economic Commission for Italy documents, Fonds AG-033 International Paris Peace Conference (1946), UNA.
34. Spencer, *Ethiopia at Bay*, 179n2. He continued, however, to play a prominent role in the negotiations: see telegram from Douglas to Marshall, dated November 19, 1947, in US Department of State, *Foreign Relations of the United States 1947* (Washington, DC: United States Government Printing Office, 1972), 3:617–619.
35. Hans Woller, *I conti con il fascismo. L'epurazione in Italia, 1943–1948*, trans. Enzo Morandi (Bologna: Mulino, 1997); and Roy Palmer Domenico, *Italian Fascists on Trial, 1943–1948* (Chapel Hill: University of North Carolina Press, 1991).
36. On the Commission and the ministries, see Chiara Giorgi, *L'Africa come carriera: Funzioni e funzionari del colonialismo italiano* (Rome: Carocci, 2012), 187–198; and Guido Melis, "Note sull'epurazione nei ministeri, 1944–1946," *Ventunesimo secolo* 2, no. 4 (2003): 17–52.
37. Claudio Pavone, *Alle origini della repubblica. Scritti su fascismo, antifascismo e continuità dello Stato* (Turin: Bollati Boringhieri, 1995), 123–146.
38. The process records can be found in the file "Procedimento n. 12 contro S. E. Enrico Cerulli," ACS MAI AGP Commissione di Primo Grado per l'Epurazione, bust. 370.
39. In comparison to the other ministries, the Ministry of Italian Africa had a relatively small number of cases: Melis, "Epurazione," 26.

40. Charge sheet signed by Mauro Scoccimarro, dated November 28, 1944, ACS MAI AGP Commissione di Primo Grado per l'Epurazione, bust. 370.
41. Unlike the rest of the north, present-day Friuli-Venezia Giulia and Trentino-Alto Adige were directly occupied by Germany.
42. On the development of this logic, see Focardi, "Italy's Amnesia."
43. Domenico, *Fascists on Trial*, 92–97; Woller, *Epurazione in Italia*, 234–238, 253–255; and Julian Jackson, *France on Trial: The Case of Marshal Pétain* (Cambridge, MA: Harvard University Press, 2023), 31–39. Caruso was appointed by RSI functionary Tullio Tamburini, who had supervised the detention of Hamärä Eshäté in Mercogliano, and who was himself sent to Dachau on suspicion of Allied collaboration: Mimmo Franzinelli, *Squadristi. Protagonisti e tecniche della violenza fascista 1919-1922* (Milan: Mondadori, 2003), 266–268.
44. Affidavits titled "Allegato 1" and "Cerulli, dott. Enrico," both in ACS MAI AGP Commissione di Primo Grado per l'Epurazione, bust. 370. The testimony of Aldo Baldari, Alberto Mario Piccioni, and Silvio Zanutto is contained in this same file.
45. Victoria De Grazia, *The Perfect Fascist: A Story of Love, Power, and Morality in Mussolini's Italy* (Cambridge, MA: Harvard University Press, 2020), 372–377.
46. "Appunto" and "Memoria difensiva," both in ACS MAI AGP Commissione di Primo Grado per l'Epurazione, bust. 370.
47. "Memoria difensiva," ACS MAI AGP Commissione di Primo Grado per l'Epurazione, bust. 370: "Circa l'asserzione del denunciante che la mia carriera si deve alla conoscenza 'di quattro fesserie sul popolo abissino di poco superiore alla scimmia,' mi limito a dire che precisamente questa di considerare le popolazioni delle Colonie come 'di poco superiori alle scimmie' è esattamente la mentalità cui dobbiamo in gran parte il fallimento totale cui il fascismo ha portato le nostre Colonie; e che proprio tutta la mia opera, nel campo scientifico come in quello pratico, rivolta allo studio delle popolazioni africane nella loro storia, nella loro cultura, e nelle loro istituzioni è stata costantemente diretta a demolire questo volgare pregiudizio, sommario culturalmente e pernicioso politicamente. E si è visto con quanta eleganza di frasi l'anonimo denunziatore adotta proprio il logoro slogan del colonialismo razzista; da un lato i popoli eletti e dall'altro le genti dominate, non uomini ma 'di poco superiori alle scimmie.'"
48. On this understanding, see Giorgi, *Africa come carriera*, 193.
49. Summary of deliberations, dated February 2, 1945, ASMAP MAI AGP Commissione di Primo Grado per l'Epurazione, bust. 370. On the composition of the Commission itself, see Woller, *Epurazione in Italia*, 201.
50. "Memoria difensiva," ACS MAI AGP Commissione di Primo Grado per l'Epurazione, bust. 370.
51. Domenico, *Fascists on Trial*, 98–101.
52. The most comprehensive study is Plesch, *Human Rights After Hitler*. The official history is *History of the United Nations War Crimes Commission and the Development of the Laws of War* (London: United Nations War Crimes Commission, 1948).
53. *History of UNWCC*, 119. Though a Briton, Wright served as the acting Australian member. On his biography and legal philosophy, see Neil Duxbury, "Lord Wright and Innovative Traditionalism," *UTLJ* 59, no. 3 (2009): 265–339.

54. Danilo Zolo, *Victors' Justice: From Nuremberg to Baghdad* (London: Verso, 2009).
55. Carsten Stahn, "Complementarity and Cooperative Justice Ahead of their Time? The United Nations War Crimes Commission, Fact-Finding, and Evidence," *CLF* 25 (2014): 223–260; Christopher Simpson, "Shutting Down the United Nations War Crimes Commission," *CLF* 25 (2014): 133–146; and Narrelle Morris and Aden Knaap, "When Institutional Design Is Flawed: Problems of Cooperation and the United Nations War Crimes Commission, 1943–1948," *EJIL* 28, no. 2 (2017): 513–534.
56. Arieh Kochavi, *Prelude to Nuremberg: Allied War Crimes Policy and the Question of Punishment* (Chapel Hill: University of North Carolina Press, 1998), 36–50.
57. On jurisdictional politics, see Lauren Benton, *Law and Colonial Cultures: Legal Regimes in World History, 1400-1900* (New York: Cambridge University Press, 2002); and on neocolonial gatekeeping and international law, see An-Naim, *Decolonizing Human Rights*, 1–20.
58. Steven Jensen, *The Making of International Human Rights: The 1960s, Decolonization, and the Reconstruction of Global Values* (New York: Cambridge University Press, 2016), 1–17.
59. The latter served as governor of Montenegro on leaving the Amhara governate in Africa Orientale Italiana.
60. Effie Pedaliu, *Britain, Italy, and the Origins of the Cold War* (New York: Palgrave, 2003), 9–34; and Woller, *Epurazione in Italia*, 55–56, 189–190.
61. Pedaliu, *Origins*, 21–32.
62. This context is discussed in Richard Pankhurst, "Italian Fascist War Crimes in Ethiopia: A History of Their Discussion, from the League of Nations to the United Nations (1936–1949)," *NEAS* 6, nos. 1–2 (1999): 92–97.
63. Wen-Wei Lai, "China, the Chinese Representative, and the Use of International Law to Counter Japanese Acts of Aggression: China's Standpoint on UNWCCC Jurisdiction," *CLF* 25 (2014): 111–132; and *History of UNWCC*, 114.
64. Letter from Leijonhufvud to Wright, dated October 8, 1947, UNWCC A.56.
65. Letter from Zivkovic to Wright, dated December 10, 1945, UNWCC Misc. 2.
66. Letter from Ambayé Wäldä Maryam to UNWCC, dated July 22, 1946, UNWCC I/76.
67. For the Commission precis, see "Jurisdiction of the Commission over War Crimes Committed Prior to 1939: Oral Answers to Questions," dated July 17, 1945, UNWCC C.212.
68. Minutes of Commission meeting, dated July 19, 1946, UNWCC M.109.
69. Note by the secretary to Committee III, dated July 23, 1946, UNWCC III/50.
70. Minutes of Committee III meeting, dated July 30, 1946, UNWCC No. 18/46; and report presented by Committee III, dated July 31, 1946, UNWCC Doc. C217.
71. Minutes of Commission meeting, dated July 31, 1946, UNWCC M.110.
72. Letter from Ambayé Wäldä Maryam to UNWCC, dated December 31, 1946, UNWCC I/76.
73. Note by Litawski, dated January 20, 1947, UNWCC I/76; Aklilu Habtäwäld, የአክሊሉ ማስታወሻ, 161-2; and *Paris Peace Conference*, 567.
74. Minutes of Committee I meeting, dated January 30, 1947, UNWCC No. 87.
75. Note by Litawski, dated February 13, 1947, UNWCC I/81.

76. Muzkat also supported the failed Albanian attempt to submit cases to the Commission: see minutes of Commission meeting, dated October 29, 1947, UNWCC M.131.
77. Minutes of Commission meeting, dated March 12, 1947, UNWCC M.124.
78. Minutes of Commission meeting, dated March 26, 1947, UNWCC M.125.
79. Letter from Éfrém Täwäldä Mädhen to Wright, dated August 12, 1947, UNWCC A.55.
80. On his work for the EWCC, see Erik Leijonhufvud, *Kejsaren och hans hövdingar* (Stockholm: Norstedt and Söners Förlag, 1948).
81. Minutes of Commission meeting, dated September 24, 1947, UNWCC M.130.
82. Satyabrata Rai Chowdhuri, *Leftism in India, 1917-1947* (New York: Palgrave, 2007), 205-206.
83. Minutes of Commission meeting, dated September 24, 1947, UNWCC M.130.
84. Harold Marcus, *The Politics of Empire: Ethiopia, Great Britain, and the United States, 1941-1974* (Lawrenceville, NJ: Red Sea Press, 1995).
85. Minutes of Commission meeting, dated September 24, 1947, UNWCC M.130.
86. Letter from Leijonhufvud to Wright, dated October 8, 1947, UNWCC A.56, which gives the first contact as July 1945. This key point was subsequently mistaken in the official history of the Commission: *History of UNWCC*, 148.
87. Letter from Éfrém Täwäldä Mädhen to Ledingham, dated October 28, 1947, UNWCC A.58. This preliminary list differed from the final version: it included Rodolfo Graziani, Pietro Badoglio, Alessandro Lessona, Guglielmo Nasi, Carlo Geloso, Sebastiano Gallina, and Alessandro Pirzio Biroli, all subsequently charged; but also Pietro Maletti (then deceased), Orlando Lorenzini (also deceased), and Pietro Pinna Parpaglia, who were not subsequently charged. Absent from the preliminary list were Cerulli, Ruggero Tracchia, and Guido Cortese.
88. Minutes of Commission meeting, dated October 29, 1947, UNWCC M.131. During the discussion of Albanian standing at this same meeting, Craigie explained that he had reversed his views on the Ethiopian cases for "practical" reasons, after realizing that they would only submit ten cases and learning "the Ethiopian Government's proposed procedure."
89. Annalisa Urbano and Antonio Varsori, *Mogadiscio 1948. Un eccidio di italiani fra decolonizzazione e guerra fredda* (Bologna: Mulino, 2019); and Ruth Iyob, *The Eritrean Struggle for Independence: Domination, Resistance, Nationalism 1941-1993* (New York: Cambridge University Press, 1995), 61-81. The other Ethiopian UNWCCC cases are described in Pankhurst, "War Crimes," 124-128, using Foreign Office materials.
90. The American representative, Earl Kintner, a State Department lawyer overseeing the publication of the Commission's official history, recused himself because of his earlier abstention during the vote on Ethiopian jurisdiction: minutes of Committee I meeting, dated March 4, 1948, UNWCC No. 139; and on his involvement generally, see *History of UNWCC*, 123, 504.
91. Drawing on the Nuremberg and Tokyo Charters, the UNWCC defined the latter category as crimes in which civilians were killed or persecuted on "racial, political, or religious grounds." For definitions, see *History of UNWCC*, 178-179.
92. Charge sheet against Enrico Cerulli, Case No. 10 A-B, dated February 23, 1948, UNWCC charge files, reel 4, UNA. For the UNWCC's framework, see *History of UNWCC*, 34-36.

93. Draft report of Committee III on "Attempts to Denationalise the Inhabitants of Occupied Territory," dated September 24, 1945, UNWCC C.149; and *History of UNWCC*, 488. This definition suggests the influence of Raphael Lemkin, the legal scholar who developed the concept of genocide and who met with Egon Schwelb, the author of the Committee III report on denationalization: Sands, *East West Street*, 188, 322. On the history of the concept of "crimes of denationalization" during the interwar period, see Mark Lewis, *The Birth of the New Justice: The Internationalization of Crime and Punishment, 1919-1950* (New York: Oxford University Press, 2014), 64–77.
94. *Ethiopian Penal Code of 1930* (Addis Ababa: 1941): preface, articles XI and XII; section 3, chapters V, VIII, and XII; and section 4, chapters I, II, and VI.
95. Minutes of Committee I meeting, dated March 4, 1948, UNWCC No. 139.
96. Letter from Leijonhufvud, dated March 19, 1948, UNWCC charge files, reel 4, UNA.
97. Leijonhufvud, *Kejsaren*, 193.
98. This point appears to have informed the erroneous but frequently repeated assertion that Cerulli was only charged as a witness: Pankhurst, "War Crimes," 128; and Karla Mallette, *European Modernity and the Arab Mediterranean: Toward a New Philology and a Counter-Orientalism* (Philadelphia: University of Pennsylvania Press, 2010), 268n53.
99. Minutes of Committee I meeting, dated March 4, 1948, UNWCC No. 139.
100. "Request by the Ethiopian government regarding Signor Enrico Cerulli," dated March 11, 1948, FO 371/73180, Z2054.
101. Confidential cypher from Foreign Office to British UN Delegation, dated March 9, 1948, FO 371/73180, Z2054; and note from Goold-Adams to Ledingham, dated March 13, 1948, UNWCC charge files, reel 4, UNA.
102. Letter from Leijonhufvud, dated March 19, 1948, UNWCC charge files, reel 4, UNA.
103. Zäwdé Rätta, በቀዳማዊ ኃይለ ሥላሴ ዘመነ መንግሥት የኤርትራ ጉዳይ 1941–1963 (እንደ አውሮፓውያን አቆጣጠር) (አዲስ አበባ: ሻማ ቡክስ, 2006), 464.
104. *Documents on Italian War Crimes Submitted to the United Nations War Crimes Commission by the Imperial Ethiopian Government* (Addis Ababa: Ministry of Justice, 1950), 2:4.
105. The 1947 trial of Haylä Sellasé Gugsa was widely covered in the local press. On the trial of Afäwärq Gäbrä Iyäsus, see Alain Rouaud, *Afä-wärq 1868-1947: Un intellectuel éthiopien témoin de son temps* (Paris: Éditions CNRS, 1991), 190–193; and on the last years of Berhanä Marqos, see Mickaël Bethe Selassié, *La jeune Éthiopie: Un haut-fonctionnaire éthiopien Berhanä-Marqos Wäldä-Tsadeq (1892-1943)* (Paris: Harmattan, 2004), 150–156.
106. Another prominent recuperable who avoided this fate was *le'ul ras* Haylu Täklä Haymanot.
107. Letter from Éfrém Täwäldä Mädhen, enclosing affidavit of Asfeha Wäldämika'él, dated March 25, 1948, UNWCC charge files, reel 4, UNA. The affidavit is in French.
108. This affidavit, preserved today at the UN Archives in New York City, appears to be distinct from the affidavit published in excerpt by the Ethiopian Ministry of Justice in its official documentation of the UNWCC cases. The published excerpt repeats some of the language from the archival affidavit, but it does not focus on Cerulli

and is less categorical in its judgment of him. For example, the published affidavit contains the following passage: "As for Cerulli I cannot remember ever having seen any orders by him to shoot captured patriots or to burn villages, etc. But on the other hand Cerulli did not to my knowledge ever attempt to interfere about or inquire into any of the atrocities that were brought to his attention." In contrast, the archival affidavit contains the following overlapping but distinct passage: "My opinion based on the words and actions of Cerulli is that he approved of the violent policies of Graziani. As vice governor of AOI Cerulli had clear authority, with Aosta being only nominally his superior. To my knowledge Cerulli never tried to intervene or inquire about any of the cases of atrocities that came to his attention." Cf. *Documents on Italian War Crimes*, 2:4–5; and letter from Éfrém Täwäldä Mädhen, enclosing affidavit of Asfeha Wäldämika'él, dated March 25, 1948, UNWCC charge files, reel 4, UNA.

109. Affidavit number 3, dated August 17, 1947, UNWCC charge files, reel 4, UNA.
110. Letter from *aläqa* Haylu to Haylä Sellasé, dated June 27, 1938, UNWCC charge files, reel 4, UNA; and for the original, "Situation in Ethiopia," *LNJ* 20 (1939): 14. This letter does not appear in the Ministry of Justice's published collection of documents.
111. Minutes of Committee I meeting, dated March 31, 1948, UNWCC No. 141.
112. This fact distinguished Cerulli from the Japanese ex-colonial administrators Seishirō Itagaki and Kenji Doihara, who were tried and executed for crimes committed in Manchuria as well as the subsequent Asia-Pacific War. I thank Wen-Wei Lai for calling my attention to this point.
113. "Italians," undated, UNWCC reel 39.
114. *Documents on Italian War Crimes*, 1:3–4.
115. *History of UNWCC*, 189.
116. Carol Anderson, *Bourgeois Radicals: The NAACP and the Struggle for Colonial Liberation, 1941-1960* (New York: Cambridge University Press, 2014), 187–192; Rossi, *Africa italiana*, 397–477; and Saul Kelly, *Cold War in the Desert: Britain, the United States, and the Italian Colonies, 1945-52* (New York: St. Martin's, 2000), 115–117.
117. UN ORTSGA, Part II, summary records of meetings, 30–32.
118. UN ORTSGA, Part II, summary records of meetings, 40–41.
119. UN ORTSGA, Part II, summary records of meetings, 98.
120. "Italy's Place in Africa," *The Times*, April 12, 1949; "Italy Asks Return of Three Colonies," *New York Times*, April 12, 1949; "Il dibattito all'O.N.U. sulle ex-colonie," *L'Unità*, April 12, 1949; and "Dieci delegati chiedono il ritorno dell'Italia in Africa," *Corriere della sera*, April 12, 1949. See also Tafarra Deguefé, *Minutes of an Ethiopian Century* (Addis Ababa: Shama Books, 2006), 113. These events played a role in the subsequent effort to reestablish bilateral Italo-Ethiopian relations in the early 1950s. According to Cora, who led this initiative from the Italian side, it was considered inadvisable to allow Cerulli to participate in the preliminary talks of 1951 since key Ethiopian players—presumably, Foreign Minister Aklilu—associated Cerulli with a dangerous colonial "mentality." For this reason, Cora felt that Cerulli's presence in a diplomatic delegation to Ethiopia would undermine trust between the two sides.

For a discussion, see Giampaolo Calchi Novati, "Italia e Etiopia dopo la guerra: Una nuova realtá, i risarcimenti e la stele rapita," *Africa* 46, no. 4 (1991): 487–488.

121. "በጋዜጣና ማስታወቂያ መሥሪያ ቤት ሊጋዜጠኞች የተገለጸ," አዲስ ዘመን, April 16, 1949. See also *New Times and Ethiopia News*, October 15, 1949.

122. Annalisa Urbano, "International Law of War, War Crimes in Ethiopia, and Italy's Imperial Misrecollection at the End of Empire, 1946–1950," *Historical Journal* 66, no. 1 (2022): 237–257.

123. "Interventions des délégués africains," *Présence africaine* 3 (1955): 35–36.

124. Pietro Badoglio, *L'Italia nella seconda guerra mondiale* (Verona: Mondadori, 1946); Rodolfo Graziani, *Una vita per l'Italia* (Milan: Mursia, 1986); and Alessandro Lessona, *Memorie* (Florence: Sansoni, 1958), *Un ministro di Mussolini racconta* (Rome: Edizioni Nazionali, 1973), and *Crepuscolo nero* (Florence: Edizioni A.L., n.d.).

125. Enrico Cerulli, "La fine del colonialismo," *Ulisse* XI, vol. v, fasc. 28–29 (1958): 1551–1559. For a contemporaneous comment, see Teobaldo Filesi, "Ulisse: il Tramonto del Colonialismo," *Africa* 13, no. 4 (1958): 175–178.

126. Fabian Klose, *Human Rights in the Shadow of Colonial Violence: The Wars of Independence in Kenya and Algeria*, trans. Dona Geyer (Philadelphia: University of Pennsylvania Press, 2013), 92–137.

127. Cerulli, "Colonialismo," 1553: "Non si fa questione dell'uno o dell'altro particolare modo, nel quale 'atrocità'—come si suol dire—sono state commesse; ma la questione fondamentale: è legittimo l'uso della forza per imporre il proprio dominio a genti straniere? Se la risposta è sì; se, cioè, si ammette con la formula di Niccolò Machiavelli che gli Stati non si governano con i Paternostri, gli eccessi e le atrocità vanno commisurate non più con i principi morali, ma con le opportunità delle singole situazioni. E giustificarli è volgare opera di abilità politica. Se invece non si ammette, anzi si giudica immorale l'uso della forza per la soggezione dei popoli, non e il grado di intensità di quella forza che possa renderla 'atrocità' od, invece, giustificata misura di governo."

128. Cerulli, "Colonialismo," 1559; and Léopold Sédar Senghor, "La décolonisation: condition de la communauté franco-africaine," *Le Monde*, September 4, 1957. Memmi's influential work appeared the previous year: Albert Memmi, *Portrait du colonisé, précédé du portrait du colonisateur* (Paris: Buchet Chastel, 1957).

129. Friedrich Nietzsche, *On the Genealogy of Morals and Ecce Homo*, trans. Walter Kaufmann (New York: Vintage, 1989), 44–46.

130. Tekeste Negash, *Eritrea and Ethiopia: The Federal Experience* (Uppsala: Nordiska Afrikainstitutet, 1997), 111–120, 132–138; and Iyob, *Eritrean Struggle*, 88–92.

131. Bärihun Käbbädä, የአዤ ኃይለሥላሴ ታሪክ (አዲስ አበባ: አርቲስቲክ ማተሚያ ቤት, 1993 ዓም), 446–447, 1317.

132. Correspondence with Ruth Iyob, June 21, 2024.

133. Zäwdé Rätta, የኤርትራ ጉዳይ, 462: "የናዚ አስተርጓሚ[፤] የሙሶሊኒ ተሸላሚ[፤] የዱካ ዳአስታ ፊታውራሪ[፤] የቸሩሊ ዋና አማካሪ[።]"

134. "Dimmi con chi vai e ti dirò chi sei" and "ንዲኻ ማን አንደሆን ንገረኝ እና አንተ ማን አንደሆንክ እነግርሃለሁ።"

11. Field Operations

1. "Remains of Blattengueta Herouy Interred," *Ethiopian Herald*, September 22, 1947.
2. "ስለ ብላቴን ጌታ ኅሩይ ሞት[፤] መዝሙር," የኤርትራ ድምፅ, Hamlé 4, 1939 ዓም.
3. On postcolonial mythmaking in Ethiopia, see Bahru Zewde, "The Italian Occupation of Ethiopia: Records, Recollections, and Ramifications," in *Society, State, and History: Selected Essays* (Addis Ababa: Addis Ababa University Press, 2008), 375–390. On sites of memory and wars of anticolonial liberation, see Emmanuel Alcaraz, *Les lieux de mémoire de la guerre d'indépendance algérienne* (Paris: Karthala, 2017); and Etienne Achille, Charles Forsdick, and Lydie Moudileno, eds., *Postcolonial Realms of Memory: Sites and Symbols in Modern France* (Liverpool: Liverpool University Press, 2020).
4. Andrea Celli, *Dante and the Mediterranean Comedy: From Muslim Spain to Post-Colonial Italy* (Cham, Germany: Palgrave, 2022), 40–74.
5. Enrico Cerulli, *Il libro etiopico dei Miracoli di Maria e le sue fonti nelle letterature del medio evo latino* (Rome: Bardi, 1943).
6. Enrico Cerulli, *Etiopi in Palestina. Storia della comunità etiopica di Gerusalemme* (Rome: Ministero dell'Africa Italiana, 1943 and 1947).
7. Enrico Cerulli, *Il "Libro della Scala" e la questione delle fonti arabo-spagnole della Divina Commedia* (Vatican City: Biblioteca Apostolica Italiana, 1949). On ensuing developments, see Vicente Cantarino, "Dante and Islam: History and Analysis of a Controversy (1965)," *Dante Studies* 125 (2007): 37–55; and Celli, *Mediterranean Comedy*, 69–74.
8. Lanfranco Ricci, "Enrico Cerulli e l'Istituto per l'Oriente," *Oriente moderno* 9, no. 70 (1990): 6.
9. Enrico Cerulli, *Storia della letteratura etiopica* (Milan: Nuova Accademia, 1956).
10. Enrico Cerulli, *Somalia. Scritti vari editi ed inediti* (Rome: Poligrafico dello Stato, 1957, 1959, and 1964).
11. Enrico Cerulli, *Scritti teologici etiopici dei secoli XVI-XVII* (Vatican City: 1958 and 1960).
12. Francesco Gabrieli, "New Light on Dante and Islam," *Diogenes* 2, no. 6 (1954): 61–73. The same article appeared the previous year in *East and West*, the ISIAO journal. On the colonial politics of Braudel's Mediterraneanism, see John Strachan, "The Colonial Cosmology of Fernand Braudel," in *The French Colonial Mind, Volume 1: Mental Maps of Empire and Colonial Encounters*, ed. Martin Thomas (Lincoln: University of Nebraska Press, 2012), 72–95.
13. The published proceedings are *Atti del convegno internazionale di studi etiopici (Roma 2-4 aprile 1959)* (Rome: Accademia Nazionale dei Lincei, 1960). For assessments, see Rita Pankhurst, "International Conferences of Ethiopian Studies," in *EA*, 3:175–179; Rita Pankhurst, "International Conferences of Ethiopian Studies: A Look at the Past," in *Proceedings of the Seventh International Conference of Ethiopian Studies: University of Lund, 26–29 April 1982*, ed. Sven Rubenson (Addis Ababa: Institute of Ethiopian Studies, 1984), 1–9; Bahru Zewde et al., "From Lund to Addis Ababa: A Decade of Ethiopian Studies (1982–1991)," *JES* 27, no. 1 (1994): 1–28; and Alessandro Bausi, "The Encyclopaedia Aethiopica and Ethiopian Studies," *Aethiopica* 19 (2016): 188–206.

14. Raffaello Morghen, *The Accademia Nazionale dei Lincei in the Life and Culture of United Italy on the 368th Anniversary of Its Foundation (1871-1971)* (Rome: Accademia Nazionale dei Lincei, 1990).
15. On the relationship between these paradigms, see Fikru Negash Gebrekidan, "Ethiopia in Black Studies from W. E. B. Du Bois to Henry Louis Gates, Jr.," *NEAS* 15, no. 1 (2015): 1–34.
16. For contemporary discussions, see "E' necessario un riordinamento degli studi africanisti in Italia," *Africa* 14, no. 1 (1959): 17–20, 41; and Carlo Giglio, "Le discipline africanistiche orientalistiche e coloniali nelle Università italiane," *Africa* 15, no. 3 (1960): 107–120.
17. Yaqob Beyene, "In memoriam: Lanfranco Ricci (1916–2007)," *Aethiopica* 11 (2008): 217–221.
18. Gianfranco Fiaccadori, "Mordini, Antonio," in *EA*, 3:1017–1019; and on Mordini and the Viceroy, see Amedeo di Savoia-Aosta, *Studi africani* (Bologna: Zanichelli, 1942), 72.
19. Giuseppe Puglisi, *Chi è? dell' Eritrea 1952. Dizionario biografico con una cronologia* (Asmara: Agenzia Regina, 1952), 228.
20. See chapter 3.
21. Report from Cerulli to the Ministry of Italian Africa, dated April 25, 1937, ASMAI AP cart. 83, fasc. 245.
22. Interview with Aklilu Habté, November 13, 2018.
23. Pankhurst, "A Look at the Past," 2; and interview with Aklilu Habté, November 13, 2018. For Cerulli's acquaintances at the college in this period, see the annotated photograph in Osvaldo Raineri, ed., *Inventario dei manoscritti Cerulli etiopici* (Vatican City: Biblioteca Apostolica Vaticana, 2004), 277; and additionally, the multilingual publication of the college, ደብረ ቅ[ዳ]ስ አስጢፋኖስ, which featured publications by some of his acquaintances.
24. Gäbrä Iyäsus Haylu, "Un manoscritto amarico sulle verità della fede," in *Atti del convegno*, 345–351, with reference on 345. On the author, see Gäbrä Iyäsus Haylu, *The Conscript: A Novel of Libya's Anticolonial War*, trans. Ghirmai Negash (Athens: Ohio University Press, 2013); and Uoldelul Chelati Dirar, "Writing WWI with African Gazes: The Great War Through the Writing of Tigrinya Speaking Expatriates," in *The First World War from Tripoli to Addis Ababa (1911–1924)*, ed. Shiferaw Bekele et al. (Addis Ababa: Centre français des études éthiopiennes, 2018), https://books.openedition.org/cfee/1379?lang=en.
25. Germachäw Täklä Hawaryat, "Allocuzione di S.E. Ghermacceu Takla Hawariat, Ambasciatore di Etiopia presso il Quirinale," in *Atti del convegno*, 4.
26. Enrico Cerulli, "Punti di vista sulla storia d'Etiopia," in *Atti del convegno*, 27.
27. Stefan Strelcyn, "Marcel Cohen," *BSOAS* 38, no. 3 (1975): 615–622.
28. Marcel Cohen, "Linguistique éthiopienne: état des travaux et perspectives pour le proche avenir," in *Atti del convegno*, 65.
29. Marcel Cohen, "Parole di chiusura dei lavori del convegno," in *Atti del convegno*, 461: "l'oubli délibéré de conflits passés."

30. Felice Ostini, "L'opera dell'istituto di studi etiopici di Asmara," in *Atti del convegno*, 255.
31. Aklilu Habté, "[ከቡር ሊቀ መንበር]," in *Atti del convegno*, 269–270.
32. Aklilu Habté, "[ከቡር ሊቀ መንበር]": "ስለዚህ ባሁኑ ጊዜ መገናኛ በአየርም ሆነ በምድር በተሰፋፋበት፤ የተማሩ ኢትዮጵያውያን በበዙበት ጊዜ፤ እንደዚህ ያለውን የሳይንስ መልክ ዘዴ ያልተመረኩዝ ድርሰት አየደጋገሙ ማውጣት ከአውነት መሪቅን መፈለግ ወይም አውነትን እንደማገራቆት ወይም የኢትዮጵያን መለዋወጥ አለማወቅን ስለሚያሳይ ታላቅ ስህተት መሰለ ይታየኛል።"
33. Enrico Cerulli, "[Reply to Aklilu Habté]," in *Atti del convegno*, 271: "Io mi richiamo a quanta abbiamo detto ieri, e cioè alla opportunità che i giovani studiosi figli dell'Etiopia pur impadronendosi dei metodi della scienza moderna, non dimentichino, anzi mettano sempre più in valore le antiche tradizioni del loro Paese nella storia, nella letteratura, nel diritto. Così l'edificio dell'Etiopia moderna sarà stabilito su solide basi e così i figli dell'Etiopia potranno continuare a dare contributi importanti alla conoscenza del loro proprio Paese." Cerulli's comments anticipated Francesco Gabrieli's reply to Anouar Abdel-Malek: Gabrieli, "Apology for Orientalism," *Diogenes* 13, no. 50 (1965): 135.
34. Interview with Aklilu Habté, November 13, 2018.
35. Interview with Aklilu Habté, November 13, 2018.
36. Frédéric Grah Mel, *Alioune Diop, le bâtisseur inconnu du monde noir* (Abidjan: Presses Universitaires de Côte d'Ivoire, 1995), 169–197; Elizabeth Foster, *African Catholic: Decolonization and the Transformation of the Church* (Cambridge, MA: Harvard University Press, 2019), 88–92; and Gary Wilder, *Freedom Time: Negritude, Decolonization, and the Future of the World* (Durham, NC: Duke University Press, 2015), 181–183.
37. "Notre politique de la culture," *Présence africaine* 24/25 (1959): 5–7; and more generally, Bernard Mouralis, "*Présence Africaine*: Geography of an 'Ideology,'" in *Surreptitious Speech: Présence Africaine and the Politics of Otherness, 1947–1987*, ed. Valentin-Yves Mudimbe (Chicago: University of Chicago Press, 1992), 3–13.
38. Cristina Brambilla, "Temi del Secondo Congresso Mondiale degli scrittori e artisti neri," *Africa* 14, no. 3 (1959): 122; and "New Appointments Are Made by the Emperor," *Ethiopian Herald*, October 27, 1956.
39. Alioune Diop, "Le sens de ce Congrès," *Présence africaine* 24/25 (1959): 40–48.
40. Lylian Kesteloot, "1956–1959. D'un Congrès à L'autre," *Présence africaine*, n.s., nos. 175/177 (2007): 125–129.
41. On the context of this vision, see Catherine Coquery-Vidrovitch, "*Présence Africaine*: History and Historians of Africa," in *Surreptitious Speech*, ed. Mudimbe, 59–94.
42. Modilim Achufusi, "Devoirs et responsabilités des historiens africains," *Présence Africaine* 27/28 (1959): 81–95.
43. Saburi Biobaku, "Les responsabilités de l'historien africain en ce qui concerne l'histoire et l'Afrique," *Présence africaine* 27/28 (1959): 96–99.
44. "Résolution soumise par le sous-comité d'histoire de la commission des sciences humaines," *Présence africaine* 24/25 (1959): 399–401.
45. Some of the Italian attendees celebrated Mediterraneanism and Catholicism as frameworks for postcolonial Italo-African fraternity. See also "Si sentono orgogliosi

della cultura nera," *Corriere della sera*, March 25, 1959; and "Scrittori e artisti neri ricevuti dal Presidente Gronchi," *Corriere della sera*, March 26, 1959.

46. Frantz Fanon, *The Wretched of the Earth*, trans. Constance Farrington (New York: Grove, 1968), 84.
47. Enrico Cerulli, "Il nuovo posto dell'Italia nel continente africano," *Africa* 14, no. 4 (1959): 175–176.
48. Mario Dorato, "Discours d'accueil à l'Istituto Italiano per l'Africa," *Présence africaine* 24/25 (1959): 25; and "Evoluzione del colonialismo," *Africa* 14, no. 4 (1959): 172–174.
49. Wilder, *Freedom Time*, 156–161.
50. Cerulli, "Nuovo posto," 176: "Le discussioni qui a Roma tra studiosi dell'Etiopia e dei più vari Paesi del mondo si sono concluse con una manifestazione veramente affetuosa di amichevole collaborazione nel campo dell'alta cultura tra l'Etiopia e l'Italia, rinverdendo la secolare tradizione degli studi italiani etiopici che rimonta al Rinascimento."
51. These positions complemented his involvement with the Brussels-based International Institute of Differing Civilizations, a Eurafrica-focused neocolonial think-tank that succeeded the International Colonial Institute: Florian Wagner, *Colonial Internationalism and the Governmentality of Empire, 1893–1982* (New York: Cambridge University Press, 2022), 320–321. For a postscript to Cerulli's RAI evaluation of ICES, see Renato Lefevre, "Tasfa'-Seyon e la concessione ufficiale di S. Stefano agli etiopi nel 1548," ዳግማ ቅ ኢትዮጵያ 8, no. 15 (1968): 62–64. Two years later, Cerulli offered further comments on the perceived epochal significance of ICES while presiding over the Accademia's 1961 conference: Cerulli, "Dalla tribù allo stato nell'Africa Orientale," in *Somalia*, 3:97.
52. Interview with Aklilu Habté, November 13, 2018.
53. Kwame Nkrumah, "Address Delivered to Mark the Opening of the First International Congress of Africanists," in *The Proceedings of the First International Congress of Africanists, Accra 11th–18th December 1962*, ed. Lalage Bown and Michael Crowder (Evanston, IL: Northwestern University Press, 1964), 6–15.
54. Kenneth Onwuka Dike, "Address of Welcome to the First International Congress of Africanists," in *First International Congress of Africanists*, ed. Bown and Crowder, 4–5. On Du Bois's years in Ghana and participation in the conference, see David Levering Lewis, *W. E. B. Du Bois: A Biography* (New York: Holt, 2009), 2:709–712. He was too ill to attend the founding event of the OAU in May the following year, and died that August.
55. "Participants at the First International Congress," *First International Congress of Africanists*, ed. Bown and Crowder, 357–368.
56. Interview with Aklilu Habté, November 13, 2018.
57. Correspondence with Christopher Clapham, March 29, 2019; correspondence with Christopher Ehret, August 18, 2021; correspondence with Herbert Lewis, August 16, 2022; and correspondence with Alessandro Triulzi, August 23, 2022.
58. On the politics of this development, see William Martin and Michael West, eds., *Out of One, Many Africas: Reconstructing the Study and Meaning of Africa* (Urbana: University of

Illinois Press, 1999); and Jean Allman, "#HerskovitsMustFall? A Meditation on Whiteness, African Studies, and the Unfinished Business of 1968," *ASR* 62, no. 3 (2019): 6–39. Privately, Cerulli disparaged the area studies approach to Italian students.

59. For recollections, see the accounts of the former directors: Abebe Ambatchew, *A Glimpse of Greatness* (Vancouver: Trafford, 2010), esp. 34–48; and Berhanou Abebe, "The Haile Selassie I Prize Trust," *NEAS* 2, no. 3 (1995): 53–66. The annual awardees are listed in የቀዳማዊ ኃይለ ሥላሴ ሽልማት ድርጅት 10ኛ ዓመት። *Haile Selassie I Prize Trust 10th Year* (Addis Ababa: Artistic Printers, 1973); and Bärihun Käbbädä, የአፄ ኃይለሥላሴ ታሪክ (አዲስ አበባ፡ አርቲስቲክ ማተሚያ ቤት, 1993 ዓም), 529–581.

60. የቀዳማዊ ኃይለ ሥላሴ ሽልማት ድርጅት ቻርተር *The Haile Selassie I Prize Trust Charter* (አዲስ አበባ፡ ብርሃንና ሰላም ማተሚያ ቤት, 1955ዓም), 5–8. The prize in education was added in 1969: Berhanou Abebe, "Prize Trust," 53.

61. Interview with Abebe Ambatchew, April 3, 2018.

62. Bärihun Käbbädä, የአፄ ኃይለሥላሴ ታሪክ, 531, 539, 573. On Hansberry's award, see the conclusion.

63. Bärihun Käbbädä, የአፄ ኃይለሥላሴ ታሪክ, 529, 535, and 539.

64. Berhanou Abebe, "Prize Trust," 55.

65. It was rumored that the emperor was involved in securing Cerulli's nomination, a point generally disputed by the directors: cf. Abebe Ambatchew, *Glimpse*, 41–45; and Berhanou Abebe, "Prize Trust," 61–63.

66. Richard Pankhurst, "The Haile Selassie I Prize," in *Von Hiob Ludolf bis Enrico Cerulli*, ed. Piotr Scholz (Wiesbaden: 2001), 234–235; and Bärihun Käbbädä, የአፄ ኃይለሥላሴ ታሪክ, 545. Pichi Sermolli had conducted research in Africa Orientale Italiana, as he noted in his acceptance speech. Another precedent for an Italian awardee was the 1965 industry prize, given to Tullio Camerino of Asmara.

67. Berhanou Abebe, "Prize Trust," 55–56.

68. Correspondence with Alessandro Triulzi, September 1, 2022; and correspondence with Bairu Tafla, October 7, 2022.

69. Edward Ullendorff, *The Two Zions: Reminiscences of Jerusalem and Ethiopia* (New York: Oxford University Press, 1988), 211–212. See also his "Professor Enrico Cerulli: Obituary," *The Times*, September 28, 1988.

70. Bärihun Käbbädä, የአፄ ኃይለሥላሴ ታሪክ, 535.

71. Lanfranco Ricci, "Luigi Fusella," *RSE* 34 (1990): 229–232.

72. On Giglio's broadly liberal assessment of colonialism, see Giampaolo Calchi Novati, "Colonialismo e indipendenza dell'Africa nell'opera di Carlo Giglio," *Africa* 57, no. 2 (2002): 225–241. His dispute with Rubenson unfolded in the newly-established *Journal of African History* over the next two years.

73. Rita Pankhurst, "Look at the Past," 3. Other accounts of the conference include Richard Pankhurst, "Alcune note retrospettive sulla III conferenza di studi etiopici," *Sestante* 2, no. 1 (1966): 95–98; and Czeslaw Jesman, "Some Impressions of the Third International Congress of Ethiopian Studies in Addis Ababa," *Africa* 21, no. 4 (1966): 407–411.

74. Correspondence with Bairu Tafla, October 7, 2022.

75. This situation developed three years later in the *Journal of Ethiopian Studies*, the leading publication in the area studies branch of the field, published by the IES. Its second 1969 issue featured a critique of Cerulli's *Folk Literature of the Galla* by Fride Hylander. The son of a Swedish missionary colleague of Onesimos Näsib, Hylander had participated in the 1935 conflict, survived a field hospital bombing, and subsequently gave evidence of atrocities to the League. By the 1960s, he worked as a teacher at Haylä Sellasé Secondary School, the future Kotebe Teachers' College. It was in this capacity that he attacked the methodological and analytic shortcomings of Cerulli's work: Fride Hylander, "Onesimos Nesib: Some Remarks on Cerulli's 'The Folk-Literature of the Galla,'" *JES* 7, no. 2 (1969): 79–87.
76. Salome Gebre Egziabeher, "The Patriotic Works of Dejazmatch Aberra Kassa and Ras Abebe Aragaye," in *Proceedings of the Third International Conference of Ethiopian Studies, Addis Ababa 1966* (Addis Ababa: Institute of Ethiopian Studies, 1969), 293–314.
77. Salome Gabre Egziabeher, "The Ethiopian Patriots, 1936–1941," *Ethiopian Observer* 12, no. 2 (1969): 63–91.
78. Correspondence with Bairu Tafla, October 7, 2022. The attendees also visited Santo Stefano: Pankhurst, "A Look at the Past," 5–6.
79. Herbert Lewis, "Anthropology in Ethiopia, 1950s–2016: A Participant's View," in *Seeking Out Wise Old Men: Six Decades of Ethiopian Studies at the Frobenius Institute*, ed. Sabine Dinslage and Sophia Thubauville (Berlin: Reimer, 2017), 36; and Pankhurst, "A Look at the Past," 5.
80. Interview with Lee Cassanelli, November 10, 2018. On the development of this field, see his "The Somali Studies International Association: A Brief History," *Bildhaan* 1 (2001): 1–10.
81. Mersha Alehegne, ዜና ጸሳሳት ኢትዮጵያውያን (አዲስ አበባ: 1996 ዓም), 41–49.
82. Mersha Alehegne, ዜና ጸሳሳት ኢትዮጵያውያን, 72–80, 104–108.
83. Ian Campbell, *The Massacre of Debre Libanos, Ethiopia 1937: The Story of One of Fascism's Most Shocking Atrocities* (Addis Ababa: Addis Ababa University Press, 2014).
84. Telegram from d'Aosta to Ministry of Italian Africa, dated March 10, 1938, ASMAI pos. 181/44.
85. Mersha Alehegne, ዜና ጸሳሳት ኢትዮጵያውያን, 81–86, with details of the colonial era ecclesiastic hierarchy on 85.
86. "Il Sabato Santo etiopico solennizzato alla presenza del Duca di Spoleto," *Corriere dell'impero*, April 24, 1938; and "የኢትዮጵያ ቄሳር እንደራሴ የደብረ ሊባኖስን ገዳም ሰለመንብያታቸው," የቄሳር መንግስት መልከተኛ, October 30, 1938. A similar celebration occurred the following year: "Alla presenza dei Duchi d'Aosta il clero della chiesa etiopica celebra solennemente la festa di 'Fasicà,'" *Corriere dell'impero*, April 9, 1939.
87. Gärima Tafärrä, ገንደሬ በጋሻው (አዲስ አበባ: 1949 ዓም), 86: "ዛሬ የደብረ ሊባኖስ ገዳም አምራና ታድሳ ለታሪኳ የተገባ ክብር ተሰጥቷት ትታያለች።"
88. "አዲሱ ሊቀ ጳጳስ," የሮማ በርሃን, September 27, 1939; list of Ethiopian detainees at Camilluccia, undated, ASMAI pos. 181/54; and ASMAI GS cart. 72. On *eçhägé* Yesehaq, see Mersha Alehegne, ዜና ጸሳሳት ኢትዮጵያውያን, 94–99.

89. "በደብረ ሊባኖስ ገዳም የአቡነ ተክለ ሃይማኖት በዓል አከባበር," የሮማ ብርሃን, February 11, 1940. See also Paolo Sacripanti, "Debra Libanos ed il Suo Santo," *Etiopia* 3, no. 9 (1939): 21–24.
90. Mersha Alehegne, "The *Mälkəʾa sämaʿətat* of Däbrä Libanos: Text and Translation," *RSE* 3a Serie, 1, no. 48 (2017): 128, 134.
91. Campbell, *Debre Libanos*, 244–249.
92. Enrico Cerulli, "Gli abbati di Dabra Libānos, capi del monachismo etiopico, secondo la 'lista rimata' (sec. XIV–XVIII)," *Orientalia* 12 (1943): 226–253; "Gli abbati di Dabra Libānos, capi del monachismo etiopico, secondo la 'lista rimata' (sec. XIV–XVIII) (Continuazione)," *Orientalia* 13 (1944): 137–182; and "Gli abbati di Dabra Libānos, capi del monachismo etiopico, secondo le liste recenti (sec. XVIII–XX)," *Orientalia* 14 (1945): 143–171. The third installment did not use the poem.
93. For the etymology, see Heruy Wäldä Sellasé, ዋዜማ፡ በማግሥቱ የኢትዮጵያን ነገሥታት የታሪክ በዓል ለማክበር (አዲስ አበባ፡ ጎሐ ጽባሕ, 1921 ዓም), 101. On Enbaqom's place of birth, Cerulli suggests the description of origins "west of Persia" (*fars*) could mean eastern Syria, while Heruy, in contrast, accepts the Yemeni origins described in Enbaqom's hagiography, but cites the dictionary of Charles William Isenberg to establish this point: Cerulli, "Abbati [II]," 150; and Heruy Wäldä Sellasé, ዋዜማ, 110.
94. Cerulli, "Abbati [II]," 140–145.
95. Cerulli, "Abbati [III]," 168; and on the ministerial involvement in ecclesiastic and monastic politics in this period, specifically in terms of the autocephaly debate and the elevation of *abunä* Abreham, see ASMAI AP cart. 72, fasc. 165.
96. Alain Rouaud, *Afä-wärq 1868–1947: Un intellectuel éthiopien témoin de son temps* (Paris: Éditions CNRS, 1991), 190–193.
97. Cerulli, *Storia della letteratura etiopica*, 255: "Il belâttenghetà Heruy Wolda Sellâse ha, letterariamente, una figura diversa da quella del suo contemporaneo Afework. Molto meno caldo di entusiasmo e perciò forse meno brillante, lo Heruy ha invece maggiore spregiudicatezza di ragionamento e piú rigorosa forza logica sí da raggiungere effetti artisticamente meno appariscenti."
98. File titled "Negadras Afeuorch," ASMAI AP cart. 79: "il primo letterato del suo paese: ha una profonda conoscenza della propria lingua, ed ama farne sfoggio, scrivendo in uno stile prezioso e pieno di parole rare, alla Daniele Bartoli."
99. File titled "Blattenghieta Herui," ASMAI AP cart. 79: "uno dei pochi letterati che l'Abissinia possegga, e si distingue per il suo stile semplice, sobrio, anglicizzante; intonato alla puerilità dei concetti."
100. Chinua Achebe, "Colonialist Criticism," in *Hopes and Impediments: Selected Essays 1965–1987* (New York: Penguin, 1988), 69–90.
101. According to Leijonhufvud, Graziani's final word regarding this affair was: "There is thus no trace left of the Debra Libanos monastery, which for centuries was a nest of murderers going by the name of monks, and which once before in the time of Negus rule, was rewarded with destruction for the identical crime." See Erik Leijonhufvud, *Kejsaren och hans hövdingar* (Stockholm: Norstedt and Söners Förlag, 1948), 159–162.
102. With respect to postcolonial historiography, this tendency is epitomized by the publications of the Comitato per la Documentazione dell'Opera dell'Italia in Africa.

Established in 1952 and sponsored by the Italian Ministry of Foreign Affairs, the Comitato aimed to authoritatively document the progressive and civilizing nature of Italian colonial rule in Africa, and its members and authors were largely alumni of the dissolved Ministry of Italian Africa. Cerulli was a founding member as well as a subject of the works themselves. For discussions, see Antonio Morone, "I custodi della memoria: Il Comitato per la documentazione dell'opera dell'Italia in Africa," *Zapruder* 23 (2010): 25–38; and Giampaolo Calchi Novati, "Italy and Africa: How to Forget Colonialism," *JMIS* 13, no. 1 (2008): 41–57.

103. On the project, see Chloé Maurel, "L'Histoire générale de l'Afrique de l'UNESCO: Un projet de coopération intellectuelle transnationale d'esprit afro-centré (1964-1999)," *CEA* 3, no. 215 (2014): 715–737. For recollections by participants, see Bethwell Ogot, *My Footprints on the Sands of Time: An Autobiography* (Kisumu: Anyange Press, 2006), 382–399; and Jan Vansina, "UNESCO and African Historiography," *History in Africa* 20 (1993): 337–352.
104. Interview with Aklilu Habté, November 13, 2018.
105. Henry Louis Gates Jr., "W. E. B. Du Bois and the Encyclopedia Africana, 1909–63," *AAAPSS* 568 (2000): 203–219.
106. Introductory document by the Committee of Experts on the General History of Africa, Abidjan, dated August 23, 1966, UNESCOA. The lone attendee representing Ethiopian studies was Carlo Giglio, who seemingly arrived uninvited.
107. Final report by the Meeting of Experts on the General History of Africa, Paris, dated August 6, 1969, UNESCOA.
108. Interview with Abebe Ambatchew, October 28, 2021.
109. Aklilu Habté, የቀዳማዊ ኃይለ ሥላሴ ዩኒቨርሲቲ ታሪክ የከፍተኛ ትምህርት መቋቋምና መስፋፋት ጉዞ በኢትዮጵያ (Tainan City: Chiachin Printing, 2017).
110. Today, Grottanelli is viewed as a founder of the Italian anthropological discipline: Mariano Pavanello, "Vinigi L. Grottanelli a cento anni dalla nascita," *L'uomo* 1/2 (2012): 7–32.
111. Haberland was an ex-Nazi who was then the director of the Frobenius Institute, Germany's oldest anthropological institute. He eventually quit the UNESCO project after attacking committee members for their description of Europe as capitalist. This summary is based on correspondence with Herbert Lewis, August 22, 2022; and Ogot, *Footprints*, 389–390.
112. Interview with Aklilu Habté, November 13, 2018.
113. Final report by Meeting of Experts on the General History of Africa, Addis Ababa, dated September 15, 1970, UNESCOA.
114. Final report by Bureau of the International Scientific Committee, Butare, dated July 26, 1972, UNESCOA.
115. Final report by International Scientific Committee, Lusaka, Annex III, dated August 3, 1973, UNESCOA.
116. Correspondence with Christopher Ehret, August 19, 2021. El Fasi was not at the meeting, and the minutes of subsequent meetings describe poor relations between the two editors.
117. Bown and Crowder, eds., *First International Congress of Africanists*, 360.

118. Interview with Aklilu Habté, November 13, 2018. On Berque's identity as a "mutineer," see Jacques Berque, *Mémoires des deux rives* (Paris: Seuil, 1989); and on his academic and UNESCO career, see George Steinmetz, *The Colonial Origins of Modern Social Thought: French Sociology and the Overseas Empire* (Princeton, NJ: Princeton University Press, 2023), 247–270.
119. Interview with Aklilu Habté, November 13, 2018.
120. Final report by International Scientific Committee, Lusaka, dated August 3, 1973, UNESCOA.
121. Enrico Cerulli, "Ethiopia's Relations with the Muslim World," in *UNESCO General History of Africa, III: Africa from the Seventh to the Eleventh Century*, ed. Mohammed El Fasi and Ivan Hrbek (Berkeley: University of California Press, 1988), 575–585.
122. The chapter was originally to be written by Sergew Hable Selassie: final report by International Scientific Committee, Lusaka, Annex III, dated August 3, 1973, UNESCOA.
123. Täklä Ṣadeq Mäkwuriya, "The Horn of Africa," in *UNESCO General History of Africa, III*, ed. El Fasi and Hrbek, 569n31; and Täklä Ṣadeq Mäkwuriya, የሕይወቴ ታሪክ (አዲስ አበባ: ኤክሊፕስ ማተሚያ ቤት, 2008 ዓም), 64–69.
124. Miranda Fricker, *Epistemic Injustice: Power and the Ethics of Knowing* (New York: Oxford University Press, 2007), 7.
125. Hannah Arendt, "Organized Guilt and Universal Responsibility," in *Essays in Understanding, 1930–1964: Formation, Exile, and Totalitarianism*, ed. Jerome Kohn (New York: Schocken, 1994), 121–132.
126. Hannah Arendt, "Collective Responsibility," in *Responsibility and Judgment*, ed. Jerome Kohn (New York: Schocken, 2003), 147–158.
127. At Nuremberg, former governor general of Poland Hans Frank famously pointed beyond his individual guilt to an indelible national stain, in what many considered a bid for leniency: Phillipe Sands, *East West Street: On the Origins of "Genocide" and "Crimes Against Humanity"* (New York: Vintage, 2017), 298–299.
128. Arendt, "Collective Responsibility," 147.
129. Another was Guglielmo Nasi, who was also charged.
130. Danilo Zolo, *Victors' Justice: From Nuremberg to Baghdad* (London: Verso, 2009), 44; and Latha Varadarajan, "The Trials of Imperialism: Radhabinod Pal's Dissent at the Tokyo Tribunal," *EJIR* 21, no. 4 (2015): 793–815. Some Commission representatives made similar points during the London deliberations. For example, at the penultimate Committee I meeting, just prior to Cerulli's decision, Muzkat raised this issue in connection to a politicized decision on a German case: minutes of Committee I meeting, dated March 25, 1948, UNWCC No. 140.
131. Cf. Mahmood Mamdani, "The New Humanitarian Order," *The Nation* (September 29, 2008): 17–22; and Kamari Clarke, Abel Knottnerus, and Eefje de Volder, eds., *Africa and the ICC: Perceptions of Justice* (New York: Cambridge University Press, 2016).
132. This situation is suggested by Ennio Flaiano's 1947 novel *Tempo di uccidere*, or *Time to Kill*, whose protagonist is absolved of his crimes by his peers' confidence in the moral rightness of empire: Flaiano, *Tempo di uccidere* (Milan: Rizzoli, 1989).

Conclusion

1. The most detailed biography is Kwame Wes Alford, "A Prophet Without Honor: William Leo Hansberry and the Origins of the Discipline of African Studies (1894–1939)" (PhD diss., University of Missouri-Columbia, 1998).
2. These included Earnest Hooton, Dows Dunham, and George Reisner.
3. On this vision, see Maghan Keita, *Race and the Writing of History: Riddling the Sphinx* (New York: Oxford University Press, 2000), 95–122.
4. Joseph Harris, *African-American Reactions to War in Ethiopia, 1936–1941* (Baton Rouge: Louisiana State University Press, 1994), 22.
5. On Mälaku and Dorothy Bäyyan, see Fikru Negash Gebrekidan, "Race, Gender, and Pageantry: The Ups and Downs of an African American Woman in Imperial Ethiopia," *NEAS* 21, no. 2 (2021): 265–300. Täsfay Zaphiro was likely related to Phillip Zaphiro, a Greek employee at the British Legation and longtime resident of Addis Ababa. The elder Zaphiro died one year before the younger Zaphiro arrived at Howard. See "ስለ ሙሴ ዛፊሮ ዕረፍት," ብርሃንና ሰላም, September 7, 1933; and Adrien Zervos, *L'empire d'Éthiopie: Le miroir de l'Éthiopie moderne, 1906–1935* (Alexandria: Imprimerie de l'École professionnelle des frères, 1936), 454.
6. On Zaphiro's January 1936 mission to the United States, see the intelligence files in ASMAI AP cart. 15. He also spoke at the 1936 National Negro Congress in Chicago: Harry Haywood, *A Black Communist in the Freedom Struggle*, ed. Gwendolyn Midlo Hall (Minneapolis: University of Minnesota Press, 2012), 226.
7. Telegram from Phillips to Hull, dated November 20, 1936, in US Department of State, *Foreign Relations of the United States 1936* (Washington, DC: United States Government Printing Office, 1953), 3:218.
8. Alford, "Prophet Without Honor," 223.
9. Marc Crawford, "The Scholar Nobody Knows," *Ebony*, February 1961; and interview with Tewodros Abebe, November 4, 2021.
10. https://www.aaiafrica.org/.
11. Interview with Gail Hansberry, November 15, 2022. More generally, see Fikru, "Race, Gender, and Pageantry," 289–290.
12. Interview with Gail Hansberry, February 10, 2023; Joseph Harris, "William Leo Hansberry, 1894–1965: Profile of a Pioneer Africanist," in William Leo Hansberry, *Pillars in Ethiopian History*, ed. Harris (Washington, DC: Howard University Press, 1974), 16–17; and Jerry Gershenhorn, "'Not an Academic Affair': African American Scholars and the Development of African Studies Programs in the United States, 1942–1960," *JAAH* 94, no. 1 (2009): 48–49.
13. Interview with Mulugeta Wodajo, October 14, 2022. Wodajo Ali worked in the Addis Ababa municipality, served as a monitor of Haylä Sellasé Gugsa in Mäqällä, and was the last Ethiopian consul in colonial Asmara.
14. Report by Cerulli for the Ministry of Italian Africa, dated April 25, 1937, ASMAI AP cart. 83, fasc. 245.

15. Letter from Ministry of Italian Africa to Ministry of the Interior, dated May 11, 1937, ASMAI pos. 181/54. The family received the news in Mercogliano from a fellow detainee: interview with Mulugeta Wodajo, October 14, 2022.
16. Mulugeta was president of the New York chapter of the African Students Association and concurrently served as president of the Ethiopian Students Association. He recalls that Du Bois advised him that Ethiopia should follow the example of China with respect to development and international affairs: interview with Mulugeta Wodajo, October 21, 2022.
17. Looking back on this formative political experience, Mulugeta recalls, "Malcolm X led the Black Muslims, and I had the Ethiopian students on my side." Interview with Mulugeta Wodajo, October 14, 2022.
18. Interview with Mulugeta Wodajo, October 21, 2022.
19. That same year, his brother Kifle Wodajo became the first secretary general of the OAU.
20. Interview with Abebe Ambatchew, October 28, 2021.
21. "Haile Selassie I Prize Trust Award Winner American Professor Hails Achievement of Emperor," *Ethiopian Herald*, July 17, 1964.
22. Bärihun Käbbädä, የአፄ ኃይለሥላሴ ታሪክ (አዲስ አበባ፡ አርቲስቲክ ማተሚያ ቤት, 1993 ዓም), 530.
23. Keita, *Race and Writing of History*, 100.
24. Interview with Abebe Ambatchew, October 28, 2021.
25. የቀዳማዊ ኃይለ ሥላሴ ሽልማት ድርጅት 10ኛ ዓመት፡፡ Haile Selassie I Prize Trust 10th Year (አዲስ አበባ፡ አርቲስቲክ ማተሚያ ቤት, 1973), 23; and correspondence with Bairu Tafla, dated October 7, 2022. At the award reception, Hansberry was also reunited with Mulugeta: interview with Mulugeta Wodajo, October 21, 2022.
26. Interview with Gail Hansberry, November 15, 2022.
27. See also Philip Curtin, "Recent Trends in African Historiography and Their Contribution to History in General," in *UNESCO General History of Africa, I: Methodology and Prehistory*, ed. Joseph Ki-Zerbo (Berkeley: University of California Press, 1981), 66.
28. Interview with Abebe Ambatchew, October 28, 2021. He recalls that the attendees lamented Hansberry's lack of recognition outside of Africa, where people "worshipped him almost."
29. Marc Crawford, "The Scholar Nobody Knows." The reference is to Mark 6:4, "A prophet is not without honor except in his own town, among his relatives, and in his own home."
30. For this reason, it is significant that the recipient of the inaugural award for Ethiopian studies was Marcel Cohen, who had been the most prominent specialist to publicly defend Ethiopia during the Italo-Ethiopian crisis. Given this criterion, the other candidates would have been W. E. B. Du Bois, who died in 1963, and Marcel Griaule, who died in 1956.
31. On this possibility, see Carlo Ginzburg, *The Judge and the Historian: Marginal Notes on a Late-Twentieth Century Miscarriage of Justice*, trans. by Antony Shugaar (New York: Verso, 1999).
32. Lanfranco Ricci, "Cerulli, Enrico," in *EA*, 1:708–709.

33. Karla Mallette, *European Modernity and the Arab Mediterranean: Toward a New Philology and a Counter-Orientalism* (Philadelphia: University of Pennsylvania Press, 2010).
34. Michel-Rolph Trouillot, *Silencing the Past: Power and the Production of History* (Boston: Beacon, 2015), xxiii. For a perceptive specialist reflection on this point, see Alessandro Bausi, "The Encyclopaedia Aethiopica and Ethiopian Studies," *Aethiopica* 19 (2016): 191–193.
35. Andrew Mitchell and Peter Trawny, eds., *Heidegger's Black Notebooks: Responses to Anti-Semitism* (New York: Columbia University Press, 2017).
36. Peter Trawny, *Heidegger and the Myth of a Global Jewish Conspiracy*, trans. Andrew Mitchell (Chicago: University of Chicago Press, 2015).
37. Mitchell and Trawny, "Editors' Introduction," in *Black Notebooks*, ed. Mitchell and Trawny, xxv.
38. Albert Memmi, *Portrait du colonisé, précédé du portrait du colonisateur* (Paris: Buchet Chastel, 1957).
39. Michael McDonnell and Dirk Moses, "Raphael Lemkin as Historian of Genocide in the Americas," *JGR* 7, no. 4 (2005): 501–529.
40. Jorge Luis Borges, *The Aleph and Other Stories*, trans. Andrew Hurley (New York: Penguin, 1998), 62–68.
41. Bonny Ibhawoh, *Human Rights in Africa* (New York: Cambridge University Press, 2018), 221–238.
42. Malika Bilal, host, *The Take*, podcast, episode 258, "Is Germany's Genocide Apology to Namibia Enough?," *Al Jazeera*, June 7, 2021, https://www.aljazeera.com/podcasts/2021/6/7/is-germanys-genocide-apology-to-namibia-enough.
43. Statement by Ethiopian delegation, undated [October 1946?], Economic Commission for Italy documents, Fonds AG-033 International Paris Peace Conference (1946), UNA.
44. The phrase is adapted from Jean Cocteau's characterization of Jacques Maritain, in *Art and Faith: Letters Between Jacques Maritain and Jean Cocteau*, trans. John Coleman (New York: Philosophical Library, 1951).

Bibliography

I. Unpublished Sources
i. ARCHIVES AND SPECIAL COLLECTIONS

Archivio Centrale dello Stato, Rome, Italy
Fondi Ministero dell'Africa Italiana
Fondo Rodolfo Graziani

Archivio Storico Diplomatico, Ministero degli Affari Esteri, Rome, Italy
Archivio Segreto del Gabinetto del Ministro dell'Africa Italiana
Archivio Storico del Ministero dell'Africa Italiana
Archivio Ordinario del Gabinetto del Ministro dell'Africa Italiana
Fondo Direzione Generale Affari Politici del Ministero dell'Africa Italiana

Biblioteca Apostolica Vaticana, Vatican City
Fondo Cerulli Etiopici

Bibliothèque Nationale de France, Paris, France
Collection Marcel Griaule

Brooklyn College Library, New York City, United States
Enrico De Leone Papers, Robert Hess Collection
Rosida Cuoco Papers, Robert Hess Collection

Evangeliska Fosterlands-Stiftelsen Arkiv, Uppsala, Sweden
Olle Eriksson Collection

Institute of Ethiopian Studies, Addis Ababa, Ethiopia
Manuscript Section

National Archives, Kew Gardens, United Kingdom
Cabinet Office Records
Foreign Office Records

Saint John's University, Collegeville, United States
Ethiopian Manuscript Microfilm Library

United Nations Archives, New York City, United States
International Paris Peace Conference Fonds
United Nations Conference on International Organization Fonds
United Nations War Crimes Commission Fonds

United Nations Library and Archives, Geneva, Switzerland
League of Nations Archives

United Nations Educational, Scientific, and Cultural Organization Archives, Paris, France
Records of the Social Sciences, Human Sciences, and Culture Sector

University of Massachusetts Amherst Libraries, Amherst, United States
W. E. B. Du Bois Papers

Yale University, New Haven, United States
Human Relations Area Files

ii. DISSERTATIONS, THESES, AND PRESENTATIONS

Alford, Kwame Wes. "A Prophet Without Honor: William Leo Hansberry and the Origins of the Discipline of African Studies (1894–1939)." PhD diss., University of Missouri-Columbia, 1998.

Asfa-Wossen Asserate. "The Emperor's Closest Friend: The Life and Work of Blattengeta Herouy." Presentation at Freedom in the City, Bath, UK, September 20, 2021.

Brook Abdu. "Taamrat Emmanuel in Post-Italian Ethiopia." Presentation at Ethiopian Jews Under Fascist Rule, New York City, October 23, 2014.

Caglioti, Angelo Matteo. "Meteorological Imperialism: Climate Science, Environment, and Empire in Liberal and Fascist Italy (1870–1940)." PhD diss., University of California at Berkeley, 2017.

Cauli, Alberto. "Italian Pioneers: Colonial Propaganda and Geographic Exploration." PhD diss., University of Auckland, 2019.

Desalegn Seyum. "E. Cerulli's *Folk Literature of the Galla of Southern Abyssinia*: A Critical Evaluation." Master's thesis, Addis Ababa University, 1985.

Ertola, Emanuele. "L'impero immaginario: i coloni italiani in Etiopia, 1936–1941." PhD diss., Università degli studi di Firenze, 2014.

Feigh, Lacy. "Abyssinia to Ethiopia: Slavery, Race, and the Transition from Empire to Nation, 1855–1974." PhD diss., University of Pennsylvania, 2022.

Guluma Gemeda. "Land, Agriculture, and Society in the Gibe Region: Southwestern Ethiopia, c. 1850–1974." PhD diss., Michigan State University, 1996.

Heran Sereke Brhan. "Building Bridges, Drying Bad Blood: Elite Marriages, Politics, and Ethnicity in 19th and 20th Century Imperial Ethiopia." PhD diss., Michigan State University, 2002.

Raz, Ronen. "The Transparent Mirror: Arab Intellectuals and Orientalism, 1798–1950." PhD diss., Princeton University, 1997.

Tesfaye Tolessa. "A History of Oromo Literature and Identity Issues, c. 1840–1991." PhD diss., Addis Ababa University, 2019.

Turtur, Noelle. "Making Fascist Empire Work: Italian Enterprises, Labor, and Organized-Community in Occupied Ethiopia, 1896–1943." PhD diss., Columbia University, 2022.

Virtue, Nicolas. "Royal Army, Fascist Empire: The Regio Esercito on Occupation Duty, 1936–1943." PhD diss., Western University, 2016.

Weissleder, Wolfgang. "The Political Ecology of Amhara Domination." PhD diss., University of Chicago, 1965.

Wildish, Mark. "Hieroglyphic Semantics in Late Antiquity." PhD diss., Durham University, 2013.

Wondwosen Admasu Woldehana. "A Catalogue of Some Manuscripts in Ankobär Mädhane Aläm Church Museum." Master's thesis, Addis Ababa University, 2011.

iii. PERSONAL COLLECTION OF AUTHOR

Dähné Wäldä Maryam. የሕይወት ታሪክ. Amharic diary shared with the author by Abebe Ambatchew, along with related family documents.

Märse'é Hazän Wäldä Qirqos. Untitled Amharic diary, in unpublished manuscript form.

II. Newspapers and Popular Periodicals

ብርሃንና ሰላም
አእምሮ
አዲስ ዘመን
የሮማ ብርሃን
የቄሳር መንግሥት መልከተኛ
የኤርትራ ድምፅ
ደብረ ቅ[ዱስ] እስጢፋኖስ
Al Jazeera
Atlantic Monthly
Baltimore Afro-American
Bath Weekly Chronicle and Herald
Corriere dell'impero
Corriere della sera
Corriere della Somalia
Courrier d'Éthiopie
The Crisis
Daily Gleaner
Ebony
Ethiopian Herald
Ethiopian Observer
Etiopia
Gazette de Lausanne
Gerarchia
Giornale d'Italia
Humanité
Italia coloniale
Journal de Genève
Labour Monthly
Le Monde
Le Temps
Mattino illustrato
The Nation
New Times and Ethiopia News

New York Sun
New York Times
Public Opinion
Quotidiano eritreo
Regards
The Times (London)
Voce dell'africa
Voice of Ethiopia

III. Published Sources

Abdel-Malek, Anouar. "Orientalism in Crisis." *Diogenes* 11, no. 44 (1963): 103–140.

Abdissa Aga. በኢጣልያ በረሃዎች። አዲስ አበባ፣ 1968።

Abebe Ambatchew. *A Glimpse of Greatness*. Vancouver: Trafford, 2010.

———. *His Share of the Universe*. Abebe Ambatchew, 2014.

Achebe, Chinua. "Colonialist Criticism." In *Hopes and Impediments: Selected Essays 1965–1987*, 68–90. New York: Penguin, 1988.

Achille, Etienne, Charles Forsdick, and Lydie Moudileno, eds. *Postcolonial Realms of Memory: Sites and Symbols in Modern France*. Liverpool: Liverpool University Press, 2020.

Achufusi, Modilim. "Devoirs et responsabilités des historiens africains." *Présence Africaine* 27/28 (1959): 81–95.

Additional Notes to the Memorandum on the Italian Territories in Africa. 1946.

Adom Getachew. *Worldmaking After Empire: The Rise and Fall of Self-Determination*. Princeton, NJ: Princeton University Press, 2019.

Afäwärq Gäbrä Iyäsus. *Manuale di conversazione italiano-amarico con la pronuncia figurata*. Rome: Tipografia Poliglotta Vaticana, 1934.

———. ልብ ወለድ ታሪክ። ሮማ፣ 1900 ዓም።

———. ኢትዮጵያ። *Grammatica della lingua amarica: metodo pratico per l'insegnamento*. Rome: Tipografia della Reale Accademia dei Lincei, 1905.

———. ኢትዮጵያ። *Guide du voyageur en Abyssinie*. Rome: De Luigi, 1908.

———. የኢትዮጵ መንግሥት አልጋ ወራሽና እንደራሴ ልሑል ተፈሪ መኮንን የደጉ መንገዳቸው አኳኋን። አዲስ አበባ፣ ተፈሪ መኮንን ማተሚያ ቤት፣ 1918 ዓም።

———. ዳግማዊ አጤ ምኒልክ። ሮማ፣ 1901 ዓም።

Agamben, Giorgio. *Means Without End: Notes on Politics*. Trans. Vincenzo Binetti and Cesare Casarino. Minneapolis: University of Minnesota Press, 2000.

Ahmed Asif, Manan. *The Loss of Hindustan: The Invention of India*. Cambridge, MA: Harvard University Press, 2020.

Ahmed Hassen Omer. "Italian Local Politics in Northern Shäwa and Its Consquences 1936–1941." *JES* 28, no. 2 (1995): 1–13.

Ahmida, Ali Abdullatif. *Genocide in Libya: Shar, A Hidden Colonial History*. New York: Routledge, 2021.

Akingbade, Harrison Ola. "The Liberian Problem of Forced Labor, 1926–1940." *Africa* 52, no. 2 (1997): 261–273.
Aklilu Habtäwäld. የአክሊሉ ማስታወሻ *Aklilu Remembers*. አዲስ አበባ፣ አዲስ አበባ ዩኒቨርሲቲ ፕሬስ፣ 2010።
Aklilu Habté. "[ከቡር ሊቃ መንበር]." In *Atti del convegno internazionale di studi etiopici (Roma 2-4 aprile 1959)*, 269–270. Rome: Accademia Nazionale dei Lincei, 1960.
——. የቀዳማዊ ኃይለ ሥላሴ ዩኒቨርሲቲ ታሪክ የከፍተኛ ትምህርት መቋቋምና መስፋፋት ጉዞ በኢትዮጵያ። Tainan City: Chiachin Printing, 2017.
Alatas, Syed Farid. *Applying Ibn Khaldūn: The Recovery of a Lost Tradition in Sociology*. New York: Routledge, 2014.
Albro, Robert, George Marcus, Laura McNamara, and Monica Schoch-Spana, eds. *Anthropologists and the Securityscape: Ethics, Practice, and Professional Identity*. Walnut Creek, CA: Left Coast Press, 2012.
Alcaraz, Emmanuel. *Les lieux de mémoire de la guerre d'indépendance algérienne*. Paris: Karthala, 2017.
Alemseged Abbay. "The Trans-Mareb Past in the Present." *JMAS* 35, no. 2 (1997): 321–334.
Allain, Jean. "Slavery and the League of Nations: Ethiopia as a Civilized Nation." *JHIL* 8 (2006): 213–244.
Alliegro, Enzo Vinicio. *Antropologia italiana: storia e storiografia, 1869-1975*. Florence: SEID, 2011.
Allman, Jean. "#HerskovitsMustFall? A Meditation on Whiteness, African Studies, and the Unfinished Business of 1968." *ASR* 62, no. 3 (2019): 6–39.
Aloisi, Pompeo. *Journal (25 Juillet 1932-14 Juin 1936)*. Trans. Maurice Vaussard. Paris: Plon, 1957.
Amedeo di Savoia-Aosta. *Studi africani*. Bologna: Zanichelli, 1942.
Amin, Shahid. "The Marginal Jotter: Scribe Chaube and the Making of the Great Linguistic Survey of India c. 1890–1920." *OPIIC* 27 (2011): 1–17.
Anderson, Benedict. *Imagined Communities: Reflections on the Origins and Spread of Nationalism*. New York: Verso, 1983.
Anderson, Carol. *Bourgeois Radicals: The NAACP and the Struggle for Colonial Liberation, 1941-1960*. New York: Cambridge University Press, 2014.
Angelini, Margherita. "Clio Among the Camicie Nere: Italian Historians and Their Allegiances to Fascism." In *In the Society of Fascists: Acclamation, Acquiescence, and Agency in Mussolini's Italy*, ed. Giulia Albanese and Roberta Pergher, 211–231. New York: Palgrave, 2012.
Anghie, Antony. *Imperialism, Sovereignty, and the Making of International Law*. New York: Cambridge University Press, 2004.
An-Naim, Abdullahi Ahmed. *Decolonizing Human Rights*. New York: Cambridge University Press, 2021.
Antonio Gramsci: Témoignages. Paris: Entente Internationale pour la Défense du Droit, de la Liberté et de la Paix en Italie, 1938.
App, Urs. *The Birth of Orientalism*. Philadelphia: University of Pennsylvania Press, 2010.
Arén, Gustav. *Envoys of the Gospel in Ethiopia: In the Steps of the Evangelical Pioneers, 1898-1936*. Stockholm: EFS Förlaget, 1999.

Arendt, Hannah. "Collective Responsibility." In *Responsibility and Judgment*, ed. Jerome Kohn, 147–158. New York: Schocken, 2003.
——. *Eichmann in Jerusalem*. New York: Viking, 1963.
——. "Organized Guilt and Universal Responsibility." In *Essays in Understanding, 1930–1964: Formation, Exile, and Totalitarianism*, ed. Jerome Kohn, 121–132. New York: Schocken, 1994.
Arielli, Nir. "Colonial Soldiers in Italian Counterinsurgency Operations in Libya, 1922–1932." *BJMH* 1, no. 2 (2015): 47–66.
——. *Fascist Italy and the Middle East 1933–40*. New York: Palgrave Macmillan, 2010.
Arthurs, Joshua. *Excavating Modernity: The Roman Past in Fascist Italy*. Ithaca, NY: Cornell University Press, 2012.
Asad, Talal. "From the History of Colonial Anthropology to the Anthropology of Western Hegemony." In *Colonial Situations: Essays on the Contextualization of Ethnographic Knowledge*, ed. George Stocking, 314–324. Madison: University of Wisconsin Press, 1991.
Asante, S. K. B. *Pan-African Protest: West Africa and the Italo-Ethiopian Crisis, 1934–1941*. London: Longman, 1977.
Asfa-Wossen Asserate. *King of Kings: The Triumph and Tragedy of Emperor Haile Selassie I of Ethiopia*. London: Haus, 2015.
Atti del convegno internazionale di studi etiopici (Roma 2–4 aprile 1959). Rome: Accademia Nazionale dei Lincei, 1960.
Atti del XIX congresso internazionale degli orientalisti, Roma 23–29 settembre 1935-XIII. Rome: Tipografia del Senato, 1938.
Augustyniak, Zuzanna. "Lij Iyasu's Marriages as a Reflection of His Domestic Policy." In *The Life and Times of Lij Iyasu of Ethiopia: New Insights*, ed. Éloi Ficquet and Wolbert Smidt, 39–47. Berlin: Lit Verlag, 2018.
Aydin, Cemil. *The Idea of the Muslim World: A Global Intellectual History*. Cambridge, MA: Harvard University Press, 2017.
Badoglio, Pietro. *L'Italia nella seconda guerra mondiale*. Verona: Mondadori, 1946.
Baer, George. *The Coming of the Italian-Ethiopian War*. Cambridge, MA: Harvard University Press, 1967.
——. *Test Case: Italy, Ethiopia, and the League of Nations*. Stanford, CA: Hoover Institution Press, 1976.
Bahru Zewde. "The Ethiopian Intelligentsia and the Italo-Ethiopian War, 1935–1941." *IJAHS* 26, no. 2 (1993): 271–295.
——. "The Italian Occupation of Ethiopia: Records, Recollections, and Ramifications." In *Society, State, and History: Selected Essays*, 375–390. Addis Ababa: Addis Ababa University Press, 2008.
——. *Pioneers of Change in Ethiopia: The Reformist Intellectuals of the Early Twentieth Century*. Athens: Ohio University Press, 2002.
——. *The Quest for Socialist Ethiopia: The Ethiopian Student Movement, c. 1960–1974*. New York: James Currey, 2014.
Bahru Zewde, Baye Yimam, Eshetu Chole, and Alula Pankhurst. "From Lund to Addis Ababa: A Decade of Ethiopian Studies (1982–1991)." *JES* 27, no. 1 (1994): 1–28.

Bairu Tafla. "Four Ethiopian Biographies: Däjjazmač Gärmamé, Däjjazmač Gäbrä-Egzi'abehér Moroda, Däjjazmač Balča and Käntiba Gäbru Dästa." *JES* 7, no. 2 (1969): 1-31.
———. "Ras Dargé Sahlä-Sellasé, c 1827-1900." *JES* 13, no. 2 (1975): 17-35.
———. "Three Portraits: Ato Aṣmä Giyorgis, Ras Gobäna Dači and Ṣähafé Tezaz Gäbrä Selassé." *JES* 5, no. 2 (1967): 133-150.
———. "A Turning Point in Ethiopian Historiography from Within." In *Die äthiopischen Studien im 20. Jahrhundert*, ed. Rainer Maria Voigt, 159-182. Aachen, Germany: Shaker Verlag, 2003.
———. "Two of the Last Provincial Kings of Ethiopia." *JES* 11, no. 1 (1973): 29-55.
Bälätä Gäbré. የጉዞ ትዝታ። አዲስ አበባ፤ ቼምበር ማተሚያ ቤት፤ 2004 ዓም።
Bandeira Jerónimo, Miguel. "'Imperial Internationalisms' in the 1920s: The Shaping of Colonial Affairs at the League of Nations." *JICH* 48, no. 5 (2020): 866-891.
Bandini, Franco. *Gli italiani in Africa: storia delle guerre coloniali 1882-1943*. Milan: Longanesi, 1971.
Bärihun Käbbädä. የአጼ ኃይለሥላሴ ታሪክ። አዲስ አበባ፤ አርቲስቲክ ማተሚያ ቤት፤ 1993 ዓም።
Barros, James. *Betrayal from Within: Joseph Avenol, Secretary-General of the League of Nations, 1933-1940*. New Haven, CT: Yale University Press, 1969.
Bausi, Alessandro. "The Encyclopaedia Aethiopica and Ethiopian Studies." *Aethiopica* 19 (2016): 188-206.
———. "Philology, research in." In *Encyclopaedia Aethiopica*, ed. Siegbert Uhlig and Alessandro Bausi, vol. 4, 142-144. Wiesbaden: Harrasowitz Verlag, 2011.
Baxa, Paul. "Capturing the Fascist Moment: Hitler's Visit to Italy in 1938 and the Radicalization of Fascist Italy." *JCH* 42, no. 2 (2007): 227-242.
Bayart, Jean-François. *The State in Africa: Politics of the Belly*. New York: Longman, 1993.
Ben-Ghiat, Ruth. *Fascist Modernities: Italy, 1922-1945*. Berkeley: University of California Press, 2001.
———. "Italian Universities Under Fascism." In *Universities Under Dictatorship*, ed. John Connelly and Michael Grüttner, 45-74. University Park, PA: Penn State University Press, 2005.
Benton, Lauren. *Law and Colonial Cultures: Legal Regimes in World History, 1400-1900*. New York: Cambridge University Press, 2002.
Bentwich, Norman. *My 77 Years: An Account of My Life and Times, 1883-1960*. Philadelphia, PA: Jewish Publication Society of America, 1961.
Berhanou Abebe. "Les Flambeurs d'Hommes. Interrogations croisées sur une réalité devenue mythe." *Annales d'Éthiopie* 20 (2004): 13-22.
———. "The Haile Selassie I Prize Trust." *NEAS* 2, no. 3 (1995): 53-66.
———. "Quelques notes sur le rôle d'abba Jérôme Gabra-Muse dans la diplomatie éthiopienne de l'entre-deux guerres." In *Proceedings of the Eighth International Conference of Ethiopian Studies*, ed. Taddese Beyene, 299-313. Addis Ababa: Institute of Ethiopian Studies, 1989.
Berque, Jacques. *Mémoires des deux rives*. Paris: Seuil, 1989.
Biedermann, Zoltán. "Querying the Origins of Orientalism: Recent Approaches to the History of Representations." *Ler História*, 74 (2019): 261-275.

Biobaku, Saburi. "Les responsabilités de l'historien africain en ce qui concerne l'histoire et l'Afrique." *Présence africaine* 27/28 (1959): 96–99.

Bliesemann de Guevara, Berit, ed. "Knowledge Production in Conflict: The International Crisis Group," special issue. *TWQ* 35, no. 4 (2013).

Boaglio, Alessandro. *Plotone chimico: Cronache abissine di una generazione scomoda*. Ed. Giovanni Boaglio and Matteo Dominioni. Milan: Mimesis, 2010.

Boittin, Jennifer Anne. *Colonial Metropolis: The Urban Grounds of Anti-Imperialism and Feminism in Interwar Paris*. Lincoln: University of Nebraska Press, 2010.

Borges, Jorge Luis. *The Aleph and Other Stories*. Trans. Andrew Hurley. New York: Penguin, 1998.

Borra, Edoardo. *Amedeo di Savoia: terzo duca d'Aosta e viceré d'Etiopia*. Milan: Mursia, 1985.

——. *Prologo di un conflitto: Colloqui col segretario del Negus (Dicembre 1934–Ottobre 1935)*. Milan: Paoline, 1965.

Borruso, Paolo. *L'Africa al confino: la deportazione etiopica in Italia (1937–39)*. Rome: Lacaita, 2003.

——, ed. *Il mito infranto: la fine del "sogno africano" negli appunti e nelle immagini di Massimo Borruso, funzionario coloniale in Etiopia (1937–46)*. Manduria: Lacaita, 1997.

Boswell, Christina. "The Political Functions of Expert Knowledge: Knowledge and Legitimation in European Union Immigration Policy." *JEPP* 15, no. 4 (2008): 471–488.

Bosworth, Richard. *Mussolini*. London: Bloomsbury, 2002.

Bottai, Giuseppe. *Quaderno affricano*. Florence: Giunti, 2016.

Bourdieu, Pierre. "Le champ scientifique." *ARSS* 2, nos. 2–3 (1976): 88–104.

——. "Understanding." In *The Weight of the World: Social Suffering in Contemporary Society*, 607–626. Stanford, CA: Stanford University Press, 1993.

Brambilla, Cristina. "Temi del Secondo Congresso Mondiale degli scrittori e artisti neri." *Africa* 14, no. 3 (1959): 122–124.

Brattain, Michelle. "Race, Racism, and Antiracism: UNESCO and the Politics of Presenting Science." *AHR* 112, no. 5 (2007): 1386–1413.

Brocades Zaalberg, Thijs, and Bart Luttikhuis, eds. *Empire's Violent End: Comparing Dutch, British, and French Wars of Decolonization, 1945–1962*. Ithaca, NY: Cornell University Press, 2022.

Brown, Ian. *The School of Oriental and African Studies: Imperial Training and the Expansion of Learning*. Cambridge: Cambridge University Press, 2016.

Brusasca, Giuseppe. *Il ministero degli affari esteri al servizio del popolo italiano (1943–1949)*. Rome: Ministero degli Affari Esteri, 1949.

Bruzzi, Silvia. *Islam and Gender in Colonial Northeast Africa: Sittī 'Alawiyya, the Uncrowned Queen*. Leiden, Netherlands: Brill, 2018.

Buelli, Arlena. "The Hands Off Ethiopia Campaign: Racial Solidarities and Intercolonial Antifascism in South Asia (1935–36)." *JGH* 18, no. 1 (2023): 47–67.

Bulliet, Richard. "Orientalism and Medieval Islamic Studies." In *The Past and Future of Medieval Studies*, ed. John Van Engen, 94–104. Notre Dame, IN: University of Notre Dame Press, 1994.

Burbank, Jane, and Fred Cooper. *Empires in World History: Power and the Politics of Difference*. Princeton, NJ: Princeton University Press, 2010.

Bureau, Jacques. *Marcel Cohen et ses successeurs, ou Cent ans d'études éthiopiennes en France*. Addis Ababa: Maison des Études Éthiopiennes, 1997.

Burke III, Edmund. *The Ethnographic State: France and the Invention of Moroccan Islam*. Berkeley: University of California Press, 2014.

Burke III, Edmund, and David Prochaska, eds. *Genealogies of Orientalism: History, Theory, Politics*. Lincoln: University of Nebraska Press, 2009.

Burke, Roland. *Decolonization and the Evolution of International Human Rights*. Philadelphia: University of Pennsylvania Press, 2010.

Burkman, Thomas. *Japan and the League of Nations: Empire and the World Order, 1914-1938*. Honolulu: University of Hawai'i Press, 2007.

Burnett, Charles, Alastair Hamilton, and Jan Loop, eds. *The Teaching and Learning of Arabic in Early Modern Europe*. Leiden, Netherlands: Brill, 2017.

Bustanov, Alfrid. *Soviet Orientalism and the Creation of Central Asian Nations*. New York: Routledge, 2014.

Calabrò, Lino. *Intermezzo africano: Ricordi di un residente di governo in Etiopia (1937-1941)*. Rome: Bonacci, 1988.

Calame-Griaule, Geneviève. "On the Dogon Restudied." *Current Anthropology* 32, no. 5 (1991): 575-577.

Calchi Novati, Giampaolo. "Colonialismo e indipendenza dell'Africa nell'opera di Carlo Giglio." *Africa* 57, no. 2 (2002): 225-241.

——. "Italia e Etiopia dopo la guerra: Una nuova realtá, i risarcimenti e la stele rapita." *Africa* 46, no. 4 (1991): 479-502.

——. "Italy and Africa: How to Forget Colonialism." *JMIS* 13, no. 1 (2008): 41-57.

——. "Studi e politica ai convegni coloniali del primo e del secondo dopoguerra." *Il Politico* 55, no. 3 (1990): 487-514.

Camilleri, Nicola. "How a Colonial Subject Became an Italian Citizen: The Life and Naturalization of Sengal Workneh Between Colonial Eritrea and Italy (1882-1929)." In *Languages of Discrimination and Racism in Twentieth-Century Italy: History, Legacies and Practices*, ed. Marcella Simoni and Davide Lombardo, 27-46. New York: Palgrave Macmillan, 2022.

Campbell, Ian. *The Addis Ababa Massacre: Italy's National Shame*. New York: Oxford University Press, 2017.

——. *The Massacre of Debre Libanos, Ethiopia 1937: The Story of One of Fascism's Most Shocking Atrocities*. Addis Ababa: Addis Ababa University Press, 2014.

——. *The Plot to Kill Graziani: The Attempted Assassination of Mussolini's Viceroy*. Addis Ababa: Addis Ababa University Press, 2010.

Canali, Mauro. *The Matteotti Murder and Mussolini: The Anatomy of a Fascist Crime*. Trans. Ann Pichey. Palgrave: New York, 2024.

Cantarino, Vicente. "Dante and Islam: History and Analysis of a Controversy (1965)." *Dante Studies* 125 (2007): 37-55.

Cassanelli, Lee. "The Somali Studies International Association: A Brief History." *Bildhaan* 1 (2001): 1-10.

Castro, Francesco. "Scritti di Martino Mario Moreno." *RSE* 20 (1964): 12-21.

Cauli, Alberto. "At Ras Tafari Malonnen's Court: The 1927 Italian Diplomatic Mission to Ethiopia and Its Colonial Implications." In *Reflections on Leadership and Institutions in Africa*, ed. Kenneth Kalu and Toyin Falola, 95-112. London: Rowan and Littlefield, 2020.

Cavallero, Ugo. *Gli avvenimenti militari nell'impero: Dal 13 gennaio 1939–XVII al 14 aprile 1939–XVII*. 2 vols. Addis Ababa: 1940.

Ceci, Lucia. "Chiesa e questione coloniale: guerra e missione nell'impresa d'Etiopia." *Italia contemporanea* 233 (2003): 617-636.

Celli, Andrea. *Dante and the Mediterranean Comedy: From Muslim Spain to Post-Colonial Italy*. Cham, Germany: Palgrave, 2022.

Cerulli, Enrico. "Canti burleschi di studenti delle scuole abissine." *RSO* 13, no. 4 (1933): 342-350.

———. "Canti popolari amarici." *RRAL* V, 25 (1916): 563-658.

———. "Ethiopia's Relations with the Muslim World." In *UNESCO General History of Africa, III: Africa from the Seventh to the Eleventh Century*, ed. Mohammed El Fasi and Ivan Hrbek, 575-585. Berkeley: University of California Press, 1988.

———. "Etiopia." *Oriente moderno* 12, no. 6 (1932): 305.

———. *Etiopia occidentale (dallo Scioa alla frontiera del Sudan)*. 2 vols. Rome: Sindacato Italiano Arti Grafiche, 1929 and 1933.

———. *Etiopi in Palestina. Storia della comunità etiopica di Gerusalemme*. Rome: Ministero dell'Africa Italiana, 1943 and 1947.

——— [Niliacus]. "Etiopia schiavista." *Nuova antologia* 1520 (1935): 161-169.

———. *Folk Literature of the Galla of Southern Abyssinia*. Cambridge, MA: African Department of the Peabody Museum of Harvard University, 1922.

———. "Francesco Gallina." *RSE* 2, no. 3 (1942): 347-348.

———. "Giuliano Cora e l'Etiopia." *RSPI* 36, no. 1 (1969): 18-24.

———. "Giusto da Urbino." In *Enciclopedia italiana di scienza, lettere ed arti*. Rome: Istituto Treccani, 1929-1938. https://www.treccani.it/enciclopedia/giusto-da-urbino_%28Enciclopedia-Italiana%29/.

———. "Gli abbati di Dabra Libānos, capi del monachismo etiopico, secondo la 'lista rimata' (sec. XIV-XVIII)." *Orientalia* 12 (1943): 226-253.

———. "Gli abbati di Dabra Libānos, capi del monachismo etiopico, secondo la 'lista rimata' (sec. XIV-XVIII) (Continuazione)." *Orientalia* 13 (1944): 137-182.

———. "Gli abbati di Dabra Libānos, capi del monachismo etiopico, secondo le liste recenti (sec. XVIII-XX)." *Orientalia* 14 (1945): 143-171.

———. *Il "Libro della Scala" e la questione delle fonti arabo-spagnole della Divina Commedia*. Vatican City: Biblioteca Apostolica Italiana, 1949.

———. *Il libro etiopico dei Miracoli di Maria e le sue fonti nelle letterature del medio evo latino*. Rome: Bardi, 1943.

———. "Il nuovo posto dell'Italia nel continente africano." *Africa* 14, no. 4 (1959): 175-176.

———. "Inni della chiesa abissina." *RSO* 12 (1929-1930): 361-407.

——— [Niliacus]. "L'Etiopia di oggi." *Nuova antologia* 1511 (1935): 43-53.

———. "La fine del colonialismo." *Ulisse* XI, vol. V, fasc. 28-29 (1958): 1551-1559.

———. "La poesia popolare amarica." *BSAI* 35 (1916): 172-178.

———. "La seconda spedizione Bottego nei racconti galla." *BSAI* 36 (1917): 24–28.
———. "L'Islam nei regni galla indipendenti." *BSAI* 35 (1916): 113–119.
———. "Muḥammad b. ʿAbd Allāh Ḥassān al-Mahdī." In *Encyclopaedia of Islam*, 1st ed., ed. M. Th. Houtsma, A. J. Wensinck, E. Levi-Provençal, H. A. R. Gibb, and W. Heffening, vol. 3, 667–668. Leiden: Brill, 1934.
———. "Note sul movimento musulmano nella Somalia." *RSO* 10, no. 1 (1923): 1–36.
———. "Notizia preliminare dei risultati scientifici del mio viaggio nell'Etiopia occidentale." *Oriente moderno* 8, no. 7 (1928): 325–328.
———. "Notizie varie." *Oriente moderno* 6, no. 10 (1926): 555–557.
———. "Notizie varie." *Oriente moderno* 7, no. 7 (1927): 353–357.
———. "Nuove idee nell'Etiopia e nuova letteratura amarica." *Oriente moderno* 6, no. 3 (1926): 167–173.
———. "Nuovi libri pubblicati in Etiopia." *Oriente moderno* 12, no. 3 (1932): 170–175.
———. "Nuovo ministro d'Etiopia a Parigi." *Oriente moderno* 13 (1933): 108.
———. "Pubblicazioni recenti dei musulmani e dei cristiani dell'Etiopia." *Oriente moderno* 8, no. 9 (1928): 429–432.
———. "Punti di vista sulla storia d'Etiopia." In *Atti del convegno internazionale di studi etiopici (Roma 2-4 aprile 1959)*, 5–27. Rome: Accademia Nazionale dei Lincei, 1960.
———. "Rassegna periodica di pubblicazioni in lingue etiopiche fatte in Etiopia. I." *Oriente moderno* 13 (1933): 58–64.
———. "[Reply to Aklilu Habté]." In *Atti del convegno internazionale di studi etiopici (Roma 2-4 aprile 1959)*, 271. Rome: Accademia Nazionale dei Lincei, 1960.
———. Review of *Ethiopian Itineraries circa 1400-1524*, ed. O. G. S. Crawford. *Orientalia* 28, no. 4 (1959): 391.
———. Review of *Genti di Somalia*, by Giuseppe Caniglia. *Oriente moderno* 2, no. 8 (1923): 510–511.
———. Review of *Storia della letteratura etiopica*, by Ignazio Guidi. *Oriente moderno* 13, no. 2 (1933): 111–112.
———. "Ricordo di Carlo Alfonso Nallino." *Levante* 20 (1973): 7–10.
———. *Scritti teologici etiopici dei secoli XVI-XVII*. Vatican City: 1958 and 1960.
———. *Somalia. Scritti vari editi ed inediti*. 3 vols. Rome: Poligrafico dello Stato, 1957, 1959, and 1964.
———. "Somaliland." In *Encyclopaedia of Islam*, 1st ed., ed. M. Th. Houtsma, A. J. Wensinck, E. Levi-Provençal, H. A. R. Gibb, and W. Heffening, vol. 4, 483–488. Leiden: Brill, 1934.
———. *Storia della letteratura etiopica*. Milan: Nuova Accademia, 1956.
———. "Una raccolta amarica di canti funebri." *RSO* 10, no. 2/4 (1923-1925): 265–280.
Cerulli, Enrico, J. H. Stafford, C. L. Collenette, William Goodenough, Barrington Brown, Charles Close, and W. A. MacFadyen. "The Anglo-Italian Somaliland Boundary." *Geographical Journal* 78, no. 2 (1931): 102–125.
Cerulli, Enrico, Carlo Conti Rossini, Mario Giordani, Ignazio Guidi, Michelangelo Guidi, Luigi Gramatica, Attilio Mori, Giovanni Negri, Mario Salfi, and Giuseppe Stefanini. "Etiopia." In *Enciclopedia italiana di scienza, lettere ed arti*. Rome: Istituto Treccani, 1929–1938. https://www.treccani.it/enciclopedia/etiopia_(Enciclopedia-Italiana)/.

Chaîne, Marius. "Un monastère éthiopien a Rome au XV et XVI siècle, Santo Stefano dei Mori." *MFO* V (1911): 1–36.
Chakrabarty, Dipesh. *The Calling of History: Sir Jadunath Sarkar and His Empire of Truth*. Chicago: University of Chicago Press, 2015.
———. *Provincializing Europe: Postcolonial Thought and Historical Difference*. Princeton, NJ: Princeton University Press, 2000.
Chambard, Olivier. "Marcel Griaule, un ethnologue français et le conflit italo-éthiopien." *Journal des africanistes* 54, no. 2 (1984): 101–106.
Ciano, Galeazzo. *Ciano's Hidden Diary: 1937-1938*. Trans. Andreas Mayor. New York: Dutton, 1953.
———. *Diario*. 2 vols. Milan: Rizzoli, 1946.
Cipriani, Lidio. "Il passato e l'avvenire degli etiopici secondo l'antropologia." *Gerarchia* 15 (1935): 916–919.
———. "Il significato degli etiopici nell'antropologia africana." In *Atti del XIX congresso internazionale degli orientalisti, Roma 23-29 settembre 1935-XIII*, 155–162. Rome: Tipografia del Senato, 1938.
Clarke, Kamari, Abel Knottnerus, and Eefje de Volder, eds. *Africa and the ICC: Perceptions of Justice*. New York: Cambridge University Press, 2016.
Clifford, James. *The Predicament of Culture: Twentieth-Century Ethnography, Literature, and Art*. Cambridge, MA: Harvard University Press, 1988.
Cocteau, Jean, and Jacques Maritain. *Art and Faith: Letters Between Jacques Maritain and Jean Cocteau*. Trans. John Coleman. New York: Philosophical Library, 1951.
Cohen, Marcel. *L'Abyssinie doit rester indépendente*. Paris: Bureau d'Éditions, 1936.
———. "Linguistique éthiopienne: état des travaux et perspectives pour le proche avenir." In *Atti del convegno internazionale di studi etiopici (Roma 2-4 aprile 1959)*, 59–73. Rome: Accademia Nazionale dei Lincei, 1960.
———. "Parole di chiusura dei lavori del convegno." In *Atti del convegno internazionale di studi etiopici (Roma 2-4 aprile 1959)*, 461. Rome: Accademia Nazionale dei Lincei, 1960.
———. "Rapport sur une mission linguistique en Abyssinie (1910–1911)." *NAMSL*, n.s. 6 (1912): 1–80.
Cohn, Bernard. *Colonialism and Its Forms of Knowledge: The British in India*. Princeton, NJ: Princeton University Press, 1996.
Conklin, Alice. *A Mission to Civilize: The Republican Idea of Empire in France and West Africa, 1895-1930*. Stanford, CA: Stanford University Press, 1997.
———. *In the Museum of Man: Race, Anthropology, and Empire in France, 1850–1950*. Ithaca, NY: Cornell University Press, 2013.
Connelly, Matthew. *A Diplomatic Revolution: Algeria's Fight for Independence and the Origins of the Post-Cold War Era*. New York: Oxford University Press, 2002.
Contee, Clarence. "Du Bois, the NAACP, and the Pan-African Congress of 1919." *JNH* 57, no. 1 (1972): 13–28.
Conti Rossini, Carlo. "Bibliografia etiopica (1927–giugno 1936)." *Aevum* 10, no. 4 (1936): 467–587.
———. "Epistolario del debterà Aseggachègn di Uadlà." *RRAL* 6, no. 1 (1925): 449–490.

———. *Fonti storiche etiopiche per il secolo xix. I, Vicende dell'Etiopia e delle missioni cattoliche ai tempi di Ras Ali, Deggiac Ubié e Re Teodoro secondo un documento abissino*. Rome: Tipografia della R. Accademia dei Lincei, 1916.

———. "La fine di Re Teodoro in un documento abissino." *Nuova antologia* 1526 (1935): 453–458.

———. *Italia ed Etiopia dal trattato d'Uccialli alla battaglia di Adua*. Rome: Istituto per L'Oriente, 1935.

———. "L'Etiopia è incapace di progresso civile." *Nuova antologia* 1524 (1935): 171–177.

———. "Lo Ḥatatā Zar'a Yā'qob e il padre Giusto da Urbino." *RRAL* 29, no. 5 (1920): 213–223.

———. *Storia d'Etiopia*. Milan: Lucini, 1928.

Coon, Carleton. *Measuring Ethiopia and Flight into Arabia*. London: Jonathan Cape, 1936.

———. "A Realist Looks at Ethiopia." *Atlantic Monthly* (September 1935): 310–315.

Cooper, Frederick. *Africa Since 1940: The Past of the Present*. New York: Cambridge University Press, 2002.

Copans, Jean. "Leiris et Balandier face à la situation coloniale des années 1950. Entre dévoilements socio-politiques et redéfinitions disciplinaires." *Raison présente* 199 (2016): 61–73.

Coquery-Vidrovitch, Catherine. "*Présence Africaine*: History and Historians of Africa." In *Surreptitious Speech: Présence Africaine and the Politics of Otherness, 1947–1987*, ed. Valentin-Yves Mudimbe, 59–94. Chicago: University of Chicago Press, 1992.

Cora, Giuliano. "Giuseppe Colli di Felizzano." *RSPI* 10, no. 4 (1943): 415–450.

———. "Il trattato italo-etiopico del 1928." *RSPI* 15, no. 2 (1948): 205–226.

———. "Un diplomatico durante l'era fascista." *Storia e politica* 5 (1966): 88–98.

Crawford, Neta. "Decolonization Through Trusteeship: The Legacy of Ralph Bunche." In *Trustee for the Human Community: Ralph J. Bunche, the United Nations, and the Decolonization of Africa*, ed. Robert Hill and Edmond Keller, 93–115. Athens: Ohio University Press, 2010.

Cresciani, Gianfranco. *Fascism, Anti-Fascism, and Italians in Australia, 1922–1945*. Canberra: Australian National University Press, 1980.

Cresti, Federico. "Il professore e il generale: La polemica tra Carlo Alfonso Nallino e Rodolfo Graziani sulla Senussia e su altre questioni libiche." *Studi storici* 45, no. 4 (2004): 1113–1149.

Curtin, Philip. "Recent Trends in African Historiography and Their Contribution to History in General." In *UNESCO General History of Africa, I: Methodology and Prehistory*, ed. Joseph Ki-Zerbo, 54–72. Berkeley: University of California Press, 1981.

Dabashi, Hamid. *Europe and Its Shadows: Coloniality After Empire*. New York: Pluto, 2019.

———. *Reversing the Colonial Gaze: Persian Travelers Abroad*. New York: Cambridge University Press, 2020.

Dästa Täklä Wäld. ዐዲስ ያማርኛ መዝገበ ቃላት። በካህናትና በገረ ሰብ ቋንቋ። አዲስ አበባ፤ አርቲስቲክ ማተሚያ ቤት፤ 1970።

Davis, Graham, and Penny Bonsall. *A History of Bath: Image and Reality*. Lancaster, UK: Carnegie, 2006.

De Carlo, Mariana. "Colonial Internment Camps in Africa Orientale Italiana: The Case of Dhanaane (Somalia)." In *Themes in Modern African History and Culture: Festschrift for*

Tekeste Negash, ed. Lars Berge and Irma Taddia, 193–208. Padova: Libreria Universitaria, 2013.
De Felice, Renzo. "Gli storici italiani nel periodo fascista." In *Federico Chabod e la "nuova storiografia" italiana del primo al secondo dopoguerra, 1919–1950*, ed. Brunello Vigezzi, 559–630. Milan: Jaca Book, 1984.
———. *Mussolini il Duce: I. Gli anni del consenso 1929–1936*. Turin: Einaudi, 1974.
De Grazia, Victoria. *The Perfect Fascist: A Story of Love, Power, and Morality in Mussolini's Italy*. Cambridge, MA: Harvard University Press, 2020.
De Lorenzi, James. *Guardians of the Tradition: Historians and Historical Writing in Ethiopia and Eritrea*. Rochester, NY: University of Rochester Press, 2015.
De Monfreid, Henri. "Abissinia." *Africa italiana* 53, nos. 1–13 (1935): 66–84.
———. *L'Avion noir*. Paris: Bernard Grasset, 1936.
De Vecchi, Cesare Maria. *Orizzonti d'impero: Cinque anni in Somalia*. Milan: Mondadori, 1935.
Debaene, Vincent. "Les 'Chroniques éthiopiennes' de Marcel Griaule." *Gradhiva* 6 (2007): 86–103.
———. *Far Afield: French Anthropology Between Science and Literature*. Trans. Justin Izzo. Chicago: University of Chicago Press, 2014.
Del Boca, Angelo. "Un lager del fascismo: Danane." *Studi piacentini* 1, no. 1 (1987): 59–70.
———. *Gli italiani in Africa Orientale: III. La caduta dell'impero*. Milan: Mondadori, 1992.
———. *Gli italiani in Africa Orientale: II. La conquista del impero*. Milan: Mondadori, 1999.
———. *The Ethiopian War, 1935–1941*. Trans. P. D. Cummins. Chicago: University of Chicago Press, 1969.
Delgado Rosa, Frederico, and Han Vermeulen, eds. *Ethnographers Before Malinowski: Pioneers of Anthropological Fieldwork 1870–1922*. New York: Berghahn, 2022.
———. "Other Argonauts: Chapters in the History of Pre-Malinowskian Ethnography." In *Ethnographers Before Malinowski: Pioneers of Anthropological Fieldwork, 1870–1922*, ed. Delgado Rosa and Vermeulen, 1–46. New York: Berghahn, 2002.
Deplano, Valeria. *L'Africa in casa: Propaganda e cultura coloniale nell'Italia fascista*. Milan: Mondadori, 2015.
Deschamps, Hubert. "Griaule, Mandel et l'Ethiopie." *JES* 4, no. 1 (1966): 71–73.
Di Lauro, Raffaele. *Come abbiamo difeso l'impero*. Rome: Casa l'Editrice Arnia, 1949.
———. *Tre anni a Gondar*. Milan: Mondadori, 1936.
Di Pasquale, Francesca. "The Other at Home: Deportation and Transportation of Libyans to Italy During the Colonial Era (1911–1943)." *IRSH* 63 (2018): 211–231.
Dike, Kenneth Onwuka. "Address of Welcome to the First International Congress of Africanists." In *The Proceedings of the First International Congress of Africanists, Accra 11th–18th December 1962*, ed. Lalage Bown and Michael Crowder, 4–5. Evanston, IL: Northwestern University Press, 1964.
Dimpflmeier, Fabiana, ed. "Antropologia italiana e fascismo: Ripensare la storia degli studi demoetnoantropologici." Special Issue. *Lares* 87, nos. 2–3 (2021).
Diop, Alioune. "Le sens de ce Congrès." *Présence africaine* 24/25 (1959): 40–48.
Diouf, Mamadou. *L'Afrique dans le temps du monde*. Sète, France: Ròt-Bòt-Krik, 2023.

Dlamini, Jacob. *The Terrorist Album: Apartheid's Insurgents, Collaborators, and the Security Police.* Cambridge, MA: Harvard University Press, 2020.

Documents on Italian War Crimes Submitted to the United Nations War Crimes Commission by the Imperial Ethiopian Government. 2 vols. Addis Ababa: Ministry of Justice, 1950.

Domenico, Roy Palmer. *Italian Fascists on Trial, 1943-1948.* Chapel Hill: University of North Carolina Press, 1991.

Dominioni, Matteo. "Le fotografie di Danane nel contesto dell'immagine coloniale." *Studi piacentini,* no. 36 (2004): 213-226.

——. *Lo sfascio dell'impero. Gli italiani in Etiopia, 1936-1941.* Bari: Laterza, 2019.

Donaldson, Megan. "The League of Nations, Ethiopia, and the Making of States." *Humanity* 11, no. 1 (2020): 6-31.

Dorato, Mario. "Discours d'accueil à l'Istituto Italiano per l'Africa." *Présence africaine* 24/25 (1959): 25.

——. "Evoluzione del colonialismo." *Africa* 14, no. 4 (1959): 172-174.

Dore, Gianni. "Antropologia e colonialismo italiano nell'epoca fascista: il razzismo biologico di Lidio Cipriani." *AFLF,* n.s. 2, no. 39 (1981): 285-313.

——. "Antropologia e colonialismo italiano. Rassegna di studi di questo dopoguerra." *La ricerca folklorica* 1 (1980): 129-132.

——. "Carlo Conti Rossini in Eritrea tra ricerca scientifica e prassi coloniale (1899-1903)." In *Linguistic, Oriental and Ethiopian Studies in Memory of Paolo Marrassini,* ed. Alessandro Bausi, Alessandro Gori, and Giuseppe Lusini, 221-242. Wiesbaden: Harrassowitz, 2014.

——. "Identity and Contemporary Representations: The Heritage of Alberto Pollera's Monograph, *I Baria e i Kunama.*" *NEAS* 10, no. 3 (2003): 71-99.

——. "Ideologia coloniale e senso comune etnografico nella mostra delle terre italiane d'oltremare." In *L'Africa in vetrina: storie di musei e di esposizioni coloniali in Italia,* ed. Nicola Labanca, 47-65. Treviso: Pagus, 1992.

——. "Scienze sociali, colonialismo e fascismo. La missione al lago Tana (1937)." *Lares* 87, nos. 2-3 (2021): 409-432.

Dorman, Jacob. *Chosen People: The Rise of American Black Israelite Religions.* New York: Oxford University Press, 2013.

Du Bois, W. E. B. *Dusk of Dawn.* New York: Oxford University Press, 2007.

——. "Inter-Racial Implications of the Ethiopian Crisis: A Negro View." *Foreign Affairs* 14, no. 1 (1935): 82-92.

Duedahl, Poul. "Selling Mankind: UNESCO and the Invention of Global History, 1945-1976." *JWH* 22, no. 1 (2011): 101-133.

Duxbury, Neil. "Lord Wright and Innovative Traditionalism." *UTLJ* 59, no. 3 (2009): 265-339.

"E' necessario un riordinamento degli studi africanisti in Italia." *Africa* 14, no. 1 (1959): 17-20.

Ebner, Michael. *Ordinary Violence in Mussolini's Italy.* New York: Cambridge University Press, 2011.

El-Ariss, Tarek. "On Cooks and Crooks: Aḥmad Fāris al-Shidyāq and the Orientalists in England and France (1840s-1850s)." In *The Muslim Reception of European Orientalism:*

Reversing the Gaze, ed. Susannah Heschel and Umar Ryad, 14–38. New York: Routledge, 2018.
Elena Sengal. "Favole e storielle abissine." *Africa italiana* 53, nos. 1–13 (1935): 124–151.
———. "In Memoria di Francesco Gallina (1861–1942)." *Oriente moderno* 22, no. 7 (1942): 301–302.
Emmanu'él Abraham. *Reminiscences of My Life*. Trenton, NJ: Africa World Press, 2010.
Emmanu'él Abraham and Luigi Villari. "Abyssinia and Italy." *JRAS* 34, no. 137 (1935): 366–377.
Emru Zälläqä. *A Journey: Memoirs*. North Charleston, NC: Createspace, 2016.
Enders, Armelle. "L'école nationale de la France d'Outre-Mer et la formation des administrateurs coloniaux." *RHMC* 40, no. 2 (1993): 272–288.
Ertola, Emanuele. *In terra d'Africa: Gli italiani che colonizzarono l'impero*. Bari: Laterza, 2017.
Ethiopian Penal Code of 1930. Addis Ababa: 1941.
Fallocco, Silvano, and Carlo Boumis. *Roma coloniale*. Rome: Commari Edizioni, 2022.
Falcucci, Beatrice. "Bringing the Empire to the Provinces: Colonial Museums and Colonial Knowledge in Fascist Italy." *CFV* 3, no. 10 (2021): 113–146.
Fanon, Frantz. *Black Skin, White Masks*. Trans. Charles Lam Markmann. New York: Grove, 1994.
———. *A Dying Colonialism*. Trans. Haakon Chevalier. New York: Grove, 1994.
———. *The Wretched of the Earth*. Trans. Constance Farrington. New York: Grove, 1968.
Fantahun Ayele. "The Life of *däǧǧač abba* Wəqaw Bərru: Some Notes on Sirak's Manuscript (Addis Ababa, Institute of Ethiopian Studies, Ms 400)." *Africa* 3, no. 2 (2021): 19–34.
Farago, Ladislas. *Abyssinia on the Eve*. London: Putnam, 1935.
Farello, Piero. "Le bande irregolari indigene a caccia di partigiani in Etiopia." *Studi piacentini* 11, no. 1 (1992): 137–162.
Federzoni, Luigi. *Italia di ieri per la storia di domani*. Milan: Mondadori, 1967.
Ferraro, Giuseppe. "I deportati dall'impero. Gli etiopi confinati in Italia durante il regime fascista." *NRS* 100, no. 1 (2016): 243–265.
———. "From the Mountains of Africa to Italy: The Experience of Ethiopian Deportees Confined in Longobucco (Calabria) in the Period 1937–1943." *Annales d'Éthiopie* 31 (2016–2017): 293–319.
Fesseha Giyorgis. *Storia d'Etiopia*. Trans. Yaqob Beyene. Naples: Istituto Universitario Orientale, 1987.
Fiaccadori, Gianfranco. "Mordini, Antonio." In *Encyclopaedia Aethiopica*, ed. Siegbert Uhlig and Alessandro Bausi, vol. 3, 1017–1019. Wiesbaden: Harrasowitz Verlag, 2007.
Fiemeyer, Isabelle. *Marcel Griaule, citoyen dogon*. Paris: Actes Sud, 2004.
Fikru Negash Gebrekidan. *Bond Without Blood: A History of Ethiopian and New World Black Relations, 1896–1991*. Lawrenceville, NJ: Africa World Press, 2015.
———. "Ethiopia in Black Studies from W. E. B. Du Bois to Henry Louis Gates, Jr." *NEAS* 15, no. 1 (2015): 1–34.
———. "Pan-Africanist in the Court: W. E. B. Du Bois and His Vision of Ethiopian Internationalism." In *Routledge Handbook of Pan-Africanism*, ed. Reiland Rabaka, 273–288. New York: Routledge, 2020.

———. "Race, Gender, and Pageantry: The Ups and Downs of an African American Woman in Imperial Ethiopia." *NEAS* 21, no. 2 (2021): 265-300.

Filesi, Teobaldo. "Ulisse: il Tramonto del Colonialismo." *Africa* 13, no. 4 (1958): 175-178.

Finchelstein, Federico. *Transatlantic Fascism: Ideology, Violence, and the Sacred in Argentina and Italy, 1919-1945*. Chapel Hill, NC: Duke University Press, 2010.

Fiorani Piacentini, Valeria. "Tra oriente e occidente: una galleria di profili della storiografia arabo-islamica italiana." *Studi storici* 50, no. 4 (2009): 965-981.

Flaiano, Ennio. *Tempo di uccidere*. Milan: Rizzoli, 1989.

Focardi, Filippo. "Italy's Amnesia over War Guilt: the 'Evil Germans' Alibi." *Mediterranean Quarterly* 25, no. 4 (2014): 4-26.

Fogu, Claudio. *The Historic Imaginary: Politics of History in Fascist Italy*. Toronto: University of Toronto Press, 2003.

Foks, Freddy. "Bronislaw Malinowski, 'Indirect Rule,' and the Colonial Politics of Functionalist Anthropology, ca. 1925-1940." *CSSH* 60, no. 1 (2018): 35-57.

Ford, James W. "An Interview with Tecle Hawariate, Ethiopian Ambassador." In *The Communists and the Struggle for Negro Liberation*, 29-33. New York: Harlem Division of the Communist Party, n.d.

———. "The Struggle for Peace and the Independence of Ethiopia." In *The Communists and the Struggle for Negro Liberation*, 41-47. New York: Harlem Division of the Communist Party, n.d.

Formento, Ettore. *Kai bandera: Etiopia 1936-1941, una banda irregolare*. Milan: Mursia, 2000.

Foster, Elizabeth. *African Catholic: Decolonization and the Transformation of the Church*. Cambridge, MA: Harvard University Press, 2019.

Foucault, Michel. "What Is an Author?" In *Textual Strategies*, ed. Josué Harari, 141-160. Ithaca, NY: Cornell University Press, 1979.

Fournier, Marcel. *Marcel Mauss: A Biography*. Trans. Jane Marie Todd. Princeton, NJ: Princeton University Press, 2006.

Franchetti, Raimondo. *Nella Dancàlia etiopica, spedizione italiana 1928-29*. Milan: Mondadori, 1930).

Franciska Rac, Katalin. "Arabic Literature for the Colonizer and Colonized: Ignaz Golziher and Hungary's Eastern Politics (1878-1918)." In *The Muslim Reception of European Orientalism: Reversing the Gaze*, ed. Susannah Heschel and Umar Ryad, 80-102. New York: Routledge, 2018.

Frank, Sarah Ann. *Hostages of Empire: Colonial Prisoners of War in Vichy France*. Lincoln: University of Nebraska Press, 2021.

Franzinelli, Mimmo. *Squadristi. Protagonisti e tecniche della violenza fascista 1919-1922*. Milan: Mondadori, 2003.

Fricker, Miranda. *Epistemic Injustice: Power and the Ethics of Knowing*. New York: Oxford University Press, 2007.

The Friends of Ethiopia in America. New York: 1935.

Fusella, Luigi, and Joseph Tubiana. "Souvenirs d'Elena Sengal." *Pount* 12 (2018): 27-35.

Gäbrä Egzi'abhér Elyas. *Prowess, Piety, and Politics: The Chronicle of Abeto Iyasu and Empress Zewditu of Ethiopia, 1909-1930*. Trans. Reidulf Molvaer. Cologne, Germany: Rüdiger Köppe Verlag, 1994.

Gäbrä Iyäsus Abbay. መሥረት ዓለት ሕዝቢ. መረብ ምላሽ ብጛንጛ ትግርኛ ዝተዳለወ። አስመራ፣ ኮከብ ጽባሕ፣ 1954 ዓም።

Gäbrä Iyäsus Haylu. *The Conscript: A Novel of Libya's Anticolonial War.* Trans. Ghirmai Negash. Athens: Ohio University Press, 2013.

———. "Un manoscritto amarico sulle verità della fede." In *Atti del convegno internazionale di studi etiopici (Roma 2-4 aprile 1959)*, 345–351. Rome: Accademia Nazionale dei Lincei, 1960.

Gäbrä Krestos Täklä Haymanot. አጭር የዓለም ታሪክ ባጭርኛ። አዲስ አበባ፣ ተፈሪ መኮንን ማተሚያ ቤት፣ 1917 ዓም።

Gäbrä Mädhen Gäbrä Musé [abba Jérôme]. "Souvenirs d'Erythrée." In *Guirlande pour Abba Jérôme: travaux offerts à Abba Jérôme Gabra Musé par ses élèves et ses amis*, ed. Joseph Tubiana, 7–46. Paris: Mois en Afrique, 1983.

Gäbrä Sellasé Wäldä Aregay. ታሪክ ዘመን ዘዳግማዊ ምኔልክ ንጉሥ ነገሥት ዘኢትዮጵያ። አዲስ አበባ፣ አርቲስቲክ ማተሚያ ቤት፣ 1959 ዓም።

Gabrieli, Francesco. "Apology for Orientalism." *Diogenes* 13, no. 50 (1965): 128–136.

———. "New Light on Dante and Islam." *Diogenes* 2, no. 6 (1954): 61–73.

———. *Orientalisti del novecento.* Rome: Istituto per l'Oriente "Nallino," 1993.

Galbiati, Giovanni. "Notizia sui manoscritti etiopici della Biblioteca Ambrosiana." In *Atti del XIX congresso internazionale degli orientalisti, Roma 23-29 settembre 1935-XIII*, 619–625. Rome: Tipografia del Senato, 1938.

Gärima Tafärrä. ጎንደሬ ቢጋሻው። አዲስ አበባ፣ 1949 ዓም።

Garretson, Peter. *A Victorian Gentleman and Ethiopian Nationalist: The Life and Times of Hakim Wärqenäh, Dr. Charles Martin.* Suffolk, UK: James Currey, 2012.

Gentilli, Roberto. *Guerra aerea sull'Etiopia, 1935-1939.* Florence: Edizioni Aeronautiche Italiane, 1992.

Gérard, Albert. "Amharic Creative Literature: The Early Phase." *JES* 6, no. 2 (1968): 39–59.

Germachäw Täklä Hawaryat. "Allocuzione di S.E. Ghermacceu Takla Hawariat, Ambasciatore di Etiopia presso il Quirinale." In *Atti del convegno internazionale di studi etiopici (Roma 2-4 aprile 1959).* Rome: Accademia Nazionale dei Lincei, 1960.

Gershenhorn, Jerry. "'Not an Academic Affair': African American Scholars and the Development of African Studies Programs in the United States, 1942-1960." *JAAH* 94, no. 1 (2009): 44–68.

Getatchew Haile. "The Discourse of Wärqe Commonly Known as *Ḥatäta zä-Zär'a Ya'eqob*." In *Ethiopian Studies in Honour of Amha Asfaw*, 51–71. New York: Getatchew Haile, 2017.

Ghobrial, John-Paul. "The Archive of Orientalism and Its Keepers: Re-Imagining the Histories of Arabic Manuscripts in Early Modern Europe." *Past and Present* 230, supplement 11 (2016): 90–111.

———. "The Life and Hard Times of Solomon Negri." In *The Teaching and Learning of Arabic in Early Modern Europe*, ed. Charles Burnett, Alastair Hamilton, and Jan Loop, 310–331. Leiden: Brill, 2017.

Giannini, Amedeo. "Riassunto della situazione." *Oriente moderno* 4, no. 7 (1924): 430.

Gibson, Mary, and Ilaria Poerio. "Modern Europe, 1750-1950." In *A Global History of Convicts and Penal Colonies*, ed. Clare Anderson, 337–370. London: Bloomsbury Academic, 2018.

Giglio, Carlo. "Le discipline africanistiche orientalistiche e coloniali nelle Università italiane." *Africa* 15, no. 3 (1960): 107–120.

Ginzburg, Carlo. *The Judge and the Historian: Marginal Notes on a Late-Twentieth Century Miscarriage of Justice*. Trans. Antony Shugaar. New York: Verso, 1999.
Giorgi, Chiara. *L'Africa come corriera: Funzioni e funzionari del colonialismo italiano*. Rome: Carocci, 2012.
Giorgis, Elizabeth Wolde. *Modernist Art in Ethiopia*. Athens: Ohio University Press, 2019.
Girard, Aurélien. "Was an Eastern Scholar Necessarily a Cultural Broker in Early Modern Europe? Faustus Naironus (1628–1711), the Christian East, and Oriental Studies." *PBA* 225 (2019): 240–263.
Giuffrida-Ruggeri, Vincenzo. "Nuovi studi sull'antropologia dell'Africa orientale: etnologia e antropometria delle popolazioni eritreo-somale-abissine e delle regioni vicine." *AAE* XLV (1915): 123–179.
Glassman, Jonathon. "Towards a Comparative History of Racial Thought in Africa: Historicism, Barbarism, and Autochthony." *CSSH* 63, no. 1 (2021): 72–98.
Go, Julian. *Policing Empires: Militarization, Race, and the Imperial Boomerang in Britain and the US*. New York: Oxford University Press, 2024.
Goglia, Luigi. "Un aspetto dell'azione politica italiana durante la campagna d'Etiopia 1935–36: la missione del senatore Jacopo Gasparini nell'Amhara." *Storia contemporanea* VIII (1977): 791–822.
———. "Propaganda italiana a sostegno della guerra contro l'Etiopia svolta in Gran Bretagna nel 1935–36," *Storia contemporanea* 15, no. 5 (1984): 845–906.
Gooch, John. *Mussolini and His Generals: The Armed Forces and Fascist Foreign Policy, 1922–1940*. New York: Cambridge University Press, 2007.
Goodwin, Ralph, Neal Petersen, Marvin Kranz, and William Slany, eds. *Foreign Relations of the United States, 1947*. 8 vols. Washington, DC: United States Government Printing Office, 1972.
Grafton, Anthony. "Foreword." In *The Hieroglyphics of Horapollo*, trans. George Boas, xi–xxi. Princeton, NJ: Princeton University Press, 1993.
Graziani, Rodolfo. *Una vita per l'Italia*. Milan: Mursia, 1986.
Grah Mel, Frédéric. *Alioune Diop, le bâtisseur inconnu du monde noir*. Abidjan: Presses Universitaires de Côte d'Ivoire, 1995.
Gran, Peter. *The Persistence of Orientalism: Anglo-American Historians and Modern Egypt*. Syracuse, NY: Syracuse University Press, 2020.
Griaule, Marcel. *Les flambeurs d'hommes*. Paris: Calmann-Lévy, 1934.
———. *La peau de l'ours*. Paris: Gallimard, 1936.
Grilli, Chiara. "Making of the Italian American Colonizer: Colonialism, Race, and the Italo-Ethiopian War." *IIJPS* 23, no. 4 (2021): 526–543.
Guariglia, Raffaele. *Ricordi 1922–1946*. Naples: Edizione Scientifiche Italiane, 1950.
Guerri, Giordano Bruno. *Giuseppe Bottai*. Milan: Mondadori, 1996.
Guha, Ranajit. *History at the Limit of World-History*. New York: Columbia University Press, 2002.
———. "The Prose of Counter-Insurgency." In *Selected Subaltern Studies*, ed. Ranajit Guha and Gayatri Chakravorty Spivak, 45–86. New York: Oxford University Press, 1988.
Guida dell'Africa Orientale Italiana. Milan: Officine Fotolitografiche, 1938.

Guidi, Ignazio. *Della sede primitiva dei popoli semitici*. Ed. Mario Liverani. Rome: Bardi Edizioni, 2015.
———. *Storia della letteratura etiopica*. Rome: Istituto per l'Oriente, 1932.
———. *Vocabolario amarico-italiano*. Rome: Casa Editrice Italiana, 1901.
Guluma Gemeda. "The Rise of Coffee and the Demise of Colonial Autonomy: The Oromo Kingdom of Jimma and Political Centralization in Ethiopia." *NEAS* 9, no. 3 (2002): 51–74.
Haddis Alämayyähu. ትዝታ። አዲስ አበባ፣ ማንኩሳ ማተሚያ ቤት፣ 2013 ዓም።
Hallaq, Wael. *Restating Orientalism: A Critique of Modern Knowledge*. New York: Columbia University Press, 2018.
Hamilton, Alastair. *The Copts and the West, 1439–1822: The European Discovery of the Egyptian Church*. New York: Oxford University Press, 2006.
Hannoum, Abdelmajid. *The Invention of the Maghreb: Between Africa and the Middle East*. New York: Cambridge University Press, 2021.
Hargreaves, John. *Decolonization in Africa*. New York: Routledge, 1996.
Harris, Joseph. *African-American Reactions to War in Ethiopia, 1936–1941*. Baton Rouge: Louisiana State University Press, 1994.
———. "William Leo Hansberry, 1894–1965: Profile of a Pioneer Africanist." In William Leo Hansberry, *Pillars in Ethiopian History*, ed. Joseph Harris, 3–30. Washington, DC: Howard University Press, 1974.
Hartog, François. "Time, History and the Writing of History: The *Order* of Time." *KVHAA Konferenser* 37 (1996): 95–113.
Hassan, Said, and Abdullah Omran. "The Reception of the Brill Encyclopedia of Islam: An Egyptian Debate on the Credibility of Orientalism (1930–1950)." In *The Muslim Reception of European Orientalism: Reversing the Gaze*, ed. Susannah Heschel and Umar Ryad, 61–79. New York: Routledge, 2018.
Haylä Sellasé [with Heruy Wäldä Sellasé]. ሕይወቴና የኢትዮጵያ እርምጃ። አዲስ አበባ፣ ብርሃንና ሰላም ማተሚያ ቤት፣ 1965 ዓም።
———. *My Life and Ethiopia's Progress, Volume 1: 1892–1937*. Trans. Edward Ullendorff. New York: Oxford University Press, 1976.
———. *My Life and Ethiopia's Progress: Haile Selassie I King of Kings of Ethiopia*. Vol. 2, *Addis Abeba, 1966 E.C.* Trans. Ezekiel Gebissa, Guluma Gemeda, Tessema Ta'a, Daniel Kendie, Harold Marcus, and Angela Raven-Roberts. East Lansing: Michigan State University Press, 1994.
Haywood, Harry. *A Black Communist in the Freedom Struggle*. Ed. Gwendolyn Midlo Hall. Minneapolis: University of Minnesota Press, 2012.
Heruy Wäldä Sellasé. ለልጅ ምክር ለአባት መታሰቢያ። አዲስ አበባ፣ ብራና ማተሚያ ቤት፣ 1997 ዓም።
———. ለአባት መታሰቢያ ለልጅ ምክር። አዲስ አበባ፣ 1910 ዓም።
———. ማኅደረ ብርሃን ሀገረ ጃፓን። አዲስ አበባ፣ ኅዳ ጽባሕ፣ 1924 ዓም።
———. ስለ አውሮጳ መንገድ የምክር ቃል። አዲስ አበባ፣ ተፈሪ መኮንን ማተሚያ ቤት፣ 1916 ዓም።
———. በኢትዮጵያ የሚገኙ በግዕዝና ባማሪኛ ቋንቋ የተጻፉ የመጻሕፍት ካታሎግ። አዲስ አበባ፣ ተፈሪ መኮንን ማተሚያ ቤት፣ 1920 ዓም።
———. በኢትዮጵያ የሚገኙ የመጻሕፍት ቁጥር። አዲስ አበባ፣ 1904 ዓም።

——. በዕድሜ መሰንበት ሁሉን ለማየት። አዲስ አበባ፣ ጎህ ጽባሕ፣ 1926 ዓም።
——. አዲስ አለም፡ የቅኖችና የደግ አድራጊዎች መኖሪያ። አዲስ አበባ፣ ጎህ ጽባሕ፣ 1925 ዓም።
——. ወዳጄ ልቤና ሌሎችም። አዲስ አበባ፣ አዲስ አበባ ዩኒቨርሲቲ ፕሬስ፣ 2000 ዓም።
——. ዋዜማ። በማግሥቱ የኢትዮጵያን ነገሮታት የታሪክ በዓል ለማክበር። አዲስ አበባ፣ ጎሐ ጽባሕ፣ 1921 ዓም።
——. የልቅሶ ዜማ ግጥም። ምስጢሩ ከመጻሕፍት ጋራ የተስማማ። አዲስ አበባ፣ 1910 ዓም።
——. የለዕልት ወይዘሮ መነን መንገድ በኢየሩሳሌምና በምስር። አዲስ አበባ፣ ተፈሪ መኮንን ማተሚያ ቤት፣ 1915 ዓም።
——. የሕይወት ታሪክ (Biographie) በኋላ ዘመን ለሚነሡ ልጆች ማስታወቂያ። አዲስ አበባ፣ ተፈሪ መኮንን ማተሚያ ቤት፣ 1915 ዓም።
——. የኢትዮጵያ ልዑካን ቡድን በአውሮጳና መካከለኛው ምሥራቅ (1903 ዓም)። አዲስ አበባ፣ የኢትዮጵያ አካዳሚ ፕሬስ፣ 2009 ዓም።
——. የኢትዮጵያ ታሪክ፡ ከንግሥተ ሳባ እስከ ታላቁ የአድዋ ድል። አዲስ አበባ፣ ሥናይት ተከለማርያም፣ 2006።
——. ደስታ ከበር የኢትዮጵያ መንግሥት አልጋ ወራሽና እንደራሴ ልዑል ተፈሪ መኮንን ወደ አውሮፓ ሲዬዱና ሲመለሱ የመንገዳቸው አኳኋን። አዲስ አበባ፣ ተፈሪ መኮንን ማተሚያ ቤት፣ 1916 ዓም።

Heruy Wäldä Sellasé, ed. መጽሐፈ ቅኔ፡ ዘቀደምት ወደጋርት ሊቃውንቲሃ ወመዕምራኒሃ ለኢትዮጵያ። አዲስ አበባ፣ 1918 ዓም።

——. መጽሐፈ ቅዳሴ። አዲስ አበባ፣ ኃይለ ሥላሴ ንጉሠ ነገሥት ዘኢትዮጵያ ማተሚያ ቤት፣ 1922 ዓም።

Heschel, Susannah. "Orientalist Triangulations: Jewish Scholarship on Islam as a Response to Christian Europe." In *The Muslim Reception of European Orientalism: Reversing the Gaze*, ed. Susannah Heschel and Umar Ryad, 147–167. New York: Routledge, 2018.

Heschel, Susannah, and Umar Ryad, eds. *The Muslim Reception of European Orientalism: Reversing the Gaze*. New York: Routledge, 2018.

Heywät Hadaru. ያቺ ቀን ተረሳች ከትምህርት ቤት ወደ ቆንስላ ሥራ። አዲስ አበባ፣ ብርሃንና ሰላም ማተሚያ ቤት፣ 1967 ዓም።

History of the United Nations War Crimes Commission and the Development of the Laws of War. London: United Nations War Crimes Commission, 1948.

Holmes, Rachel. *Sylvia Pankhurst: Natural Born Rebel*. London: Bloomsbury, 2020.

Huber, Valeska, and Jürgen Osterhammel. "Introduction: Global Publics." In *Global Publics: Their Power and Their Limits, 1870–1990*, ed. Huber and Osterhammel, 1–60. London: Oxford University Press, 2020.

Hylander, Fride. "Onesimus Nesib: Some Remarks on Cerulli's 'The Folk-Literature of the Galla.'" *JES* 7, no. 2 (1969): 79–87.

Ibhawoh, Bonny. *Human Rights in Africa*. New York: Cambridge University Press, 2018.

Ileto, Reynaldo. *Knowing America's Colony: A Hundred Years from the Philippine War*. Manoa: University of Hawai'i at Manoa, 1999.

"Interventions des délégués africains." *Présence africaine* 3 (1955): 28–38.

Isneghi, Mario. *Intellettuali militanti e intellettuali funzionari. Appunti sulla cultura fascista*. Turin: Einaudi, 1979.

Iyob, Ruth. *The Eritrean Struggle for Independence: Domination, Resistance, Nationalism 1941–1993*. New York: Cambridge University Press, 1995.

Jackson, Julian. *France on Trial: The Case of Marshal Pétain*. Cambridge, MA: Harvard University Press, 2023.

James, C. L. R. "Abyssinia and the Imperialists." *The Keys* 3, no. 3 (1936): 32–33.

———. *The Black Jacobins: Toussaint L'Ouverture and the San Domingo Revolution*. New York: Vintage, 1989.
Jarrett-Macauley, Delia. *The Life of Una Marson, 1905-1965*. Manchester, UK: Manchester University Press, 1998.
Jensen, Steven. *The Making of International Human Rights: The 1960s, Decolonization, and the Reconstruction of Global Values*. New York: Cambridge University Press, 2016.
Jesman, Czeslaw. "Some Impressions of the Third International Congress of Ethiopian Studies in Addis Ababa." *Africa* 21, no. 4 (1966): 407-411.
Jolly, Éric. "Marcel Griaule, ethnologue: La construction d'une discipline (1925-1956)." *Journal des africanistes* 71, no. 1 (2001): 149-190.
Jolly, Éric, and Marianne Lemaire, eds. *Cahier Dakar-Djibouti*. Meurcourt: Éditions les Cahiers, 2015.
Jones, Delmos. "Social Responsibility and the Belief in Basic Research: An Example from Thailand." *Current Anthropology* 12 (1971): 347-350.
———. "Towards a Native Anthropology." *Human Organization* 29, no. 4 (1970): 251-259.
Käbbädä Mika'él. የዕውቀት ብልጭታ። አዲስ አበባ፣ አርቲስቲክ ማተሚያ ቤት፣ 1956 ዓም።
Kapteijns, Lidwien. "I. M. Lewis and Somali Clanship: A Critique." *NEAS* 11, no. 1 (2004-2010): 1-23.
Karren, Stewart. "Horapollon." In *The Coptic Encyclopedia*, ed. Aziz Suryal Atiya, vol. 4, 1255-1256. New York: Macmillan, 1991.
Kässaté Berhan Täsämma. መዝገበ ቃላት። አዲስ አበባ፣ 2008።
Keita, Maghan. *Race and the Writing of History: Riddling the Sphinx*. New York: Oxford University Press, 2000.
Keller, Marcus, and Javier Irigoyen-García, eds. *The Dialectics of Orientalism in Early Modern Europe*. New York: Palgrave Macmillan, 2018.
Keller, Marcus, and Javier Irigoyen-García. "Introduction: The Dialectics of Early Modern Orientalism." In *The Dialectics of Orientalism in Early Modern Europe*, ed. Keller and Irigoyen-García, 1-16. London: Palgrave: 2018.
Kelly, Saul. *Cold War in the Desert: Britain, the United States, and the Italian Colonies, 1945-52*. New York: St. Martin's, 2000.
Kennedy, Dane. "Minds in Crisis: Medical-Moral Theories of Disorder in the Late Colonial World." In *Anxieties, Fear, and Panic in Colonial Settings: Empires on the Verge of a Nervous Breakdown*, ed. Harald Fischer-Tiné, 27-48. Cham, Germany: Palgrave-Macmillan, 2016.
Kennedy, David. *A World of Struggle: How Power, Law, and Expertise Shape Global Political Economy*. Princeton, NJ: Princeton University Press, 2016.
Kenyatta, Jomo. *Facing Mount Kenya*. New York: Vintage, 1962.
———. "Hands off Abyssinia!" *Labour Monthly* 17, no. 9 (1935): 532-536.
Kesteloot, Lylian. "1956-1959. D'un Congrès à L'autre." *Présence africaine*, n.s., nos. 175/177 (2007): 125-129.
Khalili, Laleh. *Time in the Shadows: Confinement in Counterinsurgencies*. Stanford, CA: Stanford University Press, 2013.

Klose, Fabian. *Human Rights in the Shadow of Colonial Violence: The Wars of Independence in Kenya and Algeria*. Trans. Dona Geyer. Philadelphia: University of Pennsylvania Press, 2013.

Kochavi, Arieh. *Prelude to Nuremberg: Allied War Crimes Policy and the Question of Punishment*. Chapel Hill: University of North Carolina Press, 1998.

Krebs, Edgardo. "Popularizing Anthropology, Combatting Racism: Alfred Métraux at the UNESCO Courier." In *The History of UNESCO: Global Actions and Impacts*, ed. Poul Duedahl, 29–48. New York: Palgrave, 2016.

Kropp, Manfred. "Abreha's Names and Titles: CIH 541, 4- Reconsidered." *PSAS* 21 (1991): 135–145.

"La visita degli orientalisti del congresso internazionale." *Africa italiana* 53, no. 4 (1935): 195–196.

Laachir, Karima, Sara Marzagora, and Francesa Orsini. "Significant Geographies in Lieu of World Literature." *JWL* 3 (2018): 290–310.

Labanca, Nicola. "L'amministrazione coloniale fascista: Stato, politica e società." In *Il regime fascista: Storia and storiografia*, ed. Angelo Del Boca, Massimo Legnani, and Mario Rossi, 352–398. Bari: Laterza, 1995.

———. *L'Oltremare. Storia dell'espansione coloniale italiana*. Bologna: Mulino, 2002.

Lai, Wen-Wei. "China, the Chinese Representative, and the Use of International Law to Counter Japanese Acts of Aggression: China's Standpoint on UNWCCC Jurisdiction." *CLF* 25 (2014): 111–132.

Lake, Marilyn, and Henry Reynolds. *Drawing the Global Colour Line: White Men's Countries and the International Challenge of Racial Equality*. New York: Cambridge University Press, 2008.

Lamont, Mark. "Malinowski and the 'Native Question.'" In *Anthropologists and Their Traditions Across National Borders*, ed. Regna Darnell and Frederick Gleach, 69–110. Lincoln: University of Nebraska Press, 2008.

Laurière, Christine, and André Mary, eds. *Ethnologues en situations coloniales*. Paris: Carnets de Bérose, 2019.

Lauterpacht, Elihu. *The Life of Hersch Lauterpacht*. New York: Cambridge University Press, 2010.

Lawrance, Benjamin, Emily Lynn Osborn, and Richard Roberts, eds. *Intermediaries, Interpreters, and Clerks: African Employees in the Making of Colonial Africa*. Madison: University of Wisconsin Press, 2006.

Lealem Berhanu Terega and Mahlet Solomon. "Religious, Political and Cultural Influences on the First Ethiopian Playwright, Teklehawariat Teklemariam and His Play 'Fabula: Yawreoch Commedia.'" *JACS* 26, no. 3 (2014): 276–286.

Lefevre, Renato. "Tasfa'-Seyon e la concessione ufficiale di S. Stefano agli etiopi nel 1548." ደብረ ቀ አስጢ.ፋኖስ 8, no. 15 (1968): 62–64.

Leijonhufvud, Erik. *Kejsaren och hans hövdingar*. Stockholm: Norstedt and Söners Förlag, 1948.

Leiris, Michel. *Phantom Africa*. Trans. Brent Hayes Edwards. Chicago: University of Chicago Press, 2017.

Lessona, Alessandro. *Crepuscolo nero*. Florence: Edizioni A.L., n.d.
——. *Memorie*. Florence: Sansoni, 1958.
——. *Un ministro di Mussolini racconta*. Rome: Edizioni Nazionali, 1973.
——. *Verso l'impero. Memorie per la storia politica del conflitto italo-etiopico*. Florence: Sansoni, 1939.
L'Estoile, Benoît de. "Enquêter en 'situation coloniale': Politique de la population, gouvernementalité modernisatrice et 'sociologie engagée' en Afrique équatoriale française." *CEA* 228 (2017): 863-919.
Levering Lewis, David. *W. E. B. Du Bois: A Biography*. 2 vols. New York: Holt, 2009.
Levi Della Vida, Giorgio. "Carlo Alfonso Nallino (1872-1938)." *Oriente moderno* 18, no. 9 (1938): 459-478.
——. *Fantasmi ritrovati*. Venice: Pozza, 1966.
——. "Omaggio ad Enrico Cerulli." *Oriente moderno* 43, nos. 10/12 (1963): 795-798.
——. "L'opera orientalistica di Ignazio Guidi." *Oriente moderno* 15, no. 5 (1935): 236-248.
Lewis, Herbert. "Anthropology in Ethiopia, 1950s-2016: A Participant's View." In *Seeking Out Wise Old Men: Six Decades of Ethiopian Studies at the Frobenius Institute*, ed. Sabine Dinslage and Sophia Thubauville, 27-46. Berlin: Reimer, 2017.
——. *In Defense of Anthropology: An Investigation of the Critique of Anthropology*. New Brunswick, NJ: Transaction, 2013.
——. *Jimma Abba Jifar: An Oromo Monarchy, 1830-1932*. Lawrenceville, NJ: Red Sea Press, 2001.
Lewis, Ioan. *A Modern History of the Somali: Nation and State in the Horn of Africa*. Boulder, CO: Westview, 1965.
Lewis, Mark. *The Birth of the New Justice: The Internationalization of Crime and Punishment, 1919-1950*. New York: Oxford University Press, 2014.
Li, Darryl. "From Exception to Empire: Sovereignty, Carceral Circulation, and the 'Global War on Terror.'" In *Ethnographies of U.S. Empire*, ed. Carole McGranahan and John Collins, 456-475. Durham, NC: Duke University Press, 2018.
Link, Arthur, and David Hirst, eds. *The Papers of Woodrow Wilson*. 69 vols. Princeton, NJ: Princeton University Press, 1989.
Littmann, Enno. "Arde'et: The Magic Book of the Disciples." *JAOS* 25 (1904): 1-48.
——, ed. *Philosophi abessini*. Paris: Republic, 1904.
Liverani, Mario. "Giorgio Levi Della Vida e il suo contributo agli studi africanisti." *Africa* 23, no. 2 (1968): 222-224.
Lockman, Zachary. *Field Notes: The Making of Middle East Studies in the United States*. Stanford, CA: Stanford University Press, 2016.
Louis Gates Jr., Henry. "W. E. B. Du Bois and the Encyclopedia Africana, 1909-63." *AAAPSS* 568 (2000): 203-219.
Luigi Amedeo di Savoia-Aosta. *La esplorazione dello Uabi-Uebi Scebeli dalle sue sorgenti nella Etiopia meridionale alla Somalia Italiana (1928-29)*. Milan: Mondadori, 1932.
Lundström, Karl Johan, and Ezra Gebremedhin. *Kenisha: The Roots and Development of the Evangelical Church of Eritrea, 1866-1935*. Trenton, NJ: Red Sea Press, 2011.
Lusini, Gianfrancesco. "Ignazio Guidi, Martino Mario Moreno, Enrico Cerulli: studiosi dell'Etiopia." *RSE* ser. 3, 1 (2017): 164-174.

Machiavelli, Niccolò. *The Prince.* Trans. Daniel Donno. New York: Bantam, 1981.
Mahtämä Sellasé Wäldä Mäsqäl. "የኢትዮጵያ ባህል ጥናት፡ ቼ በለው።" *JES* 7, no. 2 (1969): 195–303.
——. ዕጹብ ድንቅ። አዲስ አበባ፣ ነጸነት ማተሚያ ቤት፣ 1943 ዓም።
——. ዝክረ ነገር። አዲስ አበባ፣ አርቲስቲክ ማተሚያ ቤት፣ 1962 ዓም።
Makalani, Minkah. *In the Cause of Freedom: Radical Black Internationalism from Harlem to London, 1917–1939.* Chapel Hill: University of North Carolina Press, 2013.
Makonnen, T. Ras. *Pan-Africanism from Within, as Recorded and Edited by Kenneth King.* New York: Oxford University Press, 1973.
Malaparte, Curzio. "In guerra muiono i migliori." In *Viaggio in Etiopia e altri scritti africani,* ed. Enzo Laforgia, 164–171. Bagno a Ripoli: Passigli, 2019.
Mallette, Karla. *European Modernity and the Arab Mediterranean: Toward a New Philology and a Counter-Orientalism.* Philadelphia: University of Pennsylvania Press, 2010.
Mamdani, Mahmood. *Citizen and Subject: Contemporary Africa and the Legacy of Late Colonialism.* Princeton, NJ: Princeton University Press, 1996.
Manela, Erez. *The Wilsonian Moment: Self-Determination and the International Origins of Anticolonial Nationalism.* New York: Oxford University Press, 2007.
Marchand, Suzanne. *German Orientalism in the Age of Empire: Religion, Race, and Scholarship.* New York: Cambridge University Press, 2009.
Marcus, Harold. "The Embargo on Arms Sales to Ethiopia." *IJAHS* 16, no. 2 (1983): 263–279.
——. *The Politics of Empire: Ethiopia, Great Britain, and the United States, 1941–1974.* Lawrenceville, NJ: Red Sea Press, 1995.
Marinucci, Cesare, and Tomaso Columbano. *Il governo dei territori oltremare.* Rome: Istituto Poligrafico dello Stato, 1963.
Marrassini, Paolo. "Problems in Critical Edition and the State of Ethiopian Philology." *JES* 42, nos. 1/2 (2009): 25–68.
Märse'é Hazän Wäldä Qirqos. ቀዳማዊ ኃይለ ሥላሴ 1922–1927። አዲስ አበባ፣ አዲስ አበባ ዩኒቨርሲቲ ፕሬስ፣ 2009 ዓም።
——. የሐያኛው ክፍለ ዘመን መባቻ፡ የዘመን ታሪክ ትዝታዬ ካየሁትና ከሰማሁት 1896–1922። አዲስ አበባ፣ አዲስ አበባ ዩኒቨርሲቲ ፕሬስ፣ 1999 ዓም።
——. የአምስቱ የመከራ ዓመታት አጭር ታሪክ። አዲስ አበባ፣ ብርሃንና ሰላም ማተሚያ ቤት፣ 1947 ዓም።
——. የኢትዮጵያ የአንግሊዝ ሶማሊላንድ የወሰን መካለል ታሪክ። አዲስ አበባ፣ አዲስ አበባ ዩኒቨርሲቲ ፕሬስ፣ 2007 ዓም።
——. *Of What I Saw and Heard: The Last Years of Emperor Menelik II and the Brief Rule of Iyassu.* Trans. Hailu Habtu. Addis Ababa: Centre Français des Études Éthiopiennes, 2004.
Marson, Una. *The Moth and the Star.* Kingston, Jamaica: 1937.
Martha Nasibù. *Memorie di una principessa etiope.* Vicenza: Neri Pozza, 2005.
Martin, William, and Michael West, eds. *Out of One, Many Africas: Reconstructing the Study and Meaning of Africa.* Urbana: University of Illinois Press, 1999.
Marzagora, Sara. "History in Twentieth-Century Ethiopia: The 'Great Tradition' and the Counter-Histories of National Failure." *JAH* 28, no. 3 (2017): 425–444.
Masotti, Pier Marcello. *Ricordi d'Etiopia di un funzionario coloniale.* Milan: Pan, 1981.
Maspero, Jean. "Horapollon et la fin du paganisme égyptien." *BIFAO* 11 (1914): 163–195.
Mastrogregori, Massimo. "Sulla 'collaborazione' degli storici italiani durante il fascismo." *Belfagor* 61, no. 2 (2006): 151–168.

Matera, Marc. *Black London: The Imperial Metropolis and Decolonization in the Twentieth Century*. Berkeley: University of California Press, 2015.

Maurel, Chloé. "L'Histoire générale de l'Afrique de l'UNESCO: Un projet de coopération intellectuelle transnationale d'esprit afro-centré (1964–1999)." *CEA* 3, no. 215 (2014): 715–737.

Mauro da Leonessa. *Santo Stefano Maggiore degli Abissini e le relazioni romano-etiopiche*. Vatican City: Tipografia Poliglotta Vaticana, 1929.

Mazower, Mark. *No Enchanted Palace: The End of Empire and the Ideological Origins of the United Nations*. Princeton, NJ: Princeton University Press, 2009.

Mazzucchetti, Eugenio. *Diario somalo di Eugenio Mazzucchetti*. Ed. Guido Votano. 2002.

Mbembe, Achille. *Necropolitics*. Trans. Steven Corcoran. Durham, NC: Duke University Press, 2019.

McCoy, Alfred. *Policing America's Empire: The United States, the Philippines, and the Rise of the Surveillance State*. Madison: University of Wisconsin Press, 2009.

McDonnell, Michael, and Dirk Moses. "Raphael Lemkin as Historian of Genocide in the Americas." *JGR* 7, no. 4 (2005): 501–529.

McFate, Montgomery, and Janice Laurence, eds. *Social Science Goes to War: The Human Terrain System in Iraq and Afghanistan*. New York: Oxford University Press, 2015.

McKenzie, Donald. *Bibliography and the Sociology of Texts*. New York: Cambridge University Press, 2004.

McNamara, Laura, and Robert Rubinstein, eds. *Dangerous Liaisons: Anthropologists and the National Security State*. Santa Fe, NM: School for Advanced Research Press, 2011.

Mekuria Bulcha. "Onesimos Nasib's Pioneering Contributions to Oromo Writing." *NJAS* 4, no. 1 (1995): 36–59.

Mele, Franca. "L'Asinara e le colonie penali in Sardegna: un'isola penitenziaria?" In *Le colonie penali nell'Europa dell'Ottocento*, ed. Mario Da Passano, 189–213. Rome: Carocci, 2004.

Melis, Guido. "Note sull'epurazione nei ministeri, 1944–1946." *Ventunesimo secolo* 2, no. 4 (2003): 17–52.

Melman, Billie. *Empires of Antiquities: Modernity and the Rediscovery of the Ancient Near East, 1914–1950*. New York: Oxford University Press, 2020.

Memmi, Albert. *Portrait du colonisé, précédé du portrait du colonisateur*. Paris: Buchet Chastel, 1957.

Memorandum on the Italian Colonies. 1945.

Mersha Alehegne. ዜና ጻጸሳት ኢትዮጵያውያን። አዲስ አበባ፣ 1996 ዓም።

———. "The *Mälkəʾa sämaʿətat* of Däbrä Libanos: Text and Translation." *RSE* 3a Serie, 1, no. 48 (2017): 121–137.

———. "Towards a Glossary of Ethiopian Manuscript Culture and Practice." *Aethiopica* 14 (2011): 145–162.

Messaoudi, Alain. *Les arabisants et la France coloniale 1780–1930*. Lyon, France: ENS Éditions, 2015.

Messay Kebede. "Return to the Source: Asres Yenesew and the West." *Diogenes* 59, nos. 3–4 (2014): 60–71.

Mickaël Bethe Selassié. *La jeune Éthiopie: Un haut-fonctionnaire éthiopien Berhanä-Marqos Wäldä-Tsadeq (1892-1943)*. Paris: Harmattan, 2004.

Missiroli, Mario [Giulio Cesare Baravelli]. *L'ultimo baluardo della schiavitù: L'Abissinia*. Rome: Novissima, 1935.

Mitchell, Andrew, and Peter Trawny, eds. *Heidegger's Black Notebooks: Responses to Anti-Semitism*. New York: Columbia University Press, 2017.

Mitchell, Timothy. *Rule of Experts: Egypt, Techno-Politics, Modernity*. Berkeley: University of California Press, 2002.

Mohammed Hassan. *The Oromo of Ethiopia: A History, 1570-1860*. New York: Cambridge University Press, 1990.

Monin, Boris. "The Visit of Rās Tafari in Europe (1924): Between Hopes of Independence and Colonial Realities." *Annales d'Éthiopie* 28 (2013): 383-389.

Moreno, Martino Mario [XXX]. "Gli stranieri in Abissinia." *Nuova antologia* 1514 (1935): 443-464.

——. Review of Heruy Wäldä Sellasé, *Mahdärä berhan, hagärä japan*. *Oriente moderno* 13, no. 5 (1933): 279-280.

Morghen, Raffaello. *The Accademia Nazionale dei Lincei in the Life and Culture of United Italy on the 368th Anniversary of Its Foundation (1871-1971)*. Rome: Accademia Nazionale dei Lincei, 1990.

Morone, Antonio. "I custodi della memoria: Il Comitato per la documentazione dell'opera dell'Italia in Africa." *Zapruder* 23 (2010): 25-38.

Morris, Aldon. *The Scholar Denied: W. E. B. Du Bois and the Birth of Modern Sociology*. Berkeley: University of California Press, 2015.

Morris, Narrelle, and Aden Knaap. "When Institutional Design Is Flawed: Problems of Cooperation and the United Nations War Crimes Commission, 1943-1948." *EJIL* 28, no. 2 (2017): 513-534.

Mouralis, Bernard. "'*Présence Africaine*: Geography of an 'Ideology.'" In *Surreptitious Speech: Présence Africaine and the Politics of Otherness, 1947-1987*, ed. Valentin-Yves Mudimbe, 3-13. Chicago: University of Chicago Press, 1992.

Moyn, Samuel. *The Last Utopia: Human Rights in History*. Cambridge, MA: Harvard University Press, 2010.

Mufti, Aamir. *Forget English! Orientalisms and World Literature*. Cambridge, MA: Harvard University Press, 2016.

Mukhtar, Mohamed Haji. *Historical Dictionary of Somalia, New Edition*. Lanham, MD: Scarecrow, 2003.

Naison, Mark. *Communists in Harlem During the Depression*. New York: Grove, 1984.

Naithani, Sadhana. *In Quest of Indian Folktales: Pandit Ram Gharib Chaube and William Crooke*. Bloomington: Indiana University Press, 2006.

Nallino, Carlo Alfonso. "I principali risultati del viaggio di Enrico Cerulli nell'Etiopia occidentale nel 1927-1928." *Oriente moderno* 13, no. 8 (1933): 430-436.

Nallino, Maria. "Il XIX Congresso internazionale degli orientalisti." *Oriente moderno* 16, no. 2 (1936): 97-110.

Nemours, Alfred. *Craignons d'être un jour l'Éthiopie de quelqu'un.* Port-au-Prince, Haiti: Imprimerie du Collège Vertières, 1945.
Nicolini, Nicola. *L'Istituto orientale di Napoli. Origine e statuti.* Rome: Edizioni Universitarie, 1942.
Nietzsche, Friedrich. *On the Genealogy of Morals and Ecce Homo.* Trans. Walter Kaufmann. New York: Vintage, 1989.
Nkrumah, Kwame. "Address Delivered to Mark the Opening of the First International Congress of Africanists." In *The Proceedings of the First International Congress of Africanists, Accra 11th-18th December 1962,* ed. Lalage Bown and Michael Crowder, 6–15. Evanston, IL: Northwestern University Press, 1964.
Normand, Roger, and Sarah Zaidi. *Human Rights at the UN: The Political History of Universal Justice.* Bloomington: Indiana University Press, 2008.
"Notre politique de la culture." *Présence africaine* 24/25 (1959): 5–7.
Nurhussein, Nadia. *Black Land: Imperial Ethiopianism and African America.* Princeton, NJ: Princeton University Press, 2019.
Ogot, Bethwell. *My Footprints on the Sands of Time: An Autobiography.* Kisumu: Anyange Press, 2006.
Onesimos Näsib and Astér Ganno. ጀልቀበ ቤርሲሳ እንስ መጫፈ ዱቢሱ በርሲሱን አፋን ኦሮሞት። መንኩሎት፣ 1894።
Orsini, Francesca, and Laetitia Zecchini. "The Locations of (World) Literature: Perspectives from Africa and South Asia." *JWL* 4, no. 1 (2019): 1–12.
Ostini, Felice. "L'opera dell'istituto di studi etiopici di Asmara." In *Atti del convegno internazionale di studi etiopici (Roma 2-4 aprile 1959),* 255–257. Rome: Accademia Nazionale dei Lincei, 1960.
Ottley, Roi. *New World A-Coming: Inside Black America.* New York: Houghton Mifflin, 1943.
Paleologos, Costantino. *Tafari & Ci.* Trieste: Delfino, 1938.
Pankhurst, Richard. "Alcune note retrospettive sulla III conferenza di studi etiopici." *Sestante* 2, no. 1 (1966): 95–98.
———. "The Haile Selassie I Prize." In *Von Hiob Ludolf bis Enrico Cerulli,* ed. Piotr Scholz, 229–242. Wiesbaden: 2001.
———. "Haile Sellasie's Autobiography and an Unpublished Draft." *NEAS* 3, no. 3 (1996): 69–109.
———. "Italian Fascist War Crimes in Ethiopia: A History of Their Discussion, from the League of Nations to the United Nations (1936–1949)." *NEAS* 6, nos. 1–2 (1999): 83–140.
———. "Pro- and Anti-Ethiopian Pamphleteering in Britain During the Italian Fascist Occupation (1935–41)." *IJES* 1, no. 1 (2003): 153–176.
———. "The Short-Lived Newspaper *Abyssinia* (1935–1936): A Memory of the League of Nations." In *Varia Aethiopica in Memory of Sevir B. Chernetsov (1943–2005),* ed. Denis Nosnitsin, 257–264. Piscataway, NJ: Gorgias, 2009.
———. "Sylvia and *New Times and Ethiopia News.*" In *Sylvia Pankhurst from Artist to Anti-Fascist,* ed. Ian Bullock and Richard Pankhurst, 149–191. New York: Palgrave Macmillan, 1992.
Pankhurst, Richard, and Ian Bullock, eds. *Sylvia Pankhurst from Artist to Anti-Fascist.* New York: Palgrave Macmillan, 1992.

Pankhurst, Rita. "International Conferences of Ethiopian Studies: A Look at the Past." In *Proceedings of the Seventh International Conference of Ethiopian Studies: University of Lund, 26-29 April 1982*, ed. Sven Rubenson, 1-9. Addis Ababa: Institute of Ethiopian Studies, 1984.

——. "International Conferences of Ethiopian Studies." In *Encyclopaedia Aethiopica*, ed. Siegbert Uhlig and Alessandro Bausi, vol. 3, 175-179. Wiesbaden: Harrasowitz Verlag, 2007.

——. "The Library of Emperor Tewodros II at Mäqdäla (Magdala)." *BSOAS* 36, no. 1 (1973): 15-42.

——. "In Quest of Ankobar's Church Libraries." In *New Trends in Ethiopian Studies: Papers of the Twelfth International Conference in Ethiopian Studies, 5-10 September 1994*, ed. Harold Marcus, 198-216. Lawrenceville, NJ: Red Sea Press, 1994.

Paoli, Renato. *Nella colonia Eritrea*. Milan: Treves, 1908.

Pavanello, Mariano. "Vinigi L. Grottanelli a cento anni dalla nascita." *L'uomo* 1/2 (2012): 7-32.

Pavone, Claudio. *Alle origini della repubblica. Scritti su fascismo, antifascismo e continuità dello Stato*. Turin: Bollati Boringhieri, 1995.

——. *A Civil War: A History of the Italian Resistance*. Trans. Peter Levy. London: Verso, 2013.

Pawlos Män Amäno. የኢየሩሳሌምና የቅዳሳት ቦታዎች ታሪክ። አዲስ አበባ፤ ጎሀ ጽባሕ፤ 1925።

Paxton, Robert. *The Anatomy of Fascism*. New York: Knopf, 2004.

Pearson, Jessica Lynne. "Defending Empire at the United Nations: The Politics of International Colonial Oversight in the Era of Decolonisation." *JICH* 45, no. 3 (2017): 525-549.

Pedaliu, Effie. *Britain, Italy, and the Origins of the Cold War*. New York: Palgrave, 2003.

Pederson, Susan. "Back to the League of Nations." *AHR* 112, no. 4 (2007): 1091-1117.

——. *The Guardians: The League of Nations and the Crisis of Empire*. New York: Oxford University Press, 2015.

——. "An International Regime in an Age of Empire." *AHR* 124, no. 5 (2019): 1676-1680.

Pes, Alessandro. "An Empire for a Kingdom: Monarchy and Fascism in the Italian Colonies." In *Crowns and Colonies: European Monarchies and Overseas Empires*, ed. Robert Aldrich and Cindy McCreery, 245-261. Manchester, UK: Manchester University Press, 2016.

Peterson, Derek, and Giacomo Macola, eds. *Recasting the Past: History Writing and Political Work in Modern Africa*. Athens: Ohio University, 2009.

Phillips, Hugh. *Between the Revolution and the West: A Political Biography of Maxim M. Litvinov*. Boulder, CO: Westview, 1992.

Piccioli, Angelo. *La nuova Italia d'oltremare*. 2 vols. Milan: Mondadori, 1933.

Pigli, Mario. [Gihâd]. *La civiltà italiana e l'Etiopia*. Rome: Tipografia Editrice Italiana, 1935.

——. *L'Etiopia moderna nelle sue relazioni internazionali 1859-1931*. Padua: Antonio Milani, 1933.

——. *Italian Civilization in Ethiopia*. London: Dante Alighieri Society, 1936.

Piovan, Dino. "Ancient Historians and Fascism: How to React Intellectually to Totalitarianism (or Not)." In *Brill's Companion to the Classics, Fascist Italy and Nazi Germany*, ed. Helen Roche and Kyriako Demetriou, 82-105. Leiden, Netherlands: Brill, 2017.

Plesch, Dan. *Human Rights After Hitler: The Lost History of Prosecuting Axis War Crimes.* Washington, DC: Georgetown University Press, 2017.
Poerio, Ilaria. *A scuola di dissenso. Storie di resistenza al confino di polizia (1926–1943).* Rome: Carocci, 2016.
Pollock, Sheldon. "Philology in Three Dimensions." *Postmedieval* 5, no. 4 (2014): 398–413.
Potter, Pittman. *The Wal Wal Arbitration.* Washington, DC: Carnegie Institute, 1938.
Pouillon, François, and Jean-Claude Vatin, eds. *Après l'orientalisme: L'Orient créé par l'Orient.* Paris: Karthala, 2011.
Price, David. *Cold War Anthropology: The CIA, the Pentagon, and the Growth of Dual Use Anthropology.* Durham, NC: Duke University Press, 2016.
———. "Counterinsurgency and the M-VICO System: Human Relations Area Files and Anthropology's Dual-Use Legacy." *Anthropology Today* 28, no. 1 (2012): 16–20.
የቀዳማዊ ኃይለ ሥላሴ ሽልማት ድርጅት ቻርተር *The Haile Selassie I Prize Trust Charter.* አዲስ አበባ፣ ብርሃንና ሰላም ማተሚያ ቤት፣ 1955ዓም።
Puglisi, Giuseppe. *Chi e'? dell' Eritrea 1952. Dizionario biografico con una cronologia.* Asmara: Agenzia Regina, 1952.
Rafael, Vicente. *Motherless Tongues: The Insurgency of Language Amid Wars of Translation.* Durham, NC: Duke University Press, 2016.
Rai Chowdhuri, Satyabrata. *Leftism in India, 1917–1947.* New York: Palgrave, 2007.
Raineri, Osvaldo, ed. *Inventario dei manoscritti Cerulli etiopici.* Vatican City: Biblioteca Apostolica Vaticana, 2004.
Ranger, Terence. "The Invention of Tradition in Colonial Africa." In *The Invention of Tradition,* ed. Eric Hobsbawm and Terence Ranger, 211–262. Cambridge: Cambridge University Press, 1983.
———. "The Invention of Tradition Revisited: The Case of Colonial Africa." In *Inventions and Boundaries: Historical and Anthropological Approaches to the Study of Ethnicity and Nationalism,* ed. Preban Kaarsholm and Jan Hultin, 5–50. Roskilde, Denmark: Roskilde University, 1994.
Reese, Scott. *Renewers of the Age: Holy Men and Social Discourse in Colonial Benaadir.* Leiden, Netherlands: Brill, 2008.
Ribi Forclaz, Amalia. *Humanitarian Imperialism: The Politics of Anti-Slavery Activism, 1880–1940.* New York: Oxford University Press, 2015.
Ricci, Lanfranco. "Cerulli, Enrico." In *Encyclopaedia Aethiopica,* ed. Siegbert Uhlig and Alessandro Bausi, vol. 1, 708–709. Wiesbaden: Harrasowitz Verlag, 2003.
———. "Conti Rossini, Carlo." In *Encyclopaedia Aethiopica,* ed. Siegbert Uhlig and Alessandro Bausi, vol. 1, 791–792. Wiesbaden: Harrasowitz Verlag, 2003.
———. "Enrico Cerulli e l'Istituto per l'Oriente." *Oriente moderno* 9, no. 70 (1990): 1–6.
———. "La 'komidiyā' di Takla Hawāryāt." In *Proceedings of the Ninth International Congress of Ethiopian Studies, Moscow, August 26–29, 1986,* ed. Anatoly Andreevich Gromyko, 193–203. Moscow: Nauka Publishers, 1989.
———. "Luigi Fusella." *RSE* 34 (1990): 229–232.
———. "Martino Mario Moreno." *RSE* 20 (1964): 3–11.
———. "Ricordo di Enrico Cerulli." *RSE* 32 (1990): 5–44.

Ricci, Lanfranco, and Gianfrancesco Lusini. "Enrico Cerulli [con Bibliografia]." *RSE* 32 (1988): 4–44.
Rose, Wayne. "W. E. B. Du Bois: Ethiopia and Pan-Africanism." *JBS* 50, no. 3 (2019): 251–272.
Rosselli, Alessandro. "Appunti sul colonialismo fascista. Venti mesi di azione coloniale (1926) di Luigi Federzoni." *JMS* 26 (2017): 89–98.
Rossi, Ettore. "Silvio Zanutto (n. 1870–1946)." *Oriente moderno* 26, nos. 1/6 (1946): 55–57.
Rossi, Gianluigi. *L'Africa italiana verso l'independenza (1941–1949)*. Milan: Giuffrè, 1980.
Rota, Emanuel. " 'We Will Never Leave.' The Reale Accademia d'Italia and the Invention of a Fascist Africanism." *Fascism* 2, no. 2 (2013): 161–182.
Rouaud, Alain. *Afä-wärq 1868–1947: Un intellectuel éthiopien témoin de son temps*. Paris: Éditions CNRS, 1991.
———. "Les contacts secrets italo-éthiopiens du printemps 1936 d'après les archives françaises." *Africa* 37, no. 4 (1982): 400–411.
———. "Quelques lettres et documents concernant Afä-Wärq (2)." *Annales d'Ethiopie* 19 (2003): 189–213.
Rubenson, Sven. "The Protectorate Paragraph of the Wiçhalē Treaty." *JAH* 5, no. 2 (1964): 243–283.
Ryad, Umar. " 'An Oriental Orientalist': Aḥmad Zakī Pasha (1868–1934), Egyptian Statesman and Philologist in the Colonial Age." *Philological Encounters* 3 (2018): 129–166.
Said, Edward. *Culture and Imperialism*. New York: Vintage, 1994.
———. *Orientalism*. New York: Vintage, 1977.
Saini Fasanotti, Federica. *Vincere! The Italian Royal Army's Counterinsurgency Operations in Africa, 1922–1940*. Annapolis, MD: Naval Institute Press, 2020.
Sajid, Mehdi. "A Muslim Convert to Christianity as an Orientalist in Europe: The Case of the Moroccan Franciscan Jean-Mohammed Abdeljalil (1904–1979)." In *The Muslim Reception of European Orientalism: Reversing the Gaze*, ed. Susannah Heschel and Umar Ryad, 209–232. New York: Routledge, 2018.
Salome Gebre Egziabeher. "The Ethiopian Patriots 1936–1941." *Ethiopian Observer* 12, no. 2 (1969): 63–91.
———. "The Patriotic Works of Dejazmatch Aberra Kassa and Ras Abebe Aragaye." In *Proceedings of the Third International Conference of Ethiopian Studies, Addis Ababa 1966*, 293–314. Addis Ababa: Institute of Ethiopian Studies, 1969.
Salvadore, Matteo. "Zärᶜay Därräs." In *Encyclopaedia Aethiopica*, ed. Siegbert Uhlig and Alessandro Bausi, vol. 5, 151–152. Wiesbaden: Harrasowitz Verlag, 2014.
Salvadore, Matteo, James De Lorenzi, and Deresse Ayenachew Woldetsadik. *The Many Lives of Täsfa Ṣeyon: An Ethiopian Intellectual in Early Modern Rome*. New York: Cambridge University Press, 2024.
Samatar, Abdi Ismail. *Africa's First Democrats: Somalia's Aden A. Osman and Abdirazak H. Hussen*. Bloomington: Indiana University Press, 2016.
———. *Framing Somalia: Beyond Africa's Merchants of Misery*. Lawrenceville, NJ: Red Sea Press, 2022.
Samatar, Said. *Oral Poetry and Somali Nationalism: The Case of Sayyid Maḥammad 'Abdille Ḥasan*. Cambridge: Cambridge University Press, 1982.

Sandford, Christine. *Ethiopia Under Hailé Selassié*. London: Dent and Sons, 1946.
Sands, Phillipe. *East West Street: On the Origins of "Genocide" and "Crimes Against Humanity."* New York: Vintage, 2017.
Santoro, Marco. "Empire for the Poor: Imperial Dreams and the Quest for an Italian Sociology, 1870s–1950s." In *Sociology and Empire: The Imperial Entanglements of a Discipline*, ed. George Steinmetz, 106–165. Durham, NC: Duke University Press, 2013.
Saraiva, Tiago. *Fascist Pigs: Technoscientific Organisms and the History of Fascism*. Cambridge, MA: MIT Press, 2016.
Satta, Gino. "L'ultimo baluardo della schiavitù. La 'barbarie abissina' nella propaganda per la guerra d'Etiopia." In *Variazioni africane: saggi di antropologia e storia*, ed. Fabio Viti, 67–93. Modena: Fiorino, 2016.
Sbacchi, Alberto. "The Archives of the Consolata Mission and the Formation of the Italian Empire, 1913–1943." *History in Africa* 25 (1998): 319–340.
——. *Ethiopia Under Mussolini: Fascism and the Colonial Experience*. London: Zed, 1985.
——. "I governatori coloniali italiani in Etiopia: gelosie e rivalità nel periodo 1936–1940." *Storia contemporanea* 8, no. 1 (1977): 835–877.
——. "Italian Mandate or Protectorate over Ethiopia in 1935–1936." *RSPI* 42, no. 4 (1975): 559–592.
——. "Italy and the Treatment of the Ethiopian Aristocracy, 1937–1940." *IJAHS* 10, no. 2 (1977): 209–241.
——. *Legacy of Bitterness: Ethiopia and Fascist Italy, 1935–1941*. Trenton, NJ: Red Sea Press, 1995.
Scarfone, Marianna. "Italian Colonial Psychiatry: Outlines of a Discipline, and Practical Achievements in Libya and the Horn of Africa." *History of Psychiatry* 27, no. 4 (2016): 389–405.
Scott, William. "Black Nationalism and the Italo-Ethiopian Conflict 1934–1936." *JNH* 63, no. 2 (1978): 118–134.
——. *The Sons of Sheba's Race: African-Americans and the Italo-Ethiopian War, 1935–1941*. Bloomington: Indiana University Press, 1993.
Seidenfaden, Emil Eiby. "The League of Nations' Collaboration with an 'International Public,' 1919–1939." *CEH* 31, no. 3 (2022): 368–380.
Seligman, Charles. *Races of Africa*. London: Thornton Butterworth, 1930.
Serawit Debele. "The Politics of 'Queer Reading' an Ethiopian Saint and Discovering Precolonial Queer Africans." *JACS* 34, no. 1 (2022): 98–110.
Sergew Hable Selassie. አማርኛ የቤተ ክርስቲያን መዝገበ ቃላት። አዲስ አበባ፣ 1988።
——. "Two Leading Ethiopian Writers." *JSS* 25, no. 1 (1980): 85–93.
Shack, William. "Ethiopia and Afro-Americans: Some Historical Notes, 1920–1970." *Phylon* 35, no. 2 (1974): 142–155.
——. "Social Science Research in Ethiopia: Retrospect and Prospect." In *Proceedings of the Seventh International Conference of Ethiopian Studies, University of Lund, 26–29 April, 1982*, ed. Sven Rubenson, 411–417. Addis Ababa: Institute of Ethiopian Studies, 1984.
Shadle, Brett. "The Unity of Black People and the Redemption of Ethiopia: The Ethiopian World Federation and a New Black Nationalism, 1936–1940." *IJAHS* 54, no. 2 (2021): 193–215.

Sharkey, Heather, ed. *Cultural Conversions: Unexpected Consequences of Christian Missionary Encounters in the Middle East, Africa, and South Asia*. Syracuse, NY: Syracuse University Press, 2013.

Shiferaw Bekele. "Śahle Ṣädalu." In *Encyclopaedia Aethiopica*, ed. Siegbert Uhlig and Alessandro Bausi, vol. 4, 467–468. Wiesbaden: Harrasowitz Verlag, 2010.

Simpson, Christopher. "Shutting Down the United Nations War Crimes Commission." *CLF* 25 (2014): 133–146.

Smidt, Wolbert. "The Term Ḥabäša: An Ancient Ethnonym of the 'Abyssinian' Highlanders and Its Interpretations and Connotations." In *Multidisciplinary Views on the Horn of Africa: Festschrift in Honour of Rainer Voigt's 70th Birthday*, ed. Hatem Elliesie, 37–71. Cologne, Germany: Rüdiger Köppe Verlag, 2014.

Sollai, Michele. "How to Feed an Empire? Agrarian Science, Indigenous Farming, and Wheat Autarky in Italian-Occupied Ethiopia, 1937–1941." *Agricultural History* 95, no. 3 (2022): 379–416.

Solomon Ṣehayä. ማስን መልቀስን ቀዳሞት። አስመራ፣ ቤት ማሕተም ፍራንቸስካና፣ 2012።

Soravia, Bruna. "Ascesa e declino dell'orientalismo scientifico in Italia." In *Il mondo visto dall'Italia*, ed. Agostino Giovagnoli and Giorgio Del Zanna, 271–286. Milan: Guerini, 2005.

———. "Carlo Alfonso Nallino (1872–1938). Lineamenti di una biografia intellettuale." *Studi magrebini*, n.s. 8 (2010): 9–24.

———. "Il percorso politico di Giorgio Levi Della Vida, dall'impresa libica al rifiuto del giuramento, 1911–1931." *Rivista di storia* 10, no. 2 (2021): 175–194.

Sòrgoni, Barbara. *Etnografia e colonialismo. L'Eritrea e l'Etiopia di Alberto Pollera (1873–1939)*. Turin: Bollati Boringhieri, 2001.

———. *Parole e corpi. Antropologia, discorso giuridico e politiche sessuali interrazziali nella colonia Eritrea (1890–1941)*. Naples: Liguori, 1998.

———. "Pratiche antropologiche nel clima dell'impero." In *L'Impero fascista. Italia ed Etiopia (1935–1941)*, ed. Riccardo Bottoni, 411–423. Bologna: Mulino, 2008.

Spencer, John. *Ethiopia at Bay: A Personal Account of the Haile Selassie Years*. Algonac, MI: Reference Publications, 1984.

Stahn, Carsten. "Complementarity and Cooperative Justice Ahead of their Time? The United Nations War Crimes Commission, Fact-Finding, and Evidence." *CLF* 25 (2014): 223–260.

Steer, George. *Caesar in Abyssinia*. London: Hodder and Stoughton, 1936.

———. *Sealed and Delivered: A Book on the Abyssinian Campaign*. London: Hodder and Stoughton, 1942.

Steiner, Zara. *The Triumph of the Dark: European International History, 1933–1939*. New York: Oxford University Press, 2011.

Steinmetz, George. *The Colonial Origins of Modern Social Thought: French Sociology and the Overseas Empire*. Princeton, NJ: Princeton University Press, 2023.

———, ed. *Sociology and Empire: The Imperial Entanglements of a Discipline*. Durham, NC: Duke University Press, 2013.

Stocking, George. *The Ethnographer's Magic and Other Essays in the History of Anthropology.* Madison: University of Wisconsin Press, 1992.
Stoler, Anna Laura. *Duress: Imperial Durabilities in Our Times.* Durham, NC: Duke University Press, 2016.
Stolzenberg, Daniel. "Les 'langues orientales' et les racines de l'orientalisme académique: une enquête préliminaire." *Dix-septième siècle* 268 (2015): 409–426.
Strachan, John. "The Colonial Cosmology of Fernand Braudel." In *The French Colonial Mind, Volume 1: Mental Maps of Empire and Colonial Encounters,* ed. Martin Thomas, 72–95. Lincoln: University of Nebraska Press, 2012.
Strang, Bruce, ed. *Collision of Empires: Italy's Invasion of Ethiopia and Its International Impact.* Surrey, UK: Ashgate, 2013.
Strelcyn, Stefan. "Marcel Cohen." *BSOAS* 38, no. 3 (1975): 615–622.
Subrahmanyam, Sanjay. *Europe's India: Words, People, Empires, 1500–1800.* Cambridge, MA: Harvard University Press, 2017.
Susmel, Edoardo, and Duilio Susmel, eds. *Opera omnia di Benito Mussolini.* 36 vols. Florence: La Fenice, 1959.
Tä'amrat Yeggäzu. የስደት መታሰቢያ፡ ጠላት ኢትዮጵያን በወረረ ዘመን፤ ወደ ኢየሩሳሌም ስደት። አዲስ አበባ፣ ብርሃንና ሰላም ማተሚያ ቤት፣ 1944 ዓም።
Tabor Wami. አባ ቦሩ (1897–1958 E.C.) (የደጃዝማቾች ገረሱ ዱኪና የሌሎች አርበኞች ታሪክ)። አዲስ አበባ፣ 1986 ዓም።
Taddäsä Zäwäldé. ቀሪን ገረመው፣ የአርበኞች ታሪክ። አዲስ አበባ፣ ብርሃንና ሰላም ማተሚያ ቤት፣ 1960 ዓም።
Taddele Yidnekatchew. "Negadras Tessema the Witty Poet: Renderings of a Grandson." *IESB* 21/22 (2000): 18–24.
Tafarra Deguefé. *Minutes of an Ethiopian Century.* Addis Ababa: Shama Books, 2006.
Täklä Hawaryat Täklä Maryam. ኦቶባዮግራፊ (የሕይወቴ ታሪክ)። አዲስ አበባ፣ አዲስ አበባ ዩኒቨርሲቲ ፕሬስ፣ 1998 ዓም።
Täklä Ṣadeq Mäkwuriya. "The Horn of Africa." In *UNESCO General History of Africa, III: Africa from the Seventh to the Eleventh Century,* ed. Mohammed El Fasi and Ivan Hrbek, 559–574. Berkeley: University of California Press, 1988.
———. የሕይወቴ ታሪክ። አዲስ አበባ፣ ኤክሊ.ፐስ ማተሚያ ቤት፣ 2008 ዓም።
———. የኢትዮጵያ ታሪክ፡ ከአጼ ቴዎድሮስ እስከ ቀዳማዊ ኃይለ ሥላሴ። አዲስ አበባ፣ አርቲስቲክ ማተሚያ ቤት፣ 1946 ዓም።
Tasgaraa Hirphoo. *Abbaa Gammachiis (Oneesimos Nasib).* Trans. Magarsaa Guutaa. Hermannsburg, Germany: 1999.
Tässäma Eshäté. ሰምና ወርቁ። አዲስ አበባ፣ 1985 ዓም።
Tayyä Gäbrä Maryam. የኢትዮጵያ ሕዝብ ታሪክ ባጭር ቃል የወጣ፣ አስመራ፣ ሚሲአን ሱኤድዊ ማተሚያ፣ 1914 ዓም።
Tekeste Negash. *Eritrea and Ethiopia: The Federal Experience.* Uppsala: Nordiska Afrikainstitutet, 1997.
Terrefe Ras Warq. የአንኮበሩ ሰው በጀኔቭ። አዲስ አበባ፣ 2011 ዓም።
Tesema Ta'a. *The Political Economy of an African Society in Transformation: The Case of Macca Oromo (Ethiopia).* Wiesbaden: Harrasowitz Verlag, 2006.

Tesemma Ta'a and Alessandro Triulzi, eds. የወለጋ የታሪክ ሰነዶች ከ1880ዎቹ እስከ 1920ዎቹ (ኢ.ኢ..አ.)። አዲስ አበባ፤ አዲስ አበባ ዩኒቨርሲቲ ፕሬስ፤ 1999 ዓም።

Teshale Tibebu. "Modernity, Eurocentrism, and Radical Politics in Ethiopia, 1961–1991." *African Identities* 6, no. 4 (2008): 345–371.

Thomas, Martin. *Empires of Intelligence: Security Services and Colonial Disorder After 1919*. Berkeley: University of California Press, 2008.

Thomas, Martin, and Amanda Harris. "Anthropology and the Expeditionary Imaginary." In *Expeditionary Anthropology: Teamwork, Travel, and "The Science of Man,"* ed. Thomas and Harris, 1–36. New York: Berghahn, 2018.

Tilley, Helen, and Robert Gordon, eds. *Ordering Africa: Anthropology, European Imperialism, and the Politics of Knowledge*. Manchester, UK: Manchester University Press, 2007.

Togliatti, Palmiro [Comrade Ercoli]. "The Preparations for Imperialist War and the Tasks of the Communist International." In *VII Congress of the Communist International*, 386–451. Moscow: Foreign Languages Publishing House, 1939.

Tollardo, Elisabetta. *Fascist Italy and the League of Nations, 1922–1935*. New York: Palgrave, 2016.

Tomlinson, Lisa. *Una Marson*. Kingston, Jamaica: University of the West Indies Press, 2019.

Toynbee, Arnold. *Survey of International Affairs 1935*. 2 vols. London: Oxford University Press, 1936.

Trawny, Peter. *Heidegger and the Myth of a Global Jewish Conspiracy*. Trans. Andrew Mitchell. Chicago: University of Chicago Press, 2015.

Trevisan Semi, Emanuela. *Taamrat Emmanuel: An Ethiopian Jewish Intellectual, Between Colonized and Colonizers*. Trans. Jill Goldsmith. New York: Centro Primo Levi, 2016.

———, ed. *L'epistolario di Taamrat Emmanuel. Un intelletuale ebreo d'Etiopia nella prima metà del XX secolo*. Turin: Harmattan, 2000.

Triulzi, Alessandro. "Africani in Italia: La memoria e l'archivio." *Meridione* 2 (2010): 30–50.

———. "Neḳemte and Addis Ababa: Dilemmas of Provincial Rule." In *The Southern Marches of Imperial Ethiopia: Essays in History and Social Anthropology*, ed. Donald Donham and Wendy James, 51–68. Athens: Ohio University Press, 2002.

Trouillot, Michel-Rolph. *Silencing the Past: Power and the Production of History*. Boston: Beacon, 2015.

Trüper, Henning. *Orientalism, Philology, and the Illegibility of the Modern World*. London: Bloomsbury Academic, 2020.

Tsehai Berhane Silassie. "Women Guerilla Fighters." *NEAS* 1, no. 3 (1979–1980): 73–83.

Ullendorff, Edward. "Some Early Amharic Letters." *BSOAS* 35, no. 2 (1972): 229–270.

———. "Some Further Material from the Eugen Mittwoch 'Nachlass.'" *BSOAS* 53, no. 1 (1990): 64–76.

———. Review of *Somalia. Scritti vari editi ed inediti. I.*, by Enrico Cerulli. *BSOAS* 21, no. 2 (1958): 431–432.

———. *The Two Zions: Reminiscences of Jerusalem and Ethiopia*. New York: Oxford University Press, 1988.

Ullendorff, Edward, J. S. Trimingham, C. F. Beckingham, and W. Montgomery Watt. "Ḥabas͟h, Ḥabas͟ha." In *Encyclopaedia of Islam*, 2nd ed., ed. H. A. R. Gibb, J. H. Kramers,

E. Lévi-Provençal, J. Schacht, B. Lewis, and Ch. Pellat, vol. 3, 2–8. Leiden, Netherlands: Brill, 1986.

Umoren, Imaobong. *Race Women Internationalists: Activist-Intellectuals and Global Freedom Struggles*. Berkeley: University of California Press, 2018.

Uoldelul Chelati Dirar. "Writing WWI with African Gazes: The Great War Through the Writing of Tigrinya Speaking Expatriates." In *The First World War from Tripoli to Addis Ababa (1911–1924)*, ed. Shiferaw Bekele, Uoldelul Chelati Dirar, Alessandro Volterra, and Massimo Zaccaria. Addis Ababa: Centre français des études éthiopiennes, 2018. https://books.openedition.org/cfee/1379?lang=en.

Urbano, Annalisa. "International Law of War, War Crimes in Ethiopia, and Italy's Imperial Misrecollection at the End of Empire, 1946–1950." *Historical Journal* 66, no. 1 (2022): 237–257.

Urbano, Annalisa, and Antonio Varsori. *Mogadiscio 1948. Un eccidio di italiani fra decolonizzazione e guerra fredda*. Bologna: Mulino, 2019.

US Department of State. *Foreign Relations of the United States 1936*. 5 vols. Washington, DC: United States Government Printing Office, 1953–1954.

———. *Foreign Relations of the United States 1946*. 11 vols. Washington, DC: United States Government Printing Office, 1969–1972.

———. *Foreign Relations of the United States 1947*. 8 vols. Washington, DC: United States Government Printing Office, 1971–1973.

Van Beek, Walter E. A., R. M. A. Bedaux, Suzanne Preston Blier, Jacky Bouju, Peter Ian Crawford, Mary Douglas, Paul Lane, and Claude Meillassoux. "Dogon Restudied: A Field Evaluation of the Work of Marcel Griaule [and Comments and Replies]." *Current Anthropology* 32, no. 2 (1991): 139–167.

Van der Veer, Peter, ed. *Conversion to Modernities: The Globalization of Christianity*. New York: Routledge, 1996.

Vansina, Jan. "UNESCO and African Historiography." *History in Africa* 20 (1993): 337–352.

Varadarajan, Latha. "The Trials of Imperialism: Radhabinod Pal's Dissent at the Tokyo Tribunal." *EJIR* 21, no. 4 (2015): 793–815.

Varisco, Daniel. *Reading Orientalism: Said and the Unsaid*. Seattle: University of Washington Press, 2007.

Varsori, Antonio. *L'Italia nelle relazioni internazionali dal 1943 al 1992*. Rome: Laterza, 1998.

Vedovato, Giuseppe. *Gli accordi italo-etiopici dell'agosto 1928*. Florence: Poligrafico Toscano, 1956.

Ventresco, Fiorello. "Italian-Americans and the Ethiopian Crisis." *Italian Americana* 6, no. 1 (1980): 4–27.

Vermeulen, Han. *Before Boas: The Genesis of Ethnography and Ethnology in the German Enlightenment*. Lincoln: University of Nebraska Press, 2015.

Villari, Luigi. *Storia diplomatica del conflitto italo-etiopico*. Bologna: Zanichelli, 1943.

Virtue, Nicolas. "Technology and Terror in Fascist Italy's Counterinsurgency Operations: Ethiopia and Yugoslavia, 1936–1943." In *Fascist Warfare, 1922–1945: Aggression, Occupation, Annihilation*, ed. Miguel Alonso, Alan Kramer, and Javier Rodrigo, 143–168. New York: Palgrave, 2019.

Voigt, Rainer. "Abyssinia." In *Encyclopaedia Aethiopica*, ed. Siegbert Uhlig and Alessandro Bausi, vol. 1, 59–65. Wiesbaden: Harrasowitz Verlag, 2003.

Vrdoljak, Ana Filipa. "Human Rights and Genocide: The Work of Lauterpacht and Lemkin in Modern International Law." *EJIL* 20, no. 4 (2010): 1163–1194.

Wagner, Florian. *Colonial Internationalism and the Governmentality of Empire, 1893-1982*. New York: Cambridge University Press, 2022.

Walters, Francis. *A History of the League of Nations*. New York: Oxford University Press, 1952.

Wa Thiong'o, Ngũgĩ. *Detained: A Writer's Prison Diary*. New York: Heinemann, 1981.

———. *Moving the Centre: The Struggle for Cultural Freedoms*. New York: James Currey, 1993.

Watenpaugh, Keith David. *Bread from Stones: The Middle East and the Making of Modern Humanitarianism*. Berkeley: University of California Press, 2015.

Wempe, Sean Andrew. "A League to Preserve Empires: Understanding the Mandates System and Avenues for Further Scholarly Inquiry." *AHR* 124, no. 5 (2019): 1723–1731.

———. *Revenants of the German Empire: Colonial Germans, Imperialism, and the League of Nations*. New York: Oxford University Press, 2019.

Weststeijn, Arthur. "Egyptian Memorials in Modern Rome: The Dogali Obelisk and the Altar of the Fallen Fascists." In *The Iseum Campense from the Roman Empire to the Modern Age*, ed. Miguel John Versluys, Kristine Bülow Clausen, and Giuseppina Capriotti Vittozzi, 331–347. Rome: Edizioni Quasar, 2018.

Wilder, Gary. *Freedom Time: Negritude, Decolonization, and the Future of the World*. Durham, NC: Duke University Press, 2015.

Wilkinson, Robert. *Orientalism, Aramaic, and Kabbalah in the Catholic Reformation: The First Printing of the Syriac New Testament*. Leiden, Netherlands: Brill, 2007.

Wion, Anaïs. "L'histoire d'un vrai faux traité philosophique (Ḥatatā Zarʾa Yāʾeqob et Ḥatatā Walda Ḥeywat)." *Afriques*, online "Debates and Readings" supplement (2013). https://journals.openedition.org/afriques/1063?lang=en.

Wolk, Ewa, and Denis Nosnitsin. "Kəflä Giyorgis." In *Encyclopaedia Aethiopica*, ed. Siegbert Uhlig and Alessandro Bausi, vol. 3, 370–371. Wiesbaden: Harrasowitz Verlag, 2007.

Woller, Hans. *I conti con il fascismo. L'epurazione in Italia, 1943-1948*. Trans. Enzo Morandi. Bologna: Mulino, 1997.

Wright, Stephen. *Ethiopian Incunabula*. Addis Ababa: Commercial Printing Press, 1967.

የብርሃንና ሰላም ቀ.ኃ.ሥ. ማተሚያ ቤት የወርቅ ኢዮቤልዩ 1914–1964 [ዓም]። *Berhanena Selam H.S.I. Printing Press Golden Jubilee 1921-1971*. አዲስ አበባ፣ ብርሃንና ሰላም ማተሚያ ቤት፣ 1971።

የቀዳማዊ ኃይለ ሥላሴ ሽልማት ድርጅት 10ኛ ዓመት። *Haile Selassie I Prize Trust 10th Year*. አዲስ አበባ፣ አርቲስቲክ ማተሚያ ቤት፣ 1973።

Yaqob Beyene. "In memoriam: Lanfranco Ricci (1916–2007)." *Aethiopica* 11 (2008): 217–221.

Yaréd Gäbrä Mikaʾél. ግርማዊት እቴጌ መነን። አዲስ አበባ፣ አርቲስቲክ ማተሚያ ቤት፣ 1950 ዓም።

የተፈሪ መኮንን ትምህርት ቤት አጭር ታሪክ። አዲስ አበባ፣ ብርሃን ሰላም ማተሚያ ቤት፣ [n.d.]።

የተከበሩ ቀኛዝማች ደህነ ወልደ ማርያም የሕይወት ታሪክ ባጭሩ። አዲስ አበባ፣ 1956።

Yates, Brian. "Ethiopian Categories, British Definitions: British Discovery of Ethiopian Identities from the Nineteenth Century to the First Decade of the Twentieth Century." *NEAS* 18, nos. 1–2 (2018): 231–269.

———. *The Other Abyssinians: The Northern Oromo and the Creation of Modern Ethiopia, 1855-1913*. Rochester, NY: University of Rochester Press, 2020.

Yirga Gelaw Woldeyes. "Colonial Rewriting of African History: Misinterpretations and Distortions in Belcher and Kleiner's *Life and Struggles of Walatta Petros*." *JALHC* 9, no. 2 (2020): 133-216.

Yonas Seifu and Jan Záhořík. "Jimma Town: Foundation and Early Growth from ca. 1830-1936." *Ethnologia Actualis* 17, no. 2 (2017): 46-63.

Younis, Musab. *On the Scale of the World: The Formation of Black Anticolonial Thought*. Berkeley: University of California Press, 2022.

Zaccaria, Massimo. "La lunga strada verso Ginevra. L'Etiopia e la Conferenza della Pace di Parigi." *RISI* 2, no. 1 (2019): 31-54.

Zännäb [aläqa]. መጽሐፈ ጨዋታ። አዲስ አበባ፣ ጎህ ጽባሁ፣ 1924 ዓም።

Zäwdé Rätta. በቀዳማዊ ኃይለ ሥላሴ ዘመነ መንግሥት የኤርትራ ጉዳይ 1941-1963 (እንደ አውሮፓውያን አቆጣጠር)። አዲስ አበባ፣ ሻማ ቡክስ፣ 2006።

Zervos, Adrien. *L'empire d'Éthiopie: Le miroir de l'Éthiopie moderne, 1906-1935*. Alexandria: Imprimerie de l'École professionnelle des frères, 1936.

Zollmann, Jakob. "Ethiopia, International Law and the First World War: Considerations of Neutrality and Foreign Policy by the European Powers, 1840-1919." In *The First World War from Tripoli to Addis Ababa (1911-1924)*, ed. Shiferaw Bekele, Uoldelul Chelati Dirar, Alessandro Volterra, and Massimo Zaccaria. Addis Ababa: Centre français des études éthiopiennes, 2018. https://books.openedition.org/cfee/1311?lang=en.

Zolo, Danilo. *Victors' Justice: From Nuremberg to Baghdad*. London: Verso, 2009.

Zorzi Pugliese, Olga. "Antifascisti friulani in Canada nel periodo interbellico, con la trascrizione dell'intervista inedita rilasciata ad Angelo Principe dall'anarchico Attilio Bortolotti." *Metodi e ricerche* 32, no. 2 (2013): 133-183.

Index

A'emro (newspaper), 21, 145, 199
Aars Rynning, Jacob, 237
Abäbä Arägay, 171, 181–90, 192–96, 217, 246–47, 262, 354, 361
Abäbäch Abägaz, 156
Abäbäch Chärqosé, 154
Abärra Kassa, 147, 219, 262
Abbaa Bagiboo II, 45
Abbaa Balloo, 46
Abbaa Jifar II, 41, 43–52, 177
Abbaa Joobir Abbaa Dula, 177, 239
Abdeljalil, Jean-Mohammed, 5
Abdissa Aga, 212
Abreha Däboch, 147, 156, 164, 169
Abreham (*abun*), 176, 187, 264, 266, 388
Abyssinia (concept), 52, 71–74, 87, 91, 128, 133
Abyssinia Association (British), 130, 204
Abyssinian military colonialism (concept), 52, 88, 103–5, 159, 179
Accademia dei Lincei, 249, 251–52, 258, 263, 274
Achebe, Chinua, 267
Achufusi, Modilim, 256–57
Adal, Sultanate of, 64, 103
Addis Ababa, 141–43, 175–76, 187, 199, 219, 247–48, 258, 279–81
Addis Aläm Maryam, 21
Addis zämän (newspaper), 243
Adwa, Battle of, 1–2, 24–26, 36, 80, 94, 112, 118, 132
Adwa complex (concept), 84
Afäwärq Gäbrä Iyäsus, 36, 54, 72, 126–27, 176, 201, 239, 266–67, 355n5, 369n39
Afäwärq Täklé, 280
Afäwärq Wäldä Maryam, 165
al-Afghani, Jamal ad-Din, 5
Africa-America Institute, 278
Africa Orientale Italiana, 8, 11, 142, 144, 150, 157, 159, 171, 175, 177, 197; dissolution of, 142–43; establishment of, 141–42, 176, 195; structure of, 150–51, 176, 181, 187–88, 189–90, 237–38. *See also* Ministry of Italian Africa, specific offices and administrative units
African studies (academic field), 9, 186, 220, 249, 260, 278–79

Africana encyclopedia, planned by Du Bois, 268, 278
ag'azyan (concept), 30, 58, 73, 323n89
Agamé, 28
Agäññähu Engeda, 99, 151
Agäw people, 92
Aja Fasilädas, 241
Ajayi, J. F. Ade, 259, 278
Akkälä Guzay, 29, 245
Aklilu Habtäwäld, 96, 158, 203, 222–25, 233, 239, 242–43, 260–61, 274, 285
Aklilu Habté, 250, 252–55, 258–61, 270–71
Aksum Ṣeyon, 67, 69
Alämayyähu Goshu, 83
Albania, 27, 378
Algeria, 7, 244, 271, 273
Ali Amdé, 161
Ali Mika'él, 161
All African Peoples Conference, 255
Alliance Israélite Universelle, 62
Aloisi, Pompeo, 2, 85, 88, 94, 96–98, 101, 111–12, 201, 332
Ambayé Wäldä Maryam, 224, 231
Amdä Ṣeyon, 64
Amdé Ali, 161, 165, 362n167
Amedeo di Savoia, Duke of Aosta, 173, 175, 177–81, 183–90, 194–96, 206, 210, 226–27, 240, 246, 249, 262, 264, 273
Amhara people, 48–49, 72, 92, 124, 153, 159, 161, 171, 193, 237
Amharic language, 211, 252, 260
Amharic literature, 248, 260, 266–67, 282
Amsalä Heruy, 33, 206
Amsterdam, 143, 198, 201, 212
Angell, Norman, 130
Ankober, 142, 145, 169–73, 179, 181–89, 191, 197, 213, 261–62
anthropology (discipline), 3, 6–7, 37, 72, 99, 115–17. *See also* ethnology
anticolonialism, international, 79–83, 99, 108–9, 133–34, 225, 229, 243, 256
antifascism, 108–9, 115, 130, 203–4, 225–28

Arabic language, 15, 17, 21, 34–37, 45, 51, 71–72, 183, 213
Arabic literature, 4, 35, 63–64, 121, 248
Arat Kilo, 143
arbäñas, anticolonial guerillas, 142–43, 166, 171–72, 180, 182, 185, 190, 193
Archivio Storico del Ministero dell'Africa Italiana, 282
area studies (academic framework), 6, 249, 259, 263, 279, 386n58, 387n75
Arendt, Hannah, 272–73
Armenian, Ethiopian diaspora community, 149
Arsi, 181
art, preserving and looting, 25, 100, 186
Aryan race (concept), 131, 196
Aṣädä Wäyn Heruy, 202, 208, 210
Asfa Wässän, 369n39
Asfaw (*däjjazmach*), 172
Asfaw Gäbräyohannes, 208, 211
Asfaw Manayé, 165
Asfawässän Kassa, 184, 219
Asfeha Wäldä Mika'él, 151–53, 160, 163–64, 175–76, 187, 189–90, 206, 239–41, 245–46
Asian-African Conference. *See* Bandung Conference
Asinara, 148–61, 164–66
Askalä Maryam Gäbrä Giyorgis, 167, 169, 172–73, 181, 186, 197
askari, 15, 41, 46–47, 50, 171–72, 179, 182, 192, 197
Aṣmä Giyorgis, 170, 362n155
Asmara, 62, 152, 171, 237, 338n54, 366n66, 391n13
Asräs Yänésäw, 302n50
Assäb, 26, 38, 199
Asäggahäñ (*däbtära*), 120–21, 127, 268
assimilation, 50–52, 55, 64, 72, 127, 128, 130, 179
Astuto, Riccardo, 53, 85, 222
Athens, 143, 201, 212
author (concept), 64–70, 89–90, 106, 127, 270

Avenol, Joseph, 87–88, 111–12, 206
Awash, 196
Ayyälä Gäbrä, 176, 231
Ayyälä Haylé, 172
Ayyaléw Berru, 154, 159–61, 165, 362n167
Azikiwe, Nnamdi, 278

Badoglio, Pietro, 141–43, 170–71, 202, 230–32, 236, 241, 243, 378n87
Bafäna Wäldä Mika'él, 20
Bägémder, 83, 120
Baghdassarian, Aramast, 164
Baidoa, 38
Bäkkälä Ali, 371n73
Balad, 38
Balandier, Georges, 8, 259
Baltimore Afro-American (newspaper), 108–9
Bäqqälä Kiros, 164
Bärihun Käbbädä, 280
Barlassina, Gaudenzio, 163, 346n
Barracu, Francesco Maria, 227
Bataille, Georges, 99
Bath, 198–99, 202, 205–7, 219, 278
Bäyyänä Märed, 156, 219
Bäzabeñ (*lej*), 42
Beguinot, Francesco, 135, 355n52
behérä ag'azit (concept), 30–31, 58
Bénishangul, 42
Benyam Wärqenäh, 217, 219, 240
Berhanä Habtämika'él, 163–65, 368n18
Berhanä Marqos Wäldä Ṣadeq, 158–59, 160–61
Berhanenna sälam (newspaper), 2, 21, 49, 62–63, 65–66, 71–73, 114–16, 126, 177, 199–200
Berhanou Abebe, 260
Berlin Congress, 86
Berque, Jacques, 271
Bétä Esra'él, 62–63
Bible, 23, 49. *See also* specific books
Biblioteca Apostolica Vaticana, 282
Bibliothèque Nationale de France, 100

Biobaku, Saburi, 256
Birratu (*fitawrari*), 42
Black Americans, and Ethiopia, 17, 31, 63, 79, 82, 109, 132, 134, 203, 277–81
Black internationalism. *See* pan-Africanism
Black Israelites, 63
Boaglio, Alessandro, 191, 194
Bokkalä (*balambaras*), 172
Bolshevik, 95, 98, 235
Borra, Edoardo, 1, 174–75, 177–78, 181, 183, 186–87, 194, 199
Bortolotti, Attilio (Art), 325n31
Boshara Bidaru, 48–49
Bottai, Giuseppe, 141–42, 170, 186, 196, 202
Bottego, Vittorio, 43
Bourdet, Claude, 244
Bourdieu, Pierre, 281, 305
Brancaleone, Nicolò, 125
Breton, André, 99–100
Britain, 77, 88, 97, 99, 109–10, 201–6, 221, 229–30, 236
British Foreign Bible Society, 21, 23
British Italian Somalia border survey, 38
Brown, Francis, 238–39
Brown, W. W. (Reverend), 17
Bulga, 193
Bunche, Ralph, 277
Byzantium, 89

Cable Street, Battle of, 204
Caetani, Leone, 135
Cambridge History of Africa, 268
Campolonghi, Luigi, 130
Capuchins, 64, 67, 151
Careathers, Benjamin, 108
Caroselli, Francesco, 174–75, 211
Caruso, Pietro, 226
Catholic Church, 25, 134. *See also* specific institutions and organizations
Cavallero, Ugo, 174, 176, 181–82, 188–90, 193–96, 273

Cecchi, Antonio, 43, 45
Centro di Studi Coloniali, 117
Cerulli, Enrico: and 1928 Treaty, 2–4; and Addis Ababa Legation, 38; and antifascist sanction process, 225–28; appraisals of, 114–15, 253–55; appraisals of colonialism by, 244–45; appraisals of Heruy Wäldä Sellasé by, 55–56, 205, 266–67; appraisals of modern Ethiopia by, 52–53, 54–56, 89–92, 257–58; death of, 271; as diplomatic advisor, 222–25, 242–43; dismissal of, 195–96; education and research in Naples, 15–17, 34–37; fieldwork in western Ethiopia, 40–51; as governor of Harar, 196–97; involvement in Ethiopian studies, 249–55, 259–62, 263, 282–83; and Italo-Ethiopian crisis, 84, 88–89, 104–5, 111–12; and Ministry of Italian Africa, 53, 150–66, 201; scholarship on Ethiopian monasticism, 263–68; scholarship on Somalia, 39–40; and Somalia, 37–38; and UNESCO General History of Africa, 271–72; as vice governor general and regent, 174–94, 209–12, 264; and war crimes indictment, 237–42
Césaire, Aimé, 255–56, 274
Chacha, 182, 188, 190–91
chemical weapons, 172, 188, 194, 201, 237, 240
Chiarini, Giovanni, 43, 45
China, 82, 133, 237, 292n16
Christian Democrat Party (Italian), 221
Cipriani, Lidio, 118, 135–36, 196, 355n52
clanship, Somali (concept), 40, 179
Cohen, Marcel, 99–100, 129–30, 134, 170, 251, 258, 260, 263, 280
Cold War, 6, 221, 229, 241, 257, 274
collaboration, colonial, 143, 150, 156, 162, 164, 239, 246
collaboration, RSI/German, 226–27
collective guilt (concept), 272

Colli di Felizzano, Giuseppe, 26, 38
colonial administration, concepts of, 87, 156, 180–81, 185–86, 227
colonial exception (concept), 7, 113, 285
Colonial Museum (Rome), 25
colonial studies (academic field), 6, 35–36, 116, 186
Colson, Everett, 96, 199
Columbia University, 63, 279
Comintern Congress, 108
Comitato per la Documentazione dell'Opera dell'Italia in Africa, 388n102
Comité Internationale pour la Défense du Peuple Éthiopien et de la Paix, 130–31
communism, 102, 109, 204, 230, 236
Communist Party (American), 108
Communist Party (British), 204
Communist Party (French), 129
Communist Party (Italian), 225
complementarity (concept), 229
concentration camps, 143–44, 148, 166, 197, 208, 212, 264, 272, 285
conferences, academic. *See* specific events
confino, system of, 148, 157, 345n48
Congress of Africanists (Accra), 258–59, 274
Congress of Africanists (Addis Ababa), 263
Congress of Negro Writers and Artists (Rome), 255–57, 268
constitution (Ethiopian), 95
Contarini, Salvatore, 26–27, 30
Conti Rossini, Carlo, 63–86, 72, 106, 115, 118–23, 127, 130, 132, 135, 249, 268
Coon, Carleton, 79, 318n26, 331n57
Cora, Giuliano, 1–2, 38, 40, 162, 222–24
Corinthians (book), 68
Corio, Silvio, 204
Corriere dell'impero (newspaper), 176
Corriere della sera (newspaper), 2, 171
counterinsurgency, conceptions and doctrines of, 6–8, 157, 180–81, 185, 189–90, 268

INDEX   439

Craigie, Robert, 230, 232–33, 235–39, 274
crimes against humanity (concept), 202–3, 219–20, 244–45, 272
Cruise O'Brien, Conor, 259
cultural relativism (concept), 11, 80, 108
Cuoco, Rosida, 192
Curcio, Francesco, 228
Cushitic languages, 92
Cushitic race (concept), 19, 40, 42, 52, 73, 119
Cutelli, Stefano Mario, 196

d'Abbadie, Antoine, 65, 67, 69, 120
Däbrä Berhan, 21, 94, 169, 171–72, 181–83, 187–95, 213, 240, 273, 361n138
Däbrä Libanos, 29, 32, 58, 65, 143, 184–85, 197, 208, 213, 250, 263–68
Däbrä Qeddus Esṭifanos, 27. *See also* Santo Stefano degli Abissini
Däbrä Selṭan, 202
Däbrä Sina, 172, 190, 195
Däbrä Tabor, 241
Dähné Wäldä Maryam, 145–53, 160, 162, 165–66, 170, 260, 269
Dämissé (*fitawrari*), 45
Dän Abbo, 20
Dan'él Abäbä, 183
Daodice, Giuseppe, 174
Dässé, 38, 141, 161
Dästa Damṭäw, 41, 124, 219, 262
Dästa Täklä Wäld, 65
Davidson, Basil, 244, 260
De Baer, Marcel, 236
De Biase, Luigi, 194
De Bono, Emilio, 53, 112, 356n64
De Feo, Vincenzo, 174
De Gasperi, Alcide, 221–25
De Leone, Enrico, 244, 356n73
De Martini, Francesco, 183–84
de Sacy, Antoine Silvestre, 310n5
De Vecchi, Cesare Maria, 37–38, 40, 186, 211, 227

decolonization, cultural and intellectual, 245, 255–59, 268–70, 281–82
decolonization, political, 221, 244, 257–58
denationalization (concept), 237
Denqenäsh Täfäri, 346
Denqenäsh Täklämaryam Heruy, 208
Denti di Pirajno, Alberto, 178
Deschamps, Hubert, 79, 256–57
desert, symbolism of, 72, 212
Deutsche Aksum Expedition, 67
Dhanaane, 208–13, 264, 269, 272
Di Lauro, Raffaele, 100, 160
Dike, Kenneth Onwuka, 259, 269, 278
Diop, Alioune, 259
Diop, Cheikh Anta, 270–71, 274
direct rule. *See* colonial administration, models of
Djibouti, 24, 26, 79, 95, 99, 101–2, 193, 201–2, 314n62
Dogali obelisk, 25–26
Dorato, Mario, 257
Dov Gotein, Shelomo, 135
Drummond, Eric, 74
Du Bois, W. E. B., 17–18, 131–35, 203–4, 259, 268, 270, 274, 277–79
dual-use research (concept), 7–8, 40, 117–18, 284
Durkheim, Émile, 129
Dutt-Majumdar, Niharendu, 234

East Africa Force (British), 142
Easter (Fasika), 49, 176, 264
Ebnat, 241
École Nationale de la France d'Outre-Mer, 34
École Nationale des Langues Orientales Vivantes, 99, 129, 251
education, 31, 52, 60, 62, 116, 156, 167–68, 234, 256, 260, 268, 277–78
Éfrém Asfaw Heruy, 208
Éfrém Täwäldä Mädhen, 96, 108–10, 168, 202–3, 208, 222, 224, 234, 236, 374n17
Egyptian University (Cairo), 35

El Fasi, Mohammed, 271
Elena Sengal, 36, 127–29, 351n144
emmahoy Ṣeggé Maryam. *See* Ṣeggé Maryam
Emmañu Yemär, 164
Emmanu'él Abraham, 79, 203–4, 222, 352n8, 374n17
Emru Haylä Sellasé, 149, 156, 217
Emru Zälläqä, 224, 278, 352n8, 357n86
Enciclopedia italiana "Treccani," 35, 105
Encyclopaedia Aethiopica, 283
Endreyas (*echägé*), 265
Enfraz, 65, 67–70
Enṭoṭṭo, 17, 20–21, 27, 32, 143, 167
Enṭoṭṭo Maryam, 20, 36, 167, 169
Enṭoṭṭo Ragu'él, 20, 32, 36, 167
Eriksson, Olle, 49–50
Eritrea, 31, 36, 40, 42, 49, 85–86, 101, 105, 107, 122–25, 149–50, 159, 174, 180, 186, 221–22, 242–45, 250, 273
Estägizé'aw Yelma Heruy, 209, 212
Esṭifanos (*aläqa*), 71
Ethio-Swiss Treaty of Friendship, 96
Ethiopia: ancient and Aksumite, 31, 63–64, 71, 131, 250–51, 271, 277, 281; during colonial occupation, 169–97, 199–201, 207–8, 219–20, 263–65; during reign of Haylä Sellasé, 22, 83–85, 90–91, 94–95, 112, 145–47, 168–69; during reign of Menilek II, 20–21, 28–29, 36, 43, 45, 49–52, 91–92, 126–27, 142–43, 145, 159, 169–73; during reign of Zäwditu, 2, 24, 77, 86, 90, 126, 145, 159, 162; liberation and after, 142–43, 221, 247–48; Solomonid dynasty and, 28, 31, 64, 73, 92, 107, 123, 130
Ethiopia, "Greater" (concept), 30, 103, 282
Ethiopian exceptionalism (concept), 53, 73, 86, 119, 131, 230
Ethiopian Manuscript Microfilm Library, 270
Ethiopian Orthodox Church, 49, 58, 123–24, 176, 248, 263, 267, 287. *See also* specific topics and institutions

"Ethiopian" race, ancient (concept), 105, 135–36
Ethiopian Red Cross, 132
Ethiopian Research Council, 132, 203, 279
Ethiopian studies (academic field), 11, 35, 63–65, 104, 115–18, 131, 249–55, 257–61, 279–80, 283
Ethiopian War Crimes Commission, 224–25, 232, 234, 239, 262
Ethiopian World Federation, 203
ethnic cleansing. *See* genocide and crimes against humanity
ethnography (methodology), 40, 42–43, 117
ethnology, 34, 40, 43, 117, 177. *See also* anthropology
Eurafrique (concept), 257
Evangeliska Fosterlands-Stiftelsen, 49–50, 62
Evans-Pritchard, Edward, 278
exceptionalism, Ethiopian (concept), 53, 72–73, 86–87, 119, 130–31, 230
exoticism, 99
expeditionary anthropology (methodology), 42
extraterritorial courts, 21, 72, 122

Fairfield House, 202–6, 219
Faitlovitch, Jacques, 62–62, 70–71
Fanon, Frantz, 144, 255–57
Fäqqädä Sellasé Heruy, 33, 169, 202, 207, 212, 219, 240
Farag (*shaykh*), 38
Farello, Piero, 191
fascism (Italian), 6, 11, 24–25, 37–38, 63, 82–83, 97, 116–18, 122, 129–30, 141–42, 144, 147–48, 150, 174, 186–86, 192–93, 196, 212, 220–28, 230. *See also* Movimento Sociale Italiana, National Fascist Party
Fasika. *See* Easter
Fatuma (daughter of Abbaa Jifar), 43
Faysa (*fitawrari*), 51

Federzoni, Luigi, 40
Fesseha (*mämmeré*), 186
Fetha nägäst, 63, 104
feudalism (concept), 46, 52, 130, 204
Fileppos (*echägé*), 265
First World War, 36, 99, 132, 175
Florence, 62, 345n57
folklore (discipline), 37, 117
Ford, Arnold Josiah, 63
Ford, James, 108–9
Formento, Ettore, 179
Frank, Hans, 196, 390n127
Fusella, Luigi, 261

Gäbrä Ab (*liqä liqawent*), 149, 344n41, 348n102, 349n112
Gäbrä Egzi'abhér (*däjjazmach*), 48–49, 90
Gäbrä Giyorgis Wäldä Ṣadeq, 263–65
Gäbrä Heywät Mika'él, 149
Gäbrä Iyäsus Abbay, 30
Gäbrä Iyäsus Haylu, 250
Gäbrä Krestos Täklä Haymanot, 62, 73
Gäbrä Mika'él Germu, 309n91, 322n82
Gäbrä Sellasé Baryagabber, 24
Gäbrä Sellasé Wäldä Aregay, 21–22, 145, 169
Gäbru Dästa, 17, 132, 149, 154
gadaa, system, 42
Galaal, Muuse, 270
Gallina, Francesco, 35–36, 42, 127–28
Gambella, 42
Gännät Heruy, 149, 202, 208
Gärräsu Duki, 180, 184
Garvey, Amy Ashwood, 203
Gasparini, Iacopo, 160
Gäwé (Abbaa Balloo), 47
Gäzahäñ Afläñ, 66–70
Ge'ez language, 17, 20, 31, 99. *See also* ag'azyan, behérä ag'azit
Ge'ez literature, 21–23, 54, 56, 63–66, 70–71, 104, 119, 142, 248, 266. *See also* specific works
Gédiyon Bäyyänä, 149

Gédo, 50–52, 178–81, 183–85, 187, 262
Genesis (book), 68, 151
Geneva, 2, 11, 74, 78–88, 92–94, 96–99, 101–3, 108–11, 113–15, 118, 133–36, 143, 150, 198–99, 202, 219, 221–23, 234, 253
Geneva Protocol, 21
genocide (concept), 12, 237, 272, 285
Gentile, Giovanni, 116
George V, King, 17, 21
Germa (grandchild of Heruy), 208
Germachäw Täklä Hawaryat, 95, 149, 154, 164, 250–53, 274, 351n143
Germany, 67, 69, 82, 272–73, 285
Germé Cherfé, 186
Gétachäw (grandchild of Heruy), 208
Gétachäw Abbatä, 149, 163
Gétahun Tässäma, 374n17
Géṭu Täsämma, 264
al-Ghazi, Ahmad Ibrahim, 103
Gibb, Hamilton, 135
Gibe, 41, 43–45
Gibé River, 50
Giglio, Carlo, 261
Giovanni Afäwärq, 126
Giuffrida-Ruggeri, Vincenzo, 105, 135–36
Giusto da Urbino, 64–69
Glissant, Édouard, 255
Global War on Terror, 6
Gobäna Dachi, 43–48
Goha Ṣebah (press), 22, 33, 128
Gojjam, 24, 32, 43, 181, 189, 264
Goldziher, Ignaz, 5
Gomma, 92
Gondär, 20, 36, 38, 62, 99–100, 103, 120, 125, 142, 147, 156, 160
Goräbéla, 171–72, 186, 355n48
Goré, 42, 49
governate (colonial administrative unit), 156, 176–77, 187–88. *See also* Africa Orientale Italiana, specific locations
Governo Generale. *See* Africa Orientale Italiana

Gramsci, Antonio, 129
Grañ. *See* Ghazi, Ahmad Ibrahim al-
Graziani Massacre. *See* Yekatit 12
Graziani, Rodolfo, 147, 150–51, 153, 156, 158, 160–61, 171–75, 178, 180, 206, 208, 232, 237–38, 240–41, 244, 262, 264, 268
Griaule, Marcel, 99–105, 108, 111, 113, 115, 120, 125–26, 129–30, 134–36, 156, 392n30
Grottanelli, Vinigi, 270
Guariglia, Raffaele, 87–88, 112, 201
Guénon, René, 5
Gugsa Ar'aya, 38, 90
Gugsa Wälé, 159
Guidi, Ignazio, 63–64, 66, 68–70, 115, 118, 135–36, 170, 249, 266
Gullälé, 32, 202, 206, 208, 210, 279, 282
Guragé people, 149, 159
Guummaa, 44, 48

habash (concept), 71
habäsha (concept), 71–72
Haberland, Eike, 270
Habtä Giyorgis, 104
Habtä Maryam, 48–49, 51
Habtä Mika'él (*qäññazmach*), 50
Habtä Mika'él Yenadu, 45, 51
Habtä Sellasé, 170
Habtäwäld Wärqenäh, 170, 186
Haddis Alämayyähu, 162
Hadley, Dorothy, 132
Hagos Fessuh, 28–31
Hague Conventions, 219
Haile Selassie Prize Trust, 259–62, 269, 271, 275, 279–83
Haile Selassie University, later Addis Ababa University, 261–62, 270, 279
Haiti, 79, 82, 87, 113, 270
Halbwachs, Maurice, 129
Hamärä Eshäté, 149, 202, 208, 210–11, 247
Hamasén, 16, 31, 197
Hamitic race (concept), 105, 120, 135–36
Hampâté Bâ, Amadou, 259

Hansberry, William Leo, 12, 79, 260, 277–83
Harär, 62, 87, 92, 94, 103, 149, 158, 187, 195–96, 212, 224, 226, 228, 264
Harari people, 10
Harlem, 17, 31, 63, 79, 82, 109, 203, 279
Harvard University, 277–78, 281
Hasan, Muhammad Abdallah, 37, 40
al-Hashemi, Faysal, 18
Haud Plateau, 38
Haylä Mäläkot, 169
Haylä Maryam (*abba*), 206
Haylä Maryam Gäbrä Egzi'abhér, 42
Haylä Maryam Gugsa Dargé, 303n2
Haylä Maryam Mammo, 171–72, 181–83, 191, 246, 262
Haylä Mika'él Mäsgänna, 269
Haylä Sellasé Gugsa, 24, 165, 187, 199, 239
Haylä Sellasé: 1924 European tour as Täfäri Mäkonnen, 23–29, 145; appraisals of, 28–29, 56, 58, 86–87, 90–91, 124, 126, 129–30, 132–33; career as Täfäri Mäkonnen, 1–2, 35, 41, 43, 45, 49–50, 63, 74, 95, 99, 145, 163, 167, 169; coronation of, 22, 146; in exile, 202–4; and Heruy Wäldä Sellasé, 206–7, 247–48; and Italo-Ethiopian crisis, 83–84, 212; and liberation, 142–43
Haylé Wäldä Mäsqäl, 149
Haylu (*aläqa*), 241
Haylu Täklä Haymanot, 24, 38, 90, 99, 185, 187
Heidegger, Martin, 283–84
Herodotus, 90
Herskovits, Melville, 259
Heruy Wäldä Sellasé: 1919 visit to United States, 17–18, 132; and 1928 Treaty, 2–3; appraisals of, 55–56, 204–5, 266, 282; appraisals of foreign scholarship by, 59, 106, 115; conception of Ethiopia, 29–31, 73–74; creative writing of, 55, 60–61; death of, 206–8, 210; as director of Ministry of Foreign Affairs, 49, 145, 163; early life and

education, 19–21; efforts to prosecute war crimes by, 219–20, 241; in exile, 198–99, 202–3, 205–6, 278; as foreign minister, 83–84, 94–96, 100–101, 112, 199–202, 222; historical writing of, 22, 56–60, 128, 265–68; involvement in printing and translation, 22, 71; repatriation of, 247–48; residence of, 32–33; travel writing of, 23–31. *See also* specific family members
High Commission for Sanctions Against Fascism (Italian), 225–28, 248
historiography, 22–23, 42, 57–62, 73, 120, 124, 166, 256–57, 262, 266, 268
history (discipline), 37, 42, 256, 265, 268–70. *See also* historiography
Hitler, Adolf, 84, 150, 206
Ho Chi Minh, 18
Hoare, Samuel, 83, 109, 111, 199
Holocaust, 272
Homer, 90
Hooton, Earnest, 278, 281, 391n2
horse naming, 304n7, 343n24
Howard University, 79, 132, 203, 260, 277–81
Hrbek, Ivan, 271
Human Relations Area Files, 40
human rights, 5–7, 9, 220, 229–30, 244, 284
humanitarian interventions, 11, 80, 136, 274
Hussein, Taha, 135

imperialism (European), 26–27, 40–41, 78–82, 131, 133–34, 198–99, 212, 224–25, 230, 244, 256, 273–74, 282
India, 205, 229, 231, 235
indirect rule. *See* colonial administration, models of
Institute of Ethiopian Studies, 259–60
International African Friends of Ethiopia, 79, 203
International Alliance of Women for Suffrage and Equal Citizenship, 109
International Conference of Ethiopian Studies, Addis Ababa, 261–62

International Conference of Ethiopian Studies, Rome (1959), 249–55, 257–58, 282–83
International Conference of Ethiopian Studies, Rome (1972), 263
International Congress of Africanists, Accra, 258–59
International Congress of Africanists, Addis Ababa, 263
International Congress of Orientalists, Moscow, 259
International Congress of Orientalists, Rome, 135–36
International Criminal Court, 220, 229, 274
International Institute of Differing Civilizations, 385n51
International Military Tribunal, Nuremberg, 202, 219, 220, 233, 284
International Military Tribunal, Tokyo, 273, 284
irreducibles (concept), 153–57, 164, 180, 182, 194, 250, 279
Islamic law, 104, 195
Islamic movements, 28, 37, 40, 177, 132, 179. *See also* specific individuals
Islamic schools, 43, 196. *See also* specific institutions
Islamic studies (academic field), 35–36, 121
Issa, Abdullahi, 243
Istituto Coloniale Fascista, 117, 122
Istituto Italiano per il Medio ed Estremo Oriente, 117
Istituto Italiano per l'Africa, 257
Istituto per l'Oriente, 35, 117
Italia coloniale (periodical), 2, 123–24
Italy: fascist, 24–25, 53, 116–18, 135, 141, 148, 157, 162, 164, 177, 209–11; liberal, 34, 62–63, 148; medieval and early modern, 43, 123; republican, 221–22, 236, 241, 243, 257–58; RSI and occupied, 226–28, 236
Iyyasu (*lej*), 43, 77, 86, 95, 141, 145, 149, 159, 162, 167, 169, 172

James, C. L. R., 79, 109, 203
Japan, 82, 98, 133, 206, 220, 233, 273, 284
Jasir Bey, Shukri, 201
Jebat, 183, 189
Jérome Gäbrä Musé (*abba*), 99–101, 126, 176
Jerru, 142, 167, 189, 354n35
Jerusalem, 29, 198, 202–3, 206, 263
Jesuits, 121, 267
Jews, Ethiopian. *See* Betä Esra'él
Jèze, Gaston, 84, 96–98
Jimma, city, 146–47, 180, 264
Jimma, Sultanate of, 87, 92, 103, 177
Jiren, 44, 266
Jones, William, 108
Journal of Ethiopian Studies, 387n75
Jubba River, 38
Judaic studies (academic field), 121, 135

Käbbädä Ali, 161
Käbbädä Mika'él, 148, 154, 212, 280
Käffa, 41, 87, 92, 103, 145, 180
Käflä Giyorgis, 70, 128, 170
Kärän, 151, 273
Kassa Haylu, 21, 90, 147, 184, 202, 219, 369n39
Kassa Wäldä Maryam, 262
Kässäm, 182, 361n138
Kässaté Berhan Täsämma, 56
Kassayé Eshäté, 149
Kebrä nägäst, 64
Kenfé (*aläqa*), 319n29
Kenya, 7, 105, 134, 244, 270, 273
Kenyatta, Jomo, 79, 109, 203, 278
Ki-Zerbo, Joseph, 259, 270
Klobukowski Treaty, 122
Kolmodin, Johannes, 69
Koo, Wellington, 231–32
Kumsaa Moroda. *See* Gäbrä Egzi'abhér

La Guardia, Fiorello, 81
La Pradelle, Albert Geouffre de, 84
Lakälesh Bayyän, 172

Lanza di Scalea, Pietro, 27
Laqäch Heruy, 202, 207–12
Lauterpacht, Hersch, 202
Laval, Pierre, 83, 96–97, 199
Lazarists, 158
League of Coloured Peoples, 79, 109, 203
League of Nations: Council, 78, 83–85, 96–99, 112–13; General Assembly, 74, 78–79, 83, 85, 88, 94, 96, 108–14, 202, 212; member state delegations, 24, 79, 80, 85, 94–96, 114, 164, 250; Permanent Mandates Commission, 78, 87; Secretariat, 78, 82, 84, 88–89, 93, 109
Ledingham, George Alexander, 239
Leeqaa, 48
Leijonhufvud, Erik, 234, 236–39
Leiris, Michel, 8, 100–101
Leslau, Wolf, 260–61
Lessona, Alessandro, 53, 84–85, 93, 111, 143, 151, 153, 157–60, 164, 173–75, 186, 201, 208, 228, 237–38, 240, 244
Lessona, Silvio, 84
Levi Della Vida, Giorgio, 34–35, 135, 250, 307n63, 336n20
liberalism, 134–35, 175, 185, 199, 203, 222, 227–28, 244, 253, 263, 275, 283
Liberation Jubilee, 261–62
Liberia, 82, 87, 108
Libya, 15, 34, 102, 121–22, 148, 173–76, 180, 208, 212–13, 222, 242, 249
Lifschitz, Deborah, 100
Limmu, 45–46, 48, 180
Litawski, Jerzy, 232–33, 235
Littmann, Enno, 64–65, 67, 69, 125, 135
Litvinov, Maxim, 98–99, 108–9
London, 17, 79, 81, 95–96, 109, 143, 154, 198, 202–5, 217, 222, 229, 231, 233–34, 239, 277
London School of Economics, 278
Longobucco, 157, 164, 250, 279
Longuet, Jean, 130
Loränsiyos Wäldä Iyäsus, 16, 47
Lorenzini, Orlando, 188–90, 193–96, 273

INDEX 445

Lorenzo Ta'ezaz, 202, 222, 224, 369n39, 374n21
Lugard, Frederick, 87
Luigi Amedeo di Savoia-Aosta, Prince, 37, 40, 87–88, 92, 163, 175
Lumumba, Patrice, 255
Lyautey, Hubert, 186

Machiavelli, Niccolò, 174, 244
Mädhané Aläm, 172–73
Maghreb (concept), 73
Mahdist movement, Sudanese, 28, 132
Mahtämä Sellasé Wäldä Mäsqäl, 22, 163, 261, 362n167
Mahtämä Wärq Eshäté, 62
Makedda, 58, 67
Mäkonnen Endalkachäw, 369n39, 374n17
Mäkonnen Haylé, 79
Mäl'akä Ṣähay Iyyasu, 172, 182
Mälaku Bäyyan, 132, 203, 277
Malaku "Chips" Bayen Jr., 278
Malaparte, Curzio, 171, 189–90, 195
Malcolm X, 279
Maletti, Pietro, 181–82, 184–85, 264, 273, 378n87
Malinowski, Bronislaw, 8, 186
Mänän Asfaw, 21, 23, 169, 199, 202, 206–7
Mängäsha (däjjazmach), 172, 351n143
Männa Mäkätäwa, 241
Mänz, 181–82, 188–89, 193–94
Mäqällä, 141, 147, 199
Märäb River, 112
Marciano, Amedeo, 350n126, 368n18
Marescotti, Luigi Aldrovandi, 84–85
Märha Ṭebäb, 145
Märhabété, 19, 21, 23, 263
Marinetti, Filippo Tommaso, 186
Mark (book), 392n29
Marković, Lazar, 232
Marqos (abba), 206
Marqos Pawlos Män Amäno, 154, 176
Märse'é Hazän Wäldä Qirqos, 142–43, 145, 168, 170

Marson, Una, 109, 202–3, 205, 217–19, 222
Martin, Marguerite, 130
Marx, Karl, 130
Marxism, 11, 130, 134
Mäṣḥafä arde'et, 68
Mäṣḥafä hatäta, 64–72, 119
Mäshäsha Haylé, 255
Mäshasha Täwänd Bälay, 354n35
Maspero, Jean, 89–90
mass killings, 12, 93, 112, 144, 147–48, 184, 193–94, 219, 224, 237, 240–41, 261–62, 264–66
massä (poetic genre), 29
Massignon, Louis, 5, 135, 186
Mätafäriya Mälkä Ṣédéq, 171, 186
Matteotti, Giacomo, 24
Mattéwos (abun), 342n20
Mauss, Marcel, 99, 129
Mayçhäw, Battle of, 147, 169, 202
Mayr-Harting, Herbert, 232
Mazeingo, Nandiuasora, 285
Mazzini, Giuseppe, 107
Mediterraneanism (concept), 248, 251, 257–58. See also Eurafrique
Meli Lupi di Soragna, Antonio, 222
Memmi, Albert, 245, 284
Menassé (grandchild of Heruy), 208
Menassé Lämma, 374n17
Menilek I, 67
Menilek II, Emperor, 58, 126–27, 342n20
Menilek Palace, 143
Mercogliano, 157, 161, 163, 209–11
Mezzetti, Ottorino, 174, 181
Michigan State University, 263
Mika'él Ali, 141, 149, 161–62
Mika'él Täsämma, 208
military administrations (British and Anglo-American), 221
Military Hospital (Naples), 15–16, 36–37, 46
Ministry of Education (Italian), 116
Ministry of Foreign Affairs (Ethiopian), 2, 21, 74, 100, 158, 239

446 INDEX

Ministry of Foreign Affairs (Italian), 35, 55, 87–88, 157, 201
Ministry of Interior (Italian), 150, 157, 165, 208, 210
Ministry of the Colonies (French), 100
Ministry of the Colonies (Italian), later Ministry of Italian Africa, 26, 34–35, 37, 42, 53, 84, 88, 100, 117, 121, 153, 162, 176, 201, 204, 210, 226, 237, 249, 267
Ministry of the Pen (Ethiopian), 145
al-Mirghani, Alawiyya, 177
Mission Dakar-Djibouti, 99–101
missionaries. *See* specific groups
Missiroli, Mario, 125–26
mode of production (concept), 130
Mogadishu, 37–38, 208, 237
Mogäs Asgädom, 147, 156, 164
Montagna, Raffaele, 84
Moody, Harold, 109
Morät, 182
Mordini, Antonio, 249
Moreno, Martino Mario, 121–23, 136, 175, 181, 209–11, 226, 249, 251
Movimento Sociale Italiana, 244
Muhammad Abbaa Digga, 44–45
Mulugeta Wodajo, 279
Mulugéta Yeggäzu, 1, 24, 95
Musée d'Éthnographie, 99
Musée Nationale d'Histoire Naturelle, 100
Mussolini, Benito: and 1924 Ethiopian summit, 24–27; and Africa Orientale Italiana, 143, 172–75, 177–78, 181, 185, 193–96, 238; and Cerulli, 157, 174–75, 185, 193, 226–27, 240, 246; during Italo-Ethiopian crisis, 83–84, 93, 105, 112–13, 115; and Ethiopian detainees, 157–60, 209–11
Muzkat, Marian, 233–34

Naddäw Abba Wällo, 17, 24, 42
Nallino, Carlo Alfonso, 35, 55, 135
Namibia, 285

Naples, 15–17, 35–37, 44, 46, 104, 126–27, 161, 163, 212, 248
Naqamtee, 42, 48–52, 178–79, 183
Nardal, Paulette, 130
Nasi, Guglielmo, 195, 243, 246
Näsibu Zä'amanu'él, 124, 202, 205, 212
National Association for the Advancement of Colored People, 6, 17, 79, 108, 131–32
National Fascist Party (Italian), 24, 38, 116, 118, 178–79
National Library (Ethiopian), 248
Needham, Joseph, 244
Nemours, Alfred, 79, 113, 134, 199
neocolonialism, 27, 230, 242, 275
neofascism. *See* Movimento Sociale Italiana
New Times and Ethiopia News (newspaper), 204
New York City, 17–18, 55, 63, 81, 132, 199, 203, 242, 279
Nilotic language group, 92
Nkrumah, Kwame, 255, 258, 274, 278
Nuova antologia (journal), 89, 102, 118, 121, 123, 132, 268
Nuremberg Charter, 219
Nyerere, Julius, 278

Office of Political Affairs (Addis Ababa), 163, 176, 261
Office of Political Affairs (Mogadishu), 38
Office of Political Affairs (Rome), 8, 26, 53, 84, 88, 150, 153, 157–58, 161, 166, 175, 204, 209, 238
Ofori Atta I, King, 109
Ogaden, 41, 83, 88, 243
Ogot, Bethwell, 259, 270
Oljira Moroda, 48
Omotic language group, 92
Oncho (of Guumaa), 47
Onesimos Näsib, 49–52
Organization of African Unity, 258, 260, 268, 270

INDEX 447

L'Orientale. *See* Regio Istituto Orientale
Orientalism, debates about, 4–5, 54, 114–16
Oriente moderno (journal), 35, 55, 60, 64
Oromiyya, 42, 47–48, 50–52, 72, 130, 179–80, 196
Oromo language (Oromiffa), 47, 51
Oromo people, 43, 45–52
Ostini, Felice, 249
Ottoman Empire, 87, 122

Padmore, George, 108, 255–56
Pal, Radhabinod, 273
palaces, 21, 44, 46, 94, 142–43, 145–48, 169–73, 187, 189, 261
Palazzo Chigi, 25, 27–29, 53, 56
Palermo, 35, 157, 175, 212
Palestine, 7, 23–24, 154, 202
Pan-African Congresses, 132
pan-Africanism, 11, 109, 130–32, 134, 255, 256, 258–69, 277
Pankhurst, Richard, 259, 270
Pankhurst, Rita, 262
Pankhurst, Sylvia, 204, 231
Paris, 17–18, 31, 55, 62, 65, 67, 81, 84–85, 88, 94–97, 99, 102, 158, 170–71, 201, 203, 221–22, 224–26, 230, 233, 238, 243, 255, 269, 274, 285
Paris Peace Conference (1919), 17
Paris Peace Conference (1946), 221–25, 274, 285
Paternò di Manchi di Bilici, Gaetano, 38
Pavolini, Emilio, 135
Ṗawlos Män Amäno, 22, 346n71
Ṗeṭros (*abun*), 263, 265
philology (discipline), 5, 19, 37, 63, 66, 70, 249, 310n17
philosophy, 5, 58, 67, 69–70, 89, 116, 119, 245, 255–56, 260, 283–84
Pichi Sermolli, Rodolfo, 260
Pigli, Mario, 122–23, 125
Piotrowski, Stanislaw, 235

Pirzio Biroli, Alessandro, 171, 174, 230, 354n35
Pius XI (pope), 165
Politis, Nicolas, 85
Pollera, Alberto, 160
Pontifical Ethiopian College, 27, 250
Ponza, 156, 162–63
Popular Front, 108, 129
Potter, Pittman, 84
Présence africaine (journal), 255
Psalms (book), 71

Qeddest Sellasé, 247–48, 282
Qeddus Giyorgis, Zärrät, 241
qené (poetic genre), 56, 77–78, 90, 119
Qérellos (*abun*), 147, 368n18
Quebec Document, 222

Radcliffe-Brown, Alfred, 278
Rafanelli, Leda, 63
Ranke, Leopold von, 42
Ras Makonnen, T., 203–4
Ras Wärq Wäldä Mäsqäl, 167–73, 181, 185–86, 197, 261, 269
recuperables (concept), 154, 156–62, 177
Regia Aeronautica, 175
Regio Istituto Orientale (L'Orientale), 16, 34–37, 72, 127, 248
Repubblica Sociale Italiana, 226–27, 244
Research Office, Ministry of the Colonies/ Italian Africa, 8, 88, 117, 121
restorative justice (concept), 285
Ricci, Lanfranco, 244, 249
Ricotti, Sidney Prina, 228
Roatta, Mario, 230
Robeson, Paul, 109
Romanä Wärq Haylä Sellasé, 149, 156–57
Rome (ancient), 118, 136, 141, 198
Rome (modern), 25–30, 34–35, 37, 42, 53, 67, 88, 116, 121, 123, 126, 136, 143–44, 150, 153–54, 157–58, 162–66, 173–78, 181, 186, 188, 194, 197, 199, 225–28, 239–40, 249–56, 262–63, 266, 273, 283

Roncalli, Angelo Giuseppe, 158
Rouche, Jean, 259
Royal African Society (British), 79
Royal Air Force (British), 142
Rubenson, Sven, 261, 270
Ruiz Guiñazú, Enrique, 97
Russia, 94

Sa'id, Agha Muhammad, 16
Sägälé, Battle of, 162, 343n24
Sägänäyti, 151
Ṣägga (aläqa), 100
Ṣägga Wärädä Wärq, 186
Sahlä Sellasé, 162, 169
Sahlämaryam Negatu, 95
Sahlé (aläqa), 170
Sahlé Ṣädalu, 170, 344n41, 349n112
Said, Edward, 4, 199
Saint Peter's Basilica, 27
Sälama (abunä), 30
Sälla Dengay, 145, 188–90, 192–93, 213
Salò. See Repubblica Sociale Italiana
Salome Gebre Egziabeher, 262
Salvemini, Gaetano, 116
Sämén, 154, 160, 263
Samuel (book), 373n5
Sandford, Daniel, 207
Sängal Wärqenäh, 16, 36
Santangelo, Luigi Bruno, 228
Santini, Ruggero, 174
Santo Stefano degli Abissini, 27–30, 56, 70, 170, 249, 258
Saqqa, 45
Sassari, 149
Savoy, House of, 107, 147, 151, 175
Säyfu Mika'él, 154, 186
School of Oriental and African Studies, 34
Schwelb, Egon, 232, 379n93
scientific method (methodology), 253
Seddest Kilo, 147, 187
See of Saint Mark (Alexandria), 58, 124, 263
Ṣeggé Maryam (emmahoy), 149

Seligman, Charles, 105
Semitic languages, 249
Semitic race (concept), 71, 105, 111, 119, 133, 135–36
Semitic studies (academic field), 2, 34–35, 37, 117, 124, 129, 131, 249
Senghor, Léopold Sédar, 245, 251, 255, 257–58, 260, 263
Sergew Hable Selassie, 270
Seyyum Mängäsha, 24, 90, 124, 149
Sforza, Carlo, 242–43
Sharpeville Massacre, 279
Sheba, Queen of. See Makedda
Shebelle River, 37–38, 40, 196
She-Wolf (Roman), 143
al-Shidyaq, Ahmad Faris, 5
Sidama people, 91
Sirak Heruy, 33, 96, 199, 201–3, 206–7, 212
slavery, international debates about, 86–87, 104, 111, 123–25
socialism, 131
Società Africana d'Italia, 128
Société des Africanistes, 99
sociology (discipline), 115, 117, 131, 256
Solomonid dynasty, 28, 31, 64, 73, 92, 107, 123, 130
Somali studies (academic field), 40, 263
Somalia, 17, 37–38, 40, 42, 83, 86, 88, 105, 143, 149–50, 174–75, 178–80, 210–12, 221–22, 227–28, 242–43, 257
Somaliland. See Somalia
Sora, Gennaro, 194
Sorbonne, 84, 96
South Africa, 86, 143, 263, 279
sovereignty, 19, 43, 73–74, 78, 80, 82, 97, 108, 122, 134, 220, 230, 232, 244
Soviet Union, 108, 221, 229
Spencer, John, 158, 199, 201, 222
Stonehewer-Bird, Hugh, 177–78
strategic bombing, 172, 180
Sudan, 28, 42, 100, 105, 132, 142–43, 180–81, 244, 278
Sultan, Muhammad, 172

Sululta, 208
Susenyos, Emperor, 65, 121
Suvich, Fulvio, 96, 201

Tä'amrat Ammanu'él, 62–72, 115, 121, 199
Taddäsä Mäshäsha, 159
Taddäsä Zäwäldé, 188–89, 193
Taddesse Tamrat, 270
Täfäri Mäkonnen. See Haylä Sellasé
Täfäri Mäkonnen School, 167, 169, 186, 217, 279
at-Tahtawi, Rifa'a, 5
Takkälä Wäldä Hawaryat, 180–81, 194, 202, 246, 262
Täklä Hawaryat Täklä Maryam, 80, 94–99, 101–3, 105–15, 120, 126, 130, 134, 136, 149, 158
Täklä Haymanot, Saint, 197, 263–64
Täklä Ṣadeq Mekwuriya, 269, 271
Täklämaryam Kassahun, 208, 247
Tämbén, Battle of, 147
Tamburini, Tullio, 209–10, 376n43
tarikä nägäst (historiographic genre), 58
Täsfa Ṣeyon, 29, 31, 123
Täsfay Zaphiro, 79, 277
Täsfayé Tägäñ, 96, 154, 165, 205, 222
Täshomä Shänquṭ, 194, 240–41
Tässäw Eshäté, 77–78, 134
Ṭassäw Walälu, 165
Taṭärä Wärq Sheberé, 145
Ṭaytu Beṭul, 20
Tayyä Gäbrä Maryam, 73, 90–91, 265
Tayyé Gullelaté, 162–63
Tegray, 24, 30, 32, 67, 112, 124, 221, 239
Ṭelahun Bähabté, 154
Teruzzi, Attilio, 174, 181, 184, 195, 210, 226, 228
Téwodros Wärqenäh, 154, 351n143
The Crisis (monthly), 17
Theodoli, Alberto, 87–88, 112
Third World, 8–9, 12, 220, 255, 275
Tigray. See Tegray
Tigrayan people, 92

Tigrinya language, 124–25
Tigrinya literature, 121, 128, 245, 270
Tivoli, 157, 159–61, 177
Togliatti, Palmiro, 79, 108, 225
Tomb of the Unknown Soldier (Rome), 25
Torre del Greco, 157, 163
Toynbee, Arnold, 79
Tracchia, Ruggero, 171–72, 182, 184
trauma, colonial, 144–45, 224, 235, 275
Tucci, Giuseppe, 116, 135
Turayev, Boris, 64, 69
Turin, 35–36, 157

Ullendorff, Edward, 8, 261
Umberto, King, 91
Umberto II, King, 151
UN Trusteeship Council, 6
underdevelopment (concept), 257
UNESCO, 5–6, 9, 12, 248, 269
UNESCO General History of Africa, 6, 268–72
UNESCO History of Mankind, 268
UNESCO National Commission (Ethiopian), 269
UNHRC, 5
Union of Fascists (British), 204
UNWCC, 9, 144, 229–42, 245–46, 248–49, 251, 253, 266, 273–75, 284
University of Florence, 62, 84, 136
University of Genova, 121
University of Naples, 15, 36–37
University of Palermo, 35, 175
University of Rome, 35, 118, 125, 135, 174, 250

Venice, 34
Verchère de Reffye, Paul, 100–101
Vichy regime, 226
victors' justice (concept), 229, 273
Villabruzzi, 38, 41
Viterbo, Carlo Alberto, 63
Vittorio Emmanuele III, King, 25, 147, 169
Voice of Ethiopia (newspaper), 203
Volta Congress, 116, 186

Wäläla Wändeyyerad, 172
Wälättä Maryam, 20
Wälayta, 87, 91–92
Wäldä Gabr'él, 50
Wäldä Giyorgis Abboyé, 45
Wäldä Giyorgis Habtä Maryam, 20
Wäldä Giyorgis Wäldä Yohannes, 177, 202–3
Wäldä Heywät, 64, 67–68, 70
Wäldä Maryam Ayyälä, 158, 334n117
Wäldä Mäsqäl Tariku, 145, 176, 344n41
Wäldä Sellasé (*aläqa*), 353n12
Wäldä Sellasé (father of Heruy), 20
Wälläga, 16, 40, 42, 48–49, 52, 71, 162, 178–79, 212, 217
Wällo, 141, 161, 264
Wälwäl, 83–86, 89, 91, 94, 96, 98, 102, 142
Wänd Bäwässän Kassa, 100, 156, 219
Wändämeh Gäbrä Kidan, 172
war crimes (concept), 219–20, 237, 241, 245
war crimes, prosecution of. *See* Ethiopian War Crimes Commission, UNWCC
Wärqenäh Eshäté, 109, 154, 167, 203, 217, 277
Wečhalé, Treaty of, 36, 122, 132, 170, 261
Wentworth, Arthur Matthew, 63
Weqaw Berru, 2, 145, 362n167
White House, 17
White supremacy, 11, 18, 74, 79, 83, 108, 131, 134, 282
Williams, Eric, 255
Wilson, Woodrow, 17
World Council of Churches, 206
World Economic Conference (London), 96
world-history (concept), 43, 72, 80, 135, 257, 281
world literature (concept), 54, 70
Wright, Robert, 229, 232, 234–37, 274

Yäqésar mängest mälektäña (newspaper), 176
Yaréd, Saint, 30
Yäroma berhan (monthly), 176, 264
Yeggäzu Bähabté, 170
Yekatit 12, 147–48, 171, 184–85, 206–8, 217, 219, 237, 261–62, 264
Yelma Gäbrä Kidan, 96, 199, 207–11
Yemen, 27, 265
Yesehaq (*echägé*), 247, 264, 266
Yohannes (*echägé*), 187, 263–64
Yohannes, Emperor, 28–29, 104, 128
Yohannes Käma (*echägé*), 265
Yoséf Wärqenäh, 217–19, 240
Young Ethiopians, 90–91, 122, 153–54, 156, 180, 240
Yugoslavia, 229–31

Zä'ra Ya'eqob (*däbtära*), 65–80
Zä'ra Ya'eqob, Emperor, 64
Zälläqä (*mäl'akä ṣähay*), 169
Zännäb (*aläqa*), 22, 128
Zanutto, Silvio, 69, 115, 376n44
Zär'ay Soqwar, 29–31
Zärrät, 194, 213, 240–41
Zäwdé Asfaw Dargé, 262
Zäwditu, Empress, 1–2, 24, 77, 86, 90, 126, 145, 159, 162
Zayla, 83
Zeman, E., 237
Zervos, Adrien, 201
Zimonjic, Milivoje, 235
Zivokvic, Radomir, 230

GPSR Authorized Representative: Easy Access System Europe, Mustamäe tee 50, 10621 Tallinn, Estonia, gpsr.requests@easproject.com